Learning

*A Behavioral, Cognitive,
and Evolutionary Synthesis*

As always, for Jeanne and Elaine

SAGE was founded in 1965 by Sara Miller McCune to support the dissemination of usable knowledge by publishing innovative and high-quality research and teaching content. Today, we publish more than 850 journals, including those of more than 300 learned societies, more than 800 new books per year, and a growing range of library products including archives, data, case studies, reports, and video. SAGE remains majority-owned by our founder, and after Sara's lifetime will become owned by a charitable trust that secures our continued independence.

Los Angeles | London | New Delhi | Singapore | Washington DC

Learning

A Behavioral, Cognitive, and Evolutionary Synthesis

Jerome Frieman
Kansas State University

Steve Reilly
University of Illinois at Chicago

Los Angeles | London | New Delhi
Singapore | Washington DC

Los Angeles | London | New Delhi
Singapore | Washington DC

FOR INFORMATION:

SAGE Publications, Inc.
2455 Teller Road
Thousand Oaks, California 91320
E-mail: order@sagepub.com

SAGE Publications Ltd.
1 Oliver's Yard
55 City Road
London EC1Y 1SP
United Kingdom

SAGE Publications India Pvt. Ltd.
B 1/I 1 Mohan Cooperative Industrial Area
Mathura Road, New Delhi 110 044
India

SAGE Publications Asia-Pacific Pte. Ltd.
3 Church Street
#10-04 Samsung Hub
Singapore 049483

Printed in the United States of America

ISBN 978-1-4833-5923-6

This book is printed on acid-free paper.

Acquisitions Editor: Reid Hester
eLearning Editor: Lucy Berbeo
Editorial Assistant: Morgan McCardell
Production Editor: David C. Felts
Copy Editor: Diana Breti
Typesetter: C&M Digitals (P) Ltd.
Proofreader: Eleni-Maria Georgiou
Indexer: Kathleen Paparchontis
Cover Designer: Anupama Krishnan
Marketing Manager: Shari Countryman

SUSTAINABLE FORESTRY INITIATIVE
Certified Chain of Custody
Promoting Sustainable Forestry
www.sfiprogram.org
SFI-01268
SFI label applies to text stock

15 16 17 18 19 10 9 8 7 6 5 4 3 2 1

BRIEF CONTENTS

DETAILED CONTENTS

CHAPTER 3 • Pavlovian Conditioning Is an Inference Task   81

CHAPTER 4 • Identifying the Predictors of Significant Events   109

PART II: Learning About the Consequences of One's Behavior   213

CHAPTER 7 • The Procedures and Phenomena We Call Operant Conditioning   215

CHAPTER 10 • Life Is About Making Choices   335

CHAPTER 11 • Inference and the Representations of Knowledge in Operant Conditioning   375

PREFACE

The study of conditioning and learning has changed radically over the past 40 or so years (e.g., Schachtman & Reilly, 2011). What used to be the province of behaviorism is now home to cognitive perspectives, our views of reinforcement have changed, and we better appreciate how the mechanisms and processes of learning are reflected in the behavior of different species. As a result, we have new understandings of these processes and mechanisms. Although there is much that we still do not know about learning and conditioning, we believe it is possible to put together an integrated and coherent account of what we do know. Our intention in this book is to show students what these new understandings are and how we came to them.

Current research on conditioning and learning reflects three themes: a methodological behavioral theme that focuses on how certain experiences lead to changes in behavior, a cognitive theme that focuses on how experiences are represented in memory, and an evolutionary/adaptive behavior theme that focuses on the various kinds of learning as adaptive specializations that evolved through the mechanism of natural selection. We have attempted to interweave these themes to present an integrated and coherent account of our current state of knowledge in this area. The evolutionary/adaptive behavior theme is the central theme within which the cognitive and behavioral themes are developed here.

Some readers who favor a behavioral perspective may find this book too cognitive, and some readers who favor a cognitive perspective may find this book too behavioral. However, we hope the majority of people who teach the courses for which this book is intended will find our blending of behavioral and cognitive approaches into an evolutionary perspective to be an interesting way to think about and teach learning.

WHAT MAKES THIS BOOK DIFFERENT

We have tried to focus on our current understandings of the psychological processes involved in learning; therefore, this book is not a survey of conflicting research and theories. Although the majority of the evidence presented here involves nonhuman animals (henceforth termed *animals*), this is not a book about animal learning. We have tried to integrate into the narrative research on humans and everyday examples of human behavior. Experimental designs, the implications of what we learn from laboratory research for understanding human behavior, and the relationship between learning and other psychological constructs like motivation, perception, and memory are discussed when appropriate and not consigned to separate chapters. Likewise, the historical development of ideas and procedures is woven into the narrative.

In order to provide an integrated account of our current state of knowledge about learning, we had to deviate from the standard organization of most textbooks currently on the market and make some hard choices about what to include and not include. Some people may fault us for some of these choices. What we chose to include reflects the three themes described above, our focus on the mechanisms and processes involved in learning, and our desire to create a coherent account of the current understanding of these mechanisms and processes and of the evidence that leads to that understanding. In addition to the three core themes, the following concepts play a prominent role in this book:

- The distinction between declarative knowledge (knowing that) and procedural knowledge (knowing how) is introduced in Chapter 1 and becomes the focus of the discussions of how experiences with Pavlovian conditioning (Chapter 5) and operant conditioning procedures (Chapter 11) are encoded. This distinction also is relevant to the discussion of the difference between verbally mediated and contingency-mediated behaviors (Chapter 13).

- The distinction between instinctive knowledge (knowledge obtained through the mechanisms of heredity) and learned knowledge (knowledge obtained through experience) is also introduced in Chapter 1. Not everything can be learned with equal facility, and different species are more adept at learning some things than others. These differences reflect the influence of instinctive knowledge on the acquisition of learned knowledge. How instinctive knowledge affects learning is illustrated throughout this book.

- David Hume's three conditions that favor the formation of causal inferences (consistency, temporal and spatial contiguity, and temporal precedence) are introduced in Chapter 3. Both Pavlovian conditioning and operant conditioning involve making inferences about the causes of events. In Pavlovian conditioning situations, the individual's task is to identify external predictors (causes) of motivationally significant events (Chapter 3). In operant conditioning situations, the individual's task is to discover what one has to do to obtain what one wants or to escape from or avoid dangerous things (Chapter 11).

- An important question in the study of learning is to specify the necessary and sufficient conditions for the occurrence of learning. This question first appears in Chapter 3 for Pavlovian conditioning and is raised again in Chapters 9, 11, and 12 for operant conditioning.

- Behavior systems (interrelated sets of perceptual, central control, and motor mechanisms organized around biological functions) are described in Chapter 6 to explain the origins of Pavlovian conditioned responses. They are also integral to our understanding of operant behaviors (Chapters 7, 8, and 12).

- Hill-climbing is a basic mechanism underlying successful operant conditioning. First introduced in Chapter 8, this concept is used repeatedly in Part II of this book.

- Molar feedback and molecular feedback as possible explanations for performance on schedules of reinforcement and in choice situations are invoked in Chapters 9, 10, 11, and 13.

The following is a chapter-by-chapter summary of the distinctive content of this book:

Prologue

- Reminds students why we study psychology (to understand; predict; and, where appropriate, to change behavior) and why we use experimental methods in psychology to study behavior.

- Sets the stage for viewing the ability to learn as an adaptive specialization.

Chapter 1: Where Learning Fits Into the Big Picture

- Introduces the three central themes in this book: (1) Learning is the psychological process by which individuals acquire knowledge through experience (cognitive theme). (2) We study learning by manipulating experiences and observing how these lead to changes in behavior (methodological behavioral theme). (3) The ability to learn from experience evolved so that individuals can adjust their behavior to changing circumstances in their environment (evolutionary theme).

- Defines knowledge and distinguishes between declarative knowledge (knowing that) and procedural knowledge (knowing how) and between instinctive knowledge obtained through the mechanism of heredity and learned knowledge obtained through experience.

- Introduces the procedure/process/phenomenon distinction as it relates to the study of learning.

Part I: Learning to Predict Important Events

Chapter 2: The Procedure and Phenomena We Call Pavlovian Conditioning

- The basic concepts, procedures, phenomena, and terminology of Pavlovian conditioning are introduced through Pavlov's pioneering work on conditioned salivation, Watson's demonstration of a conditioned emotional response in a child, conditioned drug effects, conditioned taste aversions, and sign tracking.

Chapter 3: Pavlovian Conditioning Is an Inference Task

- Characterizes Pavlovian conditioning as an inference task in the context of David Hume's analysis of the conditions for forming causal inferences.

- Analyzes why although none of Hume's three conditions are necessary or sufficient for the occurrence of Pavlovian conditioned responses, we still believe that Pavlovian conditioning involves a process of causal inference.

Chapter 4: Identifying the Predictors of Significant Events

- Explores the role of salience based on instinctive knowledge (overshadowing) and prior experience in Pavlovian conditioning (CS-preexposure effect, learned irrelevance, relative validity of cues).

- Explores the role of surprise in Pavlovian conditioning (blocking).

- Shows how a mathematical model of Pavlovian conditioning based on salience and surprise (the Rescorla-Wagner model) can be developed.

Chapter 5: The Representations of Knowledge in Pavlovian Conditioning

- Describes how we can investigate the internal representations of experience with a Pavlovian conditioning procedure through the use of post-conditioning devaluation.

- Describes the role of transitive inference in second-order conditioning, sensory preconditioning, and post-conditioning devaluation.

- Describes feature-positive and feature-negative discriminations, how they are represented in memory, and how they relate to occasion setting and conditioned inhibition.

- Describes the role of context and temporal relationships and how such factors influence extinction phenomena.

Chapter 6: From Knowledge to Behavior: The Forms and Functions of Pavlovian Conditioned Responses

- Illustrates how specific conditioned responses are understood in the context of underlying behavior systems.

- Three functions of conditioned responses are described: enabling individuals to optimize interactions with the impending biologically important event, changing the individual's evaluation of events along some affective dimension (evaluative conditioning), and changing the motivational significance of the conditioned stimulus.

Part II: Learning About the Consequences of One's Behavior

Chapter 7: The Procedures and Phenomena We Call Operant Conditioning

- The basic concepts, procedures, phenomena, and terminology of operant conditioning are introduced through descriptions of Thorndike's and Skinner's early work.

- Lovaas's work with autistic children is described in some detail.

Chapter 8: How Individuals Adjust Their Behavior to Meet the Demands of the Situation

- Explores reinforcers as sources of incentive motivation for performing actions and for providing feedback.

- Introduces hill-climbing based on successive comparisons of one's current situation as the basic mechanism underlying successful operant conditioning.

- Describes how the method of successive approximations involves the judicious use of the procedures of reinforcement and extinction.

- Describes how differential reinforcement can be used to modify aspects of the topography of a behavior and the rate of production of behaviors and to promote behavioral variability and the production of novel behaviors.

Chapter 9: Adjusting to Schedules of Partial Reinforcement

- Explores the relative importance of molar and molecular feedback on schedule performance.

- Describes the effects of prior experience on schedule performance.

- Explores the variables that promote behavioral persistence.

Chapter 10: Life Is About Making Choices

- Describes the development of the empirical and theoretical matching laws.

- Evaluates evidence related to whether matching is due to melioration (molecular feedback) or optimization (molar feedback).

- Discusses implications of the matching laws for behavior modification and for understanding operant conditioning.

Chapter 11: Inference and the Representations of Knowledge in Operant Conditioning

- Characterizes operant conditioning as an inference task in the context of David Hume's analysis of the conditions for forming causal inferences.

- Illustrates why we believe that experience with an operant conditioning procedure is represented in memory as declarative knowledge.

- Explores how individuals learn the incentive value of reinforcers.

- Describes the conditions under which experience with an operant conditioning procedure can be reorganized as procedural knowledge.

- Highlights extinction effects and their relevance to relapse phenomena in humans.

Chapter 12: The Similarities Between Operant Conditioning and Natural Selection

- Explores the analogy between operant conditioning and natural selection.

- Describes the two sources of variation in operant conditioning: induced variation (behaviors generated by the situation) and behavioral variability (the inherent variability in behavior).

- Assesses the importance of temporal proximity between behaviors and reinforcing events and the behavior-outcome contingency in operant conditioning.

- Addresses whether shaping by the method of successive approximations involves the gradual molding of behavior or the creation of new behavioral programs out of existing behavioral modules.

- Addresses whether behavior is strengthened by its consequences or is retained while other behaviors drop away.

Part III: The Social Transmission of Knowledge

Chapter 13: Social Learning

- Reviews evidence for the social learning of food preferences and fears.

- Reviews evidence for imitation and directed instruction in animals.

- Discusses the importance for the distinction between verbally mediated and contingency-mediated behaviors in humans.

FEATURES DESIGNED TO FACILITATE STUDENT LEARNING

Like most areas in psychology, the study of learning has its own specialized vocabulary, and students can become overwhelmed by the vast number of technical terms we employ. To help our students master this vocabulary, we introduce **technical terms in boldface** followed by their *definitions in italics*. These terms and their definitions are also collected in the Glossary at the end of the book. Furthermore, the basic concepts, procedures, and phenomena associated with Pavlovian conditioning introduced in Chapter 2 are, given their central importance, organized and presented on the inside front cover. The same is true for the basic concepts, procedures, and phenomena associated with operant conditioning, which are collected on the inside back cover.

Sometimes we use the same term to refer to a procedure or a phenomenon or a psychological process (e.g., Pavlovian conditioning). This can be confusing to students. To help our students understand which usage is appropriate in a given context, we have attempted to be explicit about how we are using a term in the text and in the glossary.

As you can see from our description of the content of this book, we have attempted to show our students that the three themes we identify in current research on learning can be woven together to provide a coherent account of our current understanding of the mechanisms and processes that underlie Pavlovian and operant conditioning based on the small number of concepts described above. This allowed us to provide integration across chapters and to use a lot of cross-referencing to help our students see how the various pieces of the puzzle are connected.

To help our students appreciate what they are about to read, we provide short summaries at the beginning of every section and subsection. Furthermore, to aid better understanding of the material in the main body of the book, important information about applications, concepts, and historical perspective is provided throughout the book in Boxes. Finally, to benefit self-evaluation of understanding, a set of study questions is included at the end of each chapter.

Because this book is organized around three themes, there are a great many links among the chapters, and important concepts introduced early in the book reappear later. The Instructor's Manual, available on the companion website at study.sagepub.com/frieman, is designed to help you see the book's overall organization so that you can anticipate what comes next and what you need to emphasize in your classroom presentations. Important concepts are highlighted for you as they appear in the book, and their links to other chapters are noted. Because the manuscript for this book was used in class by a variety of people during its development, we have a pretty good idea of what students find difficult. These are also noted on the Instructor's Manual. Also included are suggested background readings for you and suggested additional readings for your students, who can also visit the companion website to access practice quizzes, flashcards and additional multimedia study tools.

ACKNOWLEDGMENTS

We would like to thank our editor, Reid Hester, for his advice, guidance, and encouragement during all stages of the production of this textbook. We are indebted to other SAGE personnel, including Lucy Berbeo, Diana Breti, David Felts, and Morgan McCardell, who helped bring this book to completion. We would also like to thank the following reviewers who, at the beginning of the project, provided invaluable input about the content of the book: Michael J. Beran, Georgia State University; Michael Emond, Laurentian University; Gwen Lupfer, University of Alaska Anchorage; Darryl Mayeaux,

St. Bonaventure University; Christy Porter, College of William and Mary; and Nina L. Tarner, Gettysburg College. We are grateful to Gwen Lupfer of the University of Alaska Anchorage for help with the Instructor's web page. Finally, we each wish to thank the undergraduates in our classes who, over the years, have helped refine the material and its presentation. You all have our gratitude.

Jerome Frieman
Steve Reilly

ABOUT THE AUTHORS

Jerome Frieman earned his PhD from Kent State University in Ohio. He has been at Kansas State University since 1968. Over the course of his career, he engaged in research on operant conditioning in pigeons, rats, and dwarf hamsters; Pavlovian conditioning in rats; social learning in dwarf hamsters; and extraordinary memory in a human participant. He is the author of *Learning and Adaptive Behavior* and co-author of *Memory Search by a Memorist*.

Steve Reilly obtained his D.Phil. from the University of York, England, for research concerning the neural basis of learning and memory. He has held positions in England, Canada and the United States, and is now in the Department of Psychology at the University of Illinois at Chicago. His research focuses on the neural mechanisms and functional neuroanatomy of conditioned taste aversion learning and incentive learning. Dr. Reilly is the editor of two books (*Conditioned Taste Aversion: Behavioral and Neural Processes* and *Associative Learning and Conditioning Theory: Human and Non-Human Applications*) and is currently on the editorial boards of the *International Journal of Comparative Psychology* and *Behavioral Neuroscience*.

PROLOGUE

There are three reasons for studying psychology: to understand behavior; to be able to predict the future occurrence of behavior; and, when appropriate, to change behavior. The study of learning involves all three. Current research on learning focuses on how knowledge is obtained from experience and encoded in memory and on the adaptive functions of the various types of learning.

Human beings have attempted to understand the behavior of both people and animals at least since the beginning of recorded history. We see this in the writings that have survived from the ancient world: the works of Aristotle and Plato, the various myths about the Greek and Roman Gods, and our own Bibles. Some of the insights about human behavior offered by the ancients are still relevant today. Although most psychologists take a scientific approach to the study of behavior, it is certainly true that we can also learn about human behavior through art, literature, theater, film, music, and dance. No doubt, what makes Shakespeare's plays relevant for us today is the author's keen awareness of human behavior and his ability to convey that to us.

Many of us take psychology classes (and perhaps become psychologists) because we want to *understand* the reasons why individuals behave in certain ways. Presumably, if we understand why and how a certain behavior occurs, we would be able to provide an explanation for that behavior or behavior pattern. Understanding (explaining) behavior is certainly a legitimate and worthy objective, but understanding is not the only reason we study psychology.

If our explanations are correct, we should be able to *predict* what individuals will do under certain circumstances, and through careful observation we should be able to determine whether our prediction is confirmed. We become more confident about our explanations (or at least that they are on the right track) when our predictions are confirmed. Of course, there is the possibility that we were right for the wrong reason; that is, our predictions are confirmed even though our explanation is incorrect. On the other hand, if our predictions are not confirmed, then we know there is something incorrect or lacking in our explanations.

There are many ways to test our explanations and predictions. Sometimes the only way to test an explanation is by observing individuals in certain circumstances. When predictions are based on characteristics of the individual (gender, age, social group, etc.), we can observe whether individuals with those characteristics behave the way we predicted. A more rigorous way to test explanations and predictions is through systematic experiments. Well-conceived and well-executed experiments are the best way to eliminate alternative explanations of observed behavior. In the language of experimental psychology, *our proposed explanation* is our **theory**, and *the prediction derived from that explanation* is our **experimental** hypothesis. The **independent variable** in our experiment (*what we do to the subjects*) and the **dependent variable** (*what we observe the subjects do after experiencing the independent variable*) are based on our prediction (i.e., individuals who *have* this experience will behave in a certain way under certain circumstances, and individuals who *lack* this experience will behave in other ways under the same circumstances).

If we really understand the mechanisms and processes that underlie and influence an individual's behavior, we should also be able to *affect the future occurrence* of that individual's behavior. Socializing children involves getting them to behave in certain ways, and the purpose of psychotherapy is to provide experiences that will help people change the way they behave. *The study of learning focuses on how experiences change behavior.* Therefore, understanding the mechanisms and processes that are involved in learning hopefully will (1) provide us with an *understanding* of how and why individuals behave differently after experiencing certain things, (2) help us *predict* what individuals will do after they experience these things, and (3) give us tools for *influencing and changing* behavior.

For about 100 years, psychologists have been studying the effects of procedures that we now call conditioning. *The therapeutic application of the principles of operant conditioning to effect behavior change* is called **behavior modification**, and *the therapeutic application of the principles of Pavlovian conditioning to effect behavior change* is called **behavior therapy**.

Much of the research described in this book involves the study of the behavior of animals (primarily rats and pigeons) under rather artificial conditions, and some readers might be tempted to dismiss this research as having no relevance to the behavior of humans. Rather than dismiss this research out of hand, you should approach it with a skeptical eye and reserve judgment until after you have attempted to apply the principles of learning presented in this book to human behavior. Like physicists who study balls rolling down inclined planes; chemists who isolate pure elements and combine them under controlled conditions; and biologists who use peas, fruit flies, and bacteria to study heredity, we increase our understanding of behavior by removing individuals from their natural environments and studying them under controlled conditions. This allows us to see more clearly the basic principles at work; then we can see whether what we have learned in the laboratory has relevance to the non-laboratory situation. It is an empirical question whether what we observe in animals applies to humans and whether what we observe with human subjects in the laboratory is relevant to behavior outside the laboratory.

A large part of this book is about Pavlovian and operant conditioning. Because these procedures are studied under controlled conditions in the laboratory, you may believe that they are not relevant to everyday life. If you believe this, you are in for a surprise. Pavlovian conditioning is about learning to anticipate the occurrence of important events. Operant conditioning is about learning what to do or not do to obtain things you want and what to do or not do to avoid unpleasant events. As you learn about these procedures, you should begin to see them in your everyday experiences.

The study of learning and conditioning has undergone profound changes in the last 40 or so years. We no longer think of conditioning as an automatic process to which subjects passively react; now we view conditioning as reflecting a process of causal inference about the predictors of important events in their lives. We recognize that the effects of those things we call reinforcers are relative, not absolute, and we no longer think of reinforcers as strengtheners of preceding behavior; now we understand that they are part of what subjects learn. The cognitive revolution in psychology has forced us to reassess our views of what subjects learn and how they learn. You may be surprised to see discussions of expectancies, choice, knowledge, and memory in animals.

Physics and chemistry have atomic theory to provide them with an overarching theory lending coherence and structure to our understanding of the physical environment. Physics also has Einstein's theory of relativity to aid our understanding of the cosmos and quantum mechanics to guide our understanding of subatomic particles. Biology has Darwin's doctrine of evolution by natural selection to provide coherence and structure to our understanding of living systems. What is the overarching theory for psychology? There was a time in the not-too-distant past when many of us thought that the principle of reinforcement would provide us with such a theory of behavior. We no longer believe that. Perhaps we should take our cue from biology and use the doctrine of evolution by natural selection as our overarching theory for understanding behavior.

By adopting the doctrine of evolution by natural selection, we focus on the adaptive functions of psychological processes like learning. When we do that, an individual's learning abilities are understood in the context of the environment in which that individual lives (or that individual's ancestors lived), and learning is viewed as one of the adaptations that enable members of different species to survive.

We still believe that there are general principles of learning, but we no longer believe that all species learn in exactly the same way. There are some things that members of some species learn about very rapidly, and other things that they have great difficulty learning. You will find many examples throughout this book.

It is fair to say that in psychology there is more that we do *not* know about behavior than we do know. This is true for every area of psychology, including the study of learning. Nevertheless, after 100 years of scientific study, we are at the point when we can put together a coherent account of the psychological process we call learning. You may find it disconcerting that we do not know more or that there is not universal agreement about psychological processes like learning, but those of us who study psychology enjoy the intellectual challenge of trying to understand why people and animals behave the way they do. We suspect that most of you are interested in psychology for the same reason. With that thought, we turn our attention to what we currently know about the psychological process called learning.

1

WHERE LEARNING FITS INTO THE BIG PICTURE

We tend to take the ability to learn for granted, perhaps because it is so central to our lives. What we know, how we think about ourselves, and many of the things we do every day reflect what we have learned. The ability to learn and transmit what we have learned to others has done more to shape the course of human history than perhaps any other ability we possess. Thirty thousand years ago our ancestors lived in caves, and it appears from the fossil record that they had the same cranial capacity and presumably the same intellectual capacity as we do (Bolles, 1985). Over the next 30,000 years, we humans learned to farm, domesticate animals, exploit natural resources for minerals, and build structures. We created social systems, governments, religions, cultures, and techniques to preserve and transmit what we learned. The modern, technological, urban society we inhabit is the result of the accumulation and transmission of that knowledge. Much of this accumulated knowledge is passed down to us in books. This is a book about learning, but it is not about learning from books. This is a book about learning from firsthand experience, the way our ancestors first learned to do some of the things we read about in books. We will review some of the ways knowledge can be transmitted between individuals in the last chapter of this book.

Most of what we know how to do and most of the knowledge we use in our daily lives we learned from our parents (or other caregivers), from interactions with our peers, by observing what others do and what happens to them, by direct observation of the relationships between events in our environment, by trial and error, and from the "school of hard knocks." At an early age we learned to use the "potty" and a language for communication. As we grew older, we learned what is appropriate and inappropriate behavior, proper manners, and social skills. We learned how to ride bicycles and drive automobiles, how to perform at sports and other athletic activities, how to play games, how to win friends and influence people, how to flirt, and how to get out of unpleasant situations. We learned to identify the signs that something good is about to happen and the warning signals of danger. Over time, we developed likes and dislikes and emotional reactions to various things we encounter.

At some point in our lives, we learned that the color of the traffic signal is important: a green light signifies that it is safe to cross the street; a red light signifies that it is not safe. We learned the significance of the traffic signal colors through some combination of verbal instructions (including praise and scolding) and observations of others. What we do when the light is a particular color reflects what we learned.

There is an important distinction here. Although learning is something individuals do, it is not an observable activity. We can observe what someone experiences and how he or she behaves after that experience. We attribute changes in behavior to the prior experience and infer that these new behaviors are learned behaviors. **Learning** is the name we give to *the psychological process (or processes) by which knowledge is acquired from experience*. **Learned behavior** *reflects the acquisition of that knowledge*.

WHAT IS KNOWLEDGE?

Knowledge is internally stored information about the world and about how to do things. We make a distinction between two types of knowledge: declarative knowledge (knowing that) and procedural knowledge (knowing how).

If learning is the psychological process (or processes) by which knowledge is acquired from experience, then what is knowledge? The philosopher David Pears (1971) notes that no one has yet provided a universally accepted answer to this seemingly simple and direct question. If asked to provide a list of things that we know and activities we know how to do, all of us would readily oblige with a rather long list of both, and we would be sure that the things we know are true. Now, try to write a definition of "knowledge" that separates what we identify as knowledge from beliefs, opinions, and superstitions. The difficulty with any definition of knowledge becomes apparent when we are confronted with another person who disagrees with us and is just as certain about what he or she "knows" to be true.[1]

The lack of a widely accepted definition of knowledge in philosophy does not stop us in psychology from trying to understand how individuals obtain and store knowledge. Psychologists tend to focus on how experience is encoded and stored in memory as opposed to what knowledge is, and we tend to be more concerned with what individuals *believe* to be true rather than whether what they believe is *indeed* true. Thus, for psychologists, **knowledge** is *internally stored information about the world and about how to do things*. Notice that this definition includes two types of knowledge: declarative knowledge (knowing that) and procedural knowledge (knowing how; see, e.g., Cohen & Squire, 1980; Ryle, 1949).

Declarative knowledge (knowing that) is *knowledge about the world*. This includes knowledge about attributes of objects (the sky is blue), general information (George Washington was the first president of the United States), past events (what we did yesterday), the meaning of concepts (freedom is the opportunity to behave in the absence of restraint), the significance of things (red lights mean stop, green lights mean go, amber

---

[1]The branch of philosophy called epistemology deals with what knowledge is and how we acquire it. The traditional definition of knowledge that goes back to Plato and Aristotle identifies knowledge as justified true belief; however, one person's "justified true belief" may not be another's. This is why it is not easy to answer the question "What is knowledge?"

lights mean drive faster), and the relationships between events (the sound of a siren may be followed by the appearance of an emergency vehicle). Thus, when we state a fact, explain a concept, or describe an event or the relationship between events, we are exhibiting declarative knowledge. Tulving (1972, 1985) argued that in humans, declarative knowledge is stored in two separate memory systems: *Facts, ideas, and concepts (which are conveyed to us through language) are stored in* a **semantic memory** system, and *personally experienced events and episodes are stored in* an **episodic memory** system. In this book, we are primarily concerned with knowledge obtained through personal experience (episodic memories), although in Chapter 13 we will examine how verbal instructions can sometimes influence behavior.

Procedural knowledge (knowing how) is *knowledge of how to do something*. Examples of procedural knowledge include skilled actions (driving an automobile, riding a bicycle, typing with a touch typing system as opposed to hunt and peck, playing a musical instrument) and certain cognitive abilities (speaking the English language, solving certain types of mathematical problems). Thus, we are demonstrating procedural knowledge when we do things in an efficient manner.

Another distinction between declarative and procedural knowledge is that *declarative knowledge tends to be* **explicit knowledge**; that is, we humans are usually *able to tell others what we know. Procedural knowledge tends to be* **implicit knowledge**; that is, *we can demonstrate that we can do something but may not be able to describe how we did it.* Most of us know how to drive automobiles and ride bicycles, but can you explain to someone else in detail how you do it? We learned to do these things efficiently through practice, not just by observing others or by being told how to do them. (See Figure 1.1 for a summary of the various types of knowledge.)

Throughout our lives we acquire declarative knowledge (both semantic and episodic) about events and the relationships between events. Thus we learn, for example, the names of objects and people, the meaning of things like the colors of traffic lights, and the relationships between events like the presence of certain dark clouds in the sky and impending rain. We also learn how to read, write, and speak certain languages, and we learn motor skills like driving automobiles, tying our shoes, and shooting baskets.

There is a great deal of evidence that declarative knowledge and procedural knowledge are stored in different areas of the brain. People with damage to certain areas of their brains show deficits on either declarative knowledge or procedural knowledge but not both (e.g., Cohen & Squire, 1980; Squire, 2004; Knowlton, Mangels, & Squire, 1996), and functional neuroimaging studies with non–brain damaged people indicate that declarative learning and procedural learning are stored in different locations (e.g., Brown & Robertson, 2007; Hazeltine, Grafton, & Ivry, 1997; Honda, Deiber, Ibanez, Pascal-Leone, Zhuang, & Hallet, 1998; Willingham, Salidis, & Gabrieli, 2002).

It is important for us to keep the distinction between declarative knowledge (knowing that) and procedural knowledge (knowing how) in mind because some kinds of learned behaviors appear to reflect declarative knowledge and other kinds of learned behaviors appear to reflect procedural knowledge (Mackintosh, 1985). Furthermore, some learned behaviors appear to reflect declarative knowledge early in training and procedural knowledge after prolonged training (Adams, 1982; Dickinson, 1985, 1994).

Figure 1.1   The Various Types of Knowledge

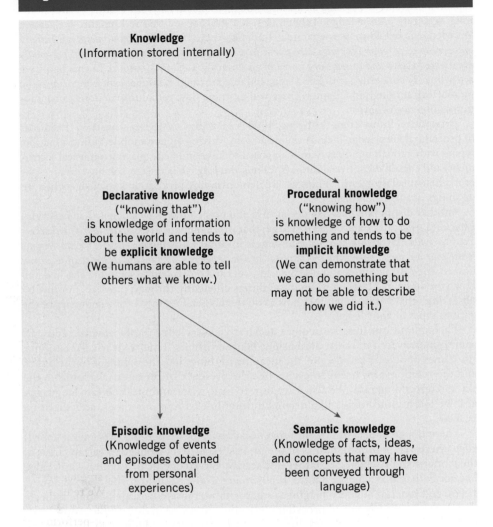

Knowledge
(Information stored internally)

Declarative knowledge
("knowing that")
is knowledge of information
about the world and tends to
be **explicit knowledge**
(We humans are able to tell
others what we know.)

Procedural knowledge
("knowing how")
is knowledge of how to do
something and tends to be
implicit knowledge
(We can demonstrate that
we can do something but
may not be able to describe
how we did it.)

Episodic knowledge
(Knowledge of events
and episodes obtained
from personal
experiences)

Semantic knowledge
(Knowledge of facts, ideas,
and concepts that may have
been conveyed through
language)

HOW CAN WE STUDY SOMETHING WE CANNOT SEE?

Learning is the psychological process by which knowledge is acquired from experience. Because we cannot observe psychological processes like learning directly, we must infer how they work by observing behavior. We study learning and other psychological processes by conducting experiments to test hypotheses about these processes.

We study psychology in order to understand why individuals do what they do. Although we can observe someone's behavior and note regularities, there is only so much we can learn from simple observation. How many times have you had a discussion with someone about a third person's behavior in which both of you had different explanations for what the subject of your conversation did? It is easy to come up with explanations for behavior, but it is much more difficult to come up with the correct explanation. Without some way to test an explanation, we have no way of deciding whether it is correct or not. That is why we bring individuals into the laboratory and observe them under controlled conditions. By systematically manipulating the experiences of our subjects and observing how they behave, we can test our explanations of learning and other psychological processes.

Learning and Performance

We study learning by giving individuals certain experiences and observing how those experiences change behavior. We infer what is learned by relating how given experiences lead to changes in behavior (performance).

How do we know that someone (perhaps you) has learned something? The only way to tell is by observing that person's behavior. For example, how will your instructor assess what you have learned from reading this book? Most likely, he or she will infer what you have learned from your performance on a test. Fundamental to using test performance to measure learning are two *assumptions:* One assumption is that students who pay attention in class, take good notes, go home and study those notes, read and study the textbook, and reflect on the information they are exposed to in the course will learn something. Even if we observe you while you are doing these things, we cannot tell whether you are learning; you may be "going through the motions" and not paying attention. (How often have you stared at a page of a textbook and not been reading it?) That leads to the second assumption: Your performance on the test reflects what you learned; that is, good grades reflect that you have learned a lot, and poor grades reflect that you did not learn much. The point is that what your instructor observes when he or she grades your test is not learning but the results of learning. Furthermore, most of us have had the experience of studying hard for a test only to receive a low score. We say we studied, and we believe we learned something, but our performance did not reflect it. We refer to this as the **learning-performance problem**: *the only way we can study learning is by observing performance, but performance may not always reflect learning.* The learning-performance problem requires us to consider carefully the tests we use to try to reveal that learning has occurred.

How We Study Learning

We study learning by giving individuals certain experiences and observing their behavior at a later point in time. We attribute long-term changes between pre- and post-experience performance to learning.

In order to study learning (which we cannot see but which may be reflected in behavior), we compare an individual's behavior at two different points in time: We provide an individual with an experience, and then at a later time we observe the behavior of that individual again. If the behavior at that later time depends on the earlier experience, we infer that the observed change in behavior is due to learning (Rescorla & Holland, 1976). We can do this in a variety of ways: We can observe the individual before and after the initial experience (repeated measurements on the same individual) or compare those who had the experience (the experimental subjects) with those who did not have it (the control subjects). Either way, *we infer that learning has occurred when an individual's behavior at a later time is changed from what it would have been if he or she had not had the earlier experience.*

A word of caution is in order: Not all changes in behavior reflect learning. Some changes in behavior can be due to other processes. For example, the experience of engaging in vigorous exercise can bring on fatigue, and exposure to viruses and bacteria can lead to fevers, aches, and pains (as well as changes in behavior), but we do not attribute any of these changes to learning. We attribute to learning some of the strategies the individual employs to overcome the physical distress brought on by the illness when the individual does these things each time he or she becomes ill. Similarly, physical injury to some parts of the body can lead to behavior changes, but we do not attribute these changes to learning, although the individual may learn to compensate for the injury. Some behavior changes may be due to changes in the availability of desirable things (like food, water, or sexual partners) or to unpleasant stimulation. We attribute these changes in behavior to changes in motivation, although motivational states can be aroused as a result of learning and individuals can learn ways to gain access to desirable things and escape from unpleasant stimulation. *We attribute changes in behavior to learning when the changes are long term and appear to reflect the acquisition of knowledge about the experience or how to deal with the experience.* Changes in behavior due to fatigue, infections, the availability of desirable things, and unpleasant stimulation typically last only as long as the precipitating factor is present (or during recovery); these are not long-term changes. Permanent injuries and chronic illnesses produce long-term effects, but these effects are due to the injury or illness, not the acquisition of knowledge.

The starting point in the study of learning is the experience of the individual; however, what an individual experiences depends on who that individual is and the nature of the event. In order for an individual to experience something, he or she must be able to sense it. Bees can sense ultraviolet light; we cannot. Dogs can sense high frequency sounds; we cannot. These are stimuli that bees and dogs can learn about; we cannot. On the other hand, there are stimuli that we do not notice even though we have the sensory capability to experience them: We may not notice a spot on an x-ray image that a radiologist recognizes as a malignant growth. We have the sensory capacity to see the spot, but only the radiologist understands what it means. Because the presence of a stimulus does not guarantee that an individual will experience it, *the study of learning involves identifying the aspects of the earlier situation that are critical to the effect we observe at a later time.* Shettleworth (1994) calls these the **conditions of learning**. We attempt to discover the conditions of learning by manipulating various aspects of the situation and observing the effects they have on the subject's behavior at a later time. *The things* *we systematically manipulate in an experiment* are called the independent variables. The independent variables are the procedures. We will use the term procedure here in a wider sense to designate *the events and arrangements between events individuals encounter or are presented with in an experiment.*

The study of learning involves relating earlier experiences (procedures) to the behavior of the subject at a later time. *When the individual behaves differently at a later time* as a result of the earlier experience, we infer that he or she learned something. We refer to this change in behavior as the phenomenon of learning. *In psychological experiments, the behavior of the subjects* is called the dependent variable. We will use the term phenomenon to refer to *the behavior of individuals after they have experienced certain events and relationships between events (procedures).*

As we noted in a previous section, the study of learning is complicated by the learning-performance problem: *The only way we can study learning is by observing performance, but performance may not always reflect learning.* When we test whether learning has occurred, the conditions determine whether one will observe behavior that reflects learning. If the situation at the time of the test is inadequate to trigger retrieval of the relevant knowledge from memory, individuals may not demonstrate what they have learned. In other words, the problem may be a problem of memory, not a lack of learning. Clearly, learning and memory go together: There can be no learning without a mechanism for storing knowledge (memory), and there can be no expression of learning in behavior unless that knowledge can be retrieved from memory. There is abundant evidence that the expression of learning depends on the relationship between the conditions at the time of the experience and the conditions at the time of the test (Spear & Riccio, 1994).

Another important factor is the motivation of the individual. Motivation is the psychological process that provides impetus and direction to behavior. Motivation can be manipulated by depriving individuals of certain things (e.g., food, water, sexual activity, sensory stimulation), by providing stimulation (e.g., stimulation that produces discomfort, stimulation that arouses), and by the presence of desirable items or opportunities to engage in desirable activities. Without adequate motivation, what has been learned may not be reflected in the individual's behavior when the test occurs. Therefore, although learning may have occurred, it might not be reflected in the individual's behavior if the situation when the test occurs is not adequate to trigger memories of what was learned, the level of motivation is inadequate to provide impetus for the performance of certain behaviors, or both.

The term *"phenomenon of learning"* could imply that the observed behavior change is learning, but that is not correct. The change in behavior between the experience and the test is the *result* of learning; it is *not* the learning itself. Our task as students of learning is to explain how prior experience produces the observed long-term changes in later behavior.

Linking Experiences to Changes in Behavior. As psychologists, we are interested in how experiences (procedures) produce changes in behavior. There are three general approaches to linking experiences with changes in behavior.

One approach is to explain the observed relationship between procedures and phenomena by specifying the conditions of that relationship in terms of a principle. A **principle** is *a statement describing the relationship between the procedure and the phenomenon* (Bitterman, 1975; Johnston, 1981; Shettleworth, 1983). It is a generally accepted principle that learning is affected by the temporal interval between events: The shorter the interval, the easier it is for subjects to make a connection between the two events. Although learning can occur with long interevent intervals, there is an advantage with short intervals (see, e.g., Smith & Roll, 1967). Sometimes we give these principles the status of laws, as in the case of what we call the "matching law": In a two-choice situation, subjects will distribute their behavior to match the relative values of the alternatives (Baum & Rachlin, 1969; Herrnstein, 1970). Principles and laws are stated in terms of observable events (procedures and phenomena). They tell us how the conditions of learning are related to the phenomenon of learning, but they do not tell us anything about the internal mechanisms or processes involved in learning. This approach is the basis for the kind of behaviorism espoused by B. F. Skinner (1945, 1950, 1974).

At the other extreme, we can try to explain learning in terms of the structure and function of the nervous system. It is obvious that the nervous system is the organ system for all psychological processes, including learning. Great strides have been made in our understanding of the nervous system and how neural functioning relates to learning. We have evidence that certain kinds of experiences produce changes in brain cells (see Rosenzweig & Bennett, 1996; Weiler, Hawrylak, & Greenough, 1995) and that NMDA receptors may be involved in learning (Faneslow, 1993). We also have evidence that the different regions of the mammalian brain, such as the amygdala, brainstem, cerebellum, cortex, hippocampus, striatum, and median temporal lobe, are involved in learning in various ways (see, e.g., Balleine & O'Doherty, 2010; Gluck & Myers, 1995; Jog, Kubota, Connolly, Hillegaart, & Graybiel, 1999; Knowlton et al., 1996; Maren, Phan, & Liberzon, 2013; Reilly, 2009; Schmajuk & DiCarlo, 1992; Squire, 1992; Steinmetz, 1998; Thompson, 2013; White, Packard, & McDonald, 2013). However, despite these advances in our knowledge of how experiences affect neural structures, we are not yet able to explain how complex experiences are encoded in the nervous system and how that encoding translates into behavior. Nevertheless, *an explanation based on changes in the structure and function of the nervous system would describe the physiological mechanisms of learning.*

A middle ground between a purely behavioral account of learning and an account in terms of neural functioning and changes in neural structures is to explain learning in terms of inferred psychological processes. This level of explanation is the most common one employed in psychology. Borrowing from Tolman (1932), we label learning and other psychological processes **intervening variables**. They are called this because they provide *a conceptual link between the independent variable (procedure) and the dependent variable (phenomenon)*. This conceptual link provides a psychological explanation of the observed relationship between the two observed variables (independent and dependent). When we invoke learning as an intervening variable, we are theorizing about how individuals extract information from sensory experiences, process that information, and store the knowledge obtained. Certainly this involves changes in neural structures and function, but even without a complete understanding of the neurophysiology involved, we can construct theories about how these psychological processes (the intervening

Table 1.1 Procedures, Phenomena, and Processes as They Relate to Learning

Procedure (independent variable)	Process Phenomena (intervening variable)	Phenomena (dependent variable)
A new experience for the individual.	**Learning** Our theoretical explanation for why an individual's behavior is affected by his or her experiences	Observed long-term changes in the individual's behavior as a result of his or her earlier experiences

variables) operate and test our theories by conducting experiments. Therefore, *learning is the psychological process we invoke to explain how experiences influence later behavior. This psychological process involves the acquisition of knowledge, and we infer that individuals have obtained knowledge based on their behavior* (see Table 1.1).

DEFINING VARIOUS KINDS OF LEARNING BY PROCEDURES AND PHENOMENA

There are a number of procedures that can produce learning, and the behavior changes that result from these procedures take various forms. We classify various kinds of learning by what the individual experiences (procedures) and the resulting behaviors (phenomena).

Learning occurs when certain experiences lead to long-term changes in behavior that reflect the acquisition of knowledge about that experience. Although learning is a psychological process (an intervening variable), we classify various types of learning in terms of both procedures (what the individual experiences) and the phenomena (observed changes in behavior). The various forms of learning described here are summarized in Table 1.2 at the end of this section.

Habituation

The procedure for producing habituation is the repeated presentation of a stimulus that is not harmful or has no bearing on an individual's welfare. The phenomenon of habituation is the reduction in responsiveness to that stimulus. Habituation is specific to the original stimulus and to stimuli that are similar to it.

The simplest procedure for producing learning is to present to individuals the same stimulus repeatedly. We have all had the experience of being distracted by sounds (e.g., conversation, music) while trying to study, but if the volume is not too high, our responses to these distractions diminish. This *diminution of responsiveness to a stimulus is* the phenomenon of habituation. The procedure for producing habituation is the *repeated presentation of a stimulus that is not harmful or has no bearing on an individual's welfare.*

Ornitz and Guthrie (1989) provided a rather nice demonstration of the development of the phenomenon of habituation in humans under laboratory conditions. Their subjects were 18- to 34-year-old males who came to the laboratory for five daily sessions. The independent variable in this experiment was the repeated presentation to these subjects of a short loud sound (105-decibel burst of white noise[2] for 50 milliseconds [1/20th of a second]) at various times during the five experimental sessions, while they watched silent movies of their choice. The dependent variable was their startle reflex to the noise, which was measured by recording the contractions of the muscles around their eyes (blinking). The results of this experiment are presented in Figure 1.2.

Each line in Figure 1.2 represents the mean amplitude of the eyeblink response across the 20 presentations of the loud noise (grouped in blocks of four trials) for each of the five

Figure 1.2   Amplitude of the startle response to a loud noise across five successive blocks of four trials each for five successive days.

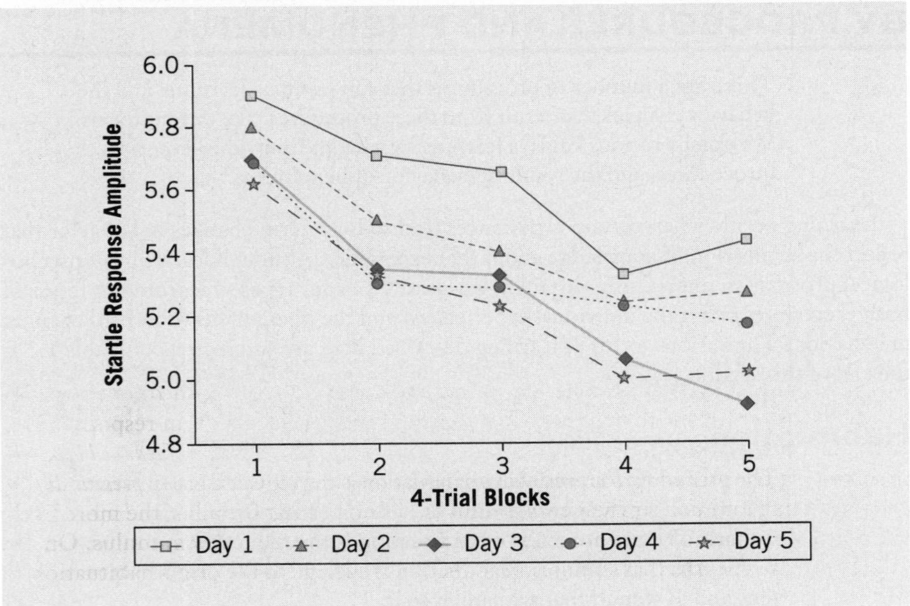

From Ornitz and Guthrie, 1989. Redrawn with permission of Cambridge University Press.

---

[2]White noise is composed of the entire range of frequencies of sounds. It sounds like radio static.

days the individuals were in the experiment. Notice that within each day, the muscle contractions involved in the startle response to the loud noise decreased in amplitude. More important, notice that the amplitude of this startle response decreased across days: The startle response was the strongest on the first block of four trials on Day 1 and was overall highest throughout the Day 1 session. The startle response was lower on Day 2, and lower yet on Days 3, 4, and 5.

These data illustrate the phenomenon of habituation: With repeated exposure to the loud noise, the startle reflex showed a long-term decline that partially carried over to the next day. This carryover is an indication that the reduction in startle cannot be due to fatigue or some other short-term process. If it were, the level of startle would have been the same at the beginning of each day, but that did not happen. However, there was some recovery of the startle response between the end of the previous day's session and the start of the next session. (The startle response was always higher on the first block of trials of a daily session than it was on the last block of the previous day). This *recovery of the target behavior after an interval of time in which there is no stimulation* is the phenomenon of **spontaneous recovery**. The amount of spontaneous recovery depends on the length of the time interval when there is no stimulation: In general, the longer the interval, the greater the amount of spontaneous recovery, and, in some situations, the recovery can be complete.

Another long-term effect of exposure to repeated stimulation can be seen in Figure 1.2. Notice that the startle response declined faster on Days 2 through 5 (particularly between blocks 1 and 2) than on Day 1. This is another indication that habituation is due to learning. If it were not, then the rates of decline on each day should be the same. Although spontaneous recovery is akin to forgetting, the more rapid rates of decline in startle on each succeeding day illustrate an important and frequently observed characteristic of learning that we have all experienced: We may not be able to recall or recognize something, or remember how to perform a skilled task, but relearning that information or skill tends to occur faster than the original learning. This is strong evidence that once you have learned something, you are always different.

Another characteristic of habituation is that it is *stimulus specific*. By this, we mean that after repeated exposure to one stimulus, the decline in responsiveness is specific to that stimulus and to stimuli that closely resemble that stimulus. For example, if the stimulus is a tone of a certain frequency presented repeatedly, the individual will develop habituation to that tone and to tones that are close to it in frequency. The closer the other tone is to the original tone, the more the reduction in response. This latter phenomenon is called **stimulus generalization**: *The occurrence of learned behavior to stimuli not present during training that are similar to the stimuli that were present during training.* The more similar the new stimulus is to the training stimulus, the more likely the learned pattern of behavior will occur in response to that new stimulus. On the other hand, if the stimulus is a specific tone, there will be little or no habituation to white noise that sounds very different from a tone.

Thompson and Spencer (1966; see also Rankin et al., 2009) observed that the phenomenon we call habituation includes (but is not limited to) the following characteristics:

1. Repeated exposure to a specific stimulus results in decreased responsiveness to that stimulus.

2. The weaker that stimulus, the more rapid the decrease in responsiveness (habituation may not occur to strong or unpleasant stimuli).

3. The response to that stimulus may return after a period of no exposure (spontaneous recovery).

4. The effect is specific to the original stimulus except that habituation of responsiveness to one stimulus may occur to similar stimuli (stimulus generalization).

5. *Presentation of another (usually strong) stimulus typically results in a temporary increase in responsiveness to the original stimulus.* This phenomenon is called **dishabituation** and is taken as evidence that habituation is the result of an active learning process, not just fatigue or sensory adaptation.

Habituation is not limited to startle responses to auditory and tactile stimuli. For example, humans exhibit more habituation of salivation to the repeated presentation of the same food cues than they do when the food cues are varied across presentations (e.g., Temple, Giacomelli, Roemmich, & Epstein, 2008). Habituation of sexual arousal to erotic materials and fantasies has been observed under laboratory conditions in both females (Meuwissen & Over, 1990) and males (O'Donohue & Plaud, 1991; Plaud, Gaither, Henderson, & Devitt, 1997). In both sexes, habituation is less when the erotic materials are varied, and arousal increases with the presentation of novel erotic stimuli (dishabituation).

Habituation has also been observed to occur in very primitive organisms. For example, Wood (1973) demonstrated habituation in the single-celled creature called *Stentor coeruleus*, and Rushforth, Burnett, and Maynard (1963) demonstrated habituation in *Hydra pirardi*, a small multi-celled creature closely related to jellyfish. The nervous system in the hydra is a loose network of neurons distributed around the body with no concentration in one spot. Both species live in water, and when disturbed, both species contract. In these experiments, the stimulation was agitating the water, and in both experiments, the animals gradually habituated to the agitation. To demonstrate that the effect is stimulus specific, a light was used as a second stimulus. There was no habituation to the light.

Being able to learn to ignore frequently occurring stimuli that are not harmful or have no bearing on an individual's welfare is clearly an adaptive specialization for that individual. Otherwise, the individual would be constantly distracted by these harmless things.

Sensitization

The procedure for producing sensitization is exposure to dangerous or painful stimulation. The phenomenon of sensitization is an increase in responsiveness to a wide variety of stimuli. Sensitization appears to be involved in posttraumatic stress disorder.

On the other hand, *exposure to dangerous or painful stimulation* can influence an individual to the point where he or she responds defensively to routine events. We call this *enhanced responsiveness* sensitization. Sensitization is not stimulus specific; in fact, it is characterized by heightened responsivity to a wide variety of stimuli. Davis (1989) provided a nice demonstration of the phenomenon of sensitization in rats. In this study, the stimulus that caused the sensitization was electric shock, and sensitization was demonstrated with a loud noise (105-decibel noise at a rate of two per minute). Davis measured the amplitude of his rats' startle responses with a device that recorded how much the rats moved after each burst of noise. Before he presented the first loud noise, he gave half of his rats 10 footshocks of moderate intensity in rapid succession. The other half of the rats received no shock. All rats then received a total of 80 presentations of the noise (at a rate of 2 per minute) over the next 40 minutes. The results of this study are presented in Figure 1.3.

The difference in level of startle between the two groups of rats in Figure 1.3 represents sensitization in the group that was shocked. Note that the startle response habituated for the nonshocked rats, and it started to habituate later in the session for the shocked rats. In another experiment reported in the same paper, Davis showed

Figure 1.3   Mean amplitude of startle responses over successive 1-minute periods following a series of 10 footshocks before the first burst of noise (solid) or no footshock (open).

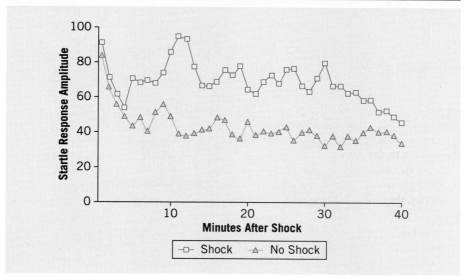

Redrawn with permission from M. Davis, 1989. Sensitization of the acoustic startle reflex by footshock. *Behavioral Neuroscience, 103,* 495–503. Copyright © 1989 by the American Psychological Association.

that this effect is not due to Pavlovian conditioning. Davis also demonstrated that this sensitization effect was more pronounced after 5 or 10 shocks than after a single shock and more pronounced after stronger shocks. Greenwald, Bradley, Cuthbert, and Lang (1998) provided a similar demonstration of sensitization in human subjects in the laboratory.

The effects of exposure to the shocks in the experiment described above were rather short term; however, when Garrick, Morrow, Shalev, and Eth (2001) gave rats 30 tail shocks over 30 minutes on one day and five more over 30 minutes the second day, they found that one-third of their rats did not show a reduction in startle responses when tested repeatedly over a three-week period. Dykman, Ackerman, and Newton (1997) presented the case that the clinical condition known as posttraumatic stress disorder is the result of sensitization resulting from exposure to chronic stressors or a single traumatic event. See Box 1.1 for how the phenomenon of sensitization helps us understand one of the mechanisms involved in posttraumatic stress disorder.

Sensitization and Posttraumatic Stress Disorder

Posttraumatic stress disorder (PTSD) is the name we give to a cluster of symptoms that occur in some people who experience severe traumas such as physical and sexual assault, natural disasters, war, and torture. A complete list of these symptoms can be found in the DSM-V (American Psychiatric Association, 2013). The diagnosis of PTSD relies heavily on self-report of the symptoms (e.g., recurrent and distressing memories and dreams, avoidance of associated activities and situations, difficulty concentrating); however, one symptom in the list, exaggerated startle response, is one of the commonly reported symptoms (Davidson, Hughes, Blazer, & George, 1991; McFarlane, 1988), and, in addition to self-report, it can be measured directly (see Pitman et al., 2012, for a review). Morgan, Grillon, Southwick, Davis, and Charney (1996) demonstrated that Gulf War veterans with PTSD have greater startle responses to bursts of white noise than Gulf War veterans without PTSD.

They subjected three groups of volunteers to a series of short bursts of randomly presented intensities of white noise (which sounds like radio static): Gulf war veterans diagnosed as having PTSD, Gulf War veterans from the same units as the subjects in the first group but without PTSD, and civilians with no combat experience and without PTSD. There are two independent variables here: The status of the subjects (veterans with PTSD, veterans from same units without PTSD, and civilians without PTSD) and the different intensities of the white noise (ranging from 90 to 114 decibels and repeatedly presented in random orders). The dependent variable was their startle reflex to the noise; this was measured by recording the contractions of the muscles around their eyes (blinking). The results of this experiment are presented in Figure 1.1.1.

These results are quite striking. On the first exposure to the loud noise (102 decibels for all subjects), the PTSD veterans exhibited a much higher level of startle, and except for

Figure 1.1.1   Magnitude of the startle response to a loud noise in Gulf War veterans with PTSD, Gulf War veterans from the same units without PTSD, and civilians without PTSD on the first exposure to the loud noise and as a function of various intensities of the noise across repeated exposures.

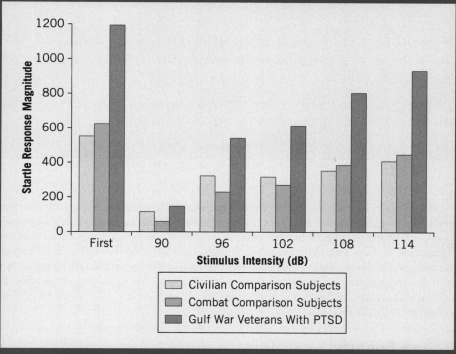

From C. A. Morgan, C. Grillon, S. M. Southwick, M. Davis, and D. S. Charney, D. S., 1996. Exaggerated acoustic startle reflex in Gulf War veterans with posttraumatic stress disorder. *American Journal of Psychiatry, 153*, 64–68. Copyright © 1996, the American Psychiatric Association. Redrawn by permission.

the lowest level of sound tested, they had higher levels of startle than the other two groups, which did not differ. Clearly there was some habituation to the loud noise as a result of repeated exposures. (Morgan et al., 1996 reported that the rate of habituation was similar for all groups, although they did not present these data.)

The veterans with PTSD said that the white noise was not reminiscent of the sounds of war; therefore, these results were not due to stimulus generalization. Therefore, Morgan et al. (1996) argued, the increased magnitude of startle reflected sensitization produced by the PTSD veterans' war experiences. In a later study, Grillon, Morgan, Davis, and

(Continued)

Southwick (1998) reported that the startle response is higher in the dark for citizens, non-PTSD Vietnam veterans, and PTSD Vietnam veterans, with the largest increase from the light to the dark condition exhibited by the PTSD veterans.

We may wonder why some people exposed to severe traumas get PTSD and others do not. Guthrie and Bryant (2005) measured physiological responses to acoustic stimuli in firefighters while they were recruits and after they had been exposed to a traumatic event. Elevated pretrauma startle responses predicted posttrauma startle responses. Pole, Neylan,

Otte, Henn-Haase, Metzler, and Marmar (2008) exposed police academy recruits to repeated 106-dB sounds under increasing levels of threat of electric shocks and took various measures of arousal and fear. They tested the same individuals after exposure to police-related trauma one year later and found that more severe PTSD symptoms were predicted by some of the measures taken earlier. These results suggest that some people may be vulnerable to anxiety disorders and PTSD. This information could help prevent PTSD by identifying those who might be vulnerable and taking remedial actions to protect them.

Sensitization typically requires fewer exposures than habituation, and a stimulus that ordinarily would result in habituation can produce sensitization in individuals who have been traumatized or aroused. In both habituation and sensitization, the procedure involves stimulation of some sort. Whether this stimulation produces habituation or sensitization depends on attributes of the stimulation and the state of the individual at the time of the stimulation: Sensitization is more likely to occur after exposure to sudden, dangerous, or painful stimulation, and individuals who are already aroused are more likely to exhibit sensitization (M. Davis, 1974).

Phase-Specific Learning

Some species appear to be sensitive to certain classes of stimulation at certain critical periods in their lives. When exposed to these stimuli during that critical period (procedure), individuals of these species rapidly learn something about the stimuli (phenomenon). One class of phase-specific learning is called imprinting. Here exposure to certain things leads to long-term attachment or responsiveness to those things. Song learning in some birds and language learning in humans are other examples of phase-specific learning.

Figure 1.4 shows three goslings (baby geese) trailing after the European biologist Konrad Lorenz. They are doing this because during a specific time after they hatched, he was present and moving around. This is one example of **phase-specific learning**, a form of learning that occurs rapidly when experiences involve *exposure to certain types of stimulation during specific times in an individual's life*. The kind of phase-specific learning

Figure 1.4 Precocial birds follow moving objects that they encounter during a certain "critical period" soon after hatching and become "imprinted" on those objects. Usually that object is their mother. The goslings in this picture became imprinted on Konrad Lorenz, the European naturalist who studied imprinting and other species-specific behaviors.

Reprinted with permission from Nina Leen/TimePix.

pictured in Figure 1.4 is called **imprinting**: *Exposure to certain things during specific times leads to long-term attachment or responsiveness to those things.* The kind of imprinting in that figure occurs in some species of precocial birds—that is, birds that are able to see and walk immediately after hatching. Most of the time, they encounter their mother soon after hatching and thus become imprinted on her, but it is obvious that they can imprint on other objects that have certain characteristics. Although there is a strong preference for objects that resemble the bird's own species, objects that move, make noise, and are not too small are likely candidates for imprinting. Konrad Lorenz "fits the bill" for these goslings.

The function of this kind of imprinting is for the birds to learn who their parents are so that they will attend to and follow them. In some species, this "filial imprinting" (imprinting to the parents) leads to "sexual imprinting," that is, learning who are appropriate mates. The attachment of baby monkeys to their mothers shares many of the characteristics of imprinting in birds: stimulus specificity (texture, temperature, size) during early periods of life (Harlow & Harlow, 1965; Harlow & Soumi, 1970). Although the situation is more complicated, there is evidence of an imprinting-like attachment process in humans (Schaffer & Emerson, 1964). Imprinting also is the process by which young salmon learn to identify the stream in which they were hatched so that they can return to it later to spawn (Hassler, Scholz, & Horral, 1978).

Song learning in some species of birds and language learning in humans are other forms of phase-specific learning. In both cases, exposure to certain stimulation during certain "critical periods" produces relatively efficient learning of specific vocal behaviors or languages (Lenneberg, 1967; Marler, 1976, 1987, 1991). For example, Newport (1990, 1991) looked at the competency with American Sign Language (ASL) of congenitally deaf individuals who learned ASL at various times in their lives. ASL is like other languages in terms of structure and grammatical complexity. Only 5%–10% of congenitally deaf children are exposed to ASL at birth because they are born into families with a deaf parent. Most deaf children are born to hearing parents, and they are typically not exposed to ASL before they are 4 years old, when they go to a residential school for the deaf where ASL is the language of daily interactions and not formally taught. However, not all deaf children attend residential schools for the deaf at that age; these people may learn ASL later, typically around 12 years of age. Newport tested adult deaf individuals (35–70 years old) who learned ASL at various ages. She found that the earlier the immersion in ASL, the more sophisticated their use of the ASL grammar and structure. Those who learned at or later than puberty showed basic word order and only the simplest aspects of grammar. Similar results were reported by Johnson and Newport (1989) with individuals whose first language was Korean or Chinese and who moved to the United States and were immersed in English from ages 3–39. The younger the immersion in English, the more complex their grammar and language morphology up to age 17. The scores on the language tests did not change after age 17. This does not mean that people cannot learn a new language after age 17. We can, and some of us are better than others at this. It does mean that most adults will not be as good as those who learned the language as young children.

In all three cases (imprinting, song learning, and language learning), there appears to be a critical period of sensitivity during which learning is highly likely to occur (although some learning can occur outside that critical period) and the individual appears to be sensitive to learn about certain types and patterns of stimulation (Immelmann & Soumi, 1981).

Pavlovian Conditioning

The procedure called Pavlovian conditioning involves presenting an individual with two events in some relationship to each other. As a result of that experience, the individual does something in the presence of one of those events that he or she did not do before (phenomenon).

No doubt you have read about Pavlov's experiments in which he trained a dog to salivate when a certain sound (ticking of a metronome) occurred (Figure 1.5). The standard procedure in his experiment was to start the metronome (event 1) and 1–5 seconds later, while the metronome was still ticking, deliver food into the dog's mouth (event 2). After a number of repetitions of this arrangement (metronome → food), the dogs salivated when the metronome was presented without the food. Dogs do not normally salivate when they hear metronomes, but they do when they learn that the metronome is a signal for something important (like food).

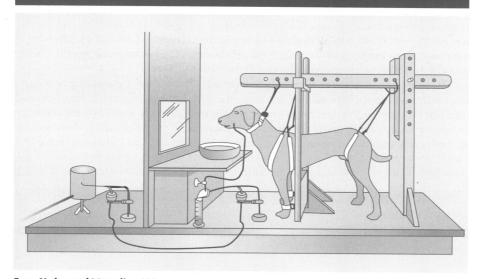

Figure 1.5 Diagram of Pavlov's apparatus for studying conditioned salivation in dogs. The tube running from the dog's cheek collected drops of saliva and conveyed the amounts to the recording device in the next room. The metronome, which was the conditioned stimulus in many of Pavlov's experiments, is not shown in this diagram.

From Yerkes and Morgulis, 1909.

The basic procedure for Pavlovian conditioning is to present two events in some relationship to each other. As a result of experiencing this relationship, the individual begins to do something to one of these events that he or she did not do before (like salivate after hearing the sound of a metronome). All of us have learned to associate signals with important events and behave accordingly when we experience those signals. Many common examples easily come to mind: What is the reason we tense up in the dentist's chair when we hear the sound of the drill motor? Why do we have an emotional reaction when we hear a siren or see a car with flashing lights coming up behind us? Why do we lose our appetite for certain foods after we have had the intestinal flu? All of these effects are due to Pavlovian conditioning, which is the subject of Chapter 2; therefore, we will postpone discussing them until then.

Operant Conditioning

The procedure called operant conditioning involves presenting or removing something when a behavior occurs. As a result, the individual is more or less likely to perform that behavior again in the future (phenomenon).

Along with Pavlov, the name that most people associate with the study of learning is B. F. Skinner, and most of us know that Skinner taught rats to press levers for food in an apparatus referred to as a "Skinner box" (Figure 1.6). Skinner's standard procedure is to reward a hungry rat with a small piece of food every time it presses the lever. The result is that the rate at which the rat presses the lever increases. As we will see in Chapter 7, there are three other varieties of operant conditioning. In addition to getting behaviors to occur more often by following them with rewards, operant conditioning can be used to get behaviors to occur more often by removing or preventing something bad (escape and avoidance). It can also be used to reduce the frequency of a behavior by following it with unpleasant events, such as something that hurts or the loss of privileges (like being grounded). These latter two procedures are forms of punishment.

Therefore, the basic procedures of operant conditioning involve presenting or removing something when a behavior occurs. The phenomenon is the change in that behavior (increase or decrease) depending on what is presented or taken away. We are all aware that rewards and punishments can affect our behavior and the behavior of others around us, but operant conditioning involves more than learning what and what not to do. It is

Figure 1.6 The "Skinner box." Every time the rat presses the lever, a pellet of food drops into the food tray.

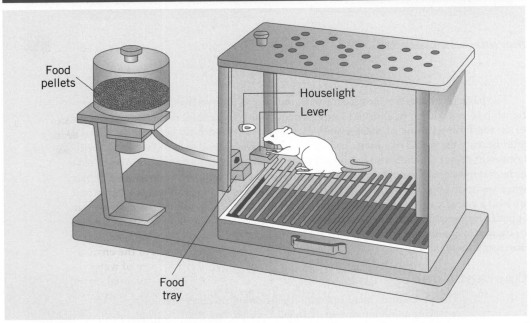

Food pellets

Houselight

Lever

Food tray

From *Learning: Behavior and Cognition*, 2nd edition, by D. A. Lieberman, copyright © 1993. Reprinted with permission of Wadsworth, a division of Cengage Learning.

through operant conditioning that we become more efficient in performing actions and learn how to adjust our behavior to meet the demands of a given situation. We will postpone a detailed discussion of operant conditioning until Part II of this book.

Social Learning

The procedures for various types of social learning involve observations of the behavior of another individual or instruction by another individual. That instruction can be spoken or written words, or it can be some form of physical guidance.

Although we humans continually learn from our exposure to the procedures of habituation, sensitization, Pavlovian conditioning, and operant conditioning, we are social beings and most of what we know we learned from others (Bandura, 1986). We call this **social learning**: *obtaining knowledge about events and the relationships between events, and how to perform actions efficiently, through interactions with others.*

There are a number of ways that we learn from others: We can learn by observing what others do or what happens to them (observational learning), through direct instruction when a teacher provides us with information (instructed learning), and by reading books (text-based learning). As we will see in Part III of this book, with the exception of text-based learning, social learning is not restricted to humans. The social learning of food preferences and aversions, what should be feared as potentially dangerous and who is a predator, and how to perform certain actions to obtain food have all been observed in a variety of species.

The various forms of learning described in this section are summarized in Table 1.2.

THE EVOLUTION OF LEARNING

The various forms of learning we observe both within and across species reflect the principle of natural selection. This principle is the basis for our understanding of why, how, and what individuals learn.

Every living being possesses a set of physical attributes and behavioral dispositions that it inherited from its parents. These attributes and dispositions are solutions to the problems of survival that an individual's ancestors faced during the course of its species' evolution. The exact nature of those problems depends on the characteristics of that species' ecological niche. A **niche** is *the set of physical and biological conditions in which the members of a species live.* These include the physical conditions of the environment (e.g., climate, moisture level, terrain for terrestrial species, salinity of water for aquatic species); sources of food, water, and shelter; the availability of potential mates; and the characteristics of predators. Most of these aspects of niches are not static; they can and do change over time. Change presents another problem for survival because the characteristics that enable survival under some conditions may not be relevant under others.

Table 1.2 Procedures and Phenomena for Various Kinds of Learning

Kind of learning	Procedure	Phenomenon
Habituation	Repeated presentation of a stimulus	Reduction in responsiveness to that stimulus
Sensitization	Presentation of a noxious stimulus	Increased responsiveness to that and other stimuli not present when the noxious stimulus occurred
Phase-specific learning (e.g., imprinting, song learning, language learning)	Presentation of a particular type of stimulus during a certain period in the individual's life	The rapid acquisition of a behavior pattern related to that stimulus. Acquisition is slower if the initial stimulus presentation is at another time.
Pavlovian conditioning	Presentation of two events in some relationship to each other	Behavior occurs in response to one of these events that did not occur in response to that event before
Operant conditioning	Presenting or removing something when a behavior occurs	Individual is more or less likely to perform that behavior in the future
Social learning		
Observational learning	Observing another individual behave in a certain way in a certain situation	Observer more likely to behave in the same way in that or similar situations
Instructed learning	A teacher provides information to pupil	The behavior of the pupil is affected by the instruction
Text-based learning	Reading about something	The behavior of the reader is affected by what is read

We observe that different species possess structures, systems, and behavior patterns that allow them to survive in specific niches. Some of the solutions are general and some are quite specific. For example, most living things are sensitive to light in some way, and many species possess specialized cells for photoreception. Many invertebrates have eyespots that allow them to do nothing more than detect light. Honeybees have compound eyes that allow them to see the patterns and colors of flowers. They can also sense ultraviolet light, which they use for navigation. The eye of the frog has cells that are sensitive to small moving objects (like bugs) and shadows (like a predator might produce). Squids and octopuses have eyes that produce clear visual images like vertebrate eyes do. Not all vertebrates can see colors, but birds and humans can. Birds have much better visual acuity than we do, no doubt because they must see objects clearly from great heights. Furthermore, homing pigeons are sensitive to the earth's magnetic field, a specialization that aids navigation, and although bats can see, they can also navigate by echolocation, an auditory solution to the problem of navigation and flight at night.

As species became more complex, organ systems evolved. Each organ system has a function: Lungs and gills developed for the exchange of gases. Stomachs and intestines developed to extract nutrients from food. Hearts, veins, and arteries developed to distribute these nutrients and gases to various parts of the body, and livers developed to remove waste products from the blood. Endocrine systems developed to regulate the internal environment with hormones. Immune systems developed to ward off pathogens. Skin, hair, or feathers developed for protection and temperature regulation. Animals developed skeletons for support, muscular systems for locomotion, sense organs to obtain information about both the internal and external environment, and nervous systems to transmit and integrate that information and issue commands to the various effector systems that mediate overt behavior. However, the exact nature of each of these structural and functional adaptations depends on the niche the species inhabits. Fish, whales, and dolphins all live in water, and their bodies reflect the medium in which they live: Most but not all fish have fins and scales and breathe through gills. Whales and dolphins have fins but no scales, and they breathe by coming to the surface for air.

In all but the simplest species, some of the functions of the nervous system are carried out by a concentrated collection of neural tissue called the brain. As species became more complex, their brains developed mechanisms and structures to carry out the psychological processes we call perception, learning, memory, thinking, and motivation. With the exception of simple reflexes, behavior reflects the interactions among those processes that an individual possesses.

The simplest behavioral mechanisms for survival evolved to deal with the most basic problems: food, predators, and reproduction (Staddon, 1988). Many species inhabit niches where food is not readily available; it must be sought out and, in some instances, captured. Many species have predators that must be avoided, and where sexual reproduction exists, mates must be found and engaged.

Even the simplest animals possess mechanisms for coming in contact with food. Whether the food comes to the animal or the animal goes to the food, the animal must possess sensory abilities to detect the presence of food and mechanisms for locomotion to increase the opportunity to encounter food, even when it waits for the food to arrive. Fortunately, food tends to occur in certain places and at certain times. Knowledge of what constitutes food and what responses to make to increase the probability of coming into contact with food increases the chances of finding it. Likewise, danger can come at any time, but some places are more dangerous than others and some times are more dangerous than others. Sometimes dangerous events come with warning signals. Knowing who predators are, having the sensory ability to detect their presence, and knowing what to do when their presence is sensed increases the chances for escape. Prospective mates give signals when sexual advances will be accepted and when they will be rejected. Knowing how to reproduce and with whom one is most likely to be successful increases the chances of having offspring. How did all this come to be?

The Doctrine of Evolution by Natural Selection

Charles Darwin provided us with the explanation for the various adaptations described above. His explanation, called natural selection, is based on transmission to their offspring of those characteristics that allow individuals to survive.

The most plausible explanation for the diversity of species adapted to survive in specific niches and for the observed changes that occur in species when they are challenged by severe changes in their niche was provided by Charles Darwin. Darwin's explanation is called the doctrine of natural selection. See Box 1.2 for the historical context of Darwin's views on evolution.

Darwin's doctrine of evolution by natural selection is based on three principles:

1. *The observed characteristics of individuals are inherited; that is, offspring tend to resemble their parents more than they resemble other individuals (mechanism of inheritance).*

2. *Within a species, individuals differ from one another in both their physical structures and behavioral dispositions (source of variation).* Although Darwin could not offer an explanation for the source of this variation, he had collected ample evidence for its existence in his journal. The later discovery of genes and mutations provided the explanation for how characteristics are inherited and the source for the observed variation between individuals.

3. *Those individuals with characteristics that favor survival in competition with others and in the face of environmental stresses or changes will be more likely to transmit their characteristics to offspring and thus tend to be preserved (method of selection).*

BOX 1.2

Charles Darwin and Evolution by Natural Selection

Charles Darwin (1809–1882) was not the first person to propose that species evolved from one another. The Greek philosopher Anaximander of Miletus (610–546 BCE) proposed that all life originated in water and later our ancestors moved to land. He also proposed that the first humans must have been children of a different animal (Kirk, Raven, & Schofield, 1983).

Later Augustine of Hippo (354–430 CE), the early Christian theologian, commented that new species may have come about through the "decomposition" of earlier forms of life (Augustine of Hippo, 1982).

At the beginning of the nineteenth century, the combined discoveries of new species in the New World and fossils of extinct species in various geological strata led naturalists, geologists, and philosophers to view the entire physical universe as a dynamic system. In 1809, Jean Baptiste de Lamarck (1744–1829), the French naturalist and philosopher, proposed the first theory for the evolution of species. Lamarck's theory included the proposal that physical characteristics acquired during individuals' lifetimes can be transmitted to their offspring. Although Lamarck is most remembered today for that now-discredited theory, he was instrumental in establishing the framework for the scientific study of evolution (Gould, 2002).

Darwin's interest in evolution was aroused during his voyage around the world from 1831 to 1836 on the H.M.S. *Beagle*. He carefully recorded his observations of the diversity of species in a journal that was published in various volumes beginning in 1839. Darwin reworked his journal and published it as *The Voyage of the Beagle* in 1845 (and revised it in 1860; Darwin, 1860/1962). By 1837, Darwin was convinced that species evolved, and by 1842 he had formulated the doctrine of evolution by natural selection to explain it; however, he only alluded to it in his 1845 book. Alfred Russell Wallace, another British naturalist, independently formulated the concept of natural selection and sent Darwin a copy of his manuscript. Papers by both Darwin and Wallace were read at the meeting of the Linnean Society of London in 1858. In 1859, Darwin laid out his doctrine of evolution by natural selection and the observations that led to it in his book *On the Origin of Species by Means of Natural Selection: Or the Preservation of Favoured Races in the Struggle for Life.*

Again, it may be asked, how is it that varieties, which I have called incipient species, become ultimately converted into good and distinct species, which in most cases obviously differ from each other far more than do the varieties of the same species? How do those groups of species, which constitute what are called distinct genera, and which differ from each other more than do the species of the same genus, arise? All these results, as we shall more fully see in the next chapter, follow inevitably from the struggle for life. Owing to this struggle for life, any variation, however slight and from whatever cause proceeding, if it be in any degree profitable to an individual of any species, in its infinitely complex relations to other organic beings and to external nature, will tend to the preservation of that individual, and will generally be inherited by its offspring. The offspring, also, will thus have a better chance of surviving, for, of the many individuals of any species which are periodically born, but a small number can survive. I have called this principle, by which each slight variation, if useful, is preserved, by the term of Natural Selection, in order to mark its relation to man's power of selection. We have seen that man by selection can certainly produce great results, and can adapt organic beings to his own uses, through the accumulation of slight but useful variations, given to him by the hand of Nature. But Natural Selection, as we shall hereafter see, is a power incessantly ready for action, and is as immeasurably superior to man's feeble efforts, as the works of Nature are to those of Art. (p. 62)

(Continued)

We may still refer to evolution by natural selection as a theory, and there may not be agreement as to all of its various nuances, but no other testable explanation exists to explain the diversity of species, the changes recorded in the fossil record, and the adaptive fit of species to their niches. Natural selection is not just an explanation of past events; it can explain, among other things, why the vaccine we develop each year to ward off the flu virus does not work the next year. Combined with the known principles of inheritance, natural selection provides us with a powerful tool for understanding living systems.

Darwin's ideas about natural selection apply to both physical attributes and behaviors. He was interested in the evolution of behavior and the role of learning in that evolution, both of which he addressed in *On the Origin of Species* (1859/1964), *The Descent of Man and Selection in Relation to Sex* (1871/1901), and *The Expression of the Emotions in Man and Animals* (1873/1979).

Natural selection describes a gradual and continuous process of evolution by which species change, new ones come into existence, and others become extinct. Species survive because some of their members can survive long enough to reproduce and pass their genetic material to their offspring. The measure of success in natural selection is called **reproductive fitness**: *the level of production of offspring that survive to reproduce themselves*. New species evolve when some individuals possess characteristics that increase their reproductive fitness relative to others, and extinction occurs when no members of a species can survive to reproduce. Thus natural selection provides us with an explanation for how characteristics of individuals are related to their niche.

Ginsburg and Jablonka (2010) suggested that the appearance of associative learning (the process that underlies Pavlovian and operant conditioning) was a driving force in the great diversification of species that occurred in what is called the Cambrian explosion, 542 million years ago when the ancestors of most of the phyla that exist today emerged. When this ability appeared, it enabled those species that possessed it to exploit and survive in new niches, which in turn increased reproductive fitness, and along with other adaptations, led to species diversification.

Knowledge and Natural Selection

Individuals can acquire knowledge from two sources. One source is through heredity (instinctive knowledge), and the other source of knowledge is from direct experience (learned knowledge). These two sources of knowledge are not as distinct as the names imply.

Natural selection appears to have created two interrelated solutions for obtaining knowledge. Both are the product of natural selection, and both provide solutions to specific problems that one's ancestors encountered during the course of evolution.

Instinctive Knowledge. The first solution is to build this knowledge into the individual. **Instinctive knowledge** is *knowledge obtained through the mechanism of heredity.* This knowledge is innate; that is, it is *not acquired through direct experience by that individual.* In some species, instinctive knowledge includes recognition of food, predators, and members of one's own species, and predispositions to behave in species-specific ways in the presence of food, predators, prospective mates, parents, and offspring. Instinctive knowledge can include both declarative knowledge (knowing that) and procedural knowledge (knowing how).

Weber, Peterson, and Hoekstra (2013) provided a demonstration of the genetic transmission of knowledge in two recently diverged and interfertile species of field mice that build distinct burrows: oldfield mice (*Peromyscus polionotus*) and deer mice (*Peromyscus maniculatus*). The former lives in open fields in the southeastern United States, and the latter lives in both prairies and forests across the United States. *P. polionotus* builds complex burrows with long entrance and escape tunnels while *P. maniculatus* builds simple burrows. The offspring of matings between these two species produce burrows with long entrance and escape tunnels similar to those of *P. polionotus*. Of interest is that the offspring of a first generation backcross (mating the first generation with one of the original species, in this case *P. maniculatus*) resulted in offspring who produced a variety of burrows: some with short and some with long entrance tunnels, and some with escape tunnels and some with no escape tunnels. These results illustrate the innate knowledge involved in constructing burrows in these species is controlled by a number of genes.

There are two common misconceptions about instinctive knowledge. One is that there is a class of behaviors called **instincts** that are not influenced by experience. At the purely descriptive level, instincts are *stereotyped behavior patterns that are performed in the same way by members of a particular species without practice;* that is, these behaviors occur pretty much in complete form the first time they are performed. The occurrence of species-specific behavior patterns does not mean that experience plays no part in their expression or that they cannot be modified by experience. Hailman (1969) investigated the feeding behavior of gull chicks in the laboratory under controlled conditions. He demonstrated that some aspects of hatchling feeding behaviors in gulls thought to be the direct expression of instincts are, in fact, modifiable by experience.

The other misconception is that humans do not possess instinctive knowledge. Most humans no longer live in a natural environment (Schwartz, 1974), and our new niche may no longer present us with the same problems our ancestors faced, but we appear to retain some instinctive knowledge of some of the hazards (Buss, 1995). For example, although many of us have been injured by electric shocks and automobiles, relatively few of us develop phobias to them. The most common phobias relate to snakes, spiders, heights, darkness, and strangers, dangerous events in our ancestors' niches. Most of us have not been injured by these, yet at certain times of our lives we may have exhibited some fear of them. No doubt these fears were learned, but they were readily learned (Marks, 1987). Rakison and Derringer (2008) provided evidence that human infants possess a perceptual template for spiders that facilitates learning to fear spiders, especially when others exhibit fear in the presence of spiders. We will explore the social learning of fear in Chapter 13.

Learned Knowledge. The second way to obtain knowledge is *through individual experience*. We call this **learned knowledge**. The ability to learn and the ease with which individuals can learn about certain things is also the result of natural selection; thus, there is not a clear demarcation between knowledge obtained through experience and knowledge that is inherited. What an individual can and does learn in a given situation depends on the situation and who he or she is (species, maturation level). All experiences do not automatically lead to learning, and when learning does occur, not everything can be learned with equal facility. Gould and Marler (1987) coined the term "learning by instinct" to characterize the influence of natural selection on the ability to learn. Thus, instinctive knowledge and prior experiences both affect what an individual can and does learn.

For example, many species that eat a wide variety of foods quickly learn to avoid a novel food that makes them sick; in fact, they can learn this on the basis of a single exposure, even when they get sick hours later. Rats avoid similar tasting foods while birds avoid similar looking foods (Logue, 1988). This difference appears related to the niche each species occupies: Rats are primarily nocturnal creatures who rely more on smell and feel than sight to navigate about their environment. Birds rely more on vision to find their food.

Maturation level also affects the ability to learn, and this, too, is the result of natural selection. Humans are quite adept at learning to talk and to speak the language they are exposed to at an early age, yet many of us struggle to learn another language when we are adults (G. A. Miller, 1981; Moskowitz, 1978). Although apes can be taught sign language (Gardner & Gardner, 1969; Patterson & Linden, 1982), they do not learn it readily without extensive training. On the other hand, human children learn language with little prompting, and untutored deaf children will invent sign language to use with each other (G. A. Miller, 1981). It is true that apes use gestures in the wild, but that form of communication never developed into a sophisticated sign language.

Language learning in humans and song learning in birds share a number of striking similarities. Human infants can recognize all of the consonant sounds that occur in human speech, even those sounds that are not present in the language spoken around them. Out of human babbling, the consonant sounds of the language to be learned emerge and the other consonant sounds drop out. We require extensive training to make those "lost" sounds again later. Babbling begins and ends in deaf children about the same time it does in hearing children; this suggests a genetically programmed sequence. Birds also learn their song at an early age. There appears to be a critical period when exposure to the song of the species will produce efficient learning. As in humans, deaf birds will also begin vocalizing at the same time as hearing birds. Although different avian species learn their songs in different ways, hearing the song at a specific age is critical to learning that song (Marler, 1987). Of course, the use of language in humans is much more advanced than the use of songs for communication in birds.

Instinctive knowledge is acquired through natural selection and transmitted through genes from parent to offspring. In some species, *learned knowledge acquired through experience can be transmitted between members of that species*; however, parents are not the only channel through which this information flows. Individuals can learn from any experienced individual: parents, grandparents, peers, and so on. This is called **cultural transmission of knowledge** when referring to humans, or **social transmission** of knowledge when referring to other species. Both genetic transmission and cultural transmission allow for changes in transmitted knowledge; however, changes through cultural transmission can be more rapid. Change is much slower with genetic transmission because it is based on the genetic mechanisms underlying natural selection, and these require the random processes of genetic recombination and mutation. On the other hand, knowledge obtained through cultural transmission (both declarative knowledge and procedural knowledge) can be more easily modified through the mechanisms of learning as individuals confront new situations in their own lives. Clearly, the processes and abilities that underlie cultural transmission are also the result of natural selection.

Transmission of information between members of the same species also occurs in other species. In Chapter 13, we will review evidence for the social transmission of food preferences, food aversions, fears, and other kinds of knowledge in a variety of species, including humans.

Finally, despite the obvious advantages the ability to learn confers to an individual, not all species of animals are capable of learning (Mayr, 1974). Relatively simple forms of learning (habituation and sensitization) tend to occur in simple species (Corning, Dyal, & Willows, 1973). As species become more complex, they require more advanced learning abilities. These more advanced abilities are more likely to occur in species that live a long time and have prolonged and intense parental care, small litter size, large body and brain sizes, and slow development (Gould, 1977; Mayr, 1974).

LEARNING IS AN ADAPTIVE SPECIALIZATION

> Because all forms of learning evolved as solutions to problems of survival, we characterize learning as an adaptive specialization.

Natural selection explains how the observed structural and behavioral diversity among species evolved as solutions to problems individuals face in their ecological niche. The ability to learn provides one of these solutions. Some problems appear in all niches, and some are specific to a given niche and require special abilities and capacities. How and what individuals can learn reflects the niche in which their species evolved (Shettleworth, 1993).

In all niches, causes precede effects and preceding events may predict future events; events that occur close together in time and place are more likely to be related than events that are separated; and things tend to occur in cycles that suggest they may occur again (Anokhin, 1974; Rozin & Schull, 1988). The mechanisms underlying Pavlovian and operant conditioning appear to have evolved so that individuals can learn about these universal aspects of the world.

However, even here some things are easier to learn than others. Rats learn more rapidly to avoid food that leads to illness based on the taste of the food than on its visual properties (Garcia & Koelling, 1966). Golden hamsters can learn through operant conditioning to rear, dig, and scratch the wall to obtain food, but they cannot learn to wash their faces, leave scent markings, or scratch themselves to obtain that same food (Shettleworth, 1975). On the other hand, face washing is suppressed when it is followed by electric shock (punished), but rearing is not (Shettleworth, 1978). Humans readily learn to fear spiders and snakes, the dark, and open spaces, and these are the most common phobias in our society. On the other hand, we rarely see individuals who have phobias about electrical appliances, from which we all have received electric shocks (Davey, 1992; McNally, 1987). Human infants also exhibit fear of heights around the time that they start to crawl (Campos, Anderson, Barbu-Roth, Hubbard, Hertenstein, & Witherington, 2000; Gibson & Walk, 1960).

All of these observations make sense when one considers the niches in which these various species evolved. Rats are primarily nocturnal animals for which vision is less important than smell, touch, and taste when seeking food. For hamsters, rearing, digging, and scratching at objects are more likely to produce food in their niche than leaving scent markings or washing and scratching themselves. Rearing serves both to increase the chances of finding food and of spotting predators; therefore, it is not surprising that rearing can be increased if it brings food but is not decreased when it brings shock (danger). For humans, snakes, spiders, open spaces, dark places, and heights were dangerous things and places for our ancestors (and they still can be today). They are among the most common phobias observed in adults in our society (Nesse, 1990). Therefore, it is not surprising that we possess evolved mechanisms to readily learn to be afraid of these things (Öhman & Mineka, 2001). Electrical appliances can deliver fatal shocks, but they are recent threats to us and therefore there has not been time for natural selection to prepare us to become readily afraid of them.

Some forms of learning appear to have evolved to deal with more restricted problems involved in parenting and social interactions. Song learning, language learning, observational learning, and instructed learning occur in species that invest time and energy in rearing their offspring because they provide mechanisms for passing information between individuals who live in social groups. This lessens the load of instinctive knowledge that must be transmitted through genes. Imprinting is a form of learning that occurs in some species of precocial birds (birds that can see and walk soon after hatching). Many precocial birds follow moving objects soon after hatching. Because most of the time this object will be a parent, imprinting provides a mechanism by which the hatchling quickly learns to distinguish its own parent from other adults.

All of these observations point to an important conclusion: *the various forms of learning are adaptive specializations that evolved as solutions to some of the problems of survival.* In species that can learn, natural selection provided a way for individuals to learn about what they are likely to encounter in their niches. Thus, all species that can learn are predisposed to recognize the importance of some cues, attend to them, and learn about them quickly, and learning will be slow or nonexistent when the individual is confronted with a situation that it is not equipped by natural selection to handle (Gould & Marler, 1987). Some forms of learning are more specialized than others because they serve rather restricted functions (e.g., imprinting, song learning, language learning); however, even in the cases of Pavlovian conditioning and operant conditioning (which are considered general learning processes), some things are easier to learn about than others.

Adaptation is an important concept in natural selection. It refers to the progressive changes that occur over successive generations as a species adjusts to its niche. Lewontin (1978) described adaption in terms of the problems faced by all individuals: "Adaptation is the process of evolutionary change by which the organism provides a better and better 'solution' to the 'problem'" (p. 213). Thus, in the broadest sense, adaptation is *a process of adjustment to the circumstances in which an individual lives*. It means more than just reproductive fitness (see The Doctrine of Evolution by Natural Selection, above). Furthermore, adaptation is a relative concept: Whether a characteristic is adaptive depends on the niche in which it evolved. Not all structures and mechanisms an individual possesses provide the *best* solutions, and there can be more than one solution that is adaptive in a given niche.

Learning is an adaptation that evolved through natural selection, but the ability to learn affords individuals with another form of adaptation: adaptation to their immediate situation through the acquisition of knowledge from direct experience. Some knowledge is programmed genetically, but it is impossible to program all knowledge. For example, members of some species are programmed genetically to recognize members of their own species, but it would be difficult to provide each individual with instinctive knowledge to identify its own parents (Bateson, 1978).

The ability to learn allows for greater flexibility to deal with new situations. Individuals can acquire knowledge that helps them adapt to their own particular situation within their species' ecological niche, but this flexibility is not without its costs. Individuals may fail to learn what is required for adaptation to a given situation, and they may learn maladaptive patterns by accident. Incorrect, inadequate, or inappropriate knowledge can be acquired even when learning is highly specialized. For example, precocial birds are programmed through instinctive knowledge to follow moving objects soon after hatching. As a result of that experience, they become imprinted on these objects. Imprinting not only affects their behavior as juveniles, it also directs their interest in mating toward members of their own species. However, imprinting on members of other species is possible (see Figure 1.4). Fortunately, there can be opportunity for correction even when learning is not confined to a specific developmental stage (as is the case with imprinting).

Finally, in humans the ability to learn and the ability to create written languages has led to what is sometimes referred to as cultural evolution, *the process by which we humans adapt to our environment by transmitting acquired knowledge from generation to generation through teaching and imitation* (Boyd & Richerson, 1985). Cultural evolution, which is based on cultural transmission of knowledge, is a more rapid process than biological evolution. Because we can learn, speak, and create written languages, the world we live in today reflects the cultural evolution of human beings over the past 30,000 years. The cultural transmission of knowledge takes learning to another level: Individuals need not discover solutions to problems by themselves because they can profit from the experience of others. The abilities that are required for cultural evolution are also the result of biological evolution.

There is also evidence of cultural evolution in other species. For example, Whiten et al. (1999) collated published observations of the behavior of chimpanzees taken at seven different spatially separated locations in Africa. They found that within this single species there are distinct local "traditions" for a wide variety of behaviors used to obtain the same foods.

LEARNING IS PART OF AN INTEGRATED SYSTEM OF PSYCHOLOGICAL PROCESSES

Although we divide the study of psychology into different areas (learning, perception, memory, motivation, cognition, and so on), the psychological processes we study do not operate in isolation. Behavior reflects the interaction of all of them.

What individuals do at any point in time depends on the situation they are in and who they are: their abilities, capacities, skills, maturation level, internal states, and knowledge. Behavior reflects an integrated set of psychological processes and systems. These include *sensory* systems (vision, audition, olfaction, etc.) for receiving information from the environment; *perceptual* processes for sifting through, attending to, recognizing, and organizing the sensory information in ways that are meaningful to the individual; *learning* abilities for incorporating that information into knowledge; *memory* systems for storing that knowledge; and *cognitive* abilities to perform mental operations on that knowledge. But knowledge alone does not produce behavior. Depending on the situation, what an individual does may require the *retrieval* of knowledge from memory, *motivation* to perform actions, and *motor skills* required for those actions. All of these processes and systems arise out of a nervous system that is the product of natural selection.

None of these systems and processes operates alone. They are *integrated* and *interrelated*, and that makes it difficult, if not impossible, to discuss any one of them in isolation. Although we characterize learning as the processes by which we acquire knowledge and skills, it is clear that the ability to learn requires the ability to remember. Without memory systems—that is, mechanisms for storing and retrieving information—there can be no learning. Learning occurs when there is something to learn about and requires information about events in our environment to come to us through our senses. After sensory information is received, it must be interpreted, and interpretation involves the mechanisms of perception. Perception and learning are intimately related: What we learn and how quickly we learn is determined, in part, by what aspects of the information we attend to, and attention is influenced by both innate knowledge and learned knowledge. Thus the perception of information can be affected by what has already been learned. Whether learning will occur, what will be learned, and when and how that information will be used can be affected by motivation. Motivations arise from physiological states of our bodies, from external stimulation, and from experience. We will have to consider all of these as we explore the ability called learning.

SUMMARY AND CONCLUSIONS

Learning is the psychological process (or processes) by which knowledge is acquired from experience. We can distinguish two types of knowledge: declarative knowledge (knowing that) and procedural knowledge (knowing how). We will keep this distinction in mind as we look at the various forms of learning.

Because learning is a psychological process, we cannot study it directly. We study learning by observing individuals under controlled conditions where we can manipulate their experiences and look for changes in their behavior that we can attribute to those experiences. The arrangement of events we present to individuals constitutes the learning procedure, and we define some forms of learning in terms of their procedures. The observed changes in behavior are the phenomenon of learning. Because we infer the process of learning as the link between the procedure (what the individual experiences) and the phenomenon (the observed change in behavior), we characterize learning as an intervening variable. The distinction is important because we should be clear about whether we are referring to the procedure, process, or phenomenon of learning.

Learning is inferred to have occurred when an individual's behavior changes as a result of having an experience. This is the learning/performance problem: The only way we can study learning is by observing performance, but performance may not always reflect learning. Learning may have occurred, but the conditions may not be adequate for that learning to be expressed in behavior. As psychologists, we are interested in trying to discover the mechanisms that produce the effects we call learned behavior and the conditions under which learning occurs.

Natural selection created two interrelated mechanisms for providing individuals with knowledge for surviving in their ecological niche: instinctive knowledge obtained through the mechanism of heredity and learned knowledge obtained through experience. The various forms of learning are adaptive specializations that evolved through natural selection. We characterize learning as specialized because what an individual can and cannot learn depends on who he or she is. Not everything can be learned with equal facility. Different species evolved dispositions to learn in species-specific ways; these include dispositions to learn certain things at various stages of development. We characterize learning as adaptive because it can provide an individual with a solution to a problem of survival. Of course, it may not be the best solution; that depends on the situation and the learning abilities of the individual. Individuals may fail to learn what is required for adaptation to a given situation, and they may learn maladaptive patterns by accident.

Behavior reflects an integrated set of psychological processes and systems: sensory, perceptual, learning, memory, cognitive, and motivational. Therefore, we cannot study learning without making reference to these other systems.

In the following chapters, we will look at a number of different forms of learning. We begin with Pavlovian conditioning, the procedure during which individuals are presented with two events in some relationship to each other. As a result of this experience, individuals may come to behave in certain ways when one of these events is experienced again. Our focus will be on the conditions under which Pavlovian conditioning occurs, the psychological processes and mechanisms underlying Pavlovian conditioning, and how Pavlovian conditioning is expressed in behavior.

STUDY QUESTIONS

1. What is the difference between learning and learned behavior?

2. What is knowledge? What is the difference between declarative and procedural knowledge? Give an example of each.

3. How do we study learning? What is the learning-performance problem? Why is this a problem, and why is it important for us to be aware of it?

4. Why do we characterize learning (and other psychological processes) as intervening variables?

5. How is the learning/performance problem related to the procedure/process/phenomenon distinction and to the independent variable/intervening variable/dependent variable distinction? Where do psychological processes like learning and motivation fit in here?

6. Describe the procedures and phenomena for the following kinds of learning (and give a human example of each):

   a. habituation

   b. sensitization

   c. phase-specific learning

   d. Pavlovian conditioning

   e. operant conditioning

   f. observational learning

   g. instructed learning

   h. text-based learning

7. What are the principles that form the basis for Darwin's doctrine of evolution by natural selection?

8. What is the difference between innate knowledge and learned knowledge? Give some examples of each.

9. What does it mean to say that learning is an adaptive specialization?

10. How are the various psychological processes (learning, perception, motivation, memory, etc.) related to each other and to the behavior of individuals?

PART I

LEARNING TO PREDICT
IMPORTANT EVENTS

2

THE PROCEDURES AND PHENOMENA WE CALL PAVLOVIAN CONDITIONING

Although sometimes our lives seem chaotic, for the most part the world is an orderly place where things happen in rather predictable ways, and being able to detect these regularities allows us to anticipate events and adjust our behavior accordingly. Identifying stimuli that predict the occurrence of good things (like food, shelter, safety, and sexual partners) increases our chances of successfully obtaining them, and identifying warning signals for bad things helps us escape or avoid them (if that is possible). Survival would be difficult, if not impossible, if we could not learn about what events lead to other events in our environment.

The ability to identify relationships between events is fundamental to the kinds of learning we call Pavlovian and operant conditioning. **Pavlovian conditioning** is *the name we use for how humans and other animals learn about and respond to signals for important events.* **Operant conditioning** *refers to how they learn to do (or not do) things to bring on or get away from these important events.* In these next five chapters, we will explore the procedures, processes, and phenomena we call Pavlovian conditioning.[1] Operant conditioning will be the subject of Part II of this book.

JAWS: HOW THEY GET YOU IN HORROR FILMS

> If you have ever seen any of the *Jaws* films, you can relate to this example of Pavlovian conditioning, although you may not have recognized it as such before.

If you have seen *Jaws*, you should get the joke in Figure 2.1. The use of music in films like *Jaws* provides us with an example of Pavlovian conditioning that we have all experienced. Early in *Jaws*, the music starts. A young woman is swimming. Suddenly there is

---

[1]Hilgard and Marquis (1940) introduced the name *classical conditioning* to designate the procedures we are referring to here as *Pavlovian conditioning*, and for many years that was the name most psychologists used (and some still use). In 1937, Skinner introduced the term *respondent* to refer to the conditioned responses in Pavlov's procedure, and many of his followers refer to that procedure as *respondent conditioning*. Because all three names refer to the same procedure, it is a matter of personal preference as to which to use. Pavlovian conditioning is the name used in this book.

Figure 2.1 "Start the music!"

THE NEW BREED

"Start the music!"

©New Breed, 1995 Distributed by King Features Syndicate, World Rights Reserved

thrashing and screaming, and then blood appears in the water. This scenario is repeated. What was your reaction when the music was played later in the film? Most of us report that when we hear that music we anticipate that something bad is going to happen, which triggers an emotional response.

Our emotional reaction to the music is a conditioned response produced by the procedure we call Pavlovian conditioning. We will examine how such conditioned emotional responses are produced by Pavlovian conditioning procedures later in this chapter.

PROCEDURES, PHENOMENA, AND PROCESSES

In Chapter 1, we discussed the procedure/process/phenomenon distinction. Pavlovian conditioning is both a procedure (something done to subjects) and a phenomenon (change in behavior after experiencing the procedure).

The sequence of events in films like Jaws is an example of the **procedure of Pavlovian conditioning**: *Two events occur in some relationship to each other*. Typically, one of the events (called the conditioned stimulus) precedes the other event.[2] The **phenomenon of Pavlovian conditioning** *occurs when an individual behaves differently in response to one of the events (the conditioned stimulus) after experiencing the procedure of the two events in combination.* How the individual behaves when the conditioned stimulus is presented again is determined by who the individual is (its species and prior experiences), what the two events are, and how they are related to each other. We infer from the change in behavior that the individual has learned something about the relationship between the two events. As psychologists, we are interested in what individuals learn, how they learn, what affects whether they learn, and how fast they learn. It is common to also refer to the theoretical mechanism or **process** we believe underlies all this as **Pavlovian conditioning**. This seems confusing, but it need not be if we are clear about whether we are referring to the procedure, the process, or the phenomenon of Pavlovian conditioning.

In this chapter, we will look at five very different examples of Pavlovian conditioning. We begin with a brief overview of Pavlov's pioneering work. Then we will look at how Pavlovian conditioning affects emotional responses, physiological responses to drugs, taste aversions, and reactions to signals for food. These examples illustrate the diversity and pervasiveness of Pavlovian conditioning in everyday experience.

Examples of Pavlovian Conditioning Before Pavlov

Pavlov was not the first person to describe what we call Pavlovian conditioning today, but he is the person who recognized the importance of the learned responses to events that signal the impending occurrence of important events and showed us how to study this form of learning scientifically.

Lope de Vega put the following story in his 1623 play *El Capellán de la Virgen* (The Chaplain of the Virgin):

> Saint Ildefonso used to scold me and punish me lots of times. He would sit me on the bare floor and make me eat with the cats of the monastery. These cats were such rascals that they took advantage of my penitence. They drove me mad stealing my choicest morsels. It did no good to chase them away. But I found a way of coping with the beasts in order to enjoy my meals when I was being punished. I put them all in a sack, and on a pitch black night took them out under an arch. First I would cough and then immediately whale the daylights out of the cats. They whined and shrieked like an infernal pipe organ. I would pause for awhile and repeat the operation—first a cough, and then a thrashing. I finally noticed that even without beating them, the beasts moaned and yelped like the very devil whenever I coughed. I then let them loose. Thereafter, whenever I had to eat off the floor, I would cast a look around. If an animal approached my food, all I had to do was to cough, and how that cat did scat! (Quoted in Bousfield, 1955, p. 828).

---

[2]Pavlovian conditioning can occur with other arrangements. Some of these will be discussed in Chapters 3 and 4.

Isacoff (2001) provided the following quote from René Descartes' *Letters to Père Marin Mersenne, Le Minime: On the Science of Sound and Music, 1629–1640*:

> What makes some people want to dance may make others want to cry. This is because it evokes ideas in our memory: for instance, those who have in the past enjoyed dancing to a certain tune feel a fresh wish to dance the moment they hear a similar one; one the other hand, if someone had never heard a galliard without some affliction befalling him, he would certainly grow sad when he heard it again. This is so certain that I reckon that if you whipped a dog five or six times to the sounds of a violin, it would begin to howl and run away as soon as it heard that music again. (p. 175)

In both of these stories, there are two events that occur in relationship to each other (a cough followed by the thrashing and the sound of a violin followed by a whipping). After experiencing that relationship with those events, the animals in the story behave (or are hypothesized to behave) differently when the sounds occur again. These are examples of conditioned emotional responses produced by Pavlovian conditioning, a topic to be covered later in this chapter.

WHY WE CALL IT PAVLOVIAN CONDITIONING

Pavlov's pioneering work provides an interesting story of how scientific study increases our knowledge and understanding of psychological processes such as learning.

Mention Pavlov and you may get comments about training individuals to respond in robot-like fashion when a certain stimulus is presented. For some, this conjures up an image of mad scientists manipulating people to respond against their will, as portrayed in the book and film *A Clockwork Orange*. Fortunately, Pavlov's work has not led to such totalitarian mind control. To the contrary, it has fostered a number of useful therapies for dealing with behavior problems and has helped us understand many interesting aspects of human and animal behavior. Pavlov showed us how to study psychological processes through careful and systematic study. Although some of the details of his quasi-physiological theory for the mechanism of conditioning are not correct, his conceptualization of conditioning as the association or connection between events is. There is no doubt that Pavlov's work on conditioned reflexes has and will continue to have an enormous influence on our understanding of behavior.

Evolution of an Idea. Ivan P. Pavlov (1849–1936) was already a famous scientist by the time he began his work on what he called "conditioned reflexes," and his earlier work on gastric secretions in dogs would earn him a Nobel Prize in 1904. A few years before receiving that great honor, Pavlov became interested in the common observation that the mere sight of food instigates salivation in hungry dogs and hungry people (Pavlov, 1903/1955). Others had demonstrated that the ability of the sight (and smell) of food to produce salivation in hungry dogs is acquired through experience. Pavlov (1927) cited the work of Dr. Zitovich, who raised puppies away from their mother with only milk. When the puppies were a few months old, Zitovich showed them solid food, but they did not salivate. Only after the puppies had been allowed to eat meat on several occasions did the sight or smell of it evoke salivation. Why does this happen? Pavlov rejected explanations in terms of the dog's thoughts, feelings, and desires as unfruitful speculations. Rather, he believed he could find an objective way to study the effects of what was called at that time "psychical stimulation." Out of his determination to study this phenomenon objectively, Pavlov developed the experimental techniques that bear his name.[3] See Box 2.1 for excerpts from Pavlov's groundbreaking book *Conditioned Reflexes*.

We are all familiar with Pavlov's basic procedure: After performing a simple surgery that allowed him to collect drops of saliva from one of the dog's salivary glands, he put his dogs in an isolation room (Figure 2.2). A stimulus (usually a metronome) was turned on and then food was delivered directly into the dog's mouth. The dog always salivated after the food was placed in its mouth. After a few of these metronome-food presentations, the dog would salivate when the metronome was presented alone.

Identifying the Unconditioned Stimulus and Unconditioned Response. Following Pavlov's lead, we refer to the food as the **unconditioned stimulus** and the salivation that occurs in response to it as the **unconditioned response**. An **unconditioned stimulus (US)** *reliably elicits a response before training begins. That response is called the* **unconditioned response (UR).**

Figure 2.2   Photographs from Pavlov's laboratory. The dog was strapped in a harness in one room while the experimenter controlled the presentation of stimuli and recorded data in an adjoining room.

From Pavlov, 1927, *Conditioned Reflexes* (G. V. Anrep, Trans.). Copyright © 1927. Reprinted by permission of Oxford University Press.

---

[3]This account of how Pavlov came to study conditioned reflexes comes from his 1927 book. Todes (1997) suggests that this account is Pavlov's attempt to rewrite history. Todes presents evidence that one of Pavlov's students (A. T. Snarski) is the originator of this "objective" view of "psychical stimulation."

Excerpts From Conditioned Reflexes

These excerpts from the 1927 English translation of Pavlov's book help us understand the importance he attached to his work.

Let us return now to the simplest reflex from which our investigations started. If food or some rejectable substance finds its way into the mouth, a secretion of saliva is produced. The purpose of this secretion is in the case of food to alter it chemically, in the case of a rejectable substance to dilute and wash it out of the mouth. This is an example of a reflex due to the physical and chemical properties of a substance when it comes into contact with the mucous membrane of the mouth and tongue. But, in addition to this, a similar reflex secretion is evoked when these substances are placed at a distance from the dog and the receptor organs affected are only those of smell and sight. Even the vessel from which the food has been given is sufficient to evoke an alimentary reflex complete in all its details; and, further, the secretion may be provoked even by the sight of the person who brought the vessel, or by the sound of his footsteps.

Food, through its chemical and physical properties, evokes the salivary reflex in every dog right from birth, whereas this new type claimed as reflex—""the signal reflex"—is built up gradually in the course of the animal's own individual existence. But can this be considered as a fundamental point of difference, and can it hold as a valid argument against employing the term "reflex" for this new group

of phenomena? It is certainly a sufficient argument for making a definite distinction between the two types of reflex and for considering the signal reflex in a group distinct from the inborn reflex. But this does not invalidate in any way our right logically to term both "reflex," since the point of distinction does not concern the character of the response on the part of the organism, but only the mode of formation of the reflex mechanism. We may take the telephonic installation as an illustration. Communication can be effected in two ways. My residence may be connected directly with the laboratory by a private line, and I may call up the laboratory whenever it pleases me to do so; or on the other hand, a connection may have to be made through the central exchange. But the result in both cases is the same. The only point of distinction between the methods is that the private line provides a permanent and readily available cable, while the other line necessitates a preliminary central connection being established. In the one case the communicating wire is always complete, in the other case a small addition must be made to the wire at the central exchange. We have a similar state of affairs in reflex action. The path of the inborn reflex is already completed at birth; but the path of the signalizing reflex has still to be completed in the higher nervous centres. We are thus brought to consider the mode of formation of new reflex mechanisms. A new reflex is formed inevitably under

BOX 2.1

a given set of physiological conditions, and with the greatest ease, so that there is no need to take the subjective states of the dog into consideration. With a complete understanding of all the factors involved, the new signalizing reflexes are under the absolute control of the experimenter; they proceed according to as rigid laws as do any other physiological processes, and must be regarded as being in every sense a part of the physiological activity of living beings. I have termed this new group of reflexes conditioned reflexes to distinguish them from the inborn or unconditioned reflexes. The term "conditioned" is becoming more and more generally employed, and I think its use is fully justified in that, compared with the inborn reflexes, these new reflexes actually do depend on very many conditions, both in their formation and in the maintenance of their physiological activity.

From Pavlov, 1927, *Conditioned Reflexes* (G. V. Anrep, Trans.), pp. 13, 24–25. Copyright © 1927. Reprinted by permission of Oxford University Press.

Pavlov argued that the chemical and physical properties of food produce an inborn or unconditioned reflex of salivation that is present at birth. Perhaps this is so, but there is the possibility that the observed unconditioned stimulus-unconditioned response (US-UR) relationship is itself the result of experience and hence due to learning. This may seem counterintuitive, but there is evidence that behaviors usually thought to be unlearned are influenced by experience. Anyone raised on a farm knows that soon after hatching, chicks get up and walk around and start to peck at objects. Kuo (1932) demonstrated that this behavior pattern is molded by experience. He devised a way to remove part of the outer shell of an egg and create a window from which to observe what the chick is doing before it hatches. He observed that pecking responses were occurring in response to stimulation within the shell. In a set of rather clever experiments, Kuo demonstrated that he could influence pecking and walking by manipulating the prehatching environment inside the egg. Thus, even species-specific behavior patterns that appear shortly after hatching are shaped by experiences inside the egg. J. A. Hogan (1973) demonstrated that chicks may peck at objects at birth, but they must learn to recognize what is and is not food. Likewise, young rats have to learn to seek water when they are dehydrated (Hall, Arnold, & Myers, 2000).

In addition to food, Pavlov used unpleasant-tasting substances (such as weak acids like dilute hydrochloric acid and vinegar) delivered directly into his dogs' mouths as unconditioned stimuli (USs). The UR to these unpleasant-tasting things is also salivation, something we all have experienced when we get something unpleasant in our mouths. Pavlov also used injections of morphine as a US. The UR to a morphine injection includes nausea, vomiting, sleep, and salivation, which illustrates that unconditioned responses need not be simple responses. The same is true of conditioned responses. Although Pavlov primarily studied salivation as the conditioned response (CR), there are a number of CRs when food is the US. Some of these will be described later in this chapter and in succeeding chapters. Conditioned reactions involving a drug as the US will be described later in this chapter.

Identifying the Conditioned Stimulus and Conditioned Response. Pavlov called the salivation that occurs in the presence of the metronome and prior to the delivery of food into the mouth a **conditioned reflex** because *it is "conditional" on the individual's experience with the metronome and the food.* Today we usually call this a **conditioned response (CR)**. He coined the term **conditioned stimulus (CS)** to refer to *a stimulus which, as a result of its juxtaposition to the US, gains the ability to produce a response.* In addition to a metronome, Pavlov used tactile stimuli (such as vibration, weak electric current, cold), visual stimuli (black square, lights, rotating objects), odors, and other auditory stimuli (buzzing electric bells, tones, motor car hooter) as conditioned stimuli (CSs).

We call *the new response that now occurs when the CS is presented* (in this case salivation) the **CR**. In Pavlov's experiments, these two responses (CR and UR) were similar but not identical; they were similar in that both were salivation, but the CR and UR differed in terms of their amplitude (number of drops of saliva and viscosity of the saliva) and how quickly salivation occurred (the latency) after the stimulus (CS or US) was presented. We will see later that *the conditioned response need not even resemble the unconditioned response.* In a number of situations, these responses may be opposites.

Frequently the CS is described as a "neutral stimulus" before the conditioning procedure begins, but that is misleading. At the beginning of the experiment, the CS frequently produces a response. Make a sound, suddenly turn on a visual stimulus, or touch someone, and that person will turn toward the stimulation as if to investigate. Pavlov called this *investigatory response to a sudden or novel stimulus* an **orienting reflex (OR)**. If the stimulus (auditory, visual, tactile, or olfactory) is presented repeatedly and is not too uncomfortable (loud, bright, irritating) or too pleasurable (in the case of touch), the OR will cease to occur when the stimulus is presented. When this happens, we say the orienting reflex has habituated (see Chapter 1).

Furthermore, an event that usually serves as a US, like shock or food, can serve as a CS when it precedes another biologically important event. For example, Tuber (1986) gave cats two brief shocks in succession, the first to one forepaw and the second to the other forepaw. The UR to such a shock is pulling back of the limb (flexion). After repeated presentations of this sequence of shocks, presentation of the first shock (to one forepaw) produced a conditioned flexion response on the other limb. In other words, the shock to one paw served as the CS and the shock to the other paw served as the US. The CR was the flexion of the limb that received the second shock.

After the individual experiences the CS followed by the US a number of times, he or she may behave differently when the CS is presented. Although the response to the US alone remains the same, a CR may emerge to the CS. *The form of that CR depends on both the CS and the US.* For example, the introduction of food or an unpleasant tasting substance (a US) directly into the dog's mouth produces the UR of salivation. If the US is regularly preceded by a CS (auditory, visual, tactile, or olfactory), the CR will also be salivation. But in rats, the CR to a light that precedes food is different from the CR to a tone that precedes the same food (Holland, 1977), and the CR to a tone that precedes food is different from the CR to a tone that precedes electric shock. Sometimes the CR to a drug is opposite to the UR to that drug (Siegel, 1985, 1999, 2005).

The Effects of Extraneous Events on the Conditioned Response. Pavlov's technique allowed him to study in a controlled and systematic way the effects of various procedures on the occurrence (and nonoccurrence) of the conditioned response. He found that salivary CRs emerged when the CS was regularly followed within 1–5 seconds by the US. However, *if an external stimulus occurred while the CS was on, the individual would stop salivating.* The salivary CR would occur on subsequent trials if there were no other interruptions. Pavlov called this phenomenon **external inhibition** and argued that the absence of a CR did not mean that the individual had lost what he or she had learned, merely that the conditioned response was temporarily disrupted or suppressed (inhibited). Pavlov performed his experiments in a controlled environment to minimize the occurrence of external inhibition from extraneous events.

Can the effects of Pavlovian conditioning be undone? After the individual was producing salivary CRs consistently, Pavlov presented the CS alone for a number of trials (without the US). We call this **extinction**. Pavlov observed that *the procedure of extinction (presentation of the CS alone after training) caused the conditioned response to decline in intensity* (that is, the number of drops of saliva decreased). Pavlov labeled this phenomenon experimental extinction. Although it is tempting to think that if the procedure of conditioning (CS followed by US) produces learning, the procedure of extinction (CS followed by no US) would undo the effects of conditioning, that is not the case. To explain the phenomenon of extinction (reduction in the conditioned response during the procedure of extinction), Pavlov argued that it reflects *a process antagonistic to the process that produces the original conditioned response.* He called this antagonistic process **internal inhibition**. In everyday discourse, we say someone is "inhibited" when we believe that person is restraining himself or herself from performing an action that seems to us appropriate in that situation. Pavlov used the term *inhibition* to refer to an internal process that blocks the execution of certain actions that an individual might otherwise perform.

Pavlov described three phenomena to support his contention that extinction does not lead to the loss of learned behavior, even though the individual is no longer making conditioned responses during the extinction procedure. The first involves the presentation of another external stimulus while his dogs were experiencing the procedure of extinction (CS presented alone). After the dogs were no longer salivating when the CS was presented alone for a number of trials, the sudden presentation of another stimulus would result in the reappearance of the conditioned response. Pavlov used the term **disinhibition** (the "negation" of inhibition) to describe *the reappearance of salivary CR when an external stimulus is presented while the individual is experiencing the procedure of extinction*. Thus, Pavlov argued that the decline in the performance of the conditioned response during the procedure of extinction was due to an inhibitory process that is temporarily disrupted when a sudden different stimulus is introduced. This is analogous to the disruption of conditioned responses by the introduction of external stimuli (external inhibition) during conditioning. In both cases (external inhibition and disinhibition), the external event disrupts the psychological process that is controlling behavior at the moment.

The second phenomenon involves the reintroduction of CS-US presentations after a period of extinction. If extinction erased the effects of conditioning, then individuals would have to relearn from scratch to make conditioned responses to the CS, but that is not what happens: *Conditioned responses can quickly resume their preextinction levels when the original CS-US relationship is restored.* This phenomenon of rapid reacquisition has been demonstrated following extinction in aversive and appetitive Pavlovian procedures (Napier, Macrae, & Kehoe, 1991; Ricker & Bouton, 1996).

The third piece of evidence is that *behavior that has been extinguished reappears when the individual is returned to that situation after a period of time has elapsed.* This well-established phenomenon, termed **spontaneous recovery**, has been obtained using humans (Franks, 1963; Hartman & Grant, 1962; Prokasy, 1958) and other animals (Brooks & Bouton, 1993; Haberlandt, Hamsher, & Kennedy, 1978; Quirk, 2002; for a review, see Rescorla, 2004). Although spontaneous recovery is not complete—that is, the individual does not perform the CR to the same level as he or she did at the end of conditioning (and the start of extinction)—the fact that the CR reappears later without intervening CS-US trials suggests that the CR was suppressed or inhibited, not unlearned, during extinction. If extinction produced unlearning, then the CR should not reappear when the individual is back in the extinction situation. All three of these phenomena (disinhibition, rapid reacquisition, and spontaneous recovery) illustrate that CRs are not unlearned during the procedure of extinction (for reviews, see Delamater & Westbrook, 2014; Lattal & Lattal, 2012; McConnell & Miller, 2014; Rescorla, 2001; Todd, Vurbic, & Bouton, 2014a). Pavlovian extinction will be revisited in Chapter 5.

The Temporal Relationship Between the CS and US. Pavlov also explored the effects of the temporal (time) relationship between the CS and US. He found that the salivary CR appeared in a few trials if the CS came on 1–5 seconds before the US and stayed on while the US was presented. Furthermore, he reported that the number of trials needed to obtain a salivary CR increased for longer CS-US intervals between the start of the CS and the presentation of the US. When the CR did emerge after a number of trials with these long CS-US intervals, initially it tended to occur soon after the CS was presented. *As the number of trials increased, the salivary CR would occur later in the interval and closer to the time that the US was scheduled to occur.* Pavlov called this a **delayed reflex**. From this we derive the name **delay conditioning** for *the procedure where the CS comes on and stays on until the US is presented* (Figure 2.3, panel a). Pavlov's basic procedure is a delay conditioning procedure because the CS commenced 1–5 seconds before the US was presented.

In delay conditioning experiments, the CS and US overlap. However, a salivary CR will emerge even when the CS and US do not overlap. *The CS can come on and go off, and the US can be presented some time later.* We call this procedure **trace conditioning** because Pavlov labeled the CR a **trace response**; that is, *a response to the memory trace of the CS (which is no longer present when the US is presented*; Figure 2.3, panel b). Pavlov reported that with both delay and trace conditioning, the salivary CR occurred during the interval between the two stimulus presentations, and with continued training, the CR tended to occur just before the US was scheduled to occur.

Pavlov believed that the appearance of conditioned responses required that the CS occur *before* the US. He based this belief on his failure to obtain conditioned responses when he *presented the CS and US at exactly the same time* (**simultaneous conditioning procedure**) (Figure 2.3, panel c) and when the *US preceded the CS* (**backward conditioning procedure**; Figure 2.3, panel d); however, as later research shows, there are situations in which simultaneous and backward conditioning procedures can produce conditioned responses.

Finally, Pavlov found that *the presentation of the US at regular intervals* also led to the occurrence of salivary CRs just before the occurrence of the US (Figure 2.3, panel e). He suggested that the passage of time served as the CS in this case. Today we call this procedure **temporal conditioning**. The similarities and differences among these procedures are presented in Figure 2.3.

As noted above, *with delay, trace, and temporal conditioning procedures, the CR tends to occur close to the time that the US is scheduled.* He labeled this phenomenon (the gradual shift in

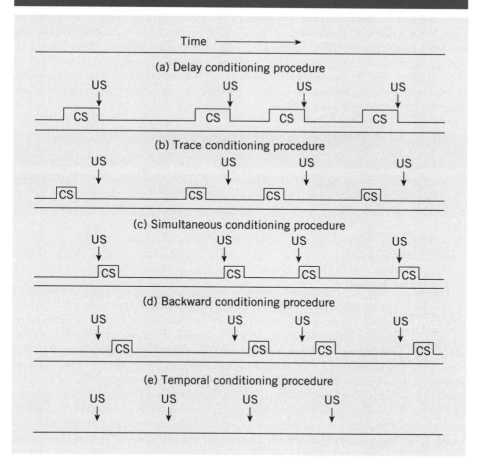

Figure 2.3 Various temporal relationships between the presentation of the CS and the US in Pavlovian conditioning. Note the relationships between the presentations of the CS and US. The occurrence of the CS is indicated by the symbol |CS| and the occurrence of the US by the down arrow (↓). In the temporal conditioning procedure in which the US occurs at regular intervals (panel e), the passage of time is the CS.

the time that CR occurs) as **inhibition of delay** because he thought that the CR was being inhibited until just before the US is scheduled to occur.

Second-Order Conditioning. With delay and trace conditioning procedures, *the CS is followed by a US.* This is called **first-order conditioning**. Pavlov also described a procedure that allowed him to *produce conditioned responses (CRs) to conditioned stimuli (CSs) that had never been presented with unconditioned stimuli (USs)*. That phenomenon is called **second-order conditioning** (Rescorla, 1980b). The procedure for producing second-order conditioning is presented in Table 2.1. The first step is first-order conditioning: A conditioned stimulus (called CS_1) is followed by a US. This produces a CR to CS_1. In Pavlov's demonstration, CS_1 was a metronome and the US was food. After the conditioned salivary response occurred readily when the metronome (CS_1) was presented, Pavlov proceeded to the second step. He presented his dogs with a black square for 10 seconds (CS_2) followed 15 seconds later by the metronome (CS_1), but *no* food was presented. After a number of these black square-metronome (CS_2-CS_1) trials, the dog also salivated when the black square (CS_2) was presented, even though the square had *never* been presented with food. Pavlov called the response to the black square a secondary conditioned reflex. The **procedure of second-order conditioning** can be summarized as follows: *Individuals are given first-order Pavlovian conditioning ($CS_1 \rightarrow US$). Then they are given Pavlovian conditioning in which a second stimulus (CS_2) is followed by CS_1. CS_2 is never followed by the US* (see Table 2.1). Second-order conditioning is a specific instance of a general phenomenon termed higher-order conditioning. By increasing the number of CSs involved, third-order conditioning, fourth-order-conditioning, and so forth are possible, but obtaining CRs to those higher-order CSs is increasingly more difficult.

Table 2.1 The Procedure for Producing Second-Order Conditioning

Phase 1	Phase 2	Test
First-order conditioning	Second-order conditioning	
$CS_1 \rightarrow US$	$CS_2 \rightarrow CS_1$	CR to CS_2
metronome → food	black square → metronome	salivation to black square

Blair and Shimp (1992) provided an interesting example of second-order conditioning in an experiment designed to demonstrate that prior unpleasant experience with a particular song or melody subsequently can affect how a person might react to a commercial on radio or television that pairs that music with a product brand. In the first stage of their experiment (first-order conditioning), participants (undergraduate students) were told they were evaluating audiotapes for use in a marketing curriculum. During each of the five daily sessions that took place over one week during non-class hours in wintery weather, they listened to a different 20-minute tape in which the introductory statement was accompanied by a particular piece of music that had been determined earlier to be neutral by a different group of students. At the end of each session, the participants evaluated the tape they just heard. (That had no bearing on the experiment and was only done to legitimize the cover story.) Listening to these tapes under those unpleasant conditions was the US, and that music was the CS_1.

Immediately after the participants finished evaluating the last tape, a second experimenter entered the room and asked if they were willing to serve in a second experiment in another room for money. Those who accepted were taken to that location and shown slides of various men's' shirts along with associated fake brand names (CS_2) followed by 25 seconds of music. For the participants given second-order conditioning, one of the fake brand names (the target) was always paired with the music from the first stage of the experiment, and the other names were paired with different musical selections.

The dependent measure in this experiment was the rating of the brand names. The only brand name that was negatively affected was the target name that always was followed by the music that introduced each audiotape in the first phase of the experiment. These results indicate that how individuals react to commercials that contain music depends on their prior experiences with that music. We will see other examples of how Pavlovian conditioning can affect preferences in Chapter 6 (evaluative conditioning).

Assessing Pavlov's Contribution. Some people find it easy to dismiss Pavlov's work as irrelevant for understanding human behavior. His dogs were strapped in harnesses in isolation rooms, and everything the dogs experienced was controlled by the experimenter who stayed in an adjoining room. Even the saliva was collected in tubes that carried it to the experimenter (see Figure 1.5 in Chapter 1). What can we possibly learn from such an artificial and sterile arrangement that is relevant to us? The answer is that we can learn a great deal. Think for a moment about the phenomenon Pavlov studied. It is a common observation that hungry dogs and people react to the sights and smells of food and to the sounds of food being dished out or prepared. Clearly, we and our four-legged friends learn to identify the signals preceding the imminent delivery of food to our plates (and bowls), and we behave in ways that reflect that knowledge. Pavlov was interested in studying "objectively" (his word) the psychological processes that are responsible for our "anticipatory" behavior. To do so, he had to create an environment in which he could control all of the stimuli that impinged on his subjects. His dogs were not raised in isolation; they had learned about the sights and smells of food. They already knew who fed them, when, and what that person did while delivering the food. In order to study the "psychical reflexes" (salivation that is triggered by an external stimulus not in the mouth), Pavlov had to isolate his subjects from extraneous events and use arbitrary stimuli as CSs. Had he not done this, his data would have been contaminated by the effects of past experience and by external inhibition and disinhibition. His careful attempts to study conditioned reflexes in isolation make it easy for all of us to see what he found.

Because of the relative simplicity of Pavlov's procedures, it is easy to overlook his contribution to the study of behavior. Pavlov showed us how we can use systematic observation and experimentation to explore psychological processes, and he provided a way to measure behavior objectively. He rejected explanations in terms of feelings, thoughts, and desires of his dogs when they salivated at sights and smells of food as unfruitful speculations. He did not deny that humans have an inner world; his objection was to those who explained the behavior of animals in terms of these mental states. Pavlov believed that we can come to understand the behavior of animals by studying how they react to their environment. His objective approach to the study of behavior preceded that of John Watson, the father of the school of thought we call behaviorism.

> A rather large number of new terms and concepts were introduced in this section, and it is easy to get overwhelmed by them. Furthermore, many of these terms and concepts will be used throughout this book to describe procedures and explain phenomena. Therefore, it is important that you become familiar with them. To aid you, the basic terms and concepts from this section are contained in the Glossary and on the inside front cover.

CONDITIONED EMOTIONAL RESPONSES

Watson and Rayner's experiment with Albert showed how Pavlovian conditioning procedures can be used to arouse emotions like fear. Fear is an inferred psychological state; its existence is inferred from behavior. We will examine how we measure such psychological states.

Reflexes like salivation are not the only things that can be influenced by the procedure of Pavlovian conditioning. The example from *Jaws* at the beginning of this chapter illustrates conditioning of emotional reactions. These conditioned responses are internal and not directly observable (as opposed to salivation, which is directly observable). When we observe people gasp or cringe during the film, we infer that they are experiencing the emotional reaction we call fear. The conditioned response is the fear, and the observed behavior is an indication of that fear. *Fear is an intervening variable—it is not something that we observe directly; we infer it from the observed behavior.* Likewise, the feelings you experience when you hear the dentist's drill motor or hear a siren behind you when driving are emotional states. You can experience them directly, but someone observing you infers how you feel by your facial expressions and body language.

Conditioned Fear (Little Albert). Little Albert is probably the most famous child in psychology. Using Pavlovian conditioning, John Watson and Rosalie Rayner demonstrated what they called a **conditioned emotional response** in a human being, that is, *a learned emotional response (fear) to a stimulus that did not evoke that response before conditioning* (Watson & Rayner, 1920). Their procedure fits the standard Pavlovian procedure: When a white rat was presented to Albert, he reached for it (orienting response). As he touched the rat, one of the experimenters created a loud noise by striking a steel rod with a hammer behind Albert's head. Albert's overt reaction to the loud noise was to jump violently and fall forward, burying his face in the mattress (Watson & Rayner, 1920, p. 4). After six more repetitions of this procedure spread over two sessions one week apart, Albert began to cry and withdraw when the rat was presented (see Box 2.2 for an excerpt from "Conditioned Emotional Reactions"). Can

BOX 2.2

Excerpt From "Conditioned Emotional Reactions"

This excerpt from Watson and Rayner's paper provides us with a description of how they conditioned Albert to be afraid of a white rat:

> At first there was considerable hesitation upon our part in making the attempt to set up fear reactions experimentally. A certain responsibility attaches to such a procedure. We decided finally to make the attempt, comforting ourselves by the reflection that such attachments would arise anyway as soon as the child left the sheltered environment of the nursery for the rough and tumble of the home. We did not begin this work until Albert was eleven months, three days of age. Before attempting to set up a conditioned response we, as before, put him through all of the regular emotional tests. *Not the slightest sign of a fear response was obtained in any situation.*
>
> The steps taken to condition emotional responses are shown in our laboratory notes.

11 Months 3 Days

1. White rat suddenly taken from the basket and presented to Albert. He began to reach for rat with left hand. Just as his hand touched the animal the bar was struck immediately behind his head. The infant jumped violently and fell forward, burying his face in the mattress. He did not cry, however.

2. Just as the right hand touched the rat the bar was again struck. Again the infant jumped violently, fell forward and began to whimper.

In order not to disturb the child too seriously no further tests were given for one week.

11 Months 10 days

1. Rat presented suddenly without sound. There was steady fixation but no tendency at first to reach for it. The rat was then placed nearer, whereupon tentative reaching movements began with the right hand. When the rat nosed the infant's left hand, the hand was immediately withdrawn. He started to reach for the head of the animal with the forefinger of the left hand, but withdrew it suddenly before contact. It is thus seen that the two joint stimulations given the previous week were not without effect. He was tested with his blocks immediately afterwards to see if they shared in the process of conditioning. He began immediately to pick them up, dropping them, pounding them, etc. In the remainder of the tests the blocks were given frequently to quiet him and to test his general emotional state. They were always removed from sight when the process of conditioning was under way.

2. Joint stimulation with rat and sound. Started, then fell over immediately to right side. No crying.

3. Joint stimulation. Fell to right side and rested upon hands, with head turned away from rat. No crying.

4. Joint stimulation. Same reaction.

5. Rat suddenly presented alone. Puckered face, whimpered and withdrew body sharply to the left.

(Continued)

(Continued)

6. Joint stimulation. Fell over immediately to right side and began to whimper.

7. Joint stimulation. Started violently and cried, but did not fall over.

8. Rat alone. The instant the rat was shown the baby began to cry. Almost instantly he turned sharply to the left, fell over on left side, raised himself on all fours and began to crawl away so rapidly that he was caught with difficulty before reaching the edge of the table.

This was as convincing a case of a completely conditioned fear response as could have been theoretically pictured. In all seven joint stimulations were given to bring about the complete reaction. It is not unlikely had the sound been of greater intensity or of a more complex clang character that the number of joint stimulations might have been materially reduced.

From Watson and Rayner, 1920, pp. 3–5.

you identify the CS, CR, US, and UR in Watson and Rayner's demonstrations with Albert? Over the next month, Albert's reactions to a number of other things were tested. When he was presented with wooden blocks, he always played with them; however, he whimpered and/or withdrew from a dog, a rabbit, a piece of fur (seal), a piece of cotton wool, and John Watson in a Santa Claus mask. Presumably, the similarities these latter objects have with the white rat produced **stimulus generalization**, *CRs to those stimuli that had something in common with the CS* (white rat).

Clinical Implications of Watson and Rayner's Demonstration. Some second-hand accounts of Watson and Rayner's work with Albert describe an extinction procedure, although none was reported in their paper because Albert left the hospital before such procedures could be carried out (Beck, Levinson, & Irons, 2009; Harris, 1979). However, Watson and Rayner did describe what they *would have done* had they had the opportunity. In 1924, Mary Cover Jones used one of Watson and Rayner's suggestions to reduce fear of rabbits in a child named Peter (Jones, 1924, 1974). In this case, the child was afraid of rabbits when he was brought for treatment. Jones's treatment was straightforward. She had Peter sit at a table and eat ice cream. The rabbit was slowly introduced into the room, first as far away from Peter as possible and then gradually brought closer and closer to him during the course of repeated sessions. At the last session, Peter let the rabbit nibble his fingers.

Watson and Rayner believed they had produced a fear (or phobia) where none had existed before. They argued that one need not invoke psychodynamic concepts to explain phobias and that phobias are the result of Pavlovian conditioning, nothing more. It is interesting that although Watson and Rayner described a number of methods for treating phobias in their 1920 paper, and Jones demonstrated that at least one of them worked in 1924, it was not until the 1950s that these techniques were applied to clinical problems (Wolpe, 1958).

Criticisms of Watson and Rayner's Demonstration. Fortunately, Watson and Rayner recorded some of their demonstration on film. By today's standards we can see that this was not very good research (Samelson, 1980). Watson and Rayner used only one subject (Albert), and there is no evidence that they employed any control conditions to eliminate other explanations of their results. Perhaps the loud noise sensitized Albert to be afraid of any object: In their film, we see the rat, dog, monkey, piece of cloth, and Santa Claus mask all presented abruptly to Albert. Other experiments with strong stimuli have demonstrated reactions that look like Pavlovian conditioned responses but are not due to the joint presentation of a CS and US.[4] In fairness to Watson and Rayner, they did not present their work with Albert as anything other than a demonstration. It would have been a better demonstration if they had demonstrated (either in other subjects or in Albert before the conditioning trials) that the loud noise they used did not sensitize Albert to withdraw when any sudden stimulus was presented.

Another problem with Watson and Rayner's demonstration is that on a number of trials they presented the loud noise when Albert either touched or was touched by the rat. One could argue that this is not true Pavlovian conditioning because Albert experienced the loud noise after he did something (reached for the rat). From that perspective, this is an example of the operant conditioning procedure called punishment (response is followed by an unpleasant event). Thus, Albert's withdrawal could be due to punishment, not Pavlovian conditioning. However, the view of most students of learning is that Watson and Rayner's procedure is Pavlovian conditioning.

Natural Selection and Conditioned Fear. Despite the criticisms of their work, Watson and Rayner's demonstration of a conditioned fear produced by Pavlovian conditioning has long been taken as an example of how the principles of learning can be used to explain phobias. It is interesting that there are a few reported attempts to replicate Watson and Rayner's demonstration, only some of which were partially successful; however, the lack of success in these experiments is instructive.

English (1929) reported three sets of observations, two based on observations at home and one that took place in the laboratory. The first case involved a 7-month-old child named Joan Katherine. At the moment that her mother offered her a black stuffed cat that Joan Katherine had played with earlier that morning, her older sister howled in protest. Joan Katherine withdrew her hand, cried, and rejected the toy cat when it was offered again during the next 10 minutes. She warily accepted it 2 hours later, but soon began to show fear. Forty-eight hours later she played with the cat and showed no sign of fear again. Given that there was only one conditioning trial, and the child had played with the cat earlier, the loss of the conditioned response two days later is not surprising. Can you identify the CS, US, and CR in this example? (The UR is not specified, but you can infer what it is from the US.)

For his second example, English attempted to condition a 14-month-old child, Helen Elizabeth, to fear a toy wooden duck that she had not seen before. The child was seated in a high chair when the toy duck was presented followed by a loud noise produced by striking a metal bar (similar to that used by Watson and Rayner). This child showed no visible sign of distress of the loud noise, and she did not exhibit fear to the toy duck. English's third

---

[4]Just presenting a strong US alone for a number of trials can evoke an emotional reaction to any sudden stimulus. This is an example of sensitization (see Chapter 1).

example involved the same child (Helen Elizabeth) at 15 months of age at home. She was fond of playing with her father's house slippers. However, when she came upon a pair of patent leather shoes lying in the sunlight, she became apprehensive and did not want to touch them. When the shiny shoes were placed with her father's shoes, she became afraid of the latter too. Thus, it appeared that the fear of the shiny shoes became attached to the house slippers. Three months later, these fears were not in evidence. English focused on the failed attempt to replicate Watson and Rayner's result with Albert, but the other two examples (although they were not controlled experiments) did illustrate the occurrence of fear to formerly unfeared objects.

Valentine (1930) described both an unsuccessful and a successful replication of Watson and Rayner's observations. Using his own 1-year-old daughter, he attempted to condition fear to an old pair of opera glasses: each time the child reached for the opera glasses, he blew a loud whistle behind her. Each time he did that, the child turned to look at him, but she showed no signs of fear. Later that same day, a caterpillar was substituted for the opera glasses. On the very first conditioning trial (after the whistle was blown), the child screamed and turned away from the caterpillar. Four more conditioning trials were given with the caterpillar. The next day the child still showed some fear of the caterpillar when it was presented without the whistle.

Bregman (1934) attempted to condition 15 infants (seven boys and eight girls, 8–16 months of age) to fear various objects (various shaped and colored blocks of wood or pieces of cloth). Each child was seated in a chair. The conditioned stimuli were presented on a small table in front of the child, and the unconditioned stimulus was an electric bell hung on the back of the chair. All of the children exhibited startle responses to the sound of the bell (the US), and they cried on 87% of the trials when the bell was presented. Some of these conditioned stimuli were followed by the bell, and others by a music box that played a simple tune. The results were mixed. Some children produced negative emotional responses to the stimuli paired with the bell and others did not.

Bregman's (1934) results appear to contradict Watson and Rayner's (1920) results, until one considers the conditioned stimuli. Watson and Rayner used a white rat while Bregman used arbitrarily chosen stimuli. English observed fear produced to a toy cat and house slippers (both furry objects), and Valentine (1930) produced fear to a caterpillar but not to opera glasses. Later research also points to the importance of the specific stimulus employed as the CS: Conditioning is more rapid when the CS is a snake or a spider than when it is a circle or a triangle (Marks, 1987; Öhman & Hugdahl, 1979). On the other hand, with arbitrary CSs like circles and triangles, verbal instructions about the CS-US relationship facilitates the acquisition of the conditioned response (Cook & Harris, 1937; Dawson & Grings, 1968), instructions that the US will no longer occur facilitates the extinction of the response (Bridger & Mandell, 1965; Cook & Harris, 1937; Dawson & Grings, 1968; Katz, Webb, & Stotland, 1971; Wilson, 1968), and providing people with false information about the CS-US contingency will lead them to behave in accordance with that false information, not the actual contingency in effect (Deane, 1969; Spence & Goldstein, 1961). This is not true when the CS is a snake or spider.

The obvious conclusion for all of these studies is that, through natural selection, members of a species acquire innate knowledge of dangerous things in their ancestors' niche.

When one is hurt or otherwise threatened in the presence of these things, one can rapidly learn to be afraid of them. That explains why humans are more likely to develop phobias to spiders, the dark, heights, open spaces, and so on, as opposed to electrical appliances from which most if not all of us have received shocks (Davey, 1992; McNally, 1987; Oehlberg & Mineka, 2011).

Conditioned Fear as an Intervening Variable. Watson and Rayner titled their paper "Conditioned Emotional Reactions" because they claimed to have made Albert afraid of something (the white rat) he was not afraid of before. Fear is both an emotion and a motivation—that is, a psychological state aroused by a signal for impending danger. We do not see fear directly; we infer it from behavior. We may feel afraid (an emotion), and that emotional state interferes with ongoing behavior; sometimes it can "motivate" us to do something (e.g., get away). Thus, we attribute Albert's withdrawal from the white rat and other furry objects as due to his being made afraid of them. Fear and other emotional states are **intervening variables**: *psychological processes that we infer exist between what is done to the individual (independent variable) and how the individual behaves (dependent variable)*. In Watson and Rayner's demonstration, the independent variable was what they did to Albert (Pavlovian conditioning), and the dependent variable was Albert's reaction (crying, withdrawal). As a result of the conditioning trials, Albert behaved in a way that leads us to say he had become afraid of the white rat. We infer that he was afraid based on his behavior; thus, his fear is classified as an intervening variable.

Conditioned Suppression as a Measure of Conditioned Fear. By identifying fear as the conditioned response, we are assuming that this psychological state exists and that its presence is reflected in behavior. Watson and Rayner used Albert's whimpering, crying, and withdrawal from objects as their index of fear. Another way to study conditioned fear is by observing *how much the presentation of the fear-provoking stimulus disrupts ongoing behavior*. This technique, called **conditioned suppression**, has the advantage of providing a quantitative measure of fear through the amount of disruption or suppression of the ongoing behavior (Estes & Skinner, 1941).

One way to study conditioned suppression in the laboratory is to use operant conditioning to train individuals to do something (press a lever) and then initiate the Pavlovian conditioning procedure while the individual is performing that behavior. For example, a rat is trained with an operant conditioning procedure to press a lever to obtain food (see Chapter 7). After the rat is pressing the lever at a stable rate that does not vary much either within or between sessions, a tone is presented. Although the tone may produce an orienting response the first few times it is presented, that orienting response habituates with repeated presentation of the tone alone. Pavlovian conditioning consists of the following sequence: The tone is presented, and a brief electric shock is delivered through the floor while the tone is still on. The unconditioned response to the shock is to jump and squeal. For a short time after the shock, the rat does not press the lever. After a while, the rat resumes performing that behavior. After a few of these tone-shock presentations, the introduction of that tone produces an immediate reduction in lever pressing. When the tone is no longer present, the rat resumes lever pressing. Can you identify the US, UR, CS, and CR here?

This procedure allows us to compute a quantitative index of fear. That index is based on the assumption that the amount of suppression of the ongoing behavior (in this case lever pressing) is related to the amount of fear conditioned to the CS (in this case the tone). There are a number of formulas one can use to compute a behavioral index of fear. All of them are based on comparing the rate of occurrence of the operant behavior when the CS is present with the rate of that behavior immediately before the CS occurs. A commonly-used measure of conditioned suppression called the **suppression ratio** is defined as follows:

$$\frac{\text{Rate of responding in presence of CS}}{\text{Rate of responding in presence of CS} + \text{Rate of responding prior to presentation of CS}} \quad (1)$$

How Equation 1 provides us with a quantitative index of fear can be seen from the following numerical example: Suppose the rate of lever pressing prior to the presentation of the tone is 40 times per minute. If the rat has never been shocked in the presence of the tone, he or she should continue to press the lever 40 times per minute when the tone sounds.[5] Substituting these numbers into Equation 1 gives us a value for the suppression ratio of 0.5 [40/(40 + 40) = 0.5]. Therefore, *the value of the suppression ratio will be 0.5 when the introduction of the CS has no influence on the ongoing operant behavior (because no fear has been conditioned to that CS).* On the other hand, if the rat has experienced a few moderate shocks in the presence of the tone, presentation of that tone while the rat is pressing a lever for food will typically result in a reduction in the rate of lever pressing during the tone. For example, if the rat is making 40 lever presses per minute before the CS is presented and that rate drops to zero lever presses during the CS, the suppression ratio in Equation 1 will be 0 [0/(0 + 40) = 0]. We infer that this suppression of ongoing behavior is caused by fear aroused by the tone as a result of Pavlovian conditioning. Therefore, *the value of the suppression ratio will be zero when the introduction of the tone produces complete suppression of the ongoing behavior.* Complete suppression of ongoing behavior when the CS is introduced indicates a high level of fear has been conditioned to that CS. An intermediate level of conditioned fear will produce partial suppression of the ongoing behavior, and the suppression ratio will be between 0.5 and 0. For example, if the rate of lever pressing falls from 40 per minute prior to the presentation of the tone to 10 per minute in the presence of the tone, the suppression ratio will be 0.2 [10/(10 + 40) = 0.2]. Therefore, *the amount of conditioned suppression and the value of the suppression ratio will reflect the level of fear conditioned to the CS; the lower the suppression ratio, the greater the suppression and the greater the fear.* These three possible scenarios (no suppression, partial suppression, and complete suppression) are summarized in Table 2.2 and Figure 2.4.

---

[5]External inhibition of lever pressing may occur the first time the tone is presented, but after a few presentations the rat should ignore the tone and maintain the same rate of lever pressing both before and during the tone.

Table 2.2 Calculating Suppression Ratios

Condition	Rate of responding during the CS (a)	Rate of responding prior to the CS (b)	Suppression ratio $\dfrac{a}{a+b}$
No suppression	40	40	$\dfrac{40}{40+40} = \dfrac{40}{80} = 0.5$
Partial suppression	10	40	$\dfrac{10}{10+40} = \dfrac{10}{50} = 0.2$
Complete suppression	0	40	$\dfrac{0}{0+40} = \dfrac{0}{40} = 0$

Figure 2.4 Graphical depiction of the suppression ratios for the three situations described in Table 2.2.

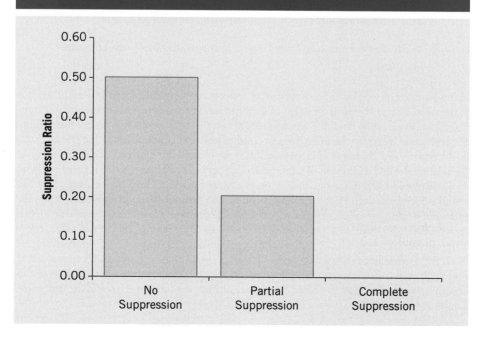

Summary: How We Use Conditioned Suppression as an Index of Conditioned Fear

1. Fear can disrupt ongoing behavior, and the greater the fear, the greater the disruption.

2. Stimuli that occur along with dangerous events can come to evoke fear as a result of Pavlovian conditioning; that is, these stimuli become Pavlovian CSs.

3. We can provide a quantitative index of fear by comparing performance during the CS with performance prior to the presentation of the CS. That index is called a suppression ratio (Equation 1). *The amount of conditioned suppression and the value of the suppression ratio will reflect the level of fear conditioned to the CS.* (Partial suppression in Table 2.2 and Figure 2.4.)

4. *The value of the suppression ratio will be zero when the introduction of the tone produces complete suppression of the ongoing behavior.* (Complete suppression in Table 2.2 and Figure 2.4.)

5. *The value of the suppression ratio will be 0.5 when the introduction of the CS has no effect on the ongoing operant behavior. This will be the case when no fear has been conditioned to that CS.* (No suppression in Table 2.2 and Figure 2.4.)

6. With this measure of conditioned suppression, *lower* values mean *more* fear.

If the amount of conditioned suppression reflects the amount of conditioned fear, it is reasonable to expect that the course of experimental extinction (reduction of the conditioned response when the CS is presented without the US) would also reflect the amount of conditioned fear; that is, the strongest conditioned fear would take the longest to extinguish. Annau and Kamin (1961) systematically investigated the effects of US intensity on the acquisition and extinction of conditioned suppression with rats. They trained rats with an operant conditioning procedure to press a lever for food. Once the response rate had stabilized for each animal, the Pavlovian conditioning procedure was initiated. While the rats were working to obtain food, the conditioned stimulus (a low volume white noise that sounds like radio static) was presented for 3 minutes. Different groups of rats experienced different intensities of a brief (0.5 second) electric shock to the paws delivered at the end of each CS presentation. After 10 days of training, the extinction procedure was instituted; that is, the CS (noise) was presented alone (no shock). The results of both phases of this experiment are presented in Figure 2.5; the acquisition data is on the left and the extinction data is on the right.

Clearly, the stronger the US (shock measured in milliamps of current), the greater the degree of suppression and the longer it takes the individuals to resume responding when the CS is no longer followed by the US. If we assume that the amount of conditioned fear

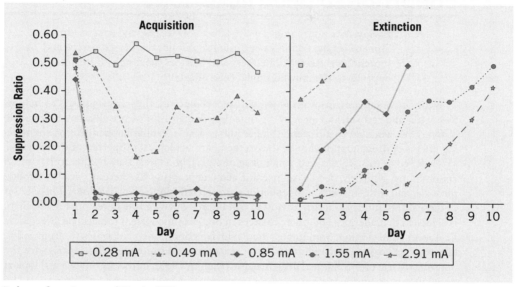

Figure 2.5 Acquisition (left) and extinction (right) of conditioned suppression to a low-volume white noise CS in rats as a function of the intensity of the unconditioned stimulus (mA of shock). The suppression ratio measures the amount of conditioned suppression. A ratio of 0.5 indicates no suppression. A ratio of 0 indicates complete suppression.

Redrawn from Annau and Kamin, 1961.

is a direct function of the intensity of the US (in this case the electric shock), then this experiment illustrates the relationship among the independent variable (shock intensity), intervening variable (fear), and dependent variable (level of response suppression in the presence of the CS).

Why Fear Produces Suppression of Ongoing Behaviors. The unconditioned response to the electric shock is to jump, but the characteristic observed response to a signal for that shock is to freeze (N. E. Miller, 1951). It is important to consider why rats stop pressing the bar while the CS is on. On the surface, conditioned suppression appears maladaptive because the rats can do nothing to avoid or escape from the shock, and by pressing the bar less, they lose food. However, the typical responses of an animal in the face of imminent danger are to either freeze or flee. Both of these responses are adaptive depending on the circumstance: flight can remove the individual from danger, and freezing can minimize the chances of detection by a predator. Flight is not possible in the conditioned suppression situation; that leaves freezing as the only remaining adaptive behavior in the face of imminent danger. Bolles (1970) argued that flight and freezing are **species-specific defense reactions**: *inherited behavior patterns evoked in response to danger*. From that perspective, conditioned suppression reflects innate knowledge in the face of danger. Fear affects behavior in a number of important ways. In the case of conditioned suppression, fear disrupts the ongoing behavior. But fear can also serve as a motivator to escape from and avoid an aversive situation (McAlister & McAlister, 1971, 1992; N. E. Miller, 1948).

CONDITIONED DRUG REACTIONS

> Pavlovian conditioning can also affect how we respond to some drugs. Sometimes the conditioned response mimics the drug's effects, and sometimes the conditioned response mirrors the drug's effects (i.e., is opposite to the unconditioned drug effects).

Many of us take medications when we are sick because they are supposed to help us feel better and recover, and most of the time they do help, but we are all aware that people also recover when given a placebo ("sugar pill"). Why does that happen? Aren't the healing effects of drugs supposed to be due to the pharmacological properties of those drugs? We will see in this section that some drug and placebo effects may be due to Pavlovian conditioning. Similarly, people can become addicted to drugs like heroin, cocaine, alcohol, nicotine, and caffeine. Although addictions are related to the pharmacological properties of these drugs, it turns out that Pavlovian conditioning plays a role here, too. Finally, there is evidence that allergies and other changes in our immune system can also be affected by Pavlovian conditioning. Sometimes, the Pavlovian conditioned responses to drugs *mimic* (are the same as) the unconditioned drug reactions, and sometimes they *mirror* (are the opposite of) the unconditioned drug reactions (Siegel, 1985). In this section we will look at both kinds of conditioned drug reactions (mimicking and mirroring).

Conditioned Drug Reactions That Mimic the Drug Effect. A rather interesting example of a conditioned drug effect that mimics the unconditioned drug reaction is called conditioned immunosuppression. Our bodies have a number of defenses that can be marshaled against viruses, bacteria, and other foreign agents. Some of our defenses are nonspecific in the sense that they are aroused when any kind of intrusion occurs. Local inflammation and fever are examples of nonspecific defenses. Our immune system creates a specific defensive response to specific invaders. Vaccinations (immunizations) against diseases like polio, rubella ("German measles"), and flu work because our bodies develop specific antibodies to these invaders when we receive a vaccination. The specificity of the immune system is apparent when we need a flu shot every year to ward off a new strain of the flu virus. (These new strains arise as a result of mutations.) Most of the time our immune system serves us well, but occasionally it can malfunction. Allergies are due to immune responses to normally harmless substances (dust, pollens, peanuts, perfumes and so on), and sometimes our immune systems turn against us in the form of autoimmune disorders. Rheumatoid arthritis is an example of an autoimmune disease. Finally, our immune systems can be weakened by exposure to the HIV virus (the virus that causes AIDS), to stress, and to certain chemicals.

Ader and his colleagues (for reviews see Ader & Cohen, 1991, 2001; Pacheco-López, Engler, Niemi, & Schedlowski, 2009) have reported a number of experiments in which they demonstrated suppression of the immune system in response to stimuli that preceded the injection of an immunosuppressive drug (cyclophosphamide). In these experiments, rats were allowed to consume saccharin (the CS) followed by an injection of cyclophosphamide (the US). Following conditioning, immunosuppression was measured by injecting subjects with a foreign substance (sheep red blood cells) and measuring the antibodies in their blood. When the subjects that were exposed to the conditioning paradigm tasted saccharin after the injection of sheep red blood cells, they exhibited lower antibody levels than subjects that did not consume saccharin during the test. The effects were small, but they were consistent across a number of experiments. Bovbjerg et al. (1990) also observed such anticipatory suppression of the immune system in women receiving chemotherapy for ovarian cancer. These women received chemotherapy treatments that suppressed immune system function in a hospital every four weeks. Blood samples were collected at home a few days prior to the hospital visit and at the hospital prior to the chemotherapy treatments. Measures of the immune system function taken in the hospital were lower than those taken at home.

At first glance, these results seem puzzling. What possible benefit can a conditioned response that lowers antibody levels confer to an individual? Ader (1985) argues that there can be therapeutic benefits. The important aspect of Ader's data is not that the conditioned response was suppression of the immune system; it was that the conditioned response mimicked the unconditioned response. This suggests a possible therapeutic benefit, namely, stimuli that accompany the administration of some drugs may acquire the ability to continue to produce the effects of those drugs after the drugs are discontinued.

Ader and Cohen (1982) demonstrated such a therapeutic benefit for the autoimmune disease called lupus. They found that a CS that accompanied the injection of the immunosuppressive drug cyclophosphamide affected the development and course of this autoimmune disease in mice. Using a strain of mice that are genetically disposed to develop lupus, Ader and Cohen gave different groups of mice different patterns of treatments. The design of their experiment and the results are presented in Table 2.3. All subjects were given access to saccharin once a week for eight weeks. Group C100 received an injection of cyclophosphamide once a week immediately after they consumed the saccharin (100% of the trials were conditioning trials). Group C50 drank the saccharin once a week for eight weeks, but they only received injections of cyclophosphamide four of the eight times (50% of the trials were conditioning trials). A third group (NC50) received the saccharin weekly, but on four of the eight weeks they received the cyclophosphamide on a different day than they received the saccharin (there were no conditioning trials because the saccharin and cyclophosphamide were not presented together on 50% of the weeks when the injections were given). Finally, there was a group that only drank the saccharin once each week; these animals never received injections of cyclophosphamide. This was called the nonconditioned control group (CONTROL). Ader and Cohen monitored the appearance of the disease and mortality rates while their animals continued on the weekly saccharin schedule.

As described in Table 2.3, mice in the control group developed the disease sooner and died soonest. Mice in Groups C100 and C50 showed delayed onset of the disease and prolonged survival relative to those in the other two groups. The therapeutic effect in Group C50 is particularly noteworthy because these mice received *half* as many injections of cyclophosphamide as the Group C100. This suggests that Pavlovian conditioning might

Table 2.3 The Different Conditions and the Results in Ader and Cohen's (1982) Experiment on the Effects of Pavlovian Conditioning on the Development of an Autoimmune Disease (Lupus)

Group	Pavlovian Conditioning	Results
C100	These mice received an injection of cyclophosphamide once a week immediately after they consumed the saccharin. (100% of the trials were conditioning trials.)	These mice showed the slowest onset of the disease and survived the longest.
C50	These mice received injections of cyclophosphamide on 4 of the 8 weeks immediately after they drank the saccharin. (50% of the trials were conditioning trials.)	These mice showed next slowest onset and next longest survival.
NC50	These mice received injections of cyclophosphamide on 4 of the 8 weeks that they drank the saccharin, but these injections occurred on a different day than the day they drank the saccharin. (There were no conditioning trials because the saccharin and cyclophosphamide were not presented together, but they received the cyclophosphamide on 50% of the weeks.)	The onset and survival were less than C50 but greater than the CONTROL.
CONTROL	These mice only drank the saccharin once each week. They never received injections of cyclophosphamide. This group is a nonconditioned control group.	These mice showed the fastest onset and shortest survival.

Note: During conditioning, all subjects received one saccharin trial per week for 8 weeks.

be used to bolster the therapeutic effects of some drugs; that is, one might even be able to gain the same effect with lower dosages, and the effects of the drug might be extended following its discontinuance.

Placebo Effects. Ader (1985, 1997) also noted the similarity between these data and what we call placebo effects, the benefit that is sometimes observed when individuals receive a treatment that has no real therapeutic component. He argued that some placebo effects could be produced by the act of taking a medication because taking the medication in the past was followed by relief: The events surrounding taking the medication become the CS and the therapeutic effects of the medication serve as the US. However, a word of caution is required here. Although some kinds of placebo effects may, indeed, reflect Pavlovian conditioning, it would be incorrect to infer that all placebo effects do. Placebo effects are due to a wide variety of factors, and Pavlovian conditioning may be one of them (Kirsch, 1997; Siegel, 2002).

Conditioned Drug Reactions That Mirror the Drug Effect. We classify a drug as addictive when it produces two effects: tolerance and withdrawal. *Tolerance* refers to the phenomenon that more and more of the drug is needed to achieve the same effect; over repeated administrations of the drug, the effect of the same dosage is less. *Withdrawal* refers to the unpleasant reactions individuals experience when they are deprived of the drug. Alcohol and the drugs derived from opium (morphine, heroin) produce both tolerance and withdrawal effects. Where addiction occurs, we attribute it to the drugs, but there is evidence that Pavlovian conditioning plays a role in addictions.

Siegel and his colleagues (for reviews see Siegel, 1999; 2005; Siegel, Baptista, Kim, McDonald, & Weise-Kelly, 2000; Siegel & Ramos, 2002) demonstrated that tolerance to morphine is partially attributed to Pavlovian conditioning. Morphine is an opiate, and one of its clinical uses is as an analgesic (to reduce pain). As tolerance to morphine develops, there is less pain relief from the drug. Siegel and his colleagues developed a procedure for demonstrating that tolerance can develop as a Pavlovian conditioned response to the stimulus events surrounding the administration of morphine. For example, Siegel, Hinson, and Krank (1978) gave rats a standard dose of morphine by injection in the presence of a set of distinctive environmental cues. Over trials, the rats developed a tolerance to the morphine; that is, they showed less pain relief than they did after the first trial. Pain relief was measured by how fast the rats would lick their paw after it was placed on a hot plate. The assumption was that the greater the felt pain, the quicker the rats would lick their paw. After the first injection of morphine, the rats took a long time before they licked their paw. With each subsequent administration of morphine, the rats licked their paw sooner. However, rats given morphine in one environment and tested for tolerance in a different environment showed a loss of tolerance; that is, they took longer to lick their paw when tested on the hot plate in the different environment. Siegel argued that this demonstrates that tolerance is in part a conditioned response to the stimuli that accompany the effects of the drug. In Siegel's experiments, morphine was the US that produced the UR of analgesia (pain reduction) and the stimuli that surround the injection of the morphine (the physical environment, the preparations for the injection, and the injection itself) became CSs for the CR of increased sensitivity to pain. Because the dose of morphine did not change over the training trials, we attribute the rats' increased responsiveness to pain to the development of tolerance to the drug. However, this tolerance was situation-specific; that is, it appeared in the training environment but not in a different environment.

This situation-specific aspect of drug tolerance suggests an explanation for deaths attributed to drug overdoses (OD) in experienced drug users: As tolerance develops, the drug user requires a larger dose to maintain the same effects. Those larger doses can be fatal to the first-time user who has no tolerance. If tolerance to a given drug is a Pavlovian CR elicited by the situation in which the drug was administered, then changing the situation will lessen the tolerance. That could be lethal to an experienced user.

Siegel, Hinson, Krank, and McCully (1982) tested this explanation for deaths from drug overdoses by giving two groups of rats injections of heroin in increasing amounts in a specific environment. The doses increased from 1 milligram of heroin per kilogram of body weight (1 mg/kg) to 8 mg/kg over the course of conditioning for both groups. A third group was given injections of dextrose (a sugar solution). On the test day, all three groups were given an injection of 15 mg of heroin per kilogram of body weight. Ninety-six percent of the group that had not received heroin previously died. The mortality rate for the other two groups depended on where they received the increased dose. Sixty-four percent of the group that received the increased dose in an environment different from where they received the earlier dose died compared to only 32% of the group that received the increased dose in the original environment. Thus, the lethality of the higher dose depended on prior experience with heroin and the conditions under which it was received.

Siegel (1984) extended this work to humans. He interviewed 10 former heroin addicts who almost died of drug overdoses. In 7 of the 10 cases, these people reported that they did something different when they almost died. Some of them took the drug in a different location and some changed their routine (see Box 2.3).

Mimicking and Mirroring: Why the Difference? As we have just seen, sometimes the conditioned response *mimics* the unconditioned response (as in conditioned immunosuppression); that is, the conditioned stimulus appears to be producing a reaction that is similar to the unconditioned response produced by the drug (the US). This is similar to what Pavlov found with salivary conditioning: the CS appears to *substitute* for the US by producing a CR that resembles the UR. However, sometimes the CR is the *mirror image* (opposite) of the UR (as in the conditioned drug tolerance experiments). In these cases, the CR appears to counteract the UR.

Excerpt From "Pavlovian Conditioning and Heroin Overdose: Reports by Overdose Victims"

Seven of the 10 survivors reported that the circumstances of drug administration were atypical on the occasion of the overdose. Two reported that they self-administered the drug in locations where they had never before injected themselves (the bathroom of a car wash and the basement of a candy store). Two other respondents reported unusual injection procedures when they overdosed: One successfully injected into her vein on the first attempt, in contrast with the usual difficulties she experienced in locating and injecting into a usable vein; the second accidentally diluted the heroin too much, and thus two injections (rather than the usual single injection) preceded the overdose. One of the other survivors reported that, in contrast with his usual practice of using no other drugs in conjunction with heroin, he took a barbiturate mixture (Tuinal) with the heroin when he overdosed. Another reported that, although he typically injected a combination of cocaine and heroin, cocaine was not available at the time of the overdose, and he injected heroin alone for the first time in over 9 months. The 7th victim reported that, when he overdosed, he "got off" with a number of other people in the living room of his house (a large crowd was present because they were celebrating the respondent's wedding earlier that day, and they used money received as wedding gifts to purchase a quantity of heroin). According to this respondent, he, but none of the other guests, suffered an overdose after injecting from the common drug supply. This victim reported that, although he had used heroin for about 10 years, he had never before taken heroin in his living room or in such a large group.

From Siegel, 1984, Bulletin of the Psychonomic Society, 22, p.429. With permission of Springer Science+Business Media.

BOX 2.3

Why the difference? Why do some CRs mimic the drug effect and some mirror it? Eikelboom and Stewart (1982) suggested that the difference probably reflects the URs to the drug, but as Ramsay and Woods (1997) pointed out, specifying the UR is not a simple task. They noted that most drugs affect a number of systems in the body, and the changes we observe no doubt reflect the interaction and contributions of these various systems; some of these effects are direct and some indirect. From this point of view, the difference between mimicking and mirroring as applied to conditioned drug effects is more apparent than real. What we see as the UR to the drug is the accumulation of adjustments from the different affected systems. Therefore, it is not surprising that some CRs resemble some URs (mimic) and other CRs will be the mirror image of other URs.

CONDITIONED TASTE AVERSIONS

Conditioned taste aversions (CTAs) are examples of efficient learning. The phenomenon of conditioned taste aversion helps us understand and treat appetite loss during chemotherapy. The critical element in the production of CTAs is gastrointestinal distress following the consumption of a distinctive-tasting substance, particularly if that distinctive-tasting substance is novel to the individual.

to be so deeply grounded in his nature that nothing in after life may be able to overcome it."

From Brontë (1848/1994, pp. 288–289).

Brontë anticipates by 100 years the use of a chemical compound (disulfiram, now called Antabuse) that causes vomiting and extreme discomfort when a person with it in his or her system also consumes alcohol. Unlike the compound used in Brontë's novel, Antabuse in the currently approved dosage has no adverse effect if there is no alcohol in a person's system (Alharbi & el-Guebaly, 2013). Jørgensen, Pedersen, and Tønnesen (2011) reviewed the results of 11 experiments in which participants were randomly assigned to treatment conditions that in some cases included other drugs used to reduce consumption of alcohol (G-hydroxybutyrate, Naltrexone, Topiramate). They concluded that treatment with Antabuse under close supervision has some effect on short-term abstinence (up to 12 months). Antabuse is one of a variety of chemical aversion treatments for problem drinking (see Revusky, 2009, for a review).

Have you ever consumed something, become nauseated, and then not wanted to eat that thing again? If so, you have lots of company. When Logue, Ophir, and Strauss (1981) asked 517 undergraduate students a similar question, 65% of their subjects reported that this happened to them at least once. In 74% of these aversions, the subjects reported getting nauseous some time after they consumed the substance in question. Developing an aversion to a particular food or beverage is a fairly common occurrence (see Box 2.4 for an example that predates the naming of the phenomenon), and the procedure is Pavlovian conditioning (for reviews, see Barker, Best, & Domjan, 1977; Braveman & Bronstein, 1985; Burish, Levy, & Meyerowitz, 1985; Milgram, Krames & Alloway, 1977; Reilly & Schachtman, 2009).

Conditioned Taste Aversions in Humans. The clearest examples of such CTAs in humans occur with cancer patients when they undergo chemotherapy or radiation therapy to arrest the cancer. One of the problems associated with chemotherapy and radiation is that these treatments produce vomiting and nausea. One consequence of this is that patients undergoing chemotherapy for cancer frequently lose their appetite and suffer weight loss. Cachexia (physical wasting) is the leading cause of death in cancer patients (Lindsey, Piper, & Blackburn, 1972; Morrison, 1976).

In the language of Pavlovian conditioning, the chemotherapy drugs and the radiation are USs that produce the URs of vomiting and nausea. Bernstein and her colleagues (Bernstein, 1978; Bernstein & Webster, 1980) related the loss of appetite to CTAs in both child and adult cancer patients by having them consume what was for them a novel-tasting ice cream (maple nut) 15 to 60 minutes before receiving chemotherapy. Bernstein (1978) divided her patients into three groups. One group ate maple nut ice cream before receiving chemotherapy. A second group was not offered ice cream prior to chemotherapy, and a third group consumed the ice cream but did not receive chemotherapy that day (because they were in for a routine check). Two to 16 weeks later, all subjects were offered a choice between the maple nut ice cream and another flavor. Bernstein reported that the patients who ate maple nut ice cream on the day they received chemotherapy were more likely to choose the other flavor 2 to 16 weeks later than did patients who had either consumed the ice cream without chemotherapy or who received chemotherapy without ice cream. In this experiment, the maple nut ice cream was the CS, the chemotherapy drug was the US, the gastrointestinal effects of these drugs was the UR, and the choice of the other flavor was taken as evidence that the subjects developed a CTA to the maple nut flavor (the CR).

These results are interesting for two reasons: Most of the subjects knew that it was the chemotherapy and not the ice cream that produced the nausea they experienced after the session, but they still exhibited a taste aversion to that flavor of ice cream. This suggests that CTAs are not the result of awareness of the true cause of the gastric distress. Second, subjects who did not report nausea from the drugs still tended to consume less of the maple nut, and not all of the patients who ate the ice cream just prior to the chemotherapy treatment avoided it later. This is a fairly common occurrence: The effects of the Pavlovian conditioning do not lead to a complete avoidance of the food.

Some individuals undergoing chemotherapy report anticipatory nausea over the course of treatment. Bovbjerg et al. (1990) asked their subjects who were receiving chemotherapy to treat ovarian cancer to rate their feelings of nausea at the time blood samples were taken. Ratings were much higher in the hospital where the chemotherapy was given than at home. Carey and Burish (1988) reviewed a number of studies that point to the conclusion that this anticipatory nausea is a Pavlovian CR to the stimuli surrounding the chemotherapy treatments.

Bernstein's (1978) experiments and Bovbjerg et al.'s (1990) observations can only go so far in helping us understand the phenomenon of CTAs because ethical considerations prevent us from exposing humans to harmful treatments unless there is a compelling reason to do so. Although taste aversions in humans are fairly common, we can learn more by studying this phenomenon in the laboratory under controlled conditions with animals.

Conditioned Taste Aversions in Rats. Consider the following demonstration: A thirsty rat is allowed to drink water flavored with saccharin. (Like most humans, rats readily consume sweet-tasting substances.) Seventy-five minutes later, the rat is injected with apomorphine (which causes nausea). A few days later (long after the nausea from the apomorphine is gone), the rat is again given access to saccharin-flavored water. Although the rat has been deprived of water for almost 24 hours, it will consume much less saccharin-flavored water than plain water. Even more interesting is the observation that if the rat experiences electric shock rather than nausea following consumption of the saccharin-flavored water, it will not avoid the saccharin when tested 24 hours later (Garcia, Ervin, & Koelling, 1966). This conditioned aversion in rats is to the taste of the food and not to its physical appearance.

Garcia and Koelling (1966) provided a more systematic demonstration of the selective nature of CTAs in rats (see Table 2.4). They had rats drink "bright-noisy-tasty" water. The water was made "bright" and "noisy" by having a light flash and a relay click with every lick of the water spout. The "tasty" water was produced by adding sodium chloride (table salt) to the water. After the rats drank bright-noisy-tasty water, one group was made sick by administration of the nausea-inducing agent lithium chloride (LiCl). Another group of rats drank the same "bright-noisy-tasty" water but experienced only electric shock while drinking. In the test, all rats were given an opportunity to drink the "bright-noisy" water and the "tasty" water. The results of this experiment are presented in Figure 2.6. The rats made nauseous by LiCl consumed less of the "tasty" water than they drank of the "bright-noisy" water. On the

Table 2.4   Design of Garcia and Koelling's (1966) Experiment Demonstrating the Selective Nature of Conditioned Taste Aversions in Rats

Group	CSs	US	Test
Nausea	Taste and Light/Noise	LiCl	"Tasty" water and "bright-noisy" water
Pain	Taste and Light/Noise	Shock	"Tasty" water and "bright-noisy" water

Note: LiCl = lithium chloride. At Test, the "tasty" water and "bright-noisy" water were presented on separate trials and trial order was counterbalanced within groups.

Figure 2.6   The effects of lithium chloride and shock USs on the development of aversions to the gustatory ("tasty") or the audio-visual aspects of the "bright-noisy-tasty" water CS. The dependent measure is the consumption of "tasty" water and "bright-noisy" water.

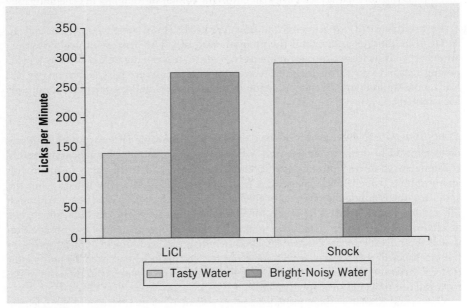

Redrawn from Garcia and Koelling, 1966. Psychonomic Science. With permission of Springer Science+Business Media.

other hand, the rats that received electric shocks when they drank the fluid in training showed no aversions to the "tasty" water, but they avoided the "bright-noisy" water.

In addition to nausea-inducing treatments (e.g., LiCl and radiation), CTAs can be induced in rats by giving them access to a distinctive tasting fluid followed by 30 minutes access to a running wheel (Lett & Grant, 1996) or a circular alley (Lett, Grant, Koh, & Parsons, 1999; for a review, see Boakes & Nakajima, 2009). Both apparatuses induce activity in rats, the running wheel more than the circular alley. After just three training trials (distinctive tasting fluid followed by access to an apparatus that induces activity), the rats exhibited a CTA to the fluid they consumed right before they were placed in the activity-inducing apparatus. The taste aversion was more pronounced after access to the running wheel, an apparatus that induces more activity than the circular alley. Lett and Grant (1996) noted the similarity between their results and activity anorexia in humans, the tendency for people exhibiting anorexia to exercise excessively. Perhaps anorectics exercise not only to burn calories but also because exercise right after eating also produces CTAs that in turn depress their desire to eat.

In Pavlov's experiment and in the conditioned emotional response experiments, the CS and US either overlapped or were separated by a short period of time (trace conditioning). Pavlov (1927) reported that the strongest conditioned salivary response occurred when the CS came on 1–5 seconds before the US. As the CS-US interval increased, more trials were needed before a salivary response appeared. In contrast, *CTAs in rats can be obtained on a single trial with delays of up to 12 hours.* For example, Smith and Roll (1967) gave different groups of thirsty rats access to saccharin-flavored water (the CS) and then exposed them to an x-ray treatment (the US) at different times after the rats consumed the flavored fluid. Other rats drank the saccharin water but did not receive an x-ray treatment (sham treatment). Twenty-four hours later, the rats were given a choice between saccharin water and plain water. Preference was measured in terms of how much of the saccharin solution they consumed relative to the plain water. The data from this experiment are presented in Figure 2.7. Although the effect of the treatment was strongest when the interval between consumption and radiation was less than 6 hours, there still was evidence of a CTA after a 12-hour CS-US delay.

The results with rats are fairly clear: Rats will form an aversion to the taste of food after just one trial if they become sick after eating that food, even if the time between when the food is consumed and the subject is made sick is as long as 12 hours. They will not form an aversion to the physical appearance of food after one trial if they become sick after eating that food. Rats will quickly learn to avoid foods and other objects in the presence of which they are shocked based on visual characteristics.

Conditioned Taste Aversions in Other Species. On the other hand, birds, with their more developed visual systems, are also likely to form aversions to the visual aspects of food (Brower, 1969; Gillette, Martin, & Bellingham, 1980; Logue, 1980; Wilcoxon, Dragoin, & Kral, 1971). This aspect of avian food-seeking behavior is exploited by some insects as an evolutionary solution to the problem of deterring predators. Insects that taste bad or produce nausea when consumed sometimes are conspicuously colored so that they can be easily identified by predators, and birds quickly learn to avoid them. Some "nonpoisonous" species evolved to resemble (mimic) the "poisonous" species' coloration. As a result, birds that learned to avoid the poisonous species will also avoid the nonpoisonous ones (see Figure 2.8). This is called Batesian mimicry (named for the nineteenth century naturalist Henry Walter Bates). The form of the mimicry depends on the species' niche, and it works because birds can readily learn not to eat insects with certain colorations that make them ill.

But some species with poorly developed visual systems also search for food visually. For example, guinea pigs search for food visually even though their visual system is no more developed than that of rats. They also develop aversions to the visual aspects of food (Braveman, 1974).

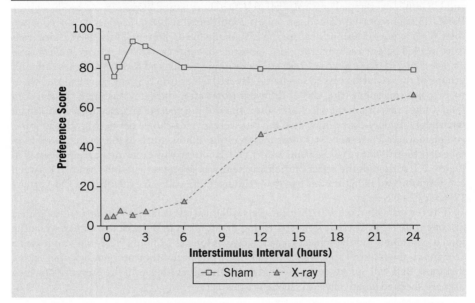

Figure 2.7 The effects of delay between tasting saccharin (the CS) and exposure to x-rays (the US). The x-ray group tasted the saccharin CS and then was given a single exposure to x-rays. Different groups received the exposure at different inter-stimulus intervals (the time period between the CS and the US). The sham group tasted the saccharin CS and was put into the x-ray chamber, but the machine was not turned on. Twenty-four hours later, all subjects were given a choice between the saccharin solution and plain water. Preference scores reflect the percentage of fluid consumption that was saccharin solution.

From Smith and Roll, 1967, *Psychonomic Science, 9*, 11–12. Redrawn with permission of Springer Science +Business Media

What is the conditioned response in conditioned taste aversions? Although it is quite clear that CTAs are the result of a Pavlovian conditioning procedure in which the CS is the taste of the food that the individual consumes, the US is what produced gastrointestinal illness (for example, LiCl, chemotherapy, radiation, poison), and the UR is that illness, the identity of the CR is not so obvious. While we observe that individuals will avoid eating something that made them sick in the past, it is a mistake to identify the CR as the avoidance of that food. Avoidance is a reflection of how the Pavlovian conditioning experience has changed that individual's evaluation of that food; it is not a CR like salivation or drug reactions.

Aversions (and their opposite, preferences) are not directly observed; they are like fear in that they are inferred from observed behavior. Just as the level of fear is inferred from the amount of conditioned suppression we observe when we present a signal for shock, CTAs

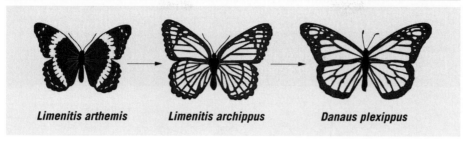

Figure 2.8 An example of Batesian mimicry. From its original form (left) the North American butterfly *Limenitis* has evolved a form (center) that resembles the poisonous monarch butterfly *Danaus* (right).

Limenitis arthemis   **Limenitis archippus**   **Danaus plexippus**

From Brower, 1969.

(and conditioned preferences) are inferred from how much an individual will consume after the conditioning experience (eating something followed by gastrointestinal illness) relative to what he or she consumed prior to that experience. Furthermore, aversions and preferences can also be inferred from an individual's facial expressions when he or she tastes something (Berridge, 2000; Steiner, Glaser, Hawilo & Berridge, 2001). Grill and Norgren (1978a; see also Grill, 1985) observed that rats exhibit distinctly different patterns of behavior when they are forced to sample naturally occurring palatable (such as sweet) and unpalatable (such as bitter or sour) substances (see Figure 2.9). When sucrose (a sweet taste) was placed directly into a rat's mouth, the animal exhibited a series of *ingestive* behaviors that included characteristic mouth movements associated with the ingestion of substances, whereas placing quinine (a bitter taste) directly into the animal's mouth produced a series of *aversive* behaviors in which the rat attempted to expel the substance (by, e.g., gaping, shaking the head rapidly from side to side, rubbing the chin across the floor, and actively spitting out the substance). Using this technique for measuring preferences and aversions, Grill and Norgren (1978b) reported that rats also exhibit aversive reactions to normally palatable sucrose paired with lithium chloride; that is, they react as if the normally palatable solution became unpleasant tasting (for reviews, see Grill & Berridge, 1985; Grill, Spector, Schwartz, Kaplan & Flynn, 1987).

The observed changes in consumption and facial expressions when an individual tastes something that in the past was followed by gastrointestinal illness are indexes of how the conditioning experience has affected the individual's evaluation of that food. Therefore, the "conditioned response" in CTAs is not really a response in the usual sense of the word; *the CR in CTAs includes a change in the individual's evaluation of that food in terms of how much he or she likes or dislikes that food.*

Taste Aversions as an Adaptive Specialization. The ability to learn to avoid food that will make one sick is an adaptive specialization that evolved in a wide variety of species to deal with the problem of identifying and avoiding poisonous foods. Procedurally, taste aversion learning is Pavlovian conditioning where the taste of the food is the CS and a substance that produces illness (which in nature typically is in the food) is the

Figure 2.9 Stereotypical action patterns shown by rats following oral infusion of taste solutions. A sequence of ingestive responses (top) are elicited by sucrose and other sweet-tasting solution and include rhythmic mouth movements, rhythmic tongue protrusions, lateral tongue protrusions, and paw licking, which all occur while the rat is motionless. Elicited by bitter and sour tasting solutions, the sequence of aversive responses (bottom) include gaping, chin rubbing, headshaking, paw wiping, and flailing of the forelimbs, all of which occur against a background of increased general activity.

From Grill, 1985.

US. The most striking aspect of taste aversion learning is that individuals can learn in one trial, even when they get sick many hours after consuming the food. Aversions are also more likely to form to novel and less preferred foods than to familiar foods, and in some species, an aversion to one taste generalizes readily to similar tastes (Parker & Revusky, 1982). Clearly, individuals have a predisposition to learn that something eaten made them sick. For most species, the best predictor of tainted food is its taste, primarily because in nature poisons and spoiled food usually have distinctive tastes. However, species with well-developed visual systems will also identify the offending food by its visual properties. Rejection on sight is even more efficient than rejection based on taste because there is no need to come in contact with the offending food (Brower, 1969).

SIGN-TRACKING (AUTOSHAPING)

This example of Pavlovian conditioning is interesting because the conditioned response involves approach to and withdrawal from signals for important events. Sign-tracking (also known as autoshaping) illustrates the relationship between Pavlovian conditioning and operant conditioning.

All the examples of Pavlovian conditioned responses we have looked at thus far (salivation, fear, immunosuppression, drug tolerance, and CTAs) might be described as conditioned *reflexes*, that is, automatic responses performed without any conscious decision on the part of the subject. In this section, we will look at the Pavlovian conditioning of approach to and withdrawal from signals for important events. At first glance, this conditioned behavior may seem rather exotic, but as we shall soon see, it reveals an important adaptive function of Pavlovian conditioning.

In 1968, Brown and Jenkins made a startling announcement: One can get pigeons to peck at a small illuminated disk (usually called a response key) by illuminating the disk (key) for 8 seconds and then giving 4 seconds of food. Pigeons will peck at the lighted disk (key) even if their pecks have no effect on the presentation of the food. In other words, pigeons will approach and peck at a light that signals the availability of food. Clearly, this procedure is Pavlovian conditioning: The food is the US for the UR of eating. The light that precedes the food is a CS, and the CR is pecking at the light (the signal for the presentation of the food).

Is it Pavlovian conditioning or instrumental conditioning? In 1968, pecking at response keys was thought of as an operant behavior, that is, a behavior that could only be influenced by an operant conditioning procedure (see Chapter 1). Pecking involves a series of actions (approach the response key and peck at it) and appears more "voluntary" than the behaviors described earlier in this chapter. Ever since Skinner first used key pecking by pigeons to study operant conditioning, hundreds of experiments had been performed in which pigeons were trained to peck at lighted response keys to obtain food (Figure 2.10). Before 1968, we thought that complex skeletal behaviors such as key pecking could be influenced only by operant conditioning procedures. How wrong we were!

Brown and Jenkins (1968) were not the first to report changes in the motor behavior of pigeons as a result of a Pavlovian conditioning procedure. Bitterman and his colleagues (Longo, Klempay, & Bitterman, 1964; Slivka & Bitterman, 1966) observed an increase in anticipatory activity during the presence of a signal for food delivery. In a rather strongly worded critique, Kimble (1964) expressed the prevailing opinion that these behaviors

Figure 2.10 Pigeons learn through Pavlovian conditioning to peck an illuminated key (CS) on the wall of an experimental chamber when such illumination signals access to food (US) from the rectangular opening (magazine) below the key.

cannot be directly affected by Pavlovian conditioning. Even Brown and Jenkins seemed hesitant to conclude that their results were due to the Pavlovian conditioning procedure they employed. They titled their paper "Autoshaping of the Pigeon's Keypeck," a title which suggests that they had uncovered another way to shape the operant behavior of key pecking.

The procedure of operant conditioning involves the relationship between a behavior and the consequences (termed an *outcome* or *reinforcer*) of that behavior: The subject does something. If the outcome is something good (presenting something good or removing something unpleasant), that behavior will be more likely to occur again. If the outcome is unpleasant (presenting something that hurts or removing something good), that behavior will be less likely to occur. We say that the individual is conditioned when the outcome influences the future occurrence of the behavior that produced it (the phenomenon of operant conditioning). This is different from Pavlovian conditioning in which the US is presented irrespective of whether the behavior occurs. *The programming of events in Pavlovian conditioning is independent of the occurrence of the CR. That is not the case in operant conditioning.*

The strongest argument that the key pecking Brown and Jenkins labeled as autoshaping is not due to operant conditioning was supplied by Williams and Williams (1969). They exposed pigeons to the following procedure: A response key was illuminated for 6 seconds after which the key light was turned off and food was presented for 4 seconds. However, if the pigeon pecked the key, the key light was turned off and no food was given. The presentation of the light followed by food is a Pavlovian conditioning procedure: A CS (key light) is followed by US (food). The loss of food following a peck at the key is an operant conditioning procedure called either **omission training** (*behavior leads to the "omission" of an otherwise expected outcome*) or **punishment by removal** (*access to the outcome is removed when the behavior occurs*). If pecking the key is an operant behavior, then pecking the key should be suppressed when the consequence of pecking is the loss of the outcome. The results in Williams and Williams' experiment were quite striking: All 13 subjects pecked the key, and 12 of them *continued to peck* through 15 days of training, even though pecking resulted in the loss of food! Clearly, the operant conditioning omission training procedure did not prevent pecking from occurring. The pigeons pecked the key because of the Pavlovian conditioning procedure (key light → food).

Characteristics of the Conditioned Response in Sign-Tracking in Pigeons. Like other forms of Pavlovian conditioning, the CR here depends in part on the US. Jenkins and Moore (1973) videotaped pigeons as they pecked the key with either food or water as the US. When food was the US, key pecks were described as sharp and vigorous; their mouths were open as they struck the key and their eyes were closed. When water was the reinforcer, pecks were slower with more sustained contact on the key; the birds' beaks remained closed and their eyes open. These CRs are similar to the URs pigeons make when they eat and drink (see Figure 2.11). Student judges who did not know the identity of the US (food or water) could correctly identify it in 87% of the cases based solely on observations of the CR (how the birds pecked).

A distinguishing feature of the CR is its directed nature. Pigeons approach and make contact with a key light that signals food, and they withdraw from a key light that signals the absence of food (Wasserman, Franklin, & Hearst, 1974). Pavlovian conditioning of directed movements to discrete signals is not restricted to pigeons. Pavlov (1932, 1934) observed that when the CS for food was the illumination of a lamp that was within reach, dogs would lick the lamp. Likewise, rats make contact with, lick, and gnaw a lever inserted into their cage if they receive a food pellet immediately after the lever is presented (Peterson, Ackil, Frommer, & Hearst, 1972), and chicks will peck a key that precedes 4 seconds of heat from a heat lamp (Wasserman, 1973). Hearst and Jenkins (1974) coined the term **sign-tracking** (also known as **autoshaping**) to describe *behavior that is directed toward or away from a stimulus that signals the occurrence or absence of a significant event (e.g., food, heat, shock).*

Sign-tracking is an appropriate term for these directed movements to signals for important things because the individual's behavior is directed toward a localized signal for something he or she would normally approach and is directed away from a localized signal for an unpleasant event. Thus, the CR "tracks" the significance of the signaled object and may reflect the species-specific behavior appropriate to that object.

In most sign-tracking experiments with pigeons, the food dispenser is located directly below the key. Would the results be the same if signals for food were in a different location than the food? Jenkins (1973) provided us with the answer. Pigeons were placed in a 6-foot-long rectangular enclosure. A response key was

Figure 2.11 Typical key pecks when the US is water (left) or food (right). Student judges who did not know the identity of the US (food or water) could correctly identify it in 87% of the cases based solely on observations of the CR (how the birds pecked).

From Jenkins and Moore, 1973, *Journal of the Experimental Analysis of Behavior, 20,* 163-181. Copyright © 1973 by the Society for the Experimental Analysis of Behavior, Inc. Reprinted by permission from John Wiley and Sons.

located at each end of this "long box," and a food dispenser was located midway between the keys on one of the long walls. Both keys were lighted briefly for various times, but only one of the lighted keys predicted the 4-second availability of food at the food dispenser. If you were a pigeon, what would you do? The keys are three feet away from the food dispenser. Since food is only available for 4 seconds, you (if you were a pigeon) cannot traverse the three-foot distance from where the key is located to get much grain before the food is withdrawn. You could maximize the amount of grain obtained if you stay in the neighborhood of the food dispenser or go to it when the predictive key light comes on. Jenkins reported that of the seven pigeons in this experiment, only one remained in the vicinity of the food dispenser. The other six pigeons approached and pecked the predictive light on almost every trial on the tenth day of training, even though pecking at the key until it went off resulted in a substantial loss of food.

Is sign-tracking adaptive? On the surface, the behavior of the pigeons in Williams and Williams' omission training and Jenkins' long box experiments appears maladaptive. The pigeons were hungry, and they could obtain food if they did *not* approach and peck the key. Why did they continue to peck when pecking decreased the amount of food they obtained? Perhaps we can answer this question if we consider how pigeons search for food in their ecological niche.

Pigeons tend to return to sites where they found food in the past (Gompertz, 1957; Goodwin, 1983). These sites are identified by landmarks, and within each site, there are specific cues indicating the location of food. Once these cues are identified, approaching them usually leads to food. In all of the experiments described above, food appeared only when the key was lit; it never appeared at any other time. Even when pecking the key resulted in the loss of food, the key light was still the best predictor of food. Pigeons appear to be disposed either from past experience or instinctive knowledge to approach signals that predict the availability of food. In the laboratory we can separate the signals from the food and observe this disposition.

The Relationship Between Sign-Tracking (Autoshaping) and Operant Conditioning. It would be a mistake to conclude that omission training has no effect on key pecking. Williams and Williams (1969, Experiment III), presented pigeons with two response keys, each illuminated with a different color. Both keys were illuminated at the same time for 4 seconds. Food was presented if a pigeon did not peck at one of the keys (the omission key); pecks at the other key (the irrelevant key) had no effect. Even if the birds were trained with the omission key first (and were pecking at it), introduction of the irrelevant key produced a shift in responding to it. When the procedures were reversed so that pecks to the original omission key had no effect (now it is the irrelevant key), and pecks to the original irrelevant key now led to the loss of food (omission training), the birds shifted responding to the new irrelevant key. Although both keys provided the same information about the occurrence of food, approaching and pecking at the irrelevant key always was followed by food. Thus, pigeons in this experiment learn about the predictors of food through Pavlovian conditioning, and they learn what to do to get it through operant conditioning.

In retrospect, it was no accident that Skinner chose key pecking in pigeons and lever pressing in rats as behaviors for operant conditioning experiments. Pecking at discrete stimuli and approaching and contacting objects are easy to train because they occur readily where food is available. In many operant conditioning experiments, a technique called shaping (see Chapter 7) is used to get individuals to perform the desired behavior. "Autoshaping" provides another method for directing the individual to the key or lever. Thus, through Pavlovian conditioning the individual learns about signals that predict important events, and the CRs to those signals may serve to promote the occurrence of the behavior that can be affected by operant conditioning. For reviews on sign-tracking see Locurto, Terrace, and Gibbon (1981).

My dog rings a bell to ask out. This relationship between Pavlovian and operant conditioning can be illustrated by the following example. Guests at our house are impressed that my dog rings a bell to go outside, and they are surprised to learn how easy it is to train: Hang a bell from the handle of the door leading to the yard. Every time the door opens, the bell rings. Dogs learn to ring the bell by either brushing against it or batting it with their paw. Let the dog outside when he or she causes the bell to ring. The relationship between the bell and the door opening is a Pavlovian conditioning procedure: The bell is the CS for the opening of the door (the US). The CR is approach and contact with the bell. Letting the dog outside for ringing the bell is an operant conditioning procedure. The two procedures work together. Pavlovian conditioning creates the association between the bell and the door opening and brings the dog in contact with the bell. Through operant conditioning, the dog learns to do something to make the door open.

A number of our friends have used this technique to train their dogs. My favorite story is of a dog who sometimes would ring the bell so that its owners would open the door to let in their cat who was waiting on the other side of the door.

SUMMARY AND CONCLUSIONS

Pavlovian conditioning is the name we give to the procedure in which subjects are exposed to two events or stimuli. By virtue of this experience, subjects may behave differently when one of these stimuli occurs again; this is the phenomenon of Pavlovian conditioning. How quickly the subjects learn and what they do when the CS is presented again depends on the subjects (species, prior experiences) and the stimuli.

In this chapter, we examined five different examples of Pavlovian conditioning: (1) Pavlov's pioneering experiments involved an arbitrary stimulus (sound of a metronome) that preceded the placement of food directly in the mouth of dogs. After experiencing a few such metronome-food presentations, the dogs salivated when the met-

ronome was sounded; (2) Watson and Rayner's demonstration that emotional states can be aroused by previously neutral stimuli by having those stimuli precede an aversive event. In this case, the CR is inferred from overt expressions of that emotional state; (3) Demonstrations that stimuli which precede the administration of certain drugs can produce physiological responses that either mimic or mirror the effects of the drug; (4) Aversions to the taste of a food produced when consumption of that food is followed by gastric distress. In this case, the learning can occur in a single trial, even when the ingestion and gastric distress are hours apart; (5) Approach and contact with signals for certain events can occur when the signals regularly precede those events.

General changes in activity frequently occur when the signals are not localized (such as with auditory stimuli).

All of the examples of Pavlovian conditioning that we have reviewed have something in common: the individual behaves differently after experiencing the CS-US relationship. This raises a number of interesting questions: What is it about the procedure that produces learning? Why does the subject make the particular CR? What are the psychological processes that underlie all of this? We will attempt to answer these questions in the next four chapters.

STUDY QUESTIONS

1. What is the basic procedure of Pavlovian conditioning? What is the phenomenon? How do we distinguish the CS from the US and the CR from the UR?

2. Identify the CS, US, UR, and CR for the following situations (and explain the reason for your identifications):

    a. The movie *Jaws*

    b. Pavlov's classic demonstration of salivary conditioning

3. Describe the following Pavlovian conditioning procedures:

    a. delay conditioning

    b. trace conditioning

    c. backward conditioning

    d. simultaneous conditioning

    e. temporal conditioning

4. Describe the following phenomena and the procedures that produce them:

    a. external inhibition

    b. experimental extinction

    c. disinhibition

    d. inhibition of delay

    e. second-order conditioning

5. Identify the CS, US, UR, and CR for the following situations (and explain the reason for your identifications):

    a. Watson and Rayner's demonstration with Little Albert

    b. English's observations with Joan Katherine and with Helen Elizabeth

    c. Valentine's observations with his own daughter

    d. Bregman's attempts to condition infants

6. Describe how conditioned suppression is used to measure the level of fear, that is, how conditioned suppression is measured and how that measurement is related to the level of fear.

7. What does it mean to say that a conditioned drug reaction "mimics" the drug's unconditioned effect? What does it mean to say that the conditioned drug reaction "mirrors" the drug's unconditioned effect?

8. Identify the CS, US, UR, and CR for the following situations (and explain the reason for your identifications):

    a. Ader and Cohen's experiment on the development of lupus

    b. Siegel and his colleagues' experiments on morphine tolerance

9. Why did Ader suggest that some placebo effects might be due to Pavlovian conditioning?

10. What is the critical element in the production of conditioned taste aversions? What is the CR in conditioned taste aversions?

11. What evidence leads us to conclude that the loss of appetite among patients undergoing chemotherapy is due to Pavlovian conditioning? In your answer, identify the CS, CR, US, and UR.

12. Describe the procedure of sign-tracking (autoshaping), and explain why it is classified as a Pavlovian conditioning procedure. Identify the CS, CR, US, and UR.

13. How does sign-tracking illustrate the relationship between Pavlovian conditioning and operant conditioning?

3

PAVLOVIAN CONDITIONING IS AN INFERENCE TASK

In our everyday lives, there is a temporal order to the flow of events in which causes precede effects (not the other way around). Usually causes and effects occur close together in time, but sometimes, as in the case of becoming ill after eating tainted food, the effect may occur hours later. Some events occur in cycles, and the time between these events is an important predictor of the next occurrence. When there is a causal connection between events, they tend to occur together rather than individually; that is, when the cause is present, usually the effect is present (and vice versa). Specifically, food is more likely to be available at certain times and in certain places than in other places and at other times, and sometimes the availability of food is predicted by specific local events (such as the rattle of the food dish or food container; the color, odor, and pattern of a flower; the scent of prey). Some places are more dangerous than others—the degree of danger may be related to the time of day (or night), and sometimes impending danger is preceded by the sound, sight, or smell of a predator or other dangerous event (such as screeching tires, roaring water, howling winds). Clearly, survival is enhanced when individuals can identify and respond to the predictors for these motivationally significant events from among the myriad other stimuli and events in their environments. This is a problem of **causal inference**: how can I identify *what caused the motivationally significant event to appear so that I can predict its next occurrence?*

Each species' niche presents specific problems for survival, and species are molded by natural selection to deal with these problems. Behavioral solutions to these problems require knowledge of the relationships between important events and the predictors of these events. Individuals can acquire knowledge about these relationships between events in one of two ways: through the mechanism of genetic inheritance (instinctive knowledge) or through experience (learned knowledge). Species with short life spans and hence little opportunity to learn from experience acquire most of this information through genetic transmission (Mayr, 1974). Instinctive knowledge is advantageous when the predictors of food and danger are few. On the other hand, the ability to obtain knowledge about these predictors from experience enables individuals to adapt to new situations. However, even when knowledge must be acquired from experience, there are some problems that require rapid learning: Individuals need to learn to recognize tainted food rapidly so that they can avoid it in the future, and individuals cannot afford the luxury of repeated confrontations with danger to learn about it. Specialized predispositions to learn evolved to meet these needs.

The procedure of Pavlovian conditioning parallels the causal texture of our world. In all of the examples of Pavlovian conditioning we reviewed in the last chapter, something (the CS) preceded with some regularity the occurrence of an important event for the individual (the US): The sound of a metronome or illumination of a spot on the wall preceded the delivery of food. The appearance of a white rat preceded a loud noise. A tone preceded an electric shock. Being in a certain place preceded the administration of a drug. Eating a certain food preceded getting sick. Clearly, the procedure of Pavlovian conditioning presents individuals with the same type of causal inference problem: *Identify the event that signals or predicts the occurrence of the motivationally significant event and behave accordingly* (e.g., salivate just prior to receiving the food to speed the process of digestion).

We view Pavlovian conditioning as an inference task because (1) the causal texture to our world as described above is a universal aspect of all niches (Anokhin, 1974; Revusky, 1977; Rozin & Schull, 1988; Tolman & Brunswik, 1935); (2) the procedure of Pavlovian conditioning parallels this causal texture; and (3) natural selection endowed some species with the ability to learn about the predictors of important events (Danks, 2009; Killeen, 1981; Mackintosh, 1977; Revusky, 1985; Shanks & Dickinson, 1987; Staddon, 1988).

THE ELEMENTS OF CAUSAL INFERENCE

The philosopher David Hume's theory of causal inference provides us with a framework for analyzing Pavlovian conditioning as a process of making causal inferences. Hume argued that individuals infer cause-effect relationships when two events occur close together in time and space, the inferred cause precedes the inferred effect, and this occurs consistently.

Inference *is the psychological process by which individuals make judgments and draw conclusions based on the information available to them.*[1] A **causal inference** is a judgment or conclusion that one event influences, affects, or causes another. For example, observing that a pattern of dark clouds is usually followed by rain might lead us to infer that there is a relationship between that pattern of clouds and rain. We may even come to the conclusion that the rain is caused by that cloud pattern, although that may or may not be the case. It could be that there is a third factor that caused both the cloud pattern and the rain, but we are predisposed to make causal inferences based on observations such as those described above (Nisbett & Ross, 1980). In this example, seeing that cloud pattern might lead you to change your plans or take rain gear with you.

---

[1]The focus of the discussion in this chapter is on drawing conclusions based on experience, observations, and prior knowledge about the world. This is called *pragmatic (inductive)* inference. Pragmatic (inductive) inference is different from logical inference and statistical inference. *Logical (formal or deductive) inference* involves drawing conclusions based on a set of premises and a prescribed set of rules; we engage in this type of inference in mathematics and when we engage in logical deduction. *Statistical inference* refers to drawing conclusions about attributes of populations based on random samples from those populations; these types of inferences are based on the laws of probability. Pragmatic inferences are the basis for attribution theory in social psychology (Kelley, 1967), medical diagnosis, and language comprehension, as well as drawing conclusions based on everyday experiences.

Perhaps no one has had a greater influence on our current understanding of how individuals form causal inferences than David Hume, the eighteenth-century Scottish philosopher (Shanks & Dickinson, 1987; Wasserman, 1990). Hume argued that when we conclude that one event caused another to occur (like the clouds and rain), it is not because we have observed a causal connection between them. *Causal connections are not directly observed; they are inferred by the individual from observations of the relationships between events.* Hume also argued that this inference process does not require deliberation; it is immediate, automatic, operates without reflection, and is not restricted to humans. *Hume concluded that we are likely to infer a causal relationship between two events when (1) the inferred cause precedes the supposed effect* (priority in time or **temporal precedence**), *(2) the two events occur close together in time and space* (**temporal contiguity** and **spatial contiguity**), *and (3) the two events occur together consistently* (**constant conjunction**; Hume, 1739/1992, 1740/1993, 1777/1993; see Box 3.1).

Excerpt From An Abstract of a Treatise of Human Nature

The publication of A *Treatise of Human Nature,* in 1739, was not well received. The next year, David Hume wrote an anonymous review of his book in which he attempted to explain what he was trying to say. The following excerpt from that review captures Hume's ideas on causal inference:

Here is a billiard-ball lying on the table, and another ball moving towards it with rapidity. They strike; and the ball, which was formerly at rest, now acquires a motion. This is as perfect an instance of the relation of cause and effect as any which we know, either by sensation or reflection. Let us therefore examine it. It is evident, that the two balls touched one another before the motion was communicated, and that there was no interval between the shock and the motion. *Contiguity* in time and place is therefore a requisite circumstance to the operation of all causes. It is evident likewise, that the motion, which was the cause, is prior to the motion, which was the effect. *Priority* in time is therefore another requisite circumstance in every cause.

But this is not all. Let us try any other balls of the same kind in a like situation, and we shall always find, that the impulse of the one produces motion in the other. Here therefore is a *third* circumstance, *viz.* that of a *constant conjunction* between the cause and effect. Every object like the cause produces always some object like the effect. Beyond these three circumstances of contiguity, priority, and constant conjunction, I can discover nothing in this cause. The first ball is in motion; touches the second; immediately the second is in motion; and when I try the experiment with the same or like balls, in the same or like circumstances, I find, that upon the motion and touch of the one ball, motion always follows in the other. In whatever shape I turn this matter, and however I examine it, I can find nothing farther.

This is the case when both the cause and effect are present to the senses. Let us now see upon what our inference is founded, when we conclude from the one that the other has existed or will exist. Suppose I see a ball moving

(Continued)

(Continued)

in a straight line towards another, I immediately conclude, that they will shock, and that the second will be in motion. This is the inference from cause to effect; and of this nature are all our reasonings in the conduct of life: on this is founded all our belief in history: and from hence is derived all philosophy, excepting only geometry and arithmetic. If we can explain the inference from the shock of two balls, we shall be able to account for this operation of the mind in all instances.

Were a man, such as *Adam*, created in the full vigour of understanding, without experience, he would never be able to infer motion in the second ball from the motion and impulse of the first. It is not any thing that reason sees in the cause, which makes us *infer* the effect. Such an inference, were it possible, would amount to a demonstration, as being founded merely on the comparison of ideas. But no inference from cause to effect amounts to a demonstration. Of which there is this evident proof. The mind can always *conceive* any effect to follow from any cause, and indeed any event to follow upon another: whatever we *conceive* is possible, at least in a metaphysical sense: but wherever a demonstration takes place, the contrary is impossible, and implies a contradiction. There is no demonstration, therefore, for any conjunction of cause and effect. And this is a principle, which is generally allowed by philosophers.

It would have been necessary, therefore, for *Adam* (if he was not inspired) to have had *experience* of the effect, which followed upon the impulse of these two balls. He must have seen, in several instances, that when the one ball struck upon the other, the second always acquired motion. If he had seen a sufficient number of instances of this kind, whenever he saw the one ball moving towards the other, he would always conclude without hesitation, that the second would acquire motion. His understanding would anticipate his sight, and form a conclusion suitable to his past experience.

It follows, then, that all reasonings concerning cause and effect, are founded on experience, and that all reasonings from experience are founded on the supposition, that the course of nature will continue uniformly the same. We conclude, that like causes, in like circumstances, will always produce like effects.

Pavlov's demonstration of conditioned salivation to the sound of a metronome satisfies all three of these conditions. On every conditioning trial the dog experienced the sound of the metronome 1 to 5 seconds before the food was delivered into its mouth (*temporal precedence* and *temporal contiguity*). The metronome was always followed by the food, and the food was never presented without the metronome preceding it (*constant conjunction*). But does successful Pavlovian conditioning require all three of these conditions; that is, are they the necessary and sufficient conditions for Pavlovian conditioning to occur? (See Box 3.2.) In this chapter, we will review the evidence for how each of Hume's three conditions affects Pavlovian conditioning. With respect to the *necessary* conditions for the occurrence of Pavlovian conditioning, we want to know

BOX 3.2

Necessary and Sufficient Conditions

As students of psychology, we are interested in determining the causes of behavior. Suppose there are two events, A and B, where B is some aspect of the behavior of an individual and A is some antecedent event. A could be a prior experience, an internal physiological event, an inherited characteristic, and so on. We try to discover whether and how A (an antecedent event) affects B (behavior); that is, is A a cause of B? The test of whether A is a cause of B requires us to ask two questions: Is A a necessary condition for the occurrence of B? Is A a sufficient condition for the occurrence of B? If the answer to both questions is yes, then A is the unique cause of B.

Necessary Conditions

In a cause-effect relationship, a **necessary condition** *is something in whose absence the effect cannot occur.* Therefore, if A is a necessary condition for the occurrence of B, then when A is not present, B will not occur. This means that the presence of A is *essential* for the occurrence of B.

Consider the following example. Those of us who were in Cub Scouts, Brownies, Girl Scouts, or Boy Scouts learned that it takes three things to make a fire: a source of fuel, oxygen, and a source of heat. If any one of these are missing, then one cannot have a fire; therefore, all of these are necessary conditions for a fire.

Sufficient Conditions

In a cause-effect relationship, a **sufficient condition** *is something in whose presence the effect must occur.* Therefore, if A is a sufficient condition for the occurrence of B, when A occurs, B automatically

follows. This means that the occurrence of A is *adequate* for the occurrence of B.

Referring back to the example of fuel, oxygen, and heat as conditions for a fire, it is clear that fuel, oxygen, and heat are all necessary conditions for a fire, but none of them are sufficient because the presence of any one of them alone will not produce a fire.

This example illustrates something important about necessary conditions: The presence of a necessary condition does not guarantee that the effect will occur, and there can be more than one sufficient condition for a given effect. For example, we know that mental retardation can be caused by a number of things: genetic disorders, anoxia (lack of oxygen at birth), extreme malnutrition early in life, rubella during the prenatal period, and so on. All of these are sufficient conditions for the occurrence of mental retardation, but none is a necessary condition. On the other hand, except when we use extraordinary means to implant fertilized ova in women, sexual intercourse is a necessary condition for pregnancy, but it is not a sufficient condition (even in the absence of birth control).

Unique Causes: Necessary and Sufficient Conditions

In a cause-effect relationship, a unique cause is both a **necessary condition and a sufficient condition;** *it is something in whose absence the effect cannot occur and in whose presence the effect must occur.* Therefore, it is the unique cause. To date we have identified only a few antecedent conditions as unique causes in psychology. Those we have identified tend to be physiological conditions that

(Continued)

produce specific effects (e.g., the chromosomal defect that produces Down syndrome).

Most of the causal factors that we have identified in psychology are neither necessary nor sufficient conditions because they do not satisfy the definitions given above. For example, we have identified the risk factors that lead to criminal behavior, but none of these factors are either necessary or sufficient conditions for criminal behavior, much less the unique cause.

Summary

If something is a **necessary condition**, then it *must be present* in order for the effect to occur. In other words, if it is *not present*, the effect *will not occur*. That is why we say that necessary conditions are *essential* for the occurrence of the effect. However, the presence of something that is only a necessary condition may not produce the effect by itself because there may be other necessary conditions (see the example of fire, above). If something is a **sufficient condition**, its *presence will produce* the effect. In other words, if it *is present*, the effect *will occur*. That is why we say a sufficient condition is *adequate* for the occurrence of the effect. However, the effect can occur for other reasons because there may be more than one sufficient condition (see example of mental retardation, above). If something is both a **necessary and sufficient condition**, then it *must be present* in order for the effect to occur and its *presence will produce* the effect. When something satisfies these two conditions, it is a *unique cause*. Something that is a necessary or a sufficient condition (but not both) is one of a number of causal factors. Something that is neither a necessary nor a sufficient condition, but is related to the effect, can be a risk factor.

whether Pavlovian conditioning can occur (1) in the absence of a consistent relationship (constant conjunction) between the CS and US, (2) when the CS and US do not occur close together in time and space (the absence of temporal and spatial contiguity), and (3) when the CS does not occur before the US (the absence of temporal precedence). With respect to the *sufficient* conditions for the occurrence of Pavlovian conditioning, we want to know if Pavlovian conditioning will always occur when (1) there is a consistent relationship (constant conjunction) between the CS and US, (2) the CS and US occur close together in time and space (temporal and spatial contiguity), and (3) the CS occurs before the US (temporal precedence). We will see that Pavlovian conditioning is enhanced when these three conditions are met, although none of these three conditions are either necessary or sufficient conditions for the occurrence of Pavlovian conditioning.

THE EFFECTS OF CS-US CONSISTENCY IN PAVLOVIAN CONDITIONING

The hallmark of a causal relationship is the consistency with which the effect follows the cause. Consistency can be quantified as the correlation between events, and a positive correlation means that the appearance of the cause predicts the effect. A negative correlation means that the appearance of the cause predicts the absence of an event (the cause makes something not occur). A zero correlation means there is no predictive relationship between events. There is no consistency, and any conjunction between these events is due to chance.

Consistency means that events occur together with regularity; that is, if one occurs, the other tends to occur, and each event does not occur alone too often. In Pavlovian conditioning, **CS-US consistency** refers to *how often the CS and the US occur in relationship to each other*, specifically, how often the US occurs when the CS has occurred and how often the US occurs when the CS has not occurred. The more often the US follows the CS and the less often the US occurs in the absence of the CS, the greater the CS-US consistency. In Pavlov's salivary conditioning experiment, the food always appeared after the metronome was turned on, and it never appeared at any other time. You cannot get more consistent than that! But consistency is a matter of degree. If the food only appeared after the metronome 50% of the time, there would be less CS-US consistency, but there would be some. Likewise, there would be less consistency if the food appeared 100% of the time after the metronome and also occasionally appeared in the absence of the metronome. Clearly, the greater the consistency, the easier it is for an observer to detect the relationship between the two events.

In Pavlovian conditioning, we use the term CS-US contingency to define the programmed relationship between the CS and US. The **CS-US contingency** is *the rule which specifies how likely the US will follow the CS and how likely the US will appear in the absence of the CS*. Because the likelihood that something occurs is measured by the probability that it occurs, contingencies in Pavlovian conditioning are specified in terms of two probabilities: the probability that the US will occur when the CS occurs [expressed symbolically as Pr (US | CS)], and the probability that the US will occur when the CS did not occur [Pr (US | no CS)]. The difference between these two probabilities defines the CS-US contingency. This contingency also tells us how well the occurrence of the CS predicts the occurrence of the US.

Positive Contingencies: When the CS Predicts the Occurrence of the US. In Pavlov's demonstration of conditioned salivation, the CS was a perfect predictor of the US because the US always followed the CS and never occurred in the absence of the CS. We can express the first part (US always follows the CS) in symbolic form as follows:

$$Pr (US \mid CS) = 1.0 \tag{1}$$

This expression is read, "The probability that the US will occur given the occurrence of the CS is 1.0." A probability of 1.0 means that the US *always* follows the CS: Whenever the CS occurs, the US always follows. The second part (the US never occurs in the absence of the CS) can be expressed in symbolic form as follows:

$$Pr (US \mid no\ CS) = 0 \tag{2}$$

This second expression is read, "The probability that the US will occur given no CS is 0." A probability of 0 means that the US will *never* occur in the absence of the CS. Together these two expressions [Pr (US | CS) = 1.0 and Pr (US | no CS) = 0] define the contingency in Pavlov's demonstration. Using the language of statistics, we can also say that in Pavlov's demonstration there was a perfect positive correlation (+1.0) between the occurrence of the

CS and the occurrence of the US. When the correlation = +1.0, the status of one variable (in this case the presence of the US) is uniquely determined by the status of the other variable (presence or absence of the CS). Once they learned the contingency, Pavlov's dogs could predict perfectly when the US would occur because the CS always preceded the US and the US never occurred without the CS—there was a perfect correlation (+1.0) between the occurrence of the CS and the occurrence of the US.

But the US *does not* need to occur every time the CS occurs in order for there to be a positive correlation and for the CS to predict the US. Suppose the US only occurred after 40% of CS presentations [Pr (US|CS) = 0.4] and *never* when there was no CS [Pr (US|no CS) = 0]. Although the correlation is less than perfect (occurrence of the CS does not always predict that the US will occur), the CS still predicts the US because there still is a positive correlation between the CS and the US (correlation = +0.5).

There can even be a positive correlation when the US sometimes occurs in the absence of the CS. Suppose Pr (US|CS) = 0.4 and Pr (US|no CS) = 0.1. The first equation is read, "The probability that the US will occur given the occurrence of the CS is 0.4." That means that 40% of the presentations of the CS will be followed by the US. The second equation is read, "The probability that the US will occur in the absence of the CS is 0.1." That means that the US will occur 10% of the time when there is no CS. Here again, there is a positive correlation between the occurrence of the CS and the occurrence of the US (correlation = +0.35).

The correlation between the occurrence of the CS and the occurrence of the US will always be positive under the following condition:

$$\text{Pr (US|CS)} > \text{Pr (US|no CS)} \tag{3}$$

We read this as, "The probability of the US occurring following the CS is greater than the probability of the US occurring following the absence of the CS." This inequality defines *a* **positive CS-US contingency.** A positive contingency means that the occurrence of the CS gives the individual information about the occurrence of the US, namely that *the US is more likely to occur when a CS has occurred than when a CS has not occurred.* If black clouds are followed by rain 50% of the time and rain occurs 2% of the time when these clouds are not present, you are more likely to be rained on when those clouds are on the horizon than when they are not. Many of us will take an umbrella or parka under those conditions rather than run the risk of getting soaked.

Negative Contingencies: When the CS Predicts the Absence of the US. We define the situation as a positive contingency when Pr (US|CS) > Pr (US|no CS). What about the situation where Pr (US|CS) < Pr (US|no CS)? Here the US is more likely to occur in the absence of the CS than in its presence. We call this a **negative CS-US** contingency because there is a negative correlation between the CS and US: *The occurrence of the CS predicts the absence of the US, and the absence of the CS predicts the occurrence of the US.* A negative contingency means that the US is more likely to occur when the CS has *not* occurred than when the CS has occurred.

The correlation between the occurrence of the US will always be negative under the following condition:

$$Pr(US|CS) < Pr(US|no\ CS) \qquad (4)$$

We read this as, "The probability of the US occurring following the CS is less than the probability of the US occurring following the absence of the CS."

A special case of a negative contingency occurs when the US will never follow a CS [$Pr(US|CS)$ = 0] *but will occur in the absence of the CS* [$Pr(US|no\ CS) > 0$]. This procedure is called **explicitly unpaired** because the CS is never followed closely by the US. With respect to prediction, in an explicitly unpaired procedure, the occurrence of the CS predicts that the US will not occur now. Thus, if the CS is a tone and the US is shock, the tone signals for the individual a period of time that is free of shock. Rather than produce fear, as is the case if there is a positive contingency between the tone and shock, a negative contingency should produce a feeling of temporary safety or relief. We will see in a few pages that the CR to a CS in a negative contingency with a US is antagonistic to the CR to a CS in a positive contingency with the same US.

Zero Contingencies: When the CS Does Not Predict Anything About the Occurrence of the US. If the CS in a positive contingency helps the individual predict the occurrence of the US, and the CS in a negative contingency helps the individual to predict the absence of the US, what would happen if the $Pr(US|CS) = Pr(US|no\ CS)$? Here the US is as likely to occur in both the presence and the absence of the CS. *They are presented randomly with respect to each other; the correlation is zero because there is no relationship between the occurrence of the CS and the occurrence of the US.* Following Rescorla (1967b), we call this the **truly random procedure** and a **zero CS–US contingency**. With a zero contingency, the values of $Pr(US|CS)$ and $Pr(US|no\ CS)$ can be anything as long as they are equal:

$$Pr(US|CS) = Pr(US|no\ CS) \qquad (5)$$

We read this as, "The probability of the US occurring following the CS is equal to the probability of the US occurring following the absence of the CS."

Rescorla (1967b) argued that the random presentation of the CS and US (zero contingency) is the proper control group against which to compare the effects of the other two contingencies. However, Rescorla also acknowledged in his 1967 paper that *individuals may learn from a zero contingency that the CS is irrelevant to the US.* Today we recognize that individuals do learn something when they experience a zero contingency between the CS and US. Mackintosh (1973) applied the term **learned irrelevance** to describe the resulting causal inference. The evidence for learned irrelevance will be described in Chapter 4.

Summary of the Various Contingencies. Contingencies are defined by the probability that the US occurs given the occurrence of the CS [$Pr(US|CS)$] and the probability that the US occurs in the absence of the CS [$Pr(US|no\ CS)$]. (See Table 3.1.)

In the case of a **positive contingency**, *the US is more likely to occur following the CS than in its absence* [that is, $Pr(US|CS) > Pr(US|no\ CS)$], and there is a positive correlation between the occurrence of the CS and the occurrence of the US; therefore, the CS

Table 3.1 Summary of Contingencies in Pavlovian Conditioning

Positive contingency (CS predicts the occurrence of the US)	$Pr(US \mid CS) > Pr(US \mid no\ CS)$
Zero contingency (CS gives no information about the occurrence of the US)	$Pr(US \mid CS) = Pr(US \mid no\ CS)$
Negative contingency (CS predicts the absence of the US)	$Pr(US \mid CS) < Pr(US \mid no\ CS)$

gives the individual information about when the US will occur. A positive contingency is also called **excitatory conditioning** because it frequently leads to the occurrence of CRs. The term *excitatory* implies an *underlying process that generates the CR.* That process is sometimes referred to as **conditioned excitation** and the *CS in a positive contingency* as a **conditioned excitatory stimulus.** We call this excitatory conditioning because it generates a CR.

In the case of a **negative contingency,** *the US is less likely to occur following the CS than in its absence* [that is, $Pr(US \mid CS) < Pr(US \mid no\ CS)$], and there is a negative correlation between the occurrence of the CS and the occurrence of the US; therefore, the CS gives the individual information about when the US will not occur. Negative contingencies are said to produce **conditioned inhibition,** *a reaction that is antagonistic to the CR that is evoked by a positive (excitatory) contingency with the same CS and US,* and *the CS that predicts the absence of the US in a negative contingency* is called a **conditioned inhibitory stimulus.** Conditioned inhibition is described as "antagonistic" to conditioned excitation because (1) a conditioned inhibitory stimulus will *depress* a CR to a conditioned excitatory stimulus and (2) the response to the inhibitory stimulus will be the *opposite* of the excitatory CR.

In the case of a **zero contingency,** *the US is just as likely to occur following a CS as in the absence of the CS* [that is, $Pr(US \mid CS) = Pr(US \mid no\ CS)$], and there is a zero correlation between the occurrence of the CS and the occurrence of the US; therefore, the CS gives the individual no information about the occurrence of the US. With extended training on a zero contingency, any CRs that initially occur disappear, and prior experience with a zero contingency can retard the acquisition of CRs when a positive contingency is introduced later.

The Effects of these Contingencies on Pavlovian Conditioning. Rescorla (1966) provided a dramatic demonstration of the effects of positive, negative, and zero Pavlovian contingencies on behavior. The design of his experiment is presented in Table 3.2.

His procedure involved training dogs to jump over a barrier to avoid shock and then presenting them with Pavlovian CSs from one of three contingencies: First he trained dogs with operant conditioning to avoid shock by jumping over a barrier in a two-chambered box.[2] The dogs learned to jump to avoid the shocks, which they fear. After three days of avoidance training, the dogs were divided into three groups and confined to one side of the box where they experienced one of the three contingencies.

Table 3.2   Design of Experiment by Rescorla (1966) on the Effects of the Contingency on Pavlovian Conditioning

Group	Pretraining	Pavlovian conditioning	Test
Positive	Jump barrier to avoid shock	Pr (Shock | tone) > Pr (Shock | no tone)	Tone
Zero	Jump barrier to avoid shock	Pr (Shock | tone) = Pr (Shock | no tone)	Tone
Negative	Jump barrier to avoid shock	Pr (Shock | tone) < Pr (Shock | no tone)	Tone

Note: Unsignaled footshocks were delivered during Pretraining and Test.

One group (Group Zero) experienced a zero contingency in which 24 5-second presentations of a tone and 24 5-second presentations of a shock were presented randomly. A second group (Group Positive) experienced a positive contingency in which only those shocks programmed to occur within the 30-second interval following the CSs were presented; all other shocks were omitted. For these dogs, the CS signaled the presence of shocks and should have increased fear. The third group (Group Negative) experienced a negative contingency in which all shocks programmed to occur in the 30-second interval following a CS were omitted; all other shocks were presented. For these dogs, the CS signaled the absence of shocks and should have decreased fear (because the tone signaled a period of safety). Following training with these contingencies, the dogs were returned to the avoidance schedule. While they were avoiding shock, the CS was presented. Rescorla recorded the rates of avoidance (jumping across the barrier) before, during, and after the CS. The results of this experiment are presented in Figure 3.1.

The dogs that experienced the **positive contingency** *increased* their avoidance responding when the CS was presented. This increase in avoidance responding represented an increase in fear, the motivational state that energized the original avoidance behavior; these dogs behaved as if they had made the causal inference that the CS caused the shock to occur. On the other hand, the dogs that experienced the **negative contingency** *decreased* their avoidance responding when the CS was presented. This decrease in avoidance responding represented a decrease in fear; these dogs behaved as if the CS caused the shocks to cease. Thus, fear was increased by a signal for shock (**excitatory conditioning**) and decreased or inhibited by a signal for no shock or safety (**inhibitory conditioning**). Finally, the CS associated with the **zero contingency** had *no effect* on avoidance responding because these dogs learned that there was no relationship between the CS and shock; in other words,

---

[2]This operant procedure is called *unsignaled (or Sidman) avoidance* (see Chapter 7). With this procedure, aversive events (e.g., shocks) occur at frequent intervals unless the target behavior (in this case, jumping over the barrier) occurs. Each jump produces an interval of time in which no shocks will occur. If the individual jumps again before that interval ends, a new shock-free interval will begin. As long as the individual continues to jump within that shock-free interval, he or she will not receive any shocks. If the shock-free interval ends without a jump, shocks will occur again until the next jump occurs and the shock-free interval begins again.

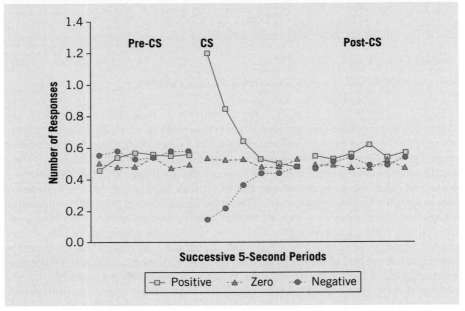

Figure 3.1 Mean number of responses in each 5-second period prior to the onset of the CS (Pre-CS), during the CS, and during the 25 seconds after the CS ended (Post-CS). Positive = positive contingency, Zero = zero contingency, and Negative = negative contingency.

Redrawn from Rescorla, 1966, *Psychonomic Science*, 4, 383–384. Redrawn with permission of Springer Science+Business Media.

the occurrence of the CS had no effect on their motivation to avoid. These data provide compelling evidence of the effects of the three CS-US contingencies (positive, negative, and zero) on behavior.

Varying the Degree of Contingency in Pavlovian Conditioning. In a 1968 study, Rescorla examined the effects of the degree of the contingency (as measured by the size of the CS-US correlation) on conditioned suppression (see Chapter 2). In the pretraining phase of the experiment, rats were trained to press a lever to receive food. Then they were given five sessions of Pavlovian conditioning in another chamber. Different groups received different correlations between the 2-minute tone CSs and 0.5-second shock USs. The contingencies and correlations for the various conditions in Rescorla's experiment are presented in Table 3.3.

Each row of Table 3.3 indicates the contingency for a different group of rats, and correlation between the occurrence of the CS and the US is in the last column. After receiving Pavlovian conditioning with the contingency for their specific group, all subjects were returned to the operant conditioning chamber to resume lever pressing for food. The rats

Table 3.3 Contingencies and Correlations for Rescorla's (1968) Experiment on the Effects of Various Contingencies and Correlations on Pavlovian Conditioning

Contingencies for the different groups		Correlation coefficients for contingencies
Pr (US|CS)	Pr (US|no CS)	
.4	.4	.00
.4	.2	.22
.4	.1	.35
.4	0	.50
.2	.2	.00
.2	.1	.14
.2	0	.33
.1	.1	.00
.1	0	.23
0	0	.00

Note: Correlation coefficient is the phi coefficient (ϕ).

were tested in extinction for the Pavlovian fear conditioning by presenting them with the tone CS (but no shocks) while they were lever pressing for food. The measure of Pavlovian conditioning was the suppression of lever pressing by the tone.[3]

The data from Rescorla's experiment are presented in Figure 3.2. Pavlovian conditioning occurred under all conditions when the Pr (US|CS) was greater than the Pr (US|no CS). The strength of the CR (measured here by the amount of suppression) was a function of the difference between Pr (US|CS) and Pr (US|no CS): the greater the difference between these two probabilities, the stronger the CR. (Compare the correlations in Table 3.3 with the data in Figure 3.2.) Note that Rescorla found no evidence of Pavlovian conditioning when Pr (US|CS) = Pr (US|no CS)—that is, when there was a zero contingency (and a zero correlation) between the occurrence of the CS and the occurrence of the US.

---

[3]With conditioned suppression, the CR is measured by the amount of suppression; *lower numbers* mean *more suppression*. A suppression ratio of 0 defines maximum suppression and a suppression ratio of 0.5 defines no suppression.

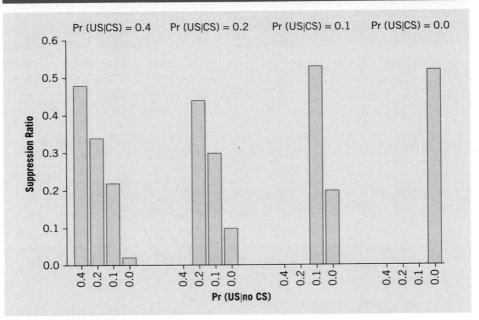

Figure 3.2 Median suppression ratios following training with the different CS-US correlations listed in Table 3.3. Each panel contains groups with the designated value of Pr (US|CS). Within each panel, the numbers identify different groups in terms of Pr (US|no CS).

Data from Rescorla, 1968.

Table 3.4 Contingencies for Hearst, Bottjer, and Walker (1980) Experiment on the Effects of Various Contingencies on Sign–Tracking in Pigeons

Group	Contingencies		Correlation coefficients for contingencies
	Pr (US|CS)	Pr (US|no CS)	
Positive contingencies			
0.4-0.0	0.4	0.0	0.50
0.4-0.2	0.4	0.2	0.22
Zero contingencies			
0.4-0.4	0.4	0.4	0.0
Negative contingencies			
0.2-0.4	0.2	0.4	−0.22
0.0-0.4	0.0	0.4	−0.50

Note: There were two groups of pigeons for each of the positive correlations. Correlation coefficient is the phi coefficient (N).

Hearst and his associates (Hearst, Bottjer, & Walker, 1980; Hearst & Franklin, 1977; Wasserman et al., 1974) found similar results with sign-tracking in pigeons (see Chapter 2). Here, the CS was the illumination of a key, and the US was the presentation of food. Different groups of pigeons received different CS-US contingencies (Table 3.4).

The effects of these various contingencies on the development of approach to and withdrawal from the key over the course of training (successive two-session blocks) are presented in Figure 3.3. The measure of conditioning used here (mean approach-withdrawal ratio) was based on how much time the pigeons spent on the side of the box with the lighted key (approach) relative to how much time they spend on the opposite side of the box away from the lighted key (withdrawal). It is clear from Figure 3.3 that the pigeons approached the lighted key when it was positively correlated with food and withdrew from the lighted key when it was negatively correlated with food. How much they approached or withdrew from the lighted key depended on the degree of correlation. They did neither when there was a zero contingency.

All of these data indicate that dogs, rats, and pigeons are able to make inferences about the predictive relationship between the CS and US. Furthermore, these animals are

Figure 3.3 Approach-withdrawal behavior during CS presentation in pigeons given various contingencies. The first number in each group designation is Pr (US|CS) and the second number is Pr (US|no CS). There were two groups with the contingencies 0.4–0.0 and 0.4–0.2.

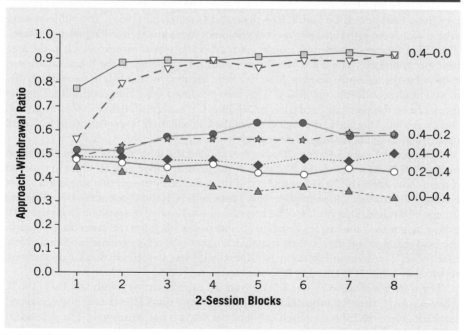

Redrawn from Hearst, Bottjer, and Walker, 1980, *Bulletin of the Psychonomic Society*, 16, 183–186. Reprinted with permission of Springer Science+Business Media.

sensitive to both the direction of the relationship (positive or negative) and to the degree of consistency in that relationship (the degree of correlation). So are we humans (Alloy & Tabachnik, 1984; Penn & Povinelli, 2007).

THE EFFECTS OF TEMPORAL AND SPATIAL CONTIGUITY ON PAVLOVIAN CONDITIONING

Hume argued that we are more likely to perceive a connection between events when they occur close together in time and space. This is true, but neither of these conditions is required for Pavlovian conditioning.

Temporal Contiguity. Events have temporal contiguity when they occur close together in time. However, the occurrence of Pavlovian conditioning does not require that the CS and US occur simultaneously. The vast majority of Pavlovian conditioning experiments are classified as either delay conditioning (the US begins some time after the CS but while the CS is still present) or trace conditioning (the US begins after the CS has terminated; see Chapter 2, Figure 2.3). Pavlovian conditioning can occur when the CS and US occur simultaneously (complete temporal contiguity) and when they occur hours apart with no overlap (as in conditioned taste aversions, CTAs). *The time between the offset of the CS and the onset of the US in Pavlovian conditioning is called the* interstimulus interval (ISI).

The effects of the ISI between the CS and US in three different Pavlovian conditioning situations are presented in Figure 3.4. In all three experiments, different groups of subjects were trained with different ISIs. The data in Figure 3.4a comes from a conditioned eyeblink experiment conducted by Smith, Coleman, and Gormezano (1969). The subjects were rabbits who were restrained so that they could not move about (like Pavlov's dogs were). The CS in this experiment was a tone and the US was a brief electric shock to the area near the rabbit's eye. The UR to the shock is a blink. Depending on the ISI, a conditioned eyeblink to the tone may develop. It is clear from Figure 3.4a that ISIs in the order of 200 to 400 milliseconds (thousandths of a second) produced the strongest conditioning (as measured by the percentage of trials on which a CR occurred). Below 200 milliseconds there was a rapid decline in the occurrence of the CR, and there is no evidence of backward or simultaneous conditioning in this experiment.

The data in Figure 3.4b come from a conditioned suppression experiment conducted by Yeo (1974). Rats were trained to poke at the door of a food tray 10 times in order to receive food. After this behavior was established, the rats were given a single Pavlovian conditioning trial in a different place with a tone as the CS and shock as the US. Different groups of rats had different ISIs. The measure of conditioned suppression in Figure 3.4b is how long it took the rats to complete 30 nose pokes when the rats were placed back in the food chamber and the tone was sounded; longer times reflect greater conditioned fear to the tone. The greatest fear occurred when the ISI was 10 seconds. Similar results were reported by Libby (1951) and by Mahoney and Ayres (1976).

The third set of data (Figure 3.4c) is from an experiment by Smith and Roll (1967). They exposed different groups of rats to x-rays at various times after the rats had consumed saccharin. Here the ISI is measured in hours, not seconds or milliseconds. The dependent variable is preference for the saccharin when given a choice between saccharin and water. Lower preference scores mean stronger aversion to the saccharin. Although the strongest

CTAs occur when the animals were made sick within 0 to 6 hours after consuming the saccharin, there is a clear effect with a 12-hour ISI. Furthermore, there does not appear to be an optimal ISI below which conditioning is reduced.

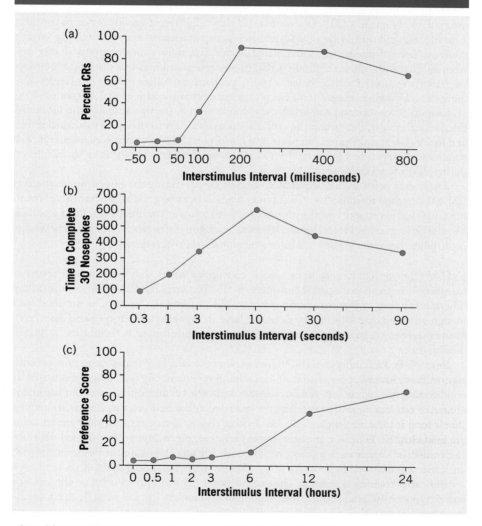

Figure 3.4 The effects of the CS-US interval on: **(a)** eyelid conditioning in rabbits (higher percentage CRs indicates stronger conditioning), **(b)** conditioned suppression (longer times indicate more conditioned fear), and **(c)** conditioned taste aversions (lower preference indicates stronger aversion). Note the different time scales along the horizontal axes.

Adapted from Smith, Coleman, and Gormezano, 1969. Data from Yeo, 1974. Reprinted with permission of the Psychonomic Society.

These data raise two questions: Why is there a different optimal ISI for different CRs? Beyond this optimal ISI, why do further increases in time have an adverse effect on the CR? The answer to the first question requires us to examine the adaptive value of making a CR in a given situation. This will be the topic of Chapter 6.

With respect to the second question, the task for the individual in Pavlovian conditioning is to identify the CS from among the other events and stimuli in the environment. To do that, the individual must remember what events occurred along with the US; therefore, an explanation of the effects of the ISI must focus on what happens during the ISI.

Two things happen with longer intervals: (1) the memory of the CS will be degraded (it is harder to remember that the CS occurred), and (2) there is more opportunity for other events to occur between the CS and US. Revusky (1971) illustrated the effects of such interpolated events in a CTA experiment. He allowed different groups of rats to consume 2 ml of saccharin. Fifteen minutes later, each group consumed water containing varying concentrations of vinegar (the interpolated event). Except for a control group, all rats then were injected with lithium chloride (LiCl) to produce gastrointestinal distress. Three days later, they were tested with a choice between saccharin and dilute coffee. The results were quite clear: Drinking vinegar between consuming saccharin and getting sick attenuated the aversion to saccharin, and the *stronger* the concentration (and presumably the more distinctive) of vinegar, the *greater* the attenuation of the CTA to the saccharin. Mackintosh and Reese (1979) and Pearce, Nicholas, and Dickinson (1981) also reported interference of conditioned suppression to a tone from a light that occurred during the tone-shock interval during Pavlovian conditioning.

These data point to the occurrence of other events during the interstimulus interval (ISI) as one of the reasons why conditioning tends to be stronger with shorter ISIs. This, in turn, adds further support for the proposition that Pavlovian conditioning reflects a process of causal inference. As Hume argued, temporal contiguity between two events increases the probability that an individual will infer a relationship between them.

Spatial Contiguity. Events have spatial contiguity when they occur close together in space. It is clear that spatial contiguity is not required for Pavlovian conditioning: The metronome in Pavlov's demonstration did not have to be next to the food, and in sign-tracking, the lighted key does not have to be next to the food (see Chapter 2). However, there is some evidence that Pavlovian conditioning is facilitated by spatial contiguity.

Rescorla and Cunningham (1979) investigated the effects of spatial contiguity on both sign-tracking (autoshaping) and conditioned suppression in pigeons using a second-order conditioning procedure (see Chapter 2). Second-order conditioning was used because it allowed the researchers to manipulate the spatial relations between two stimuli, something that is hard to do with primary USs like food or shock. The designs for their experiments are presented in Table 3.5. In their first experiment, pigeons were autoshaped with two response keys. Within each training session, each key was illuminated at various times with an X that was followed by food. After the pigeons were responding to the X on both keys, second-order training was given. The second-order CS was a green color on the key. For half the pigeons (Group Same), the green light on one key was followed by the X on the same key. For the other subjects (Group Different), the green appeared on one key immediately followed by the X on the other key.

Table 3.5   Designs of Experiments by Rescorla and Cunningham (1979) on the Effects of Temporal Contiguity on Pavlovian Conditioning

Sign-tracking experiment			
Group		First–order conditioning	Second-order conditioning
Same		X → Food (on either key)	Green → X (on same key)
Different		X → Food (on either key)	Green → X (on different keys)
Conditioned suppression experiment			
Group	Pretraining	First-order conditioning	Second-order conditioning
Same	Center key → food	Green → shock (on either key)	X → Green (on same key)
Different	Center key → food	Green → shock (on either key)	X → Green (on different keys)
Mixed	Center key → food	Green → shock (on either key)	X → Green (on same or different keys)

The acquisition of pecking to the green second-order CS is presented on the left side of Figure 3.5. Autoshaping to the green was more rapid when the green and X were on the same key. Similar results were obtained by Marshall, Gokey, Green, and Rashotte (1979).

In Rescorla and Cunningham's (1979) second experiment (bottom panel of Table 3.5), pigeons were first pretrained to peck the center of three keys to obtain food. In this experiment, the first-order CS was green and the second-order CS was the X. (Note: This is the opposite of the first experiment.) In the first-order conditioning, the green was presented on either the left or right and followed by shock. After conditioned suppression was established to the green key color, the pigeons were divided into three groups. One group had X followed by green on the same side, (Group Same) another group had X on one side followed by green on the other side (Group Different), and the third group had the X followed by green sometimes on the same side and sometimes on the opposite side (Group Mixed). No shocks occurred during the second-order conditioning phase of the experiment. The dependent measure was suppression of center key pecking when the X was presented. These results are presented on the right side of Figure 3.5. Here again, conditioning was faster and stronger when the green and X were on the same side.

Christie (1996) also reported that ring doves exhibited more approaches to the CS that was closer to food in a first-order conditioning sign-tracking experiment than to a CS that was farther away. What makes this experiment interesting is that although one CS was physically closer to the food, the time it took the subjects to reach the food was the same for both the near and far CSs. Therefore, any differences in conditioning were due to the spatial and not the temporal arrangements between CSs and USs.

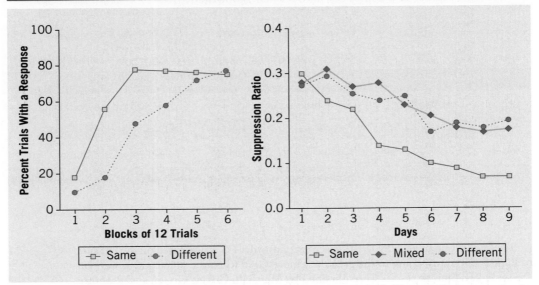

Figure 3.5 The acquisition of key pecking (left) and conditioned suppression (right) in pigeons as a function of the spatial contiguity between the stimuli. Same = both stimuli on the same key, Different = stimuli on different keys, Mixed = sometimes on same key and sometimes on different keys.

Redrawn with permission from Rescorla and Cunningham, 1979. Spatial contiguity facilitates Pavlovian second-order conditioning. *Journal of Experimental Psychology: Animal Behavior Processes*, 5, 152–161. Copyright © 1979 by the American Psychological Association.

Summary. It is a common perception that events that occur close together in time and space belong together (Michotte, 1963). Therefore, it is not surprising that *spatial and temporal contiguity facilitate Pavlovian conditioning*. However, the data on CTAs illustrates that *temporal contiguity is not a necessary condition for the occurrence of Pavlovian conditioning*. Likewise, the lack of a CR following simultaneous conditioning shows that *temporal contiguity is also not a sufficient condition for Pavlovian conditioning* (See Box 3.2). In the next section, we will see that temporal precedence (priority in time) is also not a necessary condition for Pavlovian conditioning.

THE EFFECTS OF TEMPORAL PRECEDENCE ON PAVLOVIAN CONDITIONING

In the vast majority of Pavlovian conditioning experiments, the CS precedes the US, but this is not a requirement for the occurrence of CRs.

Temporal precedence (priority in time) refers to the order of events. In nature, causes always precede effects, not the other way around, and in Pavlovian conditioning, the onset of the CS usually precedes the onset of the US. Pavlov believed that conditioning could only occur when CS onset precedes US onset, but now we know this is not the case. Pavlovian conditioning can be obtained with a simultaneous conditioning procedure (when the CS and US occur at the same time) and with a backward conditioning procedure (when the US precedes the CS). These demonstrations of backward conditioning mean that temporal precedence is *not* a necessary condition for Pavlovian conditioning.

Backward Conditioning. There have been a number of successful demonstrations of backward conditioning (see Chapter 2, Figure 2.3). In some cases, CRs occurred after a single experience with the US followed by the CS. For example, Keith-Lucas and Guttman (1975) trained rats to retrieve food pellets from a hole at each end of a rectangular chamber. On the single backward conditioning trial, a white panel consisting of two vertical stripes was inserted around one of the holes where the food was available, and the rats had to approach that panel to retrieve a food pellet. At the moment a rat grasped the food pellet from the hole surrounded by the striped panel, it received an electric shock through the floor. At the same time, the lights in the chamber were turned off for 1, 5, 10, or 40 seconds (depending on group assignment). When the lights were turned back on, a red toy hedgehog was lowered into the box next to the striped panel and remained there for 60 second before being withdrawn. Thus, there were two CSs: the striped panel was a forward CS, and the toy hedgehog was a backward CS. Additional groups of rats received either the shock and the striped panel (without the hedgehog) or the striped panel and hedgehog (without the shock). On the next day, the rats were returned to the chamber to again retrieve food pellets from both ends. While they were retrieving food pellets, the striped panel and toy hedgehog were introduced at opposite ends of the box. The dependent measure was how much time the rats spent on the side with the striped panel or the side with the hedgehog.[4] Rats in the groups in which the hedgehog was presented either 1, 5, or 10 seconds after the shock spent more time in the test on the side with the striped panel (and away from the toy hedgehog). Rats in the other three groups (shock-hedgehog ISI of 40 seconds, shock but no hedgehog, and hedgehog but no shock) spent more time during the test on the side with the hedgehog. Thus, backward conditioning occurred when there was both temporal and spatial contiguity between the shock and the hedgehog even though the hedgehog *followed* the shock. However, there was no backward conditioning when the shock and hedgehog were separated by 40 seconds.

Why did Keith-Lucas and Guttman's (1975) rats avoid the hedgehog (the backward CS) and not the striped panel (the forward CS)? Keith-Lucas and Guttman gave two reasons: (1) Predators may attack without warning, and the individual may not identify its attacker until after the attack. Most, if not all, of us have experienced a sudden "sting" and looked around to see what stung or bit us. (2) The toy hedgehog looks more like a predator than the striped panel. Thus, rats seem able to associate a novel stimulus that appears after a painful experience with that pain, especially if that novel stimulus has characteristics of a predator. This is consistent with other examples of forward fear conditioning in which the characteristics of the CS affect the ease of conditioning (Bregman, 1934; English, 1929; Marks, 1987).

---

[4]This experiment was based on an earlier paper by Hudson (1950), who reported that rats shocked while eating will avoid a bundle of pipe cleaners dropped into the chamber immediately after the shock. Hudson used few subjects, and he did not have any nonpaired control conditions.

However, Pinel, Mana, and Wilkie (1986) demonstrated that one could obtain backward conditioning with an arbitrary CS. In their study, two shock prods extended into opposite ends of the chamber. One prod was black and the other striped. One of the prods delivered an electric shock when touched. When a rat touched that prod, the shock was delivered and the lights were turned off. During the 2-second interval when the lights were off, the patterns on the prods (black or striped) were switched for one group of rats and they stayed the same for the other group. Then the lights were turned back on for 5 minutes before the animals were removed from the chamber. On the next day, the rats were returned to the chamber that now contained bedding material (ground corncob pellets) scattered over the floor. Because rats will bury inanimate objects associated with aversive experiences, the dependent measure in this experiment was the amount of time the rats spent covering the two prods. The rats in the group for which the pattern *did not change* after the shock spent more time burying that pattern while the rats in the other group (pattern *changed* after the shock) spent more time burying the second pattern, even though they were shocked for touching the first pattern. Here again, learning about the source of danger occurred after the fact.

These experiments provide convincing demonstrations that backward conditioning can be obtained with a single US-CS presentation involving an aversive US. Where danger is involved, individuals need to be able to quickly identify and learn about sources of danger and to take evasive actions in the future (Bolles, 1970). Other demonstrations of backward and simultaneous conditioning in relatively few trials using shock as the US have been reported by Ayres, Haddad, and Albert (1987), Heth (1976), Heth and Rescorla (1973), Mahoney and Ayres (1976), and Mowrer and Aiken (1954). Burkhardt (1980) found that the magnitude of this effect was a function of the intensity of the shock. However, backward conditioning is not restricted to aversive USs. Using food as the US, backward conditioning has been demonstrated with pigeons (Hearst, 1989) and rats (Silva, Timberlake, & Koehler, 1996; Silva, Timberlake, & Cevik, 1998; Silva & Timberlake, 2000; Urushihara, 2004), but in these cases more trials were required.

Although temporal precedence is one of Hume's three elements for causal inference, the existence of backward conditioning actually provides support for the proposition that Pavlovian conditioning involves causal inference: After experiencing an important event (the US), individuals appear to search for its cause. The observed CRs are best explained by assuming that the subjects have made a causal inference that the other event (the CS) caused the US, even though these two events may have been experienced in reverse order. However, with continued training, the CRs produced by backward conditioning diminish (Cole & Miller, 1999; Heth, 1976; Spooner & Kellogg, 1947), and with more extended training, backward conditioning procedures produce CRs that are antagonistic to those produced by "forward" conditioning procedures. We attribute these antagonistic CRs to the process called conditioned inhibition (Moscovitz & LoLordo, 1968; Siegel & Domjan, 1971). Thus, it is quite clear that temporal precedence is not a necessary condition for the occurrence of CRs.

Why These Seemingly Contradictory Data Support the View That Pavlovian Conditioning Is an Inference Task

Individuals can observe the temporal contiguity between the CS and US from a single experience, but it takes a number of observations to detect the CS-US contingency. Therefore, temporal contiguity is more important early in training, and when the situation is dangerous. With extended experience, individuals can learn if there is indeed a consistent relationship between the CS and US, as well as the degree and direction of that relationship.

The Problem. At first glance, the data presented in this chapter appear contradictory. Conditioned responses have been observed with both forward and backward arrangements of the CS and US, and sometimes after a single CS-US presentation. These data suggest that temporal contiguity, not temporal precedence or the CS-US contingency, is the sufficient condition for Pavlovian conditioning. On the other hand, with extended training only the positive contingency (forward CS-US arrangement) produces CRs. Extended training with zero contingencies does not produce CRs, and extended training with negative contingencies produces inhibition (an effect antagonistic to excitatory effects produced by positive contingencies). How can we resolve these apparently conflicting data?

Causal Inference Revisited. David Hume (1777/1993) argued that individuals do not directly observe the connection between events; instead they observe the occurrence of events in some order and contiguity, and with some degree of consistency. From these observations, they infer the connection between the events in question. Order and contiguity can be perceived from a single occurrence of a pair of events, but recognizing the contingency between events requires experience with a number of occurrences. However, there are times when the individual does not have the luxury of experiencing multiple occurrences of the events in question. This is certainly true when something is dangerous or life-threatening: The conjunction of events on a single trial may indeed be due to chance, but individuals may not survive long enough to learn whether a sound is or is not indicative of a predator, or whether a taste is or is not indicative of tainted food. Furthermore, temporal precedence is not that important if one is trying to learn the identity of a predator or the source of pain after having experienced a close call. Under these conditions, it is better to be safe than sorry (or dead). With additional experience, individuals can learn whether there is a causal connection between these events.

Some Data on the Respective Roles of Temporal Contiguity and CS-US Contingency in Pavlovian Conditioning. Rescorla (1972) provided data which helps us sort out the respective roles of temporal contiguity and contingency in Pavlovian conditioning. He pretrained rats to press a lever for food and then gave different groups different numbers of days of conditioned suppression training (see Table 3.6). For half of the subjects given conditioned suppression training, $\text{Pr (US|CS)} = \text{Pr (US|no CS)} = 0.1$ per 2-minute interval, and for the other half, the $\text{Pr (US|CS)} = \text{Pr (US|no CS)} = 0.4$ per 2-minute interval. With these parameters, rats in the 0.1–0.1 condition received an average of just one shock in the presence of the CS in a given training session, and rats in the 0.4–0.4 condition received an average of 4.8 shocks in the presence of the CS in a single session. A control group received no conditioning. Each group was tested once by presenting the tone CS.

Table 3.6 Design of Experiment by Rescorla (1972) on the Effects of Temporal Contiguity and CS-US Contingency in Pavlovian Conditioning

Group	Pretraining	Pavlovian conditioning Pr (US|CS) = Pr (US|no CS)	Days of conditioning	Test
0.1-0.1	Press lever for food	0.1	1	Tone
0.1-0.1	Press lever for food	0.1	3	Tone
0.1-0.1	Press lever for food	0.1	6	Tone
0.4-0.4	Press lever for food	0.4	1	Tone
0.4-0.4	Press lever for food	0.4	3	Tone
0.4-0.4	Press lever for food	0.4	6	Tone
Control	Press lever for food	None	0	Tone

Note: For all groups, CS was a 2-minute tone and US was shock.

The results are presented in Figure 3.6. The control group that received zero days of conditioning exhibited no suppression when the tone was presented. The rats that received one and three days of training with the zero contingency exhibited some conditioned suppression (which increased slightly between the one- and three-day groups), but after six days of exposure to a zero contingency, there was no conditioned suppression.

Kremer (1971) and Kremer and Kamin (1971) also reported conditioned suppression of bar pressing after five days of training with a zero contingency. Their rats received many more chance pairings of the CS and US than did Rescorla's (1972) subjects. Quinsey (1971) reported that the proportion of his rats exhibiting conditioned suppression of licking after two days of training on a zero contingency increased with the number of CS-US pairings. Clearly, conditioned suppression can occur to a stimulus presented in a zero contingency with shock after a short amount of training. However, after extended training with a zero contingency, the amount of conditioned suppression diminishes (Ayres, Benedict, & Witcher, 1975; Benedict & Ayres, 1972; Keller, Ayres, & Mahoney, 1977; Kremer, 1971; Rescorla, 1972).

The Resolution. The evidence is quite clear that individuals behave as if they are making causal inferences based on their experiences with the CS and US. This is particularly true in dangerous situations. Until individuals experience sudden painful stimulation, they have no reason to pay attention to details in their environment (unless these details involve innate or learned knowledge about predators or food). Painful stimulation evokes a search for its cause. Therefore, it is not surprising that backward conditioning can occur from a single experience with shock followed closely in time by a noticeable event. However, with repeated experience, the individual learns that the backward CS is not a predictor of the US. Repeated backward conditioning is really a negative contingency,

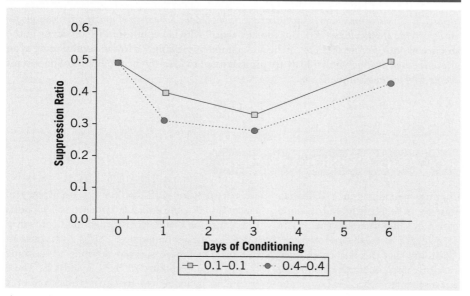

Figure 3.6 The effects of different amounts of experience with a zero contingency on conditioned suppression in rats. See Table 3.6 for descriptions of the different groups. Because this is conditioned suppression, *lower* values mean *more* suppression.

Figure redrawn with permission from "Informational Variables in Pavlovian Conditioning" by R. A. Rescorla in *The Psychology of Learning and Motivation,* Volume 6, edited by Gordon H. Bower, copyright © 1972 by Academic Press. Reprinted with permission from Elsevier Science.

and experience with a negative contingency teaches the individual that the backward CS predicts the absence of the US. Thus Hume was correct that the temporal order of events is involved in causal inference.

The research on zero contingencies where a CR emerges after a few random conjunctions of CS and US early in training also supports Hume's analysis. With sufficient exposure to the zero contingency [Pr (US I CS) = Pr (US I no CS)], individuals learn that there is no relationship between the CS and US, and the CR disappears. On the other hand, with sufficient exposure to a positive CS-US contingency [Pr (US I CS) > Pr (US I no CS)], individuals behave as if the CS causes the US. Furthermore, the CR frequently reflects the degree of correlation between the CS and US (see Figure 3.2).

Therefore, all of these data support the conclusion that individuals use both the temporal contiguity and the contingency (which involves temporal precedence) between the CS and US in Pavlovian conditioning. Because temporal contiguity can be programmed and experienced from a single CS-US pairing, the perception of a possible relationship between the CS and US requires only that the individual sense that two events occur close together in time. Therefore, temporal contiguity is important during the early Pavlovian conditioning trials when there is little opportunity to experience the contingency. On the other hand, experiencing the programmed contingency requires a number of repetitions of the CS-US relationship. The effects of the contingency (and temporal precedence) become evident with extended exposure to the pattern of CS and US presentations.

Hume was certainly correct in his identification of the conditions for causal inference. Each plays some role in Pavlovian conditioning, and Pavlovian conditioning is enhanced when all three of Hume's conditions are present; nevertheless *none of those conditions by themselves are either necessary or sufficient conditions for the formation of causal inferences (or for the occurrence of Pavlovian CRs)*. But the fact that Pavlovian conditioning can occur in the absence of one or more of them can be understood by viewing Pavlovian conditioning as an inference task in which individuals are programmed to identify the predictors of important events in their environment.

SUMMARY AND CONCLUSIONS

The task confronting individuals in a Pavlovian conditioning situation is to identify and respond to the predictors of important events. The accumulation of evidence over the past century points to the conclusion that this is accomplished through a process of causal inference. Following Hume, we view causal inference as an automatic process that requires the active processing of information. However, viewing Pavlovian conditioning as a process of causal inference does not mean that it requires verbal logic, deliberation, or reflection.

Hume argued that causal inferences are more likely to occur when there is a consistent and close temporal and spatial relationship with the inferred cause preceding the effect. Pavlovian conditioning is enhanced when all three of these conditions are present. Although none of these conditions are necessary or sufficient for the occurrence of Pavlovian CRs, the available evidence still supports the conclusion that Pavlovian conditioning involves a process of causal inference. This is most apparent in situations where survival depends on learning from a single exposure to the CS and US. These situations include post-attack identification of a predator (a backward conditioning arrangement) and learning to avoid eating tainted foods (when one might not get sick until hours later).

Although temporal precedence, temporal and spatial contiguity, and consistency all help individuals identify the predictors of important events, they are not the only factors that affect this identification. In the next chapter we will explore in more detail how natural selection has predisposed individuals to identify the predictors of important events.

STUDY QUESTIONS

1. What are Hume's three conditions for causal inferences, and how are they related to the procedures that typically produce Pavlovian conditioned responses?

2. What does it mean to say that something is a *necessary condition* for the occurrence of another event? What does it mean to say that something is a *sufficient condition* for the occurrence

of another event? What does it mean to say that something is a *unique cause* of another event?

3. Describe a positive contingency, a negative contingency, and a zero contingency in Pavlovian conditioning. What is the effect on behavior of each of these contingencies? Give an example for each contingency. How are the effects of these contingencies related to causal inference in Pavlovian conditioning?

4. What are the general effects of temporal and spatial proximity on Pavlovian conditioning? In what situations do we tend to observe Pavlovian conditioning when there are long CS-US intervals? How is this related to causal

inference in Pavlovian conditioning? Why is this adaptive?

5. Under what conditions do we tend to observe Pavlovian conditioned responses with backward and simultaneous conditioning procedures? How is this related to causal inference? Why is this adaptive?

6. Even though consistency, spatial and temporal proximity, and temporal precedence are neither necessary nor sufficient conditions for the occurrence of Pavlovian conditioning, do the data presented in this chapter support the view that Pavlovian conditioning is an inference task? Why or why not?

4

IDENTIFYING THE PREDICTORS OF SIGNIFICANT EVENTS

The problem confronting individuals in Pavlovian conditioning situations is to identify and learn what among the myriad other stimuli and events in the environment predicts the occurrence of the US. Although temporal precedence of the CS, temporal contiguity, and CS-US consistency aid in this search, they are not the only things that determine how quickly individuals learn. In this chapter we will look at other factors that influence the identification of the CS from among those events experienced when the US occurs. That identification is also influenced by what the individual brings to the conditioning situation—that is, its *inherited knowledge* about the importance of various stimulus events in relation to specific motivationally significant events and *learned knowledge* obtained through personal experience. Both kinds of knowledge affect the individual's perceptions of the various stimulus events that are potential predictors of the US.

THE SALIENCE OF STIMULI

The salience of a given stimulus is determined by attributes of that stimulus, innate knowledge, and the individual's experiences with various stimuli in that situation. All other things being equal, individuals select the stimulus with the highest salience in a given situation and learn to make CRs to that stimulus.

Stimuli differ in **salience**—that is, *the likelihood that they will be noticed, or attended to, by an individual in a given situation*. However, salience is not merely a physical attribute of a stimulus that can be measured, like intensity or wavelength. Salience cannot be measured independently of the behavior of an individual because the same stimulus may be responded to differently by different individuals and by the same individual in different situations or at different times. *The salience of a stimulus is determined in part by the physical attributes of the stimulus, in part by the situation in which that stimulus occurs, and in part by the inherited and learned knowledge the individual brings to that situation.* In some situations, a given stimulus is given high priority as a candidate for selection, and in other situations it be ignored. In Pavlovian conditioning, the emergence of CRs to a stimulus that occurs along with a US is related to the salience of that potential CS.

Salience and Discriminability

> Predictors of important events are more easily identified when they stand out from the background; that is, they are more salient.

Pavlov (1927) observed that the speed of acquisition of CRs to a given kind of CS (auditory, visual, tactile, etc.) was a function of the intensity of the stimulus: Conditioning occurred faster to the more intense stimulus. Kamin and Schaub (1963) confirmed that the rate of acquisition of conditioned suppression in rats is a function of the intensity of the noise used as the CS. However, *it is not the absolute intensity of the CS that affects the speed of conditioning; it is how discriminable (salient) that stimulus is from the background* (Logan, 1954; Perkins, 1953). Kamin (1965) demonstrated that the amount of conditioned suppression in rats is a function of how different the CS is from the background. In some groups, the noise CS increased by either 10, 20, 30, 35, or 80 decibels over the background, and in other groups the noise CS decreased by one of those amounts. The suppression ratios for all 10 groups in Kamin's experiment are presented in Figure 4.1. The effect of salience is more obvious in the left panel where the CS was a *reduction* in the intensity of the background noise. The least suppression[1] occurred in

Figure 4.1 Conditioned suppression as a function of the amount of decrease in background noise as a CS (left panel) and the amount of increase in background noise as a CS (right panel). The first number in each group designation is the background noise during the intertrial interval and the second number is the background noise during the CS.

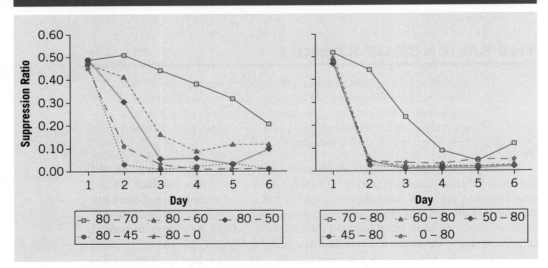

From Kamin, 1965. Redrawn with permission of the author.

---

[1]Because this is conditioned suppression, the lower the suppression ratio, the stronger the CS-US learning.

the group with the smallest change between the background and the CS (80 dB to 70 dB). As the difference between the background and CS increased, the amount of suppression increased. In the right panel, the CS was an *increase* in the level of noise over the background. Here again, the least suppression occurred in the group that had the smallest increase (70 dB to 80 dB). The other groups were not different from each other. Why should it matter whether the CS is an increase or a decrease from the background level of stimulation? One possible explanation is that a danger signal is easier to detect when it is an increase over the background. Most likely this reflects the fact that predators make noise just before they pounce or strike.

These data highlight the relationship between stimulus salience and the speed of Pavlovian conditioning: *Anything that makes a stimulus more noticeable increases its salience and thus the likelihood that an individual will attend to that stimulus and select it as a candidate CS in Pavlovian conditioning.*

The Overshadowing of One Predictor by Another

When two predictors of an important event occur at the same time, conditioning frequently occurs to only one of them. When this happens, we say that one event has overshadowed the other. We attribute overshadowing to differences in salience of these events. Those differences in salience can reflect innate knowledge or could be due to prior experience.

Pavlov (1927) also observed that when the CS consists of two events (termed a *compound CS)* that have the same temporal and contingent relationship to the US, the individual might make a CR to only one of them. He gave two examples. In his first example, the compound CS consisted of the simultaneous application of tactile stimulation of the skin and a thermal stimulus of 0°C. The US was mild acid in the mouth. Strong CRs occurred when the compound CS was presented and when the tactile stimulus was presented alone, but no CRs occurred when the thermal stimulus was presented alone. According to Pavlov, the tactile stimulus *overshadowed* the thermal stimulus. In his second example, the compound CS was a tone presented simultaneously with the illumination of a lamp (visual stimulus). The US was food. Strong CRs occurred when the compound CS was presented and when the tone was presented alone, but no CRs occurred when the visual stimulus was presented alone. Again, one stimulus (tone) *overshadowed* the other stimulus (light). In other experiments, these same lights and thermal stimuli were found to be effective CSs when they were the only CS. Pavlov coined the term overshadowing to describe the situation in which *conditioning occurs to one of the stimuli that accompany a US at the expense of other simultaneously presented stimuli.* The procedure for demonstrating overshadowing is presented in Table 4.1. The control groups are used to show that one can get CRs to occur to both CS_1 and CS_2 when each is trained separately as a CS.

Similar predispositions to select some stimuli over others have been reported in other situations. Pigeons form conditioned emotional responses more readily to auditory stimuli than to visual stimuli (LoLordo, 1979), and humans form them more readily to fear-relevant stimuli like snakes and spiders (Öhman & Hugdahl, 1979). Rats quickly form aversions to the taste rather than the visual aspects of foods that are followed by gastric distress (Garcia & Koelling, 1966), while birds are more likely to form aversions to the visual aspects of such

Table 4.1 The Procedure for Demonstrating Overshadowing

Group	Training	Test	Results
Overshadowing	$CS_1 + CS_2 \rightarrow US$	CS_1 and CS_2	Strong CR to one CS Weak CR to other CS
CS_1 control	$CS_1 \rightarrow US$	CS_1 and CS_2	CR to CS_1
CS_2 control	$CS_2 \rightarrow US$	CS_1 and CS_2	CR to CS_2

foods (Brower, 1969; Logue, 1980; Wilcoxon et al., 1971). On the other hand, rats *can* learn about environmental stimuli that accompany the consumption of foods that are followed by illness (Best, Best, & Henggeler, 1977), and birds *can* learn aversions to the taste of foods followed by illness (Gustavson, 1977). These examples point to the role of natural selection in determining the salience of certain stimuli under certain conditions.

Pavlov also reported that the overshadowing effect depended on the intensities of the various stimuli: When the loudness of a tone in a tone-light compound was reduced, the light overshadowed the tone. Kamin (1969) and Mackintosh (1971, 1976) reported similar results with conditioned suppression. Using suppression of licking, Mackintosh (1971) also demonstrated that these effects of stimulus intensity occur with a single CS-US pairing.

The occurrence of overshadowing links stimulus salience to causal inference. Individuals come to conditioning experiments with certain biases or predispositions to make inferences about some stimuli as opposed to others. One of those biases is to select stimuli that have temporal and spatial contiguity with the US. As we have seen earlier, when there is another taste closer to the time of illness, that second taste can *overshadow* the taste that preceded it (Revusky, 1971; see Chapter 3).

In the overshadowing experiments just described, although both elements of the CS provided the same information about the occurrence of the US, stronger CRs tended to occur to one element. We infer from the studies on stimulus intensity and discriminability that the stimulus selected was the more salient of the two, and we assume that the salience of a stimulus element was established either by natural selection or by the experimenter who manipulated intensity. In the next section, we will see how the salience of stimuli can be affected by experience.

SALIENCE AND PRIOR EXPERIENCE WITH POTENTIAL CONDITIONED STIMULI

Individuals can learn that something does not predict anything of importance. This interferes with later conditioning to that event when it becomes a predictor of the presence or absence of another event.

Conditioned taste aversions (CTAs) are more likely to occur to novel tastes than to familiar ones, even when the familiar taste is in closer temporal proximity to the illness than the novel taste during conditioning (Revusky & Bedarf, 1967; Wittlin & Brookshire, 1968). The evidence is quite clear that it is the familiarity with the potential CS (the taste) that is responsible for this effect. For example, Kalat and Rozin (1973) demonstrated that a single exposure to a distinctive taste 21 days before that taste is again experienced along with an illness-producing US is enough to *impede* the acquisition of a CTA. Conditioned taste aversions can be produced with highly familiar foods, but typically this requires more than one trial and a stronger dose of the US (Garcia, Kimeldorf, & Koelling, 1955; Smith, Blumsack, & Bilek, 1985).

Thus, familiarity with distinctive-tasting foods that have not produced illness makes them less likely candidates for selection when illness occurs. Broborg and Bernstein (1987) used this to reduce chemotherapy-induced CTAs in children with cancer. When children ate a distinctive-tasting candy (coconut or root beer Lifesavers) between their regular meal and the chemotherapy treatment, they consumed more of their meal on a subsequent occasion than if they had not eaten the candy between the meal and chemotherapy. Giving the children distinctive-flavored Lifesavers (coconut or root beer) after eating their evening meal at the hospital and before their chemotherapy treatment led to a greater willingness to consume items from that meal at a later time than if they had not eaten the candy. Thus, this intervention reduced the adverse impact of the chemotherapy on the children's preferences for their regular diets. All of this illustrates that salience is affected by familiarity (or lack of familiarity), but the circumstances under which the individual becomes familiar with something is the factor that affects the salience. Typically, preexposure to something that is not motivationally significant outside of a Pavlovian conditioning procedure (i.e., experiencing that event in the absence of a US) reduces its salience. That, in turn, affects the ability of that event to serve as a CS later.

The CS Preexposure Effect

> Prior experience with a potential CS outside of a Pavlovian conditioning procedure (CS alone) retards the course of later Pavlovian conditioning when that stimulus event becomes a predictor of a US.

How quickly an individual begins to make CRs to a CS depends in part on whether he or she had experienced that CS outside of the conditioning situation. *The retardation of Pavlovian conditioning by familiarity with the CS (in the absence of a US prior to conditioning)* is called the **CS preexposure effect** (or **latent inhibition**[2]). The CS preexposure effect occurs when the to-be-CS is experienced alone before presenting it in a nonzero contingency with a US. The procedure for demonstrating the CS preexposure effect is presented in Table 4.2. The No-preexposure group provides the baseline for evaluating the CS preexposure effect (in the CS_1 Preexposure group) because this group provides data on the normal course of acquisition with the chosen CS and US. The group labeled "CS_2 Preexposure" provides a control for preexposure to another stimulus, and the group labeled "CS_1 Preexposure in B" is used to demonstrate that the CS_1 preexposure effect is context (or situation) specific.

---

[2]Lubow and Moore (1959) coined the term *latent inhibition* because they thought that the presentation of the CS alone produced inhibition of responding that then interfered with subsequent excitatory conditioning. However, CS preexposure also interferes with inhibitory conditioning (Baker & Mackintosh, 1977; Rescorla, 1971a). This argues against an inhibitory mechanism as the basis for this phenomenon. Although the term *latent inhibition* is still widely used, labeling this as a "CS preexposure effect" does not imply anything about the underlying psychological processes; therefore, the latter name will be used here.

Table 4.2 The Procedure for Demonstrating the CS Preexposure Effect in CTA Learning

Group	Preexposure	Training	Test	Results
No Preexposure	Water	$CS_1 \rightarrow US$	CS_1	Normal acquisition
CS_1 Preexposure	CS_1	$CS_1 \rightarrow US$	CS_1	Acquisition of CR retarded
CS_2 Preexposure	CS_2	$CS_1 \rightarrow US$	CS_1	Normal acquisition
CS_1 Preexposure in B	CS_1 in Context B	$CS_1 \rightarrow US$	CS_1	Normal acquisition

Note: All procedures occur in Context A, except where noted otherwise.

Ginton, Urca, and Lubow (1975) use the following procedure to demonstrate the CS preexposure effect in humans. For the CS preexposure group, a white noise (which would later serve as the CS in the test phase) was presented 25 times while the subjects were engaged in another task. That task was to count how many times a list of nonsense syllables was repeated during the training phase. The white noise was occasionally superimposed on the presentation of the syllables. The No preexposure group had the same task during the training phase of the experiment, but there were no presentations of the white noise. In the test phase of the experiment, the same recording of the nonsense syllables and white noise were presented, but the task now was to predict when a counter would increment. In this phase, the white noise is the CS and each increment of the counter was the US because only the presentation of the white noise predicted the increment of the counter. The participants in the CS preexposure group took more trials to learn that it was the white noise that predicted when the counter would increment. This procedure and variations of it have been used in many different experiments to examine the CS preexposure effect in humans. The CS preexposure effect has been observed in a wide variety of situations other than CTAs and in a variety of species (see Lubow, 1989, 2009, for reviews).

There are a number of aspects of the CS-preexposure effect that point to the conclusion that it reflects a reduction in salience for the preexposed stimulus, which in turn affects the individual's bias against selecting that stimulus as a potential CS:

1. Although the CS preexposure effect can be obtained with a single trial in CTAs, it increases as a function of the number of CS preexposures (Domjan, 1972; Domjan & Siegel, 1971; Kalat & Rozin, 1973; Lantz, 1973). This indicates that individuals are learning that the preexposed stimulus predicts nothing of consequence and thus should pay less attention to it.

2. The CS-preexposure effect is specific to that CS (Carlton & Vogel, 1967; Schnur, 1971).

3. The CS preexposure effect is situation specific; that is, it is reduced when preexposure and conditioning occur in different situations

(Channell & Hall, 1983; Lovibond, Preston, & Mackintosh, 1984; Westbrook, Jones, Bailey, & Harris, 2000). Furthermore, the CS preexposure effect is also reduced if the preexposed stimulus is paired with another stimulus during preexposure (Dickinson, 1976; Lubow, Schnur, & Rifkin, 1976). When it predicts something of importance, there is less retardation of subsequent conditioning. This suggests that the individuals are making a causal inference about that stimulus, namely that it predicts nothing of consequence *in this situation*.

4. The CS preexposure effect occurs only when the motivational state under which the CS preexposure occurs and the US in the later Pavlovian conditioning are related; that is, CS preexposure when an individual is food deprived retards the acquisition of a CR when the US is food, but not when the US is water (and similarly with thirst and food; Killcross & Balleine, 1996). This suggests that during CS preexposure, individuals learn that this particular CS predicts nothing of consequence with respect to their current motivational state.

5. Preexposure to a potential CS affects conditioning with both a positive contingency and a negative contingency (Killcross & Balleine, 1996; Reiss & Wagner, 1972; Rescorla, 1971a). This provides evidence against the view that the CS-preexposure effect is simply due to inhibition. If it were due to inhibition, then it should enhance, not retard, conditioning with a negative contingency.

Therefore, the CS preexposure effect indicates that individuals learn something about stimuli that are not associated in some way with a motivationally significant event in a given situation or context. The fact that the CS preexposure effect is situation specific and is reduced if the preexposed stimulus is related to another event during preexposure suggests that the individuals are making a causal inference about that stimulus, namely that it predicts nothing of consequence *in this situation*. Therefore, when a significant event is introduced and the individual attempts to discover predictors for that event, the preexposed stimulus is a less salient choice. The obvious candidates are novel events that are experienced in close temporal proximity to the significant event (the US).

Zero Contingencies and Learned Irrelevance

Exposure to a zero contingency teaches individuals that two events are unrelated. As a result of exposure to a zero contingency, individuals take longer to acquire a Pavlovian CR with the same CS and US. We attribute this effect to the individuals making a causal inference called learned irrelevance (this stimulus is not related to the US).

Although sometimes CRs occur early in training with a zero contingency before the individual has had a chance to learn that the CS does not predict the US (see Chapter 3), these CRs disappear as training continues. However, this does not mean that there are no lasting effects from exposure to a zero contingency: experience with a zero contingency frequently retards learning with both positive contingencies (excitatory conditioning; Dess & Overmier, 1989; Linden, Savage, & Overmier, 1997) and negative contingencies (inhibitory contingencies; Baker & Mackintosh, 1977). This effect has been attributed to the formation of a *causal inference based on experience that the two events are unrelated*, and it is theorized that this inference makes it harder for individuals to learn about positive and negative contingencies involving those events (Mackintosh, 1973, 1983). This causal inference is called **learned irrelevance**. The basic experiment for demonstrating learned irrelevance is presented in Table 4.3.

Mackintosh (1973) provided a demonstration that exposure to a zero contingency retards the acquisition of subsequent Pavlovian conditioning. He trained rats to lick a tube to receive water and then subjected them to one of the treatments outlined in Table 4.3. The experimental animals (Group Learned Irrelevance) experienced eight days of training in which the CS (a tone) was presented independently of the shock US whereas the control group was placed in the apparatus for the eight days with no tones or shocks. The test consisted of Pavlovian conditioning with tone as the CS and shock as the US.

The results of this conditioned suppression experiment are presented in Figure 4.2, which shows that prior experience with a zero contingency between the CS and US retards subsequent learning that the CS is related to the US. Also notice that with extended conditioning with the positive contingency that the influence of the prior zero contingency may be overcome. Baker and Mackintosh (1977) demonstrated the effects of zero contingencies with both excitatory conditioning (a positive contingency) and inhibitory conditioning (a negative contingency) in the test.

Myers, Oliver, Warren, and Gluck (2000) demonstrated learned irrelevance in humans in a simple prediction task with college students. On each trial, a drawing was shown of a magician waving his wand at a large hat and saying a "magic word" (e.g., "blae") in the colored cartoon balloon above his head. There were 15 different words and two different colored balloons. The participants' task was to predict whether a rabbit would appear under the hat by pressing a yes or no key on the computer keyboard. In the training phase of the experiment, there was a zero contingency between the color that would be the CS in the test phase for the participants in the Learned Irrelevance

Table 4.3 The Procedure for Demonstrating Learned Irrelevance With a Zero Contingency

Group	Preexposure	Test	Results
Control	No preexposure	CS → US	Normal acquisition
Learned irrelevance	Zero contingency between CS and US	CS → US	Acquisition of CR retarded

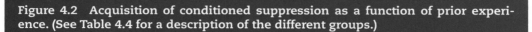

Figure 4.2 Acquisition of conditioned suppression as a function of prior experience. (See Table 4.4 for a description of the different groups.)

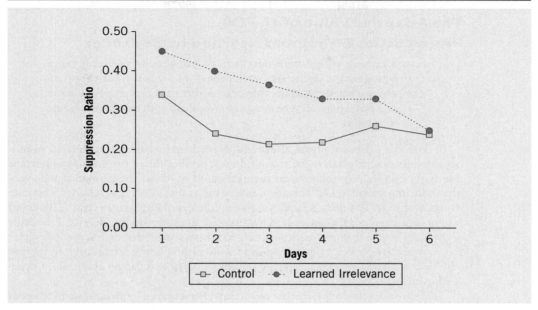

Redrawn from Mackintosh, 1973, Stimulus selection: Learning to ignore stimuli that predict no change in reinforcement. In R. A. Hinde and J. Stevenson-Hinde (Eds.), *Constraints on learning* (pp. 75–100).

group. The participants in the control group went directly to the test phase. In the test phase, the participants in the Learned Irrelevance group were told that the rules had changed. Now there were different words, and one of the colors from the training phase predicted the appearance of the rabbit (the US). The participants in the Learned Irrelevance group made more errors than those in the No Preexposure group. In other words, exposure to the zero contingency reduced how quickly those participants learned to identify the color that predicted the US.

Like the CS preexposure effect, the effects of experience with a zero contingency are context specific: A change in context reduces the effect (Matzel, Schachtman, & Miller, 1988). Furthermore, learned irrelevance can be attenuated if the individual first experiences a *positive contingency* involving the US used in the test for learned irrelevance (Nakajima, Nakajima, & Imada, 1999). All of the data reviewed here point to the conclusion that individuals exposed to a zero contingency learn that in a certain context or situation a certain stimulus is not related to the significant event (the US) that is occurring there. In other words, individuals learn that the stimulus in question is irrelevant, its salience is reduced, and they ignore it. Thus, it takes a while for them to select that stimulus as a predictor of the US when it becomes one. However, the learned irrelevance effect can be overcome if they have prior experience with the US being predicted by something.

The Adaptive Value of the CS
Preexposure Effect and Learned Irrelevance

Learning to ignore events that do not predict the occurrence of important events allows individuals to focus their attention on those predictors that do. Failure to exhibit the CS preexposure effect and learned irrelevance occurs in individuals with certain psychiatric diagnoses.

In both the CS preexposure effect and learned irrelevance effect, certain stimuli become less salient when those stimuli do not predict the occurrence of important events. As a result, individuals focus their attention on identifying stimuli that do predict those important events. The down side of this is that learning is retarded when the situation changes and those stimuli become predictors of important events. This could lead to disastrous consequences if individuals fail to recognize the cues for a predator or danger. Despite that possibility, learning to ignore stimuli that do not predict predators or other danger helps the individual to avoid responding to irrelevant information and focus limited attentional capacity on avoidance of real danger (Gonzalo, López, & Martín, 2013).

There are a number of psychiatric conditions characterized by an inability to tune out irrelevant stimuli. In the case of schizophrenia, Kapur (2003) suggested that delusions occur when the individual is trying to make sense of experiences that are abnormally salient to that person, and delusions occur as a result of a direct experience of internally salient representations. Support for this suggestion comes from a number of studies that report that individuals with acute schizophrenia do not exhibit the CS preexposure effect or learned irrelevance (for reviews, see Gray & Snowden, 2005; Lubow & Weiner, 2010). The CS preexposure effect and learned irrelevance are also reduced for individuals who exhibit schizotypal personality disorder (sometimes referred to as schizotypy), a continuum of social and interpersonal deficits that in extreme forms resemble some of the symptoms of schizophrenia (see Schmidt-Hansen, Killcross, & Honey, 2009, for a review). The failure to exhibit CS preexposure effect and learned irrelevance indicates that individuals with schizophrenia and schizotypal personality disorder do not learn how to ignore stimuli that do not predict the occurrence of important events.

RELATIVE VALIDITY IN PAVLOVIAN CONDITIONING

Where there are two predictors of the US, individuals will select the best predictor, where "best" is defined in terms of the contingency.

The task in a Pavlovian conditioning situation is not just to identify predictors of the US; it is to identify the *best* predictor. The best predictor will always be the one with the highest relative validity—that is, *the highest correlation with the US*. Wagner, Logan, Haberlandt, and Price (1968) demonstrated that CRs will occur to the stimulus with the highest relative validity, and little conditioning will accrue to other stimuli that have lesser positive correlations. Thus, the stimulus with the highest relative validity will overshadow those with lesser validity.

The design of one of their experiments is presented in Table 4.4. For one group of rabbits in this eyeblink conditioning experiment, a tone-light compound CS (designated as T_1L) always ended with a shock, while a second tone-light compound CS (T_2L) never did. This group was called Correlated because one tone CS was consistently followed by the shock whereas the other tone CS predicted the absence of the US. For the other group (called the Uncorrelated group), both tone-light compound CSs (T_1L and T_2L) were each followed by shock 50% of the time. Thus, for these rabbits, the tone CSs were not correlated with shock US.

After Pavlovian conditioning was completed, all subjects were tested in extinction to determine how much was learned about the L, T_1, T_2, T_1L, and T_2L in each group. The results, expressed as percentage trials with a conditioned response (CR), are presented in Figure 4.3.

The results in Figure 4.3 can be understood by referring back to Table 4.4. What was the best predictor of the shock in the correlated group? The answer is T_1: Every time T_1 occurred, it was followed by a shock. T_2 was never followed by a shock, and L was followed by a shock 50% of the time. Thus, shocks *always* occurred after T_1, *never* after T_2, and *half the time* after L. Therefore, T_1 (whether alone or in compound with L) was the best predictor of the shock in the correlated condition. That is why most learning (higher percentage of trials with a CR) occurred when T_1 was present and fewer CRs occurred to L and T_2. What was the best predictor of the shock in the uncorrelated group? The answer is the L: although L, T_1, and T_2 were all followed by shock 50% of the time, shocks *never*

Table 4.4 The Design of the Relative Validity Experiment by Wagner, Logan, Haberlandt, and Price (1968)		
Group	Training	Test
Correlated	$T_1L \rightarrow$ US $T_2L \rightarrow$ no US	$L, T_1, T_2, T_1L, T_2L,$
Uncorrelated	$T_1L \rightarrow$ US $T_1L \rightarrow$ no US $T_2L \rightarrow$ US $T_2L \rightarrow$ no US	$L, T_1, T_2, T_1L, T_2L,$

Note: T_1 and T_2 were, respectively, a clicking sound and a tone. L was a light.

US was a brief (0.1 second) shock delivered below the right eye.

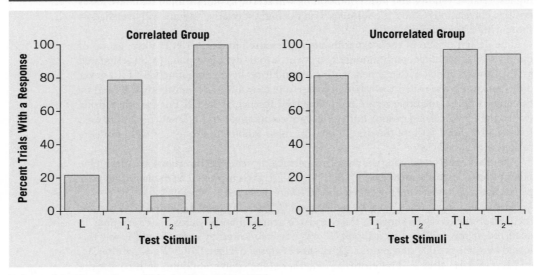

Figure 4.3 Percentage of trials with a conditioned response to different test stimuli for rabbits in the correlated condition (left) and the uncorrelated condition (right). In this figure, the higher the score, the greater the learning.

Redrawn from Wagner, Logan, Haberlandt, and Price, 1968.

occurred when L was absent, but they did occur in the absence of T_1 and in the absence of T_2. Therefore, L (whether alone or in compound with T_1 or T_2) was the best predictor of the shock in the uncorrelated group, even though the contingency between the L and shock was the same in both groups. That is why most learning (most trials with a CR) was obtained by the L in the uncorrelated group. Thus, learning occurred in both groups to the stimulus element or to the compound that *best* predicted the shock. Wagner et al. (1968) reported a comparable pattern of results using conditioned suppression in rats, as did Wasserman (1974) using sign-tracking in pigeons and Luongo (1976) using CTA in rats.

In the *uncorrelated* condition in Wagner et al. (1968), there was no difference in the percentage of reinforcement between T_1 and T_2. Both predicted the US 50% of the time (difference = 0). In the *correlated* conditions, one of those two stimuli predicted the US on 100% of the trials and the other on 0% of the trials (difference = 100). In a sign-tracking experiment with pigeons, Wasserman (1974) demonstrated that responding to the common cue (the light in the Wagner et al. experiment) is a function of the difference in percentage of reinforcement between the two other stimuli. Instead of just two groups (difference in percentage of reinforcement = 0 [uncorrelated] and 100 [correlated]), Wasserman added groups in which the differences in percentage of reinforcement by those two stimuli were 25 (62.5% - 37.5%), 50 (75% - 25%), and 75 (87.5% - 12.5%). The numbers of key pecks to the common stimulus are presented in Figure 4.4. As the predictiveness of one of the stimuli increased, responding to the common stimulus decreased.

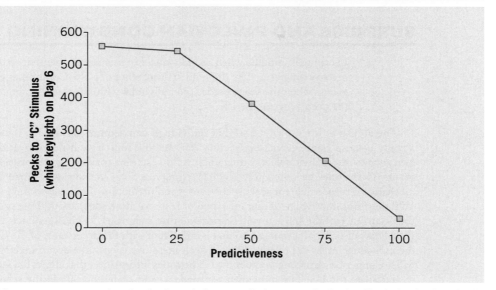

Figure 4.4 Mean number of keypecks to the white light as a function of the predictiveness of the other two stimuli (predictiveness was measured by the difference in percentage of reinforcement in the presence of the other two stimuli). Each value on the x-axis represents a different group of pigeons.

Adapted from Wasserman, E. A. (1974). Stimulus-reinforcer predictiveness and selective discrimination learning in pigeons. *Journal of Experimental Psychology, 103*, 284–297. Copyright © 1979 by the American Psychological Association. Reprinted with permission.

Relative validity of cues has also been established in video game experiments. For example, Baker, Mercier, Vallée-Tourangeau, Frank, and Pan (1993) had their participants play a video game in which the task was to guide a tank across a field guarded by visual mines that could only destroy the tank if they could see it. The participant could camouflage the tank with paint, but they did not know when they started which color paint made the tanks harder or easier to see. How likely the tank would successfully cross the field was dependent on two events. One was the color of the paint, and the other was the presence of a spotter plane, and they also did not know when they started whether the spotter plane helped or hindered the tanks in successfully traversing the minefield. Various combinations of correlated and uncorrelated procedures involving the camouflage and the spotter planes were presented in different games. The participants were asked at various times during the games to estimate the effectiveness of the camouflage and the spotter plane before, in the middle of, and after each game was finished. The findings across all games were that the estimated effectiveness of the spotter plane depended on whether the camouflage was correlated or uncorrelated with the success of the tank in traversing the field.

These data on the effects of the relative validity of events also support the proposition that Pavlovian conditioning reflects a process of causal inference. *Individuals are able to not only detect that there is a consistent relationship between events, they are able to assess those relationships and learn which has the highest correlation with the US.* The fact that this stimulus overshadows less relevant predictors suggests that its salience is affected by experience.[3]

SURPRISE AND PAVLOVIAN CONDITIONING

Learning is initiated when an individual experiences an unanticipated or surprising event like the sudden occurrence of a US. Conditioning occurs when the CS provides the individual with information about the occurrence of the US.

The ability to learn evolved so that individuals can acquire knowledge they do not already possess. Some events experienced for the first time have little motivational significance to the individual, and they elicit mild reactions (orienting responses). Other events (food, attack by a predator) produce strong reactions. In addition to these URs, the mechanisms responsible for seeking the causes and predictors of these events are invoked. Without prior knowledge (either inherited or learned knowledge) about these predictors, the occurrence of the US is unanticipated and thus surprising. With experience, the individual may discover an event (a CS) that is correlated with the occurrence of the US. After the individual learns the relationship between these two events, the occurrence of the US will no longer be surprising because the CS provides information that allows the individual to anticipate the US. The individual has made a causal inference about the relationship of the CS to the US. The key concept is **surprise**. *Individuals are surprised when something unanticipated or unexpected occurs, and learning is initiated by unanticipated or surprising events* (Kamin, 1969; Staddon, 1983).

Blocking of Pavlovian Conditioning to a Redundant Predictor of the US

If the US is already predicted by another stimulus, little or no conditioning will be observed to a second stimulus that provides redundant information. When this occurs, we say that conditioning to the first stimulus blocks conditioning to the second.

The research on relative validity tells us that individuals can identify and select the best predictor of the US from among those events that are correlated with it. Suppose, however, that an individual has already located a valid predictor of a US (such as a noise predicting shock). Under these circumstances, individuals will develop conditioned fear to that noise. If a second equally valid predictor (a light, for example) is added so that

---

[3]However, it should be noted that the effects of relative validity are reduced if both stimuli are naturally highly salient (Oberling, Bristol, Matute, & Miller, 2000).

now the noise and light both predict the shock with the same contingency, the combination CS (noise and light) will also produce fear. What will happen if the noise and the light are then presented separately? Kamin (1968, 1969) demonstrated that the prior experience with the first stimulus (noise, in this example) *blocks* conditioning to the added stimulus (a light).

The basic experimental design from Kamin (1969) is summarized in Table 4.5. Using a conditioned suppression procedure, the rats were pretrained to press a bar to obtain food and then they were separated into two groups and given the treatments shown in the table. The CSs, a noise (N) or light (L) or NL compound, were 3-minutes-long and the US was a 0.5 second foot shock. Following fear conditioning, all rats were tested for suppression to L. The suppression ratios to L are also presented in Table 4.5.[4] As expected, the control group showed strong suppression to L at test. However, when conditioning trials with the NL compound were *preceded* by conditioning trials with N, there was no suppression to L (no conditioning with L). Kamin used the term **blocking** to describe the effect of the prior conditioning with N on conditioning to L: *Prior conditioning with one element of a compound stimulus can "block" conditioning to the other element.*

Blocking occurs only when the added stimulus is redundant—that is, when the added stimulus does not provide any new information about the occurrence of the US. In Kamin's (1969) experiment (Table 4.5), the rats in the blocking group learned in Phase 1 that N was a valid predictor of the shock (N→US). The added L in Phase 2 (NL→US) was an *equally* valid predictor of the shock, but it *did not* provide these rats with any *new* information about the occurrence of the shock. Thus, *prior experience with N as a valid predictor of shock made that N a more salient stimulus than the otherwise more salient L.*

However, prior experience with N will *not* block conditioning to L if the intensity of the shock is increased when L is introduced (Kamin, 1968, 1969). Likewise, Dickinson, Hall, and Mackintosh (1976) and Mackintosh, Bygrave, and Picton (1977) showed that blocking is reduced or eliminated when any of the following changes to the US are introduced when the second element is added to a previously trained CS: adding a second shock on each trial, changing from two shocks 4 seconds apart to two shocks 8 seconds apart (postponing

Table 4.5 Design From Kamin's (1969) Experiment on Blocking

| Group | Pavlovian conditioning | | Test | Suppression ratio to light |
	Phase 1	Phase 2		
Control	None	NL → US	L	.05
Blocking	N → US	NL → US	L	.45

Note: N = noise, L = light, NL = noise-light compound, US = shock.

[4]The *lower* the suppression ratio, the *greater* the learning. A suppression ratio of 0.5 means no CS-US learning.

the second shock) on each trial, and omitting an expected second shock entirely on each trial. Thus, *blocking does not occur when the added stimulus element signals something new*. There is, however, one exception to this statement: Blocking will still occur if the magnitude of the US remains the same despite changes in some of its other properties. Rescorla (1972) reported that a 0.5 mA, 2-second shock is comparable to a 2 mA, 0.5-second shock for producing conditioned suppression. To demonstrate their comparability to produce blocking, he gave rats conditioned suppression training with a light as the CS and one of these intensity-duration combinations as the US. Then for half of the animals, the US was changed to the other intensity-duration combination when a tone was added; the shock remained unchanged for the other rats. In the test for suppression to the tone, the performance of the two groups of rats was nearly identical. Rescorla's data indicate that rats experience the two intensity-durations (0.5 mA, 2-second shock and 2 mA, 0.5-second shock) as similar in terms of how aversive they feel.

In Kamin's (1968, 1969) blocking experiment, the subjects in the blocking group learned that the shock US was predicted by N in Phase 1: when N occurred, the subjects could anticipate that the shock would follow (with a certain probability). In other words, the subjects were not surprised by the appearance of the shock. The addition of L to N in Phase 2 gave the subjects *no new information* about the occurrence of the shock because the NL compound CS predicted the shock as well as N alone did. The prior experience with N as a predictor of the shock *blocked* learning about L as a predictor of the shock because the appearance of the shock was not surprising when L was introduced.

In Pavlovian conditioning, individuals learn that a *specific* US is predicted by the CS, and it is that *specific* US that is anticipated when that CS occurs. An abrupt change in the US is unanticipated and thus surprising. Therefore, if the US changes at the same time that the second stimulus is added to the original CS, the second stimulus is not redundant because it signals a change in the US. Under these circumstances, prior experience with the first stimulus as a predictor of the US does not block learning about the second stimulus as a predictor of the US because the changes in the US are surprising.

Knowledge about blocking has implications for marketing products. How likely we are to decide which of a number of similarly-priced products to purchase from is based on our perception of quality of those products. Oxoby and Finnigan (2007) and van Osselaer and Alba (2000) demonstrated that our perceptions of quality are influenced by the sequential order in which we receive information about the attributes of the products that determine quality. In both sets of experiments, participants in one group were presented with profiles of a number of different versions of a product (e.g., white water rafts, mountain axes, or mountaineering boots) that differed in terms of brand and various relevant attributes of the products (e.g., types of compartments, hull, and floor for the rafts; length of handle, and type of steel for the axe; weight and materials used in uppers and in the heels for the boots). Also included were quality ratings.

In Phase 1 of van Osselaer and Alba's (2000) experiment, participants in the blocking groups looked at four profiles that contained brand names and some of the attributes (e.g., types of compartments and hull, but nothing about the type of floor). The high-quality rafts carried one brand name and the low-quality rafts carried the other brand name. Compartments and hull were not related to the quality ratings. The control participants did not have this experience. In Phase 2, all participants looked at 12 additional profiles that contained the same brands and components and now included type of floor that was also perfectly correlated with brand (i.e., a redundant cue). For the test, participants were presented with 8 profiles that contained all possible combinations of the two brands, types of compartments, and types of hulls. The dependent measure was the quality ratings the participants assigned to each profile. A strong blocking effect was consistently found; that is, prior exposure to the four profiles in Phase 1 where brand predicted quality blocked the assignment of high quality to the redundant cue (type of floor). Oxoby and Finnigan (2007) extended these results to price as the blocking stimulus and found that blocking can also affect judgements of quality of different products that have the same brand and similar prices. Based on these results, both sets of researchers point out the importance of understanding how prior experience with one attribute of a product can block attention to other attributes. This has implications for advertisers in terms of how they craft messages to consumers about their products.

Blocking by the Context: The US Preexposure Effect

> The US tends to occur in some situations or contexts and not others; therefore, it is reasonable to expect that those situations or contexts can become CSs for Pavlovian CRs.

Significant events that serve as Pavlovian USs do not appear in a vacuum. In the natural environment they tend to occur in some places and not others; therefore, it is reasonable to expect that these places where significant events occur can become CSs, and as CSs, they can block conditioning to other stimulus events.

As was the case with CS preexposure, *presenting the US by itself prior to Pavlovian conditioning retards the acquisition of the CR.* This is called the **US preexposure effect**. The basic design for demonstrating the US preexposure effect is presented in Table 4.6.

As is the case with the CS-preexposure effect (Table 4.2), the no-preexposure control group represents the baseline for evaluating the US preexposure effect (in the US Preexposure group) because this group provides data on the normal course of acquisition with the chosen CS and US. The control group labeled "US preexposure in B" is used to demonstrate that the US preexposure effect is context (or situation) specific.

Table 4.6   The Procedure for Demonstrating the US Preexposure Effect

Group	Preexposure	Training	Test	Results
No preexposure	None	CS → US	CS	Normal acquisition
US preexposure	US	CS → US	CS	Acquisition of CR retarded
US preexposure in B	US in context B	CS → US	CS	Normal acquisition

Note: All procedures occur in Context A, except where noted otherwise. CS = saccharin, US = LiCl.

The US preexposure effect increases as the number of US alone presentations prior to conditioning increases (Braveman, 1975; Cannon, Berman, Baker, & Atkinson, 1975; Elkins, 1973), and it weakens as the time between preexposure and conditioning is increased; however, US preexposures have been found to attenuate taste aversion conditioning as much as 28 days prior to conditioning (Cappell & LeBlanc, 1977). US preexposure effects have been reported in a wide variety of situations with a variety of species and USs (see Hall, 2009; Randich & LoLordo, 1979a, for reviews).

If the US preexposure takes place in one context and the Pavlovian conditioning with a discrete CS takes place in another context, the US preexposure effect is markedly reduced (Randich & Ross, 1985; Tomie, Murphy, & Fath, 1980). Changing the context following preexposure removes that context as a predictor of the US and eliminates the US preexposure effect. The effect is also reduced when there is a different discrete stimulus that reliably precedes the US during the preexposure phase (Randich & Ross, 1985; Mikulka, Leard, & Klein, 1977). These data suggest that the *US preexposure effect occurs because the context serves as the CS during the preexposure phase.*

The context predicts that a US will occur in this situation, but the context may not predict when. Typically the discrete CS is a better predictor of when the US will occur. Although prior conditioning to the context may retard conditioning to that discrete CS, eventually conditioning will occur to it because it provides better information about the occurrence of the US than the context does.

A MATHEMATICAL MODEL OF PAVLOVIAN CONDITIONING BASED ON BOTH SALIENCE AND SURPRISE

The mathematical model of Pavlovian conditioning proposed by Rescorla and Wagner (1972) demonstrates how one can represent psychological processes like knowledge, salience, and surprise in mathematical terms. Although the model does not provide a complete representation of the factors that underlie Pavlovian conditioning, it has generated predictions that are subject to experimental test.

Rescorla and Wagner (1972) proposed a mathematical model for Pavlovian conditioning based on both the *salience of the CS* and *how surprised the individual is at the occurrence of the US*. Surprise is determined by what the individual already knows about the occurrence of the US (the more the individual already knows, the less surprised he or she is at the occurrence of the US). These two things (salience and surprise) are assumed to combine in a *multiplicative* fashion to determine how much the individual learns about the CS-US relationship on a given trial. Although their model does not provide a complete description of Pavlovian conditioning, it is useful because it illustrates how one can use the concepts of salience and surprise to predict the course of conditioning.

By expressing knowledge, learning, salience, and surprise in mathematical terms, we can make *quantitative* predictions that potentially can be falsified when we compare our predictions to the observed behavior of our subjects. This allows us to see quite clearly both the strengths and weaknesses of our theoretical formulations. That is the power and attraction of mathematical models.

Associative Strength and Learning. In Rescorla and Wagner's (1972) model, *knowledge is represented by an intervening variable called associative strength*. In this model, associative strength is usually represented by the symbol **V. Associative strength (V)** is an intervening variable because it cannot be directly observed; it is inferred from the occurrence of the CR. Thus, the regular occurrence of vigorous CRs to a given CS after Pavlovian conditioning is presumed to reflect a high level of **V**. Because in Pavlovian conditioning individuals can learn about the relationships between various CSs in their environment and the US, there is an associative strength for each CS-US relationship. For example, if a light and a tone both predict the occurrence of the US, there can be some associative strength for the light-US relationship (V_L) and another associative strength for the tone-US relationship (V_T).

Rescorla and Wagner (1972) treated learning as synonymous with changes in associative strength between a given CS and US, represented by the symbol ΔV (delta-**V** or change in **V**). As shown in Equation 1, the change in associative strength on a given trial (ΔV) is determined by the salience of the CS and how surprising is the occurrence of the US.

$$\Delta V = \text{salience} \times \text{surprise} \qquad (1)$$

According to Equation 1, if *both* salience (of the CS) and surprise (of the US) are *high*, there will be a large change in associative strength on that trial. On the other hand, if *either* salience or surprise (or both) is *low*, then the change in associative strength will be small.

Change in associative strength is the difference in the associative strength between successive trials. If the associative strength on trial N is V_N and the associative strength on the next trial (trial N+1) is V_{N+1}, then the change in associative strength between trial N and N+1 would be represented by Equation 2:

$$\Delta V = V_{N+1} - V_N \qquad (2)$$

In Equation 2, the value of ΔV depends on the values of V_{N+1} and V_N. If V_{N+1} is larger than V_N, then ΔV is *positive* and associative strength increases from trial N to trial N+1. On the other hand, if V_N is larger than V_{N+1}, then ΔV is *negative* and associative strength decreases from trial N to trial N+1.

How the Model Treats Salience. The Rescorla-Wagner model treats the salience of a CS as a fixed quantity in a given situation. As we have already noted, the salience of a stimulus is determined in part by the physical attributes of that stimulus (such as intensity), the situation (how much it stands out from the background), and the subject's inherited knowledge (predispositions to select that stimulus). The model does not address changes in salience due to learning (based on relative validity). This points to a limitation of the model, and others have attempted to remedy this (e.g., Mackintosh, 1975; Pearce & Hall, 1980). Because those formulations introduce added complexity, it is easier to see how salience and surprise contribute to Pavlovian conditioning by staying with the original Rescorla-Wagner model.

As we have seen earlier in this chapter, the salience of a CS influences how quickly individuals learn about it. *Salience is represented by the symbol* **S** *and, when multiple CSs are present, a subscript is added that designates the particular CS under consideration.* Thus, we can represent the salience of a light as S_L and the salience of a tone as S_T. Because the context can also function as a CS, we can also represent its salience as S_C. No matter what CS we are considering, the salience of that CS is given a value between 0 and 1.0. A CS that an individual does not attend to at all (completely ignores) would be assigned a value of 0; presumably individuals do not learn anything about these stimuli. A CS that captures the individual's undivided attention to the exclusion of all other CSs would have a salience of 1.0; individuals should learn in a single trial to associate this CS with the US. In general, the more salient the stimulus, the higher the value assigned to it (up to a maximum of 1.0).

How the Model Treats Surprise. The more you know about an event and the circumstances of its occurrence, the better able you are to predict its occurrence and the less surprised you are when that event occurs. One is surprised when something unexpected or unanticipated occurs. What makes an event unexpected or unanticipated is your lack of ability to predict it. Thus, your ability (or lack of ability) to predict the occurrence of something is a function of your current state of knowledge.

In the Rescorla-Wagner model, *surprise is represented by the discrepancy between what you know at a given point in time and what you could potentially know about when an important event (the US) might occur.* In Pavlovian conditioning, the occurrence of the US is predicted by the occurrence of the CS. How much you know at any point in time about the CS-US relationship is represented by the current level of **V**. *The maximum level of associative strength is called* V_{max}, and *the value of* V_{max} *is a function of the properties of the US (its quality and quantity on each trial) and the motivational level of the individual.* Therefore, according to this model, if the US is a weak shock, a small amount of food, a bland food, or the individual is not hungry, V_{max} will be small. On the other hand, intense shock, large amounts of food, high levels of hunger, and so on increase V_{max} and thus the amount the individual can learn.

According to this model, *the current level of associative strength is the sum of the associative strengths for all CSs in the situation* (ΣV). Thus, if we have three stimuli, a light, a tone, and the context, each with associative strengths designated as V_L, V_T, and V_C respectively, ΣV will equal $V_L + V_T + V_C$.

If V_{max} represents what you could potentially know, ΣV represents what you currently know, and surprise is the discrepancy between these two, then surprise is represented by Equation 3:

$$\text{surprise} = V_{max} - \Sigma V \qquad (3)$$

At the start of conditioning, if the associative strengths for all of the stimuli are low (or zero) then the occurrence of the US will be surprising. On the other hand, if any of the associative strengths for any of the CSs in that situation (or the sum of their associative strengths) are close to the value of V_{max}, then surprise will be low and little learning will occur.

Putting All This Together Into a Mathematical Model of Conditioning. Equation 1 tells us that change in associative strength (ΔV) equals salience multiplied by surprise. *Salience* is represented by S and *surprise* is the discrepancy between what you could potentially know about the CS-US relationship (V_{max}) and the current level of learning (ΣV). By incorporating the mathematical representations of salience and surprise into Equation 1, we now have Equation 4, which tells us how much an individual learns about the CS-US relationship on a given trial.

$$\Delta V = S \ (V_{max} - \Sigma V) \tag{4}$$

Summary of the Model. Before illustrating how this model treats the various phenomena we have discussed in this chapter, it will help to summarize the major aspects of this mathematical model.

1. Knowledge is represented by an intervening variable called associative strength (**V**).

2. Learning is quantified as a change in associative strength between a given CS and US.

3. Change in associative strength is the difference in the associative strength between successive trials: $\Delta V = V_{N+1} - V_N$.

4. How much associative strength on a given trial is determined by both the salience of that CS and how surprising is the occurrence of the US: ΔV = salience X surprise.

5. Salience is represented by the symbol **S.**

6. Surprise is represented by the discrepancy between what you know at a given point in time and what you could potentially know about when the US might occur: surprise = $V_{max} - \Sigma V$

7. The maximum level of associative strength possible in a situation is called V_{max}, and the value of V_{max} is a function of the properties of the US (its quality and quantity on each trial) and the motivational level of the individual.

8. The current level of knowledge is the sum of the associative strengths for all CSs in the situation (ΣV).

9. How much associative strength changes between successive trials is a joint function of the salience of the CS and the how surprising is the occurrence of the US: ΔV = salience x surprise = $S \ (V_{max} - \Sigma V)$.

The value of any mathematical model is determined by how well that model can predict the behavior of individuals, and we should be quite impressed when the model can predict something that is not obvious. The Rescorla-Wagner model does quite well.

How This Model Handles Simple Pavlovian Conditioning. In first-order Pavlovian conditioning, it is assumed that at the beginning of the experiment the associative strength for the CS-US relationship (**V**) is zero or close to zero. If V_{max} is high relative to V, then the occurrence of the CS-US combination is surprising to the individual, $V_{max} - V$ is high, and the value of **V** increases (ΔV is large). Associative strength (V) increases each time the CS-US combination occurs, but the increase will depend on the current value of **V** on that trial relative to the value of V_{max}. As the discrepancy between V_{max} and **V** decreases, the rate of learning (ΔV) decreases. When $V = V_{max}$, $V_{max} - V = 0$, and the occurrence of the US is no longer surprising. At this point, $\Delta V = 0$ and no more learning can occur. This means that learning is most rapid at the start of conditioning, and with repeated trials the rate of learning declines.

Two computer simulations of Pavlovian conditioning based on this model are presented in Figure 4.5. The two curves represent the changes in associative strength for CSs of different saliencies as predicted by the model. S = 0.2 in one simulation, and S = 0.6 in the other. Because the same US is used in both simulations, both curves have the same asymptote, but the curve with S = 0.6 gets there quicker.

How This Model Handles Extinction. The procedure of extinction in Pavlovian conditioning involves presenting the CS in the absence of the US. On the first extinction trial, associative strength to the CS will be high (because of the prior acquisition training) and the value of V_{max} will be zero (because there is no US). Under that circumstance ΔV will be a negative number and V will decline. This implies that the procedure of extinction undoes the effects of conditioning; however, as we saw earlier (see Chapter 2), that is not the case.

On the other hand, as noted in Chapters 2 and 3, experience with a negative contingency supports conditioned inhibition, a reaction that is antagonistic to the CR produced by a positive contingency. When there is a negative contingency the value of V_{max} is a negative number, and after experience with a negative contingency, V will also be a negative number. In other words, the Rescorla-Wagner model will generate negative values for V when V_{max} is negative.

How This Model Handles Overshadowing. Overshadowing occurs when there are at least two CSs, each with a different salience and both occurring at the same time. Both are equally valid predictors of the US, but over the course of training, more CRs occur to the CS with the highest salience. Here is how the Rescorla-Wagner model predicts that this should happen.

At the start of conditioning, the associative strengths for both CSs will be zero (or close to zero). But on each trial, the CS with the *higher* salience will accrue *more* associative strength because according to the model, the higher the salience the greater the associative strength accrues to that CS. **V** will increase for both CSs, but it will increase at a faster rate for the more salient stimulus. Because increases in associative strength also depend on surprise ($V_{max} - \Sigma V$), as associative strength accrues to both CSs, the discrepancy between V_{max} and **V** decreases. When this difference reaches zero there is no more learning because

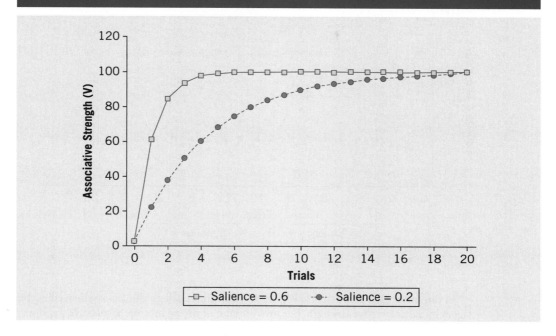

Figure 4.5 Each curve represents a different simulation of simple Pavlovian conditioning with the Rescorla-Wagner model. The difference between these curves represents differences in salience. In one simulation, salience = 0.2, in the other simulation, salience = 0.6. In both simulations, the initial values of the associative strengths (V) = 0.

the occurrence of the US is no longer surprising. This prevents associative strength from continuing to increase for both stimuli. As a result, the more salient CS will always have more associative strength than the less salient CS. Because associative strength determines the occurrence of the CR, we observe the CR to the more salient CS and say, "The more salient CS *overshadows* the less salient CS." This is simulated in Figure 4.6 with two CSs that have different saliencies (S = 0.2 and S = 0.6). The model predicts that conditioning will occur more rapidly to the CS with the higher salience. This will lead to overshadowing of the less salient CS by the more salient CS because the sum of the asymptotic associative strengths (**V**) for the two CSs cannot exceed $\mathbf{V}_{max}$ (which is 100 here).

How This Model Handles Blocking. Blocking occurs when prior experience with one CS "blocks" conditioning to a second CS. In the blocking procedure, we train the individual with one of the CSs before introducing the other. This means that the associative strength to that CS is high at the time that the second CS is introduced. Even when the second CS has high salience, little conditioning can occur to that second CS when $\mathbf{V}_{max}$ – Σ**V** is zero or close to zero because the occurrence of the US is not surprising, that is, the US is predicted by the prior-trained CS.

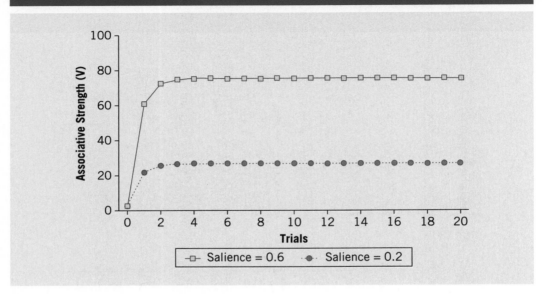

Figure 4.6 Simulation of overshadowing with the Rescorla-Wagner model. The salience of one stimulus = 0.2 and the salience of the other stimulus = 0.6. For both stimuli, the initial values of the associative strengths (V) = 0.

In the simulation presented in Figure 4.7, the stimulus with the *lower* salience has the *higher* initial associative strength. Because the sum of the asymptotic associative strengths (V) for the two stimuli cannot exceed V_{max} (which is 100 here), the associative strength of the other stimulus cannot rise above 20.

The US preexposure effect is also predicted by the Rescorla-Wagner model. During US preexposure, the US always appears in a certain context. According to the model, associative strength should accrue to that context (V_C). With sufficient training, the value of V_C should approach V_{max}. This will block conditioning to a CS that is introduced later because $V_{max} - \Sigma V$ is already zero or close to zero.

Three Unique Predictions. Perhaps the greatest value of a mathematical model is its ability to generate predictions that are not obvious. The Rescorla-Wagner makes three unique predictions: (1) combining two CSs for which the associative strengths are close to V_{max} will reduce the associative strength to both CSs (the "overexpectation effect"), (2) CRs will occur to a CS that is paired with an inhibitory CS in an extinction procedure, and (3) "superconditioning," which involves enhanced learning about an excitatory CS that is conditioned with a US in the presence of an inhibitory CS.

The "Overexpectation" Effect. Consider what would happen if you train two CSs separately with the same US. That is, suppose you teach individuals that a light predicts shock and then also train them that a tone predicts shock. Because the two CSs

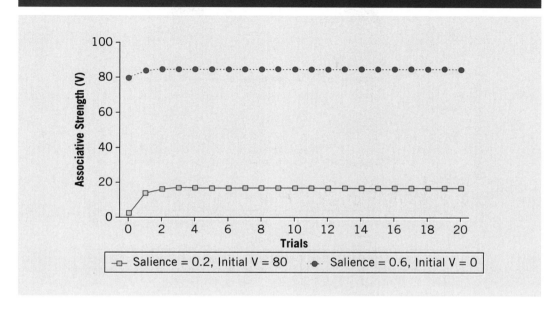

Figure 4.7 Simulation of blocking with the Rescorla-Wagner model. One stimulus had an initial associative strength (V) of 80 and the other had an initial associative strength (V) of 0. Both stimuli had saliences of 0.2.

were not presented together, each will become a valid predictor of shock (when the light appears, shock will follow; when the tone sounds, shock will follow). Therefore, the associative strengths of V_L and V_T will each be close to V_{max} at the end of training, and a strong CR should occur when either is presented. That happens. Now consider the following question: What will happen if you then present the light and tone together followed by the US? One would think that if a strong CR occurs to the tone and to the light when they are presented separately (because they are both valid predictors of the shock), a strong CR should be maintained when they are presented together, but that is not what happens. Instead of being maintained, the CR declines. Why does that happen?

The Rescorla-Wagner model predicts that the CR should decline for the following reason: At the beginning of compound training, the associative strength of the tone (V_T) and of the light (V_L) are individually close to V_{max} therefore ΣV must be higher than V_{max}. This makes $V_{max} - \Sigma V$ a negative number and, consequently, the associative strength of each CS (V_T and V_L) will decline until $V_{max} - \Sigma V$ is zero. Rescorla and Wagner called this an "overexpectation effect" because the combination of the tone and light leads the individuals to expect a larger, stronger US than actually occurs. The existence of the overexpectation effect, which is simulated in Figure 4.8, has been documented by Kehoe and White (2004), Kremer (1978), and Rescorla (1970) with aversive USs and by Lattal and Nakajima (1998) and Rescorla (1999) with appetitive USs.

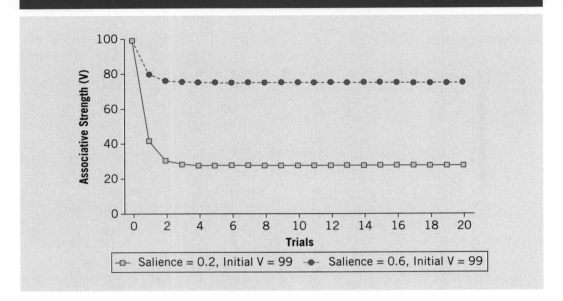

Figure 4.8 Simulation of the overexpectation effect by the Rescorla-Wagner model. Both stimuli started with associative strengths (V) = 99. One stimulus had a salience = 0.2 and the other had a salience = 0.6.

Legend: —□— Salience = 0.2, Initial V = 99   —●— Salience = 0.6, Initial V = 99

Excitatory Conditioning in the Absence of a US. A second unique prediction of the Rescorla-Wagner model involves presenting a known inhibitory stimulus (CS$_A$) together with a new, initially neutral stimulus (CS$_X$) in the absence of a US over repeated trials (procedure of extinction). Given this arrangement, it is reasonable to conclude that CS$_X$ will not accrue associative strength because it never predicted the US. However, the Rescorla-Wagner model anticipates that the associative strength for that CS$_X$ will be excitatory. According to the model, the associative strength for the inhibitory CS$_A$ is negative. Therefore, the initial ΣV for the compound CS$_{AX}$ will also be a negative number. $\mathbf{V_{max}}$ is zero during the extinction trials, but according to the model because surprise = $\mathbf{V_{max}} - \Sigma\mathbf{V}$, surprise = $0 - (-\Sigma\mathbf{V})$ is a positive number; therefore, CS$_X$ will acquire excitatory associative strength, and CRs will occur to it. This prediction was confirmed by Rescorla (1971b) and the simulation of the phenomenon is shown in Figure 4.9.

Superconditioning. A third unique prediction of the Rescorla-Wagner model, called superconditioning, results in a stronger CR than is normally produced by a US. To obtain this effect, two excitatory CSs (CS$_A$ and CS$_B$) are created by having them predict a US ($\mathbf{V_{max}} = 100$) and at the same time an inhibitory CS (CS$_N$) is created with a negative contingency. Then pair CS$_A$ with CS$_N$ in a positive contingency with a weaker level of the original US ($\mathbf{V_{max}} = 50$) and also present CS$_B$ with the same weaker US ($\mathbf{V_{max}} = 50$). It is not surprising that the CR to CS$_B$ will diminish here because now $\mathbf{V_{max}}$ is lower than it was in the original conditioning, and therefore, surprise for

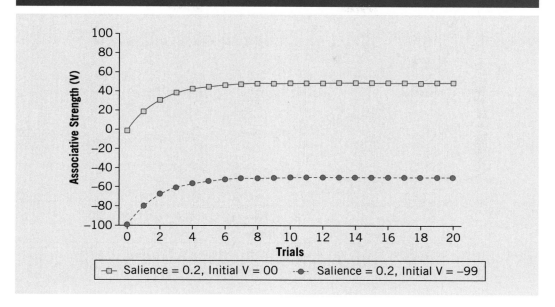

$CS_B = (V_{max} - V_B)$ is a *negative* number. That will reduce the associative strength for B. What is surprising, however, is that the CR to CS_A will *increase* even though V_{max} is now lower than it was in the original conditioning with CS_A. This will happen because combining a conditioned excitatory stimulus with a conditioned inhibitory stimulus *reduces* the value of ΣV so that now surprise for $CS_A = (V_{max} - \Sigma V)$ is a *positive* number. That leads to a stronger CR to CS_A. This prediction was confirmed using aversive (Rescorla, 1974) and appetitive (Williams & McDevitt, 2002) USs, and the simulation is shown in Figure 4.10.

The Value of the Rescorla-Wagner Model of Pavlovian Conditioning. Mathematical models are attempts to represent or summarize what we believe to be the true state of affairs in quantitative form so that testable predictions about the phenomenon under investigation can be generated. If a mathematical model can organize a set of behavioral phenomena around a small set of principles and generate a set of testable predictions, then it will be useful to us, even if the model is found to be incomplete or incorrect. In a sense, a model is like a map which attempts to represent the physical terrain and routes between locations. Maps are useful to us when they help us get from one location to another, even if the representation of the route is not accurate in every detail. Mathematical models are useful when they can provide us with testable predictions about behavior.

As we have just seen, the Rescorla-Wagner model can do that for a wide variety of Pavlovian conditioning phenomena (such as aspects of simple conditioning, overshadowing,

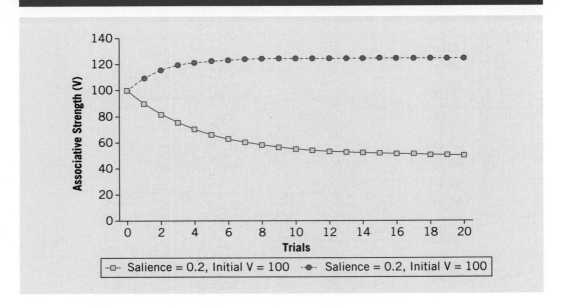

Figure 4.10 Simulation of the superconditioning effect by the Rescorla-Wagner model. Both stimuli had an initial associative strength (V) of 100 and had saliences of 0.2.

and blocking). It also produced some unique predictions about phenomena (the overexpectation effect, excitatory conditioning in the absence of a US, and superconditioning that were not observed until the model suggested that they might occur. Despite its limitations (e.g., that it treats reductions in associative strength as unlearning, does not handle changes in salience based on personal experience, and cannot predict the CS preexposure effect), this model of Pavlovian conditioning has been considered to be a major advance in our understanding of Pavlovian conditioning and has significantly influenced other areas of study (Siegel & Allan, 1996). Miller, Barnet, and Grahame (1995) reviewed 25 years of research generated by the Rescorla-Wagner model (both its successes and failures) and concluded that it is the most successful model of conditioning proposed to date.

OVERSHADOWING, RELATIVE VALIDITY, AND BLOCKING: LEARNING ABOUT THE OTHER STIMULUS

The absence of a CR when the overshadowed, less valid, or blocked stimulus is presented by itself does not necessarily mean that conditioning has not occurred to that stimulus.

Overshadowing, the relative validity effect, and blocking are phenomena in which one potential CS is selected over another. Overshadowing occurs when the two potential CSs are presented simultaneously; the result is that the CR is more likely to occur (or will be stronger) to one of them. We attribute the phenomenon of overshadowing to the relative salience of the stimuli; the more salient stimulus overshadows the less salient. The relative validity effect is a form of overshadowing due to the differences in contingency rather than the differences in initial salience of the respective stimuli; the better predictor (the one with the higher CS-US correlation) overshadows the stimulus with the lower CS-US correlation. On the other hand, blocking occurs when one stimulus is established as a CS before the other stimulus is added. Despite subsequent simultaneous presentations of both stimuli, the CR will be less likely to occur (or be weaker) to the added stimulus. We attribute blocking to prior learning; an established predictor of the US blocks conditioning to a redundant predictor.

The data on overshadowing, cue validity, and blocking reviewed this far suggest that there is little, if any, conditioning to the other less salient, less valid, or less informative stimulus. That conclusion is premature; there is good evidence that some conditioning occurs to the other stimulus. Conditioning to the less salient (overshadowed) stimulus can be demonstrated by the following procedure: after the CR is established, present the more salient (overshadowing) stimulus alone for a number of trials. This is the procedure of extinction which results in a decline in the frequency and size of the CR. Although there are no more conditioning trials with the less salient (overshadowed) stimulus, the CR to *that* stimulus will increase (Kasprow, Cacheiro, Balaz, & Miller, 1982; Kaufman & Bolles, 1981; Miller, Barnet, & Grahame, 1992). Similar results have been observed with blocking (Balaz, Gutsin, Cacheiro, & Miller, 1982; Blaisdell, Gunther, & Miller, 1999) and with relative stimulus validity (Cole, Barnet, & Miller, 1995). Thus, *decreasing the validity of one CS through extinction can increase the CR to other CSs.*

These data should remind us of the learning-performance problem: The only way we can study learning is by observing performance, but performance may not always reflect learning. Clearly, conditioning can occur to more than one stimulus, but the CR typically occurs only to the more salient, relatively valid, or informative one. Making the dominant CS a less valid predictor by presenting it alone allows the conditioning that occurred to the other CSs to become manifest. R. R. Miller and his colleagues (Miller et al., 1992; Miller & Matzel, 1988, 1989; Miller & Schactman, 1985) have argued that responding to a given CS reflects not only the level of conditioning to that stimulus, but the level of conditioning to other stimuli as well.

Natural selection may have created the bias to select the more salient or informative stimulus, but if the individual has the capacity to process information about less salient, yet equally informative stimuli, he or she may do so. Whether this is true in all species in which overshadowing and blocking have been observed remains to be determined. Thus, overshadowing, relative validity effects, and blocking reflect both stimulus selection (based on salience and the information a stimulus provides about the occurrence of the US) and the conditions under which this selection is tested.

SUMMARY AND CONCLUSIONS

Natural selection biased individuals to select some stimuli over others in the search for the predictors of significant events (i.e., USs). Thus, some stimuli are very likely to be chosen in situations involving danger or pain (spiders, snakes, white rats, hedgehogs). Natural selection also predisposed individuals to select and respond to novel events over familiar events (CS preexposure effects) as a way to avoid making responses to events that in the past have not been experienced as predictors of important events. Likewise, there are predispositions to respond to those events that have the higher relative predictive validity and those events that provide new as opposed to redundant information (blocking effects). However, this does not mean that individuals cannot learn about familiar events, less predictive events, or redundant events. When the validity of the overshadow*ing, more* valid, or block*ing* stimulus is diminished, individuals can demonstrate learning about the overshadow*ed, less* valid, or block*ed* stimulus. This suggests that causal inferences can be made at several levels.

Pavlovian conditioning lessens the load on inherited knowledge required for survival, and it allows individuals to deal with changes in their individual circumstances. All of the research reviewed in these last two chapters points to the conclusion that natural selection endowed some species with this efficient information gathering process for inferring causal relationships between events. This raises the question of how that information is represented in memory for later retrieval and use. The answers to that question are the subject of the next chapter.

STUDY QUESTIONS

1. What are we referring to when we talk about the salience of a stimulus? What determines the salience of a given stimulus? Why is salience an important concept in psychology and the study of Pavlovian conditioning?

2. What is the phenomenon of overshadowing? How do we demonstrate it? How is it related to salience and identifying the predictors of significant events?

3. What is the CS preexposure effect? How do we demonstrate it? How is it related to salience and identifying the predictors of significant events?

4. What is the phenomenon called learned irrelevance? How do we demonstrate it? How is it related to salience and identifying the predictors of significant events?

5. What are we referring to when we talk about the relative validity of cues in Pavlovian conditioning? How do we demonstrate it? How is it related to salience and identifying the predictors of significant events?

6. What are we referring to when we talk about surprise in Pavlovian conditioning? Why is it important?

7. What is the phenomenon of blocking? How do we demonstrate it? How is it related to surprise and identifying the predictors of significant events?

8. What is the US preexposure effect? How do we demonstrate it? How is it related to surprise and identifying the predictors of significant events?

9. What are the two elements in the Rescorla-Wagner model of Pavlovian conditioning? How are they represented in the model? In your own words, describe how the Rescorla-Wagner model uses these two elements to explain the following phenomena:

a. simple Pavlovian conditioning

b. overshadowing

c. blocking

d. the overexpectation effect (What is that?)

10. What evidence indicates that the absence of a conditioned response when the overshadowed, less valid, or blocked stimulus is presented by itself does *not* mean that conditioning has not occurred to that stimulus? How do we explain this?

5

THE REPRESENTATIONS OF KNOWLEDGE IN PAVLOVIAN CONDITIONING

If causal inference is the process by which individuals learn about predictors of important events, how is that knowledge encoded? Following Hume (1739/1992, 1777/1993), we believe that causal inferences are encoded as connections or associations between the **mental representations** of the inferred cause and effect, where a representation of an experienced environmental event is *a mapping of that event into a neural code* (Gallistel, 1990a, 1990b; Roitblat, 1987). Because we cannot directly observe internal representations or the associative links between them, there is continuing controversy about the nature of representations, whether they even exist, and the role they play in behavior (Anderson, 1990; Donahue & Palmer, 1994; Gallistel, 1990a, 1990b; Roitblat, 1982, 1987).

How a particular event is represented depends on the event; the sensory, perceptual, and memory abilities of the individual; and the circumstances in which the event was originally encountered. Information from the external environment is received by our sense organs and transmitted to the brain where it is filtered and interpreted. This perceptual processing creates the internal representations of environmental events that are stored as memories. When the external event is encountered again, the memorial representation of that event may be evoked and the stimulus recognized as familiar. Without these internal representations of events, we could not profit from experience.

An individual is said to possess a representation when he or she can utilize information not currently available in the environment and recognize previously encountered events (Pearce, 1987). Although human beings are capable of creating mental pictures from memory that often have behavioral effects similar to those that occur in the presence of the represented events (Finke, 1980, 1985), representations are more than mental pictures; they are encodings of both the sensory (form, color, size, texture, taste, intensity, location, etc.) and the hedonic, affective, or motivational qualities (feels or tastes good or bad) of stimulus events (Konorski, 1948, 1967). There is evidence that both of these aspects of stimuli can be represented internally.

The relationship between external events and their internal representations in Pavlovian conditioning is diagrammed in Figure 5.1. In Pavlovian conditioning, the individual experiences the two external events (the CS and the US) in some consistent temporal relationship to each other. Somehow the patterns of stimulation produced by these external events are translated into patterns of neural activity and stored in the brain as internal

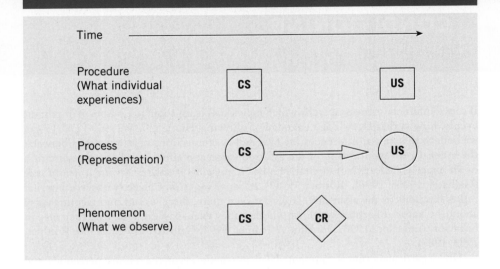

Figure 5.1 Schematic depiction of a Pavlovian conditioning procedure, the process (or internal representation of the situation), and the resulting phenomenon. Boxes signify external events and circles signify internal representations of these events. The CR is represented by a diamond.

representations. We believe that Pavlovian conditioning produces a connection or association between these representations. The arrow between the internal representations of the CS and US depicts that learned association. At a later time, the presentation of the tone will evoke the representation of that tone followed by the representation of the food. This leads to the conditioned response (CR). In this chapter, we will explore why we believe that knowledge gained from experiencing a Pavlovian conditioning procedure is represented in memory in this manner.

CS-US ASSOCIATIONS: THE REPRESENTATION OF RELATIONSHIPS IN PAVLOVIAN CONDITIONING

Declarative knowledge about the relationships among environmental events is encoded as associations between internal representations of these events.

An association *consists of the mental representations of both the external events experienced and the relationship between these events, and in Pavlovian conditioning its existence is inferred when the presentation of the CS evokes the CR in the absence of the US* (see Figure 5.1). In

Chapter 1, a distinction was made between knowing that (declarative knowledge) and knowing how (procedural knowledge). Declarative knowledge consists of information about the attributes of events and the relationships between events, and procedural knowledge is knowledge about how or what to do (a set of instructions to behave in a particular way under certain conditions). We could describe the structure of the associations underlying Pavlovian conditioning either in terms of declarative knowledge ("The metronome is followed by food") or procedural knowledge ("Salivate when the metronome sounds"). On the surface, both of these associations fit the behavior of Pavlov's dogs, but which is the correct description of what his dogs learned? Fortunately, there is an experimental design for distinguishing between these two possibilities.

Using Post-Conditioning Devaluation of the US to Study Associations in Pavlovian Conditioning

In post-conditioning devaluation experiments, we can manipulate the internal representation of the US after conditioning and observe whether this influences the CR. What happens to the CR allows us to infer the structure of the association produced by the Pavlovian conditioning procedure.

In the 1970s, an experimental procedure was developed to study the structure of associations in Pavlovian conditioning (Rescorla, 1973, 1974). This procedure, called **post-conditioning devaluation of the US**, works as follows: First we produce a CR in the conventional manner (with a positive CS-US contingency). Then we remove the individual from the training situation and *change the hedonic value (positive or negative affective value) of the US*. For example, the hedonic value of food can be changed by making the subject ill after he or she consumes that food (leading to a conditioned taste aversion or CTA to that food). In the test phase, we put the individual back in the training situation, present the CS alone (i.e., in extinction), and observe whether the devaluation of the US has changed the CR. The success of these experiments rests on the validity of two assumptions: The first assumption is that manipulating the hedonic value of the US *after* conditioning will affect the internal representation of that stimulus. The second assumption is that this manipulation will have different effects on the CR depending on whether knowledge gained from Pavlovian conditioning is encoded as declarative knowledge or procedural knowledge.

How the results of post-conditioning devaluation help us decide whether knowledge in Pavlovian conditioning is encoded as procedural knowledge or declarative knowledge is outlined in Table 5.1 using Pavlov's conditioned salivation experiment as an example.

Procedural representations are internalized instructions about what to do. In Pavlov's salivary conditioning experiment, the initial procedural instruction would be, "When the metronome sounds, salivate." After the CTA training in the post-conditioning devaluation phase, a second instruction would be learned: "Do not eat that food!" If Pavlov's dogs had simply learned to salivate when the metronome was sounded, then teaching them not to eat that food after the initial conditioning should have no effect on the first

Table 5.1 Differentiating Between Procedural and Declarative Representations With Post-Conditioning Devaluation Experiments Using Pavlov's Conditioned Salivation as an Example

Type of representation	Original conditioning (metronome → food)	Postconditioning devaluation of US (food → illness)	Test (metronome alone)
Procedural	"When metronome sounds, salivate."	"Do not eat that food."	"When metronome sounds, salivate."
Declarative	"The metronome causes food."	"The food causes illness."	"The food causes illness."

Adapted from Dickinson, 1980.

instruction because they never learned that they were not to salivate when they heard the metronome. That in turn should have no effect on what they do during the test phase when the tone is presented alone.

Declarative representations are internalized depictions of events. If both the initial salivary conditioning and the post-conditioning devaluation were encoded as declarative representations about the relationships between the metronome and food ("Sound of metronome is followed by food") and about food and illness ("That food makes me ill"), we would expect that the CTA would reduce conditioned responding to the metronome that had previously signaled the now-aversive food.

Therefore, *if knowledge in Pavlovian conditioning is encoded as a declarative association ("CS followed by the US"), the CR should be affected by manipulation of the US because the CS now signals a changed US.* On the other hand, because the manipulation comes after conditioning and in the absence of the CS and CR, there should be no change in the procedural association (i.e., "When CS occurs, respond").

Evidence That Pavlovian Conditioning Involves Declarative Knowledge About the CS and US

The strongest argument that the events experienced in Pavlovian conditioning are encoded as declarative knowledge comes from post-conditioning devaluation experiments.

Using the post-conditioning devaluation procedure, Holland (1990) provided a convincing demonstration that rats encode their experiences in Pavlovian conditioning situations as declarative knowledge. The design of his experiment is contained in Table 5.2. In Phase 1, he trained rats with two CSs (tone and noise), each leading to a different flavored food US (peppermint- and wintergreen-flavored sucrose solutions). On each day of training, the rats received randomly intermixed trials in which one CS (T_1)

Table 5.2 Design of Holland (1990) Experiment on Post-Conditioning Devaluation of the US

Phase 1	Phase 2	Test
$T_1 \rightarrow$ Flavor$_1$	Flavor$_2 \rightarrow$ LiCl	T_1 and T_2
$T_2 \rightarrow$ Flavor$_2$	Flavor$_2 \rightarrow$ LiCl	T_1 and T_2

Note: T_1 and T_2 were a tone and noise. Flavor$_1$ and Flavor$_2$ were peppermint- and wintergreen-flavored sucrose solutions. LiCl=lithium chloride. All four combinations were counterbalanced across different subjects. The conditioned response was contact with the food cup.

was followed by one of the USs (Flavor$_1$) and the other CS (T_2) was followed by the other US (Flavor$_2$). The two USs were both received in the same food cup, and the CR was contact with that cup when the CSs (tones) were presented. On the next day following acquisition (Phase 2), the rats were given 5 minutes of access to one of the USs (Flavor$_2$) followed by an injection of lithium chloride (LiCl). After the rats recovered from the effects of the LiCl, they were tested for their approach to the food cup responses in the presence of T_1 and T_2 *in the absence of the USs.*

We can see how Holland's experiment helps us to decide whether knowledge gained from Pavlovian conditioning is encoded as procedural or declarative knowledge by referring to Table 5.3. In the initial Pavlovian conditioning phase (Phase 1), the procedural instruction is to approach the food cup when T_1 and T_2 (the CSs) are presented. After the CTA training in the second phase of the experiment, the second instruction is to stop eating the Flavor$_2$

Table 5.3 Differentiating Between Procedural and Declarative Representations in the Holland (1990) Experiment

Type of representation	Original conditioning ($T_2 \rightarrow$ Flavor$_2$)	Postconditioning devaluation of US (Flavor$_2 \rightarrow$ illness)	Test (choice between flavors in presence of T_2)
Procedural	"When T_2 is present, approach the food cup."	"Do not approach the food cup when that food is there."	"When T_2 is present, approach the food cup."
Declarative	"T_2 is followed by Flavor$_2$."	"Flavor$_2$ makes me ill."	"T_2 is followed by Flavor$_2$ that makes me ill."

Adapted from Dickinson, 1980.

US. If the rats had simply learned to approach the food cup when the T_2 was presented, then teaching them not to eat Flavor$_2$ should have *no effect* on the first instruction. On the other hand, if both phases of this experiment were encoded as declarative representations (second row), we would expect that the CTA would affect conditioned responding to T_2 because it had previously signaled the now aversive Flavor$_2$ US.

The results of Holland's experiment are presented in Figure 5.2. The acquisition of the CR is presented in the left panel and the test data on the right. There is no difference in how quickly the animals learned the CR (left panel), but there was a differential effect of the devaluation of the Flavor$_2$ US (right panel). The CR to T_1 remained strong, but the CR to T_2 was markedly reduced. Thus it is apparent that creating an aversion to the US signaled by T_2 *after* the original Pavlovian conditioning with T_2 and that US (Flavor$_2$) reduced the CR to T_2. This is evidence that the Phase 1 experience was encoded as a declarative representation of the relationship between T_2 and Flavor$_2$. In showing that devaluation of the US can, subsequently, cause a change in responding to the associated CS, these results suggest that the internal representation of an absent event (the US) can be evoked by a CS. In other words, an associatively activated internal representation of an absent event can guide behavior. It has, furthermore, been suggested that such

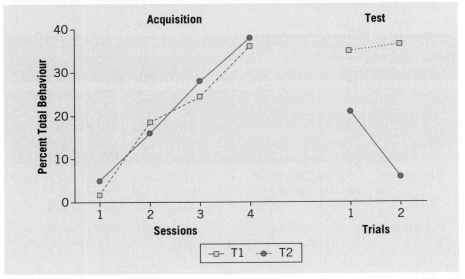

Figure 5.2 Acquisition of approach to the food delivery site as conditioned responses to the presentation of two tones (T1 and T2), each paired with a distinctive tasting sucrose solution (left panel). Responding to both tones after the animals are made sick after drinking the flavored solution presented with T2 (right panel).

Redrawn from Holland, Event representation in Pavlovian conditioning: Image and action. *Cognition, 37,* 105–131, copyright © 1990, with permission from Elsevier Science.

processing may be related to mental imagery in humans (Holland & Wheeler, 2009; Pickens & Holland, 2004) and may have clinical relevance in the treatment of, for example, anxiety disorders and posttraumatic stress disorder (PTSD; Dadds, Bovbjerg, Redd, & Cutmore, 1997).

Holland provided additional evidence that the CS-US relationship is encoded as a declarative association by observing what his rats did when T_1 and T_2 were presented to them while they were drinking a third solution. Following the tests described above, Holland, using the taste reactivity method introduced by Grill and Norgren (1978a; see Chapter 2, Figure 2.9) recorded his rat's facial and somatic responses to plain sucrose in the presence of the two CSs (T_1 and T_2). The results are presented in Figure 5.3. T_2 decreased the frequency of ingestive responses (left panel) and increased the frequency of aversive responses (right panel), while T_1 had no effect on either type of behavior when compared to sucrose alone (Sucrose). In other words, the rats reacted to the sucrose the same regardless of whether T_1 was present or not, but they reacted differently to the sucrose in the presence of T_2. These data provide additional evidence that the taste aversion conditioned to the $Flavor_2$ US is linked in memory to stimulus T_2. Thus, the rats' pattern of responding to sucrose, as aversive or not aversive, was modulated by the presence of a tone cue associated with a devalued or non-devalued US (for comparable results, see Kerfoot, Agarwal, Lee, & Holland, 2007).

Figure 5.3 Frequencies of ingestive and aversive responses to sucrose alone (SO), sucrose plus T1, and sucrose plus T2.

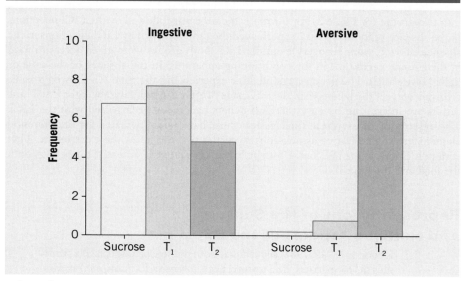

Redrawn from Holland, Event representation in Pavlovian conditioning: Image and action. *Cognition, 37,* 105–131, copyright © 1990, with permission from Elsevier Science.

Post-Conditioning Devaluation Studies With Other USs. Post-conditioning changes in the US representation are not limited to representations of food. Rescorla (1973) gave rats conditioned suppression training with a flashing light as the CS and a loud noise as the US. Then he presented the loud noise alone for several trials. He found that this treatment reduced suppression when the CS (a flashing light) was presented later. Presumably the presentations of the loud noise after conditioning reduced its aversiveness which in turn reduced the amount of conditioned suppression to the light. Randich and Haggard (1983), Randich and Rescorla (1981), and Rescorla (1974) found similar results with shock: Post-conditioning presentations of a shock US that produced conditioned suppression reduced the amount of suppression to the CS when that CS was presented alone later. These post-conditioning effects can also go in the other direction. For example, Rescorla (1974) reported that when the intensity of the shock was increased during the post-conditioning presentations, the CR was enhanced even though the rats had never experienced the more intense shock in the presence of the CS. Likewise, when the rats had extended experience with a decreased intensity of shock alone during the post-conditioning period, conditioned suppression was also reduced (Randich & Haggard, 1983; Randich & Rescorla, 1981; Rescorla & Heth, 1975).

Post-Conditioning Devaluation With the CS. In all of the experiments cited above, the CR was affected by manipulations that presumably changed the representation of the US. Holland (1981) presented evidence that a CTA can be produced by making rats ill in the presence of the CS-evoked internal representation of the food US (i.e., the food was not presented at the time that the rats were made ill). The design of this experiment is presented in Table 5.4. In Phase 1, rats were trained with a tone as the CS and wintergreen-flavored sucrose pellets as the US on some trials. On other trials, a light was presented but not followed by food. The CR (approach to the food cup) occurred to the tone but not the light. Following Phase 1 training, the rats were split into two groups for Phase 2: For Group 1, the tone was followed by the LiCl injections in the absence of food. Group 2 experienced the light followed by LiCl injections in the absence of food. After recovery from the LiCl, both groups were given access to food in their home cages (not in the conditioning apparatus) in the absence of the tone or light (Test phase). The group made ill after experiencing the tone CS showed greater reluctance to eat the pellets than the rats made ill after experiencing the light CS. These results are interesting because the food pellets had *never* been paired with the LiCl. The reluctance to eat these food pellets must have been mediated by the common element in the declarative associations from the two phases in the experiment. That common element was the tone CS (which was associated at different times with both the food and the illness).

Representations of the Sensory and Hedonic Aspects of the US

Konorski (1948, 1967) argued that both the sensory aspects of a stimulus (its form, color, size, texture, taste, intensity, location, etc.) and its hedonic aspects (it feels or tastes good or bad) can be represented in memory. The experiments described below support that argument.

Table 5.4 Design of Holland (1981) Experiment on Representation-Mediated Conditioned Taste Aversions

Group	Phase 1	Phase 2	Test
1	Tone ➝ Wintergreen-flavored pellets Light ➝ no food	Tone ➝ LiCl	Wintergreen-flavored pellets
2	Tone ➝ Wintergreen-flavored pellets Light ➝ no food	Light ➝ LiCl	Wintergreen-flavored pellets

Note: LiCl = lithium chloride. The conditioned response in Phase 1 was contact with the food cup.

As noted at the beginning of this chapter, stimuli have both sensory qualities (form, color, size, texture, taste, intensity, location, etc.) and hedonic, affective, or motivational qualities ("It feels or tastes good or bad"). The experiments described above suggest that both of these aspects of stimuli can be represented in memory. The experiments described below were designed to test that directly.

Evidence That the Sensory Qualities of the US Are Represented in Memory. Holland (1981) also demonstrated that rats can form specific internal representations of the sensory aspects of the US. The design of his experiment is presented in Table 5.5.

First he gave rats Pavlovian conditioning with two CSs, each leading to a different US: a tone CS was followed by wintergreen-flavored food pellets and a light CS was followed by sucrose solution. In both cases, the CR was approach to the food dish. After

Table 5.5 Design of Holland (1981) Experiment on Representations of the Sensory Aspects of the US

Group	Phase 1	Phase 2	Test
1	Tone ➝ Wintergreen-flavored pellets Light ➝ sucrose solution	Tone ➝ LiCl	Wintergreen-flavored pellets and sucrose solution
2	Tone ➝ Wintergreen-flavored pellets Light ➝ sucrose solution	Light ➝ LiCl	Wintergreen-flavored pellets and sucrose solution
3	Tone ➝ Wintergreen-flavored pellets Light ➝ sucrose solution	LiCl only	Wintergreen-flavored pellets and sucrose solution

Note: LiCl = lithium chloride. The conditioned response in Phase 1 was contact with the food cup.

the CR occurred reliably, he gave separate groups of rats injections of LiCl immediately after presentation of the tone, the light, or neither CS. After the rats recovered from the effects of the LiCl, consumption of the wintergreen-flavored pellets and the sucrose solutions were measured in their home cages. Those rats that received LiCl in the presence of the tone consumed less wintergreen-flavored pellets, while those rats given lithium chloride in the presence of light consumed less sucrose solution. The rats given LiCl alone showed no preference. These results provide strong evidence that the sensory qualities of the two CSs and the two USs had specific representations in memory, otherwise the LiCl would have depressed consumption to both foods equally.

Evidence That the Hedonic Qualities of the US Are Represented in Memory. Bakal, Johnson, and Rescorla (1974) demonstrated that the representation of the US also can contain general hedonic aspects that are shared by qualitatively different stimuli such as loud noise and shock. Stimuli paired with a loud noise can acquire the ability to suppress bar-pressing in rats just as stimuli paired with shock will. Bakal et al. used a blocking procedure to demonstrate that a tone paired with shock will block subsequent conditioning to a light that predicted loud noise (see Chapter 4). The basic design and results of Bakal et al.'s experiment are presented in Table 5.6.

After pretraining rats to press a lever of food, the rats were divided into different groups. Two of the groups were blocking groups; that is, they received tone → US in the first phase and tone + light → US in the second phase. For one of these groups, the US was the same in both phases of training, and for a second group, the US was different.

Thus, for the first group, the US was a loud noise in both phases. For the second group, the US was shock in the first phase and a loud noise in the second phase. A third group only received the Phase 2 training. The experiment was designed to determine if the tone → shock in Phase 1 would block conditioning to a light when light + tone →

Table 5.6 Experimental Design and Data from Bakal, Johnson, and Rescorla (1974) Blocking Experiment on Representations of the Hedonic Qualities of USs

	Pavlovian conditioning			
Group	Phase 1	Phase 2	Test	Suppression ratio to light
Blocking (US same)	T → noise	TL → noise	L	.26
Blocking (US different)	T → shock	TL → noise	L	.29
Overshadowing	None	TL → noise	L	.08

Note: T = tone, L = light, TL = tone-light compound. The lower the suppression ratio, the greater the suppression. A suppression ratio of .5 means no suppression, and a suppression ratio of .00 means complete suppression.

loud noise in Phase 2; that is, would one aversive US block conditioning with another aversive US?

The results are presented in the right column of Table 5.6. Clearly, a tone paired with a shock blocked conditioning to the light as much as did a tone paired with that same loud noise. The suppression ratio for the overshadowing group shows that without the Phase 1 experience, the light used here overshadowed the tone (which is why the suppression ratio is so low for this group). At first glance, these results seem to contradict the well-established finding that blocking occurs when the added stimulus (in this case, the light) does not signal anything new because in this case the light signaled a change in US from a shock to a loud noise. However, because both the loud noise and shock are aversive, it appears that this common hedonic property (aversiveness) is represented in memory and produces the conditioned emotional response. This is consistent with Rescorla's (1972) finding that a 0.5 mA, 2-second shock and a 2-mA, 0.5-second shock are experienced as similarly aversive (see Chapter 4).

Summary of the Evidence on the Representations of Knowledge in Pavlovian Conditioning

The data reviewed thus far provide strong evidence that *experience with a Pavlovian conditioning procedure is encoded as declarative knowledge involving associations between representations of the CS and US, and those representations contain information about both the sensory qualities of the CS and US and the hedonic qualities of the US* (see Figure 5.1). The data for these conclusions comes primarily from studies of post-conditioning devaluation of the US (for a review, see Holland & Wheeler, 2009). In those studies, individuals were exposed to two separate Pavlovian conditioning procedures, and the resulting behavior reflected a synthesis of these two separately obtained experiences. This tells us that individuals are capable of encoding complex arrangements between events. In the next section we will look more closely at how individuals combine and represent information from two separately acquired experiences.

TRANSITIVE INFERENCE AND THE LINKING OF ASSOCIATIONS IN SECOND-ORDER CONDITIONING

Individuals can combine two separately acquired pieces of information about the relationships between events to infer another relationship through the process called transitive inference. The procedures of second-order conditioning and sensory preconditioning provide two separately acquired associations that can be combined through transitive inference.

Excitatory conditioning with a positive contingency between CS and US is thought to produce the simple association diagrammed in Figure 5.1. As we have already seen in the US-devaluation experiments, individuals can learn two separate simple associations at different times and link them together. In this section, we will explore in more detail how individuals do this. We will also review evidence that individuals can form associations in which one stimulus serves as a signal that a certain CS-US relationship is in effect.

Transitive inference *occurs when individuals combine two pieces of information about the relationship between events to infer a third relationship.* For example, if you are told that an English shilling is worth more than a penny, and that an English pound is worth more than a shilling, you should have no trouble concluding that a pound is also worth more than a penny, even though you were not given that information directly. You reached the conclusion about the relative values of a pound and a penny through the process of transitive inference. The phenomena called second-order conditioning and sensory preconditioning provide examples of transitive inference in Pavlovian conditioning.

Second-Order Conditioning

Second-order conditioning is both a procedure and a phenomenon. After experiencing first-order Pavlovian conditioning with a certain CS and US, that CS can then serve as a US to produce a CR to a second CS. Second-order conditioning reflects the process of transitive inference.

The Procedure for Obtaining Second-Order Conditioning. The procedure called second-order conditioning involves two separate phases. These two phases are represented in the top panel of Table 5.7. In **second-order conditioning**, *one stimulus (CS_1) predicts the occurrence of a US* (Phase 1). *After a CR is established to CS_1, a second stimulus (CS_2) is presented with CS_1 in the absence of the US* (Phase 2). Evidence for the phenomenon of second-order conditioning comes from the test phase where CS_2 is presented alone. A CR to CS_2 is evidence of second-order conditioning. Pavlov called the CR to CS_2 a secondary conditioned reflex.

The Phenomenon of Second-Order Conditioning. Pavlov described the development of a secondary conditioned reflex with the following example: The sound of a

Table 5.7 The Procedures for Second-Order Conditioning and Sensory Preconditioning

Second-order conditioning			
Phase 1	Phase 2	Test	Results
$CS_1 \rightarrow US$	$CS_2 \rightarrow CS_1$	CS_2	CR to CS_2
Sensory preconditioning			
Phase 1	Phase 2	Test	Results
$CS_1 + CS_2$	$CS_1 \rightarrow US$	CS_2	CR to CS_2

metronome (CS_1) preceded the presentation of food (US). After the CR of salivation to the metronome was firmly established, a black square (CS_2) was presented for 10 seconds, and after a 15-second interval, the metronome (CS_1) was sounded but the food was not presented. Pavlov reported that after 10 CS_2-CS_1 trials, a dog that had never salivated when the black square was presented before the experiment began to salivate in its presence. However, the CR to the black square was not as strong as the CR to the metronome (CS_1), and Pavlov reported that he was unable to establish a third-order conditioned reflex.

A number of variables that affect the strength of a second-order CR have been identified. Rescorla and Furrow (1977) demonstrated that the CR to CS_2 is stronger when CS_2 and CS_1 are from the same stimulus dimension, and we have already discussed Rescorla and Cunningham's (1979) finding that second-order conditioning is stronger when CS_1 and CS_2 are in close spatial contiguity (Chapter 3). Thus, it appears that *second-order conditioning is enhanced when the two events are perceived as belonging together*.

Transitive Inference in Second-Order Conditioning. In Phase 1 of the second-order conditioning procedure, the declarative association between CS_1 and the US is "CS_1 predicts the occurrence of the US." In Phase 2, the declarative association between CS_2 and CS_1 is "CS_2 predicts the occurrence of CS_1." The occurrence of the CR to CS_2 (which was never experienced with the US) occurs because the individual links together these two declarative associations through the process of transitive inference: "If CS_1 predicts the occurrence of the US, and CS_2 predicts the occurrence of CS_1, then CS_2 also predicts the US." Thus, individuals can use the process of transitive inference to link the individual associations of CS_1 with the US and CS_2 with CS_1 to form the second-order association between CS_2 and the US (Rescorla, 1980b).

Sensory Preconditioning
and Within-Compound Associations

Under some conditions, individuals appear to represent the relationships between nonsignificant events that occur together as within-compound associations. The procedure for producing these within-compound associations is called sensory preconditioning. These within-compound associations may not be reflected in behavior (i.e., they are "behaviorally silent") until one of the events is paired with a significant event (US). A CR to the other event provides evidence that a within-compound association exists.

USs usually are biologically significant events for individuals. CSs, on the other hand, can be arbitrarily chosen. In that sense, CSs might be considered neutral, although even non-significant stimuli evoke orienting responses when they are first presented (see Chapter 2). The procedure called sensory preconditioning is used to produce associations between seemingly neutral events that are experienced together. The *association produced by the sensory preconditioning procedure* is referred to as a **within-compound association**. This term suggests that two events are perceived as a "compound" event because the stimuli are presented either simultaneously or close together in time.

The Procedure of Sensory Preconditioning. The procedure for sensory preconditioning is straightforward: *two* seemingly nonsignificant events are presented together in the absence of a US prior to Pavlovian conditioning with one of these events as the CS. (See Phase 1 in bottom panel of Table 5.7 where the two events are labeled CS_1 and CS_2.) No CRs are observed because there is no US. After experiencing these two nonsignificant events together, one of them is used as a CS in a positive Pavlovian contingency (excitatory conditioning) with a US. (See Phase 2 in bottom panel of Table 5.7.) A CR emerges to that CS. The evidence that the individual learned about the relationship between these two CSs comes in the test phase when the other nonsignificant event (CS_2 in Table 5.7) is presented without the US. If a CR is evoked by that second CS, we have evidence that an association was formed when the CSs were presented together without a US in Phase 1.

The Phenomenon of Sensory Preconditioning. The classic demonstration of sensory preconditioning was published in 1939 by Brogden. In Phase 1 of Brogden's demonstration, dogs experienced 200 simultaneous presentations of a doorbell and a flash of light. Other than an orienting response (that quickly habituated), there were no unconditioned responses (URs) or CRs evoked by either stimulus. In other words, at this point in the demonstration there is no evidence that the dogs had learned anything about the relationship between the doorbell and light. To demonstrate learning, Brogden used one of these stimuli as a CS signaling electric shock to one of the dog's paws in a signaled avoidance procedure.[1] The dogs soon learned to avoid the shock when the CS was presented. The test for whether the dogs had learned anything about the relationship between the doorbell and light during the 200 trials in which they occurred together involved presenting the other stimulus (the one not used as a signal for shock) and observing if a conditioned avoidance response occurred to it. Although the CR to that other stimulus was not as strong as the one to the original CS, it was reliable enough to demonstrate that the dogs had formed an association between the doorbell and light. Control subjects who did not receive the bell-light pairings showed very few avoidance responses to the other stimulus. Brogden called this phenomenon **sensory preconditioning** because the *subjects learned an association between two "sensory stimuli" prior to the introduction of the US*. Thus the name *sensory preconditioning* is used to designate both the procedure and the phenomenon.

The ease with which within-compound associations can be formed by the sensory preconditioning procedure depends on the stimuli to be associated. Brogden used a doorbell and a flash of light, two stimuli from different sensory modalities that typically do not occur together, and it took 200 trials to demonstrate sensory preconditioning with these stimuli. On the other hand, Rescorla and Cunningham (1978) and Honey and Hall (1991) demonstrated rapid learning of within-compound associations using pairs of flavors. Furthermore, Rescorla (1980a) demonstrated that within-compound associations are strongest when the two elements in the compound are experienced simultaneously rather than successively, and Lavin (1976) found no evidence of within-compound associations

---

[1] In signaled avoidance (see Chapter 7), a stimulus precedes the occurrence of an aversive event such as shock. However, if the individual makes a particular response, the aversive event is avoided. Before the avoidance response occurs reliably, there is a positive Pavlovian contingency between the signal and the aversive event [Pr (aversive event | signal) > Pr (aversive event | no signal)]. After the individual learns to avoid the aversive event, his or her response to the signal predicts the absence of the aversive event.

if the interval between the two stimuli (saccharin and coffee) was longer than 9 seconds. Finally, Rescorla and Freberg (1978) demonstrated that sensory preconditioning is disrupted if either of the two neutral stimuli are presented separately or with other stimuli following the preconditioning phase. Taken together, these results suggest that *within-compound associations are more likely to form and are strongest when the two neutral events are perceived specifically as a compound.*

The Significance of Sensory Preconditioning. The phenomenon of sensory preconditioning is interesting for a number of reasons. First, it illustrates that individuals can learn about the relationship between seemingly insignificant events; that is, Pavlovian conditioning does not require that one of the events be biologically significant. Second, because neither of the two events produces a UR, there is no CR in Phase 1 when the two nonbiologically significant events occur together. Thus, the learning that occurs in Phase 1 of the sensory preconditioning procedure is "behaviorally silent" until the conditions for exhibiting that learning occur. This is another example of the learning-performance problem we discussed in Chapter 1. As Dickinson (1980) notes, *the absence of behavioral change after exposure to the conditioning procedure does not mean that no learning has occurred.* In the case of sensory preconditioning, we have to create a reason for the individual to demonstrate that he or she learned something in Phase 1. Finally, it provides a clear illustration that individuals can integrate knowledge of two different sets of interevent relationships and use that knowledge in a meaningful way.

Transitive Inference in Sensory Preconditioning. Like second-order conditioning, sensory preconditioning also reflects encoding of experience as associations between the internal representations of the experienced events (declarative knowledge) and transitive inference. In Phase 1 of the sensory preconditioning procedure, the declarative association between CS_1 and the CS_2 is "CS_1 and CS_2 occur together." In Phase 2, the declarative association between CS_1 and the US is "CS_1 predicts the occurrence of the US." The occurrence of the CR to CS_2 (which was never experienced with the US) occurs because individuals link together these two declarative associations through the process of transitive inference: "If CS_1 and CS_2 occur together, and CS_1 predicts the occurrence of the US, then CS_2 also predicts the US." The process of transitive inference provides individuals with a way to link CS_2 and the US through the individual associations of CS_1 with CS_2 and CS_1 with the US.

What Sensory Preconditioning, Second-Order Conditioning, and Post-Conditioning Devaluation of the US All Have in Common

All three of these procedures involve transitive inferences based on combining knowledge obtained at different times.

The phenomena of sensory preconditioning, second-order conditioning, and the effects of post-conditioning US devaluation procedures all illustrate that individuals can combine knowledge from two simple Pavlovian conditioning situations. The emergence of a CR to CS_2 (a stimulus that never predicted the occurrence of the US) in both sensory preconditioning and second-order conditioning suggests that the experience with these procedures creates an association between CS_2 and the US that somehow involves CS_1 (the stimulus that does predict the occurrence of the US). A similar analysis underlies the conclusion from the post-conditioning devaluation studies. The declarative representations in the test phases of Table 5.1 and Table 5.3 represent transitive inferences based on the declarative representations from the two earlier phases of the experiments.

Representing Conditional Relationships: Feature-Positive Discriminations, Hierarchical Associations, and Occasion Setting

In a feature-positive discrimination, the presence of an event (called the "feature") signals when a CS will be followed by a US. In one arrangement (called a *simultaneous* feature-positive discrimination), the US occurs only when the feature and the CS occur together. This produces a simple association between the feature and the US. In the other arrangement (called a *serial* feature-positive discrimination), the US will occur following the CS only when the feature precedes the CS. In this hierarchical arrangement, the feature "sets the occasion" for the CS to be followed by the US. These two arrangements are represented in memory in different ways.

All of the Pavlovian conditioning procedures described thus far involve direct predictive arrangements between a CS and a US, and these simple arrangements are encoded as simple associations between representations of the CS and US (see Figure 5.1). However, individuals are capable of learning more complex relationships among events. For example, *the predictive relationship between a CS and US can depend on the presence or absence of another event (called the "feature")*. When the feature is present, the CS will be followed by the US, but when the feature is absent, the US will not occur. This type of situation is called a **feature-positive discrimination**. Thus *the presence of the feature determines whether the CS will be followed by the US*. When individuals master a feature-positive discrimination, they only make CRs when the feature is present. How a feature-positive discrimination is encoded depends on how the feature is related to the CS and the US.

Two Types of Feature-Positive Discriminations. There are two types of feature-positive discriminations in which the presence of a one event (the feature) can signal the relationship between two other events (a CS and a US). These two different types of feature-positive discriminations are presented in Table 5.8. In both cases, the US occurs only when the feature ($CS_{Feature}$) is present, and when $CS_{Feature}$ is absent, the US is also absent. Therefore, the other event (CS_A) predicts the US only when $CS_{Feature}$ is present. The procedure on the left is called a **simultaneous feature-positive discrimination** because $CS_{Feature}$ *occurs at the same time (simultaneously) with CS_A*. The procedure on the right is called a **serial feature-positive discrimination** because *the $CS_{Feature}$ precedes the CS_A-US pairing (i.e., $CS_{Feature}$ and CS_A occur in serial order)*. In both types of feature-positive discriminations, it is the combination of $CS_{Feature}$ and CS_A that signals the occurrence of

Table 5.8	Two Types of Feature-Positive Discriminations	

Simultaneous feature-positive discrimination	Serial feature-positive discrimination
$CS_{Feature} + CS_A \rightarrow US$	$CS_{Feature} \rightarrow (CS_A \rightarrow US)$
$CS_A \rightarrow$ no US	$CS_A \rightarrow$ no US

a US (while CS_A alone signals the absence of the US); however, there is an important difference in how $CS_{Feature}$ predicts the occurrence of the US. In the simultaneous discrimination, $CS_{Feature}$ is followed by the US 100% of the time, while CS_A is followed by the US 50% of the time; therefore, $CS_{Feature}$ is the better predictor of the US because it has the higher relative validity (see Chapter 4). In the serial discrimination, $CS_{Feature}$ informs the individual that the US will follow the occurrence of the next CS_A. Thus in the serial feature-positive discrimination, the situation is hierarchical: $CS_A \rightarrow US$ only when $CS_{Feature}$ has *previously* occurred.

The evidence that serial feature-positive and simultaneous feature-positive discriminations are encoded differently. The difference in roles for $CS_{Feature}$ (predict US in the simultaneous discrimination versus inform individuals when US will follow CS_A in the serial discrimination) suggests that individuals may learn different things from these two procedures. In the simultaneous feature-positive discrimination, $CS_{Feature}$ enters into a simple association with the US because it is the more valid predictor of the US. On the other hand, in the serial feature-positive discrimination where the situation is hierarchical, CS_A enters into a simple association with the US, but that association requires the presence of $CS_{Feature}$ to be activated (Holland, 1983; Rescorla, 1988, 1992).

Ross and Holland (1981) devised a clever way to demonstrate that rats encode simultaneous feature-positive and serial feature-positive discriminations as described above. They used the fact that rats exhibit distinctly different CRs to visual and auditory stimuli: When a CS signaling food is a visual stimulus, rats rear on their hind legs at the beginning of the CS and stand with their heads in the food cup, but when the CS is auditory, they exhibit a startle response to the onset of the CS followed by short, rapid side-to-side head movements (head jerks).[2] Ross and Holland trained different groups of rats with simultaneous and serial feature-positive discriminations. In both cases, $CS_{Feature}$ was a flashing house light (L) and CS_A was a tone (T). Following each type of training, the rats were tested by presenting L, T, and the LT compound stimulus. The form of the CR to these stimuli tells us how the various events involved in the two types of feature-positive discriminations are encoded. If the CR to LT is rearing, then the rats have formed an association between L ($CS_{Feature}$) and the food, but if the CR is head jerk or startle, then the rats have formed an association between T (CS_A) and the food.

---

[2]In the next chapter, we will explore in some detail the fact that the form of the CR is a function of the CS, the US, and the temporal interval between these two events.

In their *simultaneous* feature-positive discrimination, presentation of L ($CS_{Feature}$) and T (CS_A) as always followed by food, but T was never followed by food (see left panel of Table 5.8). As a result of this training, both the LT compound and L elicited rearing and orientation to the food cup, but very little head jerk or startle behavior was elicited by LT and T (see the left panel of Figure 5.4). This is what we would expect (i.e., rearing and food cup orientations) if a simple association is formed between the internal representations of L and food because L had the higher relative validity as a predictor of food.

In their *serial* feature-positive discrimination, L was presented for 5 seconds followed by a 5-second interstimulus interval (ISI) followed by a 5-second T and then by food. No food was presented when T was *not* preceded by L (see right panel of Table 5.8). As a result of this training, head jerk behavior occurred during T, but only when it was preceded by L. Head jerk behaviors also occurred during the ISI between presentation of L and T. The percentages of "L" and "T" behaviors exhibited to T when it was preceded by L are presented in the right panel of Figure 5.4. The head jerk CR during T is indicative of a

Figure 5.4 Percentage of total behaviors that are "light" behaviors (rearing and food cup orientation) and "tone" behaviors (head jerk) exhibited during light + tone combinations after simultaneous (left panel) and serial (right panel) feature-positive discriminations where the feature is a flashing light and CS_A is a tone. Data from Ross and Holland, 1981.

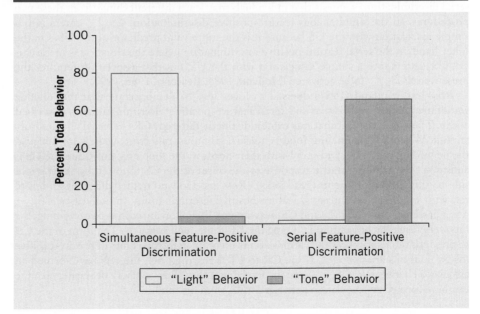

Figure from "Occasion setting in Pavlovian conditioning" by P. C. Holland in *The psychology of learning and motivation: Advances in research and theory*, Volume 28, edited by Douglas L. Medin, copyright © 1992 by Academic Press, reproduced by permission of Elsevier Science.

T-food association, and these occurred only on those trials where L preceded T. It should be noted that rearing occurred to L. That is to be expected given that L always predicted that the subsequent T would be followed by food.

Ross and Holland (1981) explained their results in terms of different representations resulting from the two procedures: In the *simultaneous* feature-positive discrimination, both the $CS_{Feature}$ and CS_A predict the US, but $CS_{Feature}$ is a better predictor (because it has a higher correlation with the US). Therefore, the feature enters into a direct association with the US. This representation is diagrammed in the left panel of Figure 5.5. On the other hand, in the *serial* feature-positive discrimination, $CS_{Feature}$ provides information about when CS_A will be followed by the US. This arrangement is hierarchical; that is, CS_A enters into a direct association with the US, and the feature signals when CS_A will be followed by the US. This representation is diagrammed in the right panel of Figure 5.5. In this hierarchical arrangement, the feature is called an **occasion setter** because *its prior occurrence "sets the occasion" for something to happen (or not happen)*. In this case, $CS_{Feature}$ sets the occasion for CS_A to be followed by the US.

A Closer Look at Occasion Setting. The term *occasion setting* describes a two-level hierarchical arrangement of events (a procedure). A serial feature-positive discrimination is one example of this type of arrangement. In a serial feature-positive discrimination, the bottom level of the hierarchy is first-order Pavlovian conditioning ($CS_A \rightarrow US$). It is important to note that the CS_A-US correlation is not +1.0; that is, sometimes CS_A is followed by the US and sometimes it is not. The second level of the hierarchy involves

Figure 5.5 Schematic depiction of associations from simultaneous (left) and serial (right) feature-positive discriminations. In the simultaneous feature-positive discrimination, the feature ($CS_{Feature}$) enters into a direct association with the US. In the serial feature-positive discrimination, $CS_{Feature}$ enters into a hierarchical (occasion-setting) relationship with the CS_A-US association; that is, the presence of $CS_{Feature}$ evokes the CS_A-US association.

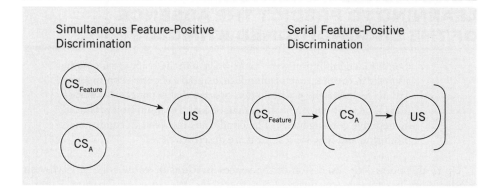

the occasion setter ($CS_{Feature}$), which is always followed by $CS_A \rightarrow US$. Thus $CS_{Feature}$ informs the individual when CS_A will be followed by the US, and we refer to the $CS_{Feature}$ as a **positive occasion setter**.

The ability to perceive this type of hierarchical arrangement has obvious advantages for individuals. When faced with a first-order Pavlovian conditioning procedure with a less than perfect CS-US correlation, an individual will waste energy and resources making CRs to a CS that is not followed by a US. It is advantageous to save those CRs for times when the US follows the CS, and the feature provides that necessary information.

Baeyens, Vansteenwegen, Hermans, Vervliet, and Eelen (2001) demonstrated that humans can learn these types of discriminations. They did this by superimposing both simultaneous and serial feature-positive discriminations on a Martian invader video game. The object of the video game was to prevent Martians from landing. Every half second one new Martian appeared, and the participants could use their laser gun to destroy them, but they only had one shot per Martian. The participant's score was determined by what percentage of the Martians they destroyed. This is an operant conditioning task, and the Pavlovian conditioning involved adding the following feature to the game: When an anti-laser shield appears, any shots will be reflected back, Martians will land, and the game is over. The appearance of the shield was preceded by either a visual stimulus, an auditory stimulus, or both (simultaneously or serially). The shield was the US, and the visual and auditory stimuli were the two CSs. One of those stimuli served as the feature and the other as CS_A. The dependent measure in this experiment was how much the participants suppressed their shooting when the stimuli appeared (using the formula for conditioned suppression in Chapter 2). When the situation was a *simultaneous* feature-positive discrimination, the participants suppressed their shooting to the visual/auditory compound and the feature alone, but not to the stimulus that was CS_A. In the *serial* feature-positive discrimination, participants suppressed shooting only when the feature preceded CS_A. These results parallel those of Ross and Holland (1981).

Ross and Holland's (1981) data indicate that in a serial feature-positive discrimination the internal representation parallels what individuals experience (compare Table 5.8 with Figure 5.5), and this internal representation consists of a declarative representation of the CS_A-US relationship that is activated by the occasion setter or feature ($CS_{Feature}$).

CONDITIONED INHIBITION: LEARNING TO PREDICT THE ABSENCE OF THE UNCONDITIONED STIMULUS

Conditioned inhibition is the name we give to the reactions individuals make in the presence of stimuli that signal a negative contingency with a US and to the psychological process that produces these reactions. There appears to be more than one kind of inhibition produced by negative contingencies. The conditions that lead to conditioned inhibition and how we test for it are described here.

Up to this point, our discussion of the representations of knowledge in Pavlovian conditioning has focused on positive contingencies. We noted in Chapter 3 that a positive contingency [Pr (US|CS) > Pr (US|no CS)] is also referred to as an excitatory contingency or as excitatory conditioning. We also refer to *a CS that elicits a CR* as a conditioned excitatory stimulus (CS+). On the other hand, we refer to a negative contingency [Pr (US|CS) < Pr (US|no CS)] as an inhibitory contingency or as inhibitory conditioning. Under some conditions, inhibitory contingencies tend to produce reactions that are antagonistic to the CR produced by an excitatory stimulus. We call a *stimulus that produces this antagonistic response* a **conditioned inhibitory stimulus** (CS–), and *we attribute the learned antagonistic response to a psychological process* called **conditioned inhibition.**[3]

In Chapter 3, Figures 3.1 and 3.3, we saw two examples of the effects of both positive and negative contingencies on behavior. Rescorla (1966) observed the effects of these contingencies on avoidance conditioning, a behavior that was motivated by fear (see Chapter 3, Table 3.2 and Figure 3.1). In Rescorla's experiment, a tone became a conditioned excitatory stimulus (CS+) when there was a positive contingency between it and the delivery of shock; the CR was an emotional response (fear) aroused by the tone. This conditioned fear was reflected in the increase in avoidance responding in the presence of the tone. On the other hand, for other dogs the tone became a conditioned inhibitory stimulus (CS–) when it predicted the *absence* of shock (a negative contingency); the effect of presenting the tone as a CS– was to reduce the level of avoidance responding in its presence—the dogs acted less afraid. In the Hearst et al. (1980) experiment (Chapter 3, Figure 3.3), the effects of the positive and negative contingencies also produced opposing reactions: the pigeons approached the signal for food (CS+) and withdrew from the signal for the absence of food (CS–), and the strength of their reactions was a function of the size of the correlations in the positive and negative contingencies.

In everyday discourse, we use the term **inhibition** to refer to the active restraining or repression of a response. ("Loosen up! Don't be so inhibited." "He would do it if he were not so inhibited.") In all of these examples, the absence of a behavior is not attributed to ignorance of what to do or inability to do it but to the individual *actively* holding back or restraining himself or herself. But to students of learning, inhibition means more than just holding back the performance of a certain behavior. Although it is true that inhibitory conditioning sometimes leads to a reduction in (or nonoccurrence of) behavior, the data described above also indicate that under certain conditions, inhibitory conditioning procedures can also lead to the occurrence of (or increase in) a behavior. In each of these situations, the increased behavior observed when the negative contingency was in effect was the opposite of that observed when the positive contingency was in effect. Therefore, *when the behavior that occurs to a signal for the absence of an important event is opposite to the behavior that occurs to a signal for the presence of that important event, we attribute that opposite behavior to the psychological process we call* **inhibition**, *and we view inhibition as antagonistic to the excitation generated by the positive contingency.* As is the case with everyday discourse,

---

[3]The terms excitation and inhibition come to us from the study of neurophysiology, and they are still used today to describe synaptic connections that increase (excitation) and decrease neuronal activity (inhibition). Pavlov (1927) was one of the first people to apply these terms to behavior, and he employed them to describe both behavioral phenomena and the underlying physiological processes he presumed produced the observed behavioral changes.

we are using the concept of inhibition here to denote an active psychological process that counteracts the process that leads to the performance of an action in a certain situation.

Procedures for Producing Conditioned Inhibition

Conditioned inhibition is produced by a negative CS-US contingency; the stimulus which predicts the absence of the US becomes a conditioned inhibitor. Negative contingencies are present in the two procedures described here: feature-negative discriminations and differential conditioning (or discrimination training).

Pavlov (1927) was the first person to study the effects of negative contingencies on CRs, although he did not employ the terminology of contingency. In one of his procedures, a CR (salivation) was first established with a perfect positive contingency between a metronome (CS_A) and food. After the CR became stable, a motor car hooter ($CS_{Feature}$) was presented along with the metronome (CS_A) on some trials, but the combination of the two stimuli was never followed by food. Food continued to be presented on trials where the CS_A was presented alone. This procedure is shown in the left panel of Table 5.9. The contingency for the CS_A (the metronome) continued to be positive even after the introduction of the $CS_{Feature}$ [Pr (food | metronome) > Pr (food | no metronome)], but the contingency for the CS_B (hooter) was negative [Pr (food | hooter) < Pr (food | no hooter)]. After experience with this procedure, his dogs continued to salivate when the metronome was presented alone, but not to the combination of the metronome and hooter. Pavlov labeled this phenomenon conditioned inhibition. Today, we call this procedure **simultaneous feature-negative discrimination** training because *an excitatory CS (CS_A in this case) is followed by a US except when the feature ($CS_{Feature}$) is present.*

Pavlov (1927) also described a second procedure involving a negative contingency: A circle was presented in a perfect positive contingency with food. Occasionally a square (CS_B) was presented by itself and never followed by food. This procedure is shown in the right panel of Table 5.9. The contingency was positive in the presence of the circle and negative in the presence of the square. After sufficient experience, dogs salivated when the circle (CS_A) was presented but not when the square (CS_B) was presented. Pavlov labeled this phenomenon differential inhibition or differentiation; today we refer to the procedure as **differential conditioning** or **discrimination training**.

Table 5.9   Two Procedures for Producing a Conditioned Inhibitory Stimulus

Simultaneous feature-negative discrimination	Differential conditioning (or discrimination training)
$CS_A \rightarrow$ US	$CS_A \rightarrow$ US
$CS_{Feature} + CS_A \rightarrow$ no US	$CS_B \rightarrow$ no US

Pavlov (1927) believed that the occurrence of CRs as a result of the CS-US pairings (behavioral excitation) and the suppression of CRs as a result of stimulus presentations in the absence of the US (behavioral inhibition) reflect, respectively, underlying processes of neural excitation and inhibition. Excitation and ionhibition were seen as antagonistic central nervous system processes in the brain centers activated by the excitatory CS (CS+) and inhibitory CS (CS–). Excitation is supposed to increase when a CS is followed by the US, and inhibition is supposed to increase when a CS is not followed by the US. The appearance of the CR was thought to depend on the relative levels of excitation and inhibition when the CS was presented. Thus, behavioral excitation and inhibition were thought to reflect underlying physiological processes of excitation and inhibition. Today we know this is not correct: Behavioral excitation and inhibition are certainly the result of physiological mechanisms, but they are not *simply* reflections of neuronal excitation and inhibition (Williams, Overmier, & LoLordo, 1992).

Tests for Conditioned Inhibition

Conditioned inhibition is antagonistic to conditioned excitation; therefore, conditioned inhibition is measured against a baseline of behavior established by conditioned excitation. Because there are other procedures that can reduce a CR, special control conditions are required to rule out alternative explanations.

Pavlov (1927) came to the conclusion that the reductions in responding observed in feature-negative discriminations and differential conditioning are due to the active suppression of the response, not the loss of excitation from omission of the US. He based this conclusion on two types of observations. The first involved *simultaneous presentations of a stimulus that had been established by one of the procedures described above as a conditioned inhibitory stimulus (CS–) along with a stimulus that had separately been established as a conditioned excitatory stimulus (CS+). The presentation of the CS– affected the CR to the CS+.* This procedure is called the summation test for conditioned inhibition because the effects look like the algebraic summation of positive and negative values. The second observation was that *it took longer to acquire a CR to a stimulus that had previously been established as a conditioned inhibitory stimulus than one that had not.* This is called the retardation of acquisition test for conditioned inhibition.

The Summation Test for Conditioned Inhibition. In a summation test, a suspected conditioned inhibitory stimulus (CS–) is presented along with a known conditioned excitatory stimulus (CS+). A reduction in the CR when the combination of stimuli is presented indicates that the suspected conditioned inhibitory stimulus is indeed inhibitory. This test is based on two premises: First, excitation and inhibition are assumed to be antagonistic processes; thus, a stimulus is defined as a conditioned inhibitor (CS–) if it counteracts the CR produced by an excitatory stimulus (CS+). Second, in order to demonstrate that a stimulus is a conditioned inhibitory stimulus (CS–), there must be something for it to inhibit. The conditioned excitatory stimulus (CS+) provides an above-zero baseline of behavior to inhibit.

The procedure for carrying out a summation test for conditioned inhibition is presented in the top panel of Table 5.10. In the conditioned inhibition group, a stimulus (CS–) is trained in a negative contingency with a US (either in a simultaneous feature-negative discrimination or as the negative stimulus in differential conditioning). During the test, the CS– is presented along with an already established excitatory stimulus (CS+). If the CR to CS+ is reduced when CS– is paired with it, we take this as evidence that CS– became an inhibitory stimulus because the inhibition conditioned to CS– counteracted the excitation conditioned to CS+.

Pavlov (1927) demonstrated the summation test with the following experiment involving the feature in a simultaneous feature-negative discrimination: A metronome predicted food, and the combination of a metronome and a whistle predicted no food. As a result, his dogs stopped salivating on those trials when the whistle and metronome were presented (the whistle was the feature in this feature-negative discrimination). To demonstrate that the whistle was an inhibitory stimulus, Pavlov also established a CR (salivation) to a tactile stimulus that predicted the introduction of mild acid in the dog's mouth. This tactile stimulus (CS+) was then used in the summation test with the whistle. When the dogs were tested for CRs to the tactile stimulus alone and to the combination of the whistle (CS–) and the tactile stimulus (CS+), the conditioned salivary response to the compound stimulus was *greatly reduced* relative to the response to the tactile stimulus (CS+) alone.

Pavlov (1927) also recognized that the summation test required control procedures to rule out alternative explanations of the results. An important control is for what Pavlov called external inhibition—that is, the reduction in conditioned responding by the introduction of a novel stimulus.[4] One could argue that observed reduction in responding to the combination of the CS+ and CS– during the test is due to external inhibition because the subjects had never before experienced the combination of the tactile stimulus and whistle. A way around this problem is to use two groups of subjects (see top panel of Table 5.10). The conditioned inhibition group is given the treatment described above. The control group for external inhibition is given excitatory training with CS+, but they have no prior experience with the stimulus that is the CS– in the conditioned inhibition group (for them that stimulus is neutral and designated as CS_N). In the summation test, the CR to the combination of CS+ and CS_N is compared to the CR to CS+ alone. One demonstrates conditioned inhibition when the CS– in the conditioned inhibition group reduces the CR to CS+ in the summation test more than does CS_N in the control group.

The Retardation Test for Conditioned Inhibition. In this test, we attempt to turn a suspected conditioned inhibitory stimulus (CS–) into a conditioned excitatory stimulus (CS+) by putting that stimulus into a positive CS-US contingency. If it takes longer to produce an excitatory CR to that stimulus than to a novel stimulus, that stimulus was previously an inhibitory stimulus (see Table 5.10 bottom). Pavlov (1927) described just such an experiment.

---

[4]Pavlov distinguished between what he called external (unconditioned) inhibition and internal (conditioned) inhibition. External (unconditioned) inhibition *is due to extraneous external stimuli that disrupt the CR.* These effects dissipate after the stimulus is removed. With repeated exposure (familiarity), the disruptive effects frequently habituate (see Chapter 1). Internal inhibition is learned through experience with a negative contingency. Today we use the term conditioned inhibition as a synonym for internal inhibition.

Table 5.10 The Tests for Conditioned Inhibition

	Summation test		
Group	**Training**	**Test**
Conditioned inhibition	CS– in a negative contingency with US and CS+ in a positive contingency with US.	CS+ and (CS- + CS+)
Control for external inhibition	CS+ in a positive contingency with US. No training with a second stimulus (CS_N).	CS+ and (CS_N + CS+)
	Retardation test		
Conditioned inhibition	CS in a negative contingency with US.	CS in a positive contingency with US.
Control	Placed in apparatus but with no CS or US	CS in a positive contingency with US

Note: In the summation test, CS- and CS_N are the same physical stimulus. CS- is the designation for that stimulus in the conditioned inhibition group, and CS_N is the designation for that stimulus in the control group.

The retardation test is based on the same two premises as the summation test: excitation and inhibition are assumed to be antagonistic processes, and in order to demonstrate that a stimulus is a conditioned inhibitory stimulus (CS–), there must be something for it to inhibit. In the retardation test, that something is the excitation generated during the test by the positive CS-US contingency.

Evidence That There Is More Than One Kind of Conditioned Inhibition

Stimuli that signal the absence of the US do not always pass both the summation and retardation tests, yet these stimuli appear to function as inhibitory stimuli. This leads us to conclude that there is more than one kind of conditioned inhibition.

Before proceeding, it will help for us to review what we have learned thus far about conditioned inhibition. Positive CS-US contingencies produce the psychological process called excitation which is reflected in the occurrence of a CR to that CS, and stimuli that generate CRs are labeled as excitatory stimuli. Negative CS-US contingencies produce the psychological process called inhibition which is reflected in behaviors antagonistic to those that reflect excitation. Rescorla (1969) suggested that a stimulus should be designated as a conditioned inhibitory stimulus only if it passes both the summation test (has the capacity to reduce CRs to a known excitatory CS) and the retardation test (it takes longer to turn that stimulus into an excitatory CS). However, there is a kind of negative contingency that clearly creates inhibitory CSs, but these CSs do not pass both the summation and inhibition test. This procedure is called a serial feature-negative discrimination.

Feature-Negative Discriminations. As we saw above, in a feature-positive discrimination, the feature is the best predictor of the occurrence of the US (Table 5.8); **in a feature-negative discrimination,** *the feature is the best predictor of the absence of the US.* As is the case with feature-positive discriminations, there are two different kinds of feature-negative discriminations (see Table 5.11). As previously noted, the **simultaneous feature-negative discrimination** is the procedure introduced by Pavlov: *an excitatory CS (CS$_A$) is followed by a US except when the feature (CS$_{Feature}$) is present.* **In a serial feature-negative discrimination,** *an excitatory CS (CS$_A$) is followed by a US except when CS$_A$ is preceded by CS$_{Feature}$.* In both the simultaneous and serial feature-negative discrimination, there is a negative contingency between the feature and the US: the US is more likely to occur in the absence of the feature than in its presence.

An impressive amount of evidence has been accumulated to show that the feature in a serial feature-negative discrimination functions as an inhibitory stimulus even though it fails the retardation test and only passes the summation test when the CS+ is from another serial feature-negative discrimination (see Holland, 1985, 1992 for reviews). This suggests that there are at least two different kinds of conditioned inhibition: One type is created by simultaneous feature-negative discriminations and differential conditioning—these inhibitory stimuli pass both the summation and retardation tests of conditioned inhibition. The other type of conditioned inhibition is produced by serial feature-negative discriminations—these inhibitory stimuli pass the summation test only when the to-be-inhibited excitatory stimulus in the test was trained in a serial feature-positive or feature-negative discrimination, and they fail the retardation test. This second type of inhibition has been characterized as a **negative occasion setter**, a term that is used to describe both the procedure and the underlying mechanism for the observed effects. The **procedure of negative occasion setting** is synonymous with serial feature-negative discrimination training because CS$_{Feature}$ *"sets the occasion" for the absence of the US; that is, it informs the individual that the next occurrence of CS$_A$ will not be followed by the US.*

Table 5.11 Two Types of Feature-Negative Discriminations	
Simultaneous feature-negative discrimination	Serial feature-negative discrimination
CS$_A$ → US	CS$_A$ → US
CS$_{Feature}$ + CS$_A$ → no US	CS$_{Feature}$ → (CS$_A$ → no US)

Representations in Conditioned Inhibition

Simple inhibition is produced by simultaneous feature-negative discriminations and differential conditioning; it involves an association between the CS– and a representation of the absence of the US. Negative occasion setting involves a hierarchical association between the feature and a CS-US association.

Simple Conditioned Inhibition. Conditioned inhibition is the name we give to the psychological process that arises from experience with negative CS-US contingencies and generates a reaction that is antagonistic to the responses generated by positive CS-US contingencies. In both differential conditioning and simultaneous feature-negative discriminations, there is a CS that has a positive contingency with a US (CS_A in Table 5.9), and a second stimulus that has a negative contingency with that same US (termed either $CS_{Feature}$ or CS_B in Table 5.9). The CS_A-US relationship is encoded as an association between these two events, but how is the negative contingency involving the second CS ($CS_{Feature}$ or CS_B) encoded?

The best answer to this question was offered by Konorski (1967): *Inhibitory conditioning results in an association between the inhibitory CS and a no-US representation* (see also Dickinson, 1980; Mackintosh & Cotton, 1985; Pearce, 1987; Pearce & Hall, 1980). At first glance, this appears to be a strange suggestion: how can the nonoccurrence of an event be represented in memory? However, it is not difficult to think of examples where the nonoccurrence of an anticipated event produces the emotional reaction of disappointment when discovering that something good will not happen or of relief when discovering that something unpleasant will not occur. Konorski viewed these emotional reactions as the result of the arousal of a no-US representation. Konorski's answer explains why $CS_{Feature}$ or CS_B passes both the summation and retardation tests for conditioned inhibition.

Negative Occasion Setting. Negative occasion setting is another name for the serial feature-negative discrimination procedure (right panel of Table 5.11). As is the case with serial feature-positive discriminations and positive occasion setting, negative occasion setting involves a hierarchical arrangement of events. At the lower level, there is a less than perfect positive correlation between CS_A and the US. At the upper level, there is a perfect negative correlation between $CS_{Feature}$ and the occurrence of the US following CS_A; in other words, the US does not follow CS_A if $CS_{Feature}$ preceded CS_A (but the US will follow CS_A if $CS_{Feature}$ has not occurred). How is this hierarchical relationship encoded?

$CS_{Feature}$ is clearly inhibitory because the CR does not occur to CS_A when $CS_{Feature}$ precedes CS_A, but the fact that $CS_{Feature}$ fails the summation test suggests that what is encoded is not simply the absence of the US. We might infer from what we already know about the representations of serial feature-positive discriminations (positive occasion setting) that these representations parallel what is experienced, but we have no experimental evidence to indicate that is the case. Perhaps you will devise an experiment to test this.

THE ROLE OF THE ENVIRONMENTAL CONTEXT IN PAVLOVIAN CONDITIONING

Pavlovian conditioning does not take place in a vacuum. The CS and US occur in a wider environmental context (in some place and at certain times). Aspects of the environmental context are represented in memory and enter into associations with the CS and US.

Although we have focused primarily on discrete CSs and USs and their relationship to each other, the CS is not the only stimulus that predicts the occurrence of the US. The events we label as the CS and US occur somewhere and at certain times. For example, in a typical Pavlovian conditioning experiment, the individual is placed in an experimental chamber, usually around the same time each day, and stimulus events (CSs and USs) are presented at various times during the experimental session typically with a set time between them. Therefore, we should expect that both the physical and temporal locations of these events will also be represented in memory and enter into associations with the CS and US.

Evidence of Context-US Associations

When the environmental context is the best predictor of the occurrence of the US, that context will function as a CS.

We have already encountered a number of instances where the environmental context in which individuals experienced a CS and a US has been implicated in Pavlovian conditioning. Both the CS preexposure effect (see Chapter 4) and the US preexposure effect (see Chapter 4) are context specific; that is, they are attenuated when the preexposure occurs in one context and Pavlovian conditioning in another. Likewise, in the case of conditioned drug tolerance (see Chapter 2), the context in which the drug was administered was identified as the CS that affected the individual's reaction to the drug.

A number of studies have demonstrated that the size of the US preexposure effect is a function of the number of presentations of the US alone (see Randich & LoLordo, 1979a and Balsam, 1982, for reviews). For example, Balsam and Schwartz (1981) demonstrated that the speed with which doves will peck a key in a sign-tracking experiment is a direct function of the number of times they experienced the food alone in the experimental chamber before conditioning: birds with more US preexposures took longer. Likewise, Randich and LoLordo (1979b) demonstrated that the size of the US preexposure effect in conditioned suppression of lever pressing in rats was affected by the number of US preexposures: The greater the number of days of US preexposure, the slower the development of conditioned suppression. With respect to drug tolerance experiments, both Siegel (1977) and Tiffany and Baker (1981) reported that the development of tolerance was retarded when their subjects were preexposed to the cues that would later be paired with morphine. These experiments are interesting because they employed the CS preexposure effect to demonstrate that the experimental context surrounding morphine administration can serve as a CS for the delivery of the morphine.

The Context as an Occasion Setter

Contexts can also enter into second-order associations with CS-US relationships that occur in those contexts.

In the majority of Pavlovian conditioning experiments, the US is signaled by a CS of short duration relative to the length of the experimental session, and the CS is a more valid predictor of the US because it provides information about when the US will occur in that context. The research on the relative validity of cues (see Chapter 4) leads us to expect that a CS will overshadow the context as long as that CS is the most valid predictor. However, this does not mean that nothing is learned about the context when a more predictive CS is present. *In addition to the predictive relationship between the CS and US, there is a hierarchical relationship between the CS-US relationship and the place and times this relationship is experienced.* The data point to the conclusion that the context can act as an occasion setter rather than a second CS. An experiment by Bouton and King (1983) provides a nice illustration of this.

The design of Bouton and King's (1983) experiment is provided in Table 5.12. They pretrained rats to bar press for food in two experimental contexts (Context A and Context B) that differed in terms of the walls (aluminum and clear plastic vs. stripes on the clear plastic, the texture of the floor (16 mm diameter bars vs. 3 mm diameter bars), odor (vinegar vs. Vicks VapoRub), food (from two different vendors), and how the rats were introduced into the chambers (through a door on the wall or from the top). After the rats pressed the bar at a stable rate in both contexts, they were given conditioned suppression training with a 60-second tone followed by a 0.5-second footshock in one of the contexts (designated as Context A). Following conditioning, for one third of the subjects (Group EXT-A), the conditioned fear to the tone was extinguished in Context A (by presenting the tone alone), for one third of the rats (Group EXT-B) the conditioned fear was extinguished in the other context (Context B). The remaining subjects (Group NE) received no extinction training. All three groups then received an extinction test with tone in context A. The results of the extinction training are presented in the left panel of Figure 5.6. Note that the course of extinction was the same in Context A and Context B. This is an example of context change not affecting behavior (see above). However, when all rats were given the extinction test in Context A (Figure 5.6, right panel), those rats that had received extinction trials in Context A showed little evidence of fear, but those rats that had received extinction trials in Context B and those that had not received any extinction trials (Group NE) showed evidence of fear to the tone. Similar results were reported by Harris, Jones, Bailey, and Westbrook (2000) and by Asem and Holland (2012) using a food US. The Asem and Holland study is also notable because they reported that exposure to a high-fat diet following acquisition and before extinction training interfered with the recovery or "renewal" of responding when the rats were tested in the original training context. Intriguingly, Asem and Holland suggested that their results might have clinical relevance for models of relapse and treatments for addiction, overeating, and phobias.

The Bouton and King (1983) results are interesting because the effects of the context on behavior were not evident (were behaviorally silent) until *after* the rats extinguished in Context B were returned to Context A. Here is yet another example of the

Table 5.12 Experimental Design for Bouton and King (1983) Study of the Context as an Occasion Setter

Group	Pretraining	Training	Extinction	Test
EXT-A	Press lever for food in Context A and Context B	T → Shock in Context A	T alone in Context A	T alone in Context A
EXT-B	Press lever for food in Context A and Context B	T → Shock in Context A	T alone in Context B	T alone in Context A
NE	Press lever for food in Context A and Context B	T → Shock in Context A	No extinction	T alone in Context A

learning-performance distinction. Furthermore, these data are best interpreted in terms of the occasion-setting function of the context (Bouton, 1991, 1993, 1994; Bouton & Bolles, 1985). Occasion setters provide information about when a CS will be followed by a US; for example, entry into the experimental chamber provides information that this is a place where a certain stimulus event (the CS) will be followed by something significant (the US). Given that placement in an experimental apparatus is followed by conditioning trials, it is not surprising that individuals still give a CR to that CS when first experiencing that CS in another context because that CS could signal danger or food in more than one place. However, when we provide something different in a different location or context (the CS without the US), the individuals will use the context to tell them when the CS will lead to the US and when it will not; that is, the context will "set the occasion" for the presence of the US.

Rescorla, Durlach, and Grau (1985) also provided a clear example of how the context can enter into second-order relationships with specific CS-US relationships. They trained pigeons in a sign-tracking task with two key light CSs: a grid of white diagonal lines on a black background slanted –45 degrees from vertical (CS_A) and a grid of black diagonal lines on a white background slanted +45 degrees from vertical (CS_B). There were two contexts, one with striped walls and the other with marbled walls. In one context, CS_A was followed by food and CS_B was not. The reverse relationship occurred in the other context. Over the course of 20 sessions, their pigeons gradually came to peck only at the pattern on the key that predicted food in each context and not to peck at the pattern that did not predict food in that context. It is quite clear from these results that the context served as an occasion-setter to inform the pigeons about which pattern on the key predicted food in that context: In Context 1, it was CS_A, and in Context 2 it was CS_B.

Finally, although the CS preexposure effect (see Chapter 4) is also context dependent (Channell & Hall, 1983; Lovibond et al., 1984; Preston, Dickinson, & Mackintosh, 1986),

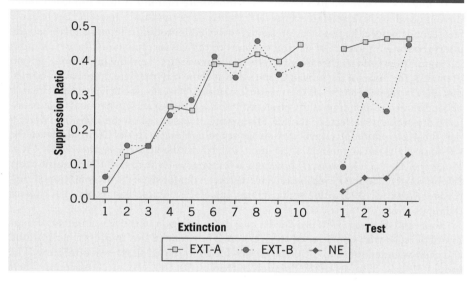

Figure 5.6 Mean suppression ratios to the tone CS during extinction and during the test. Group EXT-A had training and extinction (tone alone) in Context A. Group EXT-B had training in Context A and extinction in Context B. Group NE was trained in Context A, but they did not experience extinction. All groups were tested in Context A with tone alone.

Redrawn from Bouton and King, 1983. Contextual control of the extinction of conditioned fear: Tests for the associative value of the context. *Journal of Experimental Psychology: Animal Behavior Processes, 9,* 248–265. Copyright © 1983 by the American Psychological Association. Reprinted with permission.

this does not mean that the CS preexposure effect is the result of CS-context associations. Rather the evidence points to the conclusion that the context serves as an occasion-setter; that is, the context provides information that the CS is not followed by anything of importance in that context (Lubow, 1989). For further discussion about the roles of context in Pavlovian conditioning, see Balsam and Tomie (1985).

REPRESENTING THE TEMPORAL RELATIONSHIPS BETWEEN EVENTS

The association between the CS and US in Pavlovian conditioning includes more than just the representations of the sensory and hedonic aspects of these events—it also includes knowledge of the temporal relationship between them.

Up to this point, we have only considered the predictive relationship between the CS and US in terms of the CS-US contingency, that is, the probabilities that the US occurs in the presence or absence of the CS. The evidence reviewed suggests that this relationship is represented in memory as an association between the internal representations of these two events; however, the CS also can provide information about the time of arrival of the US. This knowledge can also be represented in memory (Miller & Barnet, 1993; Michon, 1985; Gallistel, 1990b, 1992; Gallistel & Gibbon, 2000; Gibbon, 1981).

Pavlov (1927) was the first person to demonstrate that individuals can learn about the temporal arrangement of events. He trained dogs to salivate to a CS that began a few seconds before the food was presented (delay conditioning). Then he increased the interval between the start of CS and the start of the US incrementally up to 3 minutes in length. After sufficient training with the 3-minute long CS ending in the presentation of the US, the onset of the salivation settled in at some intermediate time. Pavlov named this *delay in the onset of the CR* the **inhibition of delay** because he believed that the lack of conditioned responding to the onset of the CS was due to an active process that countered the excitatory effects of the CS. His argument was based on the additional finding that the presentation of a novel extraneous stimulus along with the CS would cause the CR to occur at the beginning of the interval. Pavlov called the *reappearance of the CR at the onset of the CS when a novel stimulus was presented along with that CS* **disinhibition**. Inhibition of delay and disinhibition have also been demonstrated with conditioned suppression (Rescorla, 1967a) and with conditioning of the galvanic skin response in humans (Kimmel, 1965).

Rosas and Alonso (1996) provided a nice demonstration of the development of inhibition of delay with conditioned suppression. They trained rats to press a bar for food and then assigned them to different groups for conditioned suppression training. The groups differed in terms of the duration of the CS: 50, 100, 150, or 200 seconds. Their data for the acquisition of conditioned suppression across five-session blocks of trials are presented in Figure 5.7. In order to compare performance across different CS durations, the data in Figure 5.7 have been expressed in terms of the suppression ratio across fifths of the time that the CS was on. Notice the systematic decrease in the amount of conditioned suppression during the earlier time segments of the CS as training progressed from sessions 1–5 to sessions 26–30 of training.[5]

Pavlov (1927) also demonstrated that *the passage of time can serve as a CS for events*. He presented dogs with food every thirtieth minute. After a number of training trials, the food was occasionally omitted. Despite omission of the food, the dogs would salivate at the 30th minute or 1–2 minutes later. Pavlov also demonstrated that the passage of time can overshadow a discrete CS like a metronome if the metronome is given just before food on a fixed time schedule: Dogs given a metronome and food every 30 minutes would not salivate if the metronome was presented 5 or 8 minutes after the last US presentation. The amount of salivation to the metronome was higher when the metronome was presented about 30 minutes after the last US presentation.

Williams, Frame, and LoLordo (1992) investigated the effects of contextual and temporal conditioning using shock as the US. A single shock was presented at a fixed time (for different groups it was either 120 or 1200 seconds) after placement in the conditioning

---

[5]Because this is conditioned suppression, the *higher* the suppression ratio, the *less* the suppression.

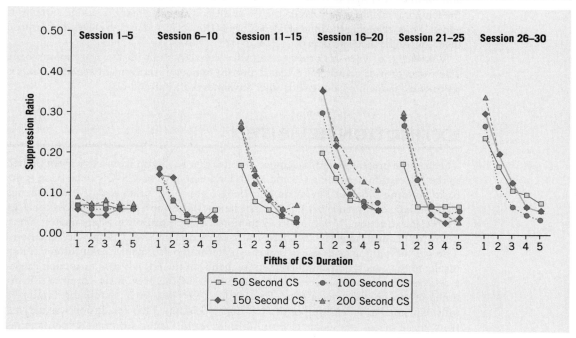

Figure 5.7 Mean suppression ratios plotted across fifths of the CS durations (50, 100, 150, and 200 seconds). Each panel represents successive blocks of five training sessions.

Figure redrawn from "Temporal discrimination and forgetting of CS duration in conditioned suppression" by J. M. Rosas and G. Alonso in *Learning and Motivation*, Volume 27, 43–57, copyright © 1996 by Academic Press, reproduced by permission of Elsevier Science.

situation in each experimental session. The CR was freezing. Typically, rats freeze when placed in the apparatus where they experienced shock, but when these rats were tested in a second context in the absence of shock, they froze at the *time* the shock had arrived in the first context. Likewise, Kehoe, Graham-Clark, and Schreurs (1989) used a conditioned eyeblink procedure to investigate temporal encoding of the occurrence of the US. They used two different CS-US intervals presented randomly during the training sessions. After sufficient experience, their rabbits blinked twice on each trial, once just before the first possible occurrence of the US and again just before the second possible occurrence. Barnet and Miller (1996) demonstrated that signals for the occurrence of a US (excitatory CSs) and signals for the omission of a US (inhibitory CSs) both provide information about the temporal location of the US.

If time can serve as a CS, then it should be capable of blocking conditioning to other stimuli. Balsam and Gibbon (1988) presented food to pigeons every 48 seconds. Later they added a tone just prior to each food delivery. They found that the passage of time served as a CS to block conditioning to the tone. Williams and LoLordo (1995) also found that shock presented at a fixed time blocked conditioning to a tone, but they also found that prior tone-shock presentations did *not* block conditioning to the temporal interval. Finally Barnet, Grahame, and Miller (1993), Goddard and Jenkins (1988), and Schreurs and Westbrook (1982) all demonstrated that blocking is attenuated if there is a change in the temporal relationship between the CS and US at the time that the second stimulus is added. Thus, changing the time of occurrence of the US introduces an element of surprise that reduces the blocking effect.

Knowledge of when important events will occur allows individuals to prepare for them. These data provide convincing evidence that the temporal arrangement between events is represented in memory along with other attributes of the CS and US.

EXTINCTION REVISITED

The material presented in this chapter indicates that Pavlovian knowledge is not limited to the association between a CS and a US. Undoubtedly, the CS-US association is the basic building block of Pavlovian knowledge, but many other events can influence learning and performance of a CS-US association. We are now in a position to reconsider Pavlovian extinction. By definition, extinction is a post-acquisition phenomenon. Thus, following acquisition with CS-US pairings, extinction involves CS only presentations. This type of training gives rise to opposite patterns of performance: acquisition training results in the generation and increased frequency of the CR whereas extinction causes a decrease in the occurrence, if not elimination, of the previously acquired CR. As noted in our previous discussion of extinction (see Chapter 2), extinction cannot be fully explained as unlearning of the CS-US association. This conclusion was derived from three pieces of evidence: disinhibition, rapid reacquisition, and spontaneous recovery, each of which could not occur if the original learning was completely erased by extinction training. Two additional pieces of evidence (reinstatement and renewal) support the view that extinction is not unlearning but, in fact, involves some new type of learning. We will first describe this evidence before moving on to the question of "what is learned in Pavlovian extinction?"

Reinstatement *occurs after extinction training and refers to the reappearance of the CR when the extinguished CS is presented following exposures to the US* (Bouton & Bolles, 1979; Delamater, 1997; Rescorla & Heth, 1975; Schachtman, Brown & Miller, 1985). The reinstatement effect occurs when US re-exposures are delivered within at least 24 hours of the test with the extinguished CS. Importantly, it has been shown that the reinstating USs must occur in the same context as the subsequent CS test trials; reinstatement does not occur if different contexts are used for the US only and CS only presentations (Bouton, 1984; Bouton & King, 1983). So, reinstatement is not an inevitable consequence of US re-exposure. Rather, it is necessary for the CS to be tested in the same context as that in which the USs were recently experienced.

Renewal *occurs after extinction training and refers to a reappearance of the CR when the extinguished CS is presented outside the extinction context* (Brooks & Bouton, 1994;

Goddard, 1999; Harris et al., 2000; Rosas & Bouton, 1997). Although we did not explicitly refer to it as renewal, we encountered this effect in our exposition of the results of Bouton and King (1983; see Figure 5.6), which demonstrated that extinction is context specific. Bouton and King used an ABA design in which the letters refer, respectively, to the different context used in acquisition, extinction, and test (see Table 5.12). Renewal also occurs with the following combinations of acquisition, extinction, and test contexts: ABC and AAB (Bouton & Ricker, 1994; Campese & Delamater, 2013; Pineno & Miller, 2004; Rosas & Callejas-Aguilera, 2006; Thomas, Larsen, & Ayres, 2003). These designs emphasize the importance of context in Pavlovian conditioning (Rosas, Todd & Bouton, 2013).

Traditionally, context has referred to the physical environment in which Pavlovian conditioning takes place (i.e., the experimental apparatus). However, other types of stimuli also can serve as the context (Balsam, 1985; Bouton, 2010; S. M. Smith, 2007). For example, the passage of time may serve as a temporal context. Indeed, when viewed in this way, spontaneous recovery can be interpreted as a renewal effect that occurs when the extinguished CS is later encountered in a different temporal context from that in which the original extinction training was administered (Bouton 1994, 2002, 2004). The internal state of the body can be conceptualized as an "interoceptive" context. This type of context might be most easily appreciated by thinking about the altered state that is experienced following administration of a drug. In these latter cases, the physical context may remain the same, but the temporal or interoceptive context changes between acquisition, extinction, and testing. As noted by, for example, Bouton and Bolles (1985), the meaning of the word "Fire!" is ambiguous in the absence of context. However, when context is taken into account (a shooting gallery at a county fair or a crowded movie theater), the meaning of the word is immediately apparent. By analogy, the context may serves to disambiguate the significance of a CS that has acquired contradictory associations, as may occur in acquisition and extinction training.

What is learned in Pavlovian extinction? Among a number of types of interpretations of extinction, three stand out as the most relevant for present purposes. The first type of account (see Figure 5.8A), which can be traced back to Pavlov's analysis of "internal inhibition," involves what might be thought of as the development during extinction training of an inhibitory connection between the internal representations of the CS and US. By this account, a parallel inhibitory link is considered to overlay, but not erase, the excitatory CS-US association that was acquired during acquisition training (Konorski, 1948). From this perspective, the disruption of internal inhibition (or the inhibitory connection) by the passage of time or a novel stimulus may reveal the original excitatory association and hence the reappearance of the CR after extinction training. Of course, if the original CS-US association remains, to some extent, intact following extinction training, then one would expect rapid reacquisition when CS-US pairings are presented again. It is not immediately clear how this "inhibitory" association account handles reinstatement, except to suggest that re-exposure to the US prior to test might serves to disinhibit performance of the original CS-US association. Because context is not encoded in the inhibitory association acquired during extinction training, this account does not predict nor can it explain the renewal effect.

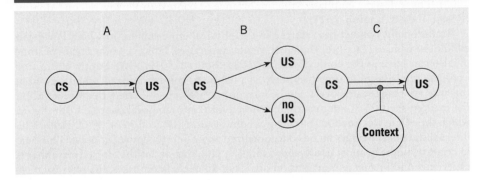

Figure 5.8 Schematic representations of three accounts of what is learned during Pavlovian extinction. Arrows indicate excitatory connections; flat-ended lines indicate inhibitory connections. (A) The development of an inhibitory link between the CS and US. (B) The development of an excitatory link between the CS and a "no US" representation. (C) The context determines when an inhibitory CS-US connection guides performance of the CR.

The second type of interpretation for what is learned during extinction training (see Figure 5.8B) was proposed by Konorski (1967), presumably following a change of mind from his earlier view, and suggests that a new excitatory connection develops between the CS and a "no US" representation when, during extinction training, the CS is followed by the absence of the expected US. This "excitatory" association account deals with the five recovery-from-extinction effects (disinhibition, rapid reacquisition, spontaneous, reinstatement and renewal) in much the same manner as the "inhibitory" association account.

The final, and most recent, account of extinction (see Figure 5.8C) differs from the first two insofar as a third stimulus (beyond the CS and the US) is encoded and this stimulus modulates expression of the originally acquired excitatory CS-US association (Bouton, 2002, 2004). As exemplified by the renewal effect, the third stimulus is typically the context that accompanies the CS when it undergoes extinction. In this way, the extinction context may become a negative occasion setter that signals the absence of the US. By this analysis, the extinction context becomes a conditioned inhibitor that governs expression of the excitatory CS-US association that developed during acquisition training. This third account readily handles the renewal effect as the expected result of the absence of the negative occasion setter at test. Spontaneous recovery is, similarly, predicted on the basis of the change in the temporal context between extinction training and test. In a rather obvious sense the presence of CS-US pairings or CS only presentations define the context, respectively, of acquisition and extinction training. Accordingly, post-extinction performance may also depend on how much the test context resembles the acquisition or extinction contexts in terms of what stimuli (CSs and/or USs) occur there. In this way, the reappearance of the CR by reinstatement or rapid reacquisition is anticipated because of the similarity, perfect in the latter case, of the test context with the acquisition context. It will not have gone unnoticed that this "context modulation" account is an extension and elaboration of the first (inhibitory connection) account of extinction. Presumably, then, each account may deal with disinhibition in the same general way (i.e., as a disruption of an inhibitory link that, consequently, reveals performance based on the original excitatory CS-US association).

We should note, although the preceding accounts emphasize the acquisition of new knowledge during extinction training, they cannot rule out the possibility that some degree of unlearning does, in fact, occur. This caveat is necessary because the recovery phenomena do not always show a full return of the CR to its pre-extinction level. Furthermore, there is evidence from research concerning the neurobiology of learning and memory that some unlearning does occur during extinction training (for a discussion of this issue, see Delamater & Westbrook, 2014).

Although procedurally simple and straightforward, extinction, as shown by the post-extinction recovery phenomena discussed above, is a complex and multifaceted process. Determining the psychological processes responsible for Pavlovian extinction is an area of active research today (see, e.g., reviews by Delamater & Westbrook, 2014; Lattal & Lattal, 2012; McConnell & Miller, 2014; Rescorla, 2001; Todd, Vurbic, & Bouton, 2014a). This research not only has intrinsic merit, but the accurate characterization of extinction processes is important for at least two other reasons. First, in noting that the recovery-from-extinction effects can also be termed relapse phenomena, this enterprise provides insight and rationale for clinical treatments and interventions that seek to eliminate unwanted or inappropriate behaviors and emotions as seen in, among many others, drug addiction, phobias, and PTSD (Crombag, Bossert, Koya, & Shaman, 2008; Laborda, McConnell, & Miller, 2011; Myers & Carlezon, 2010; Perry, Zbukvic, Kim, & Lawrence, 2014; Vervliet, Craske, & Hermans, 2013). Second, understating the neural substrates and mechanisms of extinction will not only provide insight into the behavioral processes that support extinction but also holds the potential to guide the development of pharmacological treatments for the clinical issues cited above (M. Davis, 2011; Davis, Myers, Chhatwal & Ressler, 2006; Milad, Rauch, Pitman, & Quirk, 2006; Myskiw, Izquierdo, & Furini, 2014).

SUMMARY AND CONCLUSIONS

Knowledge about the relationships between environmental events is encoded in memory as associations between and among the internal representations of these events. A positive contingency between a CS and a US can lead to an excitatory association, and a negative contingency can lead to an inhibitory association. Excitatory associations typically lead to the occurrence of CRs while simple inhibitory associations produce a reaction that is antagonistic to the excitatory CR.

The content of these associations can include representations of the sensory qualities of the CS and US, the temporal relationship between these events, and the hedonic qualities of the US. Individuals can learn two simple associations separately and later combine them (e.g., in sensory preconditioning and second-order conditioning). Individuals are also capable of encoding a hierarchical arrangement among events (as in occasion setting). Sometimes the context in which a US or a CS-US relationship is experienced can enter into associations or serve as an occasion setter.

Occasion setting occurs when there is a hierarchical arrangement in which the presence of an event (the occasion setter) signals a certain CS-US relationship (either a positive or negative contingency). The occasion setter does not enter into a direct association with the US, rather it controls the CR indirectly through the CS that is directly associated with the US. Occasion setting results in a second kind of conditioned inhibition, although we do not yet have a good understanding of the mechanism underlying it.

As revealed by post-extinction relapse phenomena (disinhibition, rapid reacquisition, spontaneous, reinstatement and renewal), extinction is a multifaceted process that involves new learning that is highly context dependent. The most complete explanation of extinction suggests that the context, acting as a negative occasion setter, signals the absence of the otherwise expected US.

Knowing that the knowledge obtained from Pavlovian conditioning involves internal representations of the events experienced does not tell us anything about the specific CR that occurs to the CS. In the next chapter we will review how the representations of the CS, the US, and the predictive relationship between them are related to the form and function of the CR.

STUDY QUESTIONS

1. What is the difference between declarative knowledge and procedural knowledge (see also Chapter 1)? Why do the experiments using post-conditioning devaluation of the US lead us to the conclusion that individuals encode the knowledge they obtain from experience with Pavlovian conditioning procedures as declarative knowledge?

2. What is transitive inference? Describe the procedures and phenomena called second-order conditioning and sensory preconditioning. How are these phenomena related to transitive inference? How are all of these related to the experiments using the post-conditioning devaluation of the US procedure?

3. What is a feature-positive discrimination? What is the difference between as imultaneous feature-positive discrimination and a serial feature-positive discrimination? What does it mean to say that a stimulus serves as an occasion setter? How is occasion setting related to serial feature-positive discriminations?

4. What is conditioned inhibition? Describe the different procedures that produce conditioned inhibition. What do all of these procedures have in common?

5. How do we test for conditioned inhibition? What evidence is there that there is more than one kind of inhibition? What are these

two types of conditioned inhibition, and how are they produced? How are these two types of conditioned inhibition represented in memory?

6. Describe how the environmental context can function as an occasion setter in Pavlovian conditioning.

7. What evidence leads us to conclude that individuals can represent in memory the temporal relationships between events?

8. Define reinstatement and renewal and explain what these phenomena tell us about extinction.

9. Describe the "negative occasion setter" account of extinction.

6

FROM KNOWLEDGE TO BEHAVIOR
The Forms and Functions of
Pavlovian Conditioned Responses

In the last two chapters, we explored the conditions under which individuals learn about the relationships between events in their environment and how that knowledge is represented in memory. The conclusions we drew about the conditions of learning and the resulting associative structures were based on the occurrence or nonoccurrence of a CR, but for the most part, the form of that response was not relevant to those conclusions. However, knowledge is not acquired for its own sake. The mechanisms involved in the processing and representation of the relationships between environmental events evolved because they have some influence on the behavior of the individual. Thus, Pavlovian conditioning involves more than the acquisition of knowledge about the environment; it also involves the translation of that knowledge into CRs. As we saw in Chapter 2, the CRs that emerge as a result of experience with a Pavlovian conditioning procedure depend on the CS, US, and species. In this chapter, we will explore the adaptive functions of Pavlovian conditioning and CRs.

CONDITIONED RESPONSES: DECIDING WHAT TO MEASURE

In any experiment, what the subjects are allowed to do and what the experimenter chooses to measure have a major impact on the results and the conclusions drawn from that experiment.

Following Pavlov, many experiments on Pavlovian conditioning involve experimenter-arranged relationships between arbitrarily selected events as the CSs and USs. By arranging a positive contingency between these events, the causal texture of events in the environment can be reproduced in the laboratory; however, what behavior is measured as the CR may not always reflect the richness of the behaviors generated by the CSs and USs employed or the adaptive functions of CRs in that type of situation. We can see this clearly when we compare Pavlov's work with later research on the effects of signals for food on the behavior of dogs.

Dogs Do More Than Salivate to Signals for Food

> When dogs are unrestrained and allowed to move about, they exhibit a variety of CRs to signals for food.

Using food as the US, Pavlov (1927) measured the amount of salivation that occurred in the presence of arbitrary stimulus events such as metronomes and black squares presented just prior to the food. His dogs were restrained and not free to move around (see Chapter 2, Figure 2.2), and his principle behavioral measure was the salivation evoked by the CS after a number of conditioning trials. Pavlov was not oblivious to the occurrence of other behaviors that occurred to the CS, but he only mentioned them in passing.[1] In two papers, he provided similar descriptions of a dog turning toward the CS (a flashing light) and licking the bulb that was within reach (Pavlov, 1932, 1934). In the 1934 paper, he also described a dog lowering its head as much as possible toward a sound that came from under the table on which the dog stood.

Pavlov never mentioned it, but Howard Liddell (see Lorenz, 1969) described an unpublished experiment he performed while working in Pavlov's laboratory. A dog that had been conditioned to salivate to an increase in the beat of a metronome was freed from its harness and allowed to move about. Lorenz provided the following description of Liddell's dog's behavior: "The dog at once ran to the machine, wagged its tail at it, tried to jump up to it, barked, and so on; in other words, it showed as clearly as possible the whole system of behavior patterns serving, in a number of *Canidae*, to beg food from a conspecific" (p. 47).[2] Lorenz used these observations to argue that conditioning involves an entire genetically programmed system, not just isolated behaviors. The reports of Pavlov and Liddell cited above are interesting, but other than the brief descriptions given above, no data were presented. Fortunately, there are a number of systematic studies of the behavior of dogs that lend support to Lorenz' conclusion.

Zener (1937) studied Pavlovian conditioning in dogs with a bell mounted on the wall 1.5 meters in front of the dog as the CS. Dog biscuits delivered into a food dish located directly beneath the dog's nose served as the US. The procedure was trace conditioning (see Chapter 2, Figure 2.3) in which the bell rang for 25 seconds followed by 15 seconds of silence before the food was delivered from a chute into the food dish. When the food arrived, the dogs seized it, raised their heads out of the food dish, and chewed it (the URs). Zener described a variety of CR patterns. The most typical patterns were: (1) orientation toward the bell followed by fixation on the food dish or the opening of the chute through which the food would be delivered, and (2) oscillation between the bell and the food dish. The dogs rarely exhibited chewing during the CS (although they did salivate to the CS). Zener likened the dog's behavior in the presence of the CS to "looking for, expecting, the fall of food with a readiness to perform the eating behavior which will occur when the food falls" (p. 393). Similar results were obtained by Wasserman (1978), who recorded both salivation and motor behavior in three dogs. His CS was illumination of a lighted panel located 14 cm above and slightly behind the food tray opening. After the CR was well

---

[1] In fairness to Pavlov, we should acknowledge that the objective of his investigations of conditioned reflexes was to answer the question of why the mere sight of food produces salivation (Pavlov, 1903/1955), not why other behaviors are also evoked by signals for food.

[2] A conspecific is a member of the same species.

established, Wasserman noted that all three dogs moved toward the lighted panel but did not make contact with it. Orientations and approaches to the light were intermixed with approaches to the food tray.

Jenkins, Barrera, Ireland, and Woodside (1978) monitored the movements of unrestrained dogs during Pavlovian conditioning within an enclosure that included a food dispenser on the top wall. Lights and speakers were mounted on the left and right walls equidistant from the food dispenser. The lights protruded into the enclosure (see Figure 6.1). On some trials (termed CS+), the speaker and light on the right side were activated for 10 seconds and followed immediately by the presentation of a small wiener from the food dispenser. On other trials (termed CS-), the speaker and light on the left side were activated, but no food was presented. Thus, the dogs had to learn from which side the light and sound signaled food. This procedure is called differential conditioning (see Chapter 5). The typical behavior of two dogs on a CS+ and a CS- trial are presented in Figure 6.2. Although the behavior of each dog was different, the overall pattern included approach to and sometimes contact with the CS+ followed by approach to the feeder. The behavior to the CS+ suggested soliciting for food. On CS- trials, the dogs also tended to approach the *inactive* CS+ and the feeder, although these behaviors did not appear to suggest anticipation of

Figure 6.1   Diagram of the apparatus in the Jenkins et al. (1978) experiment on CRs to signals for food in dogs. START indicates the location of the dog at the beginning of each trial, CS- and CS+ show the locations of the two CSs, and US indicates the location of the food dispenser.

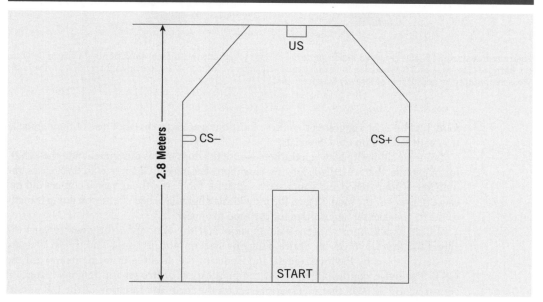

Figure redrawn from "Signal-centered action patterns of dogs in appetitive classical conditioning" by H. M. Jenkins, F. J. Barrera, C. Ireland, and B. Woodside in *Learning and Motivation,* Volume 9, 272–296, copyright © 1978 by Academic Press, reproduced by permission of Elsevier Science.

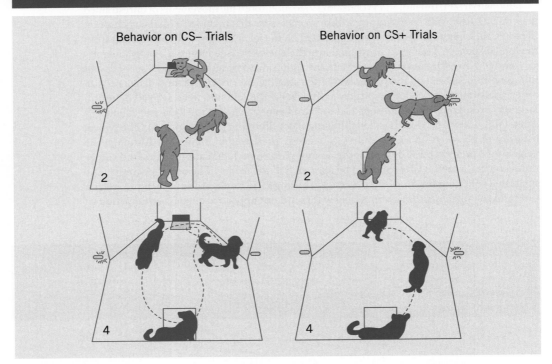

Figure 6.2 Typical behavior patterns of two dogs on CS- trials (left) and CS+ trials (right).

Behavior on CS– Trials

Behavior on CS+ Trials

Figure redrawn from "Signal-centered action patterns of dogs in appetitive classical conditioning" by H. M. Jenkins, F. J. Barrera, C. Ireland, and B. Woodside in *Learning and Motivation*, Volume 9, 272–296, copyright © 1978 by Academic Press, reproduced by permission of Elsevier Science.

food. Jenkins et al. suggested that these locations were attractive because of their association with feeding on the CS+ trials.

Note the similarity between the behavior of the dogs in this experiment and the behavior of pigeons that we called sign-tracking (autoshaping) in Chapter 2. In both cases, the individuals approached and contacted a signal for food even though such contact did not cause delivery of the food. In fact, the individuals might have been better off going directly to the food dispenser and waiting for the food to appear.

These data support Lorenz's conclusion that the actions of the dogs toward the signal for food involves an entire behavior system, not just an isolated CR. Despite the descriptions by Pavlov, Liddell, and Zener of the directed movements toward the CS in Pavlovian conditioning, it was the publication of Brown and Jenkins' paper on sign-tracking in 1968 that focused interest on the form and function of the CR and its relationship to both the CS and US (see Chapter 2). In turn, that led to an examination of the behavior systems that are activated by the US (Jenkins et al., 1978; Timberlake,

1983a; Timberlake & Grant, 1975; Timberlake & Lucas, 1989; Timberlake, Wahl, & King, 1982; Woodruff & Williams, 1976).

THE RELATIONSHIP BETWEEN CONDITIONED AND UNCONDITIONED RESPONSES

> Although Pavlov concluded that the CR was a UR elicited by the CS, we do not believe that today. The CR is a biologically pre-organized behavior pattern released by the CS in anticipation of the US.

Based on his observations of conditioned salivation, Pavlov (1927) came to the conclusion that by virtue of the relationship between the CS and US, the CS becomes a substitute or surrogate for the US; that is, the CS comes to evoke the UR. Even when he described the behavior of dogs orienting toward and licking the lamp, he interpreted this behavior as reflecting elements of the UR to food. For a long time, stimulus substitution was the dominant theory of Pavlovian conditioning (Mackintosh, 1974), and there is certainly much data consistent with it. The most compelling data comes from experiments on sign-tracking: Jenkins and Moore (1973) observed that pigeons' responses toward a localized signal depend on whether that signal predicts food or water (see Chapter 2, Figure 2.10), and Davey and Cleland (1982) observed rats biting a retractable lever when its insertion into the chamber predicted food and sniffing and licking the lever when it predicted a liquid.

On the other hand, the data described above from Jenkins et al. (1978), Liddell (Lorenz, 1969), Wasserman (1978), and Zener (1937) all indicate that the CS does *not* function merely as a substitute for the US. In each case, the dog's behavior toward the CS involved more than consummatory activities. In addition to these reports, there are numerous examples where CRs and URs bear little resemblance to each other. Some of that evidence will be reviewed in subsequent sections. Clearly, CRs are not versions of URs; rather, CRs reflect patterns of behavior that normally occur in the presence of signals for significant events (USs).

Jenkins et al. (1978) and Woodruff and Williams (1976) proposed the concept of **learned release** to characterize the function of the CS in Pavlovian conditioning; that is, *biologically pre-organized behavior patterns related to the US are released by signals for the US*. The behavior patterns that emerge as CRs reflect an underlying behavior system evoked by the US and the individual's motivational status. These behaviors are evoked in anticipation of the appearance of the US (Jenkins et al., 1978; Holland, 1984), and they prepare the individual to make contact with the US (Hollis, 1982; Woodruff & Williams, 1976).

Perhaps the clearest example of learned release in human behavior is seen in situations where people are in war zones. Our UR to a sudden intense loud noise (such as a gunshot, bomb, or mortar) is to hunch down with our arms drawn close to our body. This is a defensive reaction that minimizes being hurt. We do not think about doing that; it is a biologically pre-organized reaction, and we just do it. Because incoming rounds of bombs and mortars are typically preceded by a whistle, people adopt that same defensive reaction when they hear that whistle. This reaction is *released* by the signal for an incoming bomb or mortar round. Again, we do not think about it; we just do it.

BEHAVIOR SYSTEMS AND PAVLOVIAN CONDITIONING

> Pavlovian CRs depend on how individuals are programmed to behave to signals for biologically important events. This program, called a behavior system, involves innate and learned tendencies to react to certain stimuli in species-specific ways.

The concept of learned release described above requires that certain aspects of behavior reflect innate knowledge about what to look for or what to do first in certain situations. Without such knowledge, all stimuli would be equally salient and every individual would have to learn anew the simplest behaviors for finding food and mates and avoiding danger. Fortunately, that is not the case. We have reviewed a fair amount of evidence in this book to show that some things are more salient than others in certain situations and thus are more likely to be attended to as potential predictors. And we have just seen that the CRs we observe are relevant to the US in that situation. All of this reflects the fact that species come into the world equipped with a set of perceptual filters, behaviors, and in the case of more complex species central mechanisms to coordinate the inputs (stimuli) with the outputs (behaviors). We call this organization of input detectors and output mechanisms a behavior system.

Have you ever watched a cat when a small object is moving in the cat's visual field? If you have, you no doubt observed the cat orient toward that object, fixate on it, get into a crouching position, and perhaps lunge at it. This behavior pattern reflects the activation of the predatory behavior systems in cats.

A behavior system is *an interrelated set of perceptual mechanisms, central control mechanisms, and motor mechanisms organized around biologically important functions such as feeding, drinking, mating, defense, body care, social bonding, and care of young* (Baerends, 1976; J. A. Hogan, 1988, 1994; Timberlake, 1983a, 1994; Timberlake & Lucas, 1989). Individuals are predisposed by natural selection to perceive external events (stimuli), process these events, and behave in certain ways in response to the situation. Thus, behaviors generated by specific environmental events are organized to perform particular functions. Sometimes the same behavior may serve different functions in different systems. Which system is activated is determined by environmental events and motivational processes that prime specific behavior systems. In cats, the predatory behavior system is aroused by food deprivation and by small moving objects (even when cats are not hungry). A number of behavior systems have been identified in humans (see Box 6.1).

It is important to recognize that behavior systems are not static innate structures. Learning can occur at several points and at several levels within a behavior system and can influence the development of the various modules within the system. For example, J. A. Hogan (1971, 1973) demonstrated the role of experience in the feeding behavior of chicks, and Baerends-van Roon and Baerends (1979) described how cats learn that mice are food. Cats that are not taught by their mother to kill and eat mice will chase them and play with them, but they will not kill and eat them. Therefore, understanding the forms and functions of a CR requires knowledge of the components of the underlying behavior system.

BOX 6.1

Behavior Systems in Humans

Like the members of other species, humans possess a number of behavior systems organized around important biological functions that increase the likelihood of survival. According to Bowlby (1982), these systems govern the choice, activation, and termination of behaviors. Bowlby argued that these systems arose through natural selection to increase the likelihood of survival and were activated automatically by stimuli or situations (e.g., stimuli that might signal danger) that make a particular goal salient (need for protection) and are terminated by other stimuli that signal when the goal is reached. He identified the following behavior systems in humans: attachment, exploration, fear, and caregiving. Reviews of research on some of these behavior systems can be found in the book edited by Cassidy and Shaver (2008).

Attachment Behavior System. This system is activated in children by perceived threats and leads to a set of behaviors that are directed toward seeking proximity to individuals (e.g., parents) who can provide protection. According to Bowlby (1982), attachment in humans proceeds through a number of phases throughout an individual's life beginning in infancy when the helpless infant responds to a variety of social stimuli and over time direct their attachment behaviors toward specific individuals in their environment. As children grow older, the need for physical proximity is replaced by psychological proximity (feeling secure). In adolescence, attachment is transferred first to peers and then to romantic partners.

Exploratory Behavior System. The adaptive value of an exploratory behavior system for children is to promote the acquisition of knowledge about the environment to find food, overcome physical obstacles, and use tools to build things. The exploratory and attachment systems complement each other by providing children with both protection by maintaining proximity to attachment figures and allowing them to learn about their environments.

Fear Behavior System. Like the attachment behavior system, the function of the fear behavior system is to promote protection. Bowlby (1973) identified stimuli that are not inherently dangerous but can increase the likelihood of danger, like loud noises, darkness, sudden looming movements, and being alone, that activate this behavior system. Frightened children seek protection, and the presence of an attachment figure makes children less susceptible to fear. As we saw earlier, conditioned emotional responses in humans are relatively easy to produce to stimuli that natural selection has prepared us to consider dangerous (see Chapter 2). Bouton, Mineka, and Barlow (2001) reviewed evidence that points to the existence of a fear behavior system in humans.

Sociable Behavior System. In social species like humans, there appears to be a behavior system separate from the attachment system that leads individuals (not just children) to seek to be with other members of their own species, even with those they are not otherwise attached to. This behavior system also evolved as a means of protection because individuals in the company of others are less likely to be killed by predators.

Caregiving Behavior System. The adaptive function of the caregiving system is to protect

(Continued)

(Continued)

children and therefore increase the probability that one's genes will survive. Although both fathers and mothers participate in caregiving in humans, more research has been focused on mothers. In both humans and other mammals, maternal behaviors are triggered by the hormones involved in pregnancy and childbirth, and a great deal of evidence has been accumulated describing the differences between how human mothers and nonmothers react to newborn infants (see Fleming & Gonzalez, 2009; Olazábal et al., 2013a, 2013b for reviews). For example, human mothers are more attracted to newborn infant body odors than are non-mothers (This is also the case in other species; Numan, Fleming, & Levy, 2006). Human mothers can identify the garments worn by their own infants (in comparison to garments worn by unfamiliar infants) within

the first 20–40 hours after delivery, even when the delivery was by cesarean section and they had little or no experience with their babies prior to testing (Porter, Cernoch, & McLaughlin, 1983). Similarly, soon after delivery, human mothers are able to discriminate their own infants from other infants based on touching the back of the infant's hand (Kaitz, Lapidot, Bronner, & Eidelman, 1992). Most mothers can recognize the cries of their own infants (Formby, 1967), and they show greater sympathy in response to infant cries than nonmothers do (Stallings, Fleming, Corter, Worthman, & Steiner, 2001).

Although not all humans respond the same way to stimuli that activate these behavior systems, there exists an impressive body of research that point to their existence (Cassidy & Shaver, 2008).

The Organization of Behavior Systems

Behavior systems are organized in a hierarchical fashion around biologically important functions. Within each behavior system the particular behavioral module activated depends on the individual's motivational state, perception of stimulus events, and proximity to a goal or predator.

Behavior systems tend to be organized in a hierarchical fashion. Within the same individual there are a number of systems for processing information and guiding behavior relevant to a biologically important function (feeding, drinking, defense, mating, body care, care of young, etc.). Timberlake and Lucas (1989) described the behavioral system for feeding behavior in rats. They noted that rats feed by both scavenging for food and preying on insects and other small animals, and they suggested that the feeding system in rats includes subsystems for predation and scavenging (which they called "browsing"). Each of these two subsystems combines perceptual mechanisms, motivational states, and behavioral dispositions into a set of strategies for advancing the function of the overall system (feeding). Thus, the subsystem for predation organizes perceptual-motor structures for locating, capturing, and consuming moving prey while the browsing subsystem is organized to procure stationary food items. Each subsystem has different sensitivities to various stimuli, but they may share some common behavioral components. A system or subsystem can be aroused by both internal events (blood sugar levels, osmotic pressure, hormones, etc.) and/or external events (presence of prey or food, potential mates, predators, etc.).

Within each subsystem there may be a set of *modes* that link specific behavioral patterns or *modules* around a common purpose. For example, the search for food begins with a general search mode (see Figure 6.3). Within the predation subsystem, this mode includes behavioral modules that increase the probability that the individual will come in contact with prey. Once a potential prey is encountered, rats switch to a focal search mode in which they engage in behaviors that may lead to capture. Finally, contact with potential prey instigates the handle/consume mode that includes consummatory behaviors. The individual behavioral modules consist of the specific action patterns evoked by specific stimuli in the environment. Within the two subsystems of the feeding system, the active mode is determined by the proximity to the goal, and the shift from one mode to another depends on both spatial and temporal proximity to the goal (prey, in this example).

In addition to the system for feeding in rats described above (Timberlake, 1983a, 1994; Timberlake & Lucas, 1989), behavior systems have been proposed for nest provisioning behavior in digger wasps (Baerends, 1976), nesting behavior in herring gulls (Baerends, 1970), dust bathing in jungle fowl (J. A. Hogan, 1994; Vestergaard, Hogan, & Kruijt, 1990), feeding in chicks (J. A. Hogan, 1988, 1994), defense in rats (Davey, 1989; Fanselow, 1994; Fanselow & Lester, 1988), courtship in quail (Domjan, 1994), and, as previously noted, a variety of behaviors in humans (see Box 6.1). These behavior systems provide us with schematic representations of species-typical behaviors organized around biologically important functions like feeding, drinking, mating, and defense from predators. These schematic representations, which are based on systematic observations of behavior and experimental research, provide us with a framework for considering how behavior is organized to meet the demands of an individual's niche.

The CR that emerges from Pavlovian conditioning depends on the behavior system activated by the US, the physical characteristics of the CS in terms of its similarity to naturally occurring stimuli that elicit specific modules, and the temporal relationship of the CS to the US (Holland, 1984; Timberlake, 1994; Timberlake & Lucas, 1989). Thus, Pavlovian conditioning involves the modulation of otherwise organized behavior patterns (Holland, 1984; Jenkins et al., 1978; Woodruff & Williams, 1976).

Pavlovian Conditioning in the Predation Subsystem in Rats

> The CR depends on the characteristics of the CS (i.e., its resemblance to prey) and the temporal relationship of that CS to the presentation of food.

Predation begins with the general search mode that primarily involves the travel module to search for prey. Once a distally moving object (potential prey) is encountered, the rat shifts to the focal search mode that involves chasing and capture. Direct encounter with the prey produces the shift to the handling/consumption mode that involves testing and ingesting palatable items. Thus the particular mode and accompanying modules evoked depend on the presence of specific cues in the environment (see Figure 6.3).

Figure 6.3 Schematic depiction of the predation subsystem in rats that traces the sequence of behaviors that occur during the search for prey. The modules at the top are activated when the individual starts his or her search for prey, those in the middle are activated by the sight of prey, and those at the bottom are activated when prey is captured. Note the sequential pattern of behaviors. If the individual loses contact with the prey at any point in time, the behavior pattern will revert to a module that occurs earlier in the sequence.

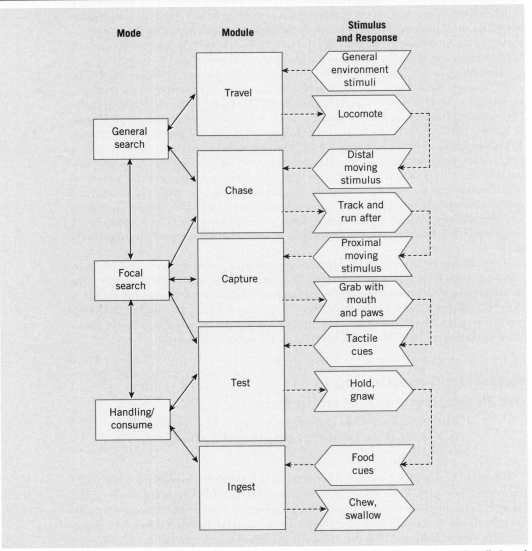

From Timberlake, 1994, Behavior systems, associationism, and Pavlovian conditioning. *Psychonomic Bulletin and Review*, 1, 405–420. With kind permission of Springer Science+Business Media.

Some species of rodents prey on insects and arthropods, and rats have been observed killing small vertebrates (Ewer, 1971; Timberlake & Washburne, 1989). Timberlake et al. (1982) provided evidence for a predation subsystem in rats by placing rats in a chamber into which a ball bearing (too big to swallow) was introduced at one end. The ball bearing rolled down a grooved channel and exited at the other side. When the exit of the ball bearing was followed by food, the rats increased their orientation, approach, and contact with the ball bearing. The typical pattern of behavior was to seize the ball bearing as it emerged into the box, stuff it into their mouth, carry it to the food tray, and then sit and turn it or gnaw it. Sometimes they would drop and retrieve it. When the ball bearing finally exited the chamber, they would move to the food tray (Timberlake, 1990; Timberlake & Lucas, 1989; Timberlake et al., 1982). Thus the CR to the ball bearing resembled the behaviors involved in the search for, and capture of, food in the predation subsystem.

In a second experiment, Timberlake et al. (1982) demonstrated that the duration of the interstimulus interval (ISI; time between the introduction of ball bearing and the presentation of food) affected the response to the ball bearing. When food was presented shortly after the ball bearing entered the chamber (1.6-second ISI), very little behavior was directed toward the ball bearing; instead, the rats tended to go directly to the food tray. When the food was delayed until after the bearing would have exited the chamber if the rats did not delay it (5.6-second ISI) or after the ball bearing *actually exited* (3.1-second ISI; as in their first experiment, described above), there was substantially more behavior directed toward the ball bearing (see Figure 6.4). Timberlake (1994) explained this in the following way: When the ISI is long, general search and some focal search behavior is the CR; that is, the rats treat the ball bearing as if it were prey—they chase, capture, and carry it before giving it up in favor of the food tray. However, when the ISI is short, handling/consumption behaviors are the most frequent CRs; that is, the ball bearing is used as a signal that food is close at hand, and the rats focused their behavior on the food tray. Thus, the behavior of the rats in this experiment reflects their learning of the predictive temporal relationship between the occurrence of the ball bearing and the food.

To demonstrate that the behaviors described above were part of a predation subsystem, Timberlake (1983b) compared the responses of rats to ball bearings that predicted food and that predicted water. Predatory behaviors are part of a feeding system not a drinking system; therefore, one would expect more interaction with a ball bearing that predicted food. That is what Timberlake found: Rats engaged in more contact and more carrying and chewing when the ball bearing signaled food. Boakes, Poli, Lockwood, and Goodall (1978) reported similar observations in an operant conditioning experiment in which rats had to obtain a ball bearing from one location and deliver it to another in order to earn food or water. The rats took longer to deliver the ball bearing when food was the reward, frequently chewing it before it was dropped. Their rats were never observed licking the ball bearing when water was the reward.

Although rats tend to be nocturnal creatures, they rely on vision as opposed to hearing to track prey; rats rarely track prey by using auditory cues (Ewer, 1971). Therefore, it is not surprising that while they approach visual signals for food, they will not approach a localized auditory signal for food; instead, they tend to direct their behavior toward the food magazine (Cleland & Davey, 1983; Harrison, 1979). Cats, on the other hand, are carnivorous predators that locate their prey through auditory signals. They readily approach a localized auditory stimulus predicting food, even

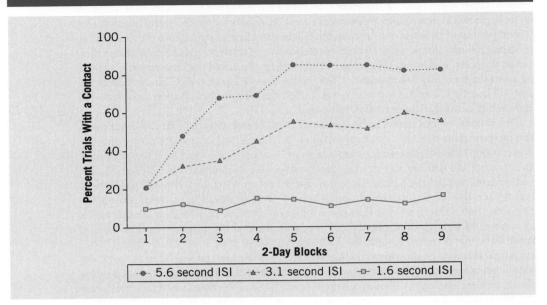

Figure 6.4 Mean percentage of trials with at least one contact with the ball bearing during two-day blocks of conditioning as a function of the duration of the ISI (time between ball bearing entry and food delivery).

From Timberlake, Wahl, and King, 1982. Stimulus and response contingencies in the misbehavior of rats. *Journal of Experimental Psychology: Animal Behavior Processes, 8*, 62–85. Copyright © 1989 by the American Psychological Association. Redrawn with permission.

when approach to the sound results in the loss of food (omission training procedure; Grastyan & Vereczkei, 1974).

Pavlovian Conditioning in the Social Module in the Feeding System in Rats

Some species of rats are social feeders; therefore, it is not surprising that the CR to the presentation of another rat signaling the availability of food is social behavior directed toward that rat.

Some species of rats feed in groups (see Galef, 1990, for a review). Timberlake and Grant (1975) and Timberlake (1983a) studied the CRs that are evoked in one rat by the presence of another rat predicting food. The basic design of their experiments was straightforward: Hungry rats were placed in a chamber that contained a food tray. One wall of this chamber was clear plastic which allowed for direct observation of the rat. The CS was always introduced into the chamber on a motorized platform through a door on the wall opposite from the food tray. When the CS was another rat, that rat was held on the platform by pipe cleaners so that it could not move off the platform. In the first experiment (Timberlake & Grant, 1975), the CS was either a rat or a rat-size block of wood. When the introduction of a live rat signaled food, the subject rat exhibited social behaviors (approach, sniffing the mouth and ano-genital area, and contact, including pawing, grooming, and crawling over the stimulus rat). A rat presented alone without food, a rat presented randomly with respect to food, and a block of wood that signaled food elicited orientation but little social behavior.

Lupfer, Egleston, and Frieman (2001) repeated Timberlake and Grant's (1975) procedure with a variety of stimuli serving as the CS: a live rat, an unscented block of wood, an unscented toy that looked like a rat, a block of wood that was put in the cage of the rat that served as the CS for 2 hours prior to training to acquire the scent of a rat, and a toy scented in the same way. After 15 conditioning trials, the most social behavior was exhibited toward the live rat, the scented toy, and the scented block of wood, in that order. The least social behavior was exhibited to the unscented wood. These results demonstrate that the social module in rats is activated by the odor of another rat. This is not surprising given that rats are nocturnal animals.

Galef (1978) and Galef and Clark (1972) studied how young rats learn food preferences from adults. Rats are omnivorous, and juvenile rats have little knowledge of appropriate foods and their locations. They gain this information by attending to the behavior of adults. Therefore one would predict that juvenile rats should make more social responses to adult rats that predict food than the other way around. That is what Timberlake (1983a) found when he systematically varied the age of the stimulus rat and the subject.

Finally, Timberlake (1983a) compared the behavior of rats to golden hamsters (*Mesocricetus auratus*) in this situation. Unlike rats, golden hamsters live alone for most of their lives (Rowell, 1961). Therefore, we should not be surprised that the behavior of golden hamsters toward a conspecific (a member of the same species) that predicts food is the opposite of rats: Instead of approaching the conspecific, the golden hamsters markedly decreased contact and remained at the food tray, often with their back to the stimulus hamster. On the other hand, golden hamsters would approach and contact a hamster-sized object that signaled food. This is in contrast to the behavior of dwarf hamsters (*Phodopus campbelli*), a social species of hamsters. These animals exhibited social behavior toward another dwarf hamster and little social behavior toward a block of wood (Lupfer et al., 2001).

Pavlovian Conditioning in the Browsing Subsystem

The other side of the feeding system involves searching for stationary food. In some species, the CR involves approach toward, and contact with, signals for food.

Browsing is the name given to the subsystem of the feeding system that is activated when individuals search for stationary food. In rats and pigeons, modules from that subsystem can be engaged by discrete, localized, stationary visual stimuli that precede the occurrence of food. In nature, both rats (Barnett, 1956, 1975; Ewer, 1971) and pigeons (Murton, 1971) approach and investigate small objects while searching for food. Therefore, it is not surprising that rats will approach and contact an illuminated or a retractable bar that is presented as a signal for food (Cleland & Davey, 1983; Davey & Cleland, 1982, 1984; Peterson et al., 1972) or a small light that protrudes into the chamber (Holland, 1980a). Likewise, pigeons will also approach and contact a discrete visual signal for food (Brown & Jenkins, 1968), but crows will not (Powell, Kelly, & Santisteban, 1975). Crows, unlike pigeons, are omnivorous and spend much of their time searching for large food items rather than pecking at small objects. The correspondence between the natural behavior of these species and their CRs to certain classes of stimuli is consistent with the behavior system approach to Pavlovian conditioning. These observations help explain the phenomenon of sign-tracking (autoshaping) in pigeons, rats, and dogs.

Conditioned Responses to Arbitrary Conditioned Stimuli Signaling Food

Most experiments on Pavlovian conditioning employ arbitrarily chosen stimuli that have little relationship to naturally occurring predictors of significant events. Nevertheless, systematic differences in the forms of CRs to different CSs may also reflect the activation of underlying behavior systems.

In the experiments described above, the CSs were either naturally occurring predictors of food (an adult rat) or stimuli that possessed characteristics of naturally occurring events (small moving objects, punctate visual stimuli), and the CRs to these stimulus events could be predicted from what we know of the natural behavior of the species under study. However, much of the research on Pavlovian conditioning in rats (and some other species) has involved arbitrarily chosen stimuli such as lights and sounds (tone or noise). How does this research fit into the behavior system analysis of Pavlovian conditioning?

In Chapter 5, we alluded to the fact that rats make different responses to visual and auditory CSs that signal food. Holland (1977) systematically investigated these CRs in a series of experiments. He used four different CSs (an 1800-Hz steady tone, a 250-Hz intermittent tone, a steady localized light, and an intermittent diffuse light) to signal food. Each CS was 10.5 seconds long, and food was delivered during the final half-second of the CS. All four CSs were presented twice on each day of training, and the behavior of the rats was videotaped. Holland observed that the visual CSs evoked CRs that involved primarily rearing and standing with their head in the food magazine. While auditory CSs evoked some magazine behavior, startle (rapid movement or jumping) and head jerks (short, rapid horizontal or vertical movements of the head) were the most frequent CRs. Rearing was more likely to occur to the localized light, and magazine behavior was more likely to occur to the diffuse light.

In another experiment reported in the same paper, Holland (1977) observed that rearing occurred most often when the light was localized above the cage. Furthermore, these four CRs tended to occur at different times during the CS. Startle and rearing occurred more often during the first 5 seconds of the 10-second tone and local light CSs respectively, while approach to the food magazine occurred more often during the last 5 seconds of the 10-second light CSs.

In subsequent experiments, Holland (1980a) reaffirmed that a localized visual CS evoked behaviors directed toward the CS while diffuse visual stimuli evoked behaviors toward the food magazine. A localized CS near the food magazine hopper evoked more CS-directed behavior but less magazine behavior than a localized CS placed farther from the place where food was obtained (Holland, 1980b). If the localized CS was a 3.5-cm diameter light that protruded into the cage, the rats would contact but not bite it (Holland, 1980b). Thus, Holland found that the stimulus modality, localizability, and location of visual stimuli all influenced the CR.

Certain aspects of these data suggest that the observed CRs may reflect rudimentary aspects of naturally occurring behaviors to the various CSs. For example, rearing tended to occur at the start of the visual CS, and it was most pronounced when that CS was localized above the cage or close to the food magazine. Furthermore, if the visual stimulus protruded into the cage, rats were likely to contact it. Thus, rearing looks more like a general search mode behavior and magazine approach more like a focal search mode behavior. On the other hand, the responses to the auditory stimuli look more like defensive behaviors than food-seeking behaviors: Startle was most evident at the beginning of the auditory CS. Furthermore, rearing rarely occurred to auditory CSs and startle rarely occurred to visual ones. Therefore, depending on the CS and its temporal relationship to the US, all or part of the relevant subsystem may be activated.

THE FUNCTIONS OF PAVLOVIAN CONDITIONED RESPONSES

Pavlovian CRs prepare individuals to optimize their interactions with forthcoming biologically important events. Pavlovian conditioning also changes the motivational significance and value of the signals for these events.

Hollis (1982, 1990, 1997) has argued that *the function of CRs is to enable the individual to optimize interactions with forthcoming biologically important events (food, predators, rivals, mates)*.[3] She called this function **prefiguring** because she viewed the CR as essentially preparatory; that is, it allows the individual to better deal with the significant events. She further argued that anticipatory responses to the stimuli that in the past reliably accompanied a significant event (US) provide a selective advantage over ignoring the signal and responding only to the presence of the US. Thus, Pavlovian conditioning involves more than just making causal inferences about the events that predict the presence or absence of the US—the ability to make anticipatory responses is the adaptive advantage that Pavlovian conditioning confers on those species that possess it.[4] Pavlov made a similar argument for the adaptive advantage

---

[3]Note the similarity of Hollis's position with an earlier one by Culler (1938): "The CR, in brief, is nature's way of getting ready for an important stimulus" (p. 136).

[4]One must be careful to distinguish between the adaptive uses of a trait and an adaptive advantage in terms of reproductive fitness. Although Hollis (1982) clearly wanted to argue for reproductive fitness, she recognized the dangers of doing so without direct evidence. Therefore, the ensuing discussion will focus on the adaptive *uses* of learning rather than adaptation in terms of reproductive fitness.

of anticipatory responding when he wrote, "It is pretty evident that under natural conditions the normal animal must respond not only to stimuli which themselves bring immediate benefit or harm, but also to other physical or chemical agencies—waves of sound, light, and the like—that in themselves only *signal* the approach of these stimuli; although it is not the sight and sound of the beast of prey which is in itself harmful to the smaller animal, but its teeth and claws" (1927, p. 14).

Defense Against Predators

The individual who can identify signals of impending danger and take evasive action has a greater chance of surviving and reproducing.

There are few species that do not have predators, and searching for food exposes individuals to the possibility of becoming someone else's meal. Therefore, it is not surprising that different species have evolved defensive strategies to avoid danger (Bolles, 1970; Edmunds, 1974). These defensive reactions are part of a behavior system that is evoked by the presence of danger (Fanselow & Lester, 1988).

Behavior Systems for Defense. Fanselow and Lester (1988) used the term **predatory imminence continuum** to describe *the relationship between the proximity of a predator to an individual and the behaviors that individual will engage in to avoid being the predator's next meal.* Various points along this continuum are characterized as pre-encounter, post-encounter, and circa-strike (contact with predator is occurring or inevitable). Pre-encounter defensive behaviors reflect behaviors designed to minimize risk of being preyed upon. Although no predator has been detected, there may be danger out there. Under these circumstances, individuals may organize their foraging for food to reduce opportunities to be detected, move about cautiously, and take other actions to minimize detection or danger.

Post-encounter defensive behaviors come into play when a predator is detected. These behaviors may involve freezing, fleeing, or some other defensive behavior. These are species-specific defense reactions (Bolles, 1970), and the behavior elicited depends on the situation and the species (Edmunds, 1974). Thus, rats and rabbits engage in what has been termed "flash behavior" which refers to a "flash of color" that occurs when animals with white backsides run away. Sometimes upon detection of a predator, the animal will run a short distance, and if the predator is not close, turn and freeze. The flash may startle the predator and induce chase, but the sudden disappearance of the distinctive object (which occurs when the prey turns and freezes) deceives the predator into believing that the prey has vanished. In the laboratory, rats have been observed to freeze when they receive shock in a distinctive box (Blanchard & Blanchard, 1969a). If the signal for that shock is localized, rats will turn and face it while they freeze (Karpicke, Christoph, Peterson, & Hearst, 1977). On the other hand, rats flee from a CS that is approaching them (Blanchard & Blanchard, 1969b); however, if the rats have had the opportunity to learn through exploration that there is no escape from the chamber, they freeze rather than flee from a moving predator (Blanchard, Fukunaga, & Blanchard, 1976). Finally, in the circa-strike mode, the individual may attempt to flee (if freezing), engage in threat displays, or turn and fight. Again, these behaviors depend on the species and the situation. Fanselow (1994) and Löw, Lang, Smith, and Bradley (2008) reviewed some of the physiological mechanisms that mediate the behavior system responsible for defense in rats.

Autonomic Nervous System Responses to Danger. In addition to the defensive behaviors described above, there are characteristic autonomic nervous system responses that prepare the individual to deal with danger, whether the defensive action is freezing, fleeing, or aggressive counteractions. These include increases in heart rate, blood pressure, respiration, and blood glucose to provide oxygenated and glucose rich blood to the muscles and brain for fleeing and aggressive counter measures. Interestingly, unlike fleeing, which is associated with heart rate acceleration (see, e.g., Perez-Cruet, Tolliver, Dunn, Marvin, & Brady, 1963), freezing is associated with heart rate deceleration (see, e.g., deToledo & Black, 1966). All of these autonomic responses can be elicited by CSs that predict dangerous events (Black, 1971).

In humans, the CR that occurs in fear conditioning situations depends on whether the CS is an arbitrarily chosen stimulus or a stimulus that natural selection has prepared us to consider as dangerous (e.g., snakes, spiders, and other crawling creatures). When the CS is an arbitrary stimulus, the CR is heart rate deceleration. On the other hand, when the CS is a slide of a snake, heart rate acceleration is observed (Cook, Hodes, & Lang, 1986).

Integrated Responses to Danger. Clearly, natural selection endows individuals with adaptive responses to those dangerous situations that their ancestors faced (Bolles, 1970). These behavior patterns are all part of the individual's defensive behavior system. Pavlovian conditioning provides a mechanism for individuals to anticipate danger and mobilize their resources to escape or avoid detection. Thus, signals for danger produce both autonomic nervous system and skeletal motor system effects that work together in tandem. Heart rate acceleration, increases in blood pressure and respiration, and release of glucose into the blood all are mobilized in the service of fleeing or fighting. On the other hand, freezing as a defense is based on avoiding detection, and the heart rate deceleration that accompanies it serves that purpose. The individual who can identify signals of impending danger and take evasive action has a greater chance of surviving and reproducing. It does not matter whether the signals come before or after the attack; natural selection provided a mechanism for individuals to make causal inferences about possible signals for danger based on a single instance (e.g., Hudson, 1950; Keith-Lucas & Guttman, 1975; Pinel et al., 1986). The bottom line is that Pavlovian conditioning shortens the reaction time for responding to a predator.

Defense of Territory

Anticipating the arrival of a rival or a raider provides an advantage to the defender.

Many species (including humans) establish and defend territories around structures in which they live, accumulate provisions, and attract mates. Like defensive reactions to danger, anticipation of an intruder should increase the owner's chances of successfully defending the territory. Hollis (1984) demonstrated this in the blue gourami, a small fish that inhabits shallow pools and streams in southeast Asia and Africa. Male gouramis establish a territory in which they construct a nest of tiny air bubbles held together with mucous. When an intruder enters a male's territory, the owner threatens the intruder by rapidly approaching with all fins erect (frontal display). If the intruder does not flee, fighting ensues until one fish is chased away. Females rarely mate with males who have not established territories; therefore, successful defense of a territory also should lead to reproductive success.

Hollis (1984) matched males on the basis of aggressive behavior and size. Training and testing occurred in an aquarium divided down the middle by both clear plastic and opaque plastic partitions. One member of each pair was given 15 Pavlovian conditioning trials on each of 24 days in which a 10-second light CS was followed by a 15 second presentation of a rival fish (the US) on the other side of the aquarium. That was accomplished by raising the opaque barrier, but no contact occurred because the clear plastic barrier was still in place. The other member of each pair received one of two control treatments (in each of two different experiments), either *explicitly unpaired* presentations of the CS and US (i.e., a negative contingency) or presentation of the US alone (termed *aggression only*). Following the different treatments, a fish receiving Pavlovian conditioning was paired with either a fish from the explicitly unpaired or the aggression only control groups. Each fish started on opposite sides of the opaque divider. The CS was presented, the divider lifted, and the fish were allowed to interact (see Figure 6.5). The Pavlovian conditioned fish (labeled Paired) approached the CS and exhibited frontal display; thus they started the interaction with their rivals (collectively labeled Control) with erect fins. The observed aggressive behaviors during encounters are presented in Figure 6.6. The fish in Group Paired always delivered more bites and tailbeats (rapid movement of the tail fin that pushes water with great force against the opponent). Hollis concluded that the CS served as a learned releaser of aggressive display that provided an advantage for the defender. This conclusion was supported in a subsequent experiment: Pavlovian-conditioned males who won their first encounter were also more likely to win subsequent encounters (Hollis, Dumas, Singh, & Fackelman, 1995).

Figure 6.5   Photograph of two male blue gourami fish fighting during the test that followed the Pavlovian training employed by Hollis (1984).

Photograph courtesy of Karen Hollis.

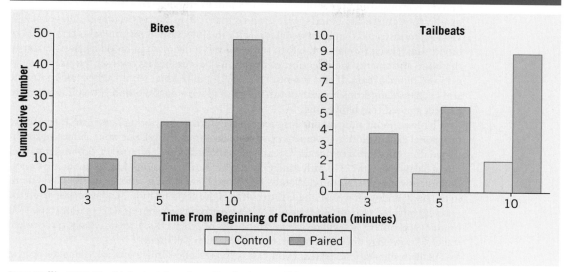

Figure 6.6 Mean cumulative number of bites (left panel) and tailbeats (right panel) of the test confrontation between fish given Pavlovian conditioning (Paired) and those given unpaired presentations of the CS and US or the US only (Control).

From Hollis, 1984. The biological function of Pavlovian conditioning. *Journal of Experimental Psychology: Animal Behavior Processes, 10,* 413–425. Copyright © 1984 by the American Psychological Association. Redrawn with permission.

Conditioned Drug Reactions

> Conditioned drug reactions that mirror the UR can be understood in terms of correcting an internal imbalance caused by administration of the drug, but not all drugs have these effects.

We reviewed some of the research on conditioned drug reactions in Chapter 2. In a few instances the CR was in the *same* direction as the UR (mimicking; Siegel, 1985). The most extreme example of mimicking is conditioned immunosuppression.[5] However, the most commonly reported conditioned drug effect is sometimes described as a **compensatory response;** that is, *the CR is opposite from the UR.* Sometimes that is referred to as mirroring (Siegel, 1985).

Hollis (1982) and Siegel and Allan (1998) have suggested that all conditioned drug reactions should be understood in the broader context of **homeostasis;** that is,

---

[5]It should be noted that there are some recent reports of conditioned immuno*enhancement* (i.e., a compensatory response) to stimuli that precede the administration of cyclophosphamide, the same drug used in the conditioned immuno*suppression* studies (Krank & MacQueen, 1988; MacQueen & Siegel, 1989). The reason for the difference is not obvious.

maintenance of the internal environment within tolerable limits. Homeostasis is a characteristic of living things. Both at the cellular and the system level, there are receptors that monitor the internal environment and take corrective action in response to imbalances. For example, there is an optimal level of glucose in the blood. If that level gets too low, hunger is aroused and the individual seeks food. In response to eating, the body secretes insulin to regulate the blood-sugar level so that it does not get too high. Siegel (1972, 1975) demonstrated that cues associated with the injection of insulin *increase* the level of blood sugar, even though the UR to the insulin is a decrease in blood sugar. Obviously, the body anticipates the injection of insulin by decreasing its own secretion of insulin into the bloodstream. If this did not happen, the individual would experience a drastic and perhaps dangerous lowering of the level of glucose in the blood. The CR appears to protect against that happening.

Thinking about anticipatory drug reactions in terms of restoring homeostasis provides a functional explanation for compensatory responses (mirroring), but what about the conditioned drug effects that mimic the UR and push the individual's internal environment further out of balance as is the case with conditioned immunosuppression? That is not an easy question to answer. As Ramsay and Woods (1997) noted, most drugs affect a number of systems in the body, and what we call the UR to a drug is the accumulation of adjustments from the different affected systems. Therefore, it is not surprising that some CRs resemble some URs (mimic) and other CRs will be the mirror image of other URs. Unfortunately, our present stage of knowledge does not allow us to predict which will occur.

Finally, it should be noted that in the cases of conditioned drug tolerance, taking the drug in a different situation can lead to death by drug overdose (Siegel, 1984), and conditioned immunosuppression reduces the body's ability to produce antibodies (Ader & Cohen, 1982). Both of these effects hardly seem adaptive. However, we need to recognize that the conditions under which these effects occur are artificial. In nature, the conditions under which chemical agents are ingested usually do not change. Drug overdoses to changes in context do occur outside the laboratory, but the ability to inject drugs only became possible with the invention of the hypodermic needle. Natural selection has had no opportunity to deal with it. Likewise, an injection of immunosuppressive drugs is not a naturally occurring event.

Conditioned Responses in Feeding Systems

The advantages of making various kinds of anticipatory responses to signals for food are reviewed.

As we saw above, feeding systems include both predation and searching for stationary sources of food. Within this system, Pavlovian CRs that range from single discrete responses involved in ingestion and digestion (such as salivation) to complex patterns of foraging behavior that include orientation, locomotion, and approach toward, and manipulation of, objects that predict the occurrence of food. If Hollis's (1984) analysis is correct, then we should be able to collect evidence that shows an advantage to making the CR.

Salivation and Other Digestive Responses. The secretion of saliva in response to the presence of food in the mouth provides lubrication for the passage of food into the digestive tract, and it is the first step in the series of chemical reactions involved in the conversion of food to energy (Pavlov, 1903/1955). Bykov (1959) noted that CSs for the occurrence of food elicit a number of other alimentary responses in addition to salivation: secretion of gastric and pancreatic juices and increases in stomach and intestinal motility. These effects increase the efficiency of the digestive process (Nicolaides, 1977). Thus anticipatory salivation (along with other anticipatory gastrointestinal responses) provides an advantage to the individual that possesses it.

Tracking Signals for Food (Sign-Tracking). In some species, modules of the browsing subsystem are activated by signals for food. Sometimes these modules involve approach toward the signal and perhaps contact. Which modules are activated depend on the similarity of the signal to naturally occurring releasers for these behaviors (Jenkins et al., 1978; Woodruff & Williams, 1976).[6] Thus, pigeons, dogs, and rats approach discrete visual signals for food (Brown & Jenkins, 1968; Jenkins et al., 1978; Peterson et al., 1972), whereas cats approach localized auditory signals (Grastyan & Vereczkei, 1974). Approach responses tend to involve general search and focal search subsystem behaviors whereas contact responses resemble those involved in handling/consumption. Therefore, it is not surprising that the form of the contact response in some cases resembles the consummatory response elicited by food (Jenkins & Moore, 1973).

Under some circumstances, sign-tracking appears to be maladaptive. Approach and contact with the signal result in the loss of food when the signal and food are spatially separated or when responses lead to the loss of food (omission training; Chapter 2). These situations rarely occur in nature; therefore, it is hardly surprising that individuals are *not* equipped to deal with them. We created these situations in the laboratory.

Finally, it should be noted that the response to signals for the absence of food is withdrawal (Hearst & Franklin, 1977; Wasserman et al., 1974). This is an efficient strategy in species like pigeons because it directs the individual away from an unproductive location and into a general search mode.

Food Consumption. Signals for the availability of food can also affect food consumption. For example, Zamble (1973) found that providing a signal for the availability of food in hungry rats increased food consumption by up to 20% over rats that received their meals unannounced at random times. These rats were maintained on a strict diet, and those that had their 30-minute access to food signaled by a 15-minute auditory or visual CS lost weight less rapidly than those that received their meal unannounced. Zamble, Baxter, and Baxter (1980) found similar effects with water in terms of amount consumed when the opportunity to drink was signaled. These data suggest that knowing when food will be available is advantageous, perhaps because it allows for the mobilization of the digestive mechanisms (see above) which makes digestion more efficient (Hollis, 1982).

Weingarten (1983) extended this finding to satiated rats. After exposing hungry rats to a 4.5-minute buzzer and light combination that signaled access to 8 ml of a liquid diet at various times during the day, he tested them while they had continuous access to the liquid diet. Presentation of the compound CS followed by the presentation of additional liquid

---

[6]These naturally occurring releasers can also be the product of learning (Hogan, 1971, 1973).

diet in a food cup elicited feeding even when the rats were satiated. In fact, they consumed 20% of their total daily intake of food in the 15 minutes following the presentation of the CS, even though they could eat at any time. Weingarten's data suggest that hunger can be aroused by signals of the impending availability of food. This is advantageous when food is not always plentiful (as it was during the training phase of this experiment).

Changing Value and Preference Through Pavlovian Conditioning

Conditioned taste aversions and preferences reflect changes in individuals' evaluations of a given food; that is, how much they like or dislike it. Therefore, a second function of Pavlovian conditioning is to change individuals' affective evaluations of things they encounter.

Many species possess innate preferences and aversions to certain tastes (see Barker et al., 1977; Capaldi & Powley, 1990), and they exhibit characteristic orofacial responses to those substances they prefer and those they dislike (Grill & Norgren, 1978a).[7] There is also ample evidence that individuals learn to prefer foods that provide nutritional benefits (Holman, 1975; Sclafani, 1990) and avoid foods that have toxic effects (Garcia & Koelling, 1966; Revusky & Garcia, 1970).

Conditioned Taste Aversions (CTAs). When consumption of food is followed by gastrointestinal illness, individuals develop an aversion to the taste of that food; that is, they not only reject it, they also make the same orofacial responses that they make to unpleasant tasting foods (Berridge, 2000; Steiner et al., 2001). Furthermore, in some species, even the sight of such foods can lead to avoidance. Sometimes the CR to foods that have been followed by illness can include rather dramatic changes in behavior. For example, Gustavson, Kelly, Sweeney, and Garcia (1976) fed wolves mutton laced with LiCl wrapped in raw sheep hide. After recovery from one exposure to mutton laced with LiCl, the wolves charged at sheep but released them after one bite. For the next half hour, the roles of the prey and predator changed: The sheep became dominant and charged the wolves, who withdrew and behaved in a submissive fashion.

Conditioned Taste Preferences. The other side of diet selection is taste preference. Here too, natural selection has provided both innate knowledge and a mechanism for learning. The taste of foods with high caloric content like sugars, starches, and fats tend to be preferred, but individuals require a learning mechanism for dietary selection when the variety of foods in their diets exceeds the limits of their innate knowledge. Like CTAs, the mechanism for conditioned taste preferences appears to be based on the postingestional consequences of consumption (Sclafani, 1990, 2004).

The basic experimental procedure for demonstrating conditioned taste preferences is to give individuals a high-calorie meal with a distinctive taste and a low-calorie meal with a different distinctive taste (see, e.g., Bolles, Hayward, & Crandall,

---

[7]These responses are described in Chapter 2 and Chapter 5.

1981). The test for conditioned preference is to observe how much of the distinctive tastes are consumed over the course of training and when the individual is confronted with both tastes at the same time. The typical finding is that individuals prefer the taste paired with or leading to the higher calorie diet. Capaldi, Campbell, Sheffer, and Bradford (1987) demonstrated that the greater the caloric value of the meal, the greater the preference for the taste paired with it. Like CTAs, conditioned taste preferences readily occur in humans (see, e.g., Baeyens, Crombez, Hendrickx, & Eelen, 1995; Baeyens, Eelen, Van den Bergh, & Crombez, 1990; Zellner, Rozin, Aron, & Kulish, 1983).

A Closer Look at Pavlovian Conditioning and Diet Selection. Clearly, taste aversions and preferences can be produced by Pavlovian conditioning procedures. However, when we look closely at the behavior of individuals who have experienced illness after eating, we observe that their reaction to that food has changed in a very interesting way: They act as if they do not like it anymore (Garcia, Clarke, & Hankins, 1973). It is *not* that the taste of that food has become a signal for illness (if I eat that I will get sick), rather that food has become less palatable to the individual (Arthurs, Lin, Amodeo, & Reilly, 2012; Garcia, Rusiniak, & Brett, 1977; for a recent review, see Lin, Arthurs & Reilly, 2014). A similar thing appears to happen with food preferences; that is, the positive effects of consuming a certain food may lead to an increase in preference for that food (Rozin & Zellner, 1985). These changes in palatability and preference as a result of a Pavlovian conditioning procedure are examples of evaluative conditioning.

Evaluative Conditioning. Affective evaluations of events in our environment in terms of dimensions such as like/dislike, good/bad, pleasant/unpleasant, and so on occur in all species, even the most primitive. In humans these affective evaluative reactions appear to be immediate and irresistible (Zajonc, 1980, 1984). The term **evaluative conditioning** was coined by Levey and Martin (1975) to *describe changes in the affective evaluative reaction to an event (the CS) that results from that event being presented in close temporal proximity to another event (the US). The result is a shift in the evaluation of the CS in the direction of the evaluation of the US.*

Levey and Martin's (1975) experiment serves as a prototype of the procedure. They presented their human subjects with 50 picture postcards of unfamiliar paintings selected to evoke a wide variety of subjective reactions. Subjects sorted these into three groups: liked, disliked, and neutral. For each subject, Levey and Martin selected the two most liked, the two least liked, and four evaluated as neutral and paired them as follows: neutral-liked, neutral-disliked, neutral-neutral, disliked-neutral, liked-neutral. Each pair was then presented to the subjects a number of times in a counterbalanced arrangement. Finally each subject sorted all cards into two categories (liked and disliked), arranged the cards within each category in order of preference, and assigned each a value between −100 and +100. Levey and Martin found changes in the ratings of the neutral pictures: The average rating for the neutral pictures paired with liked pictures became more positive and the average rating for the neutral pictures paired with disliked pictures became more negative.

Similar results have been found using photographs of faces (Baeyens, Eelen, & Van den Bergh, 1990; Baeyens, Eelen, Crombez, & Van den Bergh, 1992), photographs of faces paired with adjectives (Baeyens, Eelen, Van den Bergh, & Crombez, 1992), photographs paired with odors (Todrank, Byrnes, Wrzesniewski, & Rozin, 1995), nonsense syllables and national names paired with evaluative words (e.g., gift, sacred, happy, bitter, ugly, failure; Staats & Staats, 1957, 1958), toothpaste brand names paired with scenic photographs (Stuart, Shimp, & Engle, 1987), writing pen colors paired with music (Gorn, 1982), sounds from various sources (e.g., animals, music, nature, human nonverbal vocalizations, machines) paired with words that have positive or negative affective values (Bolders, Band, & Stallen, 2012), and the sound of a person's voice depending on the content of what the person says (Bliss-Moreau, Owren, & Barrett, 2010). See Allen and Shimp (1990), Cohen (1990), and Schachtman, Walker, and Fowler (2011) for reviews of research on evaluative conditioning in advertising.

Clearly, the procedures used to produce evaluative conditioning are Pavlovian: Two events occur in some relationship to each other. What is different here is that oftentimes the US is not a biologically significant event. Rather, the US is, for example, a photograph or a word that has some established meaning. Viewed from this perspective, such types of evaluative conditioning may be restricted to humans and, in instances where the meaning of the US was previously acquired, may be thought of as second-order conditioning (see Chapter 2).

In some ways evaluative conditioning is similar to other forms of Pavlovian conditioning, but in other ways it is different. It is similar in that one can use sensory preconditioning (Chapter 5) to produce evaluative conditioning (Hammerl & Grabitz, 1996; Walther, 2002), and post-conditioning devaluation of the US (Chapter 5) modifies earlier produced conditioned evaluations (Baeyens, Eelen, Van den Bergh, & Crombez, 1992; Walther, Gawronski, Blank, & Langer, 2009), and both the CS-preexposure (Chapter 4; De Houwer, Baeyens, Vansteenwegen, & Eelen, 2000; Stuart et al., 1987) and US-preexposure (Chapter 4; Hammerl, Bloch, & Silverthorne, 1997) effects have been obtained.

On the other hand, some of the phenomena observed in other Pavlovian conditioning situations have thus far not been observed with evaluative conditioning procedures. For example, Baeyens, Crombez, De Houwer, and Eelen (1996) could not make color an occasion-setter for a flavor-flavor association, and Campbell, Capaldi, Sheffer, and Bradford (1988) could not establish the context as an occasion-setter for flavor preferences in rats.

Conflicting results have been obtained with respect to extinction of evaluative conditioning and whether awareness of the contingency between the two events is necessary for evaluative conditioning to occur. Although there have been a number of studies that failed to show extinction of evaluative conditioning (e.g., Baeyens, Crombez, Van den Bergh, & Eelen, 1988; Blechert, Michael, Williams, Purkis, & Wilhelm, 2008; De Houwer et al., 2000; Diaz, Ruiz, & Baeyens, 2005; Hermans, Crombez, Vansteenwegen, Baeyens, & Eelen, 2003; Kerkhof et al., 2009; Vansteenwegen, Francken, Vervliet, De Clercq, & Eelen, 2006), there are a few reports where the effects of evaluative conditioning were reduced, but not completely eliminated, by an extinction procedure (e.g., Lipp, Mallan, Libera, & Tan, 2010; Lipp, Oughton, & LeLievre, 2003). Likewise, while evaluative conditioning has been observed when the participants could not describe the contingency between the two events (e.g., Baeyens, Eelen, & Van den Bergh, 1990; Dickinson & Brown, 2007; Walther & Nagengast, 2006), there have been reports of evaluative conditioning occurring only when participants became aware of the contingency between the paired events (Pleyers, Corneille, Luminet, & Yzerbyt, 2007; Stahl

& Unkelback, 2009; Stahl, Unkelbach, & Corneille, 2009). It is not clear why these differences are observed.

In a series of papers, Levey and Martin (1975, 1983; Martin & Levey, 1978, 1985, 1987, 1994) laid out what they saw as the differences between evaluative conditioning and causal inference in Pavlovian conditioning: All individuals evaluate their surroundings in terms of what is beneficial and harmful, and some likes and dislikes are based on innate knowledge as a result of natural selection in a given niche. These evaluative responses to events an individual encounters need not operate at a conscious level and may involve minimal processing. Evaluative conditioning provides a way to learn what is good or bad, pleasant or unpleasant, and so on. It is an immediate type of learning in which affective value of the CS is altered, and there really is no CR per se. What is changed by the evaluative conditioning experience is the individual's evaluation or preference for things (for reviews, see De Houwer, 2011; Field, 2005).

On the other hand, individuals also need knowledge about where and when food, water, mates, and predators are likely to occur, and Pavlovian conditioning provides a way to learn about predictive relationships between events. Causal inference is the process through which individuals organize and represent experienced relationships. Because this requires some degree of cognitive processing, evaluative conditioning is seen as the more basic or primitive form of Pavlovian conditioning.

Baeyens, Eelen, Van den Bergh, and Crombez (1992) carried this argument one step further and argued that Pavlovian conditioning involves two different functional systems. The more primitive system affects an individual's likes and dislikes; that is, the CS activates a representation of the US and nothing more, and no expectations about the occurrence of the US are generated. This would account for the extinction procedures that either do not affect evaluative conditioning or may reduce but do not eliminate evaluation conditioning effects and why occasion-setting does not occur with evaluative conditioning. Because the CS activates a representation of the US, evaluative conditioning is affected by post-conditioning devaluation of the US.

The other system involves causal inferences. This system allows individuals to detect reliable predictors of significant events (USs) and to take actions to prepare for the arrival of these events. Furthermore, this system is sensitive to the CS-US contingency such that changes in contingency (such as a shift to the procedure of extinction) are detected and the behavior of the individual changes. Finally, the context in which a CS-US relationship is detected is important because that CS-US relationship may be context specific.

Conditioned Emotional Reactions

A third function of Pavlovian conditioning is to change the emotional and motivational significance of objects and events in the environment that predict biologically significant events. This produces conditioned emotional reactions to these events.

Watson and Rayner (1920) demonstrated that emotional states could be aroused by previously neutral stimuli that precede aversive events. Fear, the conditioned emotional state evoked by danger or a signal for impending danger is an intervening variable; that is, it is not directly observable and must be inferred from behavior (see Chapter 2). The inference that Albert became afraid of the white rat was based on Albert's crying and withdrawing from it. Both of these behaviors are part of the defensive behavior system in humans: Crying is a distress signal that alerts parents and others that the defenseless child may be in danger, and withdrawal from a signal for danger is an evasive tactic. Clearly, it is possible to explain Albert's behavior in terms of species-specific defense reactions to danger and pain (Bolles, 1970; Fanselow & Lester, 1988) without invoking intervening variables like fear; nevertheless, there is evidence to suggest that one of the effects of Pavlovian conditioning is to change the motivational significance of the CS.

Mowrer (1960) presented a classification of motivational and emotional states generated by positive and negative contingencies between CSs for **appetitive events** (*things individuals will work to obtain*) and **aversive events** (*things individuals will seek to avoid*).[8] As shown in the upper left cell of Table 6.1, the CS signals the occurrence of an appetitive US (such as food). Mowrer labeled the conditioned emotional state aroused by this CS as *hope*. In the lower left cell, the CS signals the occurrence of an aversive US (such as shock). Mowrer labeled the conditioned emotional response as *fear*. In the upper right cell, the CS signals a negative contingency between the CS and an appetitive US. Mowrer labeled the conditioned emotional state here as *disappointment* because the appetitive US is more likely to occur in the *absence* of the CS than in its presence. Finally, the lower right cell is labeled *relief* because the CS signals the absence of the aversive event. Although these names are commonly used in everyday discourse to describe human emotions, they do capture the positive and negative aspects of these four Pavlovian conditioning preparations. The argument that Pavlovian conditioning affects the motivational significance of the CS as Mowrer suggests is based on two kinds of data: approach toward and withdrawal from CSs that signal these relationships, and the effects of these CSs on ongoing behavior.

Table 6.1 Motivational and Emotional States Generated by Positive and Negative Contingencies With CSs for USs That Are Either Appetitive or Aversive

US	Contingency	
	Positive (CS → US)	Negative (CS → no US)
Appetitive	Hope	Disappointment
Aversive	Fear	Relief

---

[8]Konorski (1967) provided a similar analysis, but he did not use the colloquial terms employed by Mowrer.

Approach and Avoidance as Measures of Motivational Significance. We have reviewed a number of instances when individuals have been observed to approach signals that are positively correlated with food (see, e.g., Brown & Jenkins, 1968; Grastyan & Vereczkei, 1974; Jenkins et al., 1978; Wasserman et al., 1974) and withdraw from signals that are negatively correlated with food (Wasserman et al., 1974). These reactions reflect Mowrer's (1960) conditioned *hope* and *disappointment*. There is also evidence that individuals will approach signals that are negatively correlated with shock (LeClerc, 1985) and withdraw from signals positively correlated with shock (Green & Rachlin, 1977). These reflect Mowrer's conditioned *relief* and *fear*. In all of these cases, the CRs parallel the URs to valued objects (such as food, water, sexual partners) and danger, and the URs to the absence of food and the absence of danger.

The Effects of Pavlovian CSs on Ongoing Operant Behavior. The second line of evidence that Pavlovian conditioning affects the motivational significance of CSs involves the effects of presenting a Pavlovian CS to individuals while they are engaging in behavior directed toward procuring food or avoidance of danger. Rescorla (1966) demonstrated that the effects of a Pavlovian CS presented to dogs while they were avoiding shock (which presumably is motivated by fear) depends on the CS-US relationship. When the CS signaled shock (aroused fear) avoidance behavior increased, but when the CS signaled the absence of shock, avoidance responding decreased (see Chapter 3, Figure 3.1). We also have seen that a CS signaling shock leads to conditioned suppression of behavior involved in procuring food (conditioned suppression). Thus, when the motivation for the ongoing behavior and the motivation aroused by the CS are consistent, the ongoing behavior may be enhanced. But when the motivation for the ongoing behavior and the motivation aroused by the CS are antagonistic (e.g., fear and hope or fear and relief), the ongoing behavior may be disrupted.

PAVLOVIAN CONDITIONING AS AN ADAPTIVE SPECIALIZATION

Although Pavlovian conditioning has been observed across the animal kingdom, there are differences both within and across species in terms of the speed and content of learning. These differences reflect the accumulation of adaptive specializations that evolved through natural selection.

The mechanisms underlying Pavlovian conditioning evolved because they allow individuals to acquire knowledge about the relationships between events in their environment. These include precursors of important events such as food, danger, and the presence of receptive mates.

In simple species, the ability to learn about relationships between events tends to be highly specialized (Davey, 1989; Sahley, 1984). Paramecia can learn to withdraw when vibrations are followed by electric shock (Hennessey, Rucker, & McDiarmid, 1979), the terrestrial mollusc *Limax maximus* exhibits a range of Pavlovian conditioning phenomena (such as overshadowing and blocking) with odors and the tastes of foods (Sahley, Martin, & Gelperin, 1990; Sahley, Rudy, & Gelperin, 1981), and honeybees readily learn to associate specific odors, colors, and geometric patterns with sucrose (Giurfa & Sandoz, 2012; Heinrich, 1984). In some cases, the limited range of stimuli about which these individuals can learn reflects their sensory capacities. In other cases (e.g., honeybees), this appears to reflect inherited predispositions.

In more complex species, the range of stimuli that can be used as CSs is much wider, and it is easier to demonstrate CRs to arbitrarily chosen stimuli and events (such as salivation to the sound of a metronome, withdrawal from tactile stimuli that precede electric shock). Unlike the highly specialized forms of Pavlovian conditioning, this general process learning ability *allows individuals to learn about relationships that may not have existed during the evolution of the species.* Under some conditions, general process learning can be very rapid as in one-trial backward conditioning with shock (Chapter 3). However, general process learning typically requires more trials than specializations like CTAs. This protects the individual from making CRs to every stimulus that occurs with food, predators, mates, or other important events. Repeated trials allow individuals to learn which of the myriad of stimuli in their environments consistently predicts the US.

The adaptive value of Pavlovian conditioning in terms of increased reproductive fitness has been demonstrated in two different species. Hollis, Pharr, Dumas, Britton, and Field (1997) found that blue gouramis given Pavlovian conditioning in which an intruder is signaled produced significantly more offspring than those not conditioned. Similarly, Domjan, Blesbois, and Williams (1998) gave male Japanese quail Pavlovian conditioning in which the CS was a distinctive chamber and the US was the opportunity to copulate with a receptive female in that chamber. After six conditioning trials, these males released greater volumes of semen and greater volumes of spermatozoa when placed in that chamber than males that had not received the conditioning (for a review, see Domjan & Akins, 2011).

General process learning does not replace highly specialized adaptations: Rats learn in one trial to avoid the taste rather than the visual aspects of foods that are followed by gastric distress. It takes many more trials for rats to avoid tastes that are followed by electric shock, but they can learn this (Garcia, Kovner, & Green, 1970). Similarly, it is harder to train rats to avoid a distinctive compartment where they received x-rays (and became ill) than to avoid the taste of food that precedes irradiation, but they can learn about the compartment with enough training trials (Garcia, Kimeldorf, & Hunt, 1961). Pigeons form conditioned emotional responses more readily to auditory stimuli than to visual stimuli (LoLordo, 1979).

Humans, perhaps more than any other species, reflect a full range of learning mechanisms. Although we humans obtain much of the knowledge we possess about the relationships between events in our environment through verbal communication with each other, we still retain the ability to learn about these same relationships through Pavlovian conditioning (see McLaren, Forrest, McLaren, Jones, Aitken, & Mackintosh, 2014, for a review). We possess mechanisms for both highly specialized and general process learning. In the case of CTAs, we rapidly learn to avoid tastes that are followed by illness. The rapidity with which conditioned emotional responses (such as fear) can be produced in humans depends on the CS: Conditioning is more rapid when the CS is a snake or a spider than when it is a circle or a triangle (Marks, 1987; Öhman & Hugdahl, 1979). On the other hand, with arbitrary CSs like circles and triangles, verbal instructions about the CS-US relationship facilitates the acquisition of the CR, and instructions that the US will no longer occur facilitates the extinction of the response. Instructions do not have that effect when the CS is a snake or spider. Furthermore, instructions may facilitate the acquisition of conditioned emotional responses, but instructions have little effect on the extinction of the response (Öhman & Hugdahl, 1979). In general, verbal information about the CS-US relationship has a greater effect with arbitrary CS-US combinations than with those that were encountered in our ancestors' ecological niche, and with arbitrarily chosen CSs, humans will exhibit a CR only when they have become consciously aware of the relationship between the CS and US (Dawson, Catania, Schell, & Griggs, 1979).

Thus, it appears that Pavlovian conditioning reflects at least two different systems: One system is more primitive, automatic, noncognitive, and highly specialized. For example, patients receiving chemotherapy know that it is the chemotherapy and not what they eat that makes them nauseous, yet they still develop CTAs (Bernstein, 1991). This system may also underlie evaluative conditioning. The other system involves the processing of information about the relationships between events (Baeyens, Eelen, Van den Bergh, & Crombez, 1992; Dawson & Schell, 1987; Levey & Martin, 1983; Razran, 1955). CTAs and conditioned drug effects reflect the first system, while general process Pavlovian conditioning (in which individuals can learn about the relationships between arbitrarily chosen events) appears to reflect the second level. Many forms of Pavlovian conditioning reflect both (Siegel & Allan, 1998).

General process learning mechanisms make use of the predictive relationships between events in an individual's niche, and the resulting inferences are in the form of expectations about what events are related to or predict other events. How individuals act on this information is also the result of natural selection. When the information is closely tied to important biological events, aspects of the relevant behavior systems are evoked as CRs, and these CRs are more often than not appropriate to the expectation of the significant event (Holland, 1984).

The accumulated evidence points to the conclusion that both within the same individual and across different species, the occurrence and ease with which Pavlovian conditioning phenomena can be produced reflects an interaction between the species and the events involved. It appears that the ability to learn about the relationship between events first evolved as a specialized adaptation for learning about specific events. This is what we see in species that possess simple nervous systems (such as honeybees). Species with more complex nervous systems exhibit a wide range of Pavlovian conditioning phenomena, from the highly specialized CTAs to the more general emotional response conditioning with arbitrarily chosen CSs. But even when individuals can learn about the relationship between arbitrarily chosen events, conditioning may be more rapid and more durable with some CSs than with others. In humans, verbal information and cognitive awareness can affect general process Pavlovian conditioning with arbitrarily chosen events. This does not mean that the processes and mechanisms underlying the various forms of Pavlovian conditioning in humans and other species are different; these differences may reflect the accumulation of adaptive specializations both within and across species.

SUMMARY AND CONCLUSIONS

The mechanisms underlying Pavlovian conditioning evolved because they allow individuals to acquire knowledge about the precursors (CSs) of biologically important events such as food, danger, and the presence of receptive mates (USs). One important function of the CR is to enable individuals to optimize interactions with the impending biologically important event. A given CR reflects learned knowledge of the predictive relationship, the behavior system activated in that situation, and the characteristics of the CS. Behavior systems consist of an interrelated set of perceptual, central control, and motor mechanisms organized around a biological function. The characteristics of the stimulus or event that serves as the CS and the temporal arrangement of that event with the US affect which modules in the behavior system are evoked. Thus, the CR reflects an interaction between the experimental arrangement and the species.

Another function of Pavlovian conditioning is to change the individual's evaluation of events along some affective dimension (good/bad, like/dislike,

etc.). This is reflected when we observe conditioned taste aversions and preferences, and in evaluative conditioning in humans.

A third function of Pavlovian conditioning is to change the motivational significance of the CS. This produces two consequences. First, it will affect whether an individual will approach or avoid that stimulus. Second, the presence of that stimulus can energize or interfere with ongoing behavior.

Thus, the study of Pavlovian conditioning reveals adaptive mechanisms that allow individuals to evaluate events and adjust their behavior in response to signals for impending events. These mechanisms include the ability to perceive, encode, and remember the relationships between events and response mechanisms (in the form of behavior systems) selected to deal with conditions within the individual's evolutionary niche. Pavlovian conditioning is an adaptive specialization designed to deal with the universal aspects of all niches (Anokhin, 1974) and the specific problems that require immediate solutions (such as aversions to tainted foods).

STUDY QUESTIONS

1. What evidence leads us to the conclusion that what the subjects are allowed to do and what the experimenter chooses to measure have a major impact on the results and the conclusions drawn from that experiment?

2. What is the relationship between conditioned and unconditioned responses? How is this explained by the concept of conditioned release (and what is conditioned release)?

3. What is a behavior system, and how are behavior systems related to Pavlovian conditioning? Give an example to illustrate this.

4. What are the functions of Pavlovian conditioned responses in

   a. feeding?

   b. defense against predators?

c. defense of territory?

d. conditioned drug reactions?

e. learning of preferences and aversions?

f. conditioned emotional reactions?

Give an example in each domain.

5. How are invertebrates and vertebrates alike and different with respect to Pavlovian conditioning? How are humans like other vertebrates with respect to Pavlovian conditioning? How are we different from other vertebrates?

6. What does it mean to say that Pavlovian conditioning is an adaptive specialization?

PART II

LEARNING ABOUT THE CONSEQUENCES OF ONE'S BEHAVIOR

7

THE PROCEDURES AND PHENOMENA WE CALL OPERANT CONDITIONING

The research reviewed in the previous six chapters supports the conclusion that the mechanisms underlying Pavlovian conditioning are adaptive specializations that provide individuals with the ability to identify and learn about relationships between events in their environment. Furthermore, when one of these events is a predictor for the occurrence of a biologically significant event such as food, water, a predator, or a mate, conditioned responses (CRs) may be elicited by that predictor. These CRs are part of a behavior system organized around the biologically significant event, and the forms of these CRs depend on the predictor (the CS), the significant event (the US), and the temporal relationship between them. In most situations, the CR optimizes the individual's interaction with the significant event, either by increasing the chances of contacting appetitive events (food, water, mates), reducing contact with predators, or providing anticipatory adjustments to the impending US.

The major limitation of Pavlovian conditioning as an adaptive specialization is that it does not provide a mechanism for the individual to adjust his or her behavior to the immediate outcomes of that behavior. Rather dramatic examples of this limitation were provided by Williams and Williams (1969) and Jenkins (1973) who found that the occurrence of the Pavlovian CR when pigeons pecked a key that signaled the presentation of food (sign-tracking) persisted when pecking led to the loss of that food (see Chapter 2). This does not mean that sign-tracking is not an adaptive specialization or that key pecking is never influenced by its outcomes. Most of the time sign-tracking leads individuals to food. It is in the laboratory that we separate the food from the signal or create situations where approaching a signal for food is counterproductive for obtaining that food.

The ability to learn about the relationship between behaviors and outcomes underlies the phenomena we call **instrumental learning** *and operant conditioning.*[1] Although Pavlovian

---

[1]Hilgard and Marquis (1940) introduced the term **instrumental conditioning** to refer to *those procedures where the learned behavior was "instrumental" in bringing about the occurrence of the consequence.* Skinner (1937, 1938) introduced the term **operant** to designate *behaviors that act or "operate" upon the environment to produce certain effects.* At one time, the terms instrumental learning and instrumental conditioning were reserved for studies of learning in mazes and other apparatuses in which the subjects had to move from one location to another to obtain a reward or to escape aversive stimulation. The term operant conditioning was used for those procedures in which an individual performed some action in a specified location to obtain a reward or avoid aversive stimulation. Today, many people use these terms interchangeably. In this book, the term operant conditioning will be used to designate behavior-outcome procedures in general, but studies of learning in mazes will still be referred to as instrumental learning.

conditioning allows individuals to identify the relationships between and among environmental events and make anticipatory adjustments, *operant conditioning and instrumental learning allow individuals to use the outcomes of their behavior to become more efficient in their search for desired objects and for avoiding and escaping from danger in a given situation*. Although we separate Pavlovian conditioning from operant conditioning for the purpose of understanding them, they are in fact intertwined: The declarative knowledge about events in the environment obtained from Pavlovian conditioning guides individuals in their search, and the resulting Pavlovian CRs sometimes provide the behaviors that eventually are molded by operant conditioning and instrumental learning into efficient actions. All situations in which operant conditioning occurs include elements of the Pavlovian conditioning procedure.

In these next six chapters, we will review the basic procedures and phenomena that are called instrumental learning and operant conditioning and the psychological processes we believe underlie them.

PROCEDURES, PHENOMENA, AND PROCESSES

As we saw with Pavlovian conditioning, it is important to distinguish between procedures, phenomena, and processes. Operant conditioning is a procedure (something we do to individuals) and a phenomenon (a change in behavior after experiencing the procedure). The underlying processes provide the link between the procedures and phenomena.

In previous chapters, we described the procedure of Pavlovian conditioning in terms of the predictive relationship between two events. Although both events can be neutral (i.e., not biologically significant) as in the case of sensory preconditioning (see Chapter 5), typically there is a signal (the CS) that predicts the presence (through a positive contingency) or absence (through a negative contingency) of an important event (the US). Although the behavior of the individual is not directly involved in the predictive relationship between events in Pavlovian conditioning, that behavior is an integral part of operant conditioning.

The **procedure of operant conditioning** *involves three things: (1) an environmental context, (2) a behavior in that context, and (3) an event (outcome[2]) that follows that behavior.* The behavior can be any action the individual is capable of making (e.g., pressing a lever, pecking a key, saying a specific word or phrase), or it can be the absence of that action (e.g., *not* lever pressing, key pecking, or saying that word or phrase). Likewise, the outcome can be either the *presentation or the removal of something the individual seeks* (such as food, money, approval, or safety) or the *presentation or removal of something the individual finds unpleasant* (such as shock, loss of reward or privileges, or a reprimand). *Those things an individual seeks* are sometimes referred to as **appetitive** events, and *those things the individual finds unpleasant and seeks to avoid* are referred to as **aversive** events. Whether something is appetitive or aversive depends on the individual and the situation in which the event occurs. Because individuals experience outcomes for their behavior in some contexts or situations and not others, they learn where certain behaviors have specific outcomes. These three things

---

[2]In the literature, outcomes are also termed *reinforcers, consequences* or *rewards.*

(situation/context, behavior, and outcome) comprise the procedure of operant conditioning. Simply stated, the **procedure of operant conditioning** involves *the presentation of an outcome when the individual engages in a designated behavior or behavior pattern in a given situation or context.*

The **phenomenon of operant conditioning** *is the observed change in behavior after an individual experiences the procedure of operant conditioning;* that is, *when behaviors followed by some events (such as food, money, approval, safety) are more likely to occur again, or behaviors followed by other events (such as shock, reprimands, loss of privileges) are less likely to occur again.* The terms "more likely" and "less likely" refer to the occurrences of the behavior in question after experiencing the procedure.

As was the case with Pavlovian conditioning, we also refer to the theoretical **mechanism** or **process** we believe is responsible for the observed changes in behavior as instrumental learning and operant conditioning. We believe that a similar inference process underlies both Pavlovian conditioning and operant conditioning. The data relevant to that conclusion will be presented in subsequent chapters. For the moment, we will focus on the various procedures and phenomena that are called operant conditioning (and instrumental learning).

An Example of Operant Conditioning From Ancient Times

The practical applications of instrumental learning (operant conditioning) have been known since ancient times. It is only in the last 100 years that these procedures have been studied in a systematic manner.

Turnbull (1961, p. 4) recounted the following story about the merchant and mathematician Thales (640–550 B.C.E.) of Miletus (Greece): Once Thales was responsible for delivering sacks of salt. The salt was put into sacks and conveyed to its destination on the back of a pack of mules. One of the mules slipped while crossing a river. As a result, the load was lightened because salt dissolves in water. At the next crossing, the mule submerged itself and continued to do this at each subsequent river crossing. Thales put a stop to this behavior by filling the mule's sacks with sponges.

This story about Thales and his mules illustrates the essential aspect of operant conditioning, namely that the outcomes of a behavior can influence future occurrences of that behavior. Because the outcome of submerging in water produced a lighter load, the mule continued to perform that action at every river crossing. However, when Thales substituted sponges for salt, the outcome of submerging was a heavier load, and because the mule was punished for submerging, it stopped doing that. In both cases, the outcome of the behavior influenced the future occurrence of that behavior.

The First Laboratory Experiments on Instrumental Learning

The first laboratory experiments on instrumental conditioning occurred around the same time that Pavlov was performing his experiments on salivary conditioning.

As we saw from the story about Thales, the fact that some behaviors can be influenced by their outcomes has been known for a long time; however, it was only 100 years ago that psychologists began the standardized laboratory study of what we now call operant conditioning (and instrumental learning). Before that time, published reports of how outcomes influenced behavior consisted primarily of casual and anecdotal accounts of "intelligent" behavior in animals and of descriptions of how animals were trained to perform various feats (see, e.g., Morgan, 1894; Romanes, 1882). The story about Thales's mule is illustrative of these anecdotal accounts.

Although the laboratory study of instrumental learning in the United States began around the same time that Pavlov performed his first studies of conditioned salivary reflexes in Russia, these two lines of work appear to have been carried out independently. The first English publication of Pavlov's research was the text of a lecture he delivered in England on October 1, 1906 and published in the November 1906 issue of the journal *Science*. In 1909, Yerkes and Morgulis published a systematic review of the work in Pavlov's laboratory to that point. However, it was not until the publication of *Conditioned Reflexes* in 1927 that Pavlov's work received serious attention in the United States (Hilgard & Marquis, 1940).

The Problem Box. Edward L. Thorndike (1874–1949) is generally credited with the first published laboratory experiments on instrumental learning.[3] In his 1898 monograph, Thorndike described a series of experiments conducted on hungry kittens and dogs. The animals were placed in boxes *from* which they could escape and obtain food by manipulating something within the box. A drawing of one such box is presented in Figure 7.1. Thorndike tested his animals in a variety of such boxes. In some, the door could be released by pulling a wire loop attached to a string located in various parts of the box, in others by stepping on a treadle on the floor, and in others by manipulating a knob or button on the door. (See Thorndike, 1898, 1911, for detailed descriptions of all of his boxes.) On each trial, the animal was placed in the box and the time to perform the required action to escape was measured. With repeated experience, the time to escape from the box decreased across successive trials. The data from five of Thorndike's cats in Box A are presented in Figure 7.2. Based on the data he collected in these experiments, Thorndike concluded that his cats showed little insight into the nature of the escape mechanism during their attempts to escape from these boxes. He argued instead that the reduction in time it took the cats to escape represented the gradual formation of stimulus-response (or S-R) associations between the box and the behaviors that resulted in escape from the box and access to the food. Thorndike posited that these associations were "strengthened" or "stamped in" by the resulting "pleasure" of being released from confinement and obtaining the food (see Box 7.1). In 1901, Thorndike referred to this form of learning as "learning by trial and accidental success."[4]

---

[3]Thorndike's place in the study of instrumental learning is based primarily on the impact of his work on others; however, he was not the first person to study what we now recognize as instrumental learning in the laboratory. Lubbock (1882) reported experiments with problem boxes and mazes for studying learning and sensory processes in insects.

[4]D. K. Adams (1929) repeated Thorndike's experiments with cats, using replicas of Thorndike's boxes. Based on his observations, Adams concluded that cats are capable of more intelligent behavior than Thorndike attributed to them.

Figure 7.1 Thorndike's Box A. The bolt holding the door closed was attached to the string that ran over the pulley above the door and into the box. Inside the box, the end of the string was tied to a wire loop that hung down in front of the door (not visible in the picture). By clawing, biting, or otherwise pulling the loop downward, the animal could raise the bolt and open the door. The string attached to the front of the door was tied to a weight so that the door would open outward when the bolt was raised.

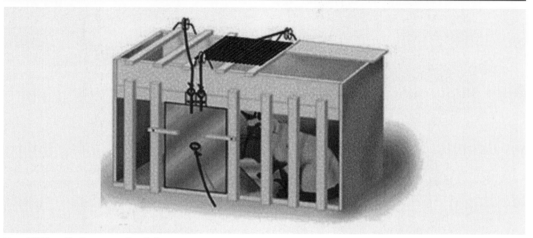

From Wikimedia Commons/Jacob Sussman.

Figure 7.2 Results from Thorndike's experiment with Box A. The vertical axis (not shown in his figures) is the time to escape. For example, cat 12 took 160 seconds to escape on trial 1 and 30 seconds to escape on trial 2. Each data point (moving horizontally from left to right) represents a successive trial. The average time to escape each trial for the five cats is given at the lower right.

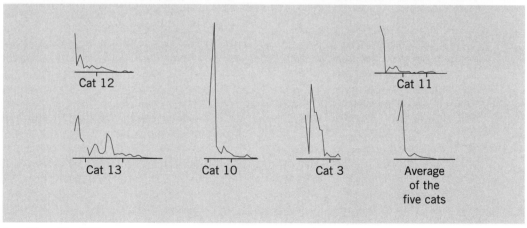

From Thorndike, 1911.

Thorndike's Description of Cats Escaping From a Problem Box

In this excerpt from his 1898 paper (reprinted in 1911), Thorndike first describes the typical behaviors he observed when he placed his cats in his problem boxes and then explains why he believes that learning involves the gradual formation of associations between the stimulus situation and the correct response:

> The behavior of all but [cats] 11 and 13 was practically the same. When put into the box the cat would show evident signs of 'discomfort and of an impulse to escape from confinement. It tries to squeeze through any opening; it claws and bites at the bars or wire; it thrusts its paws out through any opening and claws at everything it reaches; it continues its efforts when it strikes anything loose and shaky; it may claw at things within the box. It does not pay very much attention to the food outside, but seems simply to strive instinctively to escape from confinement. The vigor with which it struggles is extraordinary. For eight or ten minutes it will claw and bite and squeeze incessantly. With 13, an old cat, and 11, an uncommonly sluggish cat, the behavior was different. They did not struggle vigorously or continually. On some occasions they did not even struggle at all. It was therefore necessary to let them out of some box a few times, feeding them each time. After they thus associate climbing out of the box with getting food, they will try to get out whenever put in. They do not, even then, struggle so vigorously or get so excited as the rest. In either case, whether the impulse to struggle be due to an instinctive reaction to confinement or to an association, it is likely to succeed in letting the cat out of the box. The cat that is clawing all over the box in her impulsive struggle will probably claw the string or loop or button so as to open the door. And gradually all the other nonsuccessful impulses will be stamped out and the particular impulse leading to the successful act will be stamped in by the resulting pleasure, until, after many trials, the cat will, when put in the box, immediately claw the button or loop in a definite way.

> The starting point for the formation of any association in these cases, then, is the set of instinctive activities which are aroused when a cat feels discomfort in the box either because of confinement or a desire for food. This discomfort, plus the sense-impression of a surrounding, confining wall, expresses itself, prior to any experience, in squeezings, clawings, bitings, etc. From among these movements one is selected by success. But this is the starting point only in the case of the first box experienced. After that the cat has associated with the feeling of confinement certain impulses which have led to success more than others and are thereby strengthened. A cat that has learned to escape from A by clawing has, when put into C or G, a greater tendency to claw at things than it instinctively had at the start, and a less tendency to squeeze through holes. A very pleasant form of this decrease in instinctive impulses was noticed in the gradual cessation of howling and mewing. However, the useless instinctive impulses die out slowly, and often play an important part even after the cat has

BOX 7.1

had experience with six or eight boxes. And what is important in our previous statement, namely, that the activity of an animal when first put into a new box is not directed by any appreciation of that box's character, but by certain general impulses to act, is not affected by this modification. Most of this activity is determined by heredity; some of it, by previous experience.

From Thorndike, 1911, pp. 35–37.

About the same time, and independently of Thorndike's studies, Kline (1899a, 1899b) and Small (1900) performed experiments in which rats were required to either gnaw or dig their way *into* a box (depending on the box). One such box is depicted in Figure 7.3. Kline observed that over successive trials (one trial per day) the time it took the animals to dig into the box decreased from 1.5 hours to 3 minutes. Despite the historical significance of the problem box for the study of learning in animals, it fell into disuse.

Figure 7.3   Problem box used by Kline (1899a, 1899b) and Small (1900) to study learning in rats. Food was placed inside the box, and the rats could gain access through a section cut out of the floor by digging through the sawdust piled around the bottom.

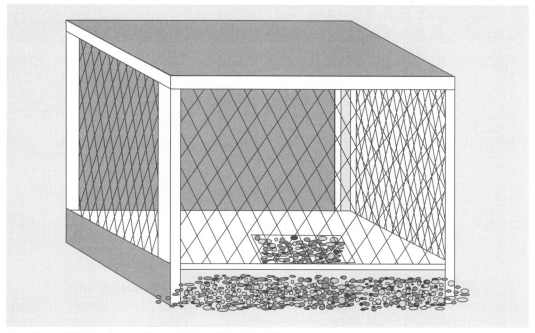

From Munn, 1950. Reprinted with permission of Peter Fernald.

These early experiments by Thorndike and Small reflected two different approaches: Thorndike developed the problem box to minimize the "helping hand of instinct" (1911, p. 30). Small, on the other hand, developed his problem box and maze so as "not to interfere with the natural instincts and predilections of the animal" (1900, p. 131). In both cases, the subjects were required to perform complex series of behaviors to reach the goal. Although the operant conditioning chamber invented by Skinner shares some features with problem boxes, Skinner's apparatus did not evolve from either Thorndike's or Kline's boxes.

The Development of Mazes to Study Learning. In his 1898 paper, Thorndike also described a set of experiments with chicks, from 2–8 days old, escaping from mazes he constructed from books set on end. On each trial, a chick was placed in the maze. Its task was to find the path to the exit that led to food and other chicks. Over the course of repeated trials, the time to successfully escape from each maze decreased.

In 1901, Small published the first paper on rats finding food in a maze. Small's maze looks like a maze. Patterned after a diagram of the Hampton Court Maze (a labyrinth constructed of hedges for humans to traverse), Small's maze was 6 feet by 8 feet and contained numerous blind alleys (Figure 7.4). Food was placed in the center of the maze, and the rats' task was to find the path from the outer opening to the center. Small trained his rats in pairs and carefully noted the times it took them to traverse the maze to the food and the number of errors they made on each trial. Over repeated trials, both the time and the number of errors tended to decrease to the point that the rats would find the food rapidly and with few or no errors.

Figure 7.4   Drawing of Small's Hampton Court–style maze.

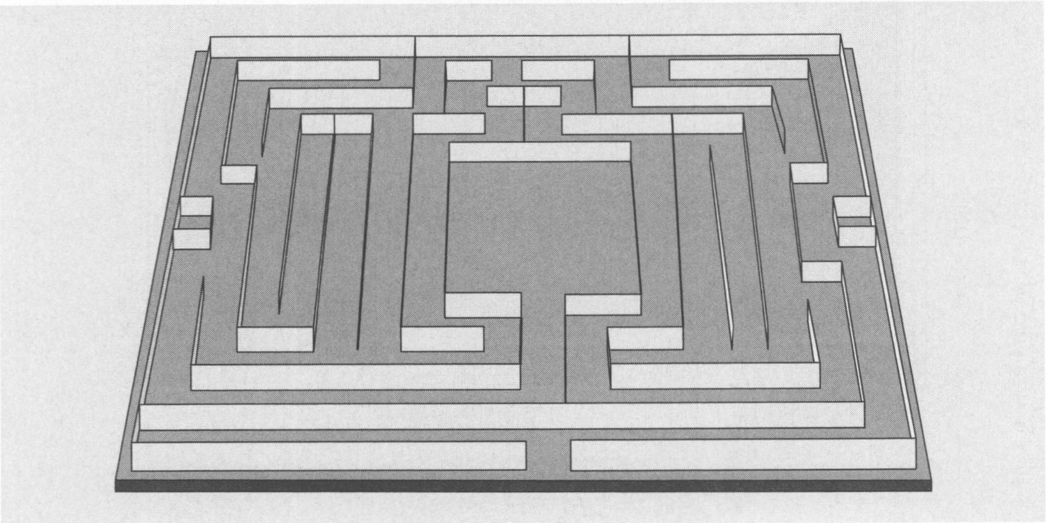

From **Munn, 1950.** Reprinted with permission of Peter Fernald.

The mazes constructed by Small (1901) became the inspiration for an enormous amount of research on the ability of rats and other animals to find food or escape to a safe place (see Box 7.2). Over time, mazes were adapted to study various aspects of instrumental learning, and some of these phenomena will be described in subsequent chapters. Although mazes are still used in some contemporary research, for the most part, the apparatus developed by Skinner has come to dominate the study of learning about outcomes.

BOX 7.2

A Short History of the Development of Mazes for the Study of Learning

In 1927, Warner and Warden published a paper titled "The Development of a Standardized Animal Maze." In this paper, they listed every published study using mazes to that time. The following excerpt contains their review of the historical development of the maze to study learning. Keep in mind that this review only goes to 1927, but it is apparent that by that early date there were a wide variety of mazes employed to study learning in a number of species.

The idea of the maze is very old—at least as old as the ancient catacombs. A number of maze patterns are described in the Encyclopedia Britannica under the heading of labyrinth. These were for the most part garden mazes constructed of shrubbery—quite popular in the later Middle Ages, and devised for the entertainment of human subjects.

The Y-shaped labyrinth, first employed it appears by Sir John Lubbock in 1882 in his study of ants, was used by him as a discrimination apparatus and not as a maze. The device was used to test the ability of ants to follow the trail of an ant that had previously traveled over one or another segment of the Y. In 1899 a somewhat similar labyrinth was used by Kline in the investigation of the discrimination capacity of the wasp.

The first labyrinths actually employed as mazes seem to have been the rather informal constructions used by Thorndike in 1898 on chicks. Books, standing on end, were used to form extremely simple patterns. The following year this writer used a maze, in the study of fishes, of the general type which we have chosen to call the compartment maze. This type has not been used much since, and as a matter of fact, exerted little influence on later maze construction.

The next year Small introduced the well-known Hampton Court maze, patterned after the famous parkway of England, modifying it only in so far as necessary in order to make it rectilinear. This pattern was widely used on a great variety of animal forms during the following decade and continued to be employed occasionally until 1915, at which time it appears to have been entirely displaced in America, at any rate, by other patterns. Small must be given the credit for or making the first maze study on a mammalian form, for

(Continued)

(Continued)

introducing the maze as a workable apparatus into the animal laboratory, and for first directing attention to the possibilities of the maze method in the infrahuman field. The influence of the Hampton Court maze still survives in various types of complex square mazes which are clearly modifications of this original pattern.

The development of the simple maze for the study of the lower forms beginning about 1901 by Yerkes marks the next genuine advance. Naturally the Hampton Court pattern was much too complex for crayfish and the like. The simple mazes developed by Yerkes, and especially the T pattern first used in 1912 on the earthworm are still widely employed.

Vincent appears to have been the first to use a wall-less maze, although Turner only a year later (1913) devised an ingenious maze for the cockroach along somewhat similar lines.

In 1914 a description of the Watson circular maze appeared. This type represented a great advance over the Hampton Court maze and soon began to displace the latter—at least in several laboratories. One advantage lay in the fact that the partitions could be easily shifted and thus different patterns, of varying degrees of difficulty arranged. It was in general much more uniform from section to section than the older maze, and with the camera lucida attachment permitted the taking of data without direct observation of the animal, thus eliminating a common source of error in the maze method....

In 1917 Carr developed a square maze in the Chicago laboratory. Like the Watson circular maze the Carr square maze represented a great advance over the Hampton Court type and aided in displacing the latter. The new maze had culs-de-sac more uniform in length and more uniformly distributed along the pathway. The partitions consisted of sliding metal panels by the manipulation of which a great variety of patterns could easily be arranged. Incidentally this year was a notable one in a number of maze studies published—a total of 28 patterns being employed in 17 experiments, if we include the alternation problem first studied by Carr during the year....

It is interesting to note the variety of animal forms that have been studied by the maze method. The white rat, of course, has been most often employed especially in the more systematic experimental work. If birds of all sorts are thrown together—hens, doves, pigeons, and songsters—this group take second place. Other rodents than the rat, including the mouse, guinea pig, squirrel and porcupine, have been used occasionally. The carnivorous group are represented by one study on the dog and two on the cat. Only two investigations of the monkey by this method have been reported to date. Of the Artiodactyls only sheep have been tested. The work of Yerkes on the turtle must stand for the reptilia while the amphibia are represented

B. F. SKINNER AND OPERANT CONDITIONING

Although Thorndike deserves the honor of being the first person to systematically study the effects of the outcomes of a behavior on the future occurrence of that behavior, many of our current procedures reflect the work of B. F. Skinner. It is fair to say that Skinner's contribution to the study of operant conditioning and instrumental learning is as important as Pavlov's contribution to the study of Pavlovian conditioning.

B. F. Skinner (1904–1990) is the person who has had the greatest impact on the study of instrumental learning and operant conditioning. Most of the language we use to describe the procedures and phenomena of operant conditioning can be directly attributed to Skinner. Although he borrowed a number of terms from others, in his hands these terms became the standard language for describing operant conditioning and instrumental learning.

The Evolution of Skinner's Methods for Studying Operant Conditioning

This brief historical sketch traces the development of Skinner's methods for studying operant conditioning.

Skinner's methods and approach to the study of operant conditioning grew out of his attempt to apply the language of reflexes to behavior in general. In the early decades of the twentieth century, many psychologists followed Pavlov and described behavior in terms of unconditioned and conditioned reflexes. Skinner's initial work involved an attempt to find a quantitative way to relate the level of motivation (hunger) to behavior, specifically to what he called the eating reflex (Skinner, 1930, 1932a, 1932b). At that time, eating was conceptualized as a "series of reflex acts by means of which an animal seizes, chews, and swallows its food" (Skinner, 1930). This series of reflexes was thought to be elicited by olfactory, visual, or tactile stimuli related to the food. Skinner's concern was with the fact that these stimuli do not always evoke eating, and he noted that eating occurs only when the individual is deprived of food. He set out to measure the strength of the "eating reflex" and to relate it to food deprivation. His method was simple yet elegant, and he devised an apparatus that allowed him to continuously monitor eating behavior in rats. His rats stood on a platform and obtained food from the well in the floor. To gain access to the food, the rats had to push a door that blocked access to the food. The door was hinged at the top, and an electrical circuit was completed each time the rat pushed the door to gain access to the food. With this apparatus, he could continuously monitor the eating behavior of an individual rat across time.

To track the eating behavior of his subjects, Skinner devised what has come to be called a **cumulative recorder**, and the records he obtained are called **cumulative records**. *In a cumulative record, the total number of behaviors that have occurred to that point in time is plotted against time* (Figure 7.5). The cumulative recorder creates this record by having a piece of paper move slowly in the direction of the arrows. Each instance of a behavior (e.g., opening the door) causes the recording pen to move one step perpendicular to the direction of the paper. With this arrangement, the *rate* of behavior as a function of time can be graphically depicted: *A shallow slope indicates that the individual is responding slowly (a), a steep slope indicates rapid responding (b), and a horizontal line indicates no recorded behavior (c).* Skinner (1932a) provided a typical cumulative record from one rat in his feeding apparatus (see Figure 7.6). Note that at the start of the session, the rat obtained food pellets at a high rate. Over the course of the 2.5-hour session, the rate at which the rat pushed the door open to get a pellet of food gradually declined. About 1 hour 45 minutes into the session, the rat stopped eating for 20 minutes and then began again, first at a high rate and again gradually more slowly.

Figure 7.5 Cumulative recorder. See text for details of its operation.

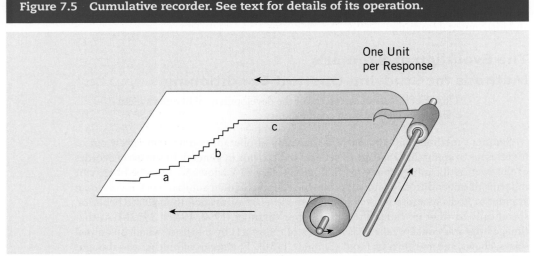

From *Learning: Behavior and Cognition*, 2nd edition, by D. A. Lieberman © 1993. Reprinted with permission of Wadsworth, a division of Cengage Learning.

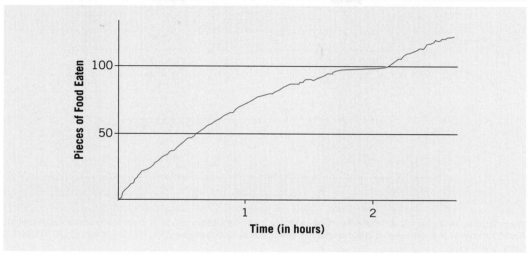

Figure 7.6 Skinner's cumulative record of the eating behavior of one rat. The vertical axis indicates the cumulative number of pellets eaten and the horizontal axis indicates time. Note that after about 1 hour and 45 minutes, the rat stops eating for about 20 minutes.

From Skinner, 1932a, *Journal of General Psychology*, Volume 6, 22–37. Reprinted with permission of the Helen Dwight Reid Educational Foundation. Published by Heldref Publications, 1319 Eighteenth St., NW, Washington, DC 20036-1802. Copyright © 1932.

Skinner (1932b) modified his food delivery apparatus so that the food pellets were dropped into a tray each time the rat pushed a horizontal lever near the food tray and changed his focus from the study of eating to the study of the acquisition of lever pressing (Skinner, 1932c).

In his original studies of the acquisition of lever pressing in rats, Skinner placed rats in an apparatus similar to the one depicted in Chapter 1, Figure 1.6, taught them to approach the feeding tray when they heard the sound of the food dispenser dropping a pellet into the tray, and waited for them to press the lever to obtain a pellet of food. *The procedure for teaching rats to approach the food tray when they hear the food dispenser (or food magazine) drop a pellet in the food tray* is called **magazine training**. Giving the rats magazine training greatly facilitates the acquisition of the behaviors such as lever pressing.

The acquisition of lever pressing for four rats is presented in Figure 7.7. Note the abrupt transition from no responding to a maximum rate of lever pressing. Over the course of the session, the rate of lever pressing shows a gradual decline—the same decline exhibited in Figure 7.6. This gradual decline in lever pressing reflects a decrease in hunger as rats consume food over the course of the experimental session (Skinner, 1932b).

Figure 7.7 Cumulative records of four rats learning to press a lever to obtain food.

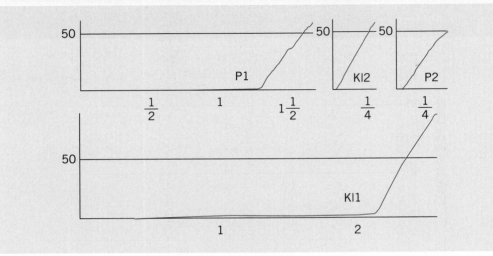

From Skinner, 1932c, *Journal of General Psychology*, Volume 7, 274–285. Reprinted with permission of the Helen Dwight Reid Educational Foundation. Published by Heldref Publications, 1319 Eighteenth St., NW, Washington, DC 200361802. Copyright © 1932.

Following Pavlov's lead, Skinner demonstrated that lever pressing is also influenced by the experimental arrangement of events. For example, Skinner demonstrated that lever pressing is maintained as long as the behavior-food contingency is in effect. *When the presentation of food ceases, the rate of lever pressing gradually decreases* (Figure 7.8). Skinner (1933a) called this phenomenon **extinction**. We use the term **extinction** here to designate both the *procedure of discontinuing the outcome* and *the phenomenon that the behavior gradually decreases when the outcome is no longer given.* Skinner also reported that *an individual who had stopped lever pressing at the end of an extended period of extinction would begin to lever press again if reintroduced back into the experimental situation 24 hours later, even if the extinction procedure was still in effect.* Skinner called this phenomenon **spontaneous recovery** (Figure 7.9). Furthermore, if the original conditioning contingency is reinstated after extinction, the behavior rapidly returns (Figure 7.10).

Shaping Patterns of Behavior. In his original demonstrations of the acquisition of lever pressing in rats, Skinner taught his hungry rats to eat from the food dispenser (procedure of magazine training) and then waited for them to press a lever to obtain food on their own. After varying amounts of time, all four rats pressed the lever without any intervention by Skinner (Figure 7.7). But that figure is deceiving because this procedure does not always result in lever pressing in rats. In 1937, Skinner described a procedure for speeding up the acquisition of lever pressing with the judicious use of food to "shape" behavior by reinforcing closer and closer approximations to the final behavior, in this case pressing the lever. This procedure is called **shaping by the method of successive approximations**, or simply **shaping**.

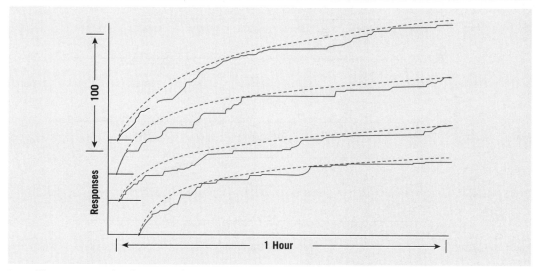

Figure 7.8 Skinner's cumulative records of four typical extinction curves. Each rat had earned 100 pellets of food for pressing the bar on the previous day. The dashed lines indicate the overall course of extinction of that response.

From Skinner, 1938. Reprinted courtesy of the B. F. Skinner Foundation

Figure 7.9 Spontaneous recovery from extinction. The cumulative record to the left of the vertical line represents lever pressing in extinction. The cumulative record to the right of the vertical line was obtained 47 hours after the one on the left. Extinction is still in effect and there is no intervening conditioning. The increase in lever pressing at the beginning of the second session is evidence of spontaneous recovery.

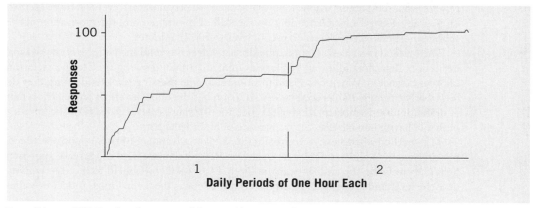

From Skinner, 1938. Reprinted courtesy of the B. F. Skinner Foundation.

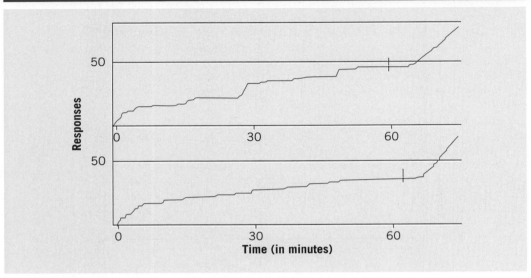

Figure 7.10 Reconditioning after extinction. Extinction is in effect for the first 60 minutes of each session. Reinforcement resumes at the vertical lines. Note the rapid recovery of lever pressing.

From **Skinner**, 1938. Reprinted courtesy of the B. F. Skinner Foundation.

The method of successive approximations works as follows when used to shape rats to press levers: After a rat has learned to eat from the food dispenser (following magazine training), food is presented when the rat approaches the lever. (Repeatedly following approach to the lever with food increases the time the rat spends in the vicinity of the lever.) After approach is established (and it does not take very long for this to happen), food is withheld until the rat makes contact with the lever. After reinforcing lever contact a few times, food is withheld again until the rat either stands over the lever or pushes on it. Gradually the criterion for what movements will be followed by the food becomes narrower and more focused on pressing-like actions. Depending on the skill of the trainer and the motivation of the subject, most rats can be shaped to press a lever within 15 minutes.

The method of successive approximations involves the combined effects of reward and extinction. Behaviors followed by pleasant outcomes tend to be repeated to the exclusion of other behaviors. When rats spend most of their time pressing levers and eating they do less of other things. The procedure of extinction has the opposite effect on behavior; that is, discontinuing the presentation of the food for pressing the lever *decreases* the occurrence of that behavior and *increases* the occurrence of other behaviors.

The method of successive approximations takes advantage of these opposite effects of reinforcement and extinction on behavior. Reinforcers are used to increase approach behaviors to bring the animal near the lever. Then food is withheld to increase activity near the lever and given again when the animal contacts the lever. Once contact becomes regular, food is again withheld to induce more variety in behavior, specifically contact with the lever more conducive to pressing it (such as standing over it). This cycle of reinforcing closer approximations and then withholding the reinforcer to induce more variations in behavior is repeated until the rat presses the lever on its own.

The method of successive approximations can also be used to shape the way behaviors are performed: rats can be shaped to press a lever with increasing force or to hold the lever down for increasing amounts of time by gradually changing the force or duration required to receive food (Skinner, 1937). The method of successive approximations can also be used to get individuals to do things they might not ordinarily do; for example, animals (dogs, porpoises, etc.) can be taught to jump by gradually increasing the height at which food is held in front of them. More examples of the processes that underlie the method of successful approximations are presented in Chapter 8.

The method of successive approximations has also been used with humans in therapeutic situation to promote variety of different behavior. For example, Wolf, Risley, and Mees (1964) shaped a preschool child with severe behavioral and social handicaps to wear his eyeglasses, Renne and Creer (1976) described how they shaped children with asthma to use their inhalation therapy equipment correctly, and Mathews, Hodson, Crist, and LaRoche (1992) described a program to teach young children with aphakia (absence or loss of the lens of the eye) and extreme nearsightedness to insert contact lenses. See Box 7.3 for another example of shaping behavior in humans.

Shaping a Catatonic Patient to Talk

In this excerpt, Isaacs, Thomas, and Goldiamond (1960) describe how they used the method of successive approximations to reinstate verbal behavior in a 40-year-old catatonic man (referred to as "S") who had become mute when he was committed to a mental hospital 19 years earlier. He was extremely withdrawn and exhibited little activity of any kind. Notice how they started with a behavior he was already doing and gradually encouraged and rewarded him for lip movements and speech.

S was brought to a group therapy session with other chronic schizophrenics (who were verbal), but he sat in the position in which he was placed and continued the withdrawal behaviors which characterized him. He remained impassive and stared ahead even when cigarettes, which other members accepted, were offered to him and were waved before his face. At one session, when E removed cigarettes from his pocket, a package of chewing gum accidentally fell out. S's eyes moved toward the gum and then returned to their usual position. This response was chosen by E as one with which he would

(Continued)

BOX 7.3

(Continued)

start to work, using the method of successive approximation.

S met individually with E three times a week. Group sessions also continued. The following sequence of procedures was introduced in the private sessions. Although the weeks are numbered consecutively, they did not follow at regular intervals since other duties kept E from seeing S every week.

Weeks 1, 2. A stick of gum was held before S's face, and E waited until S's eyes moved toward it. When this response occurred E as a consequence gave him the gum. By the end of the second week, response probability in the presence of the gum was increased to such an extent that S's eyes moved toward the gum as soon as it was held up.

Weeks 3, 4. E now held the gum before S, waiting until he noticed movement in S's lips before giving it to him. Toward the end of the first session of the third week, a lip movement spontaneously occurred, which E promptly reinforced. By the end of this week, both lip movement and eye movement occurred when the gum was held up. E then withheld giving S the gum until

S spontaneously made a vocalization, at which time E gave S the gum. By the end of this week, holding up the gum readily occasioned eye movement toward it, lip movement, and a vocalization resembling a croak.

Weeks 5, 6. E held up the gum, and said, "Say *gum, gum*," repeating these words each time S vocalized. Giving S the gum was made contingent upon vocalizations increasingly approximately *gum*. At the sixth session (at the end of Week 6), when E said, "Say *gum, gum*," S suddenly said, "Gum, please." This response was accompanied by reinstatement of other responses of this class, that is, S answered questions regarding his name and age.

Thereafter, he responded to questions by E both in individual sessions and in group sessions, but answered no one else. Responses to the discriminative stimuli of the room generalized to E on the ward; he greeted E on two occasions in the group room. He read from signs in E's office upon request by E.

From Isaacs, Thomas, and Goldiamond, 1960, p. 9. Copyright American Speech-Language-Hearing Association. Reprinted with permission.

The method of successive approximations is not the only method that can be used to get individuals to perform behaviors they are not performing. Zirpoli & Melloy (1997) described methods for **prompting** behavior in humans. These include verbal prompts (directions or instructions), gestural prompts (pointing), modeling prompts (demonstrations), and **physical guidance** (*teaching a skill by physically guiding the individual through the action*). The latter is also called "putting through." In all cases, the desired behavior is followed by a reinforcer, and later the prompt is faded or phased out. **Putting through** is commonly used to train elephants, bears, and other circus animals (Hediger, 1955).

Teaching sequences of activities. Much of our behavior and the behavior of other species involves complex sequences of behaviors. Those sequences of behavior can be trained by using a number of variations of the method called **chaining**. A variety of chaining methods have been studied, and which is most effective depends on the task being trained (Ash & Holding, 1990; Spooner & Spooner, 1984; Walls, Zane & Ellis, 1981). With **forward chaining**, *the task is broken down into a series of steps, and successful completion of each step is followed by a reinforcer*. When the individual is proficient at performing the first step, the second step is added and the reinforcer is only given after both are completed. This continues until the entire sequence is learned. See Ash and Holding (1990), Mahoney, Van Wagenen, and Meyerson (1971), and Walls et al. (1981) for examples of forward chaining in humans. Another approach is called the total-task or whole task method. Here the task is broken down into steps, but the individual performs the entire sequence with prompts along the way, and the reinforcer is only given at the end of the sequence. Horner and Keilitz (1975) demonstrated how to use this method to teach developmentally disabled adolescents to brush their teeth. Another approach is called **backward chaining**, in which *the last step in the sequence is trained first, and each preceding step is added one at a time until the entire chain of behaviors is performed*. Examples of the use of backward chaining with humans include teaching clients in a vocational rehabilitation center to assemble items like a bicycle brake, a meat grinder, and a carburetor (Walls et al., 1981), college students to play a musical score on a keyboard (Ash & Holding, 1990) and to land an airplane on a carrier deck with a flight simulator (Wrightman & Sistrunk, 1987), and a developmentally disabled boy to dress (Martin & Pear, 2003). Backward chaining is most often used to train animals to perform complex sequences of behaviors. There are many examples of such complex chains for behavior on YouTube (try "squirrel tricks," "rat tricks," or "training videos" for various animals). Other trainers, especially those with dogs, will use prompts to train the sequence in forward chaining or whole-task procedures.

It is important to note that the methods of successive approximations and chaining do *not* really create new behaviors. Rats can press levers and perform the behaviors in the chain, and Isaacs et al.'s patient was capable of speaking (see Box 7.3). Those behaviors *can* be performed; they were *not* being performed at the moment. What is taught through shaping and chaining is when, where, how, and in what order to perform behaviors. For the individual, these are new behaviors in the sense that the individual may not have performed them previously, or performed them in that situation.

The Language of Operant Conditioning

The language of operant conditioning is based on the idea that behaviors vary in strength and that there are events called reinforcers (or outcomes) that can strengthen (reinforce) the behaviors that precede them. Although we no longer view reinforcers as strengtheners of behavior, we still use that language to describe operant conditioning.

The common everyday meaning of the term *reinforce* is to strengthen. Throughout his 1927 book, Pavlov employed the term *reinforce* as a verb to describe his basic experimental procedure for producing CRs. He described the procedure of presenting a US following a CS as *reinforcing* that CS because the result of repeated CS-US presentations led to an increase in the occurrence of the CR. For Pavlov, both the consistency with which the CR occurred when the CS was presented and the number of drops of saliva evoked by the CS are measures of the *strength* of the conditioned reflex. A close reading of his papers and book indicate that his choice of the term *reinforce* reflected his belief that the mechanism underlying Pavlovian conditioning is one of strengthening of connections between sensory and motor areas of the brain (i.e., reflexes).

Skinner borrowed that language. He defined the **procedure of reinforcement** as *the presentation of a certain class of stimulus events in a temporal relation with either a stimulus or a behavior.* Those stimulus events are called reinforcing stimuli. He defined a **reinforcing stimulus** (subsequently shortened in later works to **reinforcer**) as *a stimulus or stimulus event that has the ability to produce a change in the strength of a reflex or behavior by virtue of its relationship to a CS (in Pavlovian conditioning) or a behavior (in operant conditioning).* For Skinner, the strength of a behavior is inferred from the rate of occurrence of that behavior (and represented graphically in terms of the slope of the cumulative record); stronger behaviors occur at higher rates (and the slope of the cumulative record is steeper).

In operant conditioning, a **reinforcer** is defined by its effect on behavior: A **reinforcer** is *an event that increases the rate or probability of occurrence of that behavior when that event is either presented, removed, or canceled following that behavior,* and *the procedure of arranging the temporal relationship between a behavior and a reinforcer* is called **reinforcement**. Thus, to **reinforce** a behavior as a procedure is *to create an arrangement between that behavior and a reinforcer.*

It is important to distinguish two meanings of the word reinforce. The first meaning has already been given: To **reinforce** a behavior as a procedure *is to create an arrangement between that behavior and a reinforcer.* The second meaning refers to the inferred effects of the procedure of reinforcement: To **reinforce** a behavior as a process is *to "strengthen" that behavior through the procedure of reinforcement.*

Positive and Negative Reinforcers. A **positive reinforcer** is *an event that increases the probability of a behavior when the event is presented following that behavior,* and the *procedure of presenting a positive reinforcer following a behavior* is called **positive reinforcement**. Because positive reinforcers are *things that individuals will seek out, approach, consume, or do something to obtain,* they are also called **appetitive events** or **rewards**. The terms *reward* and *appetitive event* are theoretically neutral because they do not imply that behaviors are strengthened by their outcomes. As we will see in the next section, rewards and appetitive events are better terms to describe these events.

Likewise, *an event that increases the probability of a behavior when the event is removed or canceled* is called a **negative reinforcer**, and *the procedure of removing or canceling a negative reinforcer following a behavior* is called **negative reinforcement**. *Those things that individuals will do something to get away from* are also called **aversive events**. Aversive is also a theoretically neutral term because it also does not infer any strengthening property of the event.

Summary. It is easy to become overwhelmed by the terminology we employ to describe operant conditioning. These terms are summarized here to help you see the distinctions among them and how they are employed (see the inside back cover).

In the language of operant conditioning, there exists a class of events called **reinforcers.** These events are called reinforcers because *they increase the rate or probability of occurrence of a behavior when those events are presented, removed, or canceled following that behavior.* The **procedure of reinforcement** involves *arranging a temporal relationship between the occurrence of a behavior and the presentation, removal, or cancellation of a reinforcer.*

An event that increases the probability of a behavior when the event is presented following that behavior is called a **positive reinforcer,** and *the procedure of presenting a positive reinforcer following a behavior* is called **positive reinforcement.** Because positive reinforcers are *things that individuals will seek out, approach, consume, or do something to obtain,* they are also called **appetitive events** or **rewards.**

An event that increases the probability of a behavior when the event is removed or canceled is called a **negative reinforcer,** and *the procedure of removing or canceling a negative reinforcer following a behavior* is called **negative reinforcement.** *Those things that individuals will do something to get away from* are also called **aversive** events.

Therefore, behaviors are **reinforced** if they are followed by the presentation of a **positive reinforcer** (reward, appetitive event) or the removal of a **negative reinforcer** (aversive event). **Reinforcement** is the procedure of presenting a **positive reinforcer** after a behavior has occurred (**positive reinforcement**) and removing or canceling a **negative reinforcer** after a behavior has occurred (**negative reinforcement**).

Finally, the connection between the meanings of "reinforce" and "strengthen" led to the use of the term **reinforce** to designate a **process:** To **reinforce** a behavior as a **process** *is to "strengthen" that behavior through the procedure of reinforcement.*

Do Reinforcers Strengthen Behavior?

Although we use Skinner's terminology to describe those events that individuals will perform behaviors to obtain or get away from, it is clear that reinforcers do not strengthen behavior.

As noted above, Pavlov (1927) used the term *reinforce* to describe his procedure for producing CRs to CSs by having those CSs precede USs. Although Thorndike (1898, 1911) did not use the terms *reinforce* or *reinforcer,* he articulated the idea that outcomes of actions "strengthen" or "stamp in" the connection between the stimulus situation in which these actions occur and the actions themselves (see Box 7.1). He called this the **Law of Effect:**

> Of several responses made to the same situation, those that are accompanied or closely followed by satisfaction to the animal will, other things being equal, be more firmly connected with the situation, so that when it [the situation] recurs, they [the responses] will be more likely to recur; those which are accompanied or closely followed by discomfort to the animal will, other things being equal, have their connections with that situation weakened, so that, when it [the situation] recurs, they [the responses] will be less likely to occur. The greater the satisfaction or discomfort, the greater the strengthening or weakening of the bond [situation-response connection]. (Thorndike, 1911, p. 244)

Thus both Thorndike and Skinner advocated that there is a class of events (satisfiers for Thorndike and positive reinforcers for Skinner) that strengthen something that precedes them (stimulus-response connections for Thorndike and responses for Skinner). By adopting the term *reinforcer*, Skinner avoided the subjective aspects of terms like *satisfaction* and *discomfort* and also emphasized the idea that behaviors are strengthened (reinforced) by their outcomes. But do reinforcers really strengthen behavior?

Because learning cannot be directly observed, it must be inferred from the observed changes in behavior that occur after individuals experience a particular procedure. In operant conditioning (and instrumental learning), the measure of learning is typically an increase in the occurrence of a behavior in a given situation when that behavior is followed by a positive reinforcer (or when that behavior is followed by the removal or cancellation of a negative reinforcer). This increase can be measured in a number of ways: Thorndike (1898) and Kline (1899a, 1899b) used the *time* it took their subjects to escape from their problem boxes and mazes as their measure of learning—the faster the task is completed, the stronger the learned stimulus-response connection. On the other hand, Small (1900, 1901) used both time and the *reduction in the number of errors* as the measure of learning in mazes. For Skinner (1938), the *rate of occurrence* of an operant behavior like lever pressing was the measure of learning—the higher the rate, the stronger the learned behavior. Skinner's use of rate is similar to Pavlov's use of number of drops of saliva in that the amount of behavior per unit of time is taken as an index of the strength of the learned behavior or reaction. Another index of strength and learning is called **resistance to extinction**: *how long it takes an individual to cease performing that action when the outcome no longer occurs (i.e., when the procedure of extinction is in effect)*. Resistance to extinction as an index of response strength is based on the presumption that the stronger the behavior, the longer the individual will persist in performing that behavior when it no longer produces the outcome.

All of these measures of learning are based on two premises: (1) learning involves the gradual increase in the strength of something (stimulus-response connections or behaviors) as a result of some repeated experience, and (2) this strength is reflected in how fast the individual completes the task, how many errors the individual makes on each trial, how much behavior occurs per unit time, and how long the behavior persists when it is no longer followed by the reward or positive reinforcer. In a given situation, stronger learned behaviors should be executed rapidly and efficiently with few errors, occur frequently, and persist longer than weaker learned behaviors. But what does it mean when changing the reinforcer in some way leads the individual to now take longer to complete a task, make more errors, perform less behavior per unit time, or take less time to stop behaving under the procedure of extinction? Does that mean that the individual has lost what was learned or that the learned behavior is somehow weakened? The answer to that question is an unqualified no! *If a behavior that continues to be followed by an otherwise effective positive reinforcer nevertheless becomes less efficient, frequent, or persistent, then it would be inappropriate to describe that reinforcer as originally strengthening that behavior.*

The first experiment to demonstrate that what we call reinforcers do not simply strengthen behavior was reported by Elliott (1928). He trained hungry rats to run through a 14-unit multiple T-maze (Figure 7.11) for either sunflower seeds or bran mash as the positive reinforcer. For the first nine days, one group of rats received bran mash in the food box (the experimental group) and the other group received sunflower seeds (the control group). Each subject received one trial per day. At the end of nine days, the rats receiving the bran mash were making fewer errors (Figure 7.12) and taking less time to traverse the maze to the food box; clearly, the bran mash was a more effective reinforcer than the sunflower seeds, but both groups were learning the maze. On the 10th day, the experimental group (the group that received bran mash to that point) was switched to sunflower seeds. The effect was rather dramatic; the number of errors actually increased for the experimental subjects (those switched to sunflower seeds) while the control subjects (those kept on sunflower seeds) continued to improve.[5] Furthermore, Elliott observed that on the day of the change of reward (Day 10), the rats in the experimental group divided their time in the food box between eating and random searching.

Figure 7.11 Diagram of the 14-unit multiple T-maze used by Elliott to study the effects of changing the reward on learning the maze. The door at the end of each correct alley prevented the rats from returning to the start. After entering a new section, the rats were prevented by the curtains at both ends from seeing the next door.

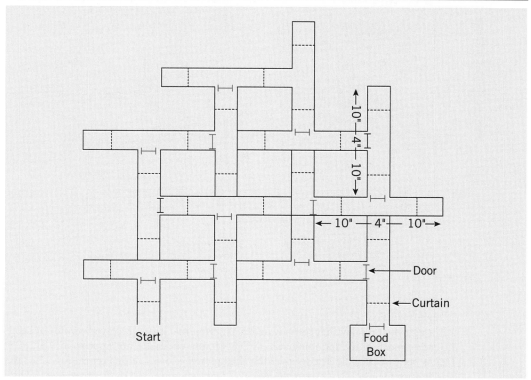

From Elliott, 1928.

Elliott's results clearly illustrate that *reinforcers do not strengthen behavior*. If reinforcers strengthened behavior, then the switch to another reinforcer should not have disrupted the rat's performance in the maze. This is another example of the learning-performance problem described in Chapter 1. Clearly the rats in Elliott's experimental group had learned something about the correct path to the food before the switch. Switching reinforcers disrupted their performance; it did not undo what they had learned. Furthermore, Elliott's

Figure 7.12 The effect of change of reward on the maze performance of rats. The rats in the control group received sunflower seeds as the reinforcer in the food box throughout the entire experiment while the rats in the experimental group received bran mash on the first nine days and sunflower seeds after that. The dependent measure is the average number of errors on each day for each group.

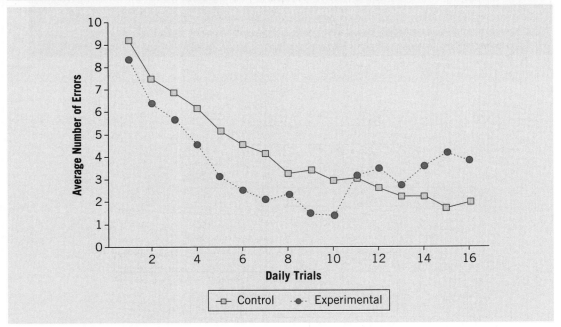

Redrawn from Elliott, 1928.

[5]Although the first day that the rats in the experimental group received sunflower seeds instead of mash in the food box was on Day 10, the effect did not appear until Day 11. That is because they did not discover the change in reinforcer until after they reached the food box on Day 10. Day 11 was the first day that they ran through the maze after having received a different reinforcer.

data illustrate that *the effectiveness of a given reinforcer on behavior is not absolute, rather it depends on what else the individual has experienced.*

Rather dramatic examples on the relativity of the effectiveness of reinforcers have been reported by others. For example, Tinklepaugh (1928) reported that he allowed a monkey to observe him place a piece of banana under one of two distinctive cups, and then while the cups were hidden from the monkey's view, he substituted a piece of lettuce for the banana; the monkey would reject the lettuce and search for the banana, even though lettuce is an adequate reward otherwise. Nissen and Elder (1935) and Cowles and Nissen (1937) reported similar observations with chimpanzees, and Pecoraro, Timberlake, and Tinsley (1999) reported that shifting rats from a 32% to a 4% sucrose solution led to an increase in search behavior. All of these data suggest that *what we call reinforcers do not "reinforce" or strengthen behavior; rather, they are what individuals try to obtain access to (in the case of positive reinforcers) or to get away from (in the case of negative reinforcers).* How reinforcers are involved in both the learning and performance of operant behavior will be discussed in more detail in Chapter 8.

But if those events that are called reinforcers do not reinforce (i.e., strengthen) behavior, then why do we continue to call them reinforcers and refer to the procedure as reinforcement? Why not use the term *reward* instead? Good questions. The reasons we use the terms *reinforce*, *reinforcer*, and *reinforcement* are both historical and practical. These terms arose out of attempts to explain behavior in terms of reflexes. The dominant theoretical position for most of the twentieth century was that behavior occurred in response to a stimulus, and learned behavior occurred when a new stimulus came to evoke that response. Pavlov argued that the presentation of the US strengthened the CR, and Thorndike (and others) argued that the presentation of the outcome for performing a response to a stimulus strengthened the connection between that stimulus and that response. Although Skinner rejected the notion that observed behavior in his experiments was evoked in a reflex-like manner by the stimulus, he still used the reflex language of response and response strength to describe operant behavior. Although we no longer subscribe to the idea that operant behavior reflects reflex-like mechanisms, we all understand what the terms *reinforcer* (a noun), *reinforce* (a verb), *reinforcement* (a noun), and *response* (a noun) mean when describing operant conditioning. We continue to use these terms because we all understand what they mean and do not mean, although "behavior" and "reward" better describe what occurs in operant conditioning and instrumental learning.

THE VARIOUS EVENTS THAT CAN SERVE AS REINFORCERS

The definitions of positive and negative reinforcers do not tell us anything about the properties that make events reinforcers. These definitions only provide us with a way to identify whether a given event is functioning as a positive or negative reinforcer in a given situation. Some events are positive reinforcers because they are important for survival (food, water, sexual partners), and others are negative reinforcers because they produce discomfort or pain. However, nonbiologically significant events and the opportunity to engage in certain activities can also serve as reinforcers. Furthermore, some events can become reinforcers because they are predictors of biologically important events through Pavlovian conditioning.

The identification of an event as a positive reinforcer or a negative reinforcer is based on the effects of presenting, removing, or canceling that event on the behavior that preceded the presentation, removal, or cancellation— that is, in terms of their effects on behavior. Typically biologically important events such as food, water, and access to mates can serve as positive reinforcers, but so can a variety of other activities and events. For some of us, praise, reading certain kinds of books, watching certain television shows or films, listening to certain kinds of music, or playing some sports or engaging in other activities also can serve as positive reinforcers. What all of these events have in common is that they can serve as positive reinforcers for some of us at some times. One thing is certain—*the ability of an event to serve as a positive reinforcer depends on the event, the individual, and the situation in which that event occurs.* What is a positive reinforcer for one individual may not be for another, and what is a positive reinforcer for an individual at one point in time may not be at another time. The same is true for negative reinforcers, and there are situations in which electric shock, which usually functions as a negative reinforcer, appears to function as a positive reinforcer (McKearney, 1969; Fowler, 1971). In other words, *there is no single property that allows us to divide events neatly into positive reinforcers, negative reinforcers, and nonreinforcers independent of their effects on behavior; the identification of reinforcers is based on their effects on behavior* (see Box 7.4).

BOX 7.4

Is It a Positive Reinforcer or a Negative Reinforcer?

Although the definitions of positive and negative reinforcers are based on the effects of presenting, removing, or canceling those events on the behaviors that precede their presentation, removal, or cancellation, sometimes it is not obvious what is serving as the reinforcer for a given behavior. For example, Weiss and Laties (1961) described a series of experiments in which rats were placed in a cylindrical Plexiglass chamber which contained a lever. A heat lamp, suspended above the chamber, was activated for a few seconds when the rat

pressed the lever (Figure 7.4.1). This apparatus was housed in a refrigerated room in which the temperature could be controlled to within 1°C. The rats' fur was removed so that they could not maintain their body temperature in a cold environment. Weiss and Laties were interested in how the rats adjusted their behavior to maintain their body temperature when given the opportunity to press the lever to turn on the heat lamp.

How quickly the rats began to press the lever consistently depended on how long they had

Figure 7.4.1 Photograph of the apparatus used to study operant conditioning of bar pressing in a cold chamber. Each bar press activated the heat lamp above the cylindrical chamber.

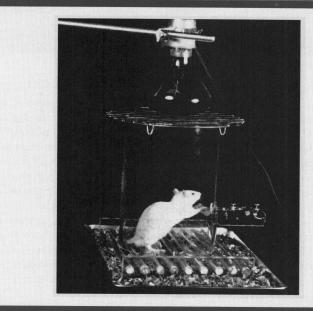

Reprinted with permission from Weiss and Laties, 1961. Behavioral thermoregulation. *Science, 133,* 1338–1344. Copyright © 1961 American Association for the Advancement of Science.

been in the cold prior to being given the opportunity to press the lever and activate the heat lamp. The critical question for us to consider here is the identity of the reinforcer that maintains lever pressing. Is lever pressing here maintained by the heat produced as an outcome of lever pressing (a positive reinforcer) or by the temporary removal of the cold (a negative reinforcer)? In this case, the motivation for pressing the lever is supplied by the aversive aspects of the cold room, and the outcome is presenting something (heat) as an outcome for lever pressing. From that perspective, the heat is a positive reinforcer just like food is a positive reinforcer. In the case of food, the motivation for behavior is supplied by the unpleasant sensations that arise when we are deprived of food for a period of time. On the other hand, we all have experienced cold as an aversive event, and we all learned behaviors to get away from it. From this perspective, the outcomes of each lever press is escape from being cold. From that perspective, we could characterize lever pressing with food as escape from hunger.

It is clear that the designation of the reinforcer depends on one's perspective. Perhaps it

(Continued)

(Continued)

does not really matter whether we view Weiss and Laties' experiments as examples of positive reinforcement (presenting a positive reinforcer contingent on a behavior) or as negative reinforcement (removing an aversive event or negative reinforcer contingent on a behavior). What does matter is that the behavior of the rat in the cold chamber is influenced by the outcomes of its actions, no matter how we characterize those outcomes.

Operant conditioning (and instrumental learning) occur in species that are able to adjust their behavior based on the outcomes of their actions. Natural selection appears to have predisposed individuals to identify some things (food, water, mates, and dangerous situations) as important with little or no experience. The importance of these things for survival of the species is obvious, and it is not surprising that they can function as reinforcers. These events can also serve as Pavlovian *un*conditioned stimuli and as positive and negative reinforcers. They are designated as **primary reinforcers** because they *function as reinforcers with little or no experience required.* However, primary reinforcers are not restricted to these few things. As we will see in the next section, there are a number of other events that function as reinforcers with little or no experience. On the other hand, there are events that *derive their ability to function as reinforcers as a result of experience, specifically as the result of a Pavlovian conditioning procedure.* We designate these events as **conditioned reinforcers**. *Events can become conditioned reinforcers when they predict the occurrence of primary reinforcers.*

Primary Reinforcers

The class of events we call primary reinforcers is not restricted to food, water, sex, and painful stimulation. Natural selection has provided different species with a variety of nonbiologically important events that can serve as primary reinforcers.

Although some experience may be necessary for an individual to identify something as food, once that thing is identified as food, the individual will readily consume it when it appears. Furthermore, there seem to be innate preferences for certain tastes. For example, many species have preferences for sweet-tasting substances, no doubt because most sugars (which are high in caloric value) are sweet tasting. Although conceivably this could be the result of experience with the post-ingestive effects (such as feelings of fullness) that result from the ingestion of sugars, sweet-tasting substances are preferred by both rats and humans immediately after birth and before there is time for any experience with taste and post-ingestive effects to become associated (Jacobs, 1964; Lipsitt, Reilly, Butcher, & Greenwald, 1976; Siqueland & Lipsitt, 1966). Many species will continue to ingest non-nutritive substances like saccharin and NutraSweet™, and these things can function as reinforcers even though they have no caloric value. Thus, it appears that individuals possess predispositions for certain types of foods, and these foods can serve as reinforcers without a great deal of experience. The ability of these substances to serve as reinforcers does not require that they predict the occurrence of anything else of significance (as is required for something to become a conditioned reinforcer).

There are also a variety of other nonbiologically important events that appear to serve as primary reinforcers (because they require minimal prior experience and do not predict anything of importance): Monkeys have been observed to work for hours on mechanical puzzles (Harlow, 1950) and to perform a behavior where the only outcome is to open a window of the test chamber to see outside (Butler, 1953). Rats will learn to run to the side of a Y-maze that leads to a large area with a checkerboard floor (Montgomery, 1954), and mice will press a lever when the only outcome is to turn a light on briefly (Kish, 1955). Clearly, primary reinforcers are not limited to food, water, sex, and painful stimulation.

In humans, simple social interactions also appear to be primary reinforcers. Fantz (1961, 1963) reported that human infants (even as young as 48 hours of age) spend more time looking at a drawing of a human face, particularly one that moves, than at other patterned or plain objects. Poulson (1983) used social interaction as a reinforcer for 3-month-old infants to increase or decrease the rate of vocalization. He placed infants and one of their parents on opposite sides of an opaque window that could be raised and lowered. In one condition, the window was raised when the infants vocalized and the parent could interact with them. In the other condition, the window was raised only when the infants had not vocalized for 8 seconds. The rates of vocalization rose and fell depending on the experimental condition. Of course, with experience, other social reinforcers (such as compliments, praise, or attention) can become important outcomes for human behavior.

Establishing Operations. The designation of food and water as primary reinforcers suggests that they can serve that function under all conditions, but that is not correct. The reinforcing value of primary reinforcers is dependent on the situation in which the food or water is given. We are well aware from casual observation that food serves as a reinforcer for hungry individuals and water for thirsty individuals. Hunger and thirst are motivational states that can be aroused in a number of ways; for example, hunger can be induced by deprivation of food, by activity, by stress, by electrical and chemical stimulation of various structures in the brain, by lesions in the lateral hypothalamus, and by the presence of food. Likewise, thirst can be aroused by similar procedures, and by the ingestion of salty or dry foods. Sexual arousal can be induced by the presence of a potential partner and by viewing erotic images. All of these procedures for arousing motivation are characterized as establishing operations. An **establishing operation** *alters how effectively something functions as a reinforcer by producing a change in an individual's internal or external environment* (Michael, 1982). Food and water will not function as reinforcers (increase or maintain a behavior when presented following that behavior) in the absence of an establishing operation like those listed above.

Perhaps the importance of establishing operations is best illustrated with heat and cold, another class of primary reinforcers. Heat is a positive reinforcer in a cold environment (see Box 7.4), and cool air is a positive reinforcer in a hot environment. Clearly, the reinforcing value of heat and cold depends on the external temperature (and our body temperature). Changes in these conditions are the establishing operations for determining the reinforcing values of heat and cold.

The Opportunity to Engage in Some
Behaviors Can Serve as a Positive Reinforcer

Positive reinforcers are typically described as objects, but the opportunity to do something can also serve as a positive reinforcer. This has important implications for how we view reinforcers and reinforcement.

Typically when we think of reinforcers we think of objects (food, water, money, cars, etc.), but the opportunity to engage in activities can also serve as a reinforcer. We saw earlier that the opportunity to look out a window can serve as a reinforcer for behavior in monkeys (Butler, 1953) and the opportunity to explore a large checkerboard floor can reinforce the correct choice in a maze with rats (Montgomery, 1954). In humans we frequently use "privileges" as reinforcers for desired behaviors. These can include watching favorite television shows, going out on the weekend, or going to special places. In each case, the reward or reinforcer is the opportunity to *do* something, not to *get* something.

Premack (1959, 1962) suggested that all reinforcement involves the opportunity to do something. He noted that the procedure of depriving an individual of food or water really involves restricting their access to these things, and the presentation of food or water to a hungry or thirsty individual gives that individual the opportunity to eat or drink. Therefore, one could argue that the opportunity to engage in eating and drinking is the reinforcing event, not the food or water. Furthermore, he noted that a hungry rat given access to food and a lever would spend most of its time eating rather than pressing the lever; that is, in this situation, eating has a high probability of occurring and lever-pressing a low probability. He argued that the reason why the presentation of food can be used to reinforce lever-pressing is because the opportunity to engage in an activity that has a high probability of occurring (eating in a food-deprived rat) is the reinforcer for an activity that has a lower probability (pressing a lever). If that is true, then if one could find an activity that has a higher probability than eating, one could use that activity as a positive reinforcer to increase eating.

Premack (1959) found such a situation in children. He gave each child in a first grade class a choice between playing with a pinball machine or obtaining candy from a dispenser. In the first test session, these two devices were placed side by side, and the children were given free access to both. Of the 33 children tested, 61% directed more of their behavior toward the pinball machine than the candy dispenser; the other 39% did the opposite. The children in the first group were labeled as "manipulators" and those in the second group as "eaters." Three to four days later, all children were again given access to both devices (second test session). However, during this second session, the two devices were wired so that one would not operate unless the child operated the other first. For half of the children in both groups ("manipulators" and "eaters"), candy could not be obtained until the child had operated the pinball machine, and for the other half, the pinball machine would not operate until he or she consumed a piece of candy. The first condition was labeled M-E (*M*anipulate pinball machine allows *E*ating candy) and the second E-M (*E*ating candy allows *M*anipulation of the pinball machine). The results of this experiment are presented in Figure 7.13. Premack presented his data in terms of the increase in the lower rate behavior between the two sessions. Note that the "manipulators" increased their consumption of candy substantially when eating was required for the pinball machine to work (left panel). There was little increase when manipulation was required for obtaining candy. Similar results were obtained for the "eaters": These children increased their playing with the pinball machine more when playing (i.e., manipulation) was required for obtaining candy. There was little increase in candy consumption when it was required for activating the pinball machine. Thus Premack demonstrated that food serves as a reinforcer for another activity only when consuming it occurs at a higher rate than the other activity.

Furthermore, Premack reasoned that if one could reverse the probabilities for two activities, the formerly low probability behavior would reinforce the formerly high probability behavior—that is, lever pressing would reinforce eating or drinking. Premack (1962) demonstrated that this is true with the following experimental arrangement: He placed rats in a running wheel. If given unrestricted access, rats will alternate running for long periods of time with resting. Premack could control their running with a brake that locked the wheel so that it could not revolve. He also had a drinking tube that could be inserted into the wheel or withdrawn from the rats' reach while they were in the wheel. Thus, he could control access to both activities (running and drinking) and manipulate their relative probabilities. When access to the drinking tube was denied, the rats became thirsty and drinking became the more probable behavior (as measured by what they chose to do

Figure 7.13 Mean increases in eating for the children labeled as manipulators (left panel) and mean increases in manipulating the pinball machine for the children labeled as eaters (right panel) when eating candy led to the opportunity to manipulate the pinball machine (E-M) and manipulating the pinball machine led to the opportunity to eat candy (M-E).

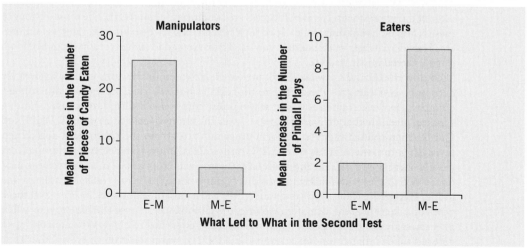

Data from Premack, 1959.

when the drinking tube was presented). When access to the water tube was unrestricted, running was the more probable behavior. Now Premack was ready to test his hypothesis. He denied access to the drinking tube and allowed the wheel to turn freely. When the rats were given access to the drinking tube after making the wheel turn a certain number of revolutions, the rats increased their running in the wheel. We would say that drinking water reinforced running in the wheel. However, if he allowed the rats free access to the drinking tube but locked the wheel until they licked the tube a certain number of times, the rats increased their rate of licking the tube. Here we would say that running reinforced drinking.

Premack's demonstrations illustrate a number of important aspects of reinforcement and reinforcers. First, they illustrate *the importance of establishing operations for determining the reinforcing value of an event*. Second, they illustrate that *the opportunity to engage in an activity can serve as a reinforcer*, and they support the contention that *reinforcement may be conceptualized as access to high-probability activities*; what makes food and water reinforcers is the opportunity to consume them under certain conditions. Finally, they demonstrate that *the ability of something to function as a reinforcer is relative to what else is available*. Even for things we classify as primary reinforcers, their ability to function as reinforcers is not absolute.

Conditioned Reinforcers (Secondary Reinforcers)

Conditioned reinforcers are created through a Pavlovian conditioning procedure: events that predict the occurrence of primary reinforcers can become conditioned reinforcers.

Although events that we classify as primary reinforcers may involve some learning, there are a wide variety of *events that derive their reinforcing ability solely as a result of learning, specifically as a result of a Pavlovian conditioning procedure (the event predicts the occurrence of a primary reinforcer)*. We call these conditioned reinforcers or secondary reinforcers. For humans, most of the events that serve as reinforcers are conditioned reinforcers. The most obvious of these is money. Even coins made of precious metals really have no intrinsic value as reinforcers. They derive their value because they can be exchanged for other commodities like food, water, entertainment, and sex.

Wolfe (1936) and Cowles (1937) provided early demonstrations of how arbitrarily chosen objects can gain the ability to function as positive reinforcers. In both studies, chimpanzees were trained to insert white poker chips (also referred to as tokens) into a vending machine that delivered a grape. After the animals learned to do this, Wolfe and Cowles then trained them to perform other tasks to obtain the tokens that could then be inserted into the vending machine. Wolfe (1936) demonstrated that the chimpanzees readily associated different food values with different colored tokens: blue tokens produced two grapes when inserted into the vending machine, white tokens produced one grape, and brass tokens produced none. After a few days of experience inserting all three types of tokens into the vending machine, the chimpanzees chose the blue tokens when given free access to all three. The chimpanzees also learned to choose the appropriately colored tokens that could be exchanged for food or water depending on whether they were hungry or thirsty and to choose the appropriately colored tokens that could be exchanged for the opportunity to engage in a specific activity (leave the experimental room and return to the home cage or play with the experimenter). Cowles (1937) also demonstrated that these same chimpanzees could learn to select the arbitrarily designated correct choice from a number of alternatives. In each problem, the correct choice was reinforced with a token that could be exchanged for a grape. In some experiments a token could be exchanged immediately, and in other experiments the animals had to collect them and make the exchange in another room after the session had ended. Both Wolfe and Cowles observed that making the chimpanzees wait to exchange the tokens for food did not appear to make too much of a difference in the animal's performance of the tasks presented to them. M. F. Smith (1939) reported a similar experiment with cats: She trained cats to push a ball into a chute in order to obtain food and then trained them to manipulate a string in order to obtain a ball.

All of these experiments with tokens parallel the acquisition of the reinforcing value of money. They also illustrate some important attributes of conditioned reinforcers (like money). First, the value of money is determined by what it will buy (the exchange rate). Second, the conditioned reinforcer can be given immediately but not exchanged for something else until later; yet it retains its ability to function as a reinforcer despite the delay. Thus, *conditioned reinforcers can help to bridge the time interval between the occurrence of a behavior and obtaining a primary reinforcer*.

The experiments of Wolfe (1936), Cowles (1937), and Smith (1939) illustrate how arbitrarily chosen objects can gain the ability to serve as conditioned reinforcers, but in all of these situations, the individuals always received food after obtaining the conditioned reinforcer. Is it possible to demonstrate that learning can occur when the only outcome is the presentation of an arbitrarily chosen event? K. A. Williams (1929) was the first person to do that. She trained rats to find food in a white compartment of a simple two-choice apparatus. Then she ran the rats for nine days in the 14-unit multiple T-maze used by Elliott (Figure 7.11) but with no food at the end. Beginning on the 10th day, the white compartment was put at the end of the multiple T-maze but with no food in it. The number of errors and time to run the maze dropped to the levels of rats that received food during all trials. Animals for whom the end of the box did not change showed no such improvement.

In 1938, Skinner provided another demonstration. He gave rats 60 presentations of the sound of the food magazine followed by the presentation of food (magazine training). This procedure is easily identified as Pavlovian conditioning because there is a positive contingency between the sound of the magazine and the appearance of food (and the Pavlovian CR is approach to the food tray).

Following this Pavlovian conditioning procedure, Skinner connected the magazine to the lever so that any depressions of the lever produced the sound of the magazine, but *not* food; therefore, the only outcome of a lever press was the sound of the food magazine that had previously predicted food. All of the rats Skinner trained in this manner pressed the lever. The results of Skinner's demonstration are presented in Figure 7.14. Because the sound of the food magazine increased the rate of behavior when presented as an outcome of that behavior, it meets the definition of a positive reinforcer (in this case a conditioned positive reinforcer). Skinner noted the parallel between his procedure and Pavlov's second-order conditioning procedure (see Table 7.1): In both cases, a stimulus is presented in a positive contingency with an important biological event (Phase 1) and a CR occurs to that stimulus. In operant conditioning, the CR is approach to the food tray when one hears the sound of it being activated (S). In the second phase, something new predicts the signal from Phase 1 (CS_2 predicts CS_1 in Pavlovian second-order conditioning, and the behavior predicts S in operant conditioning). In Pavlovian second-order conditioning, the individual makes a CR to CS_2 even though CS_2 was *never experienced* with the US. In operant conditioning, the individual performs the behavior (B) that brings on S, even though that behavior is *never followed by* the primary reinforcer (O).[6] Both procedures endow a previously neutral stimulus with the ability to increase behavior.

Skinner (1936, 1938) also demonstrated that a stimulus in the presence of which an individual's behaviors are reinforced can become a conditioned reinforcer. After training rats to press a lever for food, Skinner changed the situation in the following manner: A light was presented for 3 minutes during which the rats could obtain food by pressing the lever. These periods alternated with 3-minute periods during which the light was absent

Figure 7.14   The acquisition of lever pressing when the only outcome is the sound of the food magazine. All four rats had been trained earlier to associate the sound of the food magazine with the appearance of food.

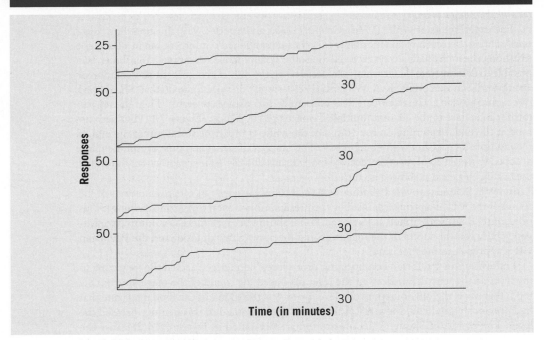

From Skinner, 1938. Reprinted courtesy of the B. F. Skinner Foundation

---

[6]A reinforcer is also known as an outcome (O). To minimize confusion with the "R" in S-R (stimulus-response) learning, we will use O as the symbol for outcome or reinforcer. Outcome and reinforcer can be used interchangeably.

Table 7.1. Comparing Second-Order Conditioning to Conditioned Reinforcement

	Second-order conditioning		Conditioned reinforcement	
	Procedure	Result	Procedure	Result
Phase 1	$CS_1 \rightarrow US$	CR occurs to CS_1	$S \rightarrow O$	CR occurs to S
Phase 2	$CS_2 \rightarrow CS_1$	CR occurs to CS_2	$B \rightarrow S$	B more likely to occur in the future

Note: B = behavior, O = outcome (or reinforcer), S = stimulus.

and no food was given for lever pressing. The rats soon learned to press the lever in the presence of the light and refrained from lever-pressing in the absence of the light. Skinner now changed the procedure again so that lever presses in the absence of the light produced the light. Under this circumstance, the rate of lever pressing increased. This is hardly surprising given that there was a positive Pavlovian contingency between the light and the occurrence of food during discrimination training.

Such positive Pavlovian contingencies can also be used to produce conditioned negative reinforcers. For example, Brown and Jacobs (1949) gave one group of rats Pavlovian conditioning by presenting a 9-second tone and light compound CS with a shock US. The shock coincided with the last 6 seconds of the CS. The second group was not given any Pavlovian conditioning; they only experienced the CS. Following this training, both groups of rats were placed in a two-compartment box in which the two sides were separated by a low hurdle. Periodically the CS came on and stayed on until the rats crossed the barrier; as soon as a rat crossed the barrier the CS was terminated. The rats given the Pavlovian conditioning learned to quickly cross the barrier. The other rats did not learn. Clearly, the Pavlovian conditioning endowed the CS with the ability to become a negative reinforcer; that is, an event the rats would do something to remove.

The strength of a conditioned reinforcer (measured in terms of how well it can increase the probability of a behavior) is a function of the number of times the stimulus is paired with a primary reinforcer, the size and quality of the primary reinforcer, and the delay between the conditioned reinforcer and the primary reinforcer. (See Wike, 1966, for a review of these studies.)

THE FOUR VARIETIES OF OPERANT CONDITIONING

There are four basic types of operant conditioning procedures. Each type of procedure involves a contingency (positive or negative) between a behavior and an outcome, and there are two types of outcomes (appetitive/positive reinforcers and aversive/negative reinforcers).

Operant conditioning involves a relationship between a behavior and its outcome, where the outcome involves either an appetitive event (positive reinforcer), an aversive event (negative reinforcer), or a signal for either of these (a conditioned reinforcer). We can define four different varieties of operant conditioning in terms of the type of the reinforcer (positive or negative) and the contingency between the behavior and that reinforcer.

Contingencies in Operant Conditioning. Operant conditioning also involves a contingency between two events, in this case between a behavior and a reinforcer (or outcome). In operant conditioning, the **behavior-outcome (B-O) contingency** *is the rule that specifies the relationship between a behavior and the occurrence or nonoccurrence of an outcome.*

When there is a **positive behavior-outcome contingency,** *the outcome is more likely to occur following the behavior than if the behavior did not occur.* This can be expressed in symbolic form as follows, where O stands for the outcome (positive or negative) and B the behavior:

$$Pr\,(O\,|\,B) > Pr\,(O\,|\,no\;B) \tag{1}$$

This expression is read, "The probability that the outcome will occur given the occurrence of a behavior is greater than the probability that the outcome will occur given the absence of that behavior."

We call the procedure where there is a *positive contingency with a positive reinforcer* **reward training** or **positive reinforcement.** The expected effect of positive reinforcement is an *increase* in the occurrence of the effective behavior in the future. When there is a *positive contingency with a negative reinforcer*, the procedure is called **punishment by application** or simply **punishment.** The expected effect of punishment is a *decrease* in the occurrence of that behavior in the future.

A **negative behavior-outcome contingency** describes the situation in which *the outcome is more likely to occur in the absence of the behavior than in its presence.* This can be expressed in symbolic form as follows:

$$Pr\,(O\,|\,B) < Pr\,(O\,|\,no\;B) \tag{2}$$

It is read, "The probability that the outcome will occur given the occurrence of a behavior is less than the probability that the outcome will occur given the absence of that behavior."

A *negative contingency with a negative reinforcer* is called **negative reinforcement.** There are two varieties of negative reinforcement. *If the negative reinforcer is present and the behavior terminates it*, the procedure is called **escape conditioning.** However, *if the behavior will postpone or cancel a negative reinforcer that might ordinarily occur if there is no behavior*, the procedure is called **avoidance conditioning.** In both varieties of negative reinforcement, the expected effect is an increase in the occurrence of the effective behavior in the future.

The expected effect of a negative contingency with a positive reinforcer is the opposite; that is, the behavior should be less likely to occur in the future. This procedure is called **omission training** because *the occurrence of the behavior leads to the omission of the positive reinforcer that would otherwise occur*, or **differential reinforcement of other behavior (DRO)** because *the positive reinforcer is more likely to follow any other* *behavior than the targeted one*, or **punishment by removal** because *the behavior results in the loss of a positive reinforcer*. Most of us experienced this last procedure when we were "grounded" for doing something we should not have done.

These four types of operant conditioning procedures are diagrammed in Table 7.2.

Procedures That Typically Increase the Future Occurrence of Behavior

With an effective positive reinforcer, the procedure of positive reinforcement leads to increases in the future occurrence of the behavior that produced that reinforcer, and with an effective negative reinforcer, the procedure of negative reinforcement leads to increases in the future occurrence of the behavior that removed or canceled that reinforcer. There are two varieties of negative reinforcement, escape conditioning and avoidance conditioning, and there are at least two varieties of avoidance conditioning, signaled avoidance and unsignaled avoidance.

Positive Reinforcement. The procedure of positive reinforcement or reward training involves a *positive contingency between a behavior and a positive reinforcer (appetitive event)*. Therefore, with positive reinforcement, the individual is more likely to receive the appetitive event (positive reinforcer) following a given behavior than in the absence of that behavior [Pr (positive reinforcer | behavior occurred) > Pr (positive reinforcer | behavior did not occur)]. The effect of this positive contingency with a positive reinforcer is to *increase the likelihood* of the target behavior occurring in the future (Table 7.2, top left panel).

Table 7.2 The Four Basic Operant Conditioning Procedures and Their Typical Effects on Behavior

Outcome	Contingency	
	Positive	Negative
Appetitive	$B \rightarrow O^+$ Positive Reinforcement $B \uparrow$	$B \rightarrow$ Absence of O^+ Omission Training $B \downarrow$
Aversive	$B \rightarrow O^-$ Punishment by Application $B \downarrow$	$B \rightarrow$ Absence of O^- Negative Reinforcement $B \uparrow$

Note: B = behavior, O^+ = positive reinforcer, O^- = negative reinforcer.

We have already reviewed a number of examples of positive reinforcement. Kline (1899a, 1899b) and Small (1900) reported that rats become more efficient in gnawing or digging their way into a box that contains food with repeated experience, and Skinner (1932c) presented the first data on the acquisition of lever pressing by rats for food (see Figure 7.8). In each of these examples, there was a positive contingency between the target behavior and the food [Pr (food | behavior occurred) > Pr (food | behavior did not occur)], and in each case the target behavior was more likely to occur in the future (as measured by the decrease in time it took to occur on each trial or by the rate at which the animals performed that behavior).

Sometimes it is easy to forget that the procedure we call positive reinforcement was not discovered in the laboratory. People have known for a long time how to use rewards (positive reinforcers) to increase behavior (see Box 7.5).

Negative Reinforcement. The procedure of negative reinforcement involves a *negative contingency between a behavior and a negative reinforcer (aversive event).* That is, with negative reinforcement, the individual is less likely to receive the aversive event following a given behavior than in the absence of that behavior [Pr (negative reinforcer | behavior occurred) < Pr (negative reinforcer | behavior did not occur)]. The effect of this negative contingency with a negative reinforcer is to *increase the likelihood* of the target behavior occurring in the future (Table 7.2, bottom right panel).

BOX 7.5

A Comment on the Use of Positive Reinforcement From the Twelfth Century

Moses Maimonides (1135–1204) was a Rabbi, philosopher, and court physician. He was born in Cordoba, Spain, where he spent his early years. He and his family were forced by religious persecution to flee first to Morocco and then to Egypt, where he lived until his death. In this excerpt from his Commentary on the *Mishnah* (Oral Law of Judaism), Maimonides provides an analogy concerning learning for tangible reinforcers rather than for its own sake. From the last sentence of this excerpt it is obvious that Maimonides recognizes why sometimes it is necessary to promote with extrinsic reinforcers a given behavior that might not ordinarily occur. Notice the progression from primary to conditioned reinforcers as the student gets older.

You, however, who read this book thoughtfully, must understand the analogy which I am about to draw for you. Prepare your mind to understand what I tell you about all this. Imagine a small child who has been brought to his teacher so that he may be taught the Torah, which is his ultimate good because it will bring him to perfection. However, because he is only a child and because his understanding is deficient, he does not grasp the true value of that good, nor does he understand the perfection which he can achieve by means of the Torah. Of necessity, therefore, his teacher, who has acquired greater perfection than the child, must bribe him to study by means of things which the child loves in a childish way. Thus, the teacher may say, "Read and I will give you some nuts or figs; I will give you a bit of honey." With this stimulation the child tries to read. He does not work hard for the sake of reading itself, since he does not understand its value. He reads in order to obtain the food. Eating these delicacies is far more important to him than reading, and a greater good to him. Therefore, although he thinks of study as work and effort, he is willing to do it in order to get what he wants, a nut or a piece of candy. As the child grows and his mind improves, what was formerly important to him loses its importance, while other things become precious. The teacher will stimulate his desire for whatever he wants then. The teacher may say to the child, "Read and I will give you beautiful shoes or nice clothes." Now the child will apply himself to reading for the sake of new clothes and not for the sake of study itself. He wants the garment more than the Torah. This coat will be the end which he hopes to achieve by reading. As his intelligence improves still more and these things, too, become unimportant to him, he will set his desire upon something of greater value. Then his teacher may say to him, "Learn this passage or this chapter, and I will give you a *denar* or two." Again he will try to read in order to receive the money, since money is more important to him than study. The end which he seeks to achieve through his study is to acquire the money which has been promised him. When his understanding has so improved that even this reward has

ceased to be valuable to him, he will desire something more honorable. His teacher may say to him then, "Study so that you may become the president of a court, a judge, so that people will honor you and rise before you as they honor So-and-So." He will then try hard to read in order to attain his new goal. His final end then will be to achieve the honor, the exaltation, and the praise which others might confer upon him.

Now all this is deplorable. However, it is unavoidable because of man's limited insight, as a result of which he makes the goal of wisdom something other than wisdom itself, and assumes that the purpose of study is the acquisition of honor, which makes a mockery of truth. Our sages called this learning not for its own sake.

Maimonides raises an interesting question about the use of positive reinforcement to encourage people to do things they *should* do but are *not* doing. In his first paragraph he uses the term "bribe" to describe what is occurring, and he concludes by commenting that this is deplorable. Perhaps it is. Ideally we learn for the intrinsic rewards we obtain from learning, but when confronted with a child who does not do his or her school work, one must ask which is worse: for a child to study for the wrong reason (treats or money) or for the child not to study at all because we refuse to use extrinsic rewards to motivate the child? The reason for using extrinsic reinforcers is to get the behavior to occur. Hopefully the child will come to experience the intrinsic rewards.

Reprinted with permission from Maimonides Heritage Foundation.

There are two basic procedures that satisfy the definition of negative reinforcement. One is escape conditioning, and the other is avoidance conditioning. With **escape conditioning,** *the negative reinforcer (aversive event) is present and the individual does something to terminate it.* All of us have had experiences in which we have learned to become more efficient in getting out of unpleasant situations, for example, learning what to say to end a conversation we do not want to continue to participate in. Likewise, Thales's mule who submerged in the river to lighten the load of salt on its back was exhibiting escape conditioning. The procedure for escape conditioning is presented in the top panel of Table 7.3.

An early experiment by Mowrer (1940) illustrates escape conditioning (and negative reinforcement). Mowrer placed his rats in a wooden box that contained a floor made of metal rods through which electric shock could be delivered. On one wall of the box there was a metal plate, hinged at the bottom. Pressing this plate would immediately terminate a shock delivered through the floor.

In this experiment, Mowrer (1940) started the shock at a low level. Over the course of 2.25 minutes, the shock intensity gradually increased until it reached its full level, where it remained until the animal pressed the panel on the wall. Mowrer reported that as the intensity of the shock increased, the rats became more active and agitated. With their first experience in this situation, most rats would accidentally press the plate within 3 to 6 minutes. By the third trial, the rats exhibited little random behavior and went directly to the plate as the shock began to feel uncomfortable. By 10 trials, the plate pressing behavior was prompt and swift. This is negative reinforcement because the outcome of pressing the plate (termination of the shock) produced an increase in that behavior. Shock occurred when the rats were not pressing the plate, and it never

Table 7.3 Negative Reinforcement Procedures
1. Escape conditioning procedure
aversive event ➙ target behavior ➙ remove aversive event
2. Signaled avoidance conditioning procedure
Signal ➚ no target behavior ➙ aversive event occurs Signal ➘ target behavior ➙ aversive event canceled
3. Unsignaled (nondiscriminated) avoidance procedure
Aversive event can occur without warning, but target behavior occurring at appropriate time can cancel next occurrence of aversive event

occurred immediately after a press; therefore, Pr (shock | plate press) < Pr (shock | no plate press). The target behavior of pressing the plate allowed the rats to escape from the shock. The experiment by Brown and Jacobs (1949) described above is also an example of escape conditioning. In that case, the aversive event was a conditioned negative reinforcer.

The other procedure that satisfies the definition of negative reinforcement is avoidance conditioning. With **avoidance conditioning**, *the aversive event will occur unless the individual does something to cancel it*. This is different from escape because an individual who learns what to do need never experience the aversive event again. There are a number of procedures used to study avoidance conditioning. Two will be described here.

The first procedure for studying avoidance conditioning is called **signaled avoidance** (or **discriminated avoidance**). In signaled avoidance, *the impending aversive event is signaled and the target behavior cancels the next occurrence of that event*. The aversive event occurs if the individual fails to execute the target behavior in time, and in some situations the aversive event does not terminate until the individual escapes by executing the target behavior. Signaled avoidance learning consists of two parts: (1) identifying the signals for aversive events, and (2) learning what actions to take to avoid them. You should recognize the first part (identifying the signals for aversive events) as a Pavlovian conditioning task. Thus, after learning that certain dark cloud patterns typically precede rain, we can avoid getting soaked by taking an umbrella or raincoat with us. Likewise, people in the military and those who live in war zones learn to identify the sounds of incoming artillery rounds and take cover. Finally, we respond to our monthly credit card statements by sending a payment to avoid late charges. In all of these situations, we learn to identify the signal for the aversive event and a behavior to avoid that event. The procedure for signaled avoidance conditioning is presented in the middle panel of Table 7.3.

In 1938, Brogden, Lipman, and Culler reported an experiment that illustrates the essential nature of avoidance conditioning. They placed two groups of guinea pigs in a running wheel. For both groups, a buzzer sounded for 2 seconds followed by an electric shock which evoked running. This is a Pavlovian conditioning procedure in which the buzzer is the CS, the shock is the US, and running is the CR. However, for one of these groups, running during the 2 seconds of buzzer canceled the impending shock. For the other group, running had no effect on the occurrence of the shock; it always occurred after the buzzer had been on for 2 seconds. There were 25 such trials a day for both groups. The results are plotted in Figure 7.15. The guinea pigs with the avoidance contingency rapidly learned to avoid the shock by turning the wheel. The guinea pigs with only the Pavlovian conditioning procedure made some conditioned wheel turning behaviors during the buzzer, but for the most part, they exhibited anticipatory behaviors described as agitation (which caused the wheel to turn occasionally).

Brogden et al.'s (1938) experiment provides a vivid demonstration of the importance of the behavior-outcome contingency. There was a negative contingency between running and shock [Pr (shock | running) < Pr (shock | not running)]. By running on every trial, the animals with this contingency were able to avoid all subsequent shocks. Despite the fact that successful avoidance produces the Pavlovian conditioning procedure of extinction (CS no longer followed by the US), running continued to occur. Clearly, the instrumental

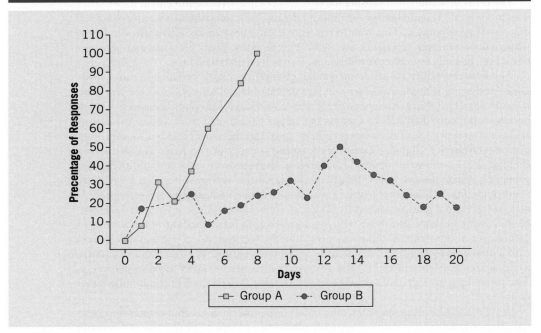

Figure 7.15   Percentage of trials on each day in which the two groups of guinea pigs rotated the wheel during the 2-second buzzer. For Group A, the shock did not occur if they rotated the wheel during the buzzer. For Group B, the shock always followed the 2-second buzzer.

behavior of avoiding shock took precedence over the extinction of Pavlovian CRs to the signal for shock.

On the other hand, the animals in the other group continued to have a positive contingency between the buzzer and shock [Pr (shock|buzzer) > Pr (shock|no buzzer)], but they had a zero contingency between running and shock [Pr (shock|running) = Pr (shock|not running)]. For these individuals, the Pavlovian contingency produced conditioned agitation in anticipation of the shock. Although Brogden et al. (1938) did not attempt to train these animals to avoid later, it is well established that *prior experience with a zero contingency involving aversive events retards the subsequent acquisition of successful avoidance behavior*. This phenomenon is called **learned helplessness** and is similar to the learned irrelevance effect described in Chapter 4.

The second type of avoidance conditioning procedure is called **unsignaled avoidance** (or **nondiscriminated avoidance**). In unsignaled avoidance, *the impending aversive event is not signaled, and the target behavior cancels the next occurrence of that event*. As is the case with signaled avoidance, the aversive event may stay on until the individual escapes from it, but that is not required. There are many situations in which unpleasant events that can occur without warning can be avoided through preventive actions. For example, we fasten our seat belts in automobiles to avoid injury in the unlikely (but possible) event of an accident. Likewise, if our word processor does not have an automatic timed backup feature, we learn to save our work from time to time to avoid losing the fruits of our labors. In both cases, typically there is no warning of an accident or a power failure. The safest course of action is to always buckle up and to periodically save our work. Likewise, the "pop quiz" can be thought of as an unsignaled avoidance procedure in which keeping up with the assigned readings avoids a failing grade on any unannounced quizzes. The procedure for unsignaled avoidance is briefly described in the bottom panel of Table 7.3.

The most commonly used procedure for studying unsignaled avoidance was devised by Sidman (1953a, 1953b). This procedure is also called **free operant avoidance** or **Sidman avoidance** (the latter after its originator). With this procedure, the subject is placed in an experimental chamber that contains a method of delivering aversive events (e.g., metal rods on the floor through which shock can be delivered to rats) and a way to record the target avoidance behavior (e.g., a lever). In Sidman's procedure, brief shocks are delivered at regular intervals unless the subject presses the lever, and each lever press postpones the next shock for a given interval of time. Sidman's procedure requires two clocks. The interval between shocks is programmed with one clock (the shock-shock or S-S clock), and the shock-free interval after a lever press is programmed with a second shock clock (the response-shock or R-S clock). In the absence of the target behavior, the S-S clock continues to cycle and deliver shocks, and each shock resets the S-S clock. When the target behavior occurs, the S-S clock stops and the R-S clock starts. While the R-S clock is running, no shocks are delivered. Each occurrence of the target behavior resets the R-S clock and prolongs the shock-free interval. However, if the R-S clock is allowed to time out (i.e., no target behaviors occur during that R-S interval), a shock is delivered and the S-S clock begins again. Note that Sidman's procedure maintains the essential feature of unsignaled avoidance (the target behavior cancels the next occurrence of the unsignaled aversive event). This procedure is described in Table 7.4.

All procedures for unsignaled avoidance (including Sidman's procedure) program a negative contingency between the target behavior and the aversive event. In Sidman's procedure, the subject is *less likely* to receive a shock when he or she presses the lever than when he or she *does not* [Pr (shock I lever press) < Pr (shock I no lever press)] because lever pressing creates a shock-free period of time (Table 7.4).

Procedures That Typically Reduce the Future Occurrence of Behavior

There are two ways to punish individuals: apply an aversive event when the target behavior occurs (punishment by application) or deny access to a desired event when the target behavior occurs (punishment by removal or omission training).

Table 7.4 The Sidman Procedure for Unsignaled Avoidance

- Aversive events are scheduled to occur periodically. The interval between these aversive events is called the S-S (shock-shock) interval.

- Each behavior (response) postpones the occurrence of the next aversive event for a given period of time. This second interval is called the R-S (response-shock) interval.

- Each behavior (response) restarts the R-S interval.

- If the R-S interval elapses without a response, the S-S interval is activated until a response occurs.

- In the diagram below, the top line indicates when shocks were given and the bottom line when the individual performed the target response. At the start of this segment, the S-S clock was operating and the individual received two shocks before performing the target response. At that point, the R-S clock started. Because he or she did not perform that response again before the R-S interval elapsed, another shock occurred and the S-S clock started again. The individual started responding before that S-S interval elapsed and continued to do so six times in rapid succession. Each of those responses restarted the R-S clock, producing the long shock-free interval. But then the individual paused again long enough for the R-S interval to elapse. This produced the final shock (and started the S-S clock again).

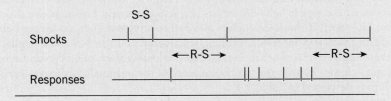

Punishment by Application. The procedure of punishment by application involves a *positive contingency between a behavior and a negative reinforcer (aversive event)*, and the individual is more likely to experience the aversive event (negative reinforcer) following a given behavior than in its absence [Pr (negative reinforcer | behavior occurred) > Pr (negative reinforcer | behavior did not occur)].[7] The typical effect of this positive contingency with a negative reinforcer is to *decrease the likelihood* of the target behavior

---

[7]Because punishment by application involves a positive contingency, some people use the term positive punishment to designate this procedure.

occurring in the future. When Thales substituted sponges for salt, he was employing the procedure of punishment by application to stop his mule from submerging at each river crossing (Table 7.2, bottom left panel).

Because punishment by application, like avoidance conditioning, involves aversive events, there is the possibility that the observed effects of the procedure on behavior reflect either unconditioned effects of the aversive event or Pavlovian conditioned responses to the context in which these aversive events are experienced (see Chapter 5). Bolles, Holtz, Dunn, and Hill (1980) provided unambiguous evidence that the reduction in a behavior can be due to the instrumental punishment contingency. They trained rats to obtain food in two different ways, sometimes by pressing down on a lever and sometimes by pulling the lever toward them. To ensure that the rats learned to perform both behaviors, each successive reward required the other behavior; that is, when the rat obtained a pellet of food by pulling the lever, it had to press the lever for the next pellet and vice versa. After these two behaviors were well established, one of them was punished by the delivery of foot shock for every tenth instance of that behavior (press or pull depending on group assignment). The effects on both the punished behavior and the unpunished behavior are presented in Figure 7.16. Clearly, punishment influenced both behaviors in the first 15 minutes of the punishment sessions, but the unpunished behaviors recovered to their prepunishment levels while the punished behaviors remained suppressed. These data illustrate that aversive events can suppress behavior directly or through Pavlovian conditioning where the context serves as a CS. But they also illustrate that the punishment by application procedure (a positive contingency with a negative reinforcer) also influences behavior beyond the unconditioned and Pavlovian conditioned effects of the aversive event. Goodall (1984) provided similar evidence using a different procedure.

Omission Training (Punishment by Removal). When we think of punishment, we typically think of punishment by application, but we have all experienced another kind of punishment which involves the removal of access to an appetitive stimulus (or the removal of the opportunity to engage in some pleasurable activity). That is what being "grounded" is all about. The procedure of omission training (punishment by removal, "grounding") involves a *negative contingency between a behavior and a positive reinforcer*.[8] With this arrangement, the individual is less likely to retain access to the positive reinforcer following the target behavior [Pr (positive reinforcer | behavior occurred) < Pr (positive reinforcer | behavior did not occur)]. The typical effect is to *decrease the likelihood* of the target behavior occurring in the future because the target behavior is punished by the *omission* of the positive reinforcer. The individual can retain access to the positive reinforcer by not exhibiting the target behavior (Table 7.2, top right panel).

---

[8]Punishment by removal is also referred to by some people as **differential reinforcement of other behavior (DRO)** because any behavior *other* than the target behavior can be followed by a positive reinforcer.

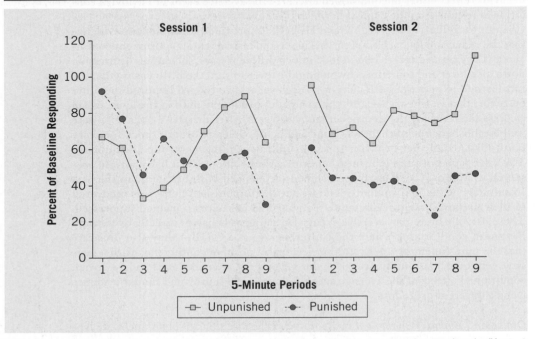

Figure 7.16 Punishment by application. Mean rates of behavior (relative to the prepunishment levels) for the punished and unpunished behaviors across two 45-minute sessions. Every 10th occurrence of the punished behavior was followed by shock.

Figure redrawn from "Comparison of stimulus learning and response learning in a punishment situation" by R. C. Bolles, R. Holtz, T. Dunn, and W. Hill, in *Learning and Motivation*, Volume 11, 78–96, copyright © 1980 by Academic Press, reproduced by permission of Elsevier Science.

In most omission training situations, the original behavior is established with a positive contingency between the behavior and the positive reinforcer *before* the omission training procedure is introduced. Thus, with the introduction of omission training, the contingency changes from positive to negative, and the target behavior is no longer followed by the positive reinforcer. Behaviors no longer followed by positive reinforcers are extinguished. This presents a problem in interpretation: does the individual cease performing the target behavior because it is no longer followed by the positive reinforcer (the procedure of extinction) or because not performing that behavior produces a positive reinforcer (the negative contingency)? Wilson, Boakes, and Swan (1987) provided rather convincing evidence that the observed changes in behavior produced by the omission are due to the negative contingency between the target behavior and the positive reinforcer.

The design of Wilson et al.'s (1987) experiment is presented in Table 7.5. Their subjects were hungry rats. Pretraining consisted of occasional presentations of food while running in a wheel. The food was presented at random times whether or not the rats turned the wheel (a zero contingency). Nevertheless, after a number of days on this zero contingency, the rats developed a fairly stable level of running. No tones or lights were present during pretraining. Then the rats were divided into two groups. The experimental group (omission training) then received six 2-minute long presentations of a distinctive stimulus (for some subjects it was a tone and for others a light) alternating with 2-minute long periods of no stimulus (as in the pretraining condition). The omission training contingency was in effect during the stimulus periods. During the no-stimulus periods, the number and distribution of food presentations were matched to that received during the preceding stimulus period. Any differences in wheel running between the stimulus and no-stimulus periods would be due to the negative contingency in the stimulus periods and not the reduction in food. There was also a yoked-control group that received the same pattern of food presentations as the experimental group subjects during training when the stimulus was present and when it was absent. Thus, for the control group, there was no programmed contingency between their behavior and the presentations of food; those presentations were determined by the behavior of the experimental group during both the stimulus and no-stimulus periods (see Box 7.6). The results of this experiment are presented in Figure 7.17. Wheel running declined only in the presence of the stimulus for the experimental (omission training) group. This is the only condition that contained

Table 7.5 Design of Wilson, Boakes, and Swan (1987) Experiment on Omission Training

Group	Pretraining	Training
Experimental (omission training)	Free food (zero contingeny) while running in a wheel	In the *presence* of a stimulus (tone or light), food given when rat does **not** run for 10 seconds (omission training).
		In the *absence* of the stimulus, food presentations matched to those during stimulus (VT or variable time).
Control (yoked)	Free food (zero contingeny) while running in a wheel	Each rat in the control group was yoked to a rat in the experimental group so that they received the same number and patterns of food as the experimental subjects in the presence and absence of the stimulus.

the omission training contingency. These data illustrate that a negative contingency with a positive reinforcer has the effect of reducing the behavior involved in that contingency.

A large number of terms and concepts have been introduced in this chapter, and many of these will be used in the rest of this book. It is important that you become familiar with them. To help you, the basic terms and concepts covered in this chapter to this point are contained in the Glossary and on the inside back cover.

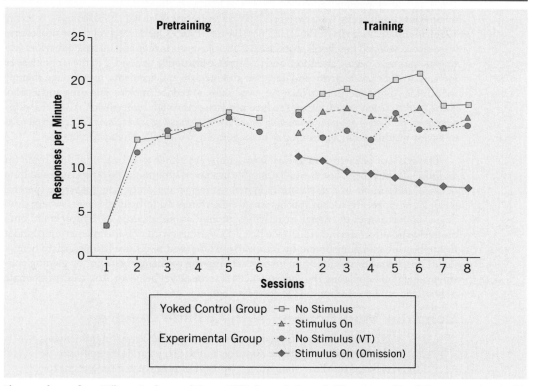

Figure 7.17 Wheel running during pretraining and during training (between stimulus and no stimulus). VT means that food is delivered at variable times (determined by the pattern of food presentations on the omission schedule during the immediately preceding stimulus period). The control group is called "yoked."

Figure redrawn from Wilson, Boakes, and Swan, 1987, *Quarterly Journal of Experimental Psychology* B. Reprinted with permission of Psychology Press Ltd.

BEHAVIOR MODIFICATION

Behavior modification involves the systematic application of the procedures of operant conditioning as therapeutic interventions to reduce inappropriate behaviors and to increase appropriate behaviors. Although not all behavior modification programs have been successful in producing therapeutic gains, there are a number of areas in which behavior modification is the preferred treatment.

Although people have known how to use reinforcers and punishments to influence behavior since ancient times, the systematic application of the procedures we now call operant conditioning began in the 1950s. In his 1953 book *Science and Human Behavior*, Skinner suggested that inappropriate behaviors are maintained by reinforcement and that the absence of appropriate behaviors is due to the lack of reinforcement for those behaviors. Beginning in the mid-1950s, operant conditioning procedures were applied to modify the behavior of psychotic patients (see, e.g., Lindsley, 1956; Ayllon & Michael, 1959), normal children (Azrin & Lindsley, 1956; Bijou, 1955), autistic children (Ferster, 1961; Ferster & DeMyer, 1961, 1962), and developmentally disabled children (Orlando & Bijou, 1960), and treatments based on operant conditioning were developed to treat stuttering (Flanagan, Goldiamond, & Azrin, 1958), thumb sucking (Baer, 1962), and tics (Barrett, 1962). Operant conditioning procedures were also developed in schools to increase academic performance and on-task behaviors (sitting in one's seat, paying attention) and to decrease disruptive behaviors, in the work place to increase worker productivity and decrease absenteeism and accidents, in marriage therapy to increase communication, to increase social skills, to reduce smoking and drug and alcohol abuse, and to teach relaxation and reduce headaches through biofeedback. All of these *systematic applications of operant conditioning procedures as therapeutic interventions* are referred to as behavior modification, contingency management, and applied behavior analysis.[9]

The goals of behavior modification programs are either to get an individual to do (or do more of) some behavior deemed desirable in a given situation or to do less of something deemed undesirable in that situation. When the individual is not doing what we (parent, teacher, therapist, etc.) deem appropriate, we use things the individual wants (sweets, privileges, opportunities to engage in activities, money, attention, etc.) as reinforcers to both motivate and direct the individual (see Box 7.5). Various forms of punishment (punishment by application and punishment by removal) are also used to reduce inappropriate behaviors. Thus, behavior modification involves attempting to change behavior by gaining control over and manipulating the consequences of some target behavior. An excellent example of how this can be accomplished is described below.

Behavior Modification With Autistic Children

No other therapeutic procedure has been as successful in influencing the behavior of autistic children as the program described here. It is based on the systematic application of positive reinforcement for appropriate behavior and punishment for inappropriate behavior.

The *Diagnostic and Statistical Manual of Mental Disorders, Fifth Edition* (DSM-5; American Psychiatric Association, 2013) classifies Autism Spectrum Disorder as a neurodevelopmental disorder characterized by "persistent deficits in social communication and social interaction across multiple contexts" and "restricted, repetitive patterns of behavior, interests, or activities." These symptoms are present from early childhood and cause significant impairment of everyday functioning (pp. 50–53). Although not all children classified as autistic display the same patterns of behavior, in general autistic children have deficits in both verbal and nonverbal communication (e.g., eye contact, communicative gestures). Where language has developed, these children may only repeat back what is said to them (echolalia) rather than use these words for interactive communication. Many autistic children engage in excessive self-stimulation (e.g., rocking, repetitively twirling objects, finger flapping) rather than creative play either by themselves or with others. Sometimes the self-stimulation takes the

---

[9]The term behavior therapy is reserved for *procedures that are based on Pavlovian conditioning.*

form of self-hitting and self-mutilation. This severe disorder in the development of social interactions is estimated to occur in 4 to 5 of every 10,000 children, and traditional psychodynamic therapies have not been found to be effective in treating children with autism (e.g., Kanner & Eisenberg, 1955; Kanner, Rodriguez, & Ashenden, 1972; Rutter, 1966). O. Ivar Lovaas and his colleagues developed the following intensive program for autistic children that is successful in reducing self-destructive and other self-stimulatory behaviors, increasing social behaviors, and teaching these children to use language for communication.

Because it is difficult to teach a child anything when he or she is engaged in self-stimulation or is having a tantrum, Lovaas and his colleagues first used extinction and punishment to reduce these behaviors (Lovaas & Simmons, 1969). Extinction was carried out by placing the children in a 12-foot by 12-foot room for 90 minutes each and allowing them to engage in self-destructive behaviors uninterrupted.[10] The data from two children treated in this manner are presented in Figure 7.18. Clearly, in both cases ignoring

Figure 7.18 Extinction of self-destructive behaviors in two autistic boys placed in a room and allowed to hit themselves without intervention. Starting on Day 18, a series of additional interventions were tried with Gregg. These included complete social deprivation (DEP), continual attention (SAT), and pleading for him to stop when he engaged in self-destructive behavior (REI = reinforcement with social attention). Note that self-destructive acts worsened the first two times social attention was introduced.

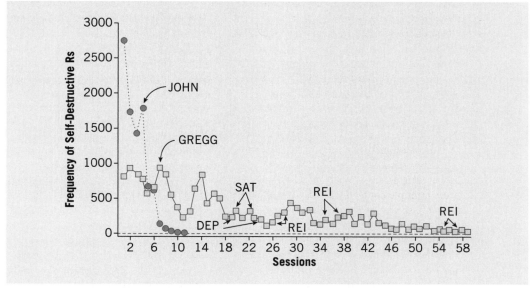

From Lovaas and Simmons, 1969. Reprinted with permission of John Wiley and Sons.

---

[10]The remainder of the time they were restrained in their beds to prevent them from hurting themselves. This was the method used to control their self-destructive behaviors before Lovaas introduced extinction and punishment.

self-destructive actions resulted in their reduction. This suggests that self-mutilation may have been maintained by the attention received from others while attempting to stop it. However, the reductions in self-mutilation observed in Figure 7.18 did not carry over into other situations. Furthermore, a more significant problem is that a great deal of self-destructive behavior occurred during the course of extinction before the individuals stopped. In some cases, that could lead to severe damage or even death. For these reasons, Lovaas and his colleagues also used punishment to suppress self-destructive behaviors (see Box 7.7).

The Use of Aversive Stimulation in Behavior Modification

Probably one of the most controversial areas in behavior modification is the use of aversive stimulation. Most of us are uncomfortable with the thought of using electric shock to control another person's behavior, but we are equally uncomfortable with images of children living in restraints or drug-induced stupors because they would inflict grievous injury to themselves if left unrestrained. Given that choice, most of us would accept the brief use of electric shock where other methods have failed to stop serious and life-threatening behaviors. However, the use of aversive stimulation should be the treatment of last resort (Lovaas & Favell, 1987).

In the following excerpt, Lovaas describes how he came to use behavior-contingent aversive stimulation in his program. Beth was a 13-year-old autistic girl who had engaged in self-destructive behavior for 10 years. As a result, she had major scar tissue on her scalp from banging her head against objects and on her hands and face from biting and scratching herself. Traditional psychotherapy had been ineffective in stopping these behaviors.

One more accidental observation may be worth mentioning, and that concerns the "decision" to use contingent aversives. Persons often ask me how that came about. When one sees a client

(or "subject") once or twice a week, one develops a relationship with that person that is very different from seeing a person 6 hours a day, 5 days a week over most of a year. Also, by the time I saw Beth, I had helped raise four children and learned a great deal about how to raise them. By now I was spending much more time with Beth than I had with my own children, and I had come to consider her as one of my own. One day, while I briefly interrupted Beth and her teacher's play to make a short comment, Beth walked away from us to a steel cabinet, bent over, and violently banged her head against the sharp corner. I would not let any of my own children act like that. Quite impulsively and without any contemplation, I reached over and gave her a whack on her behind with my hand. She stopped suddenly and looked at me, as if to ask, "Is this a psychiatric clinic or isn't it?" I experienced intense fear and guilt as to what I had done. However, Beth paused for about 1 minute, then as if to test me, hit her head once more. I mustered up enough courage to give her one more slap on the behind. At that point, Beth came back over to the teacher and me, and acted very affectionate and sociable.

BOX 7.7

There were no other acts of self-injury that day, or in my presence thereafter. This incident was never planned, and in fact, I would not have planned to do what I did. It was experiences like these that gradually led us to use the average environment and average children as a model for how to construct a treatment program. These experiences also taught us to change the natural environment only enough to isolate those variables which would make it both therapeutic and educational. As we were learning more about how to help these children, we became increasingly certain that Freud, Bettelheim, and others had, by their comprehensive, popular, and easy-to-understand theories, led themselves and others into an enormous blind alley.

Lovaas, 1993, p. 621. Reprinted with permission of John Wiley and Sons.

A more detailed description of Beth's treatment by Lovaas's team can be found in the paper by Lovaas, Freitag, Gold, and Kassorla (1965).

Lovaas used electric shock delivered by a hand-held shocker as the punishment for self-destructive behaviors. The shocks were described as painful (like a dentist drilling on an unanesthetized tooth), but they did not produce any tissue damage when applied for brief periods of time. Punishment in the form of a brief shock was applied to the child's leg within one second of a self-destructive action. The data from one individual in two different situations is presented in Figure 7.19. In the top panel, John was observed for 5 minutes each day sitting on someone's lap. Contingent shock for self-hitting was applied during those sessions indicated by an *S.* In the bottom panel, John was observed for 15 minutes in a different room from where the extinction recorded in Figure 7.18 occurred, but this time other people were in the room. In both situations, there were immediate and prolonged effects of the behavior-contingent shock. Furthermore, whining and avoiding people both declined in a similar manner, even though neither of those behaviors was punished, and the suppression of these behaviors eventually generalized to other people, even though the child was never shocked when with them (Experimenters 2 and 4 in the top panel of Figure 7.19). These results were replicated with other children.

As soon as the interfering behaviors began to decline, Lovaas and his colleagues used positive reinforcement to teach the children to use language for communication. This was accomplished by gradually shaping the children's verbal behaviors. The first step was to get the children to sit quietly and look at the teacher. These behaviors were rewarded with ice cream and other edible treats. Then any vocalizations irrespective of their content were encouraged, again by reinforcing them with edible treats. After that was accomplished, the treats were only given for making sounds within 5 seconds of a vocalization by the teacher. The next step was to require that the child make the same sound as the teacher (e.g., "ah"). After the child learned to imitate the first sound, the teacher added a second sound (e.g., "mm") that the child had to imitate in order to receive a reward. This was repeated to build a repertoire of imitative behaviors (Lovaas, Berberich, Perloff, & Schaeffer, 1966). The next step involved imitation of words and then the use of words to ask for things. The program

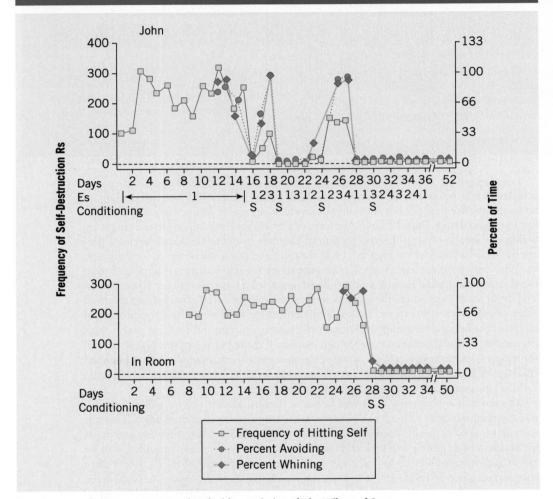

Figure 7.19 Frequency of a boy's self-destructive behaviors in two situations. Data in the top panel were recorded for daily 5-minute sessions while he sat on the lap of various experimenters (Es; labeled 1, 2, 3, and 4 under the horizontal axis). Data in the bottom panel were recorded during 15 minutes in another room with some adults present. Sessions in which shocks were administered for each self-destructive act are indicated below the horizontal axes with an S.

From Lovaas and Simmons, 1969. Reprinted with permission of John Wiley and Sons.

was structured to promote the use of language as a communication tool. Thus, in the final steps of the program, the correct uses of pronouns, tense, and abstract concepts (e.g., before and after, larger and smaller, same and different) were rewarded. Along the way, food was replaced by social approval ("good," hugs, etc.; Lovaas, Freitag, Kinder, Rubinstein, Schaeffer,

& Simmons, 1966). Finally, at the same time as the verbal communication program was being carried out, the children were also learning other social and self-help skills (dressing, personal hygiene, etc.; Lovaas, Freitag, Nelson, & Whalen, 1967).

This program involved a major expenditure of time, effort, and money (40 hours per week for 2 or more years) on each child, and although the program produced dramatic effects in some children, it was not successful in every case. Over the ensuing 30 years, Lovaas and his colleagues conducted a number of follow-up studies on their patients, and they have learned a great deal about what works and does not work. First, an intensive program with young children produces the best and most lasting results (Lovaas, 1987; McEachin, Smith & Lovaas, 1993). Second, gains from the program are more likely to last when the children are placed in environments that support those gains; otherwise the effects of the treatment are situation specific. Therefore, the program is moved out of the hospital and into the child's house where the parents are trained to become skilled teachers of their own children. It became obvious that the program is effective only as long as the reinforcers and punishments are maintained (Lovaas, Koegel, Simmons, & Long, 1973).

This last point should give us cause to reflect on the limits of behavior modification. As is the case when rats press levers and pigeons peck keys for food, operant behaviors are sustained only as long as they produce successful consequences. Normally the environment we live in provides consequences that maintain our behavior. As Maimonides suggested in the twelfth century (see Box 7.5), the range of rewards for humans expands to include social approval, recognition, and an appreciation for the inherent satisfactions we can gain from our activities. Unfortunately, it appears that autistic children (and others) require more environmental support than the rest of us. Although we may be dismayed that some people require tangible reinforcers and highly structured environments to sustain their appropriate behavior, that should not deter us from using operant conditioning procedures. In some cases, the best we can do is to offer a treatment that maintains appropriate behavior rather than a cure. In a sense, behavior modification with autistic children may be like insulin for diabetic individuals: Insulin does not cure diabetes, but it allows the individual to lead a productive life.

THE DIFFERENCES BETWEEN PAVLOVIAN CONDITIONING AND OPERANT CONDITIONING

Pavlovian conditioning and operant conditioning are different procedures. However, the distinction between them is more than procedural; the effects on behavior are different.

Although the differences between Pavlovian conditioning and instrumental learning (operant conditioning) were noted by Thorndike in 1911,[11] in the early decades of the twentieth century psychologists tended to adopt Pavlov's language and to describe most kinds of learning in terms of conditioned reflexes or CRs (Cason, 1925; Smith & Guthrie, 1921; Watson, 1919).

---

[11]In 1901, Thorndike described the behavior of his subjects as "trial and accidental success," and in 1911 as "trial and error learning." He described what we now call Pavlovian conditioning as "associative shifting." That term reflected Thorndike's view that Pavlovian conditioning involves one stimulus (the CS) becoming a substitute for another (the US).

Miller and Konorski (1928/1969) appear to be the first people to point out the important differences between these two procedures and the resulting behaviors that are produced. They restrained dogs in a standard Pavlovian conditioning apparatus (see Chapter 2, Figure 2.2). The dog's hind leg was passively flexed while a tone was presented. This was followed by food delivered directly into the dog's mouth. After a number of these tone–flexion–food presentations, the dog would actively flex its leg when the tone was presented.[12] Konorski and Miller (1937a) designated this learned response as a Type II conditioned reflex, to differentiate it from the standard Pavlovian conditioned reflex that they called Type I.

Without making reference to Miller and Konorski's 1928 paper, Skinner (1935b) also argued that there are two types of conditioned reflexes: In one case, the occurrence of the CR does not influence the occurrence of the US (Konorski & Miller's Type I), and in the other case, the response is *required* for the occurrence of the US (Konorski & Miller's Type II). Konorski and Miller (1937b) accepted Skinner's analysis as being consistent with theirs, but they took issue with some of the details. These need not concern us here.

In his response to Konorski and Miller's first 1937 paper, Skinner (1937) introduced the term **respondent** to describe behaviors that are elicited by a stimulus (Konorski & Miller's Type I responses) and the term **operant** for behaviors that emerge as the result of the relationship between the behavior and US. According to Skinner, an **operant** is *a behavior that occurs "spontaneously in the absence of any stimulation with which it may be specifically correlated."* He elaborated on this definition in his 1938 book, in which he described operants as *units of behavior that act upon the environment to produce certain effects.* Skinner defined a **respondent** as *a "response that is made to specific stimulation, where the correlation between response and stimulus is a reflex in the traditional sense"* (Skinner, 1937, p. 274). In 1940, Hilgard and Marquis introduced the term *classical conditioning* for Pavlov's "classical" procedure. Although some people still follow Skinner and use the term *respondent conditioning*, and others follow Hilgard and Marquis and use the term *classical conditioning*, today the most commonly used term is *Pavlovian conditioning*.

The Role of the Stimulus in Pavlovian and Operant Conditioning (and Instrumental Learning)

The CS in Pavlovian conditioning evokes the CR in a reflex-like manner. In operant conditioning, the stimulus functions as an occasion setter, similar to a Pavlovian occasion setter.

In the Pavlovian conditioning situation, a biologically important event (the US) *evokes* a species-specific action (UR). As a result of the positive contingency between some other

---

[12]Miller and Konorski noted that this effect depended on the US. The dog actively flexed its leg when food was the US but not when the US was a slap, an irritating puff of air, or acid in the mouth, even though all of these could be used as USs to produce defensive CRs. They reported that following flexion with a "negative stimulus" produced response inhibition, that is, active withholding of the behavior.

[13]There are also Pavlovian conditioning preparations in which the CR will occur to CSs that are presented simultaneously or in a negative contingency with the US. Some of these were described in Chapter 3.

event (the CS) and the US, that CS comes to *evoke* a CR.[13] It is quite clear that in Pavlovian conditioning, the resulting CR is a direct response to the presence of the CS. This is not true in operant conditioning.

Although Thorndike (1898, 1911) argued that the conditioned behaviors his cats made to escape from his problem boxes reflected the formation of an S-R association between the stimulus situation and the successful behavior, it is quite clear that such instrumental and operant behaviors are not simply responses *evoked* by stimuli. Skinner (1935b, 1938) pointed out the difference between a Pavlovian CS and what he labeled a **discriminative stimulus**. Discriminative stimuli are *events that signal a behavior-outcome relationship*; that is, they function as occasion setters, informing the individual about what behaviors lead to what outcomes. For example, Skinner (1938) trained rats to press a lever for food. After lever pressing was well established, Skinner changed the situation in the following way: He turned on a light in the chamber and continued to provide food when the rat pressed the lever. However, when the light was not illuminated, no food was given for lever presses (the procedure of extinction). As a result of this arrangement, his rats continued to press the lever in the presence of the light but not in its absence. Skinner argued that the light did not evoke lever pressing in the same way that a Pavlovian CS evokes a Pavlovian CR; the discriminative stimulus in operant conditioning "sets the occasion" for the behavior-outcome relationship; that is, it informs the individual that in this situation (light on) pressing the lever will be followed by food. This is similar to the information provided by Pavlovian occasion setters. In Pavlovian conditioning, occasion setters inform the individual about the current CS-US relationship (see Chapter 5); in operant conditioning, the discriminative stimulus informs the individual about the current behavior-outcome (B-O) relationship.

Despite this difference between Pavlovian CSs and operant discriminative stimuli in terms of how they influence behavior, an operant discriminative stimulus can *also* serve as a Pavlovian CS for conditioned emotional states. Every operant conditioning situation contains a Pavlovian conditioning procedure because the outcome occurs in some physical location (context) that has identifiable characteristics (spatial, visual, auditory, tactile, olfactory). These characteristics predict that the important event (outcome) will occur here. Thus they serve as both Pavlovian CSs for motivational states like hope and fear (see Chapter 6) and as discriminative stimuli when a given behavior is followed by the *hoped for* or *feared* event. This dual role for the stimuli that accompany significant events illustrates how operant conditioning and Pavlovian conditioning are intertwined.

Demonstrating That a Change in Behavior Is Due to Instrumental Learning or Operant Conditioning and Not Pavlovian Conditioning

In Pavlovian conditioning, the form of the CR depends on the CS, the US, and the relationship between these events. In operant conditioning, the form of the behavior depends on the relationship between that behavior and the outcome. Thus, manipulation of the behavior-outcome relationship should have no effect on behavior in Pavlovian conditioning; it should have a dramatic effect on behavior in operant conditioning.

Davey (1989) noted that any behavior that is directed toward some aspect of the environment like approaching the end of a maze or operating a lever to obtain food could result from sign-tracking, which we identify as a Pavlovian conditioning procedure. Therefore, to conclude that a behavior is due to operant conditioning, one must be able to demonstrate that the observed changes in behavior are due to the behavior-outcome relationship. This can be done by manipulating that relationship and observing the resulting changes in behavior (see the story of Thales earlier in this chapter).

Grindley (1932) provided the first clear evidence that satisfies Davey's (1989) condition for a demonstration that operant behavior is influenced by its consequences. Grindley restrained guinea pigs so that the only movement they could make was to turn their heads from side to side (Figure 7.20). The procedure was straightforward. A buzzer sounded while the guinea pig was facing straight ahead. If the animal turned its head in the correct direction (left or right depending on group assignment), the carrot would be raised and the animal was allowed to take one bite before the carrot was lowered. Over the course of repeated trials, the time it took the guinea pigs to initiate the head turn decreased (Figure 7.21). By itself,

Figure 7.20 Grindley's apparatus for measuring head movements in guinea pigs. Movements were recorded by displacement of the bar marked S. Movements were rewarded by raising a carrot (F) so that the guinea pig could eat it.

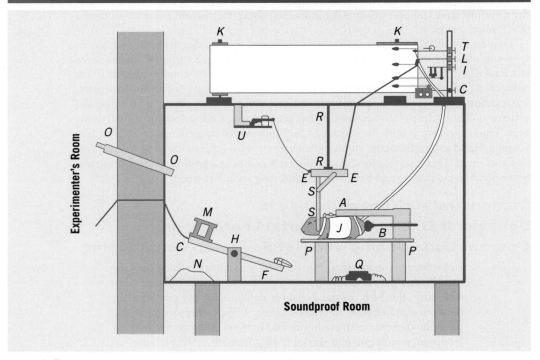

From Grindley, 1932.

these results do not provide convincing evidence that the head turning behavior was due solely to the reward. Grindley provided such evidence by *reversing* the behavior-outcome relationship. If the animal had learned to turn its head to the right, it now had to turn it to the left (and vice versa). The results of this reversal of the behavior-outcome relationship are presented in Figure 7.22. Note that over repeated trials, the old response becomes less likely to occur. Therefore, the head turning behavior must have been due to the behavior-outcome relationship because the only thing that changed when the behavior was reversed was that relationship. The buzzer served as a discriminative stimulus (see above) for the particular behavior-outcome relationship in effect during the different stages of this experiment.

Clearly, Grindley's (1932) demonstration satisfies Davey's (1989) condition for demonstrating that a behavior change is due to operant conditioning. Not only did his subjects learn to turn their heads more quickly in the direction Grindley selected for them through the behavior-outcome contingency he imposed, they also reversed the direction they turned their heads when Grindley reversed the direction required to obtain food. Turning one's head in one direction or another has no natural relationship to obtaining food in guinea pigs. On the other hand, the behaviors Skinner used (lever pressing for food in rats and key pecking for food in pigeons) require the individual to approach something that is related to the occurrence of food; this suggests sign-tracking. Furthermore, both lever pressing and key pecking are not arbitrarily chosen behaviors because they arise out of these species' food-seeking behavior systems. Despite the simplicity of Grindley's

Figure 7.21   The acquisition of a head turn response in a single guinea pig. The measure of learning is a decrease in the time to respond, expressed here as the logarithm of the number of seconds.

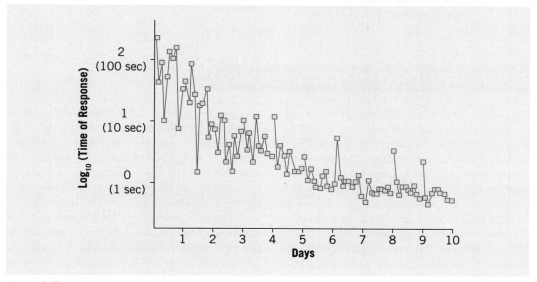

From Grindley, 1932.

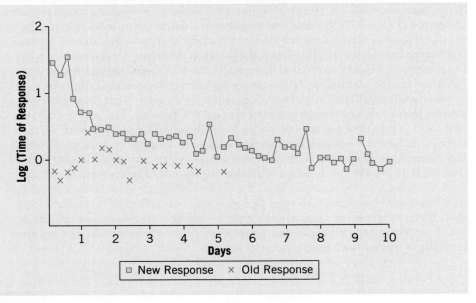

Figure 7.22   A typical curve for the reversal of the head turning response.

From Grindley, 1932.

demonstration, his work has been virtually ignored in most presentations of operant conditioning despite the fact that he provided a more convincing demonstration of operant conditioning than Skinner.

SUMMARY AND CONCLUSIONS

The *procedure of operant conditioning* involves a contingency between a behavior and some event (outcome for performing that behavior). The *phenomenon of operant conditioning* is the change in behavior that is observed after experiencing the procedure. Typically, behaviors followed by hedonically positive (appetitive) events (such as, food, money, approval, or safety) are more likely to occur, and behaviors followed by hedonically negative (unpleasant or aversive) events (such as shock, loss of rewards or privileges, or reprimands) are less likely to occur. In the language of

operant conditioning, hedonically positive events are commonly called *positive reinforcers*, and hedonically negative events are called *negative reinforcers*. Reinforcers (also termed outcomes, rewards and consequences) can involve either the occurrence of something after a behavior (a positive contingency) or the absence of something after a behavior (a negative contingency). The outcome need not involve only biologically important events. There are many outcomes that influence behavior that are not essential for survival (like the opportunity to do something), and in some cases, an outcome derives its ability to influence behavior through a Pavlovian conditioning procedure. We call these outcomes *conditioned reinforcers*. Outcomes that influence behavior with little or no learning involved are called *primary reinforcers*.

There are four basic procedures for operant conditioning that involve the two kinds of contingencies (positive and negative) and two classes of outcomes (positive and negative reinforcers). Thus, we can define *positive reinforcement* as a positive behavior–outcome contingency with a positive reinforcer, *punishment (by application)* as a positive behavior–outcome contingency with a negative

reinforcer, *omission training (punishment by removal)* as a negative behavior–outcome contingency with a positive reinforcer, and *negative reinforcement (escape, avoidance)* as a negative behavior–outcome contingency with a negative reinforcer.

Although we use terms like *reinforce, reinforcer,* and *reinforcement* to describe the procedures of operant conditioning, it is obvious that the mechanism underlying operant conditioning does not involve strengthening of behaviors by those things we call reinforcers. In subsequent chapters, we will examine other effects of behavior-outcome relationships and the psychological processes that we believe underlie these phenomena.

STUDY QUESTIONS

1. What is the procedure of operant conditioning? What is the phenomenon of operant conditioning? How is operant conditioning (instrumental learning) different from Pavlovian conditioning?

2. How does a cumulative recorder work? How are the following patterns of behavior represented on a cumulative record:

    a. rapid performance of the target behavior?

    b. slow steady performance of the target behavior?

    c. no performance of the target behavior?

3. Define the following terms as they apply to operant conditioning:

    a. extinction (procedure)

    b. extinction (phenomenon)

    c. spontaneous recovery

    d. shaping by the method of successive approximations

    e. chaining

    f. prompting

4. What is the difference between a positive reinforcer and a negative reinforcer? What is the difference between a reinforcer and reinforcement?

5. In your own words, what is the Law of Effect as Thorndike and Skinner applied it to instrumental learning and operant conditioning? Why do we believe the Law of Effect as formulated by Thorndike and Skinner is not correct?

6. What is the difference between a primary reinforcer and a conditioned reinforcer? How are conditioned reinforcers produced, and what roles do they serve in operant conditioning?

7. With respect to reinforcers, what is an establishing operation and why is this concept important? How is this related to Premack's research illustrating that the opportunity to

engage in a behavior can serve as a positive reinforcer for other behaviors?

8. Describe the basic procedure of instrumental (operant) conditioning. Be able to describe the following variations in terms of the reinforcers (positive or negative) and the contingencies (positive or negative):

a. positive reinforcement

b. negative reinforcement

c. omission training

d. punishment by application

What are the effects of these procedures on behavior?

9. How can we demonstrate that a behavior is due to operant conditioning and not Pavlovian conditioning? Give an example.

8

HOW INDIVIDUALS ADJUST THEIR BEHAVIOR TO MEET THE DEMANDS OF THE SITUATION

In an ideal environment, food, water, and mates are readily available whenever the individual seeks them, and there are no predators or other dangers. But life is not like that for most species (including us humans). Food, water, and mates must be found, and danger must be avoided. Even when food is located, sometimes it is not readily accessible, and the individual must do something to gain access to the edible parts (e.g., crack things open, capture prey, climb to get it). This lack of accessibility imposes a barrier between the individual and his or her goal. Many species have innate knowledge of how to overcome these barriers, and innate knowledge is an economical solution to the problem so long as the barriers are constant, but new challenges require new solutions. Operant conditioning involves learning how to overcome these barriers.

Operant Conditioning
From Two Different Perspectives

In the laboratory, the procedures of operant conditioning impose barriers that the individual has to overcome to reach his or her objective. The phenomena we call operant conditioning reflect how individuals adapt their behavior to try to overcome these barriers. Therefore, we should approach the study of operant conditioning from both points of view: what we do to the individual, and what the individual does in response.

Operant Conditioning From the Point of View of the Experimenter and the Behavior Modifier. We study operant conditioning in the laboratory by imposing artificial barriers or constraints on individuals (requiring them to do something like press a lever or peck a key to obtain food or avoid shock) so that we can discover how they learn to overcome these barriers. Likewise, behavior modification involves attempting to change an individual's behavior by gaining control over and manipulating the consequences of a certain behavior. If we are successful, our subjects will adapt to these manipulations as we intended. Whether we are manipulating the outcomes of behavior to study how individuals adapt to our manipulations or manipulating the outcomes to modify behavior, *we* know what the individual has to do (and when and where it has to be done) to obtain the positive reinforcer or avoid the negative reinforcer. *The individual has to discover these things.*

Operant Conditioning From the Point of View of the Individual. **From the point of view of the individual, operant conditioning** is a problem-solving task: Discover where the things one wants are and what is required to get them. Success is obtaining the goal. For example, in Thorndike's experiments with cats in the problem box and Skinner's original experiments on rats pressing levers, a hungry animal was required to do something to obtain food. In both situations, the animals engaged in a variety of behaviors until they performed the one designated correct by the experimenter. With repeated experience, the behavior designated by the experimenter as correct was performed quicker and more often, and unsuccessful behaviors dropped out. This is our evidence that the animals learned something. They could have performed the correct behavior the first time they were in the situation, but they did not because they did not know what was required of them. The animals learned from their experience in the situation what behavior designated by the experimenter would produce food.

It is common to describe the behavior of individuals in operant conditioning tasks as engaging in "trial and error" as they attempt to overcome the barriers we place in front of them, but that description masks the fact that individuals do not come into the situation empty-handed. How they go about solving the problems imposed on them by the environment, the experimenter, or the behavior modifier depends on the evolutionary history of their species, the structure of the situation, and their past experiences in similar situations or when seeking similar objectives. Operant conditioning does involve trial and error, but not in a haphazard way. Individuals first try those things that worked in similar situations in the past, either their own or their ancestors' past, and the successful individual discovers that a given behavior produces the desired outcome. Thus, from the individual's point of view, operant conditioning is also an inference task where the best predictor of the outcome is the individual's own behavior. The task is to figure out what that behavior is so that the next time that situation is encountered, he or she can behave quickly and efficiently.

THE FUNCTIONS OF REINFORCERS IN OPERANT CONDITIONING

Reinforcers (both positive and negative) serve two functions in operant conditioning. One function is to provide a reason for doing something. In that capacity, reinforcers serve as sources of incentive motivation, the goal toward which behavior is directed. The second function is as a source of feedback for selecting the behavior that will achieve the goal.

Every operant conditioning situation consists of three elements: the context and events in that context that inform the individual that this is a place where certain behaviors lead to certain outcomes, the required behaviors, and the outcomes of those behaviors. These outcomes are called reinforcers when the individual's behavior changes as a result of the contingency between his or her behavior and that outcome.

Thus, events are identified as reinforcers because of their effects on the behaviors that produce them: Positive reinforcers increase the probability of behaviors that produce them, and negative reinforcers increase the probability of behaviors that cancel or remove them. Events that do neither are not reinforcers. Reinforcers have these effects in operant conditioning because they serve two functions. The first function is motivational: Reinforcers are the goals of operant behaviors; that is, they are the things that individuals try to obtain (positive reinforcers) or get away from (negative reinforcers). The second function is to provide feedback as to the correctness of a given behavior for obtaining the outcome.

Reinforcers as Sources of Incentive Motivation

The psychological process we call motivation influences operant conditioning and the performance of operant behaviors. There are two kinds of motivation: drives that are aroused by changes in internal conditions or aversive stimulation, and incentive motivations that are aroused by the goal or signals for the goal. Deprivation of food or water is typically used to arouse a drive, and the food or water also serves as the incentive or goal for certain behaviors.

Motivation is *the psychological process we invoke to explain both the activation and goal-directedness of some behaviors*. Motivation, like learning, is an intervening variable. Motivations cannot be directly observed; we infer them from the individual's behavior. For example, we infer that individuals are hungry when we observe them seek and eat food, are thirsty when we observe them seek and drink fluids, are sexually aroused when we observe them seek sex partners or other means of sexual gratification, are afraid when we observe them tremble and seek safety when certain stimuli are present, and are motivated to achieve when we observe them engage in activities that lead to success and recognition. Thus *the impetus to perform behaviors directed toward some desired goal is attributed to the psychological process called motivation*.

Motivations can be aroused in a number of ways. Sometimes motivations are aroused by changes in internal conditions. For example, the behaviors involved in ingestion have their origin in the maintenance of the internal environment at constant levels (homeostasis). This internal balance can be upset by deprivation of food and water, increases in activity, increases in levels of insulin in the blood, and ingestion of dry or salty foods, and the consumption of food and water restore that balance. Likewise, people become addicted to drugs when these drugs disturb the internal environment and taking these same drugs provides temporary relief from the resulting discomfort. But not all motivation is due to simple regulation of the internal environment. Some motivations are induced by external factors. Eating can be induced by the presence of food in nondeprived individuals; sexual arousal can be induced by reading about, seeing, or hearing sexually-oriented activities; and escape and avoidance are triggered by pain or perceived danger. Learning can also play a role in motivated behavior: As a result of Pavlovian conditioning, signals for food can produce food-oriented behaviors, signals of impending sexual activity can evoke sexual arousal, and signals for danger can evoke fear (see Chapter 2). Thus, *motivated behaviors are aroused by changes in internal states, by external stimulation, or by some combination of both* (Colgan, 1989; Toates, 1986).

Drives. It is common to attribute increased behavior that results from deprivation to an internal state called a drive (hunger, thirst, sex, curiosity). Some of these drives can also be aroused by injecting chemicals. A **drive** is an *inferred psychological process that arises from some internal need or bodily state. It is an intervening variable invoked to provide a link between the conditions (independent variables) that produce the internal state and the resulting activated behaviors (dependent variable).* For example, how fast and how long rats will press a lever to obtain water, how much water they will drink, and how much quinine (a bitter taste) in that water will deter them from drinking (all dependent variables) are a function of how long they are deprived of water, how much dry food they are allowed to eat, and how much saline they are injected with (all independent variables). N. E. Miller (1959) argued that invoking a thirst drive was a convenient way to summarize the relationships between these various independent variables and their common effects on behavior (dependent variables). Although not all of these independent variables will have the same effects on all of these dependent variables, it still seems useful to invoke a thirst drive as the common factor underlying consumption of water as a result of these various manipulations. The intervening variable of a thirst drive provides a conceptual link between the various independent and dependent variables.

The concept of drive has a long and complicated history in psychology (Smith, 1984). Although there is no universally accepted definition of drive that satisfies everyone, and not everyone agrees that the concept is of value for understanding behavior (e.g., Hinde, 1960), we continue to use it because it appears to be a useful construct (see, e.g., MacFarland, 1970; Smith, 1984).

Incentive Motivation. Sometimes motivations are aroused by external events. Most of us will eat a piece of candy that is offered to us or is readily available even after we have eaten a full meal. Likewise, the smell of fresh baked bread or the sound of a clock striking noon can arouse our desire to eat. In all of these situations, the motivation for eating does not arise from deprivation or disturbances in our internal environment; it comes from the sight of the candy, the smell of the bread, or the association of eating with certain times of the day. The taste (hedonic value) and the caloric value of food are two things that influence how *attractive* that food is to an individual. But attractiveness is not a static attribute of an object. Although the attractiveness of something is influenced by its physical characteristics, attractiveness is determined by the individual and depends on his or her species, personal experiences, and physical and psychological states at the moment. We cannot measure attractiveness independently of how the individual behaves toward that object or event; we infer the attractiveness of something by observing how much individuals consume (in the case of things that can be ingested like food and fluid) or how hard they work to obtain those things. *Another term for attractiveness* is incentive value, and *the things that individuals work to obtain* are called incentives. *Positive reinforcers are also referred to as* incentives because individuals will perform behaviors to obtain them, and how hard individuals work for a given positive reinforcer depends on its incentive value to the individual at that time.

Therefore, we also attribute our desire to eat to incentive motivation when that desire is aroused by the presence of food or by a signal for impending food. Incentive motivation is an *inferred psychological process that is aroused by the reinforcer (or a signal for the reinforcer). The independent variable is the presentation of something of hedonic value or a signal for that something, and the dependent measure is the accompanying change in behavior involving that hedonic event.* Thus incentives, like drives, also provide impetus and direction to behavior.

There is no doubt that *operant behavior is goal-directed and influenced by the incentive value of the goal.* In Chapter 7, we reviewed the observations by Elliott (1928) and Tinklepaugh (1928) on the effects of changing the expected outcome after conditioning had occurred. In both cases, changing from a preferred outcome to a less-preferred, but otherwise adequate, outcome-induced search behavior. Crespi (1942) and Zeaman (1949) demonstrated that shifting the incentive value of the outcome (defined in terms of the number of food pellets) on rats running down an alley to obtain food produced abrupt changes in the speed of running on each trial (see Figure 8.1). An interesting aspect of these data is the "overshooting" that occurred; that is, rats shifted from 1 or 4 pellets to 16 pellets ran faster than rats trained with 16 pellets from the start (Figure 8.1, left panel), and rats shifted from 256 or 64 pellets to 16 pellets ran slower than those trained with 16 pellets from the start (Figure 8.1, right panel). This *overshooting* is called incentive contrast because the effect *depends on the individual experiencing a change in the incentive value of the outcome.*

A related effect called behavioral contrast occurs when the individual is working for two different outcomes and one of the outcomes is changed (made larger or smaller or provided more or less often). The result is that as *the behavior that produces the changed outcome increases or decreases (depending on the change in the outcome), the behavior that produces the unchanged outcome goes in the opposite direction.* For example, when pecking at a red key and pecking at a green key both lead to the same amount of food, pigeons will peck at the same rate at both colored keys. When the amount of food obtained by pecking at the red key is reduced, pigeons will peck less at that key and peck *more* at the green key, even though the amount of food obtained for pecking at the green key does not change.

The phenomena of incentive contrast and behavioral contrast indicate that individuals can learn about the value of outcomes, and this incentive value of the outcome influences the vigor with which they execute instrumental and operant behaviors. In the case of incentive contrast, an increase in the incentive value of the outcome produces more vigorous behavior than would be produced by that same outcome in the absence of a shift, and a decrease in the incentive value of the outcome produces less vigorous behavior than would be produced by that same outcome in the absence of a shift. In the case of behavioral contrast, the shift in the amount or frequency of an outcome for one behavior influences the performance of both that behavior and the performance of other behaviors for which the outcome was not shifted. In the case of a downshift in incentive value or amount of food, the behavior of rats shifts from a consume/handle mode to a search mode (see Chapter 6; Pecoraro et al., 1999).

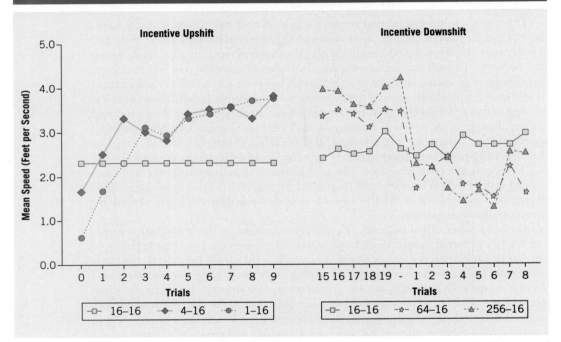

Figure 8.1 The effects of shifting the value of the incentive (number of food pellets) on the speed of running in a straight alley for various groups of rats. For group designation, the first number is the number of pellets in training and the second number is the number of pellets after the shift. The number of pellets was shifted upward in the left panel (shift data only). The number of pellets was shifted downward in the right panel (preshift and shift data are both presented). One group in the right panel (16-16) was not shifted.

Redrawn from Crespi, 1942, *American Journal of Psychology*. Copyright © 1942 by the Board of Trustees of the University of Illinois. Used with permission of the University of Illinois Press.

Signals for food and other biologically significant events can also acquire incentive value. In Chapter 7, we distinguished between primary and conditioned reinforcers. Primary reinforcers are events that serve as reinforcers with little or no experience required, whereas conditioned reinforcers derive their ability to serve as reinforcers as a result of Pavlovian conditioning where they predict the occurrence of primary reinforcers. For example, Skinner (1938) demonstrated that the sound of the food magazine (which precedes the delivery of food) can function as a conditioned reinforcer for lever pressing in rats even when no food is presented during lever press training (see Chapter 7). Williams (1994b) argued that conditioned reinforcers are effective because they acquire the incentive value of the primary reinforcer that they precede.

Reinforcers and Feedback

The second function of reinforcers is to provide feedback as to how successful various behaviors are in obtaining the goal.

In addition to being the goal of instrumental activities, the appearance of the reinforcing event soon after a behavior occurs also provides feedback to the individual that this is the correct behavior. Although individuals can learn to perform operant behaviors when there is a delay between the behavior and the outcome (Dickinson, Watt, & Griffiths, 1992; Lattal & Gleeson, 1990; Reed & Reilly, 1990; Wilkenfield, Nickel, Blakely, & Poling, 1992), operant conditioning proceeds most rapidly when there is little or no delay. (See Renner, 1964, for a review of the earlier studies on delay of reinforcement.) However, even in those situations where there is a delay between the operant behavior and the presentation of the outcome, successful conditioning is enhanced when there is a stimulus change immediately following the target behavior. In most operant conditioning situations, that stimulus change is provided by a sound that accompanies the mechanical operation of the manipulandum (lever or key), a programmed signal that the lever is depressed or the key pecked (a loud click or short blinking of the lights), or the sound of the food magazine when it is activated.

Bolles and Popp (1964) illustrated the importance of feedback in operant conditioning in the following experiment: They trained rats to avoid shock using an unsignaled avoidance procedure (see Chapter 7). With this procedure, shocks were presented every 5 seconds unless the rat pressed the lever, and each lever press postponed the next shock for 15 seconds. To investigate the effects of behavior-produced feedback, Bolles and Popp used a lever that was both silent (switch closure made no sound) and damped down so that there was no "feel" when it was depressed or released. Two groups of 10 rats each were then exposed to the unsignaled avoidance contingency. The rats in the first group used the lever described here. The rats in the other group also used that lever, but every lever press produced immediate sensory feedback in the form of a click from an outside device. Thus for the first group of rats, the only consequence of a lever press was the reduction in the frequency of shock following a lever press, whereas for the second group, there was the click and a reduction in shock frequency. Seven of the 10 rats in the group with the behavior-produced click learned to press the lever while only two of the 10 rats in the other group did. Clearly, the immediate feedback from each lever press made the difference.

In the Bolles and Popp (1964) and Skinner (1938) experiments, feedback provided by a stimulus change immediately after the target behavior occurred facilitated the learning of that behavior. But in both cases, an event of hedonic value (food or shock reduction) eventually followed. It is possible to demonstrate that pure feedback alone can serve as an effective reinforcer.

Trowbridge and Cason (1932), in a classic study of the effects of feedback on motor behavior in humans, demonstrated that different kinds of feedback have different effects on performance. The participants were given the task of drawing a 3-inch line on a piece of paper. After each attempt, three of the four groups of participants were given different kinds of feedback as to the accuracy of their performance on that trial. Subjects in the group labeled *RW* were merely told "right" when their line was within 1/8 inch of

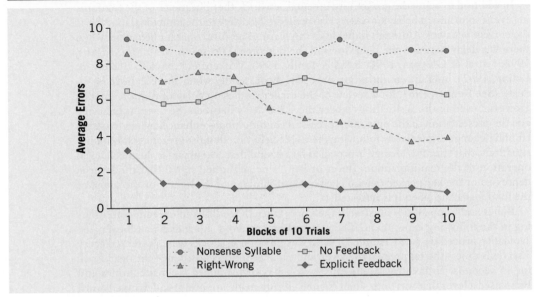

Figure 8.2 The effects of different types of feedback on the acquisition of a motor behavior (drawing a 3-inch line on a piece of paper). The descriptions of the four groups are given in the text.

From Trowbridge and Cason, 1932.

the required length and "wrong" otherwise. A second group (labeled *Correct*) was given quantitative knowledge of results; that is, they were told how far off they were in terms of the number of eighths of an inch they were over or under (e.g., minus 3 for 3/8 inch too short). A third group (*Nonsense*) received a nonsense syllable that had no relation to the outcome after each attempt. This feedback was irrelevant to the task. A fourth group (*NF*) received no feedback at all. The results of this experiment are presented in Figure 8.2. Subjects showed little improvement with no feedback (NF) and irrelevant feedback (Nonsense). The quantitative feedback (Correct) produced the greatest effect on performance, but the group with the less informative qualitative feedback (RW) also showed improvement. Thus, individuals can adjust their behavior based on feedback as to the correctness of their behavior. In the next section, we will look at how individuals can use feedback to improve their situation.

ADAPTIVE BEHAVIOR BY HILL-CLIMBING

In operant conditioning, individuals can use feedback from their behavior to determine which behavior is more efficient for obtaining the outcome through the process called hill-climbing. Hill-climbing is a fundamental adaptive process that helps individuals improve their situation based on feedback.

Successful operant conditioning requires the individual to do three things. First the individual must *classify the situation in terms of its motivational significance*—this classification can be based on either innate knowledge or learned knowledge (e.g., Pavlovian conditioned emotional and motivational states), and it involves the incentive value of the outcome for that individual. Second, *depending on that classification, the individual engages in a variety of behaviors.* These behaviors may involve behavior systems aroused by the outcome or a signal for it. Finally, the *individual must determine based on feedback whether their behavior improved or worsened their situation.* This influences how likely he or she will perform the same behavior again in that situation. Individuals tend to repeat those behaviors that better their situation; that is, produce positive reinforcers (positive reinforcement) or reduce or cancel the occurrence of negative reinforcers (negative reinforcement). Likewise, they tend not to repeat those behaviors that worsen their situation; that is, produce negative reinforcers (punishment by application) or the elimination of expected positive reinforcers (omission training or punishment by removal). With repeated experience in a situation, the individual may find that certain behaviors are more efficient than others and adjust his or her behavior accordingly (Staddon, 1975, 1983). Individuals can do this by the process called hill-climbing.

What Is Hill-Climbing?

Hill-climbing is a process individuals can use to improve their situation based on successive comparisons of their current situation. Hill-climbing is the basis for a variety of adaptive behavioral solutions to problems of survival.

Hill-climbing is *a process individuals can use to adjust their behavior based on successive comparisons of their situation. The adjustment is based on whether the behavior improves or worsens the situation* (see Box 8.1). Hill-climbing is an adaptive mechanism that occurs in a variety of forms throughout the animal kingdom. The simplest form of behavior based on hill-climbing is the orientation mechanism called kineses. Kineses do not require learning and thus do not lead to long-term increases in efficiency as a result of repeated experience in a given situation. Operant conditioning represents a more advanced solution, but both solutions are based on hill-climbing.

Kineses are *movements guided by feedback from successive comparisons of one's position based on purely local clues.* All animals, even the simplest single-cell animals, have developed the ability to move about in various ways in search of nutrients and to get away from danger. In simple creatures like bacteria that can only sense their immediate environment, movement usually results in the individual getting to a more suitable location. This is not just due to chance (Benhamou & Bovet, 1992). Bacteria can sense diffuse chemicals in their environment and orient toward increasing concentrations of these chemicals (MacNab & Koshland, 1972). They do this by the process called "myopic hill-climbing"

BOX 8.1

The Metaphor of Hill-Climbing

The name "hill-climbing" is derived from the following hypothetical metaphor: Imagine you are blindfolded and on a plateau on the side of a hill. Safety and food are at the top of that hill. How would you find your way to the top if you cannot see? As long as you can sense that you are climbing up or down, you can move around until you start to move either upward or downward. If you feel yourself moving downward, turn around and go in another direction. When you feel yourself moving upward, deviate slightly from side to side with each step and try to gauge which direction feels the steepest. If you reach another plateau along the way, you may have to change direction if the top of the hill is no longer straight ahead. Finding the top of the hill requires only that you can sense whether you are makng progress (still moving upward). You will know when you get to the top of the hill by the presence of food.

Hill-climbing is more than a metaphor, however. Did you ever play "hot and cold" when you were a child? In that game, one player hides something and the other player tries to find it. Because the second player initially has no idea where the object is hidden, he or she moves about searching for clues which come in the form of statements about how "hot" or "cold" you are. When the second player moves toward the hiding place, the first player says, "You are getting warm." If the second player starts to move away from the hidden object, the first player says, "You are getting cold." As the second player gets closer, the clues may change to "You are getting warmer," "You are getting hot," or "You are on fire."

The first player is guiding the second player toward the hidden object by providing information about whether the second player is improving his or her position relative to the hidden object. That information is valuable only so far as it helps the second player evaluate his or her position relative to the hidden object and use that information to get closer to it. The hot and cold game illustrates how individuals can use hill-climbing to improve their situation by making successive comparisons and adjusting their behavior accordingly.

(McFarland, 1989; Staddon, 1983). In bacteria, hill-climbing works as follows: The bacteria sense the concentration of chemicals in their immediate environment, move to a new location, and sense the concentration there. If the concentration is higher at the new location, they continue in that direction; if it is lower, they change direction. Through successive comparisons of concentrations at the current location and the previous one, the bacteria move toward the source of the chemical gradient (food). Thus, the bacterium seeking food is like the second player in a game of hot and cold, and the chemical gradient is like the first player's clues (see Box 8.1). Although humans have the ability to remember that certain locations visited earlier were cold, that ability is not needed to reach the goal.

Hill-climbing is possible when the individual has the sensory capacity to detect and compare differences between two levels of a gradient. There are lots of variations on the basic process of hill-climbing, but in all cases, there must be a gradient that can be sensed (steepness of ascent or descent, "temperature," chemical concentration, increased probability of being rewarded, and so forth). These gradients can be represented visually as lines of equal contour (on a contour map) and lines of equal temperature (or equal barometric pressure on a weather map). Silby and McFarland (1976) demonstrated how this type of simple feedback mechanism can produce an adaptive response to the problem of finding food or moving away from a noxious chemical. Kineses have been described in a variety of species including mammals (Benhamou & Bovet, 1989).

Kineses only require the ability to move, a sensory apparatus that can distinguish differences in stimulation at different locations and times, a simple storage system to hold the two samples of information long enough to compare, and a mechanism for comparison. Such hill-climbing is "myopic" (i.e., near-sighted) because only short-term considerations are taken into account. No long-term memory is needed. Simple species that do not live very long (like bacteria) have no need to get more efficient at locating food with practice (i.e., learn). Nevertheless, both kineses and operant conditioning represent behavioral adjustments based on outcomes. Learning requires that individuals remember the results of the hill-climbing experience and use that information to guide behavior in the future. Long-term memory allows the individual to make comparisons across longer periods of time, make comparisons across a greater number of instances, and use that information at a later time. Thus, long-term memory allows for more sophisticated hill-climbing and for improvement in performance with repeated experience. Bacteria and other species that exhibit only kineses cannot do these things; individuals capable of operant conditioning can. In complex species, kineses guide individuals to food initially, and the route or location is stored as a spatial memory for future use (Benhamou, Sauvé, & Bovet, 1990).

Reinforcement and Hill-Climbing

Individuals in operant conditioning experiments behave as if they are hill-climbing. Positive and negative reinforcement provide feedback and decrease the variability in target behaviors, while the procedure of extinction increases variability in these behaviors.

One of the characteristics of operant conditioned behavior is that it is self-correcting. With repeated success, the target behavior becomes less variable and more efficient. One of the earliest demonstrations of this was provided by Muenzinger (1928). He taught guinea pigs to press a lever in order to gain access to food in a three-chambered apparatus. The animals started in the first chamber. On each trial the experimenter opened the door to allow the animals access to the second chamber where the lever was located. Pressing the lever provided them with access to the third chamber where they received food. After the animals ate the food, they returned into the first chamber for the next trial. There were 15 trials each day. Muenzinger recorded how the animals pressed the lever over the course of 600 to 1000 trials. He observed nine different successful patterns for lever pressing: three involved the right paw, three the left paw, one both front paws, one a head movement, and one by biting the lever. All but one of his 13 subjects exhibited all nine patterns over the course of the study. There was a decrease in the number of patterns displayed by individual subjects so that by the end of training most of the lever presses involved one or two of the nine patterns; however, no animal displayed exclusively one pattern at the end of the experiment. Furthermore, over the course of training the predominate pattern never occurred exactly the same way, and sometimes it would suddenly be displaced by a different pattern.

Likewise, Vogel and Annau (1973) and Schwartz (1980) both found that the sequence of behaviors that pigeons used to advance a light from one corner of a square matrix to the opposite corner became less variable as training progressed. The specific task used by Vogel and Annau is presented in Figure 8.3. The pigeons had to use the two directional keys on the side to advance the light from the start position on the upper left to the goal position at the lower right in order to receive food. Any sequence of exactly three pecks on each key would accomplish the task. (If the pigeon pecked either key four times, that trial ended with no food and a short blackout until the next trial.) The data from one pigeon are presented in Figure 8.4. Notice that after 100 sessions the pigeon settled in on the efficient pattern *rrrddd*.

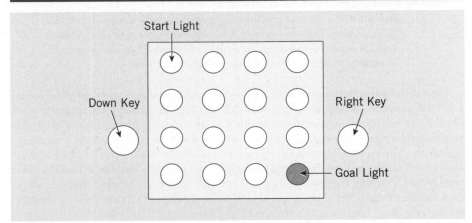

Figure 8.3 Diagram of stimulus panel used in the experiment on behavioral variability by Vogel and Annau (1973). Each trial started with the upper left light lit. Each peck on the "down" key (left side) moved the light down one position. Each peck on the "right" key advanced the light one position to the right. The pigeon's task was to move the light to the goal position (bottom right) in order to receive food. More than three pecks on the same key resulted in a short blackout and no food.

From Vogel & Annau, 1973 *Journal of the Experimental Analysis of Behavior*, 20, 1–6. Copyright © 1973 by the Society for the Experimental Analysis of Behavior, Inc. Reprinted by permission of John Wiley and Sons.

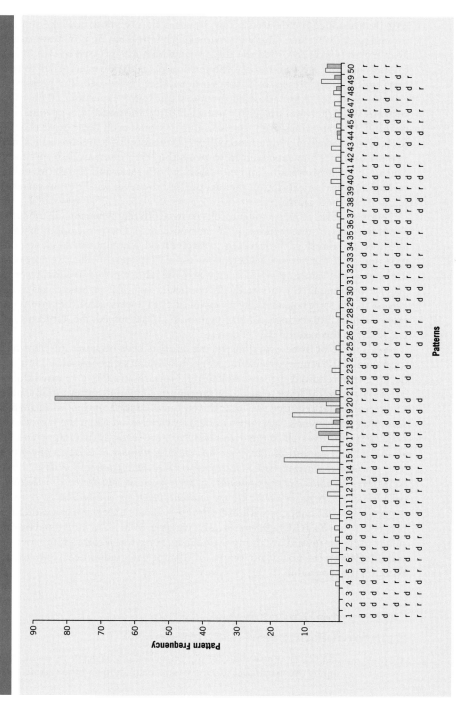

Figure 8.4 Changes in the patterns of pecks to advance the light from the start position to the goal position by one pigeon. The filled bars are the frequency of various patterns of pecking at the two keys ("down" and "right") on training days 4 and 5. The unfilled bars are the frequency of various patterns of pecks at the "d" and "r" keys on sessions 102 and 103. Any of the patterns labeled 1–20 in the left panel could end in food. All of the patterns labeled 21–50 ended in a blackout and no food.

From Vogel and Annau, 1973, *Journal of the Experimental Analysis of Behavior*, 20, 1–6. Copyright © 1973 by the Society for the Experimental Analysis of Behavior, Reprinted by permission of John Wiley and Sons.

These data establish that over time individuals settle in on a few behavioral variants that produce the desired result, but they do not show how the subject's behavior changed over time. There are two experiments that demonstrate these changes. Notterman (1959) recorded the force with which rats pressed a lever over a number of sessions. The minimum force required to press the lever in order to receive food was 3 grams. Any presses over that amount were reinforced; any presses under that amount were not. After allowing them to explore the experimental chamber for two sessions with the food dispenser not operating, followed by a session of magazine training, the rats were given four sessions in which each lever press over 3 grams of force was reinforced with a food pellet followed by two sessions of extinction. The amount of force the rats exerted to press the lever decreased to just over 3 grams during acquisition training and increased in both force and variability during extinction; that is during extinction the rats pressed the lever with a great variety of forces, many way over 3 grams.

Antonitis (1951) found similar results using a different behavior. He trained rats to exit a start box into the test chamber, poke their nose into a slot on the opposite wall of the test chamber, and return to the start box to receive food. The slot was 24 inches long, and the rats could poke their nose anywhere along those 24 inches. An effective nose poke resulted in the click of a camera that recorded where the rat had poked its nose. Over five days of acquisition training, the rats gradually confined most of their nose pokes to the location closest to the start box, and during extinction the locations of the nose pokes became more variable. Interestingly, when conditioning was resumed, the rats displayed even less variability in the location they chose.

In all three of these experiments, the animals became more efficient in their performance of the required behavior. Vogel and Annau's pigeons settled into a pattern of pecking that required the least switching, Notterman's rats decreased the effort they exerted to press the lever to just over the required amount, and Antonitis rats settled on the location that required the least travel. Furthermore, in the Notterman and in the Antonitis experiments, variability in behavior increased when the target behavior was no longer effective. All of the data reviewed here leads to two important conclusions about operant conditioning: *When any one of a number of variants of a given behavior leads to the same outcome, with repeated experience, individuals will settle on a limited number of these variants, and the variability in their behavior will decrease. If the chosen variant is no longer successful in producing the outcome, behavior will become more variable.* This is precisely what happens with hill-climbing. In the absence of a gradient indicating progress toward a goal, behavior is quite variable. When the individual begins to experience progress toward obtaining the goal, its behavior becomes more focused and less variable. When the goal is no longer present, or the gradient ceases to exist, behavior becomes more variable.

Differentiation of Behavior by Reinforcement and Extinction

We can do more than simply get behaviors to occur by using shaping by the method of successive approximation and the various forms of prompting. We can also modify specific aspects of behavior. The procedure for doing this is called differential reinforcement and the result is called differentiation.

In all of the operant conditioning experiments reviewed thus far, the experimenter or behavior modifier required their subjects to do something in order to earn positive reinforcers, and with or without the guidance provided by the method of shaping by successive approximations or prompting, the subjects eventually performed that behavior. Furthermore, when observations were made of the target behavior over the course of training, that behavior tended to become less variable and more efficient (i.e., with repeated experience, the individuals performed the required behavior quickly and most of the time apparently with minimal effort).

Suppose, however, that we not only require performance of a behavior, but we also require that the individual perform that behavior within very narrow boundaries. We can accomplish this by a procedure called **differential reinforcement** in which *behaviors that satisfy certain criteria are reinforced and all other behaviors are not. When differential reinforcement is successful in modifying specified aspects of behavior*, we say that the resulting behavior has been differentiated, and we refer to this phenomenon as **differentiation**.

Differentiation of the Topography of a Behavior

The topography of a behavior refers to how the individual performs that behavior. Differential reinforcement can be used to mold behavioral topographies so that the individual performs the target behavior in a very circumscribed manner.

The **topography of a behavior** is a *description of how an individual performs a behavior*. For example, rats can press a lever in various ways. Normally, we do not care how the rat does it as long as he or she is successful. Each variation in lever pressing is topographically distinct because each has a different description. As Muenzinger (1928) observed, with repeated experience, rats tend to restrict their lever pressing to topographically distinct variations. Through the use of differential reinforcement, we can speed up this process and select the variant we want to occur.

An excellent example of differentiation was provided by Herrick (1964). He devised a lever with a continuous sweep that would allow him to measure how far a rat pressed it. After magazine training his thirsty rats to drink from a water dipper, for 2 days he reinforced them for any presses they made. Then over the next 14 days he systematically restricted the range of presses that would be reinforced. The results for one of these rats are presented in Figure 8.5. The sweep of the lever was divided into positions 1 through 8 with 1 being the least movement and 8 the most. The percentages of the total number of lever presses at the reinforced positions are indicated by the closed bars, and presses at nonreinforced positions are indicated by the open bars. The greatest variability in lever displacement occurred when all presses were reinforced (two panels in the upper left), and the least when only position 5 was reinforced (two panels in the lower right). Although there was still variability (which means that not every lever press was reinforced), there

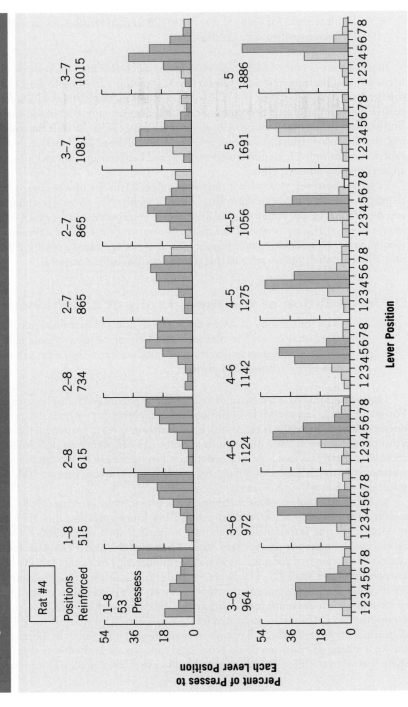

Figure 8.5 The distributions of the vertical displacement of the lever as a function of the size of the zone of reinforced lever presses for a rat (#4) across different experimental sessions. The data are represented by two rows of histograms. Each histogram is from a different day of training. On the first 2 days of training (two panels in the upper left), lever presses at all eight positions were reinforced. On successive days, the reinforced positions were restricted as indicated in each panel. By the end of training, only position 5 was reinforced (two panels in the lower right). The percentage of lever presses at the reinforced positions are indicated by the filled bars, and the percentage of lever presses at the unreinforced positions are indicated by the open bars.

From Herrick, 1964, *Journal of the Experimental Analysis of Behavior*, 7, 211–215. Copyright © 1964 by the Society for the Experimental Analysis of Behavior, Inc. Redrawn by permission of John Wiley and Sons.

was an obvious constriction in the distributions of the vertical displacements of the levers. *The use of differential reinforcement resulted in the differentiation of that behavior.*

Differential reinforcement has been used, for example, to restrict the direction that rats pushed a rod suspended from the ceiling (Davis & Platt, 1983), the location where pigeons pecked (Eckerman, Heinz, Stern, & Kowlowitz, 1980), the force applied to a lever by rats (Notterman & Mintz, 1965; Skinner, 1938), the duration that rats held down a lever (Platt, Kuch, & Bitgood, 1973; Skinner, 1938), and the duration of vocalizations in humans (Lane, Kopp, Sheppard, Anderson, & Carlson, 1967).

In everyday life, many of our behaviors are molded by differential reinforcement from our environment. For example, we adjust how we pick up things based on our experience with them and with similar items; inefficient methods for lifting give way to efficient ones. Anyone who has experienced a sticking door or a temperamental lock soon learns where to apply pressure on the door or how far to push in the key and turn it. The feedback you get from observing the effects of your behaviors molds the skilled performance of behaviors like shooting baskets, spiking volleyballs, and hitting golf balls. This kind of feedback is called "knowledge of performance" or "kinematic feedback" (Schmidt & Young, 1991). This reflects the process of hill-climbing and can legitimately be seen as "self-shaping."

Differentiation of Interresponse Times

Interresponse times are the times between successive behaviors. Differential reinforcement can be used to increase or decrease the interresponse time.

All of the studies reviewed thus far involve the differential reinforcement of some specific behavior, but an important aspect of behavior that has been neglected thus far is the time interval between the performance of successive behaviors. Sometimes it is necessary to perform behaviors in rapid succession in order to be successful. For example, you are more efficient at blowing up a balloon or pumping a bicycle tire when you perform the required behaviors rapidly. When a number of different behaviors are required to reach the end of a sequence and earn the outcome, faster performance gets you there sooner and more efficiently. On the other hand, sometimes it is better to space one's behaviors. When you have flooded the engine of your automobile, it is better to wait before cranking the engine again. Although "scarfing down" one's food gets the job of eating done sooner, heartburn may be the consequence. In all of these examples the consequence depends on how slowly or quickly one behaves. We call the *time between successive behaviors* the **interresponse time (IRT)**.[1] Interresponse times (IRTs) are also subject to the effects of differential reinforcement.

Differentiation of Longer Interresponse Times With IRT > t Schedules. Skinner (1938) described a method to slow down the rate of lever pressing in rats by providing food only if the rat waited at least 15 seconds between successive lever presses. His

---

[1] The use of *response* here instead of *behavior* reflects the history of operant conditioning described in Chapter 7.

rat had been pressing the lever at a high rate before shifting the contingency. With the new contingency, the rat had to press the lever, wait 15 seconds, then press the lever again in order to receive food. Any lever presses in that intervening 15 seconds reset the clock timing the 15-second interval. Skinner's description of his subject's behavior was sketchy, but he did report that it took a while for the rat to slow down long enough to earn food. With repeated training across a number of days, the rates of lever pressing continued to fall until a relatively stable level of performance was reached. In 1957, Ferster and Skinner labeled this procedure a **differential reinforcement of low rates (DRL) schedule.** Although that name is still commonly used, it is misleading because the procedure targets the time between successive behaviors, not the rate of behavior; the effects of this procedure on the rate of behavior are byproducts of the differential reinforcement of interresponse times (Wilson & Keller, 1953). Thus, it is more appropriate to refer to this procedure as an **IRT > t** schedule (interresponse time greater than time *t* schedule; Morse, 1966).

With an **IRT >** *t* schedule, *the individual must perform a behavior, wait at least some specified amount of time* (t), *and then perform the behavior again in order to receive the outcome.* Thus, the outcome will occur only if the individual waits the specified time (*t*) before performing the behavior a second time. If the individual behaves before that specified time has elapsed, the clock timing the required interval is reset to zero before starting to time the waiting period again. This schedule puts individuals in a somewhat awkward situation: They get the outcome for performing the required behavior, but only if they do not do it too quickly. Patience is a virtue when on an IRT > t schedule!

A consistent finding in studies of IRT > t schedules is that the most common IRT is close to the time specified by the schedule (see Kramer & Rilling, 1970, for a review). As a result, this schedule influences the overall production of behavior: The longer the required pause *(t),* the lower the overall rate of occurrence of the behavior that follows the pause and produces the outcome (Wilson & Keller, 1953). This is certainly true of rats (Malott & Cumming, 1966), monkeys (Hodos, Ross, & Brady, 1962), and adult humans (Kapostins, 1963). However, even when the individuals are doing well, sometimes there is a second peak in the distribution of interresponse times at the low end. This occurs when individuals make "bursts" of the target behavior with very short IRTs between them (Conrad, Sidman, & Herrnstein, 1958; Sidman, 1956); but it does not always occur (see, e.g., Kelleher, Fry, & Cook, 1959). Furthermore, with extended training, overall performance tends to improve and the short IRTs occur less frequently.

On the other hand, pigeons have great difficulty adjusting to IRT > t schedules when the required waiting time is greater than 20 seconds (IRT > 20 seconds) and key pecking is the required behavior. This is true even after extended training (over 200 sessions under various IRT > t schedules; Staddon, 1965). They do much better with longer values of *t* when the required behavior involves stepping on a treadle or hopping on a perch (see, e.g., Hemmes, 1975; Lejeune & Jasselette, 1986). This peculiarity in pigeon behavior probably reflects the conflict between the strong tendency to peck at signals for food (sign-tracking) and the demands of the IRT > t schedule that require pausing between pecks.

Successful performance on IRT > t schedules requires individuals to wait between successive responses, and they appear to adopt a number of strategies for how to space their behavior. Sometimes individuals have been observed to develop a stereotyped chain of behaviors that takes time to execute and thus fills the interval (Laties, Weiss, Clark,

& Reynolds, 1965; Laties, Weiss, & Weiss, 1969; Wilson & Keller, 1953). For example, Laties et al. (1965) observed a rat develop the pattern of gnawing on its tail (without breaking the skin) during the interval between successive lever presses, and Kapostins (1963) observed that human subjects uttered sequences of words or changed the pitch of their voices in a cyclical fashion during the interresponse interval (the target behavior was saying a specific word). Some of Kapostins's subjects reported that they counted or daydreamed during the interval. All of these activities are called collateral behaviors because they *are not required for the occurrence of the outcome.* Collateral behaviors do not have to be stereotyped. Hemmes, Eckerman, and Rubinsky (1979) trained pigeons to peck at a small portion of a long horizontal strip on one wall of the chamber. They worked their subjects up to an IRT > 28 seconds and recorded both pecks at the location that produced reinforcement and at all other locations. They observed that the occurrence of collateral behaviors (pecks at other locations) improved performance, but the pattern of collateral pecking was quite variable across the experimental sessions. Others have observed that performance on IRT > t schedules is disrupted when individuals are prevented from engaging in collateral behaviors during the waiting period (e.g., Laties et al., 1969; Schwartz & Williams, 1971). Thus *anything the individual does to occupy its time during the waiting period increases the chances of obtaining the outcome when the required time has elapsed.*

Differentiation of Shorter Interresponse Times With IRT < t Schedules. The opposite of an IRT > t schedule is an IRT < t schedule. In this case, *the outcome occurs when the individual performs the target behaviors in rapid succession with less than the specified time* (t) *between them.* Ferster and Skinner (1957) called this procedure a differential reinforcement of high rates (DRH) schedule. Performance on a differential reinforcement of high rates (DRH) schedule could be characterized as "beat the clock" because the individual must perform two or more behaviors within a certain time limit to obtain the consequence. This schedule generates high rates of behavior (Zeiler, 1970b).

Increasing Behavioral Variability and Novelty With Differential Reinforcement

Instead of requiring the individual to do the same thing each time for the outcome, one can require that each behavior be different from the last one. This increases variability in behavior and encourages novel activities.

We have reviewed a number of experiments in which the procedure of differential reinforcement produced rather stereotyped behavior patterns. This occurred because individuals tend to settle in on activities that involved the least expenditure of effort to obtain the outcome. Suppose, however, that instead of reinforcing the same behavior each time, the requirement is that each behavior pattern has to be *different* from the previous few patterns.

Pryor, Haag, and O'Reilly (1969) described in some detail the behavior of two porpoises subjected to that requirement. These porpoises had already been trained with the method of successive approximations to perform a variety of behaviors on command.

Then the rules were switched, and the outcome was only given for a swimming move-ment *not observed* in a prior session. Over a number of sessions, the animals displayed a great variety of behaviors, some of which were characterized to be as complex as those developed through the method of successive approximations (shaping). As interesting as these observations are, this situation does not lend itself readily to detailed experimental analysis. Therefore, most of the other studies of differential reinforcement of behavioral variability and novelty have taken place in more restrictive settings.

Goetz and Baer (1973) provided verbal reinforcement to children for using building blocks to create different structures. Each novel structure within a given session was reinforced with verbal comments praising the child for making something different. The number of novel forms increased over the course of the session. Holman, Goetz, and Baer (1977) found that children generalized the tendency to create new things to other tasks (e.g., drawing, painting, and building with other kinds of blocks).

Page and Neuringer (1985) used a two-key apparatus to study the reinforcement of behavioral variability.[2] In their experiments, pigeons were reinforced for any pattern of eight pecks at two keys (left key and right key) if they did not repeat the pattern from the previous eight pecks. When they were successful in generating two different eight-peck patterns they received food. If they were not successful, there was a 3.5-second black-out (keys and houselights turned off for 3.5 seconds). Over the course of training, the required number of prior eight-peck patterns that the prior pattern had to be different from increased from 1 to 50. Page and Neuringer reported that variability in these eight-peck patterns increased as the required number of different patterns increased. Machado (1989, 1992) reported similar results. In another experiment reported in the same paper, Page and Neuringer (1985) demonstrated that pigeons could learn to produce variable patterns and stereotyped patterns on command: Variable patterns were reinforced when the key lights were one color, and a stereotyped pattern (same pattern each time) when the key lights were another color.

In a variation on this task, Neuringer (1986) asked people to try to generate a random sequence of 100 presses of two keys on a computer. Most of us cannot do this readily (Wagenaar, 1970). However, Neuringer found that his subjects learned to generate random sequences when he provided feedback about the degree of randomness after each 100-press sequence generated by his subjects.

IDENTIFYING THE OPERANT IN OPERANT CONDITIONING

We identify operant behaviors by their function, not by their typography. All behaviors that produce the same outcome in a par-ticular situation are classified as the same operant behavior. Thus the same behavior can be an operant behavior in one situation, a Pavlovian conditioned response in another situation, and also be elicited by the periodic presentation of certain events.

---

[2]This is the same apparatus used by Vogel and Annau (1973) and Schwartz (1980) to study the develop-ment of behavioral stereotypy in pigeons.

Skinner (1937, 1938) distinguished between two classes of behaviors: respondents and operants. He defined **respondents** as *behaviors elicited by stimuli*; they are the CRs and URs in Pavlovian conditioning. For Skinner, the distinguishing feature of a respondent is its elicitation by an identifiable stimulus; that is, *a respondent requires an eliciting stimulus, and it is not influenced by its consequences.* Like Pavlov, Skinner viewed respondents as reflexes that occur only when the eliciting stimulus is present; that is, they are responses to the stimuli that evoke them. As we saw in Chapter 6, the CRs that occur in Pavlovian conditioning are directly related to the CSs and USs in that situation.

Skinner defined a second class of behaviors that he called **operants**; these are *behaviors that are not elicited by a prior stimulus and are influenced by their consequences.* For Skinner, the distinguishing features of operants are their nonreliance on a stimulus for their occurrence and the fact that they are influenced by their consequences. Although the situation can be structured so that reinforcement of a certain behavior occurs only in the presence of a certain stimulus, Skinner argued that such a stimulus does not elicit the operant behavior that occurs in the presence of that stimulus; rather, he argued that the stimulus sets the occasion for that behavior to be followed by the reinforcing event. Skinner called *a stimulus that signals a behavior-outcome relationship* a **discriminative stimulus**. Thus, Skinner divided behaviors into respondents and operants depending on their origin (elicited by an identifiable stimulus or not) and whether they are influenced by the outcomes they produce.

Skinner's recognition that there are behaviors that are not evoked by identifiable stimuli represented a break with the prevailing views of behavior at that time. Most psychologists in the early part of the twentieth century had adopted the language of reflexes to describe most forms of learned behavior (Cason, 1925; Smith & Guthrie, 1921; Watson, 1919). Skinner (1953, p. 64) pointed out that the term *response* is really not appropriate when applied to operants; however, he continued to use the term *response* in his writing because it had become so well established as a designation for both respondent and operant behavior. Many people continue to refer to CRs when referring to operant behaviors.

It is to Skinner's credit that he recognized that the language of reflexes is inadequate for describing and understanding all behavior. Reflexes are narrowly prescribed by the stimuli that evoke them. Operant behaviors are less constrained because they are not tied to any particular stimulus; they can occur in the absence of the discriminative stimulus that signaled the behavior-outcome relationship, and the presence of a discriminative stimulus does not guarantee that they will occur.

Skinner (1938) described another important characteristic of operants: "The operant must *operate* upon nature to produce its reinforcement" (p. 178). In other words, the individual has to do something to obtain the outcome. That something could be moving to a new location, pressing a lever, pecking a key, tying one's shoe, and so on. It really does not matter how one does it, as long as one is successful at obtaining the outcome. Therefore, in operant conditioning, lever presses and key pecks are defined by the displacement of the lever or key, not by the movements that produce that displacement. It does not matter whether the rat depresses the lever with his or her left paw, right paw, snout, or tail; all of these are counted as lever presses because they all produce the same result (Skinner, 1935a). Thus, *all behaviors that produce the same outcome in a particular situation are classified as instances of the same operant.* However, as Muenzinger (1928) observed, although any of these movements will produce the outcome, over time the individual will settle on a limited number of movements and there will be some variability in how the lever is depressed. On the other hand, it is possible to use differential reinforcement to restrict the definition of acceptable behavior so that the required behavior must be performed at *specific locations*, with *specified forces*, for *specified durations*, at *specified times*, and in *specific ways*. Differential reinforcement can also be used to restrict the times between successive behaviors (interresponse times) to a certain range and to increase variability by requiring variety in performance. Therefore, *the basic unit of behavior (the operant) in operant conditioning is whatever aspect of behavior produces the outcome (or is designated by the experimenter to produce the outcome). Operant behaviors are identified by their function (e.g., depress the lever or move the key far enough to close the switch connected to the counting device), not by their topography. All behaviors that produce the same outcome in a particular situation are classified as instances of the same operant.*

Three Different Kinds of Key Pecking, but Only One Is an Operant

Key pecking is commonly used in the laboratory as an operant behavior, but key pecking can also be increased through Pavlovian conditioning and through the presentation of food on a regular basis. This means that the identification of key pecking (or any behavior) as an operant behavior depends on the conditions under which it occurs: key pecking is an operant behavior only when it operates on the environment to produce an outcome.

In the laboratory, the most commonly studied behaviors in operant conditioning experiments are lever pressing (typically used with rats) and key pecking (typically used with pigeons). These behaviors were chosen for convenience: with the presentation of food as the outcome, it is relatively easy to get them to occur, and their occurrence can be detected mechanically through the depression of the lever and the key. However, in some cases, the same behavior can be produced by Pavlovian conditioning procedures, by operant conditioning procedures, and by the simple presentation of a significant event repeatedly. Key pecking in pigeons provides a clear example of a behavior pattern that can be produced by all three procedures.

Operant Conditioning of Key Pecking. In 1940, Skinner conceived of a guided missile with a pigeon providing the guidance system (Skinner, 1960). Pigeons were given food when they pecked at pictures of boats (the targets), and the movements of their heads as they pecked operated the steering mechanism to move the missile toward its target. We identify key pecking as an operant behavior here because pecks at the target produced food for the birds. A secondary consequence of pecking was to guide the missile toward the target, but that is not what makes this operant conditioning; obtaining food was the primary reason the pigeons pecked at the targets. Although the system was never employed during World War II, it became the starting point for the use of pigeons in operant conditioning research (Breland & Breland, 1966; Ferster, 1953; Ferster & Skinner, 1957; Skinner, 1950).

Pavlovian Conditioning of Key Pecking. As we saw repeatedly in Chapters 2 through 6, key pecking in pigeons can be elicited as a Pavlovian CR. This occurs when some aspect of the illumination of the key signals the impending occurrence of food. This use of a Pavlovian conditioning procedure to induce pecking at signals for food on keys was originally called autoshaping[3] because up to that time, key pecking was thought to only be modified through operant conditioning procedures. The strongest evidence that the pecks produced in the sign-tracking (autoshaping) situation are Pavlovian CRs is their resistance to the omission training contingency (see Chapter 2).

Schedule-Induced Key Pecking. Pecking can also be induced by the periodic presentation of food. *Behaviors that emerge when significant events are presented periodically* are called **schedule-induced behaviors.** Staddon and Simmelhag (1971) described the generation of pecking over the course of a number of sessions in which 2 seconds of access to food was presented to pigeons under one of two conditions: every 12 seconds independently of what they did (fixed time 12 seconds), and on the average of once every 8 seconds (with a range from 3 to 21 seconds) independently of what they did (variable time 8 seconds). Some pigeons received the fixed schedule for a number of sessions before receiving the variable schedule, and the others received the variable schedule for a number of sessions before receiving the fixed schedule. Each session lasted until the bird had received 64 opportunities to eat the food. Under both schedules of food delivery, pecking at the wall that contained the food magazine emerged over the course of repeated sessions in all pigeons. Although the fixed-time schedule resembles Pavlovian temporal conditioning (see Chapter 2), the outcome is different: there was no evidence of inhibition of delay over the course of the training sessions, and pecking emerged even under a variable condition when the time of the next food delivery could not be predicted from previous one. Furthermore, Pavlovian conditioned pecks are directed toward the signal for food while the schedule-induced pecks are more variable in their locations.

The Adaptive Significance of These Three Kinds of Pecking. It should be obvious from the descriptions of sign-tracking and schedule-induced pecking that pecking in pigeons is part of a behavior system that is aroused by the presence of food or signals for food. Nevertheless, pecking can also be modified by its consequences. Although Williams and Williams (1969) found that pecking produced by Pavlovian conditioning (sign-tracking) is resistant to the operant omission training contingency, it is not completely unaffected: when there are two illuminated keys and the omission contingency is placed on one of them, pigeons will shift their pecking to the other key and not lose access to the food (see Chapter 2).

Pecking is not the only behavior that is evoked by the presence of food; over time, the repeated periodic delivery of food evokes general activity with the greatest activity occurring immediately after each food presentation and tapering off over time (Killeen, 1979; Killeen, Hanson, & Osbourne, 1978; Staddon & Simmelhag, 1971). This is not surprising: The appearance of a small portion of food typically indicates that more food may be close at hand. Thus, the presence of food evokes behaviors like general activity and pecking that increase the opportunity for finding more food.

---

[3]The term *sign-tracking* is more descriptive than *autoshaping* because the former term reflects the role of Pavlovian conditioning in the generation of these pecks.

Therefore, Skinner's definition of an operant as a behavior (or aspect of behavior) influenced by its consequences means that *to understand why an individual does something requires us to look beyond the form (topology) of the behavior and consider both the circumstances that produce that behavior and the function of the behavior.* Key pecking provides us with a clear example of why one must look beyond the behavior itself to understand why that behavior occurs in a given situation. We identify key pecks as operants only when they are influenced by their consequences.

SUMMARY AND CONCLUSIONS

In operant conditioning, the events we call reinforcers (both positive and negative) serve as incentives for performing certain behaviors. Thus, reinforcers provide a source of motivation for performing these behaviors; we call this source of motivation *incentive motivation.* Reinforcers also provide feedback, which allows the individual to adjust his or her behavior to become more efficient at obtaining a given positive reinforcer or getting away from a given negative reinforcer in a particular situation; this reflects the process called *hill-climbing.* Hill-climbing is used by a wide variety of species to adapt to specific situations. Hill-climbing need not involve learning, but individuals who can learn can profit from the prior hill-climbing experience and use the information obtained at a later time and in other situations.

With continued reinforcement of a behavior, individuals tend to become less variable in their performance of that behavior (unless specifically reinforced for displaying variability). On the other hand, behavior becomes more variable when that behavior no longer produces the expected outcome (procedure of extinction). These changes in variability reflect the process of hill-climbing.

Operant conditioning can also be used to "fine-tune" behavior through the procedure of differential reinforcement. With differential reinforcement, the range of behaviors that produces the positive reinforcer is restricted: Only those behaviors that satisfy some criterion are reinforced; all other behaviors are not. The result is called *differentiation.* Through differential reinforcement, various aspects of the topography (form) of a behavior can be modified. Differential reinforcement can also be used to modify the times between successive behaviors (the interresponse times). The procedures for doing the latter are called *interresponse time (IRT) schedules:* Individuals will lengthen the time between performing successive behaviors when they are reinforced for doing so. The schedule for increasing the interresponse time is called an IRT > t schedule. The time between successive behaviors can be shortened with an IRT < t (interresponse time less than time t) schedule. Differential reinforcement can also be used to promote behavioral variability and the production of novel behaviors.

The procedures of operant conditioning influence any aspect of behavior that can be modified by its consequences. Therefore, the class of behaviors called operants are identified by their function, not by their form. Operants are behaviors that operate on the environment to produce consequences. The consequences in turn influence operant behaviors.

In the next chapter, we will look at how individuals adjust to situations in which not every instance of a behavior is reinforced.

STUDY QUESTIONS

1. How is the point of view of the experimenter and behavior modifier different from the point of view of the individual subject in operant conditioning situations? Why is it important that we view operant conditioning from these two perspectives?

2. What are the two functions of reinforcers in operant conditioning? Give an example to illustrate each.

3. Describe the metaphor of hill-climbing. How does it relate to reinforcement and operant conditioning?

4. What are the effects of reinforcement and extinction on behavioral variation?

5. How can we use differential reinforcement to influence

   a. the typography of a behavior?

   b. the spacing of behavior (differentiation of interresponse times)?

   c. the performance of novel behaviors?

6. What is the defining characteristic of an operant?

9

ADJUSTING TO SCHEDULES OF PARTIAL REINFORCEMENT

The procedure of operant conditioning involves *a programmed relationship between some behavior and an outcome for performing that behavior in a certain situation and at a certain time*. We refer to this relationship as a **behavior-outcome contingency**. The behavior can be defined broadly (lever press or key peck) or narrowly (within a specified range of forces, durations, or locations, or in a specified manner, e.g., only with the left paw). If it is within the individual's ability to detect the relationship between the prescribed aspect of his or her behavior and the occurrence of the outcome, the individual can use hill-climbing to become more efficient at obtaining the sought-after outcome. A special class of behavior-outcome contingencies is called a **schedule of reinforcement**. A schedule of reinforcement specifies *the conditions the individual has to satisfy in order to obtain the outcome*. These conditions can include how many times the individual must perform the behavior, when the behavior has to be performed, or what pattern of behaviors must be performed. In this chapter, we will look at how individuals adjust their behavior to the various schedules of reinforcement.

CLASSIFYING SCHEDULES OF REINFORCEMENT

In most of the examples we have discussed thus far, each instance of the target behavior was followed by the reinforcing event. This is called continuous reinforcement. But in real life, that typically is not the case. Most of the time reinforcement occurs on what we call a partial reinforcement schedule. How individuals adjust to various arrangements (schedules) of partial reinforcement provides us additional information about how outcomes influence behavior.

The simplest schedule of reinforcement is to *provide the outcome for each occurrence of the target behavior*. This is called a **continuous reinforcement schedule**. Skinner used continuous reinforcement in his first studies of operant conditioning. The data from his first subjects are presented in Chapter 7, Figure 7.10. The cumulative record in that figure illustrates that once the individual learns what behavior produces the outcome, continuous reinforcement generates a rather steady rate of behavior as long as that individual is motivated to perform and the outcome is available.

But in real life, each instance of a particular behavior does not always produce the outcome. Sometimes we are reinforced for our efforts and sometimes we come up short. Over the long run, whether we persist or give up depends on a variety of things such as the value of the outcome to us, the rate of payoff, our level of motivation, past experience in that situation or in a similar situation, and the cost to us of doing what is required. When *not* every instance of the target behavior is followed by the outcome, we say that the individual is working under a schedule of partial or intermittent reinforcement. A partial (intermittent) reinforcement schedule *specifies which instances of the target behavior are followed by the outcome*. Most schedules of partial reinforcement require that the individual either perform the target behavior a certain number of times, perform that behavior after a certain time interval has elapsed, or some combination of these two requirements. When individuals can detect the requirements of the schedule, they adapt their behavior in rather predictable ways.

The people who run lotteries take advantage of the fact that some individuals will continue to play even though they win only occasionally. The various games are designed to attract players by either offering small outcomes (another ticket or a small amount of money) with high probabilities of winning or large outcomes (millions of dollars) with low probabilities of winning (1 chance in 50 million). Typically the cost of a ticket is kept low ($1). Lotteries and other forms of gambling involve schedules of partial reinforcement because not every play results in a win; however, occasional wins (by you or someone else) may sustain your continued participation. The schedules employed in gambling can be modeled in the laboratory, and the behavior of rats and pigeons on these schedules looks remarkably like the behavior of people playing slot machines; however, it is important to recognize that the schedules of partial reinforcement studied in the laboratory are idealized procedures and are not always represented in the natural environment. Nevertheless, the behavior patterns that appear when individuals are confronted with these schedules tell us a lot about how individuals adjust their behavior to meet the demands of the situation they are in.

Although Skinner deserves the credit for recognizing the importance of schedules of partial reinforcement, he was not the first person to study the effects of partial reinforcement on behavior. That honor goes to Pavlov, who described a salivary conditioning experiment in which the US was not presented on every trial. Pavlov reported that CRs were readily obtained when the US was presented on every second or third trial, but not on every fourth trial (Pavlov, 1927). Later, Brogden (1939) found that a leg flexion CR developed when shock to the leg (the US) was delivered only 20% of the time. Humphreys (1939) found similar results with eyelid conditioning.

Skinner (1933a, 1933b, 1933c) trained rats to press a lever for food and then changed the situation so that food was available for lever pressing only after a certain time had elapsed since the last reinforcement. Thus, if the interval was 8 minutes, the first lever press after 8 minutes was followed by food. When this schedule was first introduced, the rate of lever pressing declined (phenomenon of extinction) because lever presses during that 8-minute interval were not followed by food. However, because lever pressing did not completely cease, when the 8-minute interval elapsed and the next lever press produced food, the rate of lever pressing increased. Eventually his rats maintained a regular pattern of lever pressing and earned the food pellets as they became available. Skinner called this procedure periodic reconditioning because of the alternation between positive reinforcement of a single lever press and the procedure of extinction during the 8-minute interval. Ferster and Skinner (1957) named this procedure a fixed-interval (FI) schedule, the name we still use today. In 1938, Skinner described a second procedure for partial reinforcement. In this procedure, the rats had to make a certain number of lever presses to obtain food. His rats also adjusted to this schedule that he called a fixed-ratio (FR) schedule. We still call it that. Skinner demonstrated two important effects of schedules of partial reinforcement, namely, how behavior is adjusted to the schedule and the partial reinforcement extinction effect (that behavior takes longer to extinguish after partial reinforcement). We will look at both of these effects of partial reinforcement in this chapter.

The most widely used system of classification of schedules of reinforcement was developed by Ferster and Skinner (1957), although alternative classifications of schedules have been proposed by others (Mechner, 1959; Schoenfeld & Cole, 1972; Schoenfeld, Cumming, & Hearst, 1956). A great variety of schedules have been devised and studied in the laboratory and employed in various ways in behavior modification programs. *The three most commonly studied classes of schedules are based on the number of individual behaviors required to obtain a reinforcer (ratio schedules), behaving after a certain time interval has elapsed in order to obtain a reinforcer (interval schedules), and spacing individual behaviors a certain time apart in order to be reinforced (interresponse time [IRT] schedules).* We reviewed the effects of IRT > *t* and IRT < *t* schedules in the last chapter. In this chapter, we will focus on how individuals behave when confronted with ratio and interval schedules.

RATIO SCHEDULES

> Ratio schedules require an individual to perform the target behavior a certain number of times in order to obtain the outcome. These schedules encourage very high rates of behavior.

A ratio schedule of reinforcement *specifies the number of times an individual has to do something in order to obtain a certain outcome.* That is the only requirement. The outcome occurs each time the requirement is satisfied. Zeiler (1977) referred to such formally imposed requirements of a schedule as a *direct* variable. He also noted that all schedules have unstated requirements, which he called *indirect* variables. Both the direct and the indirect variables in a schedule affect how the individual adjusts to it. For example, in all ratio schedules, the faster the individual gets through the ratio, the faster he or she earns the outcome. Thus, *ratio schedules tie the rate of reinforcement directly to the rate of behavior.* This is an indirect variable in all ratio schedules.

This relationship between rates of behavior and rates of reinforcement in ratio schedules is represented in the top panel of Figure 9.1. In that panel, each line represents a different ratio requirement. If the individual has to perform the target behavior 20 times to receive an outcome, and he or she does this 10 times per minute, then in one hour the individual will earn 30 outcomes. If the individual can increase the rate of behavior to 20 times per minute, then the number of outcomes earned in an hour jumps to 60. The same holds for the other ratios: The faster the individual performs the target behavior, the more is earned. These lines define a family of **molar feedback functions** for different ratio schedules, which define the *relationship between the rate of performance of the target behavior and the rate at which the outcome is earned.* These are called *molar* functions because they relate the *overall* rate of reinforcement to the *overall* rate of behavior. Each function reflects

Figure 9.1 (Top) Set of molar feedback functions for various ratio schedules. Each line represents a different ratio requirement. (Bottom) Set of molar feedback functions for various interval schedules. Each line represents a different interval. See text for how to interpret these functions.

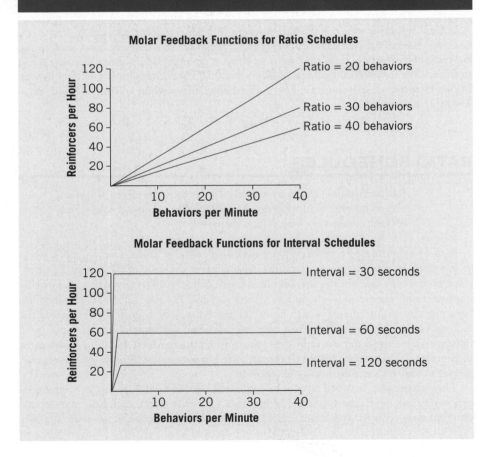

the correlation between behaviors and outcomes over time. It is clear that the molar feedback functions for ratio schedules encourage high rates of behavior because pausing and dawdling delay earning the next outcome.

Ratio schedules also encourage high rates of behavior in another way. Because the individual must perform the target behavior a certain number of times to earn the outcome, it is most likely that he or she satisfies the ratio requirement while in the middle of a run of behaviors. For example, if the individual must perform the target behavior 10 times to earn the outcome, it is unlikely that he or she consistently does it only 9 times, pauses, and then does it once more. It is more likely that the ratio requirement will be satisfied and the outcome occur while the individual is performing a series of behaviors in rapid succession. Thus, ratio schedules are more likely to reinforce short interresponse times (IRTs) rather than long ones because the IRT that is followed immediately by reinforcement is likely to be a short one, and short IRTs are synonymous with rapid behavior.

This reinforcement of short IRTs is an example of a *molecular* feedback process. A **molecular feedback function** *involves the moment-to-moment relationship between behaviors and outcomes*. A continuing controversy in the study of ratio schedules is which is more important for generating the high rates of behavior observed with ratio schedules, molar feedback or molecular feedback. This will be explored later in this chapter.

There are a number of ways that the ratio requirement can be specified. The most common types of ratio schedules are called fixed ratio (because the ratio requirement is the same for each reinforcer earned) and variable ratio (because the ratio requirement varies unsystematically across successive reinforcers). Obviously these are not the only possibilities, but they are the most commonly used in research on ratio schedules.

Fixed-Ratio Schedules (FR *n*)

> Fixed-ratio schedules require the individual to perform the target behavior the same number of times to obtain the outcome. The resulting behavior pattern is characterized by a pause and then an abrupt transition to a high rate of behavior.

On a fixed-ratio schedule of reinforcement (FR *n*), *the number of times the target behavior must occur is the same across successive reinforcers*. For example, the schedule would be designated as an FR 5 schedule when the individual must always perform the required behavior five times in order to obtain a certain outcome. For convenience, we refer to fixed-ratio schedules by the abbreviation **FR *n*** where *n* specifies the required number of times the target behavior must occur in order to obtain the outcome. Continuous reinforcement is a special case of an FR schedule in which the ratio requirement is 1 (FR 1).

Typical Performance on Fixed-Ratio Schedules. The behavior pattern that most commonly occurs on an FR schedule is presented in Figure 9.2. This pattern is typically described as "break and run." The "break" refers to a *pause for a period of time after the presentation of each outcome*. The length of this pause (called a **post-reinforcement pause; PRP**) is typically an increasing function of the FR requirement: The longer the required ratio, the longer the pause. Following the PRP (or "break"), the individual typically

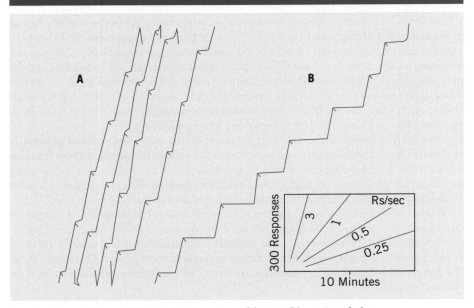

Figure 9.2 Cumulative records of patterns of performance by pigeons on an FR 200 schedule of reinforcement (Panel A) and an FR 120 schedule of reinforcement (Panel B).

From Ferster and Skinner, 1957. Reprinted courtesy of the B. F. Skinner Foundation.

makes an abrupt transition into the "run," a high steady rate of behavior that ends with the delivery of the outcome.

Fixed-ratio performance typically requires a shaping process in which the individual is gradually introduced to the final ratio requirement: Starting with an FR 1 (continuous reinforcement), the ratio is gradually increased after the behavior becomes stable. *If the steps are too large, or the outcome earned is too meager,* the individual will show what is called ratio strain; that is, a prolonged PRP, a prolonged pause in the middle of a ratio run, or both. An example of ratio strain is presented in Figure 9.3. Ratio strain indicates that from the individual's point of view, the outcome is not adequate to maintain the amount of behavior required to earn it. However, by gradually increasing the ratio requirement (a form of shaping), we can get subjects to work on FR schedules requiring 600–700 repetitions of the target behavior to earn a single outcome.

Why There Is a Post-Reinforcement Pause on Fixed-Ratio Schedules. FR schedules require the individual to perform a certain number of behaviors in order to obtain the outcome. This *direct* variable is the formally imposed requirement on an FR schedule (Zeiler, 1977). On FR schedules, the time between the receipt of successive reinforcers (called the *interreinforcer interval*) is another *indirect* variable that occurs as a byproduct of the formal schedule requirement (the direct variable). The interreinforcer interval depends on how long the individual takes to complete the ratio that in turn depends on

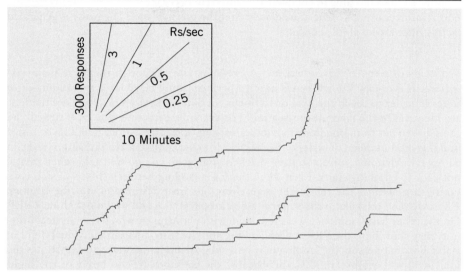

From Ferster and Skinner, 1957. Reprinted courtesy of the B. F. Skinner Foundation.

how long it takes to complete each behavior and the number of behaviors required by the schedule.

The interreinforcer interval affects the length of the PRP: *The longer the interreinforcer interval, the longer the PRP.* Killeen (1969) demonstrated that the PRP is determined by the time to the next reinforcer. He trained one group of pigeons on an FR schedule. A second group of pigeons was yoked to the first; that is, when a pigeon in the first group earned a reinforcer, a pigeon in the second group could also earn one (see Chapter 7, Box 7.6). This procedure made the interreinforcer interval for the two pigeons (and both groups) similar. Although the rate of pecking by pigeons in the second group was less (because there was no ratio requirement for them), the PRPs were the same. When Killeen added a short FR requirement for the pigeons in the second group, the rates of pecking increased toward the rate in the first group and the PRPs increased slightly (because the interreinforcer interval increased slightly). From this, Killeen concluded that the PRP (the break part of the break-and-run pattern) develops on FR schedules as a result of the indirect variable of interreinforcement interval.

Why Individuals Abruptly Switch to a Run of Behaviors on Fixed-Ratio Schedules. The high stable run part of that pattern can be explained by both the molar feedback function (that relates overall rate of reinforcement to the overall rate of behavior) and the molecular feedback function (short IRTs being more likely to be followed by a reinforcer than long IRTs). Both of these feedback functions encourage individuals to complete the ratio quickly.

Therefore, the break-and-run pattern of behavior generated by FR schedules is the result of indirect variables associated with this schedule. The run is generated by the feedback functions (molar and molecular) that encourage rapid rates of behavior, and each run requires a minimum time to complete (the interreinforcer interval). That means that the next reinforcer cannot occur immediately after the previous one. The pause is generated by this latter aspect of FR schedules.

Examples of Fixed-Ratio Schedules in Everyday Life. Although there are many situations in everyday life where we have to perform some behavior a given number of times in order to reach the goal or to obtain an outcome, very few of these situations are identical to the laboratory situation. For example, each time you have to walk up the stairs to get from one floor to another in your home, classroom building, or office building, the number of stairs is the same. However, unlike a rat pressing a lever in an operant chamber, once you have reached your goal, you go on to do other things, not back to climbing stairs. Even when there is a landing between flights of stairs, we rarely stop because the reinforcer is reaching our final destination, not the landing. Thus, we tend to walk up the stairs at a quick steady pace and we do not show a PRP. On the other hand, someone weighed down with packages or who has a physical infirmity may show both the PRP at each landing and the "run" up each individual flight of stairs. For that person, the landing may be a subgoal along the way, and sometimes the individual will exhibit "ratio strain" because the packages are too heavy or the flight of stairs too long.

Frequently cited examples of FR schedules in everyday life are working on commission, being paid for the number of tasks or objects completed (piece work), or receiving a bonus for each item or task above some minimum number. It is true that in all three cases, the amount of pay earned depends on the number of items sold (or made) based on a pay schedule which specifies how much is earned per sale or item produced. Although this looks like an FR schedule, the similarity is superficial. People are paid at set times, not when they complete the number of sales or items. Nevertheless, these situations share some things in common with FR performance observed in the laboratory. Gradually reducing the commission for each item sold or increasing the piecework rate (number of items to be completed) typically generate more performance because the individual must work more to receive the same amount of pay. This is similar to increasing the ratio requirement on a rat or pigeon. If the item to be produced takes a long time to complete (because it involves a lot of labor), people typically rest after completing one and before starting another; this is similar to the PRP.

No doubt you can think of many situations where a set number of behaviors is required to reach a goal or subgoal. In these situations, individuals tend to work hard until the goal is reached. If the task requires lots of work, they may rest before starting again. However, the laboratory situation is unique in that the only reinforcer is at the end of the fixed ratio, subjects have no other activity to perform to obtain the reinforcer, and the amount of reinforcer for completing each ratio is generally too small to satisfy them. Therefore, these subjects must complete many ratios in order to receive an adequate amount of food. This affords us the opportunity to observe both the ratio run and the PRP in the laboratory. These may not always be apparent outside the laboratory.

Variable-Ratio Schedules (VR *n*)

Variable-ratio schedules require the individual to perform the target behavior a number of times to obtain the outcome, but that number is not the same each time. The resulting behavior pattern is characterized by a high rate of behavior with little or no post-reinforcement pauses.

A second type of ratio schedule is called variable ratio. In a **variable-ratio schedule of reinforcement (VR *n*)** the individual is required to *perform the target behavior a certain number of times to obtain the outcome, but that number varies around a certain average (n)*. Thus, in a VR 5 schedule, the individual will obtain the outcome after performing the target behavior a number of times, but the number of times required to obtain the outcome will vary each time the individual works on the ratio. Sometimes a single instance is sufficient, sometimes 3, sometimes 10, and other times perhaps 15 may be required. These numbers would be selected from a distribution of ratio requirements that had *n* (in this case, 5) as the average.[1]

Figure 9.4   Cumulative record of the pattern of performance by a pigeon on a VR 110 schedule of reinforcement after 12 sessions of training.

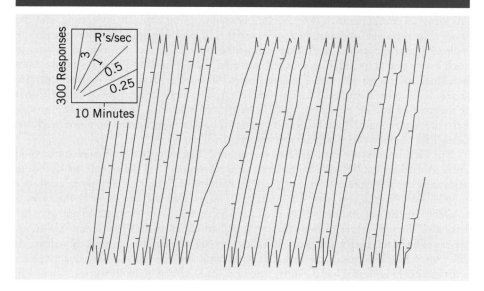

From Ferster and Skinner, 1957. Reprinted courtesy of the B. F. Skinner Foundation.

---

[1]A variation of the VR schedule is called a **random-ratio schedule of reinforcement (RR *n*)**. In a random-ratio schedule, *each occurrence of the target behavior has a probability of 1/n of being followed by a reinforcer where* n *is the mean of the ratio requirement*. With a random-ratio schedule, the probability of the next instance of the target behavior occurring is always constant at 1/*n*. The behavior patterns generated by VR and random-ratio schedules are similar enough for us to consider them together (Mazur, 1983).

Typical Performance on Variable-Ratio Schedules. Like FR schedules, VR schedules also generate high rates of behavior. An example of VR performance is given in Figure 9.4. This high rate of behavior reflects the molar and molecular feedback functions inherent in all ratio schedules. However, unlike FR schedules, VR schedules typically show little systematic pausing either after reinforcers are obtained or at other times, although PRPs have been observed in VR schedules as a function of the length of the ratio and the magnitude of the reinforcer. For example, using pigeons, Blakely and Schlinger (1988) systematically varied the ratio requirement from VR 10 to VR 70, the distribution of individual ratios within each schedule that defined the average ratio, and the magnitude of the reinforcer (2 seconds access to grain versus 8 seconds access to grain). They found more PRPs with longer ratios and when there were no short ratios within the ratio series. Furthermore, the PRP disappeared when the pigeons occasionally could get access to food on the very next peck after the previous reinforcer. These data indicate that the interreinforcement interval can also have an effect in VR schedules. Finally, the PRP was longer when the magnitude of reinforcement was smaller. This latter effect was most pronounced with the longer ratios. Thus it appears that performance on ratio schedules reflects both the schedule requirements and the value of the outcome.

Examples of Variable-Ratio Schedules in Everyday Life. The VR situations encountered in everyday experience are a lot like the VR schedules studied in the laboratory. All forms of gambling are VR schedules because winning depends on betting, and the more times you bet, the more likely you are to win. Slot machines and other gambling devices are programmed as random ratio schedules to control the rate of payoffs in such a way that the overall payout slightly favors the house, and humans playing slot machines look a lot like rats pressing levers for food on a variable or random ratio schedule. In both situations, the individuals exhibit a high steady rate of behavior that is maintained by the occasional payoff. With slot machines, the high steady rate of behavior is also maintained by near misses (two bars or two cherries on a slot machine, being one number off on a lottery ticket, etc.).

But VR schedules are not restricted to gambling. Salespeople working on commission are also working on VR schedules. The more customers they see or call on, the more sales they should make, even though the probability of a sale with any given customer may be low. Here again, that occasional sale maintains the behavior. If the ratio is too lean (or the pay too low), then the salesperson may show ratio strain and give up. Likewise, in many athletic events (baseball, basketball, football) where not every swing, shot, or run is successful, the more you shoot, swing, or run, the more likely you are to get a hit, score, or advance the ball. Of course, skill and concentration have a lot to do with success in athletics, but the more attempts made, the more likely a given player will be successful.

These examples illustrate that many VR schedules encountered in everyday experience have more in common with the schedules studied in the laboratory than do any of the other schedules described here (except continuous reinforcement). The reason is that in many of these examples, the individual continues to work on the schedule after receiving an outcome. In all of the everyday examples of other schedules, once the outcome is earned, the individuals typically go on to perform other tasks.

INTERVAL SCHEDULES

Interval schedules require the individual to perform the target behavior after a certain time has elapsed. It does not matter what the individual does before that time. These schedules encourage lower rates of behavior than ratio schedules.

Interval schedules of reinforcement *specify an interval of time after which the next occurrence of the target behavior will produce the outcome.* Note that it is not merely the passage of time that produces the outcome —the individual has to do something after that interval has elapsed in order for the outcome to occur. Any behavior that occurs before that time neither advances nor delays the outcome, but if the interval elapses and the individual does not perform, there will be no outcome until he or she does. As long as the individual is performing the target behavior some minimum number of times over the course of the experimental session, he or she will earn the maximum number of reinforcers possible, but more rapid behavior will not earn any more. Therefore, unlike ratio schedules, after a certain point, the rate of reinforcement is *independent* of the rate of behavior. This produces a molar feedback function that rises to some asymptote as the rate of behavior increases and then is flat with further increases in behavior. A set of molar feedback functions for interval schedules is presented in the bottom panel of Figure 9.1. Each line in that panel represents a different interval requirement. Thus, if the schedule specifies an interval of 30 seconds, then over the course of an hour, the individual cannot earn more than 120 reinforcers no matter how rapidly he or she produces the target behavior. With a very low rate of behavior the individual would earn less than 120 reinforcers. Increases in performance produce increases in the rate of reinforcement up to the asymptote of 120 reinforcers per hour. Beyond the point that the rate of reinforcement is at 120 reinforcers per hour, further increases in the rate of the target behavior do not increase the rate of reinforcement. Thus, *on interval schedules the overall rate of reinforcement is constrained by the schedule.* This does not encourage high rates of behavior the way ratio schedules do (compare the two panels of Figure 9.1).

At the molecular level, interval schedules also encourage an intermediate rate of behavior. Unlike the ratio schedules where pausing delays meeting the demands of the schedule and a series of behaviors performed in rapid succession is more likely to be followed by the outcome (and hence short IRTs are more likely to be reinforced), on an interval schedule pausing and low rates of behavior do not appreciably delay the outcome. However, *on an interval schedule, the longer the individual pauses, the higher the probability that the next performance of the target behavior will produce the programmed outcome.* Thus, both long and short IRTs are likely to be reinforced. As a result, interval schedules produce lower rates of behavior than ratio schedules when interreinforcer intervals are matched.

As was the case with ratio schedules, there are a number of ways to program the interval schedule requirement. Here again, the most common ways are to require the same interval for each reinforcer (fixed interval) or to unsystematically vary the interval across successive reinforcers (variable interval). These are not the only possibilities, but they are the most commonly used in research on interval schedules.

Fixed-Interval Schedules (FI *t*)

> Fixed-interval schedules require the individual to perform the target behavior after a certain time has elapsed; that time is the same for each reinforcer. These schedules usually generate post-reinforcement pauses and higher rates of behavior closer to the time of reinforcement.

In a fixed-interval schedule of reinforcement (FI *t*), *the first occurrence of the target behavior after a specified interval of time has elapsed will produce the outcome; that interval is the same across successive reinforcers.* Thus, an FI 1-minute schedule programs the outcome following the first instance of the target behavior that occurs after 1 minute has elapsed since the last outcome. For convenience, we abbreviate fixed-interval schedules as **FI** *t*, where *t* specifies the time interval in whatever units are appropriate (seconds, minutes, etc.). Fixed-interval schedules have been studied over a wide range of times from a few seconds to 100,000 seconds (27.75 hours; Dews, 1965).

Typical Performance on Fixed-Interval Schedules. Performance on FI schedules is characterized by a post-reinforcement pause (PRP) followed by either a progressively increasing rate of behavior (sometimes described as a scallop) or an abrupt transition to the terminal rate of behavior (break and run). Although both patterns have been observed in the same individual within the same session (Figure 9.5), break-and-run patterns are observed more often in short FI (*t* less than 300 seconds) after extended training (Dews, 1978; Schneider, 1969). These bifurcated patterns of behavior generated by FI schedules are commonly observed in animals and humans under the age of four. Humans aged four and older show one of two patterns: Some people exhibit continuous rapid rates of behavior throughout the interval that resembles FR performance, and these people are insensitive to changes in the interval. Other people perform the target behavior only once or twice near the end of the interval. Lowe attributes the performance of adult humans and children over the age of 4 years to their ability to construct rules about what they believe the schedule requires. In this situation, a rule is useful when it leads to efficient performance (perform the target behavior only at the end of the interval when it is likely to be reinforced). However, a rule can be counterproductive as when it leads to extremely high rates of behavior that are not tied to a corresponding increase in the rate of reinforcement. It is interesting that animals and young children appear more sensitive to the schedule requirements (Lowe, 1979, 1983). On the other hand, humans can be made to perform like animals by embedding the FI in another task (see, e.g., Laties & Weiss, 1963), and animals can be made to perform like humans by exposing the animals to a VR schedule prior to working on the FI schedule (Wanchisen, Tatham, & Mooney, 1989). We will explore rule-governed behavior in more detail in Chapter 13.

Unlike ratio schedules, which require the individual to perform the target behavior a certain number of times in order to receive the outcome, interval schedules only require one instance of that behavior (which must occur after the interval has elapsed). Thus the number of target behaviors performed during the interval has no effect on the outcome in an FI schedule. As a result, performance on FI schedules is quite variable across successive

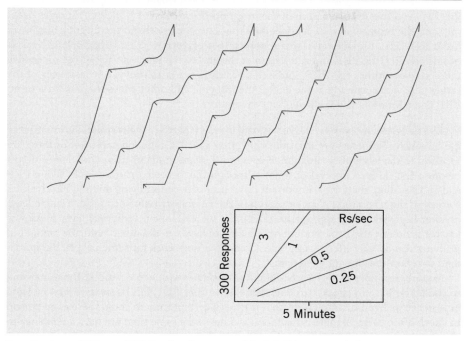

Figure 9.5 Cumulative record of the pattern of performance by a pigeon on an FI 4-minute schedule of reinforcement.

From Ferster and Skinner, 1957. Reprinted courtesy of the B. F. Skinner Foundation.

intervals; that is, sometimes the individual performs the target behavior many times and other times only a few times (see Figure 9.5). However, there do seem to be some regularities in FI schedule performance. First, most intervals contain a large number of instances of the target behavior. Second, there is a tendency for the length of the PRP to oscillate between short and long pauses across successive intervals (Shull, 1971); however, for a wide variety of the values of *t*, the average length of the PRP is around one-half of *t* (Schneider, 1969). Third, the terminal rate of behavior (i.e., at the end of the interval) is a decreasing function of *t*: when *t* is short, the terminal rate is high, and with increases in *t*, the terminal rate decreases (Catania & Reynolds, 1968). Finally, the longer the interval, more of the target behavior is generated during each interval (Dews, 1965).

Why There Is a Post-Reinforcement Pause on Fixed-Interval Schedules. The occurrence of the PRP in FI schedules is hardly surprising given that reinforcement cannot occur until a fixed time has elapsed (followed by the target behavior). This suggests that the PRP reflects a temporal discrimination on the part of the individual, but rats and pigeons are more accurate at estimating time than appears to be the case here. If the PRP reflected only a timing mechanism, then the PRP should approximate the fixed interval with sufficient practice, but it does not: individuals start to perform the target behavior much earlier than they should (Dews, 1978), and the length of the PRP in FI schedules is about the same as it is in FR schedules where the interreinforcer intervals are equated (Killeen, 1969). This suggests that FI performance in animals reflects a conflict between the discrimination of the interreinforcer interval (which encourages pausing) and the requirement of the schedule that one must perform the target behavior in order to receive the outcome (which encourages performing that behavior). As a result of this conflict, the PRP and run length at the end of the interval vary across successive intervals: sometimes the PRP dominates performance with only a few instances of the target behavior occurring at the end of the interval, and other times there is little or no PRP and a lot of behavior throughout the interval.

Fixed-Interval Schedules in Everyday Life. Although there are many situations in everyday life in which reinforcers are available only after specified time intervals, few of these are identical to the laboratory situation. For example, many students delay studying until just before a test (a fixed interval of time). Although this behavior pattern looks like a PRP and an FI scallop, there is an important difference between studying and the FI schedules studied in the laboratory: A rat or pigeon in the laboratory only need make a single lever press or key peck at the appropriate time to be successful, and additional lever presses or key pecks do not affect the amount of outcome earned. On the other hand, the amount of studying you do may affect your grade. Cramming may work for some people, but grades tend to reflect the amount of studying.

Another example of an FI schedule in everyday experience is waiting for something to cook. You have to check it to determine when it is done, but because you know from experience or from the directions that it takes a certain time to cook, there is no reason to check it too early. Because not all food is done at the same time, we have a tendency to check it close to the time we expect it to be done. If you check it before it is done, you have wasted some effort. You are reinforced for checking when it is done. This looks more like an FI schedule except that we can use clocks and kitchen timers to remind us to check. Animals do not have that luxury.

Variable-Interval Schedules (VI *t*)

Variable-interval schedules require the individual to perform the target behavior after a certain time has elapsed, but that time is not the same for each outcome. These schedules also generate slow, steady rates of behavior with little or no postreinforcement pauses.

In a variable-interval schedule of reinforcement (VI *t*), *the first occurrence of the target behavior after a specified interval of time has elapsed will produce the outcome; that interval varies around a certain average (t)*. For example, in a VI 1-minute schedule, the individual can obtain the outcome for the first occurrence of the target behavior after a certain time has elapsed, but the required time will vary across successive reinforcers with an average interreinforcer time of 1 minute. There are a number of ways to generate the various intervals that are used in a VI schedule in the laboratory. The most commonly used method in research generates a sequence of intervals that are spaced so that over the course of an experimental session the probability that the next instance of the target behavior being reinforced is a constant (Fleshler & Hoffman, 1962).[2]

Typical Performance on Variable-Interval Schedules. Subjects on a constant probability VI schedule of the kind devised by Fleshler and Hoffman (1962) produce a relatively constant rate of the target behavior with only a few brief PRPs (Figure 9.6). However, the rate of behavior is a function of the temporal parameter of the schedule (*t*). When *t* is low, the individual can earn a great number of reinforcers in a short period of time. As a result, low values of *t* tend to produce higher rates of behavior. As *t* increases, the overall rate of behavior decreases (Catania & Reynolds, 1968). This makes adaptive sense. In order to obtain the outcome, the individual has to behave. When *t* is short, the outcome is more likely to be available in the next instance of time, but when *t* is long, there will be long periods in which it is not available. The best strategy for the subject is to perform

Figure 9.6   Cumulative record of the pattern of performance by a pigeon on a VI 3-minute schedule of reinforcement.

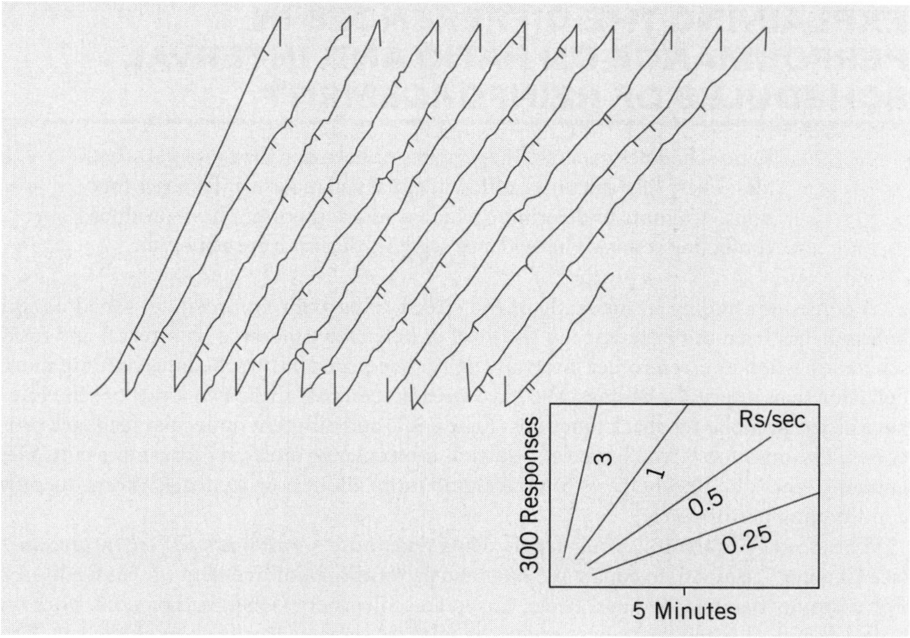

From Ferster and Skinner, 1957. Reprinted courtesy of the B. F. Skinner Foundation.

---

[2]A closely related schedule is called a **random-interval schedule of reinforcement (RI *t*)**. In random-interval schedules, *the probability of reinforcement becoming available in the next instance of time is determined in the following manner: The probability that the reinforcer will be available in the next 0.5 second interval for the next target behavior is equal to 1/*t*. Over an extended period of time, the average time between reinforcement availability will equal* t.

the target behavior at a slow steady rate, fast enough to earn all of the available outcomes, but not too fast to waste time and energy. Individuals appear to adopt such a strategy.

Variable-Interval Schedules in Everyday Life. Variable-interval schedules occur whenever the opportunity to obtain an outcome or success depends on the passage of time, but that time interval is unpredictable to the individual. For example, if you are trying to call a friend on the telephone and the line is busy (because that person does not have call waiting), you tend to wait for some time and then try again. Repeatedly pressing the redial button does not speed up your getting through. However, in this situation, if you wait too long, that person may hang up and then take another call. This can be simulated in the laboratory by imposing a **limited hold**, *a limited time after the interval has elapsed during which the target behavior must occur. If that behavior does not occur during that limited time, the opportunity to obtain the outcome is canceled.* Limited holds promote more rapid behavior because long pauses are *less* likely to be followed by the next instance of the target behavior being reinforced.

EXPLAINING THE DIFFERENCES IN PERFORMANCE ON RATIO AND INTERVAL SCHEDULES OF REINFORCEMENT

Ratio schedules generate higher rates of behavior than interval schedules. These schedules have different molar and molecular feedback functions. Attempts to determine which is more important have produced conflicting results. The evidence suggests that both are important.

A consistent finding in the study of the effects of partial reinforcement schedules on behavior has been the difference in the level of behavior generated by interval and ratio schedules: when interreinforcer intervals (IRIs) are equated, ratio schedules result in more behavior than interval schedules. We have already seen that these two kinds of schedules have different molar feedback functions (Figure 9.1) and different molecular feedback processes. The question is which type of feedback, molecular or molar, is more important. The answer to that question helps us to understand more about how feedback affects operant conditioning performance.

The strategy in the following experiments was to use a *within-subjects yoking procedure* (see Chapter 7, Box 7.6) to equate the rates and patterns of reinforcement (molar feedback). For example, Baum (1993) and Peele, Casey, and Silverberg (1984) had pigeons work on both VR and VI schedules, where each schedule was signaled by the color of the key. The time that a reinforcer was available after the next peck on the VI schedule was determined by when the bird collected a reinforcer during a previous VR schedule; that is, the availability of reinforcers on the VI schedule was yoked to the VR schedule. This equated the rate and pattern of reinforcers on both schedules.

In both studies, the pigeons had higher rates of pecking on the VR schedules than the VI schedules over a wide range of reinforcement rates. The difference disappeared when the rate of reinforcement was very high (corresponding to VR 2, VR 4, and VR 8). Most likely this reflects the fact that at high rates of reinforcement, the two schedules may be indistinguishable.

Equating Molecular Feedback. After demonstrating that a VR 200 schedule produces a higher rate of pecking than a yoked VI, Peele et al. (1984) manipulated the molecular feedback by requiring that the next reinforcer on the VI schedule have an interresponse time (IRT) that approximated the reinforced IRT on the VR schedule (see Table 9.1). When they did this, the difference in rates of pecking on the VR and VI was greatly reduced. In another experiment reported in the same paper, Peele et al. found that they could also eliminate the VR/VI difference by going in the opposite direction: They added an IRT requirement based on a preceding VI schedule to a VR schedule. *The results of these experiments suggest that it is the differential reinforcement of IRTs (molecular feedback) that produces the difference in the rates of behavior maintained by VR and VI schedules.*

Equating Molar Feedback. Using a different approach, McDowell and Wixted (1986) developed a VI schedule that simulated the molar feedback of a VR schedule; that is, faster rates of behavior produced more reinforcers per unit time. With this schedule, slower performance increased the time between the next reinforcer and the following one while faster performance reduced that interreinforcer time. Thus fast performance increased the overall rate of reinforcement (as in a VR schedule), but short IRTs were not reinforced because the time to reinforcement was set before the interval started. Using humans, they found that the rates at which their subjects pressed a panel to earn points that would be exchanged for money *did not differ* between the VR schedule and the special VI with molar feedback schedule *when the molar rates of reinforcement were equated* (i.e., faster rates of pressing the panel produced faster rates of reinforcement on both schedules). These results are interesting because the VR/VI difference disappeared even though there still was a difference in the molecular feedbacks for the two schedules (the VR still differentially reinforced short IRTs; the special VI did not). *These data suggest that*

Table 9.1   Experimental Design and Results From the Peele, Casey, and Silverberg (1984) Experiment

Phase 1	Phase 2
Color 1 ➝ VR 200 Color 2 ➝ Yoked VI	Color 3 ➝ VR 200 Color 4 ➝ VI-Yoked IRT
Result: Faster rates of pecking on VR schedule	Result: Rates of pecking on VR and VI converged

Notes: In each Phase, key colors alternated after every reinforcer.

In Phase 1, reinforcer availability on VI determined by how long it took the pigeon to be reinforced on a previous VR part of the cycle.

In Phase 2, reinforcer availability on VI determined by how long it took the pigeon to be reinforced on a previous VR part of the cycle and when IRT in range of VR IRTs.

it is the relationship between the rates of behavior and the rates of reinforcement (molar feedback) that produces the difference in the rates of behavior maintained by VR and VI schedules.

Explaining the Differences in Performance on Ratio and Interval Schedules of Reinforcement. What are we to make of the data described above? Clearly, any explanation of the differences in performance on ratio and interval schedules must deal with the fact that when either molar feedback or molecular feedback on ratio and interval schedules of reinforcement is equated, the difference in performance on these two types of schedules disappears.

If one or the other type of feedback is more important or is sufficient to account for the difference in performance, then equating that type of feedback for both types of schedules should eliminate the difference while equating the other kind of feedback should not. But that is not what happens—equating either type of feedback eliminates the difference. This leads to the following conclusion: *Both types of feedback are necessary conditions, but not sufficient conditions, for producing the differences in performance between ratio and interval schedules of reinforcement* (see Chapter 3, Box 3.2). This means that the performance of individuals on ratio and interval schedules reflects how they utilize *both* types of feedback to adjust to the demands of these schedules: Both the molar and molecular feedback functions for ratio schedules encourage high rates of behavior while the molecular and molar feedback functions for interval schedules encourage slower rates of performance of the target behavior (because rapid performance is not differentially reinforced on interval schedules).

THE EFFECTS OF PRIOR EXPERIENCE ON HOW INDIVIDUALS ADJUST TO SCHEDULES OF REINFORCEMENT

How an individual adjusts to a schedule of partial reinforcement is usually affected by his or her prior experiences. Individuals working under one schedule of reinforcement and then shifted to a second schedule may perform differently on the second schedule than individuals who did not have that prior experience with the first schedule. These carryover effects provide another perspective on how individuals adjust to changing circumstances.

Research on the effects of the various schedules of partial reinforcement illustrates how individuals adjust to the requirements of these schedules. With sufficient experience, most individuals come to behave in characteristic ways that reflect both the direct and indirect requirements of these schedules. However, we know from our own experience that how we deal with a new situation is determined by our experiences in similar situations. In all of the experiments on schedules of partial reinforcement reviewed above, the subjects were placed on a schedule soon after they had been taught to perform the target behavior and with little prior experience earning reinforcement for performing that behavior. In this section, we will look at how individuals perform on some schedules after having experience with other schedules. These studies show us that *current behavior reflects both the demands of the current situation and the effects of prior experiences in similar situations.*

The Effects of Prior Experience With a Ratio Schedule on Performance on an Interval Schedule. Baron and Leinenweber (1995; see also Wanchisen et al., 1989) investigated the effects of prior experience with a VR schedule on the performance of rats shifted to an FI schedule. This shift is interesting because the two schedules are so different in terms of their direct and indirect requirements and in their molar and molecular feedback functions. As a result of these differences, these two schedules generate very different patterns and rates of behavior (see Figures 9.4 and 9.5).

The design of both of these experiments was straightforward: There were two groups of rats. One group received a large number of sessions on a VR 20 schedule (between 48 and 80 sessions) before being shifted to an FI 30-second schedule. The second group of rats was trained only on the FI 30-second schedule. Some of the data from this study are

Figure 9.7 Results from Baron and Leinenweber's experiment on prior experience. (Left panel) Cumulative records of three control rats pressing a lever on an FI 30-second schedule. These rats were trained initially on the fixed interval schedule and had no prior experience with a variable ratio schedule. The middle 14 intervals from sessions 5, 15, 30, 60, and 90 are presented. (Right panel) Cumulative records of three rats pressing a lever on an FI 30-second schedule following a history of training with a VR 20 schedule. The middle 14 intervals from sessions 5, 15, 30, 60, and 90 are presented.

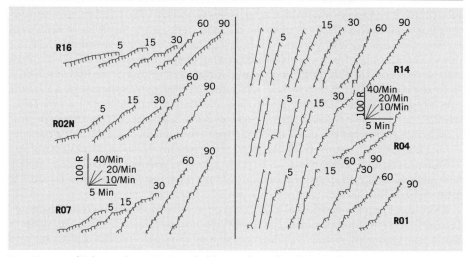

From Baron and Leinenweber, 1995, *Journal of the Experimental Analysis of Behavior*, 63, 97–110. Copyright © 1995 by the Society for the Experimental Analysis of Behavior, Inc. Reprinted by permission of John Wiley and Sons.

presented in Figure 9.7. In the left panel are sample cumulative records for three rats trained on the FI 30-second schedule (with no prior experience with a VR schedule) taken from sessions 5, 15, 30, 60, and 90. These cumulative records illustrate the development of the typical patterns of performance on an FI 30-second schedule. Note the development of the scallop in the earlier sessions which was replaced by the break and run pattern in the later sessions. The cumulative records for three rats switched from VR 20 to FI 30 seconds are in the right panel. Note that the pattern of lever pressing during the early sessions looks like VR performance; however, with extended experience the pattern gradually shifts to the typical FI performance in the left panel. The results from the Wanchisen et al. (1989) study were similar.

These data indicate that the effects of the prior experience with a VR schedule for obtaining food by lever pressing affects performance on an FI schedule, but these carryover effects progressively diminished with longer exposure to the FI schedule. Thus it appears that the subjects were insensitive to the abrupt shift in schedule, no doubt because their high rate of lever pressing continued to produce food. However, with continued exposure to the FI schedule, both the molar and molecular feedback from the FI schedule gradually took hold because slowing the rate of lever pressing would *not* diminish the rate at which food was earned (molar feedback), and pauses would be *more likely* to be followed by food for the next lever press (molecular feedback). These forms of feedback start to take hold as the mechanism of hill-climbing comes into play. When individuals exhibit some variability in their rate of lever pressing, they are more likely to experience the new schedule contingency and adjust to it.

However, the effects of prior experience with a ratio schedule on interval performance has not always been found to persist for as long as it did in the experiment described in the previous paragraph. Freeman and Lattal (1992) found rapid shifts to a new schedule of reinforcement when they compared the effects of prior experience with FR and IRT > t schedules on later FI and VI schedules: First they trained pigeons to peck a key for food on FR and IRT > t schedules where the two schedules alternated. When the key was one color, the FR schedule was in effect, and when the key was a second color, the IRT > t schedule was in effect. Over the course of 50 sessions, the pigeons came to exhibit the patterns of behavior that are characteristic of each schedule in the presence of the corresponding color—the break and run pattern on the FR schedule and the peck-pause-peck pattern on the IRT > t schedule. In the test phase of this experiment, both schedules were changed to either the *same* FI or the *same* VI (depending on the particular experiment). Although the FR and IRT > t (or DRL) schedules produce very different rates of pecking (as you might expect), the rates of pecking quickly converged when the pigeons were shifted to the same FI schedules in the presence of both key colors. The same thing happened when the shift was to identical VI schedules. Thus, in this experiment, the effects of the prior experience with an FR schedule and an IRT > t schedules rapidly dissipated within a few sessions when their subjects were switched to identical FI or VI schedules.

Why did Freeman and Lattal (1992) obtain results so different from Baron and Leinenweber (1995) and Wanchisen et al. (1989)? One possibility is the choice of subjects: Baron and Leinenweber and Wanchisen et al. used rats, and Freeman and Lattal used pigeons. Another possibility is a difference in procedure: Freeman and Lattal exposed their subjects to two schedules that produce very different patterns of behavior (FR and IRT > t).

This may have made their subjects more sensitive to the schedule in effect and thus help them detect the change to interval schedules.

Cole (2001) attempted to resolve this discrepancy. He placed different groups of rats on either a single schedule (FR or IRT > *t*) or two different schedules (FR followed by IRT > *t* or IRT > *t* followed by FR) before putting all subjects on an FI schedule. Cole found that individuals subjected to two prior schedules shifted to the FI pattern sooner, but the shift took longer than was reported by Freeman and Lattal (1992). Cole ran his subjects for at least 80 sessions on the FI schedule and found that there was no evidence of the prior schedule history in his subjects' FI performance after that extended period of time.

The Effects of More Distant History on Performance on Interval Schedules. In the study by Freeman and Lattal (1992) described above, the effects of prior experience with FR and IRT > *t* schedules was found to persist for a short time when their subjects were shifted to identical VI schedules. Ono and Iwabuchi (1997) investigated what would happen when there was a delay between the prior experience with one schedule and performance on a different schedule. First they trained three pigeons to peck for food on an IRT < *t* schedule (DRH) when the key light was green and peck for food on an IRT > *t* schedule (DRL) when the key light was red. Over time the pigeons pecked at a high rate in the presence of green (IRT < *t*) and at a slow rate in the presence of the red light (IRT > *t*; see left panels of Figure 9.8). After 30 sessions with these two schedules, the key light was made white and the pigeons worked on a VI schedule for 15 additional sessions (Figure 9.8, center panels). In the third phase of the experiment, the red and green key lights were reinstated, but the schedules were changed to identical variable intervals (the same as in the presence of the white key light). Thus, in this phase there were three key lights (white, red, and green), but the same VI schedule was in effect in the presence of all three. It is apparent in the right panels of Figure 9.8 that the effects of the original training with the IRT schedules (DRL and DRH) persisted across the intervening VI training on the white key. Note that as was the case in the Freeman and Lattal (1992) study, the effects of the prior experience dissipated as the pigeons gained experience with the VI schedules on the red and green keys.

The results depicted in Figure 9.8 indicate that the effects of the prior conditioning history with DRL and DRH survived the intervening experience with the VI schedule: when the key lights from the first phase were reinstated, the pigeons went back to what they had learned in their presence. These data point to an important aspect of learning: *Once you have learned something, you are different. The fact that you might not now be performing what you learned earlier does not mean that you forgot it. Under the right set of circumstances, the previously learned behavior may reappear.*

Ono and Iwabuchi (1997) repeated this procedure with the same pigeons two more times. They found that each time they repeated the procedure, the effects of the earlier experience was further reduced. This indicates another important aspect of learning: *Repeated experience with change makes individuals more sensitive to change so that they more readily adapt to it.*

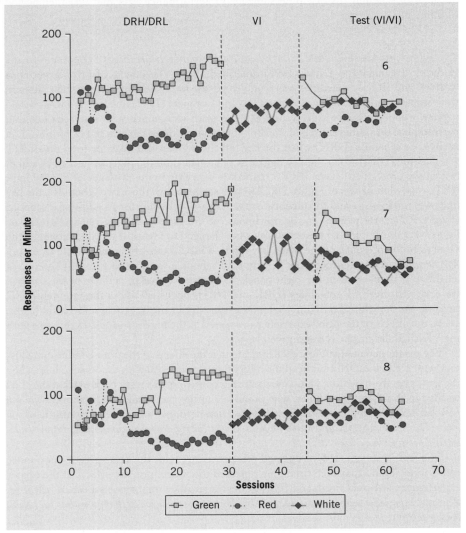

Figure 9.8   Results from Ono and Iwabuchi's experiment on prior experience. Rates of pecking under three conditions. In the left panel, when the key is green, the schedule is a DRH (IRT < t) and when the key is red, the schedule is a DRL (IRT > t). In the center panel the key is white and the schedule is a variable interval. In the right panel, the keys are red and green again with identical variable interval schedules.

From Ono and Iwabuchi, 1997, *Journal of the Experimental Analysis of Behavior*, 67, 311–322. Copyright © 1997 by the Society for the Experimental Analysis of Behavior, Inc. Reprinted by permission of John Wiley and Sons.

BEHAVIORAL PERSISTENCE

Behavioral persistence refers to the tendency to continue to perform a behavior when that behavior no longer produces a reinforcing event. There are a number of factors that influence behavioral persistence. Experience with schedules of partial reinforcement is one of them.

In the last section, we saw how prior experience with one kind of schedule of partial reinforcement influences the transition to another schedule. In this section we will examine how a variety of experiences, including partial reinforcement, influences how long an individual will persist in performing a behavior when the availability of the reinforcer for that behavior is reduced. *The conventional measure of behavioral persistence* is called **resistance to extinction**; that is, *how long it takes an individual to cease performing a behavior when that behavior no longer produces the reinforcing event (the procedure of extinction). The longer it takes the individual to cease performing a behavior when that behavior no longer produces the reinforcing event, the greater the resistance to extinction.*

Persistence is a double-edged sword. When the reinforcer will no longer be available, persistence is counterproductive because continuing to perform the formerly reinforced activity prevents the individual from moving on to more productive activities. On the other hand, persistence is productive when it eventually leads to reinforcement; in that case, giving up is counterproductive.

Persistence at performing a behavior depends on three factors. The first is how much success the individual has experienced obtaining the outcome by performing the target behavior: *The greater the amount of success, the more persistent the behavior.* The second factor is how discriminable the change in procedure is to the individual; that is, how quickly the individual can detect that the outcome is no longer available. Discriminability is determined by how similar the two situations are: *With respect to persistence, the more similar (less discriminable) extinction is to training, the greater the persistence (the more resistance to extinction).* The third is having had prior experience in which persistence has been reinforced: *Experience with partial reinforcement produces resistance to extinction.*

Amount of Training and Persistence

Up to a point, the greater the amount of training, the greater the resistance to extinction. This fits nicely with an analogy between behavioral persistence and the concept in physics of momentum. In physics, momentum = mass × velocity, and objects with greater momentum require more force to stop. Persistence is conceptualized as reflecting behavioral momentum.

Early in training when individuals are not very proficient at performing the target behavior, they will experience times when that behavior does not seem effective (because they are not doing it well enough to be successful). As they become more proficient, they experience more success, and as we saw in Chapter 8, behaviors followed by reinforcing events tend to occur more often to the exclusion of other (nonreinforced) behaviors, and these reinforced behaviors become more stereotyped and less variable (unless variability is the aspect of behavior being reinforced). Therefore, the more reinforced experience an individual has at performing a certain behavior, the more persistent he or she should be when reinforcement is discontinued.

Nevin, Mandell, and Atak (1983) attributed the greater persistence of behaviors that have been reinforced many times to **behavioral momentum**. The term "behavioral momentum" is derived from Newton's second law of motion, which can be characterized as follows: Objects have a certain mass. The greater the mass of an object, the greater the force required to change the movement in that object. Thus, it takes more force (effort) to slow down (or speed up) a massive (heavy) object than a less massive (light) object. Likewise, it takes more force to slow down an object that has a high velocity (is moving fast) than one with low velocity (is moving slowly). The combination of mass times velocity defines the momentum of an object (momentum = mass × velocity), and the greater the momentum of an object, the greater the force required to slow it down (or speed it up). With respect to behavior, Nevin et al. argued that reinforcement increases the strength of a behavior, and strength is analogous to mass in Newton's second law. Likewise, the rate of occurrence of a behavior is analogous to the velocity of on object, and the change in the reinforcement contingency (to extinction) is analogous to the force applied to the object. By analogy, behavioral momentum refers to *the tendency for a behavior to persist when the reinforcement contingency is changed. Behaviors that are more resistant to change have more momentum.* From this perspective, amount of acquisition training increases persistence (resistance to extinction) because successful behaviors acquire more momentum and thus become more resistant to change when extinction is introduced.

One thing successful individuals learn from their experiences early in acquisition training is that persistence pays when trying to produce the reinforcing event. However, there is a law of diminishing returns here: As the amount of training increases, the amount of persistence only increases up to a point. Continued training in acquisition beyond that point does not lead to more persistence. In fact, the opposite happens: With a great deal of acquisition training, resistance to extinction (persistence) decreases (see Mackintosh, 1974, for a review). These data appear to contradict the notion that training produces behavioral momentum, but that conclusion is premature. The reduction in resistance to extinction that occurs with extended acquisition training can be explained by invoking discriminability of the change in procedure.

Discriminability and Persistence

Persistence is a function of how discriminable the conditions of acquisition training are from the conditions of extinction: Extinction occurs faster (there is less persistence) when these two are more easily discriminated.

Discriminability is related to salience (see Chapter 4) and is determined, in part, by the physical attributes of the stimulus and in part by what the individual brings to the situation (sensory capacities, knowledge). We say that two events are discriminable when the individual can tell them apart. Both salience and discriminability affect *how easily an individual detects a stimulus against the background in which that stimulus occurs*. In the context of this discussion, the conditions during acquisition training define the background onto which the change to extinction is the stimulus that must be detected. There is an abundance of evidence that resistance to extinction is a function of how easy it is for the individual to detect that the situation has changed from acquisition (the background) to extinction.

Extended Training and Discriminability. After extended acquisition training in which the individual has a long record of success obtaining the outcome, the shift to extinction should be easier to detect than after only a short period of success (i.e., early in acquisition training). Thus, *behavioral momentum* that develops during acquisition accounts for the *increase* in resistance to extinction (persistence), and *discriminability of the change in procedure* accounts for the *decrease* in resistance to extinction (persistence) after extended training.

Magnitude of the Reinforcer. Whether magnitude of the reinforcer is determined by the size of the reinforcer (e.g., the number of food pellets or the length of time food is available for eating) or the quality of the reinforcer (e.g., the sweetness of the food), the general rule is that behaviors trained on a continuous reinforcement schedule when reinforcer magnitude is high are *less* resistant to extinction. This inverse effect of magnitude of the reinforcer on persistence (resistance to extinction) can be easily explained in terms of the discriminability of the change: it is easier to detect the change from a large reinforcer to no reinforcer than it is from a small reinforcer to no reinforcer. However, the opposite is true when the behavior is trained on a partial reinforcement schedule; that is, the larger the magnitude of the reinforcer, the greater the resistance to extinction. The reasons for the difference will be examined when we consider the effects of partial reinforcement on resistance to extinction.

Free Reinforcers During Extinction. The obvious difference between the procedure of positive reinforcement during acquisition and the procedure of extinction is the occurrence of reinforcers in the former and their absence in the latter. The sooner the individual realizes that their behavior will not produce the reinforcer, the sooner he or she ceases performing that behavior. However, the target behavior takes longer to extinguish when noncontingent reinforcement is presented occasionally in extinction (Boakes, 1973; Reid, 1958; Rescorla & Skucy, 1969). This should not be surprising because the occurrence of noncontingent reinforcers in extinction makes extinction look like acquisition training.

Prior Experience With Extinction. Individuals can learn from previous experience to discriminate between extinction and acquisition training (Bullock, 1960; Bullock & Smith, 1953; Clark & Taylor, 1960). In these experiments, individuals were alternated between acquisition and extinction, and each successive acquisition and extinction of the operant behavior occurred more rapidly. This suggests that individuals can learn to discriminate the difference between acquisition and extinction. This is similar to what Ono and Iwabuchi (1997) found when they had their subjects recycle through the experimental procedure a number of times. This is further evidence for the conclusion that *repeated experience with change makes individuals more sensitive to change so that they more readily adapt to it.*

Signaling the Transition From Acquisition to Extinction. Extinction will always occur faster if there is a change in the prevailing stimulus conditions at the time extinction is implemented. For example, if a pigeon is trained to peck a key for food with a green light on the key and then the procedure is changed to extinction, the pigeon will show more resistance to extinction (greater persistence) if the key light remains green than if it changes to another color. In fact, the greater the change in color (e.g., red is farther from green than yellow on the color spectrum), the less the resistance to extinction. Mackintosh (1974) reviewed a large number of experiments in which the transition from acquisition to extinction was accompanied by various changes in the procedure (in addition to the termination of reinforcement). In all of these experiments, there was *less resistance to extinction when the transition from acquisition to extinction was accompanied by another discriminable change in the situation.*

Extinction of Avoidance Learning. If we define extinction as the discontinuance of the reinforcing event, then the extinction of avoidance conditioning presents a special problem: in avoidance learning the reinforcing event is the *absence* of an aversive event that would have occurred if the avoidance behavior did not occur because the individual who is avoiding successfully rarely experiences that aversive event (see Chapter 7). The only way that individuals can discover that the aversive event will not occur in the absence of the avoidance behavior is to stop avoiding, but why should he or she do that and risk being hurt? This makes avoidance behavior quite resistant to extinction unless something is done to alert the individual that the avoidance behavior is no longer required. One way is to prevent the individual from performing the behavior. This can be done by *placing the individual in the situation in which an aversive event had previously occurred and preventing him or her from performing the avoidance behavior* (a procedure called **flooding**). Typically flooding produces rapid extinction when the individual is given the opportunity to perform the avoidance behavior later (see, e.g., Baum, 1970; Baum & Poser, 1971). Flooding makes extinction less like avoidance learning and thus reduces resistance to extinction with avoidance behaviors. The behavior therapy called **implosion therapy** employs flooding to reduce fear of objects and places (Stampfl & Levis, 1967).

Persistence and Partial Reinforcement

Behaviors maintained by partial reinforcement persist longer in extinction than behaviors maintained by continuous reinforcement. We call this the partial reinforcement extinction effect. The partial reinforcement extinction effect is due in part to the fact that it is easier for individuals to discriminate the difference between continuous reinforcement and extinction than between partial reinforcement and extinction, and in part to the fact that experience with partial reinforcement teaches individuals to tolerate frustration.

Individuals on partial reinforcement schedules learn that not every instance of a particular behavior will result in reinforcement, but they also learn that eventually they will receive the reinforcer for performing that behavior. In other words, they learn that they will be successful, but not every time they try. As a result, individuals who experience partial reinforcement are more persistent than individuals who only experience a continuous reinforcement schedule. This *increase in resistance to extinction following experience with partial reinforcement* is called the **partial reinforcement extinction effect (PREE)**.

Clearly extinction and partial reinforcement share the characteristic that individuals will perform the target behavior without receiving reinforcement (all of the time in extinction and some of the time under partial reinforcement). This shared characteristic makes it more difficult for the individual to detect that partial reinforcement has ended and extinction has begun. Clearly, it is easier to tell the difference between continuous reinforcement and extinction than between partial reinforcement and extinction. It is also easier to tell the difference between a regular pattern of reinforcement (e.g., what one would encounter on an FR or FI schedule) and extinction than between a variable pattern (e.g., VR or VI) and extinction. Therefore, it is hardly surprising that extinction occurs more rapidly after a regular pattern of reinforcement.

But discriminability between conditions by itself cannot explain the partial reinforcement extinction effect (PREE). If that were the only factor, then giving individuals a period of continuous reinforcement before extinction should reduce persistence and speed extinction (i.e., reduce resistance to extinction). It does, but it does not completely abolish the PREE (see, e.g., Jenkins, 1962; Zarcone, Branch, Hughes, & Pennypacker, 1997). This suggests that once established, the effects of partial reinforcement cannot be completely undone. But what is it about the experience with partial reinforcement that builds persistence?

What Individuals Learn From Experience With Partial Reinforcement. In order to understand why individuals who have experienced partial reinforcement exhibit more persistence during extinction, we have to first understand the emotional effects of extinction. The procedure of extinction produces failure because what used to work to obtain the reinforcing event no longer does. There is abundant evidence that the omission of an otherwise expected outcome produces frustration (Amsel, 1958, 1992). Frustration has two properties: *It energizes ongoing behavior, and it can produce competing behavior.* We are all familiar with what happens when we become frustrated because of our inability to achieve our objectives. Animals are no different. A rat who runs down an alley for food, but does not find any, runs faster down the next alley (Amsel & Roussel, 1952), and when individuals in an operant conditioning situation are placed on extinction, the rate of the target behavior *increases before it decreases.* Both of these effects (increased running speed and the initial increase in the rate of behavior) are attributed to the energizing effects of frustration: When we are frustrated by our inability to do something we try harder. However, as our level of frustration rises, it may reach a point where competing behaviors are induced (swearing, throwing things, etc.). Similarly, rats have been observed biting the lever and pigeons have been observed flapping their wings and stamping around during extinction. These competing behaviors interfere with performance.

Subjects on partial reinforcement learn to persist in the presence of nonreinforcement because they are reinforced for doing so. The frustration that results from occasional nonreinforcement energizes them to persevere, not to engage in disruptive behaviors. Subjects on continuous reinforcement do not have the opportunity to learn this. This explains why resistance to extinction is lower with larger outcomes following continuous reinforcement but higher following partial reinforcement. The loss of a larger outcome is not only easier to discriminate, but it is also more frustrating. The individual who was earning that larger outcome on a partial reinforcement schedule will persist in the face of the additional frustration while the individual who earned it under continuous reinforcement will become frustrated sooner and engage in competing behaviors.

Therefore, if you want to encourage behavioral persistence, you should place the target behavior on a schedule of partial reinforcement. On the other hand, if you want to decrease persistence and speed extinction, you are more likely to succeed if you maintain the individual on continuous reinforcement before placing him or her on extinction. Thus, the parent who eventually gives in to tantrums or other disruptive behaviors encourages their children to be persistent. It is better to indulge an infant's crying because the child will stop crying sooner when he or she is completely ignored for crying (the procedure of extinction). Once an individual experiences partial reinforcement, he or she is likely to be more persistent, even if the most recent experience has been with continuous reinforcement.

SUMMARY AND CONCLUSIONS

Schedules of reinforcement specify the conditions under which an individual can obtain an outcome. Sometimes every instance of a certain behavior produces the outcome (*continuous reinforcement*), but that is not always the case. When not all occurrences of the target behavior produce the reinforcing event, we say that the individual is on a *schedule of partial reinforcement*. Schedules of partial reinforcement typically require the individual to perform a given number of behaviors (*ratio schedules*), behave after a certain interval of time has elapsed (*interval schedules*), or space behaviors a certain time interval apart (*interresponse time [IRT] schedules*) in order to receive the reinforcing event. In the case of ratio and interval schedules, the specified number of behaviors or time interval can be the same between successive reinforcers (*fixed*) or different (*variable or random*). Each of these schedules produces a characteristic pattern of behavior. In general, when the number and distribution of reinforcers is equated, ratio schedules tend to generate

higher rates of behavior than interval schedules, and fixed schedules (both ratio and interval) tend to produce pauses after the receipt of a reinforcer (*post-reinforcement pause*).

These characteristic patterns of behavior are determined by both the molar and molecular feedback functions from each schedule. *Molar feedback* refers to the relationship between the rate of performance of the target behavior and the rate at which the outcome is earned. *Molecular feedback* involves the moment-to-moment relationship between behaviors and outcomes. By manipulating these two types of feedback, we can see how behavior is influences by its consequences.

How individuals adjust their behavior to the demands of the various schedules depends on their prior experiences. Sometimes the effects of those prior experiences can last for some time; however, with sufficient experience under a given schedule, most of the time the effects of the prior experiences fade and individuals come to exhibit the behavior patterns characteristically generated by the schedule they are on currently.

Finally, experience with partial reinforcement increases persistence: individuals who experience partial reinforcement, even if their most recent experience is with continuous reinforcement, show more resistance to extinction (persistence) than individuals who only experience continuous reinforcement of that behavior. This occurs because partial reinforcement increases frustration tolerance.

STUDY QUESTIONS

1. What is the difference between molar feedback and molecular feedback? What is the difference between ratio and interval schedules with respect to these two types of feedback?

2. For each of the following schedules of reinforcement, describe the contingency and the behavior pattern exhibited by a typical individual on each type of schedule:

   a. fixed ratio

   b. variable ratio

   c. fixed interval

   d. variable interval

   e. IRT $< t$ (see Chapter 8)

   f. IRT $> t$ (see Chapter 8)

   How do we explain these behavior patterns?

3. What is the major difference in performance on variable ratio and variable interval schedules? What is the explanation for this difference?

4. What have we learned about how prior experience with schedules of reinforcement affects how individuals adjust to other schedules of reinforcement?

5. What are the factors that promote behavioral persistence (and what are the effects of those factors on behavioral persistence)?

6. How do we explain the partial reinforcement extinction effect (PREE)?

10

LIFE IS ABOUT MAKING CHOICES

Up to this point, we have discussed operant conditioning in terms of how consequences (also termed outcomes, reinforcers, and rewards) affect single behaviors. Whether the discussion was about rats pressing levers, pigeons pecking keys, autistic children engaging in disruptive behaviors, encouraging mute individuals and autistic children to speak, or rewarding people for studying, the focus was on a single target behavior and the effects of the consequences for that behavior on its future occurrence. But behaviors and consequences do not exist in isolation. At any moment in time, we can engage in any number of activities that may have different consequences: studying or watching television, going to a movie or going to a bar, staying in school or dropping out and going to work, purchasing brand X, brand Y, or brand Z. This is even true for a rat in an operant chamber that contains a single lever connected to a food dispenser: At any point in time, the rat can press or not press the lever. Whether the rat presses or does not press the lever depends not only on the consequences of lever pressing but also the consequences of other activities the rat could engage in (grooming, exploring, resting, etc.). In this chapter, we will focus on the determinants of these choices. We will see that *how much time and effort individuals allocate to the various activities they can perform in a given situation depends on the values of the various consequences for these activities.* In other words, life is about making choices between activities that can have different valued outcomes.

There are a number of ways to study choice. One way is to collect data on a large number of individuals who have similar characteristics and look at how many of them choose X over Y. This is what is done in survey research and in focus groups. One can even ask people to make a choice and then rate the strength of their preference, but what you get are single discrete measures of choice and strength of preference. In the research reviewed in this chapter, individuals can choose between simultaneously available activities that lead to different outcomes, and they can switch back and forth among these activities. This gives us a continuous measure of choice and preference collected over a period of time. You face this type of choice situation when you sit in front of the television set with the remote control and channel surf, when you choose which stores to visit in the mall and how long to spend in those stores, and when you choose between studying and leisure activities. How you allocate your time and effort in these situations gives us information about the relative values of the outcomes of those choices for you. But as students of learning, we are more interested in how individuals arrive at their choices than in the choices themselves; that is, *we are interested in how individuals learn about the various outcomes and adjust their behavior accordingly*. We assume that the choices they make reflect what they learned.

CHOICE AND THE EMPIRICAL MATCHING LAW

The empirical matching law describes how individuals allocate their effort and time among two or more simultaneously available alternatives. Under certain conditions, individuals match their relative rates of behavior and time devoted to each alternative to various attributes of those alternatives. The empirical matching law was derived from how individuals adjust their behavior to concurrent schedules of performance.

Consider the choice between studying or engaging in some recreational activity. We can switch between these activities, allocating various amounts of time to each activity. What determines how much effort and time we allocate to different behaviors (like studying or watching television) that lead to different outcomes (grades or relaxation)? The answer to this question is straightforward: *When two or more choices are continuously available, individuals allocate their time and effort to each based on the relative values of the consequences or outcomes*. This is called the **theoretical matching law**. It is a theoretical law because value (like salience—see Chapter 4) is a psychological construct; that is, it is not a directly measurable property of something. The value of something is determined in part by its physical attributes, in part by the situation, and in part by the individual who is seeking it. In other words, the value of something depends on who is evaluating it.

The theoretical matching law involves an individual's subjective appraisal of the values of the various outcomes available to that individual. Although value is subjective, it is affected by *measurable* attributes of outcomes (e.g., their *relative rates of occurrence*, *relative amounts*, and *relative immediacies*). When we describe the relationship between observable behaviors and measurable aspects of outcomes, we are describing an empirical relationship. The observation that *individuals match the relative allocation of their behavior to the relative rates, amounts, or immediacies of the alternative outcomes* is called the **empirical matching law**. The empirical matching law describes relationships between the behavior of individuals and measurable outcomes; **the theoretical matching law** *relates the observed relationships described by the empirical matching law to the psychological construct of value*.

In order to understand and appreciate the theoretical matching law, we have to begin with the empirical matching law, which describes the relationship between behaviors (their rates of occurrence and how much time individuals devote to performing them) and measurable aspects of reinforcers (schedules of reinforcement, amounts or sizes of reinforcers, how soon the reinforcers appear after a behavior occurs [immediacy], etc.). Although we talk about "the empirical matching law" as if it is a single relationship, it is actually a set of relationships between different aspects of behaviors and outcomes. All of these relationships have a common property: Relative allocations of time and effort are related to relative rates, amounts, or immediacy of reinforcers. Because the measurable aspects of reinforcers affect their value, the theoretical matching law attempts to summarize all of these relationships in terms of how individuals allocate their behaviors based on the relative values of outcomes.

The matching laws (both empirical and theoretical) are statements about what affects our choices of one alternative over another. The data described by the empirical matching law comes from experiments utilizing concurrent schedules of reinforcement. Concurrent schedules of reinforcement are a good way to study choice because they allow us to manipulate aspects of simultaneously presented outcomes and observe how the manipulations influence the behavior of a single individual. Furthermore, the dependent measure is not a single binary value (whether the individual chooses A or chooses B); it gives us a measure of the relative strength of the choice (how much time and effort is directed toward obtaining each outcome).

Concurrent Schedules of Reinforcement

We can study choice by presenting individuals with two or more schedules of reinforcement running concurrently and observing how they distribute their time and effort across these alternatives.

With a **concurrent schedule of reinforcement**, *two or more different schedules of partial reinforcement are running concurrently, and the individual can choose which to work on at any given time. Reinforcement occurs when the individual satisfies the requirements of one of the schedules.* By switching between the two schedules, the individual may be able to collect outcomes from all of the schedules. Concurrent schedules can contain any combination of the four simple interval and ratio schedules (FR, VR, FI, VI). The schedules can all be of the same kind (e.g., concurrent FR FR or concurrent VI VI) or they can be different (e.g., concurrent VI VR or concurrent FI VI). A concurrent schedule can be composed of any number of simple schedules, but most research involves just two schedules. The two most commonly used concurrent schedule procedures are called the side-by-side procedure and the schedule-control procedure.

Side-by-Side Procedure. A side-by-side procedure provides the individual with *two or more different behaviors to perform (peck at different keys, press different levers, etc.), each of which occasionally produces reinforcement on a partial reinforcement schedule* (Ferster & Skinner, 1957; Skinner, 1950). For example, a pigeon may have access to two keys placed side by side (Figure 10.1, left panel). Pecks on the left key are rewarded on one partial reinforcement schedule (Schedule 1) and pecks on the right key are rewarded on another partial reinforcement schedule (Schedule 2). These two schedules operate simultaneously and independently. Thus, the individual is free to choose which schedule to work on at any given point in time. Choice is defined on a moment-by-moment basis (which key was pecked) and in terms of the relative distributions of time and effort directed toward each alternative. This procedure is also referred to as a **two-key** or **two-lever concurrent schedule** (depending on the specific manipulanda available to the individuals). This is similar to when you are walking in a mall and can choose which store to enter.

Schedule-Control Procedure. Findley (1958) described a second concurrent schedule arrangement called a schedule-control procedure, in which *individuals can do something in one location to select which schedule they want to work on in another location* (Figure 10.1, right panel). This is accomplished with pigeons by again having two keys available. One of the keys (the schedule-control key) controls the color and associated schedule of reinforcement on the other key. For example, the schedule-control key might always be white, and each peck (or small number of pecks) at it changes the color of the other key. Schedule 1 is in effect when the other key is red, and Schedule 2 is in effect when that key is green. Thus, the pigeon can change the color of the other key and the associated schedule of reinforcement by pecking at the schedule-control key. With this procedure, one can easily measure how long subjects spend on each schedule as well as the rate and pattern of behavior on each. Here again, choice is defined both on a moment-by-moment basis and in terms of the relative distributions of time each color is on and how much behavior occurs with each color. This procedure is also referred to as a **switching-key** or **switching-lever concurrent schedule** (depending on the specific manipulanda available to the individuals), or the **Findley procedure** (after the person who developed it). The remote control on your television set is a schedule-control device because it allows you to switch between the things you might spend time watching.

Figure 10.1 Two different ways to study behavior on concurrent schedules of reinforcement. The pigeon on the left is confronted with the side-by-side concurrent schedule procedure. Schedule 1 and Schedule 2 represent two simple schedules of reinforcement that are simultaneously available to the pigeon. The pigeon on the right is confronted with the schedule-control procedure. Pecks at the schedule-control key on the left change the schedule in effect on the right key. This pigeon can choose which schedule (1 or 2) is in effect on the right key.

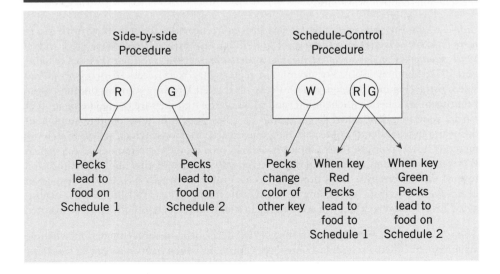

The Problem of Indiscriminate Switching Between Alternatives. With both types of concurrent schedule procedures, a frequent problem occurs when the individual ignores the schedules and switches back and forth among the alternatives. This occurs with concurrent *interval* schedules because on these schedules a reinforcer is earned for the first occurrence of the target behavior after a specified interval of time has elapsed. It does not matter what the individual does during the interval; reinforcement is delivered for the first instance of the target behavior that occurs after the interval has "timed out." Therefore, while the individual is working on one interval schedule, the other interval schedule is still advancing. The longer the individual stays on the first schedule, the more likely the next instance of the target behavior on the other schedule will be reinforced. Thus, not only are the target behaviors on both schedules reinforced, so is switching between schedules (Catania & Cutts, 1963). This encourages the subjects to ignore the schedules and simply alternate between them (e.g., peck left, peck right, peck left, and so on with the side-by-side [two-key] procedure).

To eliminate this pattern of behavior, a changeover delay (COD) is typically imposed. With a **changeover delay (COD)**, *after switching to the other schedule, the individual must spend some time working on that schedule before earning a reinforcer.* Thus, even if a reinforcer is available if the individual switches and makes a single instance of the target behavior on the other schedule, that reinforcer cannot be obtained until the end of the changeover delay (typically a few seconds). The next instance of the target behavior after the changeover delay ends is reinforced. The changeover delay (COD) eliminates reinforcement for switching and produces behavior patterns on each schedule that are similar to those generated when individuals are working on a single schedule (Catania, 1962).

The Development of the Empirical Matching Law

Skinner and others described performance that fits the empirical matching law, but Richard Herrnstein was the first person to identify it as a basic relationship between behaviors and outcomes on concurrent schedules of reinforcement.

The behavior of subjects on concurrent interval schedules was first described by Skinner (1950). He presented pigeons with two keys where pecks on each were reinforced on unspecified interval schedules. When the rates of reinforcement were the *same* on both keys, the pigeons distributed their pecks *equally* to the two keys; that is, the ratio of pecks on the left to pecks on the right equaled.[1] When the situation was changed so that reinforcement was delivered for pecks only on one key (the maintained reinforcement key), the rate of pecking on that key increased (even though the schedule of reinforcement on that key did not change), and the rate of pecking on the other key (extinction key) declined. This shifted the ratio of pecks on the two keys toward the key with the maintained reinforcement schedule, but the combined rate of pecking on both keys remained the same;

---

[1]Because there were only two behaviors that produced reinforcement in this situation (pecking at key A and pecking at key B), it also must be true that *the relative rate of pecking at key B equals the relative rate of reinforcement obtained on key B.*

that is, as the number of pecks on the extinction key declined, the number of pecks on the maintained key increased. Furthermore, if the schedules of reinforcement on both keys were changed to extinction at the same time, the *ratio* of pecking at both keys stayed the same as the overall rates of pecking on both declined.

In their 1957 book *Schedules of Reinforcement*, Ferster and Skinner devoted an entire chapter to the performance of pigeons on two-key concurrent schedules involving a variety of combinations of ratio and interval schedules, but their focus was on the patterns of behavior generated and the interactions between ratio and interval schedules in terms of performance. In 1958, Findley introduced the schedule-control procedure described above to study behavior in a concurrent choice situation. Although both Skinner and Findley observed that changes in one schedule affect behavior on the other schedule, and Skinner observed that the ratio of the rates of pecking on the two keys was preserved during extinction, neither researcher recognized the basic relationship between the relative rates of behavior and the relative rates of reinforcement on the two alternatives. That relationship was first described by Herrnstein in 1961.

Matching Relative Rates of Behavior to Relative Rates of Reinforcement. Herrnstein (1961) trained pigeons with a two-key concurrent VI VI schedule until they reached a stable level of performance on both schedules. Then the pigeons were shifted to another concurrent VI VI schedule with different values for the two VI schedules where they remained until their behavior became stable again. Herrnstein repeated this procedure a number of times for each pigeon. He chose his VI values so that the overall average rate of reinforcement from both schedules was 1.5 reinforcers per minute. In addition, he programmed a changeover delay (COD) of 1.5 seconds. The various combinations of schedules he used with one of his pigeons are presented in Table 10.1, columns (1) and (2). The relative rate of reinforcement on key A is in column (3), and how many sessions he ran his subject on each combination of schedules is in column (4). Combining the data from the last five sessions on each pair of VI schedules, Herrnstein plotted the relative rate of pecking [column (7)] against the relative rate of reinforcement earned for pecking on key A [column (3)]. These data are presented in Figure 10.2. The data for all pairs of VI schedules tested fell close to the diagonal line; that is, *the relative rates of behavior on the two VI schedules matched the relative rate of reinforcement obtained from these schedules.*

The data in Figure 10.2 can be described as follows: *The relative rate of pecking at key A equals the relative rate of reinforcement obtained on key A.* This relationship between the relative rates of pecking and the relative rates of reinforcement can be expressed by the following equation:

$$\frac{\text{Rate of pecking on schedule A}}{\text{Rate of pecking on schedule A } + \text{ Rate of pecking on schedule B}} = \frac{\text{Rate of reinforcement on schedule A}}{\text{Rate of reinforcement on schedule A } + \text{ Rate of reinforcement on schedule B}} \tag{1}$$

The expression on the left side of Equation 1 is the *relative rate of pecking on schedule A*, and the expression on the right side is the *relative rate of reinforcement earned from schedule A.*

Table 10.1 The Sequence of Concurrent VI VI Schedules, the Number of Sessions on Each Pair, and the Estimated Rates of Pecking for One of the Pigeons in Herrnstein's (1961) Experiment Demonstrating Matching

Schedules				Behavior		
1	2	3	4	5	6	7
VI on key A (min)	VI on key B (min)	Relative rate of reinforcement on key A $\dfrac{R_A}{R_A+R_B}$	No. of sessions	Pecks on key A	Pecks on key B	Relative rate of pecking on key A $\dfrac{B_A}{B_A+B_B}$
2.25	4.5	0.67	43	3100	1650	0.65
3	3	0.50	44	2250	2250	0.50
9	1.8	0.17	35	900	3900	0.19
1.5	∞ (EXT)	1.00	37	17500	0	1.00
9	1.8	0.17	20	1200	3900	0.23
1.8	9	0.83	39	3900	1150	0.77

Note: The numbers in columns 5 and 6 were extrapolated from Herrnstein (1961) Figure 2.

These are *relative* measures because they are ratios of what happens on schedule A divided by the total number of events (pecks or reinforcements) on both A and B. If the pigeon pecks equally on both schedules, the ratio is 0.5, and if he or she pecks twice as much on schedule A as schedule B, the ratio is 0.67, and so on. For ease of exposition, Equation 1 can be abbreviated as

$$\frac{B_A}{B_A + B_B} = \frac{R_A}{R_A + R_B} \qquad (2)$$

where B_A and B_B represent rates of behaviors (pecking) directed at the keys that produced schedules A and B respectively, and R_A and R_B represent the rates of reinforcement obtained on schedules A and B respectively. An algebraically equivalent form of Equation 2 (i.e., an equation which is derived from Equation 2 through application of the rules of algebra) is

$$\frac{B_A}{B_B} = \frac{R_A}{R_B} \qquad (3)$$

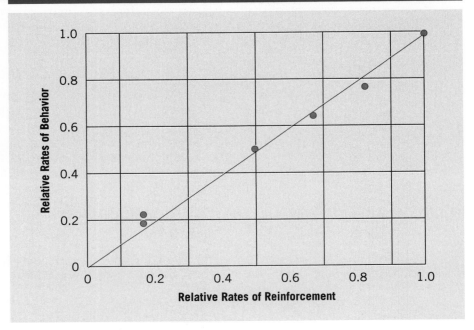

Figure 10.2 Matching of relative rates of behavior to the relative rates of reinforcement by a pigeon working on various concurrent VI VI schedules (data from Table 10.1).

From Herrnstein, 1961.

Equations 2 and 3 provide two different symbolic representations of the **empirical matching** law: *The relative rates of behavior (**B**) directed at the two alternatives matches [equals] the relative rates of reinforcement (**R**) obtained for these behaviors.*

Catania (1963) replicated Herrnstein's (1961) results with the schedule-control procedure. The matching relationship between relative rates of behavior and relative rates of reinforcement on concurrent VI VI schedules has been observed with a variety of species, including humans, in a variety of situations (see Davison & McCarthy, 1988; de Villiers, 1977; Fisher & Mazur, 1997; McDowell, 2013a; Pierce & Epling, 1983; Williams, 1988, 1994a for reviews).

It is important to note that matching of relative rates of behavior to relative rates of reinforcement requires extensive experience on each pair of schedules (see Table 10.1), and the data in Figure 10.2 are based on the last 5 days of training on each pair of schedules. Thus, *the empirical matching law describes maintenance performance, not the acquisition process itself.* Later in this chapter we will explore the processes that underlie the empirical matching law.

Extending the Empirical Matching Law

On concurrent VI VI schedules, individuals match their relative rates of behavior and the relative amounts of time they spend working on the two schedules to relative rates of reinforcement and (under certain conditions) to relative amounts of reinforcement and relative immediacy of reinforcement on two or more alternatives. Matching also occurs with concurrent ratio schedules and with concurrent arrangements of both ratio and interval schedules.

The independent variable in Herrnstein's (1961) experiment was the relative rates of reinforcement available on VI schedules for pecking at the two keys, and the dependent variable was the relative rates of pecking at the two keys. But matching is not restricted to those independent and dependent variables. It has been observed with a number of other independent variables and with how much time individuals will allocate to the different alternatives as the dependent variable. We will consider the dependent variable of time allocation first.

Matching With Relative Time Allocation as the Dependent Variable. Baum and Rachlin (1969) noted that the number of times that discrete behaviors such as key pecking and lever pressing occur (i.e., the rate of behavior) is not the only measure of performance. These behaviors are relatively discrete and of short duration, but many of the things we do (like studying, watching television, exercising, etc.) typically occupy large blocks of time; it is the time spent at these activities, not the number of times we do them that is important.

As noted above, using the control-key procedure Catania (1963) observed matching of the relative rates of pecking to the relative rates of reinforcement on concurrent VI VI schedules. In 1966, Catania presented a second analysis of data collected from these same pigeons. In this second analysis, he compared the relative time spent in the presence of the two key colors to the relative rates of reinforcement for pecking at each key. The results of both analyses are presented in Figure 10.3. The data on the left depicts the relationship between the relative rates of pecking and the relative rates of reinforcement for three pigeons, and the data on the right depicts the relationship between the relative allocation of time and the relative rates of reinforcement for the same three pigeons. The diagonal lines represent perfect matching. It is clear from this figure that *individuals also match the relative amounts of time* (**T**) *they will spend performing activities to the relative rates of reinforcement for these activities.*[2] This allows us to incorporate temporally extended behaviors into the matching law.

Using relative allocation of time as the dependent variable, Conger and Killeen (1974) demonstrated matching in a social situation. Their subjects thought they were volunteering for a study of student attitudes about drug abuse. Each subject was seated

---

[2]This can be expressed symbolically as $\dfrac{T_A}{T_A + T_B} = \dfrac{R_A}{R_A + R_B}$ and $\dfrac{T_A}{T_B} = \dfrac{R_A}{R_B}$ where T_A and T_B represent time spent working on schedules *A* and *B* respectively and R_A and R_B represent the rates of reinforcement obtained on schedules *A* and *B*.

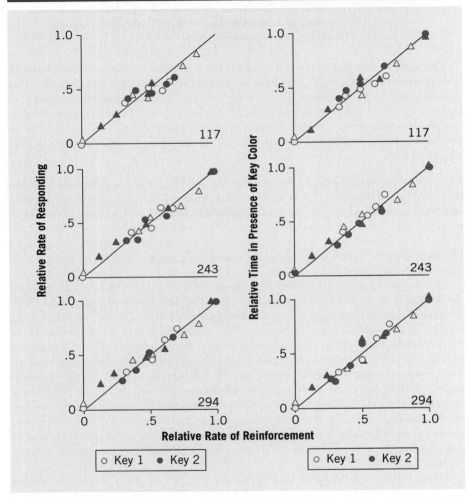

Figure 10.3 (Left panel) Matching of relative rates of responding to relative rates of reinforcement. (Right panel) Matching of relative time allocation (relative time in presence of a key color) to relative rates of reinforcement.

From Catania, 1963, *Journal of the Experimental Analysis of Behavior, 6*, 253–264. Copyright © 1963 by the Society for the Experimental Analysis of Behavior, Inc. Reprinted by permission of John Wiley and Sons.

around a table with three other people. The experimenter sat across from the subject, and the other two people (who were actually confederates of the experimenter) sat on each side of the table. The experimenter's task was to facilitate the discussion among the other three people (the subject and the two confederates). The confederates each provided verbal approval for what the subject said on a VI schedule of reinforcement. Confederates were cued by a light behind the subject as to when reinforcement was supposed to be given for the next statement by the subject. Verbal approval consisted of statements like "good," "that's a good point," and so on. For the first 15 minutes of the session, confederate 1 reinforced the subject on one VI schedule when the subject was talking to him or her, and confederate 2 reinforced the subject on a different VI schedule when the subject was talking to him or her. These schedules, which produced different rates of reinforcement, were reversed during the second 15 minutes of the session. The dependent variable was how much time each subject (there were five subjects) looked at each confederate during the last 5 minutes of each 15-minute period. The results are presented in Figure 10.4.

Figure 10.4 Proportion of time spent talking with confederate 1 as a function of the proportion of verbal approvals given by confederate 1 by five different subjects in Conger and Killeen's experiment. Different points plotted for each subject correspond to when confederate 1 reinforced the subject at a high rate and when confederate 1 reinforced the subject at a low rate.

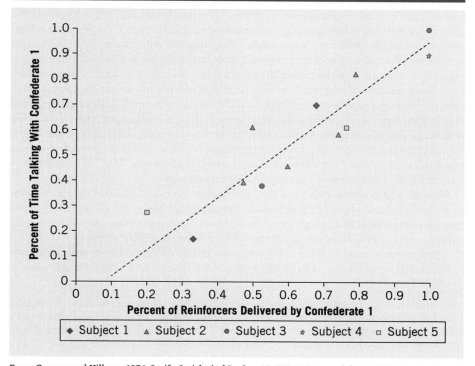

From Conger and Killeen, 1974. *Pacific Sociological Review, 17,* 399–416. Copyright © 1974. Reprinted with permission of Sage Publications, Inc.

These data show that the relative time the subjects spent talking to confederate 1 was a function of the relative rates of reinforcement (verbal approval) delivered by that confederate. None of the subjects reported being aware of what was occurring.

These experiments extend the matching law to a second dependent variable: time allocation. Next, we look at the possibility that the empirical matching law can be extended to the magnitude and immediacy of reinforcement.

Matching With Relative Magnitudes of Reinforcement as the Independent Variable.
Premack (1965) pointed out that rate of reinforcement and the magnitude of reinforcement are related in the sense that both can be expressed in terms of access to the reinforcer per unit time: Because it takes longer to consume a large reward than a small one, an individual could spend the same amount of time consuming many small pieces of food as he or she could spend consuming a few large pieces. This led Premack to suggest that both rate of reinforcement and size (magnitude) of reinforcement should have similar effects on behavior.

Brownstein (1971) demonstrated that individuals match the relative amounts of time they spend performing activities to the relative magnitudes of reinforcement for these activities. He used a Findley schedule-control procedure with pigeons, but with only one key (the schedule-control key). Pecks at that key changed the color of the house light. When the house light was one color, one variable-time (VT) schedule was in effect, and when the house light was the other color, a second VT schedule was in effect.[3] In this situation, there was only one measure of behavior: how much time each pigeon spent in the presence of each house light color. Brownstein maintained the same VT 1.5-minute schedule in the presence of the two house lights throughout the experiment. The independent variable was the magnitude of reinforcement in the presence of the two house lights. With pigeons, food is presented by raising the food tray so they can eat from it. This provides a fairly good measure of magnitude of reinforcement because the longer the food is available, the more the pigeons can eat each time the food is presented. Brownstein's pigeons matched the relative allocation of time they spent in the presence of each house light to the relative magnitudes of reinforcement available in the presence of each house light. These results extended the matching law to magnitude of reinforcement: *Individuals match the relative allocation of time* (**T**) *to the relative magnitudes of reinforcement* (**M**).[4] Neuringer (1967) reported similar results using a more complicated procedure.

Vollmer and Bourret (2000) analyzed the relative allocation of two- and three-point shots for individual players in men's and women's college basketball games. They found that the relative rates of attempts matched fairly well the relative rates for which the individuals were successful at these two shots that have different reward values.

Despite these results, there have been a number of experiments which did not report matching of relative rates of behavior or time allocation to relative magnitudes of

---

[3]On a time schedule of reinforcement, *a reinforcer is delivered after a certain time has elapsed independently of the individual's behavior.* When the schedule is a variable-time (VT), the time varies around some average value. This is different from a variable-interval (VI) schedule, which requires the individual to do something (e.g., peck a key or press a lever) after the time has elapsed.

[4]This can be expressed symbolically as $\dfrac{T_A}{T_B} = \dfrac{M_A}{M_B}$ where T_A and T_B represent the times spent on alternatives A and B respectively and M_A and M_B represent the magnitudes of the reinforcers obtained from alternatives A and B.

reinforcement. These failures to find matching of relative allocations of behavior to relative magnitudes of reinforcement appear to reflect problems some subjects have in discriminating between the magnitudes of reinforcement when the magnitudes are both very large or very small (Williams, 1988, 1994a). The matching law assumes that there is a linear relationship between physical scales (size of a reinforcer or length of time it is available) and psychological scales (perceived magnitude); however, that may not be the case. While individuals will always choose the larger of two positive reinforcers (when the difference is discriminable), the perceptions of the sizes of these objects may not be linear functions of the physical sizes; that is, doubling the size may not be perceived as creating an object twice as large. This could account for some of the deviations from matching. Despite this problem, Williams (1994a) concluded that the matching law accurately describes the results of many studies investigating the relationship between magnitude of reinforcement and behavior.

Attempts to Demonstrate Matching With the Relative Immediacy of Reinforcement as the Independent Variable. The evidence reviewed thus far shows that under certain conditions individuals match the relative allocations of their behavior and time to the relative rates of reinforcement and the relative magnitudes of reinforcement. A third attribute of reinforcers is their immediacy, that is, how soon they occur after the target behavior that produces them. Common sense tells us, and experimental research confirms, that given the choice between two identical reinforcers, one that occurs after a short delay and one that occurs after a longer delay, individuals prefer the more immediate one. Therefore, it is reasonable to also ask if individuals will match the relative allocation of their behavior to the relative immediacy of the reinforcers.[5]

Chung and Herrnstein (1967) provided data suggesting that pigeons match their rates of pecking to the relative immediacy of reinforcement. Using the two-key procedure, they presented pigeons with identical VI schedules, but the reinforcers were delayed for different amounts of time after the peck that satisfied the VI requirement occurred. During all delays, the lights in the experimental chamber were turned off until after the food was delivered. Chung and Herrnstein observed that *the relative rates of behavior matched the relative immediacy* (I or $1/$Delay) *of the reinforcers.*[6]

As appealing as this last statement is in terms of extending the generality of the matching law to immediacy of reinforcement, it has not fared well when subjected to experimental scrutiny (Williams, 1988, 1994a). With few exceptions, most studies of behavioral allocation on concurrent schedules where immediacy of reinforcement is the independent variable have not produced matching over a wide range of values of immediacy (or delay). For example, Logue and Chavarro (1987) reported that pigeons' preferences for the shorter of two delays decreased as the absolute values of these delays decreased; that is, when both delays

---

[5]One can talk here about either immediacy of reinforcement or delay of reinforcement because one is the reciprocal of the other: Immediacy = 1/Delay. Whether we are talking in terms of immediacy or delay, we are describing the time between the occurrence of the target behavior and the presentation of the reinforcer. Although it is customary to describe this as delay of reinforcement, it is less confusing to use immediacy in the matching law.

[6]This can be expressed symbolically as $\dfrac{B_A}{B_B} = \dfrac{I_A}{I_B}$ *or* $\dfrac{B_A}{B_B} = \dfrac{1/D_A}{1/D_B}$ where B_A and B_B represent rates of behaviors, and I_A and I_B represent how quickly the reinforcers are presented (immediacy) after the requirements of the respective schedules are satisfied. D_A and D_B represent the delay between the reinforced behavior and the presentation of the reinforcer $I = 1/D$.

were relatively long (5.25 seconds and 15.75 seconds), the pigeons allocated slightly *more* pecks to the shorter one than the matching law predicts, but when both delays were relatively short (0.75 seconds and 2.25 seconds), the pigeons allocated *many fewer* pecks to the shorter delay than the matching law predicts. Here again, the problem appears to be one of scaling, but it is more complicated than simply mapping the physical scale of delay in a linear fashion into a psychological scale; it involves a process called **temporal discounting**: *In some situations, the value of something for an individual decreases in a nonlinear manner the further away it is in time.* The conclusion that temporal discount functions are not linear is based on the following observations: When given a choice between two items of equal value, one that can be obtained immediately and one that *only* can be obtained later, most individuals will choose the more immediate one; however, if the *more immediate one is smaller* (less valuable) and the *more delayed one is larger* (more valuable), which is selected depends on the delay. With increasing delays imposed on obtaining the larger (more valuable) item, individuals shift their preference toward the smaller (less valuable) item, and the points at which the switch in preference tends to occur suggests that the temporal discount functions are not linear (Rachlin, 1970). Obviously, choice depends on both relative magnitudes and delays, but individuals tend to discount the value of delayed rewards in a nonlinear manner.

Extending the Matching Relationship to Other Concurrent Schedules. Up to this point, we have only considered the behavior of individuals on concurrent VI VI schedules. It is clear that under certain conditions (same target behavior on both schedules, presence of a changeover delay) individuals working on concurrent VI VI schedules match their relative allocation of effort (rate of behavior) and time to the relative rates of reinforcement. How do individuals allocate their behavior with other schedules of reinforcement?

One should not be surprised to learn that subjects on concurrent FR FR and concurrent VR VR schedules eventually direct all of their behavior to the schedule with the lower ratio requirement (Herrnstein, 1958; Herrnstein & Loveland, 1975). This makes sense when one considers the molar feedback functions for ratio schedules where the rate of reinforcement is directly tied to the rate of behavior; that is, the faster one performs the target behavior, the more reinforcement is earned (see Chapter 9, Figure 9.1). Furthermore, while an individual is working on one ratio schedule, no progress is being made toward obtaining reinforcement on the other schedule. Therefore, there is no advantage to switching between schedules, and the individual can gain the most reinforcement by finding the schedule with the lowest ratio requirement and staying on it. This is different from interval schedules where the interval clock is running on both schedules even though the individual is working on only one of them. By occasionally switching between interval schedules, the individual can obtain *all* of the available reinforcers on both schedules.

At first glance, this exclusive preference for the ratio schedule with the lower ratio requirement does not appear to be an example of matching, but it is. The matching relationships represented in Equations 1–3 are between the relative rates of behavior and the relative rates of reinforcement *obtained*. But in ratio schedules, the rate of *obtained* reinforcement is directly tied to the rate of behavior; therefore, an individual who exhibits exclusive preference is indeed matching his or her relative rates of behavior to the relative rates of *obtained* reinforcement because both the absolute and relative rate of behavior and rate of reinforcement on the nonpreferred schedule are both zero. When the two ratio schedules are the same, individuals usually switch between them, and because the rates of behavior are directly tied to the rates of reinforcement, matching is always observed (Herrnstein & Loveland, 1975). This is neither surprising nor interesting.

A more interesting situation is the concurrent VI VR schedule. Here two very different feedback functions are pitted against each other: on the ratio side, rates of reinforcement are directly tied to rates of behavior, and on the interval side, the rates of reinforcement are constrained by the schedule. Herrnstein and Heyman (1979) trained four pigeons on a variety of concurrent VI VR schedules using the switching-key procedure. This allowed them to examine both relative rates of pecking and relative time allocation as dependent variables. They found that the relative *rates* of behavior matched the relative rates of obtained reinforcement fairly well except that there was a slight bias in favor of the ratio schedules. This is not surprising given that ratio schedules encourage high rates of behavior. On the other hand, when relative *time allocation* was the dependent variable, there was a bias in favor of the interval schedules. This too is not surprising given that interval schedules encourage slower rates of behavior (which translates to more time spent making the same number of pecks). Thus, pigeons' performance on concurrent VI VR schedules approximates the matching relationship, although the fit of the data to strict matching is not perfect. Similar results were reported by Vyse and Belke (1992) with pigeons and by Savastano and Fantino (1994) with humans. The observed deviations from perfect matching should not be overlooked. These will be discussed more fully below.

Summary of the Empirical Matching Relationships. The behavior of individuals in concurrent choice situations involving concurrent schedules of reinforcement *when there is a changeover delay (COD) and when the target behavior is the same on both schedules* can be summarized as follows:

1. Individuals match their *relative rates of behavior* to the *relative rates of reinforcement* obtained from the alternatives.

2. Individuals match the *relative amounts of time they spend with each alternative* to the *relative rates of reinforcement* obtained from the alternatives.

3. Individuals match their *relative rates of behavior* and *relative amounts of time they spend with each alternative* to the *relative magnitudes of reinforcement* obtained from the alternatives; however, a number of experiments have reported deviations from perfect matching. These deviations may reflect the fact that the relationship between the physical size or magnitude of a reinforcer and the psychological scale of perceived magnitude may not be linear for all magnitudes.

4. Individuals match their *relative rates of behavior* to the *relative immediacy (1/delay) of the reinforcers* obtained from the alternatives. However, despite its intuitive appeal, this equation has not been found to hold in a rather large number of experiments. This may be due to temporal discounting (the tendency to devalue something that cannot be obtained right away). Thus the relationship between the immediacy with which a reinforcer occurs after a behavior and the perceived value of that reinforcer does not appear to be linear.

5. The empirical matching relationship has been applied successfully to concurrent schedules involving other combinations of simple schedules (e.g., concurrent FR FR, concurrent VI VR), although some deviations from perfect matching have been observed.

The Generalized Empirical Matching Law

The empirical matching relationships described thus far occur under rather restricted conditions. When we relax these restrictions, perfect matching as described by the empirical matching law does not always occur. However, these deviations from perfect matching can be accommodated by the generalized matching law which extends the matching law to a wide variety of choice situations.

It is clear from the experiments described above that *perfect matching* occurs under the following situations:

1. Individuals are working on concurrent VI VI schedules with a change-over delay of a few seconds.

2. The target behavior (e.g., pecking at a key or pressing a lever) is the same on both schedules.

While it is not expressly stated, perfect matching *also* requires:

3. The same effort to perform the target behavior on both schedules; that is, it is not harder to peck one key or press one lever than the other.

4. The individual does not have a preference for one key or lever over the other; that is, the individual does not prefer the left side or prefer the color on the left key.

5. The physical scales on which the relative aspects of the reinforcers (rate, magnitude, immediacy) map in a linear fashion into the psychological scales that the individual uses to assess those reinforcers.

But real life is not so restricted. More often than not, the choice is between performing two different activities that require different amounts of effort (e.g., studying versus watching television), and most outcomes differ in other ways, not just in terms of their rates of occurrence, magnitudes, and immediacies. Furthermore, sometimes the cost of switching from one activity to another is so great that even if the other activity seems particularly appealing, we may not want to switch because the cost of switching is prohibitive. For example, one may stay at a boring party because what you think might be a more interesting party somewhere else may take too long to get to because it is so far away. In this section, we will look at what happens when the restrictions described above are lifted. We will see that the empirical matching law can be modified to accommodate more realistic concurrent choices. The result is called the generalized matching law.

Deviations From the Empirical Matching Law

Deviations from perfect matching occur when an individual's behavior is influenced by something other than the attributes of the reinforcers. Bias toward one or the other alternative can be due to differences in difficulty in performing the different behaviors or a preference for some nonreinforcer aspect of that alternative. Deviations from perfect matching can also occur when the cost of switching between the alternatives is relatively low or relatively high. In the first case, individuals ignore the attributes of the reinforcers and switch back and forth. In the second case, they select one of the alternatives and stay with it.

Bias. With concurrent schedules of reinforcement, **bias** means that *the individual prefers one alternative more than would be predicted from the empirical matching law.* McDowell (1989) noted that bias is likely when the concurrent arrangements are asymmetrical: One behavior is harder to perform than the other, qualitatively different behaviors are required, the schedules are different kinds, the reinforcers are of different types, and so on. In their study of the relative allocation of two- and three-point shots for individual players in men's and women's college basketball games, Vollmer and Bourret (2000) found a slight amount of bias against three-point shots which are more difficult than two-point shots. McDowell (1989) also noted that deviations can occur with symmetrical arrangements when, for example, the subject favors one side or one color.

Bias is observed when the individual's behavior departs from perfect matching in the manner depicted in Figure 10.5. The thick diagonal line represents perfect matching. There is a bias toward behavior A (B_A) when the data fall along the thin curve above the diagonal and a bias toward behavior B (B_B) when the data fall along the thin curve below the diagonal. The degree of bias is represented by how far the data deviate from the thick diagonal line.[7]

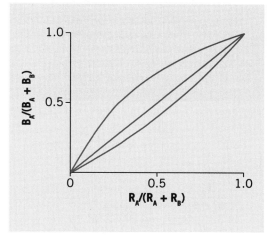

Figure 10.5 Bias and matching. The thick line depicts perfect matching and the thin lines depict deviations from matching due to bias for one or the other alternatives. The direction of the bias is reflected by whether the thin line is above or below the line for perfect matching. The degree of bias is reflected in how far the thin line is from the thick diagonal line.

From McDowell, 1989.

---

[7]The thin lines in Figure 10.5 can be represented by the following equation: $\dfrac{B_A}{B_B} = b\left(\dfrac{R_A}{R_B}\right)$.

When **b** is positive (>1), the individual favors the behavior designated as B_A, and when **b** is negative (<1), the individual favors B_B. When **b** = 1, there is no bias.

Herrnstein and Heyman (1979) observed systematic deviations from perfect matching in their study of performance on concurrent VI VR schedules: When relative rates of pecking was the dependent variable, the pigeons favored the ratio schedules, and when relative allocation of time was the dependent measure, the pigeons favored the interval schedules.

Sensitivity to the Attributes of the Choices. We noted earlier that when there is no changeover delay, individuals on a concurrent VI VI schedule tend to ignore the VI schedules and switch back and forth. This pattern is called **undermatching**. *Individuals are said to undermatch when the relative allocation of behavior is less than is predicted from the empirical matching law.* The behavior pattern of undermatching is depicted in the left panel of Figure 10.6. Here the individual allocates his or her behavior equally to the two VI schedules over a wide range of schedule values (which translates into different relative rates of reinforcement). It is only when the relative rates of reinforcement approach 0 or 1 that he or she becomes sensitive to the difference between the two schedules.

The other extreme is to *favor the schedule with the higher rate of reinforcement.* This pattern is called **overmatching**. Overmatching is depicted in the right panel of Figure 10.6. In that figure, the individual tends toward exclusive choice of the schedule with the higher rate of reinforcement. Thus, when the relative rate of reinforcement $[R_A/(R_A + R_B)] > 0.5$, the individual chooses schedule A, and when $[R_A/(R_A + R_B)] < 0.5$, the individual chooses schedule B.

Baum (1982) noted the similarity between the changeover delay (COD) and travel between the alternative sources of reinforcement. When there is little or no COD on

Figure 10.6 Undermatching and overmatching. In the left panel, the individual alternates between the two alternatives across a wide range of values of $R_A/(R_A + R_B)$. This pattern is called undermatching. In the right panel, the individual stays on the side with the greater relative rate of reinforcement longer than one would expect if individuals match. This is called overmatching.

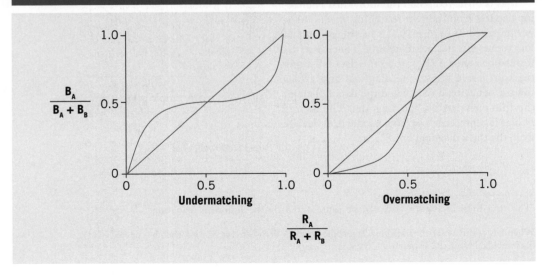

concurrent VI VI schedules, individuals can rapidly switch between the alternatives and collect all of the available reinforcers. But when there is a COD, the individual will have a period of time during which no reinforcers can be collected, even if they would be otherwise available. This "down time" is similar to what happens when the individual must physically travel to another location. Baum (1982) and Boelens and Kop (1983) investigated what would happen when barriers of different heights or lengths were interposed between the two keys so that pigeons would have to scale these barriers or go around them to switch to the other alternative. When the barriers were low (and there was no programmed COD), pigeons tended to undermatch. However, as the height or length of the barriers increased, the pigeons shifted to overmatching. Aparicio (2001) reported similar results with rats. Thus *undermatching occurs when the cost of switching to the other alternative is minimal as is the case when there is a minimal COD or minimal travel required. Overmatching occurs when the cost of a changeover is high (as is the case with a long COD and difficult travel requirement).* Channel surfing with a remote from your favorite chair is an example of undermatching; not channel surfing because the remote is broken and the television set is across the room is an example of overmatching.

We can modify the empirical matching law to incorporate bias and sensitivity to the attributes of the scheduled reinforcers. The result is the **generalized empirical matching law**: *The relative rates of behavior are a function of the relative rates of reinforcement. The exact relationship depends on the individual's bias for one of the alternatives and sensitivity to the attributes of the choices.* We can represent the exact nature of this relationship by the following equation:

$$\frac{B_A}{B_B} = b\left(\frac{R_A}{R_B}\right)^S \tag{4}$$

where **b** describes individual's bias, and **s** describes the individual's sensitivity to the attributes of the scheduled reinforcers. When **b** is greater than 1, the individual favors the behavior designated as B_A, and when **b** is less than 1, the individual favors B_B. When **b** = 1, there is no bias. When **s** is greater than 1, the individual is overly sensitive to the choices and overmatches, and when **s** is less than 1, the individual is less sensitive to the attributes of the choices and undermatches. When **s** = 1 and **b** = 1, the individual exhibits strict matching, and Equation 4 reduces to Equation 3 (the basic matching law).

Equation 4 is called the **generalized empirical matching law** because *it incorporates the deviations from strict matching.* By doing so, it extends the scope of the empirical matching relationship to a wider range of situations than required to obtain strict matching. Equation 3 (which describes strict matching) is a special case of Equation 4.[8]

The empirical matching law describes the relative allocation of behavior on concurrent VI VI schedules when the same behavior is directed toward obtaining the different alternatives. *There are many ways individuals can distribute their behavior and still obtain all*

---

[8]Separate versions of Equation 4 can be written to relate relative rates of behavior and relative time allocation to the independent variables of relative magnitudes and immediacy of reinforcement as well as to the rate of reinforcement.

of the reinforcers; but matching as described by the generalized matching law is what we tend to observe (Williams, 1988, 1994a). For example, Pierce, Epling, and Greer (1981) and Borrero et al. (2007) used procedures similar to those of Conger and Killeen (1974; see above) but with longer experimental sessions. Both sets of researchers found that the generalized empirical matching law provided a better fit to their data than the simple empirical matching law.

The generalized empirical matching law has been observed in a variety of natural situations. As noted earlier, Vollmer and Bourret (2000) observed a slight amount of bias against three-point shots in women's basketball. Alferink, Critchfield, Hitt, and Higgins (2009) found undermatching when they collected data from NCAA Division I, II, and III men's teams. Romanowich, Bourret, and Vollmer (2007) extended their analysis to the National Basketball Association where changes in the distance of the three-point line was decreased in 1994 and then changed back to its former range extended in 1997. They observed that with the shorter distance, the three-point shots were more successful and this was matched by more three-point shots being attempted. The generalized matching law described the data with both distances, and undermatching was also observed. Reed, Critchfield, and Martens (2006) and Stilling and Critchfield (2010) found that the generalized matching law also describes play selection in NFL games. Here, too, undermatching was observed. As noted above, undermatching suggests less sensitivity to the reinforcement schedules than the strict empirical matching law predicts.

McDowell and Caron (2010a) analyzed recordings of "predelinquent" boys talking with their friends in 25-minute sessions. The conversations were transcribed and coded into two categories: rule-break talk (violation of legal or normative rules of conduct like lying to parents, cheating at school, engaging in criminal behavior, or behaving defiantly) and normative talk (talking about friends, school, family, or what to do for fun). They also coded both positive social (making approving statements, smiling, nodding, laughing, etc.) and nonpositive social behaviors (anything else, including remaining silent) by the other child to those two categories of conversation. McDowell and Caron reported both undermatching and a bias in favor of normative talk. In a second study, McDowell and Caron (2010b) analyzed data from a subset of the boys in their first study who were also classified into one of four groups in terms of child deviance according to a standard measure based on self-reported delinquency. They found that the amount of undermatching increased and the bias for normative talk decreased with higher scores on the deviance measure. McDowell and Caron (2010b) attributed the increase in undermatching to a decline in the rewarding value of positive social behaviors and the decrease in bias for normative talk to different histories of reward and punishment for rule-breaking and normative behaviors for boys with higher deviance scores.

THE GENERALIZED THEORETICAL MATCHING LAW

The generalized empirical matching law (Equation 4) is a description of behavior under certain conditions. The generalized theoretical matching law relates the phenomenon of matching to the psychological construct of value.

The generalized empirical matching law is a description of how individuals allocate their time and effort (rate of behavior) in a concurrent choice situation in relation to various attributes of the consequences of their choices (rate of occurrence, magnitude, immediacy, etc.). Baum and Rachlin (1969) suggested that matching occurs because *these attributes of reinforcers enter into the determination of the value of a reinforcer, and matching reflects the relative values of reinforcers.* To the list of reinforcer attributes, Rachlin (1971) added another variable (**X**), which stands for all other aspects of a reinforcer that can also affect its value. Baum and Rachlin also suggested that the **value (V) of a reinforcer** is defined as *the product of its rate of occurrence* (**R**), *magnitude* (**M**), *immediacy* (**I**), *and all other attributes that affect the value of a reinforcer* (**X**). This can be expressed symbolically as follows:

$$V = R \times M \times I \times X \tag{5}$$

Equation 5 is a theoretical statement about how the observable and measurable attributes of a reinforcer combine to determine something that is neither observable nor measurable, namely the value of that reinforcer to an individual. If the value of a reinforcer is the product of these things, when *any one* of them is low, then the value of the reinforcer is low. All reinforcers possess the measurable attributes in the right side of Equation 5, and if any one of them is varied while the others are held constant, we should observe a behavior pattern described by the generalized empirical matching law (Equation 4) in a concurrent choice situation. Therefore, we can substitute value (V) for the measurable variables that determine value in the generalized empirical matching law to produce the **generalized theoretical matching law**: *Individuals match the relative allocation of their time and effort to the relative values of the alternative outcomes.* The generalized theoretical matching law can be expressed by the following equations:

$$\frac{B_A}{B_B} = b\left(\frac{V_A}{V_B}\right) \text{ and } \frac{T_A}{T_B} = b\left(\frac{V_A}{V_B}\right)^S \tag{6}$$

The equation on the left relates relative *rates* of behavior (effort) to the relative values of the alternatives, and the equation on the right relates relative *allocations of time* to relative values of the alternatives.

The generalized theoretical matching law is a statement about how individuals allocate their behavior in terms of the values of the outcomes of those behaviors. In many respects, the theoretical matching law is like Newton's laws of motion in physics that describe how external forces affect objects (see Box 10.1). No one doubts the validity of Newton's laws of motion, despite the fact that they are theoretical statements about unseen forces and objects.

Tests of the Generalized Theoretical Matching Law

> If the generalized theoretical matching law is correct, then we should be able to use it to determine the relative values of reinforcers.

The generalized theoretical matching law is a statement about how behavior is affected by the values of reinforcers. H. L. Miller (1976) described a way to test the theoretical

Newton's Laws of Motion and the Matching Law

Sir Isaac Newton was not the first person to ponder the causes of motion of objects. Serious attempts to understand principles that govern the motion of objects began in ancient Greece, but our current conceptions of forces and motion developed in the seventeenth century based on the work of Galileo Galilei (1564–1642) and Isaac Newton (1642–1727). Galileo performed experiments and took accurate measurements of the velocity and acceleration of falling objects and projectiles (e.g., cannon balls). On the basis of these observations, he developed equations to describe this motion but provided no theoretical explanations of his observations. That task was taken up by Newton, who was born the year Galileo died (1642). Galileo's focus was on describing the motion of projectiles and falling objects, but Newton was interested in the motion of all objects, those on earth as well as those in the heavens (planets and stars). Newton provided us with a framework for understanding all motion in terms of the interactions of forces acting on objects. His conclusions about motion are summarized in his three laws of motion, which are paraphrased here:

First law: An object persists at rest or in a state of uniform motion (steady velocity) in a straight line until acted upon by some external force (Principle of Inertia).

Second law: The acceleration (change in velocity or speed) of an object is directly proportional to the external force acting on that object.

Third law: For every action there is an equal and opposite reaction. Force results from the interaction of two objects, each exerting an equal and opposite effect on the other.

It is impossible to observe an object in the absence of an external force, yet we believe the first law is correct because we can observe the effects of applying external forces to objects and how that changes the position and velocity of those objects. For example, when we are in a train, subway or bus, we are traveling at the same velocity as the vehicle. But we lurch backward or forward when the vehicle suddenly accelerates or decelerates (which is due to an external force). But Newton's first law states that if there were no external forces, we would continue to move indefinitely in a straight line. That can only be observed in a frictionless environment in the absence of other bodies (which according to the third law would exert forces on us). We accept Newton's laws as correct explanations for what we observe because they lead to predictions that can be verified through experimentation. Physicists have been able to perform experiments to test these laws by creating special situations and using extremely sensitive measuring instruments. Similarly, the generalized theoretical matching law is a fundamental law of behavior because it too appears to lead to predictions that are confirmed through experimentation.

matching law and at the same time demonstrate how it can be used to scale the value of qualitatively different reinforcers (attribute **X** in Equation 5). His method is described in Table 10.2.

In H. L. Miller's (1976) experiment, the reinforcers were different types of grain (buckwheat, hemp seeds, and wheat). Pigeons have preferences among these three grains just like they have preferences for larger rewards, rewards that occur at higher rates, and rewards that occur sooner. But while magnitude, rate of occurrence, and immediacy are measurable attributes of reinforcers (even if there is not always a linear relationship between the physical and psychological scales), there is no obvious physical scale for *subjective quality*. Using the procedure outlined in Table 10.2, Miller derived a psychological scale for the qualities of these three grains.

In the first phase of H. L. Miller's (1976) experiment, pigeons worked on various two-key concurrent VI VI schedules with buckwheat as the reinforcer on one side and hemp seed as the reinforcer on the other. Using both relative rates of pecking and relative time allocation, Miller found deviations from perfect matching (bias) in favor of the side on which the buckwheat was obtained. In the second phase of the experiment, he repeated the same procedure but with wheat on one side and buckwheat on the other. Here he found a bias in favor of the wheat. From these data, Miller derived a prediction of the amount of bias he should observe when he repeated the experiment in the third phase with hemp and wheat. The obtained and predicted results were very close. Finally, Miller derived scales of grain quality based on the biases (b) observed in all three phases (Figure 10.7). Although the two scales do not match perfectly, the correspondence is quite close.

Cliffe and Parry (1980) used H. L. Miller's (1976) procedure to construct a psychological scale of the value of what aroused a 36-year-old incarcerated male pedophile. The "reinforcers" in this study were the opportunity to observe for 3 minutes slides of men ("pin-up" pictures taken from magazines supplied by homosexual males), slides of women (pictures taken from soft porn magazines), and slides of children (pictures from the newspaper that were collected by the participant). After giving the participant experience pressing a key to produce these slides on a VI schedule, Cliffe and Parry used the procedure outlined in Table 10.2 to investigate the relative values of these three classes of stimuli. In the first phase, slides of men were available for presses on the left key, and

Table 10.2 Using the Theoretical Matching Law to Scale the Value of Various Reinforcers

Phase 1: Choice between A and B	Phase 2: Choice between A and C	Derive prediction of choice between B and C	Phase 3: Test prediction of choice between B and C
Subjects work on various combinations of concurrent VI VI schedules to derive value for *b* (bias) for A or B using the generalized empirical matching law	Subjects work on various combinations of concurrent VI VI schedules to derive value for *b* (bias) for A or C using the generalized empirical matching law	Use results from Phases 1 and 2 to derive a prediction of bias for B and C in Phase 3	Subjects work on various combinations of concurrent VI VI schedules to derive value for *b* (bias) for B or C using the generalized empirical matching law

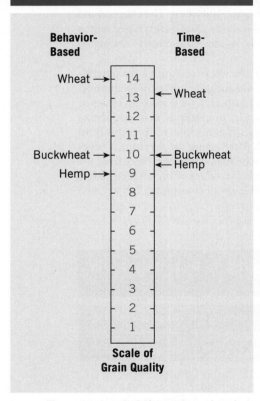

Figure 10.7 Psychological scales of the values of wheat, hemp, and buckwheat derived from the generalized theoretical matching law for the pigeons in Miller's (1976) experiment. The scale on the left is based on the relative allocation of pecking (behavior based) and the scale on the right is based on the relative allocation of time (time based). The value of buckwheat was arbitrarily set at 10 units.

From Miller, 1976, *Journal of the Experimental Analysis of Behavior, 26,* 335–347. Copyright © 1976 by the Society for the Experimental Analysis of Behavior, Inc. Reprinted by permission of John Wiley and Sons.

slides of women were available for presses on the right key. By varying the rates of reinforcement on sides, they were able to plot the relative rates of key pressing against the relative rates of reinforcement generated by the schedules. The participant exhibited a preference (bias) toward slides of women. The procedure was repeated with slides of men on the left and children on the right. Here the participant exhibited a preference (bias) toward the slides of men. From this, they were able to derive a prediction of how the participant would perform when slides of children were on left and slides of women were on the right. Their prediction was confirmed when they presented their participant with these reinforcers on a concurrent VI VI schedule (Phase 3). The match between prediction and data was very close—the subject had a bias for the slides of women.

At first glance, these results appear strange given that the participant was incarcerated for sexual offenses against young girls. However, Cliffe and Parry noted that in addition to being sexually attracted to young girls, he was also attracted to adult women but had not been successful establishing relationships with women. They also noted that he was in a program to improve his social interaction skills with adult women. In addition to providing a test of the generalized theoretical matching law, the results of their experiment suggest that the treatment program may be working.

WHY MATCHING OCCURS

Matching appears to reflect a process called melioration (making better) that involves molecular feedback. An alternative to melioration, called optimization (finding the optimal solution), is based on molar feedback. The available data favors melioration as the explanation for matching.

The empirical matching law provides a description of a set of phenomena: under certain conditions, individuals match the relative allocations of their effort and time to the relative values of certain attributes of the reinforcers they can obtain. The theoretical matching law relates the phenomenon of matching to the inferred value of reinforcers, and although the value of a reinforcer cannot be measured directly, it is hypothesized that value is related to various attributes of reinforcers. But neither the empirical nor the theoretical matching law explains why matching occurs.

In order to understand why matching occurs, we have to go back to the concept of molar and molecular feedback functions (see Chapter 9). On a concurrent schedule, **molar feedback** involves *the relationship between how individuals allocate their behavior to the alternatives and the total amount of reinforcement they obtain from that allocation.* Depending on the situation (schedules, attributes of the reinforcers, etc.), different allocations of time and effort can produce different total amounts of reinforcement. If molar feedback governs the individual's behavior, then he or she should settle into a behavior pattern that produces the maximum amount of reinforcement over the long run. On the other hand, **molecular feedback** involves *a continuing adjustment of the allocation of time and effort based on the moment-to-moment relationship between behaviors and outcomes.* If molecular feedback governs how individuals allocate their time and effort, then these local, not global, factors should be more important.

Molar Feedback as the Possible Mechanism Producing Matching. Molar feedback as a mechanism underlying choice behavior and matching is called optimization or molar maximizing. **Optimization (molar maximizing)** *is based on the assumption that individuals attempt to allocate their behavior to obtain the maximum gain for the least amount of effort, and that if an optimal allocation exists, they will find it* (Rachlin, Battalio, Kagel, & Green, 1981; Rachlin, Green, Kagel, & Battalio, 1976). Therefore, if molar maximizing (optimization) is the mechanism producing matching, then matching will maximize (optimize) the total value of the outcomes available in that situation.

Using a computer simulation, Rachlin et al. (1976) demonstrated that matching relative rates of behavior and relative allocations of time to relative rates of reinforcement results in the individual obtaining the maximum amount of reinforcement in concurrent schedules. Furthermore, as we saw earlier, individuals will obtain the maximum amount of reinforcement on concurrent FR FR or concurrent VR VR when they choose the richer schedule exclusively, a pattern consistent with the empirical matching law. Finally, optimization (molar maximizing) has been applied successfully to predict behavior when the choices are not symmetric (e.g., different qualities; Rachlin et al., 1976, 1981). However, as appealing as optimization is as an explanation of matching, there are situations in which matching does not maximize the total amount to reinforcement.

Molecular Feedback as the Mechanism for Matching. Another possibility is that matching is based on molecular feedback—that is, the moment-to-moment relationship between behavior and outcomes. At any given point in time, one alternative may be more attractive for any of a number of reasons. For example, with concurrent VI VI schedules, the probability of a reinforcer being available increases with the passage of time. Therefore, while the individual is working on one schedule, the probability is increasing that a switch to the other schedule will be reinforced (after the changeover delay); that is, at some moments in time, the probability of being rewarded is *higher* for performing the alternative behavior. This form of molecular feedback is called **momentary maximizing** because *the momentary probability of being reinforced governs the individual's behavior* (Shimp, 1966, 1969; Silberberg, Hamilton, Ziriax, & Casey, 1978). Unfortunately, despite its intuitive appeal, momentary maximizing based on the momentary probability of reinforcement has not been found when one looks closely at the local patterns of choices (Heyman, 1979; Nevin, 1969, 1979).

A better explanation for matching based on molecular feedback is called **melioration** ("making better"); Herrnstein, 1982; Herrnstein & Prelec, 1991; Herrnstein & Vaughn, 1980). Melioration is based on two assumptions. The first is that *individuals are sensitive to the current behavioral cost of obtaining reinforcers.* Behavioral cost is measured in terms of how much time and effort is expended to obtain each reinforcer. When the individual invests little time and effort, the behavioral cost is low, but when he or she invests considerable time and effort, the behavioral costs are high. The second assumption is that *individuals attempt to equalize the behavioral cost of obtaining reinforcement across the various choices and outcomes, and matching reflects the point at which these behavioral costs are roughly equivalent.*

On a concurrent VI VI schedule of reinforcement, melioration works as follows: The *longer* the individual works on one VI schedule (call it schedule A), the *more* time and effort (behavior) is invested in obtaining each outcome on that schedule. Furthermore, while the individual is working on VI schedule A, the probability of an outcome being available on the other concurrently available VI schedule (schedule B) is increasing, and switching to schedule B may earn an outcome quickly and with little effort expended. Thus when the prevailing behavioral cost of reinforcement is *lower* on schedule B, it pays to switch to schedule B. However, the longer the individual works on schedule B, the *higher* the behavioral cost for the obtained outcomes becomes there and the *lower* the cost for obtaining an outcome on schedule A. Individuals appear to be sensitive to this cost, and they switch between schedules A and B to try to keep the overall behavioral cost as low as possible on both. Matching provides the allocation of behavior that maintains the behavioral cost in terms of both time and effort roughly equal across all choices and the overall cost lowest. Melioration is a form of hill-climbing in which individuals are trying to better their situation by always moving toward the alternative that has the lowest behavior cost for obtaining the valued outcome.

A Test of Melioration as the Mechanism Underlying Matching. Vaughn, Kardish, and Wilson (1982) devised a direct test that pitted melioration against optimization. In Phase 1 of their experiment, pigeons were trained on a concurrent VI 3-minute schedule until they were matching their rates of time allocation to the rates of reinforcement (50% of the time spent pecking at each alternative). Then a special VI 1-minute schedule was added. This VI schedule operated when the pigeons worked on key A, but the outcomes were delivered when the pigeons worked on key B. Their procedure is outlined in Table 10.3.

In order to maximize the total number of outcomes earned, pigeons *should* peck on the side that causes the third schedule to advance because this increases the overall amount of food delivered, but they did the opposite: They spent more time on the side where the extra outcomes were delivered even though this *reduced* the total number of reinforcers they could earn. In other words, they shifted in the direction of melioration; that is, equalizing

Table 10.3   Experimental Design for the Vaughn, Kardish, and Wilson (1982) Experiment Testing Melioration as the Mechanism Underlying Matching

Phase	Schedules in effect on each key	
1	Key A VI 3-minute	Key B VI 3-minute
2	VI 3-minute + advance VI 1-minute	VI 3-minute + collect reinforcers set up by VI 1-minute schedule on other key

the number of pecks per outcome delivered. Herrnstein and Vaughn (1980), Mazur (1981), and Vaughn (1981) all described situations where matching reduced the overall amount of reinforcement the individual earned.

Similar results have been reported with humans using a laboratory procedure sometimes referred to as the Harvard Game. With this procedure, participants are confronted with repeated choices between two alternatives that vary in terms of their immediate versus long-term payoffs; that is, on any trial one alternative had a higher immediate payoff, but across all trials the other alternative had a higher overall payoff. (Herrnstein, Loewenstein, Prelec, & Vaughan, 1993). Sims, Neth, Jacobs, and Gray (2013) provided their participants with prospective feedback of the form, "If you continue the same strategy you can expect to win X dollars on the trials, but by adopting the optimal strategy, you could expect to win Y dollars instead." Despite this rather explicit feedback, their participants continued to meliorate.

Herrnstein and Prelec (1992) argued that drug addiction parallels the situation in the Vaughn et al. (1982) experiment because drug addiction involves a choice between two alternatives: taking the drug that initially produces a short-term high, and engaging in other behaviors that are not as reinforcing in the short-term. As a result, individuals shift their behavior toward taking the drug at the expense of other activities that also produce outcomes. Although tolerance develops from repeated exposure to the drug (which reduces its reinforcing value), the individual is trapped like the pigeons in the Vaughn et al. (1982) experiment: Taking the drug reduces the overall amount of reinforcement, but to increase the rate of reinforcement, the individual has to do something that does not have as high a momentary reinforcing value.

However, it would be a mistake to conclude on the basis of the results of these experiments that individuals *never* optimize (make choices that maximize the total amount or value of the available outcomes). Tunney and Shanks (2002) reported that the participants in their experiments meliorated when payoffs varied in probability and optimized when payoffs varied in terms of the size of the monetary payoff. Kagel, Battalio, and Green (1995) reviewed and synthesized much of the research in psychology, economics, and behavioral biology relevant to the study of choice behavior. They present a convincing argument that individuals often can and do behave in a manner that maximizes the total value of the available outcomes in a variety of situations.

Is melioration maladaptive? At first glance, melioration does not appear to be an adaptive strategy. We would expect individuals to behave in a way that maximizes the overall amount of reinforcement they receive, but we have just reviewed in detail an experiment in which they did not. In order to answer the question of whether melioration is maladaptive, we must take a closer look at both optimization and melioration.

Optimization (molar maximizing) provides an explanation of behavioral allocation based on a *long-term* perspective of the final outcome of choice; that is, the resulting allocation of behavior is directed toward obtaining the maximum possible total value of the outcomes that the situation allows. It is assumed that over time the individual will acquire sufficient knowledge of the relationship between the distribution of their time and effort and the resulting outcomes to determine the optimal allocation. In the concurrent choice situation involving interval and ratio schedules of reinforcement, an individual can optimize by keeping track of the overall rates of reinforcement from the alternatives (molar feedback), trying various allocations of behavior, and adjusting his or her behavior through a process of hill-climbing to obtain the maximum amount or value of reinforcement.

Melioration, on the other hand, is based on an individual's assessment of the *current* cost of obtaining reinforcement (molecular feedback) and his or her attempts to equalize these costs across the various alternatives. Here again, the individual can use hill-climbing to make these adjustments, but unlike optimization, melioration involves a continuous process of keeping track of the behavioral costs for each alternative. A switch to the other alternative may reduce the cost of obtaining the next outcome, but staying with that alternative will eventually drive up that cost. Matching will always be the result of melioration because matching is the distribution of time and effort that equalizes this cost.

Dreyfus (1991) demonstrated that pigeons are indeed sensitive to short-term changes in the relative rates of reinforcement on concurrent VI VI schedules. Using the schedule-control procedure, Dreyfus investigated what would happen when the relative allocations of reinforcement were switched at various times during a daily session. This switch was not signaled; that is, at the designated time, the schedule associated with green at that time was switched to red, and the schedule associated with red was switched to green. At a later designated time, the schedules switched back. Using a pair of schedules that delivered 90% of the outcomes on one schedule and 10% on the other, Dreyfus found that within 10 minutes of the switch, the pigeons were matching their relative allocation of time to the new relative rates of reinforcement. Davison and Baum (2000) found similar results using a side-by-side procedure in pigeons, as did Mark and Gallistel (1994) using electrical brain stimulation as the outcome with rats. Clearly, rats and pigeons are sensitive to the local rates of reinforcement, which is a prerequisite for melioration.

Most of the time matching also leads to optimization, but when melioration and optimization are pitted against each other, the usual result is matching and a reduction in the overall amount of reinforcement. This suggests that individuals are more sensitive to short-term molecular feedback than to the more distant molar feedback. However, Herrnstein (1982) pointed out that as the window in time in which the individual calculates the behavioral cost of reinforcement increases, melioration approaches optimization. Thus, melioration is adaptive because it provides the individual with a way to improve its situation based on the immediate effects of its behavior. This led Herrnstein to argue that melioration, not optimization, is the more basic process in choice and human decision making (Herrnstein, 1990a, 1990b; Herrnstein & Prelec, 1991). Likewise, Sims et al. (2013) argued that melioration is a reasonable strategy for an individual who is trying to obtain the maximum outcome when they have limited experience in an uncertain environment. It is hard to argue that such short term sensitivity is maladaptive. Simon (1956) pointed out that it is not necessary to find the optimal solution in a decision making or choice situation. All that is required is that the individual find a satisfactory solution; Simon calls this "satisficing." Melioration is that kind of solution.

THE SIGNIFICANCE OF THE MATCHING LAWS

The matching laws are not just descriptions of how individuals perform on concurrent schedules. They are statements about the fundamental relationship between behaviors and outcomes.

It is easy to underestimate the significance of the matching laws for our understanding of learning and behavior. *The phenomenon of matching illustrates that outcomes do not strengthen the behaviors that produce them as implied by the Law of Effect* (see Chapter 7). Clearly, the effects of outcomes on behavior depend on what other outcomes are available. Catania (1963) provided an early demonstration of this. He trained pigeons on concurrent VI VI schedules with the schedule-control procedure. The various combinations of schedules and number of sessions with each combination are presented in Table 10.4 and the results are presented in Figure 10.8. In this experiment, the schedule associated with the yellow key (key 2) stayed the same throughout the experiment while the schedule associated with the red key (key 1) was systematically varied.

If the law of effect was correct and outcomes strengthened the behaviors that produce them, then the rate of pecking when the key light is red should rise and fall with changes in the prevailing VI schedule because that schedule determines the rate of reinforcement for pecking the red key. But the rate of pecking when the key light is yellow (key 2) *should not change* because when the key was yellow, the VI schedule *did not change* throughout the experiment. On the other hand, the empirical matching law leads to a different prediction for the rate of pecking when the key is yellow. According to the empirical matching law, the rate of pecking in the presence of the yellow key should be *inversely* related to the rate of reinforcement when the key is red; that is, as the rate of reinforcement *increases* when the key is red, the rate of pecking at the yellow key should *decrease*, even though the schedule of reinforcement in the presence of the yellow key does not change.

Table 10.4   The Sequence of Concurrent VI VI Schedules and the Number of Sessions on Each Pair of VI Schedules for Catania's (1963) Experiment

Key 1 (Red)		Key 2 (Yellow)		No. of Sessions
Schedule	Reinf/hr	Schedule	Reinf/hr	No. of Sessions
Extinction	0	VI 3 min	20	9
VI 6 min	10	VI 3 min	20	12
VI 2 min	30	VI 3 min	20	10
VI 3 min	20	VI 3 min	20	10
VI 1.5 min	40	VI 3 min	20	9

Note: The COD was always 2 seconds.

Catania (1963) plotted the rates of pecking on both keys as a function of the rates of reinforcement on key 1 (which had the different VI schedules; Figure 10.8). The rate of pecking on key 1 (red key) increased as the rate of reinforcement obtained for pecking that key increased. This is predicted from both the law of effect and the matching law. On the other hand, the rate of pecking on key 2 (yellow key with VI 2-minute schedule throughout the experiment) decreased as the rate of reinforcement on key 1 increased. This result is contrary to the law of effect but is consistent with the empirical matching law.

Ruddle, Bradshaw, Szabadi, and Bevan (1979) reported the same results in humans. Their subjects could earn money by pulling two different levers. Reinforcement on both levers was programmed according to a concurrent VI VI schedule. When the schedule on one lever changed, the rate of lever pulling on both levers changed as predicted by the empirical matching law. Their data look like the data in Figure 10.8.

These data provide further evidence that outcomes do not simply strengthen the behaviors that precede them. *Performance of an operant behavior depends on the consequences of that behavior and the consequences of all other behaviors that can occur in that situation.*

The Empirical Matching Law Applied to a Single Behavior

The empirical matching law also describes the effects of outcomes on a single behavior and provides us with an equation that describes how the rate of reinforcement influences that behavior. It also tells us that we can influence the rate of occurrence of that behavior by manipulating or controlling other outcomes that are not directly tied to the target behavior.

We noted at the beginning of this chapter that all behavior involves choice. At any point in time, we can perform any one of a number of behaviors, each of which has a consequence.

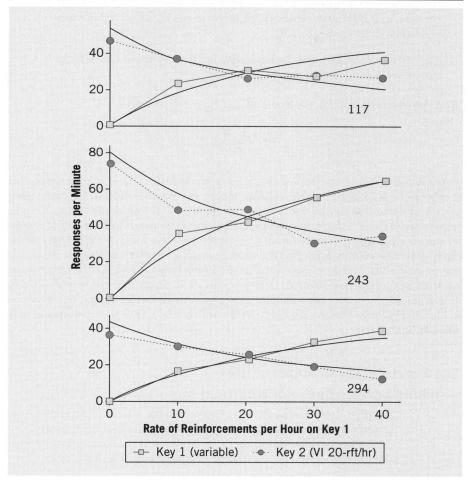

Figure 10.8 Data from Catania's 1963 experiment. Rates of pecking on each key as a function of the rates of reinforcement on key 1 (open circles) for three different pigeons. The rate of reinforcement on key 2 (solid circles) was always 20 reinforcers per hour.

From Catania, 1963, *Journal of the Experimental Analysis of Behavior, 6,* 253–263. Copyright © 1963 by the Society for the Experimental Analysis of Behavior, Inc. Reprinted by permission of John Wiley and Sons.

The empirical matching laws tell us that the relative occurrences of these behaviors are related to the relative rates of reinforcement for each of them (Equation 3). Thus, if the rate of reinforcement for behavior A increases relative to the rate of reinforcement for other behaviors, the rate of occurrence of behavior A will increase. But, if the rate of reinforcement for one of the other behaviors increases relative to the rate of reinforcement for behavior A, the rate of occurrence of behavior A will decrease. This is illustrated in Figure 10.8.

Herrnstein (1970) showed that the empirical matching law (Equation 3) can be transformed to describe the effects of the rates of reinforcement on a single behavior. To do that, he made two assumptions:

1. The total amount of behavior that occurs in a given situation is *constant*, even though the rates of reinforcement for some of those behaviors change.[9] If **B** stands for the target behavior and $\mathbf{B_O}$ stands for all other behaviors, then $\mathbf{B} + \mathbf{B_O} = \mathbf{k}$.

2. *All other behaviors* other than the target behavior also have a certain rate of reinforcement associated with them $(\mathbf{R_O})$.

With these two assumptions, the empirical matching law reduces to:

$$B = k\left(\frac{R}{R + R_o}\right) \tag{7}$$

where **B** is the rate of occurrence of the behavior, **R** is the rate of reinforcement for that behavior, $\mathbf{R_O}$ is the rate of all other outcomes for all other activities the individual performs in that situation, and **k** is a constant that is the sum of all the things the individual does in that situation. According to Equation 7, *the rate of occurrence of an operant behavior is a function of both the rate of reinforcement for that behavior* (**R**) *and the rate of reinforcement for all other behaviors* $(\mathbf{R_O})$ *in that situation.* Herrnstein (1970) showed that this equation fits data from individual pigeons working on various VI schedules as reported by Catania and Reynolds (1968; Figure 10.9). Equation 7 has been applied to data generated by humans in a number of situations with similar success (see Davison & McCarthy, 1988; McDowell, 1988, 2013a, for reviews). One such example is provided in Box 10.2.

The Practical Implications of the Matching Law for Behavior Modification

Equation 7 tells us that the rate of occurrence of a behavior depends on both the rate of reinforcement for that behavior and the rate of occurrence of other outcomes in the situation. Therefore, one can affect behavior through manipulating either or both quantities.

---

[9]This assumption has been called into question. McDowell and Dallery (1999) found that the value of **k** changes as a function of water deprivation, and Dallery, McDowell, and Lancaster (2000) found that the value of **k** varies with sucrose concentration. However, this does not affect the overall form of the resulting curve relating rate of behavior to the rate of reinforcement. After reviewing the literature on this topic and conducting a series of computer simulations, McLean (2006) concluded that the value of **k** is invariant over a wide range of changes in outcome quality, but the value of **k** decreases under extremely low values of outcome quality.

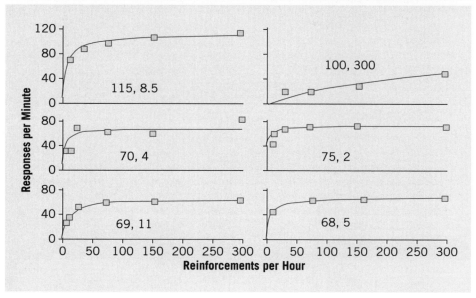

Figure 10.9 Rate of pecking as a function of the rate of reinforcement. The data were generated by Catania and Reynolds (1968). The smooth curves were fitted to the data by Herrnstein based on equation 7. The two numbers in each graph are the values of k and Ro used to fit the curves to the data.

From Herrnstein, 1970; *Journal of the Experimental Analysis of Behavior, 13*, 243–266. Copyright © 1970 by the Society for the Experimental Analysis of Behavior, Inc. Reprinted by permission of John Wiley and Sons.

McDowell (1982) noted that the matching law applied to single behaviors (Equation 7) has practical implications for behavior modification. The most common methods used to decrease undesirable behavior are extinction and punishment. Equation 7 indicates that we can also *decrease* unwanted behaviors by *increasing* the rates of reinforcement for other behaviors (R_o). Likewise, the most common method used to increase desirable behavior is by increasing the rate of positive reinforcement for that behavior, but Equation 7 also indicates that we can *increase* desirable behavior by *decreasing* the rates of reinforcement for other behaviors (R_o).

Manipulating Reinforcement for Other Behaviors to Decrease Unwanted Behavior. McDowell (1981) provided an example of how one can apply the matching law to decrease an undesirable behavior by manipulating alternative outcomes. The participant was a 22-year-old mildly retarded man who engaged in a great deal of oppositional behavior (temper tantrums, noncompliance, argumentativeness). Sometimes his temper tantrums escalated into assaults on others. Although his oppositional

BOX 10.2

Using Equation 7 to Describe Naturally Occurring Human Behavior

In 1980, Carr and McDowell published a study in which they successfully treated a 10-year-old boy who engaged in self-injurious scratching. As a result of this behavior, the boy had approximately 30 lesions all over his body. Their treatment consisted of two forms of omission training (punishment by removal; see Chapter 7), but that is not the focus of our interest here. Before they began their treatment, they recorded the naturally occurring rates of scratching and the rates of verbal reprimands by family members for his scratching in an attempt to identify the conditions under which self-injurious scratching was most likely to occur. These data were collected during four 20–30 minute observational sessions carried out on different days. They found that he was most likely to scratch himself when he and his family were watching television in their living room. Subsequently, McDowell (1981) plotted the relationship between the rates of

Figure 10.2.1   Fit of Equation 7 to the data collected by Carr and McDowell (1980) on the relationship between the rate of self-injurious scratching by a 10-year-old boy and the rate of verbal reprimands for scratching by his family. The percentage of variance accounted for by Equation 7, and the estimated values of k and R_o (called r_e here) are provided.

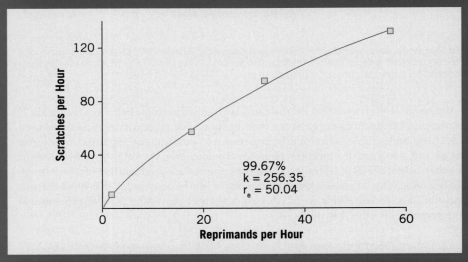

99.67%
k = 256.35
r_e = 50.04

From McDowell, 1981. Reprinted with permission of the author.

scratching and the rates of reprimands the boy received for scratching and fit Equation 7 to the data (Figure 10.2.1). These data illustrate that the empirical matching law is not just a laboratory phenomenon. It also operates in real life.

McDowell (2005) created a generalized version of Equation 7 by adding the bias and sensitivity parameters to it to obtain the following equation:

$$B = \frac{kR^a}{R^a + \frac{R_o^a}{b}}$$ (8)

Adding these parameters does improve the fit to data, but the improvement is quite small (McDowell, 2013a). While Equation 8 may be the theoretically correct version, Equation 7 fits the data so well that for practical purposes there is no need to include the additional parameters.

behavior was clearly reinforced by attention, putting him on extinction (i.e., ignoring him when he became oppositional) would not work because ignoring him rapidly led to aggression. Therefore, rather than use punishment or extinction, a point (token) system was instituted whereby he could earn points for doing routine activities (personal hygiene, helping with dinner, reading, etc.). These points could then be exchanged at the end of the week for money. Before the program was instituted, the baseline rate of oppositional behavior was collected for one week. That number is on the left of Figure 10.10. The point system was instituted for the next 8 weeks (middle of Figure 10.10). Finally, McDowell added a response cost (omission training or punishment by removal) procedure whereby the participant lost points for oppositional behaviors (right side of Figure 10.10). Note that this last procedure did not reduce the oppositional behavior further. Providing reinforcement for other behaviors has been successfully applied in a number of situations (see Carr, Severtson, & Lepper, 2009; McDowell, 1988; Petscher, Rey, & Bailey, 2009 for reviews).

Manipulating Reinforcement for Other Behaviors to Increase Desired Behaviors. Sajwaj, Twardosz, and Burke (1972) described how they increased the social behavior of a 7-year-old developmentally disabled boy in a remedial preschool classroom. Although he presented no conduct problems in school and rarely was disobedient, he spent a lot of time attempting to talk to the teacher. As a result, he did not interact much with other children. After the baseline rates of his attempts to initiate conversations with the teacher, her responses to him, and the rates of his interactions with other children were established, the teacher was instructed to ignore him completely. The result was a decrease in his attempts to initiate conversations with the teacher and an increase in social behaviors directed toward other children. Clearly, by reducing one source of reinforcement, other behaviors increased as is predicted by Equation 7.

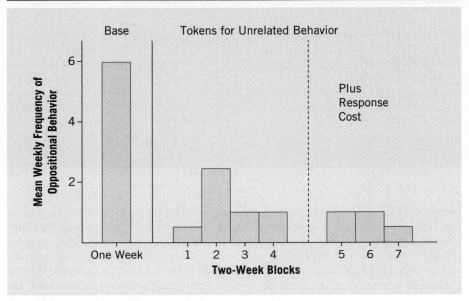

Figure 10.10 Mean weekly frequency of oppositional behavior when token reinforcement (points) was given for unrelated behaviors.

From McDowell, 1981. Reprinted with permission of the author.

The Significance of the Matching Laws

> The matching laws are statements about the fundamental relationship between behaviors and outcomes.

The empirical and the generalized empirical matching laws do more than describe the behavior of individuals in choice situations. *The phenomenon of matching illustrates that outcomes do not strengthen the behaviors that produce them as implied by the Law of Effect.* In Chapters 7 and 8, we saw that changing the outcome for a given behavior affects the performance of that behavior. The matching laws tell us that we can also affect the performance of a behavior by manipulating the schedule, magnitude, and delay of reinforcement for other behaviors. This means that *the performance of a single operant behavior depends on the consequences of that behavior and the consequences of all other behaviors that can occur in that situation.*

Finally, the theoretical matching law tells us that *choices reflect the relative values of the available alternatives in a given situation. This gives us a way to construct psychological scales of value of different events for a single individual.*

All of this suggests that the matching laws are fundamental laws of behavior. Life is indeed about making choices.

SUMMARY AND CONCLUSIONS

All operant behavior involves a choice between performing one behavior as opposed to another (including doing nothing), and choice appears to be determined by the relative values of the outcomes of the behaviors available to an individual. We can study how individuals choose between activities that lead to different outcomes with procedures called concurrent schedules. Whether we use the side-by-side procedure or the schedule-control procedure, under certain conditions individuals match their relative allocations of effort (rates of behavior) and time to the relative rates, magnitudes, and immediacy of reinforcement for each choice. This is called the *empirical matching law*. If we assume that the rate, magnitude, immediacy, and other attributes of an outcome (e.g., quality) multiply to determine its value, we can make a theoretical statement about the relationship between choice and value: Individuals match their relative allocations of time and effort to the relative values of the outcomes available. This is called the *theoretical matching law*.

But strict matching is not always observed. Individuals exhibit deviations from strict matching when they have a systematic *bias* for performing one activity over another or a preference for one choice unrelated to the attributes of the outcomes. Furthermore, when switching is relatively easy, individuals tend to ignore the attributes of the outcomes and switch back and forth readily, a phenomenon called *undermatching*. When switching is very difficult or costly in terms of time and effort to switch, individuals tend to select the behavior that produces the higher valued outcome and stay with it. That phenomenon is called *overmatching*. These deviations from strict matching can be incorporated into the matching laws to produce generalized empirical and theoretical matching laws. The *generalized empirical matching law* provides us with a way to estimate these biases and how sensitive the individual is to the attributes of the reinforcers. The *generalized theoretical matching law* allows us to scale the values of different reinforcers.

Matching occurs through a process called *melioration* ("making better") whereby individuals attempt to equalize the behavioral cost of obtaining reinforcement across the various choices and outcomes. This equalization process is based on molecular feedback as to the current behavioral cost of obtaining outcomes across the various choices. This does not always lead to optimization (obtaining the most value), but it seems to suffice.

The phenomenon of matching provides additional evidence that outcomes do not strengthen behavior and that the effects of outcomes on behavior are relative, not absolute. This has implications for behavior modification.

STUDY QUESTIONS

1. How does a concurrent VI VI schedule work? Describe how the two variations (side-by-side procedure [two-key or two-lever] procedure and the schedule-control [switching-key or switching-lever] procedure) work.

2. What function does the changeover delay (COD) serve with concurrent VI VI schedules?

3 What is the empirical matching law? To what do individuals match their relative rates of behavior and relative allocations of time?

4. Describe the conditions under which strict matching occurs.

5. What conditions lead to systematic deviations from strict matching, and how can these deviations be incorporated into the generalized matching law? What is the practical importance of these deviations?

6. What is the theoretical matching law and what does it tell us about operant conditioning and the effects of outcomes on behavior?

7. How can the theoretical matching law be used to scale the relative value of outcomes?

8. Describe optimization and melioration. How are these related to molar and molecular feedback (see Chapter 9)? Which of these provides the best explanation for why matching occurs? What evidence leads to that conclusion?

9. What does the matching law tell us about the relationship between reinforcers and individual behaviors? What is a practical application of this fact?

11

INFERENCE AND THE REPRESENTATIONS OF KNOWLEDGE IN OPERANT CONDITIONING

In Chapters 3 and 4, we reviewed a great deal of evidence that points to the conclusion that Pavlovian conditioning presents individuals with the task of discovering the predictors of important events in their environment. The process by which they obtain knowledge about the predictive relationship between these events is called causal inference, and that knowledge is encoded in associations involving these events, the temporal relationship between these events, where they occur, and hierarchical arrangements involving these events and other predictors (see Chapter 5). Learning these things helps individuals prepare for the occurrence of significant events (see Chapter 6).

Operant conditioning also presents individuals with an inference task. Here the task is to discover what they can do to make things happen; the predictors are their own behavior, and the significant events are the occurrence or disappearance of reinforcers or outcomes (Os). Unlike Pavlovian conditioning, in which individuals must draw inferences from observations of events that are out of their control, in operant conditioning they can test their inferences directly by performing or not performing behaviors and observing whether that has any effect on the outcome. In this chapter, we will explore the evidence for causal inference as the process that underlies operant conditioning and how the knowledge individuals gain from their experiences with an operant conditioning procedure is encoded.

OPERANT CONDITIONING IS ALSO AN INFERENCE TASK

> In operant conditioning, the individual's task is to discover what aspects of his or her behavior will produce a certain outcome and when and where this will occur. As is the case with Pavlovian conditioning, contingency and temporal proximity are neither necessary nor sufficient conditions for the formation of causal inferences in operant conditioning.

In Chapter 3, we recounted David Hume's (1739/1992, 1777/1993) three conditions for promoting causal inferences: temporal proximity between events, a consistent relationship (correlation or contingency) between these events, and temporal precedence (the inferred cause precedes the inferred effect). Like Pavlovian conditioning, operant conditioning is also influenced by these three conditions, and like Pavlovian conditioning, *neither contingency nor temporal contiguity are necessary or sufficient conditions for the occurrence of conditioning*.

Consistency

In operant conditioning, *consistency* refers to how likely it is that the behavior is followed by the outcome, and it is expressed as a behavior-outcome contingency. Although operant conditioning and operant behaviors can be influenced by this contingency, consistency is neither a necessary nor a sufficient condition for the occurrence of operant conditioning.

As we noted in Chapter 7, the behavior-outcome contingency in operant conditioning is determined by two probabilities: Pr (outcome | behavior) and Pr (outcome | no behavior). The first probability statement [Pr (outcome | behavior)] defines the likelihood that a given occurrence of the target behavior will be followed by a given outcome. When the Pr (outcome | behavior) = 1, that behavior is *always* followed by that outcome, and when the Pr (outcome | behavior) = 0, that behavior is *never* followed by that outcome. The other probability [Pr (outcome | no behavior)] defines the likelihood of getting outcomes for not performing the target behavior. In a sense, it defines the likelihood of obtaining the outcome for free. When the Pr (outcome | no behavior) = 0, the outcome will *never* be given in the absence of the target behavior. The higher that probability, the more likely that "free" outcomes will be given. Thus, *there is a high degree of consistency when Pr (outcome | behavior) ≈ 1, and the Pr (outcome | no behavior) ≈ 0*.

Hammond (1980) demonstrated that the degree of contingency (the difference between these two probabilities) affects the rate of lever pressing in rats with water as the outcome. He found that when the Pr (water | lever pressing) was higher than the Pr (water | no lever pressing), the rate of lever pressing was high. By systematically raising the Pr (water | no lever pressing), the rate of lever pressing declined, even though the Pr (water | lever pressing) stayed the same. When both probabilities were equal, the rate of lever pressing declined toward zero. The same was true when the contingency was negative, that is when Pr (water | lever pressing) < Pr (water | no lever pressing; see Figure 11.1).

At first glance, Hammond's (1980) data seems to provide strong evidence that consistency is necessary for the occurrence of operant conditioning. But there is an alternative interpretation of his data that must be considered: The animals had to be doing something when the "free" water was delivered. Perhaps other behaviors that were followed by water also were conditioned, and these behaviors competed with lever pressing. Colwill and Rescorla (1986; see also Dickinson & Mulatero, 1989) devised a rather ingenious way to test that alternative interpretation (Table 11.1). Rats were initially trained to perform two different behaviors (press a lever or pull a chain) to receive two different outcomes (sucrose pellets or food pellets). On the 15 test days, both behaviors were allowed to occur and to be rewarded appropriately, but in addition, free outcomes of one kind were also given. The results of Colwill and Rescorla's experiment are presented in Figure 11.2. The "free" outcomes on the test days reduced performance of both behaviors (no doubt because the added opportunities to eat took time), but the detrimental effect on the performance of the behavior previously trained with the now "free" outcomes was *greater*. The other behavior

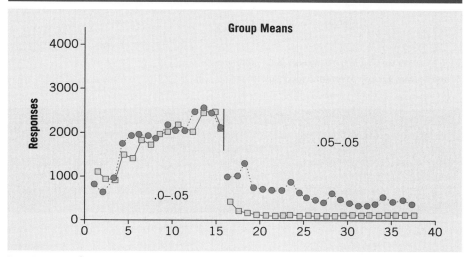

Figure 11.1 Responses per hour for two groups of rats. Both groups were trained with a positive contingency between lever pressing and water [Pr(water|lever press) = 0.05 and Pr(water|no lever press) = 0]. One group of rats was shifted to a zero contingency [0.05–0.05], and the other group of rats was shifted to a negative contingency [0–0.05].

From Hammond, 1980, *Journal of the Experimental Analysis of Behavior, 34*, 297-304. Copyright © 1980 by the Society for the Experimental Analysis of Behavior, Inc. Reprinted by permission of John Wiley and Sons.

was not affected as much. These results indicate that the effects of changes in contingency observed by Hammond (1980) are *not* the result of competition from other behaviors. Individuals are sensitive to the contingency between their behavior and outcomes.

Operant Conditioning in the Absence of a Behavior-Outcome Contingency. Zeiler (1970a) observed both the maintenance of existing behavior and the acquisition of new behavior in the *absence* of a behavior-outcome contingency. He placed 4- and 5-year-old children in a narrow room that contained two buttons on the wall, one red and the other blue. Candy could be obtained by pressing either or both buttons a total of 30 times (FR 30) in any order. Over time, the children all settled in on some pattern of behavior in which they pressed both buttons about the same number of times (i.e., they matched their relative rates of behavior to the relative rates of reinforcement). Some children made all 30 presses on one button and switched to the other, and others alternated buttons with each press. After their behavior had stabilized, the contingency was changed. Now presses on the red button had no outcomes, but the contingency on the blue was changed to omission training; that is, the children would get food only if they had not pressed the blue button for 60 seconds. Thus any presses of the blue button reset the timer and delayed the delivery of the next piece of candy (see Chapter 7). Over time the

Table 11.1	Design of the Colwill and Rescorla (1986) Experiment
Training (Diffferent days)	Test (Same days)
$B_1 \rightarrow O_1$ $B_2 \rightarrow O_2$	$B_1 \rightarrow O_1$ $B_2 \rightarrow O_2$ O_1 or O_2

Note: B_1 and B_2 were lever pressing and chain pulling.
O_1 and O_2 were sucrose pellets and food pellets.

Figure 11.2 The effects of presenting "free" outcomes on two operant behaviors; each behavior produces a specific outcome. On the test days (right panel), one of these outcomes was presented while the rats could perform both behaviors. "Same" refers to the effects on the behavior trained to produce that free outcome, and "Different" refers to the effects on the behavior trained to produce the other (different) outcome.

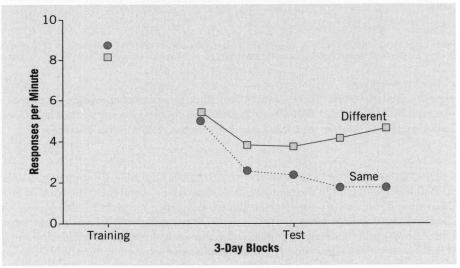

From "Associative structures in instrumental learning" by R. M. Colwill and R. A. Rescorla in *The psychology of learning and motivation*, Volume 20, edited by Gordon H. Bower, copyright © 1986 by Academic Press, redrawn by permission of R. M. Colwill

children stopped pressing the blue button, but most of them continued to press the red button even though there was no programmed outcome for doing so. The behavior of the two children who did not press the red button was especially interesting: One sat quietly and waited for the food to appear. The other crawled on the floor while waiting for the candy to appear. Zeiler attributed both behavior patterns to the accidental temporal proximity between a behavior and the delivery of the candy; in other words, the children were engaging in what we would call "superstitious behavior." These data indicate that a behavior-outcome contingency is not a necessary condition for the occurrence of operant conditioning.

Failure to Produce Operant Conditioning in the Presence of a Behavior-Outcome Contingency. On the other hand, the presence of a contingency does not automatically produce conditioning. For example, Hineline and Rachlin (1969) found it difficult to teach a pigeon to peck a key to avoid electric shock but easy to teach it to peck for food. Likewise, Shettleworth (1975) found that there were some classes of behaviors (rearing, digging, and scratching the wall) in hamsters that she could easily increase with positive reinforcement. On the other hand, her hamsters could not learn to wash their faces, leave scent markings, or scratch themselves when rewarded with food. Walters and Glaser (1971) found that a signal for shock presented contingent on digging *suppressed* digging in gerbils but *increased* alert posturing, and Blough (1958) reported that it is difficult to get a rat to stand still to receive food.

These data indicate that the effects of a behavior-outcome contingency on behavior depend on the behavior system aroused in that situation. Approaching and pecking localized objects for food is part of the feeding system in pigeons, but pecking at these same objects is not part of their defense system. Thus, we should not be surprised that pigeons easily learn to peck a key for food and have difficulty learning to peck that same key to avoid shock. Likewise, in hamsters, rearing, digging, and scratching the walls are behaviors that are part of the feeding system; face washing, scent marking, and scratching oneself are not. On the other hand, Pearce, Colwill, and Hall (1978) were able to use food as a reward for self-scratching in rats if they provided an "itch" (a collar around the rat's neck to induce scratching), and Morgan and Nicholas (1979) were able to influence the occurrence of face washing, rearing, and scratching by providing an opportunity for rats to press a lever after performing these activities. In these latter two cases, the itch provided an inducement to scratch, and the lever provided some distance between the food and the grooming activities by being interposed between them. In the case of Walters and Glaser's (1971) gerbils, activation of the defense system elicited defensive behaviors (alert posturing) at the same time it suppressed digging. Some rather humorous examples of situations in which the behavior system aroused by the outcome interfered with the behavior-outcome contingency are presented in Box 11.1.

The examples of "misbehavior" described in Box 11.1 illustrate that *it is a mistake to think of operant conditioning as automatically producing changes in arbitrarily chosen behaviors associated with arbitrarily chosen stimuli and arbitrarily chosen outcomes.*[1] *The success of operant conditioning as a technique for changing behavior requires some understanding of the unconditioned*

---

[1] For a long time, the dominant view was that instrumental learning and operant conditioning procedures could be used to modify any nonreflexive behavior. Thorndike (1911) devised his problem box because he wanted to minimize the influence of innate knowledge (instinct) on his cats' escape from his puzzle boxes, and Skinner used lever pressing in rats and key pecking in pigeons because he viewed them as arbitrarily chosen behaviors. On the other hand, Kline and Small constructed their problem boxes and mazes with the natural behavior of the species in mind. It is interesting that Thorndike's and Skinner's approach prevailed for so long.

Examples of "Misbehavior" in Operant Conditioning Situations

In 1947, Keller and Marian Breland, former students of B. F. Skinner, founded Animal Behavior Enterprises, a business devoted to using the principles of operant conditioning to train animals for commercial purposes. They described their work enthusiastically in an article in the *American Psychologist* in 1951, but 10 years later they reported a number of failures. The two failures described here are from their paper "The Misbehavior of Organisms," an obvious play on the title of Skinner's first book (*Behavior of Organisms*; Breland & Breland, 1961). They labeled these as "misbehaviors" because the animals did not perform as expected. In both cases, the "misbehavior" caused the animals to lose outcomes.

The Miserly Raccoon

The response concerned the manipulation of money by the raccoon (who has "hands" rather similar to those of the primates.). The contingency for reinforcement was picking up the coins and depositing them in a 5-inch metal box.

Raccoons condition readily, have good appetites, and this one was quite tame and an eager subject. We anticipated no trouble. Conditioning him to pick up the first coin was simple. We started out by reinforcing him for picking up a single coin. Then the metal container was introduced, with the requirement that he drop the coin into the container. Here we ran into the first bit of difficulty: he seemed to have a great deal of trouble letting go of the coin. He would rub it up against the inside of the container, pull it back out, and clutch it firmly for several seconds. However, he would finally turn it loose and receive his food reinforcement. Then the final contingency: we put him on a ratio of 2, requiring that he pick up both coins and put them in the container.

Now the raccoon really had problems (and so did we). He could not let go of the coins, and he spent seconds, even minutes, rubbing them together (in a most miserly fashion) and dipping them into the container. He carried on this behavior to such an extent that the practical application we had in mind—a display featuring a raccoon putting money in a piggy bank—simply was not feasible. The rubbing behavior became worse and worse as time went on, in spite of nonreinforcement.

The Uncooperative Chicken

The observer sees a hopper full of oval plastic capsules that contain small toys, charms, and trinkets. When the SD (a light) is presented to the chicken, the chicken pulls a rubber loop which releases one of these capsules onto a slide measuring 16 inches long and inclined at about 30 degrees. The capsule rolls down the slide and comes to rest near the end. Here, one or two sharp, straight pecks by the chicken will knock it forward off the slide and out to the observer at which point the chicken receives reinforcement by means of an automatic feeder. Most chickens are able to master these contingencies in short order; the loop pulling presents no problems and the chicken simply needs to peck the capsule off the slide to get its reinforcement.

However, 20% of all chickens do not succeed at being able to perform this set of contingencies. After they have pecked a few capsules off the slide, they begin to grab at the capsules and

BOX 11.1

drag them backward into the cage. Here they pound the capsules up and down on the floor. Of course, this results in no reinforcement for the chicken, and yet some chickens will pull in over half of all the capsules presented to them.

Almost always this problem behavior does not appear until after the capsules begin to move down the slide. Conditioning begins with stationary capsules placed by the experimenter.

When the pecking behavior becomes strong enough, so that the chicken is knocking them off the slide and getting reinforced consistently, the loop pulling is conditioned to the light. The capsules then come rolling down the slide to the chicken. At this point, most chickens will start grabbing and shaking, even if they did not have this tendency before.

(Breland & Breland, 1961, p. 682)

effects of the outcome on behavior—that is, what behavior systems (if any) might be activated by those outcomes.

Temporal Proximity

Temporal proximity occurs in operant conditioning when the outcome occurs soon after the target behavior. Although operant conditioning is influenced by temporal proximity between behavior and outcomes, proximity is neither a necessary nor a sufficient condition for the occurrence of operant conditioning.

Operant behaviors are influenced by the temporal proximity of the outcome to the target behavior. In general, operant conditioning occurs more rapidly when the outcome follows the target behavior with little delay. For example, Wilkenfield et al. (1992) magazine-trained rats and then placed them in an operant conditioning chamber for an 8-hour session. Different groups of rats experienced different delays between pressing the lever and the delivery of food (0, 4, 8, 16, and 32 seconds). When a lever press occurred during the delay interval, the delay clock was reset; thus food was never given sooner than the programmed delay for the last lever press. A sixth group (NO FOOD) never received food in that situation. The results of this experiment are presented in Figure 11.3. Each curve represents the performance of 9 rats. There is an inverse relationship between the length of the delay and the slopes of the group cumulative records at the start of the session; that is, the shorter the delay, the faster they learned. Most important, all animals in the 0-, 4-, 8-, and 16-second delay conditions, and 6 of the 9 animals in the 32-second delay condition pressed the bar consistently within 100 minutes of the start of the session. There was very little lever pressing in the NO FOOD group. Dickinson et al. (1992) reported similar results with rats, and Lattal and Gleeson (1990) with pigeons. This illustrates that temporal proximity is

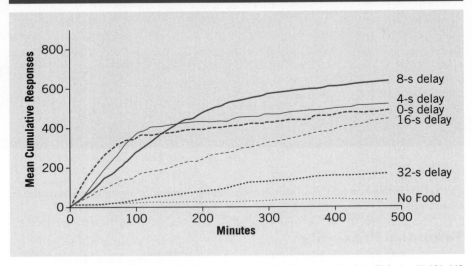

Figure 11.3 Cumulative records for groups of rats trained with different delays (0, 4, 8, 16, 32 seconds) between lever presses and food. The No Food group never received food for lever pressing. Each curve represents the performance of 9 rats.

From Wilkenfield, Nichel, Blakely, and Poling, 1992, *Journal of the Experimental Analysis of Behavior, 58*, 431–443. Copyright © 1992 by the Society for the Experimental Analysis of Behavior, Inc. Reprinted by permission of John Wiley and Sons.

not a necessary condition for the occurrence of operant conditioning. The examples of "misbehavior" described above also illustrate that temporal proximity is not a sufficient condition.

Temporal Precedence

Temporal precedence is inherent in the operant conditioning procedure because the behavior always occurs before the outcome. This means that temporal precedence is a necessary condition for the occurrence of operant conditioning.

An important *procedural* difference between operant conditioning and Pavlovian conditioning involves the scheduling of events. In Pavlovian conditioning, both the CS and US occur at the discretion and direction of the experimenter. In operant conditioning, the experimenter can determine when the outcome occurs, but he or she cannot directly determine when the subject will perform the target behavior; therefore, it is not possible to manipulate temporal precedence in operant conditioning as we can in Pavlovian conditioning. Furthermore, the investigation of temporal precedence is complicated by the fact that presenting the outcome independent of behavior can induce behaviors that have the same topography as operant and Pavlovian conditioned behaviors (see Chapter 8). Therefore, until we find evidence to the contrary, we assume that temporal precedence is a necessary condition for operant conditioning.

Reconciling the Data on the Effects of Temporal Proximity and Contingency on Causal Inference and Operant Conditioning

Despite the fact that temporal proximity and contingency are neither necessary nor sufficient conditions for the occurrence of operant conditioning, there is a striking similarity between how variations in temporal proximity and behavior-outcome contingencies affect operant conditioning in both animals and humans, and in human judgements of causality: As temporal proximity declines, operant behaviors take longer to learn, and judgements of causality become less certain. Likewise, reductions in behavior-outcome contingencies toward zero decrease rates of behavior and the certainty of causality judgements (see Dickinson & Shanks, 1985, 1995; Shanks, 1994; Shanks & Dickinson, 1987; Wasserman, 1990, for reviews).

THE REPRESENTATIONS OF KNOWLEDGE IN OPERANT CONDITIONING

Operant conditioning procedures teach individuals when and where they can perform certain behaviors to obtain good things and avoid bad things. As psychologists we are interested in how this knowledge is represented in memory.

Is the knowledge individuals obtain from experience with an operant conditioning procedure encoded as declarative knowledge or as procedural knowledge? The answer to that question is both: Individuals encode experience with an operant conditioning procedure as declarative knowledge about representations of the situation (discriminative stimulus), their behavior, and the outcome. However, under certain conditions, this knowledge can become reorganized as procedural knowledge involving representations of the situation and behavior. It took a long time for us to recognize this.

Contrasting Views of What Is Learned in Instrumental Learning and Operant Conditioning

Thorndike's Law of Effect characterizes knowledge gained from experience with instrumental learning and operant conditioning procedures in terms of stimulus-response (S-R) associations (procedural knowledge). The alternative view was championed by Tolman (1932), who argued that experience with instrumental learning and operant conditioning procedures is encoded as B-O associations (declarative knowledge).

Instrumental Learning and Operant Conditioning as Procedural Knowledge. Thorndike's Law of Effect depicts instrumental and operant conditioning as reflecting procedural knowledge: *Of several responses made to the same situation, those that are accompanied or closely followed by satisfaction to the animal will, other things being equal, be more firmly connected with the situation, so that when it* [the situation] *recurs, they* [the responses] *will be more likely to recur; those which are accompanied or closely followed by discomfort to the animal will, other things being equal, have their connections with that situation weakened, so that, when it* [the situation] *recurs, they* [the responses] *will be less likely to occur.* The greater the satisfaction or discomfort, the greater the strengthening or weakening of the bond [situation-response connection] (Thorndike, 1911, p. 244). In other words, the individual learns to perform a particular behavior in a given situation, and the outcome (the event that causes satisfaction) serves to strengthen the link between the stimulus situation and the response that occurs just prior to the presentation of the outcome. *This procedural knowledge is sometimes called* a **stimulus-response (S-R) association**. It is important to note that according to Thorndike, the outcome is **not** encoded here as part of what gets learned.

Skinner also described outcomes as strengthening behavior, but he did not conceptualize operant conditioning in terms of S-R associations. For Skinner, the stimulus is an occasion setter, not an elicitor of behavior as hypothesized by Thorndike in his Law of Effect (Skinner, 1935b, 1938). However, like Thorndike before him, Skinner did not include the outcome in what gets learned: Skinner argued that the outcome strengthens the behavior (response) that produced it. Whether the stimulus situation is viewed as an occasion setter (Skinner) or as part of an S-R association (Thorndike), in both cases, the knowledge obtained would be classified as procedural knowledge: *In this situation, perform that behavior*. For most of the twentieth century, this conceptualization of instrumental learning and operant conditioning as procedural knowledge was the dominant one. In addition to Thorndike and Skinner, Guthrie (1935, 1942) and Hull (1943, 1952) presented theories of learning that characterized instrumental learning and operant conditioning as procedural knowledge.

Instrumental Learning and Operant Conditioning as Declarative Knowledge. The alternative view is that knowledge obtained from experience with an instrumental learning or operant conditioning procedure is encoded as declarative knowledge that includes the outcome as part of the knowledge structure (Bolles, 1972; Mackintosh & Dickinson, 1979; Konorski, 1967; Tolman, 1932).

Edward Chase Tolman (1886–1959) was the intellectual grandfather of the view that experience with the instrumental learning and operant conditioning procedures is encoded as declarative knowledge. As early as 1920, Tolman argued that individuals' behaviors are goal-directed; that is, hungry individuals do things to obtain food and thirsty individuals do things to obtain water, and so on. Tolman's position was that through interactions with their environment, individuals acquire knowledge of "what leads to what," that is, declarative knowledge about the experienced relationships between events (Tolman, 1932). Some of this knowledge is about predictors of important events (CS-US associations), and some is knowledge of what to do in certain situations to obtain outcomes or escape from or avoid danger: *in this situation, performing that behavior will produce a certain outcome*. Konorski

(1967) suggested that this knowledge is encoded as an *association between representations of the behavior and the outcome* (a behavior-outcome [B-O] association). The *representation of the stimulus situation serves as the occasion setter informing the individual that the outcome will follow a certain behavior in that situation* (S→[B-O] association).

Evidence That Operant Conditioning Involves Declarative Knowledge About Representations of Behaviors and Outcomes

If experience with operant conditioning procedures is encoded as procedural representations (S-R associations), then post-conditioning devaluation of the outcome should have no effect on the behavior that originally produced that outcome. On the other hand, if experience with operant conditioning procedures is encoded as declarative knowledge (B-O associations), then post-conditioning devaluation of that outcome should affect the behavior that originally produced it.

In Chapter 5, we examined the use of post-conditioning devaluation of the US to test whether knowledge obtained from experience with Pavlovian conditioning procedures is encoded as declarative knowledge or procedural knowledge. The logic of those experiments was as follows: If experience is encoded as procedural knowledge, then changing the value of the US by making it unattractive (e.g., following the eating of food with lithium chloride [LiCl]–induced illness) should have *no* effect on the CR because procedural knowledge involves representations of the CS and CR, not the US. But if experience is encoded as declarative knowledge, devaluation of the food *should* influence the CR because declarative knowledge involves representations of the CS and US. The same logic can be applied to determine how knowledge is encoded in operant conditioning (Rozeboom, 1958).

How post-conditioning devaluation can be used to differentiate procedural from declarative representations in operant conditioning is presented in Table 11.2. In the first phase of the experiment (operant conditioning), individuals learn to perform a behavior for food. The two types of representations of knowledge from operant conditioning are described in the table. In the second phase of the experiment (post-conditioning devaluation), the subjects are made ill after eating the food. This is the standard Pavlovian conditioning procedure for producing conditioned taste aversions (CTAs) and should be carried out so that the subjects associate illness with the food, not the operant behavior they learned in the first phase of the experiment. The test occurs when the subjects are given the opportunity to perform the operant behavior. If individuals form procedural (S-R) representations of operant conditioning experiences, post-conditioning devaluation should have no effect on performance of the operant behavior because the food (the outcome, O) is not part of that representation. On the other hand, post-conditioning devaluation should reduce performance of the operant behavior if operant conditioning experiences are encoded as declarative (B-O) representations because the individual combines the two declarative associations learned in each phase of the

Table 11.2 Procedural and Declarative Representations in Operant Conditioning

Phase of Experiment	Procedural Representations	Declarative Representations
Behavior ➡ food (operant conditioning)	"In this situation, perform that behavior."	"In this situation, performing that behavior produces food."
Food ➡ illness (post-conditioning devaluation)	"Do not eat this food."	"This food causes illness."
Test	"In this situation, perform that behavior."	"In this situation, performing that behavior produces a food that causes illness."

experiment through transitive inference: "in this situation, performing that behavior produces a food that causes illness."

Colwill and Rescorla (1985) conducted such an experiment in rats (see Table 11.3). In the first phase of their experiment, rats were trained to press a lever and pull a chain for different outcomes. For half the rats, lever pressing was followed by food pellets and chain pulling by a drop of sucrose solution. For the other half, the outcomes for the two behaviors were reversed. Both the food pellets and the sucrose solution were delivered on identical VI 60-second schedules to the same food cup, and the two different behaviors were trained on different days. After the rats had learned to produce both behaviors to receive the designated outcome, they were divided into two groups. For one group, the chain and lever were not available and the animals received food pellets without having to do anything. After the rats consumed all of the pellets, they were given injections of LiCl. On the next day, they received the sucrose solution but were not made ill. This cycle was repeated five times. By that point, they would not eat any of the pellets, but they would drink the sucrose. For the other group, drinking the sucrose solution was followed by injections of LiCl and eating the pellets was not. Colwill and Rescorla took care to present these two outcomes during this second phase of the experiment the same way they were presented in Phase 1 (in same chamber and at times that matched their delivery during conditioning, but without the chain and lever present). The test involved allowing the rats access to the lever and chain, but neither lever pressing nor chain pulling produced any outcomes (i.e., the test was conducted in extinction). The question is, which behavior would the rats perform more of in extinction, the one that produced an outcome that was devalued after the original operant conditioning or the behavior that produced an outcome that remained safe?

The results of this experiment are quite clear (see Figure 11.4). When given the opportunity to perform both behaviors, the rats performed *less* of the behavior that was trained with the now-devalued outcome. Because the test was conducted in extinction, the animals had no opportunity to experience the now-devalued outcome with

Table 11.3   The Design of the Colwill and Rescorla (1985) Experiment

Phase 1 (Different days)	Phase 2 (Different days)	Test (Same session)
$B_1 \rightarrow O_1$ $B_2 \rightarrow O_2$	$O_1 \rightarrow$ illness $O_2 \rightarrow$ no illness	B_1 vs. B_2

Note: B_1 and B_2 were lever pressing and chain pulling.
O_1 and O_2 were food pellets and sucrose pellets.

the behavior that originally produced it before devaluation. These results are what one would expect to see if individuals encode their experiences with operant conditioning procedures as declarative knowledge between the behavior and outcome (see Table 11.2). Adams (1980) and Adams and Dickinson (1981) found similar results using outcome devaluation based on CTAs, but Colwill and Rescorla's (1985) experiment provides a stronger test.

Figure 11.4   Data from Colwill and Rescorla's experiment on post-conditioning devaluation of the outcome. Mean number of responses per minute during the extinction test shown separately for responses that had been reinforced in Phase 1 by sucrose (left panel) and pellets (right panel). The solid circles are for responses that in Phase 1 produced an outcome that was devalued in Phase 2. The open circles are for the outcome not devalued.

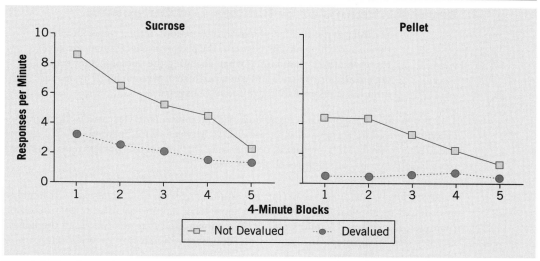

From Colwill and Rescorla, 1985. Post-conditioning devaluation of an outcome affects instrumental responding. *Journal of Experimental Psychology: Animal Behavior Processes, 11*, 120–132. Copyright © 1985 by the American Psychological Association. Redrawn with permission.

In a second experiment reported in the same paper, Colwill and Rescorla (1985) used satiation to devalue an outcome. Hungry rats were trained to press a lever and pull a chain, each for a different outcome (food pellets or sucrose pellets) as in the first experiment (see Table 11.3, Phase 1). After 10 days of training, half the rats were given free access to the food pellets and the other half to the sucrose pellets. Then they were placed in the operant chamber with both the lever and chain available. Satiating the animals with one outcome (sucrose or food pellets) had more of an effect on the behavior that produced that outcome in Phase 1. In another paper, Colwill and Rescorla (1986) reported a similar selective depression effect when they provided one of the outcomes on a zero contingency during testing. Here again, rats were trained to press a lever and pull a chain, each for a different outcome (food pellets or sucrose pellets) as in the first experiment (see Table 11.3, Phase 1). During the test, each behavior continued to produce its corresponding outcome on a partial reinforcement schedule; however, one of the outcomes was also given with the same probability in the absence of the behavior (i.e., on a zero contingency). The other outcome was only given for performing the required activity. Colwill and Rescorla reported that the zero contingency during the test had a greater effect of the behavior associated with that outcome.

All of these experiments involved devaluing an outcome in one way or another (through CTAs, satiation, or noncontingent reinforcement). In each case, the effects of the devaluation were selective; that is, the behavior that produced the now-devalued outcome was more affected by the devaluation. Colwill and Rescorla performed other experiments designed to distinguish between encoding operant conditioning as procedural or declarative knowledge. *In all cases, the data were consistent with the conclusion that experience with operant conditioning is encoded as declarative knowledge involving representations of behaviors and outcomes (B-O associations;* see Colwill, 1994; Colwill & Rescorla, 1986; Rescorla, 1987, for reviews of these experiments). These data provide a striking parallel to what is observed in Pavlovian conditioning.

Representations of Behaviors and Outcomes

We infer that individuals have representations of their behavior when they can recall what they just did. We also infer that individuals have representations of outcomes when changing the outcome after training affects performance and when performance is enhanced by having different outcomes follow different behaviors.

It is one thing to suggest that experience with an instrumental learning or operant conditioning procedure is encoded as an association between representations of the behavior and the outcome, but it is another to demonstrate that individuals possess representations of their behavior and outcomes of those behaviors.

Evidence That Individuals Form Representations of Their Own Behavior. Presumably, in order to recall what you just did, you must have a representation of that behavior. Beninger, Kendall, and Vanderwolf (1974) demonstrated that rats can recall the behavior they just performed. To demonstrate this, they trained rats to press one of four levers when a buzzer sounded in order to receive a small amount of sweetened milk. Which lever was correct depended on the behavior the animal was performing when the buzzer sounded: If the rats were immobile when the buzzer sounded, presses on lever 1 produced milk; if they were walking around when the buzzer sounded, pressing lever 2 produced milk, if they were face-washing when the buzzer sounded, pressing lever 3 produced milk, and if they were rearing when the buzzer sounded, pressing lever 4 produced milk. These four behaviors were selected because they all occur quite frequently. It is important to note that milk was not given for performing these four behaviors; it was given for pressing the lever assigned to each behavior—that is, for reporting what they were doing when the buzzer sounded. For all four behaviors, the rats selected the correct lever more than one would expect from chance alone. Morgan and Nicholas (1979) found similar results. These results suggest that individuals possess representations of just-completed behaviors.

Representations of Outcomes. If individuals learn B-O associations, they must also have a representation of the physical attributes that distinguish one outcome from another and whether that outcome is good or bad (its hedonic value; Konorski, 1967; Trapold, 1970; Trapold & Overmier, 1972). The evidence of this comes from two kinds of experiments. In the first kind of experiment, the outcome is changed after conditioning and subsequent changes in performance are observed. The consistent finding is that changing the outcome after conditioning affects the performance of the conditioned behavior. For example, when Elliot (1928) substituted sunflower seed for bran mash after 10 days of training to run through a maze for the latter outcome, his rats' performance deteriorated, even though sunflower seeds was an adequate outcome for the control group (see Chapter 7), and when Crespi (1942) increased or decreased the number of pellets, his rats showed striking changes in running speeds (see Chapter 8). When Tinklepaugh (1928) substituted lettuce for banana, his monkeys rejected the lettuce and searched for the banana, even though lettuce can be an adequate outcome for monkeys (see Chapter 7). The simplest interpretation of these data is that the original instrumental or operant training taught the animals to expect certain outcomes after running through the maze or pressing the lever.

There are a number of more recent demonstrations that rats can encode the sensory aspects of outcomes. Using the basic procedure he and Colwill used to demonstrate that experience with operant conditioning is encoded as declarative knowledge (see Table 11.3 above), Rescorla (1990) trained rats to press a lever and pull a chain for water. For one of these behaviors, the water used as an outcome was given a slightly bitter taste by adding a small amount of quinine, and for the other behavior, the water was made slightly sour by adding a small amount of acid. Thus both behaviors produced water, but each produced a different tasting water. After this training, the rats were allowed to consume one of the flavored waters and then given an injection of LiCl to induce a CTA. In testing (which occurred in extinction), both the lever and chain were available. The dependent measure was how often the rats performed each behavior in extinction. The rats performed *less* of the behavior that in the original operant conditioning training had produced the taste paired with LiCl in Phase 2 of the experiment.

Balleine and Dickinson (1998) reported similar results using satiation as the method of devaluation with different tasting foods. Each food was given a distinctive taste by the addition of salt or lemon. When they satiated their rats with one of the distinctively tasting foods prior to the choice test in extinction, their rats performed *less* of the behavior that in the original operant conditioning produced the distinctively tasting food with which they were satiated during testing. This result is quite interesting because the satiation of one food should have made them less hungry for any food and reduced all operant behaviors that produced food, but the effect of the satiation was selective.

Rescorla (1990) also reported that enhancing (rather than devaluing) one of the flavored waters by pairing it with sucrose during Phase 2 also affected performance during the choice extinction test. This time the rats performed *more* of the behavior that in the original operant conditioning had produced the flavor paired with sucrose in Phase 2. All of these data illustrate that individuals capable of operant conditioning are capable of encoding both the sensory and hedonic aspects of outcomes.

The second type of evidence comes from experiments in which subjects are taught to perform different behaviors in the presence of different stimuli. Performance on this task is *enhanced* when each behavior is followed by a qualitatively *different* outcome. For example, Trapold (1970) trained rats to press the right lever in the presence of a tone and press the left lever in the presence of a clicker. Both behaviors were trained with positive contingencies to receive outcomes. For subjects in the experimental group, the outcomes for correct lever presses were different (food pellet or liquid sucrose), and for subjects in the control groups, the outcomes were the same. For half of the experimental subjects, correct presses in the presence of the tone were reinforced by a food pellet, and correct lever presses in the presence of the clicker by liquid sucrose. For the other experimental subjects, correct presses in the presence of the tone were reinforced by sucrose, and correct lever presses in the presence of the clicker by a pellet of food. For the control subjects, correct lever presses in the presence of both the tone and clicker were reinforced by the same outcome (food for half of them and sucrose for the other half). The experimental group performed better than the control group.

This "differential outcomes effect" has been replicated many times in both rats and pigeons (e.g., Brodigan & Peterson, 1976; Peterson, Wheeler, & Armstrong, 1978). Linwick, Overmier, Peterson, and Mertins (1988) found that pigeons performed poorly on a memory task with a 4-second peck-outcome delay when the same outcome followed correct responses but performed very well when different outcomes were tied to different correct behaviors, and Williams, Butler, and Overmier (1990) reported that the performance of pigeons in these types of tasks was also facilitated when the locations of the outcomes were also tied to the different correct choices. Williams et al. concluded that individuals not only know where to collect the outcomes, they also know what they will find when they get there.

Learning the Incentive Value of Outcomes

The performance of operant behaviors is mediated by both a representation of the behavior-outcome relationship and a representation of the current incentive value of the outcome. Individuals come to most operant conditioning situations with knowledge of the value of the outcome for them, but how do they obtain this knowledge? It appears that they must learn it.

The preceding discussion points to the conclusion that individuals in operant conditioning situations have representations of their own behaviors and of the outcomes they are working to obtain, but how do they know, for example, that some things are edible and have nutritive value? How do they know that food will satisfy their hunger and water their thirst? Although we might assume that this knowledge is innate because infant rats and humans have preferences for sweet tasting substances immediately after birth and before there is time for them to experience any post-ingestive effects (Jacobs, 1964; Lipsitt et al., 1976), we also know that through Pavlovian conditioning individuals come to prefer foods that provide nutritional benefits (Sclafani, 1990) and avoid foods that have toxic effects (Garcia & Koelling, 1966). Similarly, Hogan (1973) demonstrated that baby chicks learn to recognize food.

Tolman (1949a, 1949b) argued that the performance of instrumental and operant behaviors is mediated by both a representation of the behavior-outcome relationship and the representation of the current value of the outcome for that individual, and both of these representations are acquired through experience. Thus, hungry individuals must learn that food will satisfy their hunger and what to do to get food, and thirsty individuals must learn that certain fluids will quench their thirst and what they need to do to obtain those fluids. According to Tolman, *individuals obtain knowledge about the incentive values of foods, fluids, and other things by consuming them and experiencing the aftereffects of these things. If the aftereffects of consumption are experienced as positive, then the consumed object gains positive value, and if the effects are experienced as negative then the consumed object gains negative value.* Furthermore, the incentive value that accrues will depend on the individual's state at the time of the consumption. Thus, food develops positive incentive value when individuals are deprived of food (and presumably hungry) because food reduces hunger, and water develops positive incentive value when individuals are deprived of water (and presumably thirsty). Dickinson and Balleine (1994) called this incentive learning.

Dickinson and Balleine (1994, 1995) noted that after individuals learn what things satisfy their hunger and thirst, the *current* incentive value of these things depends on the individual's *current* motivational state. Thus, the incentive value of food is much less when individuals are sated than when they are hungry; that is, individuals will work harder to obtain food when they are deprived of it for a period of time. The same applies to fluids. Fluids have higher incentive value for thirsty individuals than they do for sated individuals. Dickinson and Balleine (1994) described examples of incentive learning in other behavior systems such as thermoregulation and sex. As noted in Chapter 7, deprivation and satiation are establishing operations for the reinforcing values of things; that is, they *produce changes in the internal or external environment that alter the effectiveness of things to serve as outcomes.*

Balleine and his colleagues (e.g., Balleine, 1992; Dickinson, Balleine, Watt, Gonzalez, & Boakes, 1995) have demonstrated how the incentive value of outcomes under different motivational states is learned. The basic design of their experiments is presented in Table 11.4. In Phase 1, rats were trained to press a lever (B) to obtain food pellets (O) under a high level of deprivation. Following this experience, the animals were divided into four groups for Phase 2. Two of these groups (High/Low and High/High) were taken out of the training situation and given free access to the same food pellets under the same conditions of deprivation as in training (i.e., high level of deprivation) while the other two groups

(Low/Low and Low/High) were given free access to the food pellets under low levels of deprivation (i.e., not deprived). After this experience, all rats were tested by returning them in the training situation and allowing them to press the lever, but no food was given (i.e., the test was in extinction). Half of the animals were tested this way under high levels of deprivation and half under low levels of deprivation. The dependent measure was how often they would press the lever in extinction.

Table 11.4   The Design of the Dickinson, Balleine, Watt, Gonzalez and Boakes (1995) Experiment

Group	Phase 1	Phase 2	Test
Low/Low	High deprivation: B ➡ O	Low deprivation: O	Low deprivation: B
High/Low	High deprivation: B ➡ O	High deprivation: O	Low deprivation: B
Low/High	High deprivation: B ➡ O	Low deprivation: O	High deprivation: B
High/High	High deprivation: B ➡ O	High deprivation: O	High deprivation: B

Note: B and O were lever pressing and food pellets.

One would expect that the rats tested under high levels of deprivation would press the lever a lot because they were hungry, and the rats tested under low levels of deprivation would not press the lever much because they were not hungry, but that was not entirely the case (see Figure 11.5). Only the rats in Group Low/Low did not press the lever much during the test. Rats in the other three groups (Groups High/Low, Low/High, and High/High) all performed about the same in extinction. The surprising result is Group High/Low. Why did the low level of deprivation in the test *not* affect their performance like it did for the rats in Group Low/Low? The answer given by Balleine and his colleagues is that the rats in Group Low/Low had an opportunity to learn during the reexposure phase (Phase 2) of the experiment that these food pellets have less value to them when they are not deprived of food. The rats in group High/Low did not have an opportunity to learn this. Of course, rats in Group Low/High also learned that the food pellets have less value when not deprived, but this did not affect their test performance because they were tested while hungry, and they had learned during the original lever pressing training that the pellets were valuable to them when they are hungry. These data illustrate that individuals learn that food is valuable when they are hungry and is less valuable when they are not hungry. The same is true for other outcomes.

THE ROLE OF THE STIMULUS IN OPERANT CONDITIONING

In operant conditioning, the stimulus (including the context) in the presence of which a certain behavior reliably leads to a certain outcome

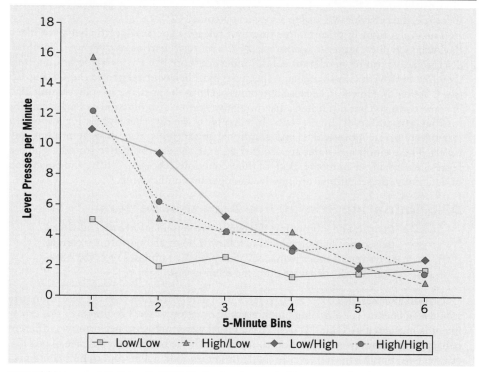

Figure 11.5   Mean lever presses per minute during extinction test for rats tested either under high levels of deprivation (Groups Low/High and High/High) or under low levels of deprivation (Groups Low/Low and High/Low). Rats in Groups High/Low and High/High obtained free pellets under high levels of deprivation after conditioning (during reexposure), and rats in Groups Low/Low and Low/High obtained free pellets under low levels of deprivation after conditioning (during reexposure).

From Dickinson, A., & Balleine, B. (1995). Motivational control of instrumental action. *Current Directions in Psychological Science, 4,* 162–167. Reprinted with permission from Sage Publications, Inc.

is called a discriminative stimulus. Discriminative stimuli serve two functions: as occasion setters (i.e., they inform the individual when and where a behavior will be effective in producing an outcome) and as Pavlovian predictors of significant events.

Operant conditioning, like Pavlovian conditioning, does not occur in a vacuum. Food, water, mates, and predators are more likely to be found in some situations and not others, and behaviors for producing or reducing those things may be effective in some situations and not in others. In operant conditioning, *an event that signals that a specific behavior will produce a certain outcome* is called a **discriminative stimulus**. Discriminative stimuli can be anything the individual is capable of detecting: sound, color, shape, object, facial expression, and so on. They can be localized like a small colored object or global like the color of the entire room. What makes them discriminative stimuli is that they indicate when certain behaviors will obtain certain outcomes. For example, we all have learned that usually one can safely cross the street when the traffic light is green, or the pedestrian control signal indicates "WALK," or when there are no cars in sight. Each of these events (green light, WALK, and the absence of cars) are discriminative stimuli that inform you that crossing the street leads to the outcome of safely getting to the other side. You can probably think of many things you do where the occurrence of some event (like the green light) tells you that a specific behavior will lead to a specific outcome.

The green light in this example does not release a species-specific behavior like a Pavlovian CS does; rather it *informs you about a behavior-outcome relationship*. Therefore, discriminative stimuli in operant conditioning are more like Pavlovian occasion setters than like Pavlovian CSs that elicit a species-typical behavior related to the CS and US (see Chapter 6). However, because outcomes occur in the presence of some stimuli (and in some contexts) but not others, discriminative stimuli also function as Pavlovian CSs for the anticipation of these events. In Chapter 6, we saw that signals for important events can arouse motivational and emotional states (hope, fear, disappointment, and relief). These emotional states are aroused because the discriminative stimulus elicits a representation of the outcome. Both of these functions (occasion setting and elicitation of outcome representations) are involved in operant conditioning.

Discriminative Stimuli Are Occasion Setters

> In operant conditioning, discriminative stimuli inform the individual that a specific outcome may follow if he or she performs a certain behavior. In other words, the discriminative stimulus "sets the occasion" for the behavior-outcome relationship.

Colwill and Rescorla (1990) provided a nice demonstration that the discriminative stimulus in operant conditioning functions as an occasion setter. The design of this experiment is presented in Table 11.5. In Phase 1, rats were trained to perform two different behaviors to obtain two different outcomes. For half the rats, in the presence of one discriminative stimulus (noise) lever pressing produced food pellets and chain pulling produced sucrose solution, but in the presence of a second discriminative stimulus (light) the

Table 11.5 The Design of the Colwill and Rescorla (1990) Experiment

Phase 1 (same sessions)	Phase 2 (different days)	Test (same session)
NOISE: $B_1 \rightarrow O_1$ and $B_2 \rightarrow O_2$	$O_1 \rightarrow$ no illness	NOISE: B_1 vs. B_2
LIGHT: $B_1 \rightarrow O_2$ and $B_2 \rightarrow O_1$	$O_2 \rightarrow$ illness	LIGHT: B_1 vs. B_2

Note: B_1 and B_2 were lever pressing and chain pulling.
O_1 and O_2 were food pellets and sucrose solution.

behavior-outcome relationships were reversed; that is, lever pressing produced sucrose solution and chain pulling produced food pellets. For the other rats, lever pressing produced sucrose solution and chain pulling produced food pellets in the presence of the noise and the opposite in the presence of the light. Following this training, the rats were divided into two groups (Phase 2). In the absence of the chain and lever, one group was injected with LiCl after they drank sucrose and the other group was injected with LiCl after they ate food pellets. After recovery from the LiCl-induced illness, both groups were allowed to eat the other food without being made sick. The noise and light were presented at various times during the test (which occurred in extinction with the lever and chain simultaneously available). The dependent measure was how often these rats would press the lever and pull the chain in the presence of the noise and light. Specifically, would they perform less of the behavior that in Phase 1 produced the now devalued outcome? The results of this experiment are presented in Figure 11.6. The effects of the devaluation of an outcome on the behavior that produced it depended on the stimulus in the presence of which that behavior produced the now-devalued outcome. These data

Figure 11.6 Mean number of responses per minute during the extinction test for the two behaviors (B_1 and B_2) in the presence of the two discriminative stimuli (NOISE and LIGHT). In initial training (Phase 1), the now-devalued outcome (O_2) reinforced B2 during NOISE and B1 during LIGHT.

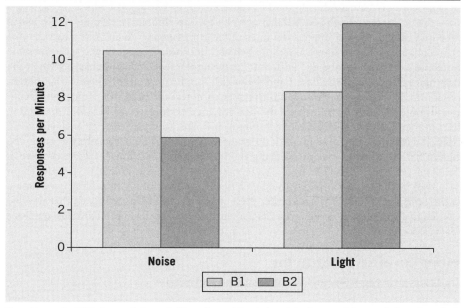

From Rescorla, 1991, *Quarterly Journal of Experimental Psychology B*. Redrawn with permission of Psychology Press Ltd.

are strong evidence that the discriminative stimulus in operant conditioning functions as an occasion setter informing the individual that performance of a certain behavior leads to a specific outcome.

Discriminative Stimuli Can Elicit Representations of Outcomes

Because outcomes must occur in some context, or in the presence of some stimulus, these things can elicit representations of the outcomes.

Colwill and Rescorla (1988) and Rescorla (1994) showed that rats can form an association between the discriminative stimulus and the outcomes in operant conditioning and that this S-O association influences operant behavior. The design of their experiment is presented in Table 11.6. In Phase 1, all rats were trained to perform the same behavior (poking their nose into a circular hole in the wall of the chamber) in the presence of two different discriminative stimuli (a light and a noise) to obtain two different outcomes (pellets and sucrose solution). Each discriminative stimulus signaled that a specific outcome could be obtained for nose poking. In the second phase of the experiment, the rats were trained to perform two new behaviors, lever pressing and chain pulling, each uniquely tied to the two outcomes from Phase 1, but neither the light nor the noise were present in Phase 2. In the test (performed in extinction), the light and noise were occasionally presented. The rates for behavior in the presence of the light, the noise, and when neither was present (the intertrial interval or ITI) were recorded. These data are presented in Figure 11.7.

The rates of behavior during the ITI represent a baseline against which we can compare the performance of these behaviors when the discriminative stimuli were present. The line labeled "Same" depicts the rates of lever presses and chain pulls when the discriminative stimulus in Phase 1 and the behavior in Phase 2 were trained with the same outcome, and the line labeled "Different" depicts the rates of these behaviors when the discriminative stimulus in Phase 1 and the behavior in Phase 2 were trained with different outcomes. It is clear that throughout the extinction test the presence of the discriminative stimulus selectively influenced the performance of the operant behavior depending on whether both the discriminative stimulus in Phase 1 and the operant behavior were trained with the same outcome or a different outcome: When they were the same, the rate of behavior was higher than during the ITI. When they were different, the rate of behavior was equal to the ITI level. What connects a given discriminative stimulus (light or noise) in Phase 1 to a specific behavior (lever pressing or chain pulling) in Phase 2 is the outcome (O_1 or O_2). Therefore, these data provide strong evidence that the discriminative stimulus elicits a representation of the outcome through a stimulus-outcome (S-O) association.

How Operant Behavior Is Generated From Representations

Any explanation of operant conditioning must be able to explain how the individual translates the knowledge he or she obtains into performance. The data suggest that discriminative stimuli can elicit representations of outcomes, and this activates the behavior that produced that outcome in the past.

Table 11.6 The Design of the Colwill and Rescorla (1988) Experiment		
Phase 1	**Phase 2**	**Test**
LIGHT: $B_{NP} \rightarrow O_1$ NOISE: $B_{NP} \rightarrow O_2$	$B_1 \rightarrow O_1$ and $B_2 \rightarrow O_2$	LIGHT: B_1 vs. B_2 NOISE: B_1 vs. B_2

Note: B_{NP}, B_1 and B_2 were nose poke, lever pressing and chain pulling.
O_1 and O_2 were food pellets and sucrose solution.

Figure 11.7 Mean number of responses per minute during the extinction test when the discriminative stimulus signaled the same outcome as was trained with the behavior (filled circles), when the discriminative stimulus signaled a different outcome than was trained with the behavior (open circles), and rates of performance of these behaviors during the ITI (*s) when the discriminative stimuli where absent.

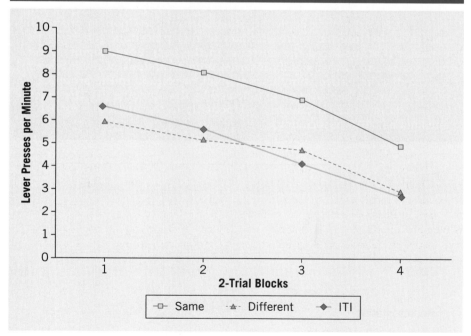

From Colwill and Rescorla, 1988. Associations between the discriminative stimulus and the outcome in instrumental learning. *Journal of Experimental Psychology: Animal Behavior Processes,* 14, 155–164. Copyright © 1988 by the American Psychological Association. Redrawn with permission.

It is clear from the above discussion that experience with operant conditioning procedures is encoded as an association between representations of the successful behavior and the outcome (B-O association). The stimulus situation or context (discriminative stimulus) in the presence of which that behavior is successful in obtaining the outcome appears to be encoded as a predictor of that outcome in a discriminative stimulus-outcome association (S-O association), and that discriminative stimulus serves as an occasion setter informing the individual that if he or she performs a certain behavior, a specific outcome may follow. But how does this knowledge translate into performance?

Rescorla (1994) argued that the best explanation for how individuals employ this knowledge was first offered by Pavlov (1932) and later expanded by Asratyan (1974): After experience with a discriminative stimulus-[behavior-outcome] relationship, subsequent presentation of the discriminative stimulus elicits a representation of the outcome. Using this representation, the individual recalls the behaviors that produced this outcome (through the B-O association) and then performs a previously successful behavior. That is, *the discriminative stimulus informs the individual that this is a place where something of value had been found in the past, and that in the past performing some behavior produced that something.* The observed behaviors reflect the individual's *expectations* about the outcome in this situation. Figure 11.8 depicts the procedure of operant conditioning (discriminative stimulus-[behavior-outcome]) and how experience with that procedure is represented in memory. The discriminative stimulus (or the context)

Figure 11.8 Schematic depiction of an operant conditioning procedure and how the internal representation of this procedure generates the behavior that produced the outcome in the past. Boxes signify external events and circles signify internal representations of these events. S = the discriminative stimulus, situation, or context in the presence of which a certain behavior (B) is followed by the outcome (O). The brackets surround behavior-outcome relationship in the procedure (which is encoded as a B-O association).

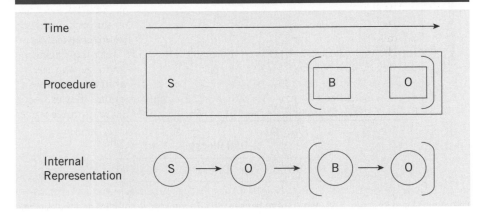

elicits the representation of the outcome that in turn elicits the representation of the behavior that produced that outcome in the past (as part of the B-O association). These representations generate the operant behavior.

Refer back to Table 11.6 and Figure 11.7 to see how this works. In that experiment, the rate of occurrence of the operant behavior was enhanced over the ITI level when a discriminative stimulus in Phase 1 was trained with the same outcome (O) as the behavior in Phase 2. The link between the discriminative stimulus in Phase 1 and the behavior in Phase 2 was the outcome common to both. Thus, in the test, the presentation of that discriminative stimulus evoked the representation of the outcome that, in turn, evoked the representation of that behavior and the B-O association.

OPERANT BEHAVIOR AS PROCEDURAL KNOWLEDGE

Operant behavior is first encoded as declarative knowledge, but under certain conditions this knowledge can become reorganized as procedural knowledge. This reorganization tends to occur after extended experience with an unchanging contingency and when wide variations in performance produce the same outcome. In both cases, there is little effect of devaluing the outcome on performance of the target behavior.

Although the experiments employing post-conditioning devaluation of the outcome point to the conclusion that experiences with operant conditioning procedures are encoded as declarative knowledge about the relationships among the various aspects of the operant procedure (i.e., the discriminative stimulus, behavior, and outcome), we all have had the experience of performing some behavior "automatically." For example, have you ever started out to get or do something and suddenly found yourself in the wrong place or doing something different than you intended to do? Norman (1981) calls these "action slips." Such action slips appear to be triggered by stimuli and contexts in which the behavior had occurred repeatedly in the past. Tolman (1932) called behaviors that through repetition become mechanical "fixations," and Dickinson (1985, 1989) used the term *behavioral autonomy* to refer to behaviors that become separated from their original outcome. Dickinson (1985) argued that behavioral autonomy occurs when the individual no longer experiences a correlation between variations in his or her behavior and variations in the outcomes of that behavior. He identified two situations where that is likely to occur: after extended training with an unchanging contingency and when wide variations in performance lead to the same outcome.

Extended Experience Can Become Encoded as Procedural Knowledge. It is not surprising that extended practice can lead to behaviors becoming habitual (see Kimble & Perlmuter, 1970, for a review). As we saw in Chapter 8, one of the effects of reinforcement on behavior is a reduction in behavioral variability and an increase in behavioral stereotypy. Adams (1982) presented evidence that extended training with an operant conditioning procedure can result in the reorganization of knowledge from declarative to procedural knowledge. The design of this experiment is outlined in Table 11.7. Adams trained two groups of rats to lever press to receive sucrose pellets. This training lasted until they had received 100 pellets. Following this training, one group (100D) was allowed to eat the pellets and then received an injection of LiCl; the other group (100N) ate the pellets but received their injection of LiCl 24 hours later. After the rats recovered from the effects of the LiCl, they were placed back in the operant chamber and allowed access to the lever (in extinction). As you might expect, the group that ate the pellets and then received the injection of LiCl immediately afterward (Group 100D) pressed the lever less than the other group (100N). Clearly, the effects of this devaluation procedure on the rats in Group 100D indicates they encoded their experience as declarative knowledge about the relationship between lever pressing and sucrose pellets. Adams also ran two additional groups of rats until they obtained 500 pellets before giving each of them one of the experiences with LiCl described above. There was *no* effect of the devaluation procedure on the rats with the extended training. The results for all four groups are presented in the left panel of Figure 11.9.

The data presented in the right panel of Figure 11.9 illustrates that the devaluation of the pellets was effective for the rats given extended training even though it did not affect their performance on the extinction test (left panel). On the day after the extinction test, all rats were placed back in the operant chamber, but this time each lever press produced a sucrose pellet. The first 5 minutes of this "reacquisition" looks like the results of the extinction test, but by the second 5 minutes, both groups given the devaluation treatment ceased pressing the lever. The other two groups exhibited increases in lever pressing (as you might expect). The fact that the now-devalued pellets could not sustain lever pressing when presented as contingent outcomes indicates that the devaluation treatment worked.

In another experiment reported in the same paper, Adams (1982) found that the effects of extended training were due to the number of earned outcomes *not* the number of lever presses performed. In addition to the four groups in his first experiment, Adams added two

Group	Phase 1	Phase 2	Test 1	Test 2
100N	100 B → O	O → no illness	B	B → O
100D	100 B → O	O → illness	B	B → O
500N	500 B → O	O → no illness	B	B → O
500D	500 B → O	O → illness	B	B → O

Table 11.7   The Design of the Adams (1982) Experiment

Note: B and O were lever pressing and sucrose pellets.

more groups that first received 50 sucrose pellets on continuous reinforcement (CRF) and then 50 more on a variable ratio (VR 9) schedule. Thus, both groups of rats earned 100 outcomes but performed 500 lever presses to earn them. After giving one of these groups post-conditioning devaluation training and the other the pellets and LiCl on separate days, Adams tested both groups in extinction and for reacquisition with the sucrose pellets. The performance of these groups was more similar to the groups given 100 CRF outcomes than the groups given 500 CRF outcomes (see Figure 11.9 above). Thus, *the transition from declarative to procedural knowledge appears to depend on how many behaviors are reinforced, not the amount of behavior that occurs in that situation.*

Molar Feedback and Procedural Knowledge. The second variable that seems to influence whether experience with an operant conditioning procedure will be reorganized

Figure 11.9 Mean rates of lever pressing during the extinction test (left panel) and during reacquisition of lever pressing following extinction (right panel). Half the subjects earned 100 sucrose pellets on a continuous reinforcement schedule and the other half earned 500 pellets. Within each of these groups, half the subjects subsequently consumed pellets followed by injections of LiCl (Devalued) and the other half consumed the pellets on one day and received the LiCl on another day (not devalued).

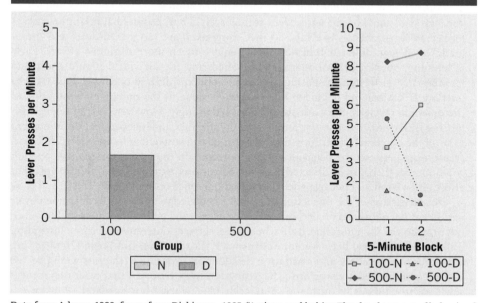

Data from Adams, 1982; figure from Dickinson, 1985, "Actions and habits: The development of behavioral autonomy." *Philosophical Transactions of the Royal Society (London), B308*, 67–78. Redrawn with permission of the Royal Society.

as procedural knowledge depends on the correlation between variations in behavior and outcomes. This correlation depends in part on the molar feedback functions for the prevailing schedules of reinforcement (see Chapter 9, Figure 9.1): On a ratio schedule where one must perform the target behavior a certain number of times to obtain the outcome, the more times you perform that behavior, the more outcomes you earn. On the other hand, on an interval schedule where outcomes are earned for the first instance of the target behavior after the interval has elapsed, wide variations in rates of performance produce the same number of outcomes per unit time. Thus, there is a stronger correlation between rates of behavior and rates of reinforcement on ratio schedules than on interval schedules. Dickinson, Nicholas, and Adams (1983) showed that post-conditioning devaluation of an outcome had a greater effect with rats that earned that outcome on a ratio schedule than on rats that earned that outcome on an interval schedule. In other words, the experience with the interval schedule became encoded as procedural knowledge. Dickinson et al. attributed this difference to the differences in molar feedback between these two classes of schedules.

Overview of Operant Knowledge. The foregoing discussion indicates that two processes underlie operant conditioning: (i) goal-directed learning that is encoded as declarative knowledge and (ii) habit learning that is encoded as procedural knowledge (Dickinson, 1985, 1989, 1994). The first process involves the development of a behavior-outcome (B-O) association, the performance of which is driven by the current value of the outcome (O, or goal). The second process involves the development of a stimulus-response (S-R) association, which does not incorporate information about the outcome, and where behavior is dictated by the antecedent stimulus (S). Thus, habits (that might be characterized as sensorimotor "see this, do that" responses) are more "reflexive" and "automatic" than goal-directed behaviors (that require much more cognitive effort). Early in learning, operant behaviors are goal-directed, and the individual is voluntarily and intentionally performing a specific response to obtain a desired outcome. This form of learning is flexible and is guided by the current value of the outcome. If the value of the outcome changes, the behavior changes accordingly. However, as training continues, performance can become stimulus-bound, inflexible, and independent of the current value of the outcome, a transition that is likely due to a weakening in the perceived causal relationship between the behavior and the outcome. In the normal progress of operant conditioning, then, a goal-directed behavior transforms seamlessly and without apparent effort into a habit and performance becomes more efficient but less flexible.

Our discussion of the dissection of operant knowledge by means of outcome devaluation has been focused on natural rewards such as food pellets and sucrose. However, not only do the basic findings hold when drugs serve as outcomes but some intriguing differences have also been found. For instance, Corbit, Nie, and Janak (2012), using alcohol as the outcome and a satiation devaluation procedure (the rats were pre-fed with alcohol immediately prior to the extinction test), reported that performance was sensitive to changes in outcome value early (1–2 weeks) but not later (4–8 weeks) in training. That is, the initially flexible goal-directed drug seeking became habitual as the value of the outcome became less relevant to performance. Using a different devaluation procedure, Zapata, Minney, and Shippenberg (2010) reported that cocaine seeking shifts from a goal-directed to a habitual behavior with extended training. Returning to the Corbit et al. (2012) study, when sucrose solution served as the outcome, the acquired operant behavior was still sensitive to devaluation after 8 weeks of training, which suggests that the transition from B-O to S-R performance occurred more rapidly for alcohol than sucrose. Furthermore, "free" access to alcohol during the 8 weeks of sucrose-reinforced lever pressing rendered that behavior insensitive to outcome devaluation. Similar results have been obtained with noncontingent exposure to amphetamine (Nelson & Killcross, 2006; Nordquist et al., 2007) and cocaine (Corbit, Chieng, & Balleine, 2014; LeBlanc, Maidment, & Ostlund, 2013). Together, these latter findings suggest that exposure to drugs can cause the abnormally rapid acquisition of response habits by accelerating the loss of voluntary control over natural reward seeking. In passing, we note that recent research found a similar enhancing effect of noncontingent "binge-eating" of a highly palatable food (Furlong, Jayaweera, Balleine, & Corbit, 2014) and stress (Dias-Ferreira et al., 2009) on the transition from B-O to S-R learning. Undoubtedly, drug taking and addiction are multi-dimensional and involve many different processes. It is also clear that recreational drug use can becomes habitual and compulsive over time. The two-process account of operant conditioning may explain, at least in part, the transition from controlled drug use (where expectancy of the drug state guides behavior) to inflexible and compulsive drug taking (the hallmarks of addiction) that is triggered by antecedent stimuli (for reviews, see Everitt & Robbins, 2013; Hogarth, Balleine, Corbit, & Killcross, 2013; Ostlund & Balleine, 2008).

Considerable evidence indicates that the two operant conditioning processes are subserved by distinct neural substrates (for reviews, see Balleine & O'Doherty, 2010; Gasbarri, Pompili, Packard, & Tomaz, 2014; Yin & Knowlton, 2006). In brief, the acquisition of goal-directed behaviors is governed by neurocircuitry that involves the dorsomedial striatum and related structures whereas dorsolateral striatum and related areas are essential for habit-controlled responding. For example, lesions of the dorsomedial striatum render rats insensitive to outcome devaluation suggesting that this brain area is essential for the acquisition and expression of goal-directed (B-O) learning (Yin, Ostlund, Knowlton, & Balleine, 2005). On the other hand, rats with lesions of the dorsolateral striatum are sensitive to outcome devaluation even after overtraining indicating that this structure is necessary for habit (S-R) learning (Yin, Knowlton, & Balleine, 2004). In addition, post-training temporary inactivation of the dorsolateral striatum causes an otherwise habitual alcohol seeking (Corbit et al., 2012) or cocaine seeking (Zapata et al., 2010) response to become, after outcome devaluation, goal-directed. These and other studies indicate that the transition from B-O to S-R performance is not necessarily permanent. Finally, it has been suggested that an overdependence on habitual responding and/or an impaired ability to shift back to goal-directed behaviors from habitual responding may be responsible, in part, for behavioral dysfunctions such as drug addiction, eating disorders, and obsessive-compulsive disorder (Gillan et al., 2011; Ostlund & Balleine, 2008).

EXTINCTION REVISITED

> A number of relapse phenomena indicate that extinction does not erase original learning of the operant contingency. Rather, extinction appears to be context specific and modulated by an inhibitory association.

In operant acquisition training, a voluntary behavior is associated with an outcome (or reinforcer) and the frequency of the behavior increases. In operant extinction, when the behavior no longer obtains the outcome (see Chapter 7), the frequency of the behavior gradually declines until, eventually, the behavior no longer occurs. As with our discussion of Pavlovian extinction (see Chapter 5), there is abundant evidence that extinction of operant behavior does not involve unlearning of the underlying associative structure. Indeed, there are a number of strong parallels between Pavlovian and operant extinction. We will first describe some relapse phenomena (spontaneous recovery, resurgence, rapid reacquisition, reinstatement, and renewal), then move on to consider the patterns of behavior that occur during extinction before addressing the issue of what is learned in operant extinction.

Spontaneous recovery (see Figure 7.9) refers to the reoccurrence of an extinguished operant behavior that is occasioned by the mere passage of time (Di Ciano & Everitt, 2002; Graham & Gagne, 1940; Peters, Vallone, Laurendi, & Kalivas, 2008; Skinner, 1938). Thus, spontaneous recovery involves a three-phase procedure: the acquisition of the target behavior in Phase 1, the extinction of that behavior in Phase 2, and, some time later, a Phase 3 test involving a second period of extinction during which the extinguished behavior reappears at a level significantly higher than seen at the end of Phase 2. As with the Pavlovian phenomenon of the same name, spontaneous recovery indicates that operant extinction does not completely erase the original learning. Spontaneous recovery shows that the behavioral effect of extinction (the elimination of a previously acquired response) dissipates with the passage of time. This is particularly problematic in therapeutic settings where the intention is to eliminate unhealthy or maladaptive voluntary behaviors (e.g., drug taking, overeating, smoking), and where spontaneous recovery results in a relapse back to the original, unwanted behavior.

Resurgence is *the return of a previously extinguished behavior during extinction of a second behavior* (Cançado & Lattal, 2011; Epstein & Skinner, 1980; Leitenberg, Rawson, & Bath, 1970; Leitenberg, Rawson, & Mulick, 1975; Lieving & Lattal, 2003; Reed & Clark, 2011; Winterbauer, Lucke, & Bouton, 2013). Resurgence is similar to spontaneous recovery except that in resurgence a second behavior is acquired in Phase 2 and then extinguished in Phase 3. The design of the Leitenberg et al. (1970) experiment is shown in Table 11.8. Food deprived rats were trained in Phase 1 to press a lever (B_1) to obtain food pellets on a VI 30-second schedule. In Phase 2, the rats were reinforced for pressing a second lever (B_2; not available during Phase 1) on an FR 10 schedule while B_1 was extinguished. In Phase 3 neither B_1 nor B_2 were reinforced. The results showed that when B_2 was in extinction, the rats resumed B_1 (i.e., they showed resurgence of the previously extinguished behavior).

Table 11.8 Design and Results From the Leitenberg, Rawson, and Bath (1970) Resurgence Experiment

	Phase 1	Phase 2	Phase 3 (test)
Procedure	$B_1 \rightarrow O$	$B_1 \rightarrow \emptyset$ and $B_2 \rightarrow O$	$B_1 \rightarrow \emptyset$ and $B_2 \rightarrow \emptyset$
Result	B_1 rate increases	B_1 rate decreases B_2 rate increases	B_1 rate increases B_2 rate decreases

Note: B_1 and B_2 were left lever pressing and right lever pressing.
O and $\emptyset$ were food pellets and no food pellets

Importantly, resurgence is found when the alternative behavior (B_2) is reinforced with a different outcome than that used to reinforce the original behavior (B_1). For example, extinction of a food-reinforced behavior causes resurgence of previously extinguished drug-seeking behaviors, as shown for outcomes such as alcohol and cocaine (Podlesnik, Jimenez-Gomez, & Shahan, 2006; Quick, Pyszczynski, Colston, & Shahan, 2011). Resurgence indicates that therapies that go beyond extinction and encourage the acquisition of an alternative, healthier behavior do not facilitate erasure of the original learning. Thus, when the replacement behavior is no longer practiced, the individual will likely relapse back to the unwanted or maladaptive behavior. For reviews of resurgence research and applications, see Doughty and Oken (2008) and Lattal and St. Peter Pipkin (2009).

Rapid reacquisition (see Figure 7.10) occurs when *after a period of extinction, the behavior-outcome contingency is reintroduced and behavior is reacquired more quickly than during original acquisition training* (Bullock & Smith, 1953; Skinner, 1938; Willcocks & McNally, 2011). The procedure for rapid reacquisition is identical to that of spontaneous recovery, except that Phase 3 involves a second period of acquisition training. Clearly, the occurrence of rapid reacquisition indicates that the original B-O learning was not completely erased by extinction. The implications for relapse back into clinically treated unwanted behaviors are readily apparent.

Reinstatement is the *recovery of the target behavior that occurs consequent to noncontingent (i.e., free) deliveries of the outcome after extinction* (Baker, 1990; Franks & Lattal, 1976; Reid, 1958; Rescorla & Skucy, 1969). As with Pavlovian reinstatement, reinstatement of operant behavior occurs when the post-extinction outcomes are presented noncontingent of behavior within at least 24 hours of the reinstatement test. Reinstatement has been obtained with a number of outcomes including drugs of abuse such as alcohol, amphetamine, cocaine, heroin, and nicotine (Chiamulera, Borgo, Falchetto, Valerio, & Tessari, 1996; Chiamulera, Valerio, & Tessari, 1995; de Wit & Stewart, 1981, 1983; Gerber & Stretch, 1975).

Renewal refers to the *reappearance of the extinguished behavior when testing occurs outside the extinction context* (Nakajima, Tanaka, Urushihara, & Imada, 2000). Table 11.9

Table 11.9 Experimental Design for the Nakajima, Tanaka, Urushihara, & Imada (2000) Renewal Study

Group	Phase 1	Phase 2	Phase 3 (test)
AAA	B ➝ O in Context A	B ➝ Ø in Context A	B ➝ Ø in Context A
ABA	B ➝ O in Context A	B ➝ Ø in Context B	B ➝ Ø in Context A

Note: B was lever pressing.
O and Ø were food pellets and no food pellets

shows the design of the basic renewal effect; the letters in the group names refer, respectively, to the context used during acquisition, extinction, and test. In a three-phase procedure, hungry rats were first trained with a behavior-outcome contingency (Phase 1) and then extinguished (Phase 2) in the same (Group AAA) or a different context (Group ABA). Finally, the renewal test (Phase 3), administered in the acquisition context (Context A), revealed that Group ABA shows significantly more of the previously extinguished behavior than Group AAA. Of clinical interest, ABA renewal has been obtained when drugs such as alcohol (Hamlin, Newby, & McNally, 2007; Marinelli, Funk, Juzytsch, Li, & Le, 2007; Zironi, Burattini, Aicardi, & Janak, 2006), cocaine (Crombag, Grimm, & Shaham, 2002; Hamlin, Clemens, & McNally, 2008), and heroin (Bossert, Liu, Lu, & Shaham, 2004; Bossert, Poles, Wihbey, Koya, & Shaham, 2007) are employed as outcomes. Furthermore, in addition to the standard ABA protocol, renewal has been obtained using AAB and ABC designs (Bouton, Todd, Vurbic, & Winterbauer, 2011; Todd, 2013; Todd, Winterbauer, & Bouton, 2012). These results are important because they demonstrate that testing in a context other than that of extinction (and not necessarily the acquisition context) will lead to the reoccurrence of the extinguished behavior. In other words, operant extinction appears to be specific to the context within which it occurred.

Patterns of Behavior During Extinction. Although the procedure of extinction leads to a reduction in the rate of occurrence of prior reinforced behaviors, the patterns and topology of the behaviors that produced the outcome are preserved, albeit at a lower rate. How can extinction increase variability of behavior and, at the same time, not undo the effects of positive reinforcement?

Neuringer, Kornell, and Olufs (2001) provided a resolution to this apparent paradox about the effects of extinction. They trained hungry rats to perform a sequence of three behaviors that could occur at three different locations (lever on the left of the food hopper [L], lever on the right of the food hopper [R], and a pigeon response key on the opposite wall of the box [K]). In order to receive food, the rats had to perform a sequence of three behaviors involving any of these three locations. For the variable group, any one of the 27 possible three-unit sequences (e.g., RRR, RKL, LLR) could earn food as long as that sequence had not occurred recently. For the repeat group, a single sequence (LKR) was selected by the experimenter for reinforcement 75% of the time, and all other

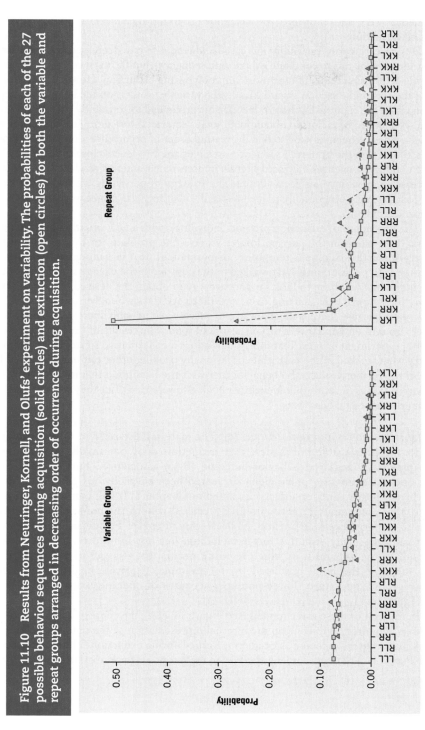

Figure 11.10 Results from Neuringer, Kornell, and Olufs' experiment on variability. The probabilities of each of the 27 possible behavior sequences during acquisition (solid circles) and extinction (open circles) for both the variable and repeat groups arranged in decreasing order of occurrence during acquisition.

Reprinted from Neuringer, Kornell, Olaf, 2001, *Journal of Experimental Psychology: Animal Behavior Processes, 27, 79–94*. Copyright © 2001 by the American Psychological Association. Reprinted with permission.

sequences were not reinforced. After extended training, all subjects in both groups were put on extinction.

During extinction, variability increased and response rate decreased (as measured by how long it took rats to complete a three-unit sequence), but the most common sequences during acquisition remained the most common during extinction. How did this happen? The answer can be seen in Figure 11.10. The variable group is on the left and the repeat group is on the right. Even though the variable group had to constantly change the three-unit sequence of behaviors to obtain food, some sequences were more likely to occur than others. These sequences are listed in decreasing order of occurrence along the horizontal axes. (Note that the preferred sequences involved the two levers close to the food.) The least common sequences increased slightly in occurrence, and this produced the observed increase in variability. Subjects adopted the strategy of persisting with what worked in the past, but they occasionally probed to see if something else might work (when the old sequences did not).

The procedure of extinction presents individuals with a new situation in which what worked for them in the past no longer works. The problem for the individual is to determine if this change is temporary or permanent. If it is temporary then the best strategy is to persist doing what worked in the past, but if the change is permanent then the individual will have to look for another way to obtain the desired outcome. Trying something new means starting over, and there are risks whenever one embarks on a new quest because there is no guarantee of success and possibly increased danger if one has to go into unfamiliar territory in search of food. The results of the Neuringer et al. (2001) experiment suggest that individuals adopt a conservative strategy of continuing to try what worked in the past while occasionally probing other options. Repeated failure of the formerly successful behavior increases the likelihood that individuals will do different things (a result that Neuringer et al. also reported), but they still persist at the formerly successful behaviors.

What is learned in operant extinction? The material discussed in this section leads us to the inescapable conclusion that extinction does not involve unlearning of the previously acquired behavior-outcome (B-O) association. Furthermore, all of the operant extinction phenomena presented here have obvious parallels with the Pavlovian post-extinction effects discussed in Chapter 5. It will come as no surprise, then, that contemporary accounts give a central role to the context in the expression of performance in extinction. As previously noted for Pavlovian extinction, context can take many stimulus forms including, but not limited to, the background stimuli of the apparatus in which learning occurs, the passage of time, and internal states of the body produced by, for example, deprivation, drugs, hormones, mood, and temperature. Three potential accounts of operant extinction are shown in Figure 11.11.

In the first of these three models (see Figure 11.11A), the context is thought to exert a direct inhibitory influence on the internal representation of the outcome. That is, an inhibitory context-outcome association is formed during extinction. The second account (see Figure 11.11B), conceptually identical to that proposed for Pavlovian extinction, views

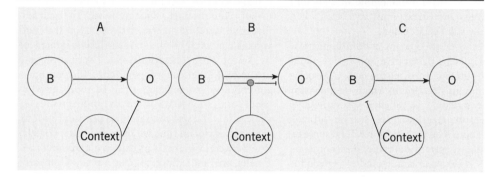

Figure 11.11 Schematic representations of three potential accounts of what is learned during operant extinction. Arrows indicate excitatory connections; flat-ended lines indicate inhibitory connections. (A) The development of an inhibitory link between the context and the outcome (O). (B) The context determines when an inhibitory behavior-outcome (B-O) connection guides performance of the behavior (B). (C) Performance is guided by an inhibitory connection between the context and the behavior (B).

the context as a negative occasion setter that signals the absence of the outcome. That is, the extinction context becomes a conditioned inhibitor that modulates expression of the B-O association that was acquired during acquisition training. The third view of extinction (see Figure 11.11C) suggests that the context inhibits the operant behavior. That is, an inhibitory association is formed between the internal representations of the context and the response (Rescorla, 1993, 1997; Todd, 2013, Todd et al., 2014b). According to this analysis, when we put individuals on extinction, we are telling them that those behaviors no longer work in *this* situation at *this* time. In a recent review of the issue, Bouton and Todd (2014) suggested that a direct inhibitory context-behavior association might, on the balance of currently available data, be the best analysis of operant extinction. However, irrespective of interpretation, context is viewed as the critical element in operant extinction, as it was for Pavlovian extinction. For both types of learning, context disambiguates what is relevant at the present moment.

The study of the psychological processes responsible for extinction is an active area of research, not least because extinction is fundamentally about behavioral change. We all have to learn to modify our behavior when an outcome or resource is no longer available or is entirely depleted. Furthermore, a complete understanding of extinction will have wide-reaching implications for the treatment of maladaptive, unhealthy, and unwanted operant behaviors and practices as seen in, for example, drug seeking and relapse back into addiction and overeating and obesity. For reviews of operant extinction, see Bouton (2014); Bouton, Winterbauer, & Vurbic (2012); Lattal, St. Peter, and Escobar (2013).

SUMMARY AND CONCLUSIONS

Operant conditioning, like Pavlovian conditioning, is an inference task. In operant conditioning, individuals attempt to discover what aspects of their own behavior produce a particular outcome. But important events do not occur in a vacuum; they are found in certain locations and at certain times. Thus, in order to be successful in obtaining (or avoiding) important events, individuals must also learn when and where they will be successful.

Experience with an operant conditioning procedure is encoded as declarative knowledge about the behavior-outcome relationship (a B-O association). The stimulus situation in which the behavior produces the outcome is called a discriminative stimulus. Because discriminative stimuli provide information about when a behavior will be successful in obtaining a certain outcome, discriminative stimuli serve as occasion setters and as signals for the availability of certain events. This latter function is the result of Pavlovian conditioning. As a result of that Pavlovian conditioning, individuals come to expect that certain outcomes will happen in certain situations (an S-O association). Therefore, the discriminative stimulus evokes a representation of the outcome, which then evokes the operant behavior that had been successful in the past for obtaining that outcome. Individuals must learn that outcomes have value. That learning is called incentive learning, and it too involves Pavlovian conditioning. Furthermore, the current incentive value of outcomes depends on the individual's current motivational state that is influenced by establishing operations like deprivation and satiation. The effects of experience with an operant conditioning procedure can be reorganized as procedural knowledge when the individual experiences the operant conditioning procedure for an extended period of time while there is little correlation between variations in behavior and outcomes. Finally, operant extinction does not cause unlearning of the previously acquired behavior. Rather, extinction is context specific, and the extinguished response may return when the individual is tested in another context.

STUDY QUESTIONS

1. How are Hume's three conditions for causal inferences related to operant conditioning? Are any of them necessary or sufficient conditions for the occurrence of operant conditioning? What evidence leads to this conclusion?

2. What evidence points to the conclusion that experience with operant conditioning procedures are encoded as declarative knowledge involving associations between representations of behaviors and reinforcers?

3. What evidence points to the conclusion that rats have representations of their own actions?

4. What evidence points to the conclusion that rats have representations of the reinforcers in operant conditioning situations?

5. How do individuals learn that reinforcers like food and water are valuable under conditions of deprivation (i.e., how do we learn the incentive values of reinforcers)? How can we show that this is the case?

6. What are the roles of discriminative stimuli (situations, contexts) in operant conditioning? Why do we believe this?

7. What is the current thinking on how operant behaviors are generated from representations?

8. Under what conditions does declarative knowledge become reorganized as procedural knowledge?

9. What evidence points to the conclusion that extinction does not erase original learning?

10. What is learned in operant extinction?

12

THE SIMILARITIES BETWEEN OPERANT CONDITIONING AND NATURAL SELECTION

As noted in Chapter 1, Darwin's explanation of the evolution of species by natural selection is based on three mechanisms: *sources of variation* among individuals, a *method of selection* for those characteristics that would be passed onto future generations, and a *mechanism for retaining changes and transmitting them across successive generations* through the inheritance of observed characteristics. Today we know enough about genetics, mutations, and ecology to see that Darwin was essentially correct in his analysis of the origins of different species.

Genetic diversity within species arises through mutations that are not lethal and from sexual reproduction between genetically different individuals *(source of variation)*. That genetic diversity may be reflected in differences in physical and behavioral traits and abilities. In the competition for food, water, and mates, and with respect to escaping from and eluding predators, some of these traits and abilities will lead to more success than others. Those traits that allow individuals to survive and reproduce will be passed on to future generations. This is called reproductive fitness and is the *method of selection*. The transfer of genetic material is the *mechanism for retaining changes and transmitting them across successive generations*. Natural selection creates new species when mutations and new genetic combinations (as a result of sexual reproduction) produce individuals who are able to survive and reproduce. This leads to diversity of species, each adapted to survive in the niche in which it evolved. However, dramatic changes in the environment will lead to the extinction of a species that does not possess characteristics needed to survive the changes.

It has not escaped the attention of psychologists and biologists that evolution of species by natural selection and operant conditioning share common features (e.g., Broadbent, 1961; Campbell, 1956, 1960; Gilbert, 1970; Herrnstein, 1964; Postman, 1947; Skinner, 1953, 1981, 1984; Staddon & Simmelhag, 1971; Staddon, 1975). In an operant conditioning situation, the individual performs various behaviors when attempting to obtain some objective (e.g., food, a mate, or another positive event) or when attempting to escape from or avoid danger. With repeated attempts, unsuccessful actions tend to drop out and successful actions tend to be repeated and come to predominate in that situation. Like natural selection, this involves *sources of variation*, *methods of selection*, and *a mechanism for retaining information* (memory). Although the analogy is not perfect, it does provide us with a framework for understanding some of the processes underlying operant conditioning.

SOURCES OF BEHAVIORAL VARIATION

In order for operant conditioning to occur, the individual must do something. Therefore, like natural selection, operant conditioning requires sources of variation. Two sources of behavioral variation in operant conditioning are described here.

In evolution by natural selection, the two principle sources of variation are genetic mutations and recombinations of genes during sexual reproduction. The expressions of these new genetic forms in both structures and behaviors provide the raw materials for natural selection.

In the case of operant conditioning, variation in behavior provides the raw material for selection. Behaviors occur for a number of reasons: Some behaviors are modules from the underlying behavior systems aroused by motivational factors and aspects of the situation. Other behaviors are Pavlovian CRs to the stimuli in that situation (although the Pavlovian conditioning might have occurred in another situation). Still other behaviors occur because previously they were successful in that situation, in similar situations, or when seeking the same goal; these behaviors are the result of prior operant conditioning. All of these sources of behavioral variation are called induced variation because they are *generated or induced by the situation*. A second source of behavioral variation is inherent in all behavior: *Individuals do not perform the same action exactly the same way each time they do it*. Even when the individual is well-practiced and the stimulus situation is identical on each occasion, there will still be some variability in how a behavior is performed. That kind of behavioral variation is called **behavioral variability**. Both kinds of variation are important in operant conditioning.

Induced Variation

Many of the behaviors that an individual performs in a given situation are generated by aspects of that situation. We call this induced variation.

Induced variation refers to *behaviors generated by the situation* (Balsam, Deich, Ohyama, & Stokes, 1988; Marr, 2009; Segal, 1972; Staddon & Simmelhag, 1971). The particular behaviors that are induced depend on the species of the individual, his or her motivational state and past history, and the attributes of the situation. Many induced behaviors arise out of underlying behavior systems activated in that situation (see Chapter 6). A given system (or subsystem) can be aroused by both internal events (depletion of nutrients, hormones, etc.) and external events (the presence of food, water, or mates, or signals for these things).

In most operant conditioning experiments, subjects are motivated by restricted access to or deprivation of something (food, water, etc.). However, deprivation is not necessary for operant conditioning. In most species, individuals search for food and water in anticipation of extreme need, and in many cases these food seeking behaviors (general search) are entrained onto a daily (circadian) rhythm and to times when food has been obtained in the past (Gallistel, 1990a). Likewise, animals tend to become active when signals for food are encountered and in places where they have obtained food in the past (see, e.g., Baumeister, Hawkins, & Cromwell, 1964). The presence of food in a given location typically arouses the focal search mode in the browsing subsystem and produces exploratory behavior in the vicinity of the food tray and the lever (Timberlake & Lucas, 1989). This arousal increases the individual's chances of coming in contact with food and other objects during focal search. It also provides behaviors to shape. Some of the knowledge about these signals for food is innate knowledge and some is learned knowledge from past experience. For example, magazine training is used to provide subjects in operant conditioning experiments with a signal for food in the food tray, but that procedure also teaches subjects that the experimental chamber is a place where food can be found. Finally, in many species, presentations of small amounts of food induce activity immediately after that food is consumed (Killeen, 1975, 1979; Killeen et al., 1978).

Killeen (1975) provided a striking demonstration of how the presence of food induces behavior. He placed pigeons in an experimental chamber equipped with a feeder. The floor of the chamber was covered by a number of panels that activated switches when the pigeons stepped on them. This allowed Killeen to measure the pigeons' activity as they moved around and from panel to panel. The pigeons were given food at regular intervals, and they did not have to do anything to get it. For example, if the interfood interval was 25 seconds, each presentation of food occurred 25 seconds after the last one. There was one restriction: To ensure that activity was not specifically rewarded by the occurrence of food, an omission training procedure was in effect; that is, they had to stay on the same panel for 5 seconds after the food was scheduled to occur. After receiving 60 presentations of food per day for 10 days on one interfood interval schedule, the pigeons were given 10 days each of experience with other schedules (25, 60, 120, 200, and 400 seconds). Half of the pigeons experienced these schedules in ascending order and half in descending order. The data from this experiment are presented in Figure 12.1; activity is measured by the number of panels stepped on per minute as a function of the proportion of the interfood interval. The greatest level of activity occurred immediately after a food presentation, and the size of the effect was a function of interfood interval: More activity was induced by the shortest interfood interval (25 seconds) and the least by a 400-second interfood interval. Except for the longest interval (400 seconds), the periodic presentation of food was always *followed* by an increase in activity. This is not surprising. Food tends to occur in clumps, and an increase in activity following the consumption of small amounts of food increases the chances that more will be found. This source of behavioral variation is highly adaptive.

In most species, the initial response to a novel situation is hesitancy and reluctance to explore followed by exploratory and manipulative behaviors of objects in the environment (Renner, 1988; Renner & Seltzer, 1991). How much exploration and manipulation occurs and the forms that these take depend on the species and the particular objects present in that environment (Glickman & Sroges, 1966). For example, pigeons are likely to peck at protruding objects (Lattal & Gleeson, 1990; Wesp, Lattal, & Poling, 1977), and rats are likely to manipulate them. Lever pressing can also be encouraged by anything that draws a rat's attention to the lever: rattling it, using a larger lever initially, or putting food on the lever. Rats, pigeons, and other species will also approach and contact objects

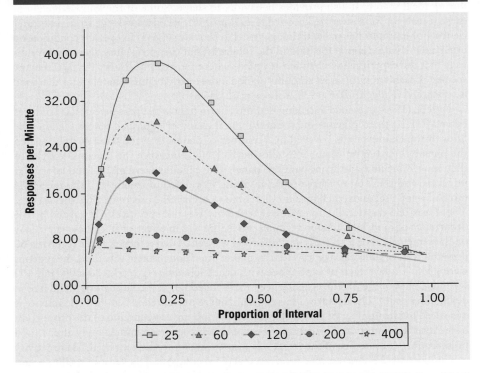

Figure 12.1 The effects of periodic presentations of small amounts of food on activity in pigeons. Activity was measured by the rate of stepping on different floor panels. The intervals between successive presentations of food (25, 60, 120, 200, and 400 seconds) are standardized on the same scale as proportions of the interfood interval.

From Killeen, 1975. On the temporal control of behavior. *Psychological Review, 82,* 89–115. Copyright © 1975 by the American Psychological Association. Reprinted with permission.

whose presence has in the past signaled food (sign-tracking; Brown & Jenkins, 1968; Peterson et al., 1972).

In behavior modification, a variety of techniques are used to induce behavior. For example, Isaacs et al. (1960) held up a stick of gum to induce looking at the therapist and later said "gum" to induce vocalizations (see Chapter 7, Box 7.3). Similarly, Lovaas, Freitag, et al. (1966) used edible treats like ice cream to induce their patients to look at the trainer in the first step of their language acquisition program. In later stages of that program, the trainers provided sounds for the children to imitate.

Variation in behavior can also be induced by the withholding of or reduction in the level of reward (Balsam et al., 1988; Pecoraro et al., 1999). As we saw in Chapter 8, the successful application of the method of successive approximations for the shaping of behavior involves the use of both positive reinforcement and extinction: The effect of withholding positive reinforcement is to increase variation in behavior, and the effect of receiving the positive reinforcer following a specific behavior is to increase the tendency to repeat the behavior that produced the reward (and reduce variation; Antonitis, 1951; Stokes, 1995). The increased variation in behavior that results from the withholding or reduction in reward can be attributed to the activation of search behaviors generated by the search modes in the underlying behavior system (see Chapter 6, Figure 6.3; Pecoraro et al., 1999).

Finally, variability in behavior can also be the result of a prior history of experience with reinforcement for behavioral variation. In the natural environment, predators encounter prey in various locations and at various distances, and the successful hunter has to employ a variety of actions to be successful. Evidence that such prior experience affects the variability of future behavior has been observed under controlled laboratory conditions. Not only can individuals be explicitly reinforced for engaging in variable behavior (see Chapter 8), but experience with explicitly reinforced variability promotes later learning (Grunow & Neuringer, 2002; Neuringer, Deiss, & Olsen, 2000). Furthermore, Stokes (1995) and Stokes, Mechner, and Balsam (1999) found in both rats and people that a stringent criterion for the shaping of an operant behavior (e.g., press the lever only with the right paw or press a certain sequence of keys on a computer keyboard) produced greater variability in behavior when the task was changed than shaping that allowed a variety of actions to produce the reward. This occurred because the subjects who encountered the stringent criterion had to engage in more variable behavior in order to find the correct one.

Thus, from the individual's point of view, induced behaviors reflect a combination of innate and learned knowledge that may increase the likelihood of overcoming the barriers imposed by the situation, experimenter, or behavior modifier.

Behavioral Variability

> But even induced behaviors do not occur the same way every time they occur. The inherent variability in all behavior is called behavioral variability.

The second kind of behavioral variation is **behavioral variability**: *Even in an unchanging environment, individuals do not perform actions exactly the same way every time they have the opportunity to perform them.* One of the earliest demonstrations of behavioral variability in operant conditioning was done by Muenzinger (1928) who recorded the various ways that guinea pigs pressed a lever in order to gain access to food (see Chapter 8). The strength of Muenzinger's study was the systematic manner in which he recorded his animals' behavior. Observations of other species in other situations reveal similar variability. For example, successive lever presses by well-trained rats differ in terms of the force exerted on the lever and the duration of time that the lever is held down. Although one can use the procedure of differentiation (see Chapter 8) to set rather narrow limits for how hard the rat must press the lever or how long he or she must hold it down in order for that lever press to qualify as successful for earning reinforcers, behavioral variability does not completely disappear (Notterman & Mintz, 1965). This behavioral variability may reflect the principles embodied in chaos theory (Gleick, 1987). According to that theory, seemingly random variation in behavior is the result of simple deterministic systems; for example, small changes in the starting conditions (e.g., how a rat approaches the lever or how one finds one's shoelaces) can result in different outcomes (how the rat presses the lever or how one holds the laces while tying them together). This suggests that behavioral variability is inherent in all living organisms.

The Importance of Both Sources of Variation in Operant Conditioning

Operant conditioning affects behaviors after they occur. Many of these behaviors are generated by the situation (induced variation), but through hill-climbing, individuals can become more efficient in their performance. Hill-climbing requires behavioral variability.

Behavioral variability and induced variation contribute to operant conditioning in different ways. *Induced variation* produces motor patterns that have been useful to the species and the individual in the same or similar situations. Because operant conditioning requires the individual to do something in order to obtain a positive reinforcer (or get away from a negative reinforcer), increases in activity, exploratory behaviors, and manipulatory behaviors all increase the probability of performing the correct actions. It is these induced motor patterns that are molded by the behavior-outcome contingency in operant conditioning. Likewise, once the individual comes to perform the correct action repeatedly, *behavioral variability* in that performance will increase the chances that more efficient versions of the action (i.e., those variations that require less effort) will be selected through hill-climbing. This leads us to the question of how the correct action (and its more efficient variants) is selected.

THE MECHANISM OF SELECTION IN OPERANT CONDITIONING

As is the case with natural selection, there must be a mechanism by which behaviors are maintained and increased by reinforcing events. We have identified hill-climbing as an important aspect of operant conditioning, there is still debate about the mechanism of selection.

The selection in natural selection refers to the mechanism for determining who will survive long enough to reproduce. We call this mechanism reproductive fitness: Individuals who possess traits (phenotypes) that allow them to live long enough to reproduce pass the genes that contribute to those phenotypes on to their offspring.

Thus, where genetic variation produces different phenotypes, and some of those phenotypes are more successful at reproducing than other phenotypes, the next generation will contain more individuals with the successful phenotypes (and the genes that determine them). Over time, the more numerous variations may crowd out the less numerous ones.

Reproductive fitness comes into play when there is a dramatic change in a niche. A variety of individuals and species may have been able to live in the old niche, but not everyone may be able to adapt to the change. If members of a species cannot survive long enough to reproduce, the species will become extinct. That is what happened to the dinosaurs. Because they could not adapt to the climatic changes that occurred, they died out as a species. On the other hand, antibiotic-resistant strains of bacteria evolve when a few individual organisms with mutations that confer resistance to antibiotics survive and pass that resistance onto their offspring who can survive and multiply in the presence of antibiotics. Reproductive fitness favors those bacteria that develop resistance to antibiotics.

Similarly, behaviors that are consistently successful (i.e., followed by positive reinforcers or by reduced contact with negative reinforcers) in a certain situation come to predominate in that situation in the future, while those behaviors that are unsuccessful (i.e., *not* followed by positive reinforcers or by reduced contact with negative reinforcers) tend to be less likely to occur in the future so long as some behavior is successful. Following the analogy with natural selection, we say that *successful behaviors are selected by their outcomes* so that in the future those behaviors will be more likely to occur again in that situation.

It is important to recognize that selection by reproductive fitness is not an automatic process. Some individuals are in a more favorable position than other individuals to survive and pass their genetic material to their offspring, but not every individual with the same genetic endowment will be successful in surviving and reproducing. The same is true with selection by outcomes: Sometimes experiencing a single outcome for a behavior will produce learning, and sometimes it will take many more than one. Furthermore, some behavior-outcome relationships are easier to learn about than others. Thus, providing an outcome does not automatically produce selection of the behavior that produced that outcome.

It is one thing to say that behaviors are selected by their outcomes in operant conditioning, and another to specify the mechanism by which this occurs. The two obvious candidates for the mechanism of selection are temporal proximity and the behavior-outcome contingency. In operant conditioning, **temporal proximity** refers to the *time between the behavior and the reinforcing event (the outcome)*. There is ample evidence that operant conditioning precedes most rapidly when there is little or no delay between the target behavior and the outcome (see, e.g., Renner, 1964). **Contingency** refers to *the predictive relationship between the target behavior and the outcome* in operant conditioning. In standard operant conditioning situations, temporal proximity and contingency are confounded; that is, there is a behavior-outcome contingency and the outcome occurs immediately after the behavior occurs. Therefore, the question is, does selection occur because the outcome closely followed a behavior in time or because there is a behavior-outcome contingency?

Temporal Proximity Between a Behavior and Outcome as the Mechanism of Selection ("Superstitious Behavior")

Temporal proximity between a behavior and outcome was the mechanism for selection identified by Thorndike in his classic statement of the Law of Effect. Skinner also identified temporal proximity as the mechanism for selection when he demonstrated that noncontingent presentations of food appeared to select certain behaviors. He called this phenomenon "superstition." However, later experiments showed that the behaviors Skinner observed were not the result of selection by temporal contiguity; they were induced by the periodic presentation of food. Therefore, although the chance occurrence of an outcome in close temporal proximity to a behavior can produce superstitious behaviors, temporal proximity is neither a necessary nor a sufficient condition for the occurrence of operant conditioning.

For much of this century, the Law of Effect proposed by Thorndike was considered to provide the mechanism for selection of operant behavior (see Chapter 7). The Law of Effect proposes the existence of a class of events (now called outcomes or reinforcers) that have the capacity to strengthen what immediately precedes them (stimulus-response associations for Thorndike and responses for Skinner). The Law of Effect made *temporal proximity* between the behavior and outcome, not the *behavior-outcome contingency*, the mechanism of selection.[1]

Temporal Proximity as the Explanation for Superstitious Behavior. There are a number of ways to test whether temporal proximity is a necessary or sufficient condition for operant conditioning. If it is a sufficient condition, then the mere occurrence of temporal proximity (without a contingency) will produce conditioning. Skinner (1948) reported an experiment in which he thought that occurred. He placed pigeons in a chamber and taught them to eat from a food tray. After magazine training, he presented food every 15 seconds independently of what the birds did. After a number of these noncontingent presentations of food, he observed that each bird exhibited what looked to him to be idiosyncratic patterns of behavior. These behavior patterns and Skinner's explanation of them are presented in Box 12.1. Skinner labeled this behavior "superstition" because "the bird behaves as if there is a causal relation between its behavior and the presentation of food, although such a relation is lacking" (p. 171). He was making the obvious analogy with superstitious behavior in humans. Zeiler (1970a) also observed the acquisition of new behavior in the absence of a behavior-outcome contingency (see Chapter 11).

In Skinner's experiment, the behavior that came to predominate was not chosen by the experimenter. Morse (reported in Herrnstein, 1966) investigated what would happen if a

---

[1] The Law of Effect implies that temporal contiguity between a behavior and an outcome is both a necessary and a sufficient condition for the selection of that behavior by the outcome (and hence for operant conditioning); however, as we saw in Chapter 11, temporal proximity is neither necessary nor sufficient.

BOX 12.1

Skinner's Description of "Superstition" in Pigeons

In 1948, Skinner reported that pigeons developed idiosyncratic and stereotyped patterns of behavior when they are given repeated presentations of food spaced at short regular intervals and independent of behavior. He labeled this phenomenon "superstition" because he believed that it reflected the same causal mechanisms as superstitions in humans, namely the accidental conjunction of a behavior with a reinforcer. In this excerpt from his paper, Skinner described the behaviors of some of his pigeons and why he believed these behaviors developed.

If a clock is now arranged to present the food hopper at regular intervals *with no reference whatsoever to the bird's behavior*, operant conditioning usually takes place. In six out of eight cases the resulting responses were so clearly defined that two observers could agree perfectly in counting instances. One bird was conditioned to turn counter-clockwise about the cage, making two or three turns between reinforcements. Another repeatedly thrust its head into one of the upper corners of the cage. A third developed a "tossing" response, as if placing its head beneath an invisible bar and lifting it repeatedly. Two birds developed a pendulum motion of the head and body, in which the head was extended forward and swung from right to left with a sharp movement followed by a somewhat slower return. The body generally followed the movement and a few steps might be taken when it was extensive. Another bird was conditioned to make incomplete pecking or brushing movements directed toward but not touching the floor. None of these responses appeared in any noticeable strength during adaptation to the cage or until the food hopper was periodically presented. In the remaining two cases, conditioned responses were not clearly marked.

The conditioning process is usually obvious. The bird happens to be executing some response as the hopper appears; as a result it tends to repeat this response. If the interval before the next presentation is not so great that extinction takes place, a second "contingency" is probable. This strengthens the response still further and subsequent reinforcement becomes more probable. It is true that some responses go unreinforced and some reinforcements appear when the response has not just been made, but the net result is the development of a considerable state of strength.

With the exception of the counter-clockwise turn, each response was almost always repeated in the same part of the cage, and it generally involved an orientation toward some feature of the cage. The effect of the reinforcement was to condition the bird to respond to some aspect of the environment rather than merely to execute a series of movements. All responses came to be repeated rapidly between reinforcements—typically five or six times in 15 sec.

From Skinner, 1948, pp. 168–169.

target behavior were trained by conventional means before eliminating the contingency and leaving only temporal proximity to maintain the behavior. To do this, pigeons were trained to peck at a key for food on an FI 11-second schedule where the first peck that occurred 11 seconds after the last food presentation resulted in food. In this situation, there was both a positive contingency between pecking and food (i.e., food always occurred after the peck that occurred after the designated time and never occurred at any other time) and temporal proximity of food to the peck that produced it. After nine sessions in which the pigeons obtained 40 outcomes on this schedule, the behavior-outcome contingency was dropped and food was given every 11 seconds no matter what the pigeons did. Because of the prior training, the pigeons tended to peck at a high rate 11 seconds after the previous delivery of food; this maintained temporal proximity between pecks and food in the absence of a programmed contingency. Over repeated sessions, the rate of pecking declined, but the birds *did not stop* pecking. When the contingency was reinstated, the rate of pecking increased. When food was discontinued (procedure of extinction), the birds stopped pecking. Similar data were reported by Appel and Hiss (1962).

On the surface, these data appear to provide strong support for the proposition that temporal proximity of an outcome to a behavior is sufficient to select and maintain behavior. However, subsequent data cast doubt on that conclusion.

Skinner (1953) commented that the interval between successive food presentations in his 1948 superstition experiment was important:

> At sixty seconds the effect of one reinforcement is largely lost before another can occur, and other behavior is more likely to appear. Superstitious behavior is therefore less likely to emerge, though it may do so if the experiment is carried on for a long time. At fifteen seconds the effect is usually immediate. (p. 85)

There is, however, another explanation for the results Skinner reported in 1948 and for his observation that longer interfood intervals did not generate what he took to be superstitious behavior.

Schedule-Induced Behavior as the Explanation for Superstitious Behavior. Staddon and Simmelhag (1971) repeated Skinner's 1948 experiment on the effects of noncontingent presentations of food to pigeons with some minor variations. In addition, they kept detailed records of the behaviors that occurred over the course of a number of sessions in which 2 seconds' access to food was presented to pigeons under one of two conditions: every 12 seconds independently of what they did, and on the average of once every 8 seconds (with a range from 3 to 21 seconds) independently of what they did. Some pigeons received the fixed schedule for a number of sessions before receiving the variable schedule, and the others received the variable schedule for a number of sessions before receiving the fixed schedule. Each session lasted until the bird had received 64 opportunities to eat the food. Under both schedules of food delivery, a variety of behaviors emerged over the course of repeated sessions in all pigeons. Some of these behaviors tended to occur early in the interfood interval and some later. For example, pecking the floor, turning quarter circles, flapping wings, moving along the walls, and moving around the chamber with beak pointed toward the ceiling tended to occur early in the interval, while orienting toward the magazine wall and pecking at the magazine wall tended to occur late in the interval. Staddon and Simmelhag labeled *the behaviors that occurred early in the interval* **interim behaviors** and *those that occurred late in the interval* **terminal activities**. Clearly, the interim behaviors were not the result of temporal proximity with food because they occurred early in the interval.

Killeen's (1975) observations that the periodic presentation of food induces activity as measured by movement around the chamber are described above. Killeen et al. (1978) argued that these data are due to an arousal effect of the food which decays with time since the last food presentation and summates over repeated presentation (as long as some arousal from the last food presentation is still present). Thus, increases in behavior due to repeated presentations of food do not represent the reinforcement of behaviors; rather, they reflect behaviors that are evoked by the schedule of food presentation.

Innis, Simmelhag-Grant, and Staddon (1983) studied the effects of a variety of interfood intervals (5, 12, 60, and 300 seconds). With the short intervals (5 and 12 seconds), most of the observed behaviors were terminal behaviors (directed toward the feeder and localized in the vicinity of the feeder). In contrast, the longer intervals (60 and 300 seconds) evoked more locomotion around the chamber. Although they tended to be in the vicinity of the feeder at the end of the intervals, no distinct feeder-directed terminal behavior emerged. Timberlake and Lucas (1985) repeated Staddon and Simmelhag's (1971) experiment with some variations and found similar results, although their differentiation of behaviors into the classes interim and terminal was not as clear. They argued that both interim and terminal behaviors are modules of the underlying feeding system that is aroused by the presence of food in this situation.

These studies all demonstrate that the mere presentation of food to hungry pigeons produces a variety of stereotyped behaviors that are *not* the result of the accidental presentation of food following these behaviors. In fact, interim behaviors rarely occurred at the time of the food presentations, and terminal behaviors did not appear until after a number of sessions. Staddon and Simmelhag (1971) concluded that Skinner had not demonstrated that temporal proximity between the occurrence of a behavior and the presentation of an outcome is sufficient for the strengthening of that behavior. It appears that Skinner was seeing behaviors from pigeons' browsing subsystem that are induced by the periodic presentation of food.

What about superstitious behavior in humans? It is obvious that Skinner's identification of temporal proximity between a behavior and the reinforcing event is not the mechanism of selection in operant conditioning. However, as Zeiler (1970a) demonstrated (see Chapter 11), and we know from everyday observations, people do perform superstitious rituals. Why does that happen? Superstitions are causal inferences based on the chance conjunctions of events, and as David Hume observed over 200 years ago, temporal proximity provides one of the conditions that favors causal inferences (see Chapter 3). And although temporal proximity is not the only condition Hume identified, there is ample evidence that humans are greatly influenced by the chance conjunction of random events (Nesbitt & Ross, 1980). One of the differences between us humans and most other species is our capacity to generate rules that come to guide our behavior, and formulating rules makes us less sensitive to the contingencies of reinforcement. Thus, superstitious behavior in humans may reflect rule-governed behavior, while other species may be more sensitive to behavior-outcome contingencies. This distinction will be discussed in some detail in Chapter 13.

Operant Conditioning Without Temporal Proximity Between the Behavior and Outcome. Thus far, we have shown that temporal proximity is *not* a sufficient condition for the occurrence of operant conditioning, and in Chapter 11, we reviewed data showing that temporal proximity is also not a necessary condition for the occurrence of operant conditioning.

Is temporal proximity the mechanism for selection in operant conditioning? The obvious conclusion from all of the data reviewed is that temporal proximity is neither a necessary or a sufficient condition for the occurrence of operant conditioning. While there are some situations in which the chance juxtaposition of a reinforcing event with a behavior produces superstitious behavior, *temporal proximity cannot be the sole mechanism of selection in operant conditioning.* That leaves the behavior-outcome contingency as the remaining candidate.

Contingency Between Behaviors and Outcomes as the Mechanism of Selection in Operant Conditioning

Although accidental temporal proximity between behaviors and outcomes can produce superstitious behavior, there is abundant evidence that individuals are sensitive to the contingency between behaviors and outcomes. However, there is also evidence that the mere presence of a contingency does not guarantee that a behavior will be selected by that contingency. Thus, the behavior-outcome contingency is also neither a necessary nor a sufficient condition for the occurrence of operant conditioning.

Killeen (1978, 1981) demonstrated that pigeons are sensitive to the presence of a behavior-outcome contingency; for example, they can tell the difference between whether a given key peck they made turned off a key light (there was a contingency between that peck and the light going off) or whether the key light was turned off independently of their behavior (but in close temporal proximity to the peck). Killeen's experiment is quite ingenious. He presented his pigeons with three keys. Pecks at the center key turned off that key light with a probability of 0.05; that is, over the course of a session, on the average, only one out of every 20 pecks at the center key turned off the light. At the same time that the pigeon was pecking at this key, a computer was generating "pecks" at about the same rate as the pigeon. Five percent of these "computer pecks" also turned off the light. When the center light went off, the two side keys were lit. If a real peck turned off the center key, then a peck at the left key would result in food. However, if a "computer peck" turned off the center key light, a peck at the right key would result in food. Incorrect classifications of the cause of the center light going off led to a 5-second blackout (the box was completely dark and no food was given). Killeen reported that all pigeons learned this discrimination and within a few weeks were performing with

80% to 90% accuracy— this shows that they were sensitive to the difference between behavior-produced and behavior-independent events. However, just because individuals can differentiate contingent from noncontingent events does not mean that they always do so (Nesbitt & Ross, 1980).

Reconciling the Data on the Effects of Temporal Proximity and Contingency on the Occurrence of Operant Conditioning

It is tempting to conclude that neither temporal proximity nor behavior-outcome contingency is involved in the selection of operant behaviors. That is a mistake. Both are involved. As we noted in Chapter 11, operant conditioning is an inference task in which individuals are confronted with the problem of determining whether the occurrence of a significant event was due to chance or to something he or she did, and if that action is performed, whether the significant event will occur again. Unlike Pavlovian conditioning, where the individual can only observe the occurrence of events, in operant conditioning the individual can test whether the reinforcing event is due to chance or is in fact brought on by his or her behavior (Staddon, 1975). Thus *it appears that both temporal proximity and behavior-outcome contingency are both involved in the selection of behavior in operant conditioning.*

Does Selection Involve Gradual Molding of Behavior or the Creation of New Behavioral Programs?

> Shaping behavior by the method of successive approximations and the procedure of differentiation suggests that operant conditioning involves the gradual molding of behaviors by their outcomes. That is not correct. Operant conditioning creates new behavioral programs that involve the rearrangement of existing behavior modules.

Most species evolved gradually over time as groups of individuals from the same species drifted apart and became isolated from each other so that they eventually accumulated enough genetic differences which prevented them from interbreeding successfully. At that point, they became different species. It is tempting to view selection in operant conditioning in the same way, but recent data casts doubt on the notion that selection in operant conditioning is a gradual process.

The notion that behavior is *gradually molded* or shaped by outcomes was expressed succinctly by Skinner (1953):

> Operant conditioning shapes behavior as a sculptor shapes a lump of clay. Although at some point the sculptor seems to have produced an entirely novel object, we can always follow the progress back to the original undifferentiated lump, and we can make the successive stages by which we return to this stage as small as we wish. At no point does anything emerge that is very different from what preceded it. The final product seems to have a special unity or integrity of design, but we cannot find a point at which this suddenly appears. In the same sense,

an operant is not something which appears full grown in the behavior of the organism. It is the result of a continuous shaping process. (p. 91)[2]

The alternative to a gradual molding interpretation of operant conditioning is to conceptualize operant behavior as the *arrangement of preexisting behavior modules* to produce the successful action (see, e.g., Gould & Marler, 1984; Staddon, 1983; Timberlake & Lucas, 1989). From this point of view, operant conditioning reflects the building of a behavioral program out of existing modules (that may be either innate or learned) in much same way one combines subroutines in a computer program.

Stokes and Balsam (1991) provided an interesting test of the two views of how operant behavior is selected by reinforcement. They trained rats to drink from a water dipper and then divided the rats into two groups for the shaping of lever pressing by the method of successive approximations (see Chapter 7). The groups differed in terms of the approximations to lever pressing that were reinforced prior to the first lever press: Early in the shaping process, rats in the first group were given water when they reared anywhere in the chamber and then when they reared over the lever. Rats in the second group were given water when their snout was close to the lever and then when they contacted the lever with their snout during shaping. These contingencies were discontinued following the first lever press; that is, lever pressing was rewarded no matter what other behavior preceded it. Stokes and Balsam observed that although rearing or contact with the snout were no longer required for the delivery of water, these behaviors persisted depending on which was rewarded early in training (more so in the case of rearing). Stokes and Balsam repeated this procedure with a second set of rats. This time there was a single group in which initially water was given for approaching the light over the lever and pressing the lever with a single paw. Once lever pressing began, only sequences that included lever presses with a single paw and approach to the light were rewarded. This continued until the rats had collected 100 water outcomes. Then the requirements of approach to the light and using a single paw were dropped so that any behavior that produced depression of the lever was rewarded. Despite the relaxation of the requirement for reward, three of the four rats continued to approach the light and press with a single paw throughout training. Stokes and Balsam concluded that operant behavior is a discrete unit composed of a sequence of subunits.

Are Selected Behaviors Strengthened or Retained?

The words we use when we describe operant conditioning (e.g., reinforcers) suggest that behaviors are strengthened by their consequences, but in natural selection, traits are retained (not strengthened) by selection.

A persistent unresolved problem is to specify exactly how the selection mechanism affects the selected behavior. Following Thorndike, one could say that behavior is

---

[2]Compare Skinner's statement to an earlier one by Lloyd Morgan (1894): "Just as a sculptor carves a statue out of a block of marble, so does acquisition carve an activity out of a mass of given random movements" (p. 23).

strengthened by its favorable outcome. The alternative is to say that behavior is *retained* because of its favorable outcome. There is a subtle and important distinction between these two viewpoints.

The *strength of a behavior is inferred from the probability or frequency of its occurrence*: Stronger behaviors occur more often and weaker behaviors less often. If there are two or more behaviors that the individual might perform at a given time in a given situation, the one that occurs more often is inferred to be the stronger one. Thorndike's Law of Effect is based on the assumption that the connection between the stimulus situation and the effective behavior is strengthened by the occurrence of the outcome. Skinner (1938) adopted a similar approach, but he argued that the effective behavior itself (not its connection to the stimulus situation) is strengthened by the action of the reinforcer. Likewise, behaviors that are not followed by positive reinforcers (or the removal of negative reinforcers) are thought to be weakened. Thus, for both Skinner and Thorndike, the effective behavior comes to predominate because it becomes stronger relative to other behaviors that might occur in that situation. If that behavior is no longer followed by a reinforcing event (procedure of extinction), it will become weakened to the point that other formerly weaker behaviors will now appear.

The alternative is to say that the reinforcer *retains* the successful behavior for the future and unsuccessful behaviors are suppressed: Following a behavior with a positive reinforcer (or the removal of a negative reinforcer) retains that behavior for the next occasion when it might be needed, and behaviors that consistently are not followed by a positive reinforcer (or the removal of a negative reinforcer) will be suppressed (but not eliminated).

Thus, the target behavior predominates not because it becomes stronger, but because other unsuccessful behaviors are suppressed (Harlow, 1949; Staddon & Simmelhag, 1971). If the effective behavior becomes ineffective (procedure of extinction), these formerly ineffective behaviors may reappear.

In either case, the behavior that eventually predominates does so because of its status *relative* to other behaviors the individual could perform in that situation. The unresolved question is whether behaviors that are followed by favorable outcomes are selected because they are *strengthened*, because they are *retained*, or because *both occur*. To date there has not been a convincing set of experiments that differentiate these explanations.[3]

However, one thing is clear: selection of behavior by its outcomes requires a *feedback mechanism* to integrate information about the behavior and its outcome. Such a feedback mechanism in turn requires *sensory mechanisms* for monitoring both behavior and outcomes, a *short-term memory* to hold both pieces of information long enough to relate them, and a *long-term memory* to store the relationship. The critical element is the feedback an outcome provides to the individual as to the effect of his or her behavior (Dennett, 1975; Staddon, 1975, 1988). The sensory mechanisms make feedback possible, and the memory mechanisms are required for that feedback to be processed and translated into future action. How quickly the target behavior comes to predominate in that situation (i.e., be selected) depends on the individual's motivation, the motivational significance of the outcome, and the appropriateness of the target behavior (what is required) relative to the aroused behavior system (Hogan & Roper, 1978).

---

[3]Because the strengthening explanation was the first offered, it is common for people who espouse the retention view to also speak in terms of the strength of the selected behavior.

Putting This All Together

McDowell (2004, 2010, 2013b) and Baum (2012) have provided comprehensive models for how the principles of natural selection apply in operant conditioning. The starting point for McDowell's (2004, 2010, 2013b) model is the entire behavioral repertoire that an individual can generate at any moment in time. Similar behaviors are grouped into classes based on their topographies. From this population of behaviors, the "fitness" of any class of behaviors that are followed by either a positive reinforcer or the absence or removal of a negative reinforcer is enhanced, and that class of behaviors is more likely to be emitted again in that situation. McDowell (2013b) described this in terms of parents, children, and generations:

> After a behavior is emitted, pairs of parent behaviors are chosen from the population and are recombined to produce child behaviors, which constitute the next generation of potential behaviors. If the behavior that was emitted from the population resulted in the acquisition of a resource or the escape from or avoidance of a threat, then parent behaviors are chosen on the basis of their similarity to the behavior that produced the outcome, which is to say, on the basis of what may be referred to as their fitness. . . . If the emitted behavior did not result in resource acquisition or threat escape or avoidance, then parent behaviors are chosen at random from the population of potential behaviors. . . . Stronger selection events result in fitter parents being chosen for mating. (p. 732)

With respect to the issue raised in the previous section as to whether selected behaviors are strengthened or retained, McDowell comes down on the side of retention. He mentions two mechanisms commonly used for genetic selection: population truncation and tournament competition. With population truncation, a proportion of the least fit in the population is discarded and parent behaviors are chosen from those that remain. With tournament selection, behaviors selected from the population are selected at random, and they compete on the basis of fitness to be parents. Either way, reinforcement keeps those behaviors in the population.

MacDowell created a computational model that can be run on a computer to test his model. He found that the model generates behaviors that match those observed with live subjects during acquisition and extinction and in choice situations.

Baum (2002, 2004, 2012) focused on the role of what he called "Phylogenetically important events" (PIEs) in behavioral selection. These are events that directly affect survival and reproductive fitness: for example, food, water, mating opportunities, predators, parasites, and extreme weather. As we saw earlier in this chapter, induced variation is due to what Baum calls PIEs and to signals for PIEs. Baum argued that PIE-induced activities compete in time with other activities; therefore, an increase in one activity reduces the opportunity for an individual to engage in other activities. This also produces matching when two activities are measured concurrently.

According to Baum, when there is a contingency between a behavior and a PIE, the behavior becomes connected to the PIE. Every behavior-outcome contingency specifies a molar feedback function that describes the dependence of the outcome and the behavior. In this model, outcomes (PIEs) do not strengthen behavior, rather they induce more of the same behavior, and the presence of the outcome (PIE) following a behavior induces more of the same behavior. Baum (2012) summarized the basic concepts in his model as follows:

1. Phylogenetically Important Events (PIEs) are unconditional inducers.

2. A stimulus correlated with a PIE becomes a conditional inducer.

3. An activity positively correlated with a fitness-enhancing PIE becomes a PIE related conditional induced activity—usually called "operant" or "instrumental" activity.

4. An activity negatively correlated with a fitness-reducing PIE becomes a PIE-related conditional induced activity—often called "operant avoidance."

5. A PIE induces operant activity related to it.

6. A conditional inducer induces operant activity related to the PIE to which the conditional inducer is related. (p. 112)

Although different in their details and emphases, the models of McDowell and Baum describe operant conditioning in terms of mechanisms for variation, selection, and retention, and both models also provide outputs similar to what is observed in experiments on matching when applied to individual behaviors and to concurrent behaviors. Neither model is based on the strengthening of behaviors by reinforcement.

OPERANT CONDITIONING AS AN ADAPTIVE SPECIALIZATION

During the course of our waking hours we engage in a variety of activities, many of which are directed toward achieving some goal. These activities include self-care and hygiene, eating, going to work or school, working, studying, playing, entertaining ourselves and others, and communicating. Many of these activities become so routine that we do them effortlessly with little thought to what and how we are doing them. However, if one observes a small child struggling with buttons or shoelaces, or trying to ride a bicycle, one can appreciate the difference between unskilled and skilled performance. Clearly, much of what we do in our everyday lives reflects accumulated knowledge (both declarative and procedural) obtained from our own experiences. And with experience, we become more efficient in performing these everyday tasks.

The mechanisms underlying instrumental learning and operant conditioning evolved so that individuals can use the outcomes of their actions to discover what works and does not work in order to become more efficient in the future. In order to do this, one must be capable of performing a variety of actions, recognizing that a given action has a specific outcome, and then modifying one's behavior as a result of those outcomes. In this respect, operant conditioning is also an inference task: Find an efficient behavioral solution to the problem at hand so that the next time that situation is encountered, one can behave quickly and efficiently. Such learning is reflected in the reduction in behavioral variability, and with practice the effective behavior becomes routine and automatic.

As is the case with Pavlovian conditioning (see Chapter 6), operant conditioning may exist at two levels. At its most basic level, operant conditioning is hill-climbing with long-term memory. Hill-climbing provides a mechanism for evaluating feedback, and long-term memory allows individuals to make comparisons across longer periods of time and use the information obtained through hill-climbing at the later time. With repeated success, individuals become less variable in their performance of those successful actions and thus more efficient at performing them. The second level involves the acquisition and representation of knowledge of behavior-outcome relationships. During the early stages of conditioning, individuals acquire representations of their behavior and of the outcomes they are working to obtain. But with sufficient practice, operant behaviors can become habits that are on the one hand quite efficient and effortless to perform, but on the other hand are less susceptible to changes in the outcomes and thus harder to change.

Operant conditioning occurs more rapidly when the behavior is related to the reinforcing event (by virtue of an underlying behavior system). In nonhuman species the list of reinforcing events is quite narrow; in humans it is broader. Likewise, individuals bring to the pursuit of their objectives a set of possible behaviors, some of which are more likely to occur than others. Thus, the success of operant conditioning as a technique for changing behavior requires some understanding of the unconditioned effects of the reinforcing event on behavior—that is, what behavior systems might be activated by those events. For example, the presence of food elicits unconditioned behaviors such as general activity that should increase the chances that individuals find more food (Killeen, 1975), and sign-tracking may bring individuals into contact with the food, but if the operant contingency requires *in*activity as the target behavior, operant conditioning may be difficult or impossible (Blough, 1958). Likewise, when the operant contingency involving the avoidance of danger requires a species-specific behavior like fleeing, that behavior is learned rapidly, but if the operant contingency requires an activity like lever pressing or key pecking to avoid danger, learning is very slow (Bolles, 1970). The phenomenon labeled as "misbehavior" provides further illustrations of the nonarbitrary nature of operant conditioning (Breland & Breland, 1961).

Individuals can do a variety of things, and typically the things that bring on the desired effect are repeated in the future; however, performing any action has a cost. Individuals seem to make a cost-benefit analysis of what behavior to perform. Where there are two possible outcomes, individuals distribute their behavior among them according to some scheme that weighs the alternatives. All operant behavior involves choice in terms of what to do or not do.

As an adaptive specialization, operant conditioning is a more sophisticated form of learning than Pavlovian conditioning for the following reasons: While Pavlovian conditioning allows individuals to make causal inferences about the relationships between events in their environment, operant conditioning allows them to exploit that learning. Although Pavlovian CRs can prepare individuals for the occurrence of significant events, operant conditioning provides a way for individuals to use the outcomes of their behavior to become more efficient in procuring food, water, and mates, and avoiding danger. Finally, Pavlovian conditioning has been observed in one-celled organisms, but bees (Heinroth, 1976, 1979; Laverty, 1980) and locusts (Forman, 1984) appear to be the simplest organisms in which operant conditioning has been clearly demonstrated to occur.

SUMMARY AND CONCLUSIONS

Although the analogy between natural selection and operant conditioning is not perfect, there are enough similarities to make the comparison useful for understanding the mechanism of operant conditioning. Operant conditioning, like natural selection, involves *sources of variation* and *mechanisms for selection*. In operant conditioning, the two sources of variation are *induced variation* (behaviors generated by the situation) and behavioral variability (the inherent *variability* in behavior). The first source of variation produces behaviors that are likely candidates for success in certain situations, and the second source of variation allows for individuals to become more efficient through hill-climbing.

Both temporal proximity between behaviors and outcomes and the behavior-outcome contingency contribute to operant conditioning, although neither is a necessary or sufficient condition for the occurrence of operant conditioning Superstitious behaviors are behaviors that continue to occur because of accidental temporal proximity between those behaviors and a reinforcing event in the absence of a contingency. On the other hand, operant conditioning can increase behaviors when there is a delay between a behavior and a contingent outcome. Finally, there are some situations where the contingency promotes a different behavior than the one intended because the behavior system aroused by the reinforcing event induces a behavior incompatible with the behavior programmed to bring on that reinforcing event.

It is quite clear that operant conditioning does not work by gradually molding behavior; it works by fostering the creation of new behavioral programs out of existing behavioral modules. It is not clear whether behavior is strengthened by its outcomes or is retained while other behaviors drop away; however, the models proposed by McDowell and by Baum both favor an explanation of operant conditioning based on retention, which is in line with how Darwin described biological evolution.

STUDY QUESTIONS

1. How is operant conditioning similar to natural selection?

2. Give an example of the two sources of behavioral variation. How do these sources of variation contribute to operant conditioning?

3. What is "superstitious behavior"? Under what condition does it occur? Why does it occur?

4. What do we know about the contributions of temporal proximity and behavior-outcome contingencies to operant conditioning? Are

either necessary or sufficient conditions for the occurrence of operant behaviors? Why or why not?

5. What is the mechanism that produces the behavior patterns that emerge when we use the method of successive approximations to "shape" behavior?

6. Are operant behaviors that are followed by positive reinforcers *selected* or *retained* by these reinforcers?

7. What is the adaptive value of operant conditioning?

8. What evidence points to the conclusion that all behaviors are *not* equally susceptible to modification by operant conditioning? Why is that the case?

PART III

THE SOCIAL TRANSMISSION OF KNOWLEDGE

13

SOCIAL LEARNING

Up to this point, we have focused on how individuals learn about the relationships between events through Pavlovian conditioning and about the relationship between their behavior and certain outcomes through operant conditioning, but a great deal of what we humans know we learned from other people either by observing what they did, listening to what they told us, or reading what they wrote. The ability to pass information from one member of a species to another confers an obvious adaptive advantage to the members of that species because individuals can profit from others' experiences and thus short-cut the discovery process. This is especially advantageous for obtaining information about dangerous situations, the locations of food, what is edible and inedible, and how to obtain food efficiently. *Obtaining knowledge about events and the relationships between events, and about how to perform behaviors efficiently through interactions with others* is called social learning. Social learning leads to the cultural transmission of knowledge: *knowledge and skills passed from one generation to another through learning.*

Social learning is *not* restricted to humans. For example, bees pass information about the location of food to the other inhabitants of a hive through a highly ritualized "dance." While the information about the direction and distance to the food is learned by the "dancer" who conveys it to the observers, the underlying mechanisms for encoding and translating the important information are innate (Von Frisch, 1974). Even in more complex species, social learning can be influenced by innate knowledge. Juvenile monkeys who observe another monkey acting afraid in the presence of a snake and a flower will readily learn to fear snakes but not flowers (Mineka & Cook, 1988). The same appears to be true in humans: We are more likely to develop fears of "little creepy-crawly things" like spiders, rodents, and snakes than of electrical outlets, even though most of us have received electric shocks but have not been hurt by those small critters (Seligman, 1972). These are examples of what Gould and Marler (1987) referred to as "learning by instinct." Cultural transmission of knowledge has also been documented in chimpanzees (Hobaiter, Poisot, Zuberbühler, Hoppitt, & Gruber, 2014; Whiten et al., 1999).

The social transmission of knowledge can occur in one of two general ways: (1) *intentionally through some form of instruction*, or (2) *inadvertently through observation of another individual*. The dancing bee is programmed through natural selection to return to the hive to transmit what it has learned about the location of food, and the other bees are programmed to be sensitive to what the messenger conveys. This is a highly specialized example of social learning through *instruction*. We tend to think of instruction as a human activity, but there is evidence of instruction in other species (Caro & Hauser, 1992). On the other hand, the transmission of fear of snakes by observing another individual acting afraid is *inadvertent*: There is no attempt on the part of the individual supplying the information to transmit it to another—he or she would do the same thing in the presence of a snake with or without the observer being present. This is an example of social learning through *observation*. Much of what we classify as social learning occurs through observation.

Various attempts have been made to categorize and classify different types of social learning (e.g., Galef, 1988a; Heyes, 1994; Hoppitt & Laland, 2008; Whiten & Ham, 1992; Zentall, 1996, 2001). Unfortunately, none is wholly satisfactory. As Galef (1996) noted, trying to create a classification system of social learning phenomena should not be our major concern. The real issues are to understand the functions of social learning and the mechanisms that underlie it. Lefebvre and Palameta (1988) suggested three questions that should be addressed in studies of social learning: (1) What is the nature of the information transmitted from demonstrator to observer? (2) How does the information spread in the population? (3) What ecological variables favor social learning? Keep these in mind as we review some different examples of social learning.

LEARNING FOOD PREFERENCES FROM OTHERS

Rats, birds, and humans (and probably other species) can learn to prefer and to avoid certain foods through social learning. Furthermore, social learning can also attenuate food aversions in rats. All of these are examples of the inadvertent transmission of information by observing others.

Members of all species are faced with the problem of identifying what to eat and what not to eat. Natural selection has provided most species with some innate knowledge to guide that search. For example, humans come into the world with a preference for sweet things, an initial dislike for bitter things, the ability to associate flavors with both positive and negative consequences, and a combination of suspicion and curiosity about novel foods (Rozin, 1976).[1] Furthermore, we are able to learn through personal experience to avoid foods that make us ill and to consume many different foods that provide necessary nutrients. The efficiency with which individuals learn to identify good and bad foods is enhanced through social learning.

Demonstrating the Social Learning of Food Preferences

Rats who smell a distinctive food on the breath of other rats develop a preference for that food. The food preferences of children can be modified by having them eat with a group of other children all of whom choose the same food.

---

[1]It is interesting that humans do not appear to have innate aversions to the smell and taste of decaying objects and feces. Our aversions to these things are culturally determined and clearly learned (Rozin & Fallon, 1987).

The most comprehensive program for studying how social learning affects food preferences was carried out by Galef and his colleagues on Norway rats (see Galef 1977, 1985b, 1988b, 1996, 2005 for reviews). Norway rats live in colonies in a system of interconnected burrows. They leave the colony individually to search for food, and upon finding food, consume it before returning to the colony (Calhoun, 1962). Unlike bees who return to the nest and *instruct* the others where to find food, rats communicate *inadvertently* to other members of the colony through the odor of the food on their breath and snouts of what they found (Galef, Mason, Preti, & Bean, 1988).

Galef and his colleagues use the following procedure to study the social transmission of food preferences (see Figure 13.1): Two rats (designated as the demonstrator [D] and the observer [O])[2] are housed together in either the same cage or adjoining cages for a few days (Steps 1 and 2). Then one of the rats (the demonstrator) is removed to another location and fed a distinctive tasting and smelling food (e.g., cinnamon or cocoa flavored; Step 3). This step simulates the demonstrator leaving the colony in search for food. The demonstrator was then returned and allowed to interact with the other rat (the observer; Step 4). This step simulates the demonstrator returning after successfully finding food. To test for the social transmission of food preferences, the demonstrator is removed and

Figure 13.1 Procedure used by Galef and his colleagues to study the social transmission of food preferences. During Steps 1 and 2, two rats (designated as the Demonstrator and the Observer) are housed together in either the same cage or adjoining cages for a few days. In Step 3, the demonstrator (D) is removed to another location and fed a distinctive tasting and smelling food (*either* Diet Cinnamon *or* Diet Cocoa). In Step 4, D is returned and allowed to interact with O for 15 minutes. In the test (Step 5), D is removed and O is given a choice between two food cups, one containing the food D consumed in Step 3 and another distinctively flavored food.

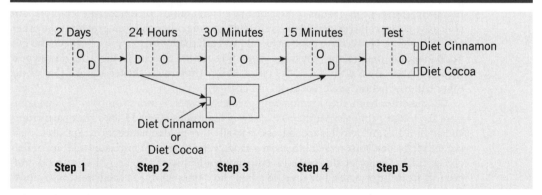

Redrawn from *Animal Behaviour*, 31, B. G. Galef, Jr. and S. W. Wigmore, Transfer of information concerning distant foods: A laboratory investigation of the "information-centre" hypothesis, 748–758, 1983, by permission of Elsevier Science.

---

[2]The terms *demonstrator* and *observer* are somewhat misleading here because the demonstrator did not "demonstrate" anything; that is, he or she did not eat the flavored food in the presence of the observer. Galef acknowledged this in his early work but for consistency retained these terms.

the observer is given access to two food cups, one containing the food the demonstrator had just consumed in another location and the other containing a different distinctively flavored food (Step 5).

The results of one such experiment are shown in Figure 13.2. The data in Figure 13.2 are the mean amounts of the cocoa-flavored food consumed as a percent of total consumption by observers whose demonstrators ate either cocoa- or cinnamon-flavored food. These data are quite clear: observers whose demonstrators ate cocoa-flavored food consumed more of it than did observers whose demonstrators ate cinnamon-flavored food, and this preference was still evident 48 to 60 hours later (Galef & Wigmore, 1983). Similar effects have been found with house mice (*Mus musculus;* Valsecchi & Galef, 1989), spiny mice (*Acomys cahirinus;* McFayden-Ketchum & Porter, 1989), Mongolian gerbils (*Meriones unguiculatus* Galef et al., 1998; Valsecchi, Choleris, Moles, Guo, & Mainardi, 1996), dwarf hamsters (*Phodopus campbelli;* Lupfer, Frieman, & Coonfield, 2003), dogs (Lupfer-Johnson & Ross, 2007), and bats (Ratcliffe & ter Hofstede, 2005), all social species. In later work, Galef and his collaborators demonstrated that knowledge of what the demonstrator ate was transmitted through the smell of the food on the demonstrator's head (Galef, Kennett, & Stein, 1985; Galef & Stein, 1985; Galef & Wigmore, 1983), specifically on its breath (Galef et al., 1988).

Galef and Wigmore (1983) demonstrated that rats can use this information to help them determine where a specific food is currently available. They trained rats to find three distinctively flavored foods in different arms of a maze. During training, only one food was available on a given day. When these rats interacted with another rat who had just eaten one of those foods, they tended to go directly to the arm where they had found that flavored food previously. Lupfer-Johnson, Hanson, Edwards, Elder, & Evans (2009) extended this research design to an open field where male dwarf hamsters had previously learned the location of three distinctively flavored foods. Following this training, they tended to go to the site from which their mate had hoarded food that day.[3]

Birch (1980) provided a similar demonstration of social learning of food preferences in preschool children. After determining which of two vegetables each child preferred, she had the children sit in groups of four or five around tables for lunch. At each table, one child (the target child) preferred one vegetable and the other children preferred the other. On each of four consecutive days each child was offered in turn a choice between the two vegetables. On the first day, the target child was offered the choice first, and on the next three days last. By the third day, the target child's preference shifted toward that of the other children (whose preferences did not change).

On the other hand, the situation with golden hamsters is more complex. Golden hamsters are solitary animals: Mothers chase away their pups about 35 days after parturition, and adult males and females are aggressive to all other golden hamsters except while mating. Adult golden hamsters fail to learn a food preference from unrelated and unfamiliar conspecifics (Lupfer et al., 2003). Juvenile golden hamsters also do not learn food preferences from littermates, but they do when the demonstrator is their mother (Lupfer, Frieman, Wiens, & Bennett, 2000).

---

[3]Male and female dwarf hamsters share a burrow when raising pups and take turns leaving to forage for food that they bring back to the burrow to hoard and provide for their pups while the other mate stays with the pups to keep them warm.

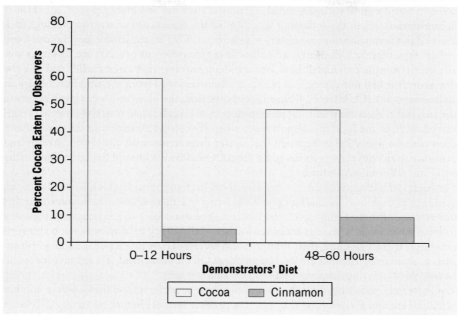

Figure 13.2 Mean amounts of the cocoa-flavored food consumed as a percent of total consumption by observers whose demonstrators ate either cocoa- or cinnamon-flavored food 0–12 and 48–60 hours earlier.

Redrawn from *Animal Behaviour, 31*, B. G. Galef, Jr. and S. W. Wigmore, Transfer of information concerning distant foods: A laboratory investigation of the "information-centre" hypothesis, 748–758, 1983, by permission of Elsevier Science.

Social Learning to Avoid Certain Foods

Although rats appear not to be able to learn to avoid foods they smell on sick rats, they can learn to avoid foods they observe a rat who becomes sick eat. Rats who get sick themselves will tend to prefer a food a demonstrator had not eaten. Blackbirds readily learn to avoid foods when they observe another bird eat it and get sick.

The adaptive value of learning what to eat from another member of your species is obvious, and it is also reasonable to expect that rats should be able to learn to avoid the food they smell on the breath of another rat who is ill or unconscious. But that is not what happens. The same rats who so readily learn what to eat by smelling the food on another rat cannot learn to avoid foods they smell on other rats who are ill (Galef, Wigmore, & Kennett, 1983; Galef, McQuoid, & Whiskin, 1990). In fact, the opposite occurs: the observers show a preference for the food the demonstrators just consumed, even though the demonstrators were ill.

However, social learning to avoid certain foods has been demonstrated under two conditions: One condition requires two rats to consume the same novel food followed by one getting sick. In these experiments, both rats drank from the same water spout and then one was removed long enough to receive an injection of LiCl before being placed back in the cage with the other rat who could continue to drink the fluid. When tested later, both rats avoided drinking that fluid, although the one poisoned drank less (Coombes, Revusky, & Lett, 1980; Lavin, Freise, & Coombes, 1980). Likewise, rats will learn to avoid a food through social learning if they get sick themselves. Galef (1987) demonstrated this in the following way: He fed the demonstrator a novel diet and then allowed the demonstrator and observer to interact. The demonstrator was removed and either immediately, 1 day later, or 8 days later (for different groups) the observer was allowed to sample two novel diets, one the demonstrator had eaten earlier and one the demonstrator had not eaten. The observers were removed from the situation and given an injection of LiCl. After a 24-hour recovery period, the observers were given access to the two novel diets they had sampled earlier. In this preference test, the observers consumed more of the food the demonstrators had *not* consumed earlier in the experiment, even with an 8-day delay between the earlier interaction with the demonstrator and exposure to the novel diets followed by illness. Galef (1986a) found the same thing using a slightly different procedure.

Galef (1985a) suggested that the inability of rats to learn to avoid foods associated with sick members of their own species (as opposed to being sick themselves) may be due to the fact that rats already have highly developed innate mechanisms for avoiding poisons (a tendency to avoid novel foods, a bias against bitter foods, and the ability to learn to develop aversions on a single trial). Therefore, there is little reason for rats to have developed the ability to learn what to avoid from smelling the food on a sick rat. On the other hand, it is adaptive for rats to be capable of inferring that what other rats are eating is safe.

Conversely, red-winged blackbirds readily learn to prefer a food they observe another blackbird eat and avoid a food they observe another bird eat before becoming ill (even a bird of another species; Mason, Arzt, & Reidinger, 1984; Mason & Reidinger, 1981, 1982). The ease with which these birds learn preferences and avoidance, and the ease with which preference and avoidance can be reversed depends on the visual aspects of the foods (see Mason, 1988, for a review). For example, blackbirds more readily learn to avoid brightly colored striped objects when they observe another consume them and get sick. This is not surprising when we consider that monarch butterflies and other poisonous species tend to be brightly colored and striped (see Chapter 2, Figure 2.8). This is another example of how innate knowledge affects learning. Furthermore, birds, unlike rats and humans, tend not to shy away from novel foods; therefore, social learning of what to avoid may be more important to them.

Social Learning Can Attenuate Food Aversions

> An ill rat will start to consume a diet it smells on a healthy demonstrator. Food aversions are also less likely to occur when the demonstrator did not get sick by eating a certain food.

The evidence is quite clear that rats, birds, and humans can learn food preferences from members of their own species. Furthermore, birds can learn food aversions by observing another bird eating something and getting sick, and rats who either eat the same food as another rat who becomes sick or become sick themselves can learn to avoid that food. Galef and his colleagues also demonstrated that social learning can be used both to reduce existing food aversions and can also prevent the development of a food aversion.

Reducing Existing Food Aversions. Galef (1985b, 1986b) allowed observer rats to eat a novel diet followed by an injection of LiCl. Two days later they were placed with demonstrators who had just consumed the same diet (or a different diet). The demonstrator and observer were then placed together for a short time (0.5 hours or 1 hour) before the observer was given a preference test (Step 5, Figure 13.1). The food aversion to the diet that preceded the LiCl injection was attenuated when the demonstrator consumed *that* diet too. This attenuation of the food aversion was not found if the demonstrator consumed a *different* diet. Thus, interaction with another rat who consumed the same novel diet and did *not* get sick appears to provide information that the diet is safe.

Preventing the Development of an Aversion. Galef (1989) and Heyes and Durlach (1990) found that one could attenuate the development of a food aversion by having a demonstrator who just consumed the novel diet and the observer interact *before* the observer eats that diet and receives the LiCl. The critical factor here is the fact that the demonstrator who ate the same diet *did not* get sick.

All of these findings illustrate that one function of social learning in rats is to transmit information about what *is* safe to eat, *not* what *is not* safe. Rats have other mechanisms for learning to avoid unsafe foods (e.g., bias toward familiar foods). On the other hand, birds can transmit information to each other through observational learning about both what is palatable and what is unpalatable.

LEARNING WHAT TO FEAR THROUGH OBSERVATIONAL CONDITIONING

Observing a member of your own species being afraid of something will lead to the social transmission of fear of that thing. This is a form of Pavlovian conditioning in which the US is fearful behavior in another individual and the CS is the thing that made the other individual fearful.

As long as no new predators enter a species' niche, natural selection could suffice to provide instinctive knowledge about who and what to avoid. And if that is not sufficient, Pavlovian conditioning can provide a mechanism for learning to fear novel objects and situations through direct experience. A form of Pavlovian conditioning called observational conditioning allows individuals to learn about threatening things from each other. In observational conditioning, *the conditioned stimulus (CS) is something to which a member of one's own species (a conspecific) exhibits fearful behavior. The unconditioned stimulus (US) is the observed fearful behavior in the conspecific, and the conditioned response (CR) is fear of that thing by the observer* (Mineka, Davidson, Cook, & Keir, 1984).

Social Transmission of Fear of Snakes in Monkeys

Fear of snakes in monkeys and recognition of predators in birds are not innate. Both are readily learned through observational conditioning. However, instinctive knowledge affects how likely an individual will learn these.

Mineka, Keir, and Price (1980) observed that while captured rhesus monkeys exhibit fearful behaviors in the presence of both real and toy snakes, laboratory-reared rhesus monkeys do not. Mineka and her colleagues proposed that the captured monkeys acquired this fear through observational conditioning in the wild. To test this hypothesis, Mineka et al. (1984) tested both captured monkeys and their laboratory-reared offspring with different objects. The wild-reared adults exhibited fear to a real snake, a toy snake, and a model snake, but not to a black cord, yellow cord, or neutral objects (square, triangular, cross-shaped, or round wood blocks painted various colors). Fear was measured both by outward signs of disturbance (e.g., facial expressions, vocalizations), how long it took them to reach past the object to obtain food, and how quickly they withdrew from the object. In contrast, the laboratory-reared juvenile monkeys showed little hesitation to reach past all of these objects to obtain food or to remain in the presence of these objects with no outward signs of fear. After demonstrating that the juveniles exhibited little fear to any of the live or toy snakes, each one was allowed to observe their parent's behavior in the presence of each of the objects described above in one laboratory room. Following this experience, the juveniles were tested for their responses to the objects in a different room.

Five of the six juveniles exhibited fearful behaviors to the snakes and not to the other objects, even when their parents were not present. This behavior pattern persisted in subsequent tests 3 months later. In a follow-up experiment using unrelated laboratory-reared juveniles and captured adults, Cook, Mineka, Wolkenstein, and Laitsch (1985) found that 7 of 10 juvenile observers became fearful of the snakes after exposure to fearful members of their own species in the presence of snakes, and Cook & Mineka (1990) demonstrated that these same effects occur when the rhesus monkeys watched videotapes of other monkeys behaving fearfully to both live and toy snakes.

This is clearly an example of Pavlovian conditioning: The US is the fearful reaction of the adult, and the UR is the fear aroused in the juvenile by observing a fearful adult. The CS is the object to which the adult exhibits fear, and the CR is fear in the juvenile observer.

Mineka and Cook (1988) demonstrated that such fears are not readily conditioned to biologically irrelevant objects such as flowers by presenting both a flower and a snake together on all conditioning trials. On test trials, the juvenile observers became fearful of the snakes and not the flowers. This is an example of overshadowing (see Chapter 4) of a less salient stimulus for conditioned fear (the flower) by a more salient stimulus for conditioned fear (the snake). This is another example of what Gould and Marler (1987) called "learning by instinct."

Finally, Mineka and Cook (1986) showed that prior experience with a snake (CS-preexposure) or prior experience observing an adult behaving nonfearfully with a snake reduces the effects of observational conditioning when those given the prior experience later encounter an adult behaving fearfully to a snake. This "immunization" against the observational learning of fear was greatest for those monkeys that observed an adult behaving nonfearfully with a snake.

Social Transmission of Fears and Phobias in Humans

Fear can also be transmitted through observational conditioning in humans. This helps explain why people with anxiety disorders (phobias, panic attacks) do not report having directly experienced the events they fear.

Watson and Rayner's (1920) demonstration of the Pavlovian conditioning of fear in Little Albert (see Chapter 2) was influential in terms of both the development of theory for understanding the acquisition of anxiety, fears, phobias, and panic disorders in humans and behavior therapy approaches for treating these disorders (e.g., Mowrer, 1939; Rachman & Costello, 1961; Wolpe & Rachman, 1960). However, many people who directly experience traumatic events do not develop these conditions (see Murray & Foote, 1979; Rachman, 1977; Rimm, Janda, Lancaster, Nahl, & Dittmar, 1977), and many people with these conditions do not report having directly experienced the traumatic event that they fear (see Marks, 1987; Kleinknecht, 1994; Merckelbach, Arntz, & de Jong, 1991; Munjack, 1984; Taylor & Deane, 1999).

One of the ways that attentional bias for threat can be assessed in humans is with the emotional Stroop color-naming task where participants are presented with words that may differ in their emotional or threat value printed in different colors (e.g., SNAKE printed in red), and they are asked to name the colors quickly while ignoring the word. People who exhibit anxiety reactions (phobias, panic disorders, and so forth) take longer to name the colors of words that have negative emotional meaning to them (Williams, Mathews, & MacLeod, 1996).

Kelly and Forsyth (2007a) used an observational fear conditioning procedure to produce emotional reactions to neutral words in people who had no past or present psychological problems and no medical problems that would pose a risk for the carbon dioxide (CO_2) challenge procedures (e.g., asthma or possibility of being pregnant) they would observe as the US, and were not color blind. All participants in this experiment were females. The CSs were semantically neutral words (e.g., CLERK, CLOUD, PRIZE, GUEST). During conditioning, two of these words (designated as CS+) appeared on the bottom of a video showing a female confederate exhibiting a mock panic attack (the US) from breathing 20% CO_2-enriched air administered through a mouth breathing respiratory mask. Two other words (designated as CS-) appeared when the confederate was supposed to be breathing room air and exhibiting neutral, calm reactions. During the Stroop task, the CS+, CS-, and two neutral previously unseen control words were presented individually in either yellow, green, blue, or red color ink. The participants' task was to name the colors of the words as quickly as they could. Following the Stroop task, the participants experienced two more CS+ and CS- observational conditioning trials followed by 16 extinction trials that consisted of presentation of the CS+ and CS- words alone.

The mean reaction time to name the colors in the Stroop task was highest for the CS+ words followed by the neural words followed by the CS- words. Following the extinction procedure, the mean reaction time to name the colors of CS+ words diminished, but the mean reaction time to name the colors of the CS+ words did not; however, the difference in reaction times still remained indicating that the extinction procedure did not completely remove the effects of observing the mock panic attacks.

In addition to measuring performance on the Stroop task, Kelly and Forsyth (2007a) also measured electrodermal responses and administered a number of scales to measure distress and fear. Participants also exhibited greater magnitude CRs to the CS+ words relative to the CS- words on these measures too.

Kelly and Forsyth (2007b) repeated their earlier experiment, this time with both males and females but only measuring electrodermal responses to the CSs and scales to measure distress and fear. They found that both males and females exhibited greater magnitude electrodermal and verbal-evaluative responses to CS+ over the CS-. Females reported more distress to the CS+, but not greater electrodermal responses than males. Taken together, these experiments provide evidence that human anxiety and phobias can be transmitted via observational conditioning.

Social Transmission of Predator Recognition in Birds

Recognition of who is a predator can be transmitted throughout a population of blackbirds by observational conditioning.

Mobbing is a defense used by blackbirds and other nesting birds to frighten away predators. In response to a mobbing cry, others take up the cry and "mob" the predator to drive it away. Curio (1988) demonstrated that observational conditioning is the basis for the social transmission of predator recognition in blackbirds. His experiment was quite ingenious. He placed two blackbirds in facing cages (see Figure 13.3). Between the two birds was a presentation box that allowed each bird to see a different stuffed model of a bird. The teacher could only see a stuffed owl (a natural predator) and the learner could only see a stuffed honeyeater (a nonpredator). The owl evoked mobbing cries in the teacher. This in turn evoked mobbing cries in the learner. Because the only model the learner could see when it heard the mobbing call was the stuffed honeyeater, it started to produce mobbing cries to honeyeaters. Once having learned this, the teacher-learner roles were reversed: Both birds were presented with models of honeyeaters, and the former learner (who now gave mobbing cries to honeyeaters) trained the former teacher to do the same. Before the experiment was carried out, neither bird feared honeyeaters; afterward, both birds feared them. Curio, Ernst, and Vieth (1978) were able to train up to six birds in this fashion, with each learner becoming the teacher for a new learner. They reported that there was no decrement in responding when the information was passed from bird to bird.

In this situation, the CS was the honeyeater and the US was the mobbing cry of one of the birds (a fear response to a perceived predator). The CR was mobbing cries to the honeyeater. This experiment demonstrated how birds can transmit information to each other about new predators in their niche.

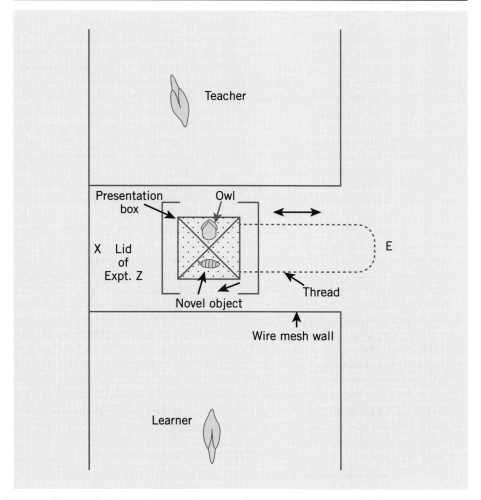

Figure 13.3 Apparatus used by Vieth, Curio, and Ernst to study the cultural transmission of predator identification in blackbirds. The presentation box between the teacher and learner contained a stuffed owl on one side and a novel object (model of a honeyeater) on the other. Each bird saw only one model at any one time. Here the teacher sees the stuffed owl (a natural predator) and the learner sees the stuffed honeyeater (a nonpredator). See text for a description of the experiment.

Reprinted from *Animal Behaviour, 28,* W. Vieth, E. Curio, and U. Ernst, The adaptive significance of avian mobbing. III. Cultural transmission of enemy recognition in blackbirds: Cross-species tutoring and properties of learning, 1217–1229, 1980, by permission of Elsevier Science.

LEARNING WHAT TO
DO BY OBSERVING OTHERS

Members of some species can learn to perform behaviors through imitation by observing others perform those behaviors. However, there are a number of instances of what looks like imitation that on closer inspection can be explained by other mechanisms. Among these are social (local) enhancement, social facilitation, goal emulation, and even Pavlovian conditioning.

In the situations described above, the observers learned what to be afraid of or what foods to seek out, but they did not learn to perform any specific behaviors. *Learning how to perform a behavior by observing another individual performing that behavior* is called imita-tion. Of the various types of social learning that have been identified, none has been more thoroughly studied and more hotly debated than imitation (see Byrne, 2002; Davis, 1973; Galef, 1988a, 1998; Heyes, 1994; Hoppitt & Laland, 2008; Whiten & Ham, 1992; and Zentall, 1996, 2001, for reviews). There is no doubt that humans learn by imitation, but there is no uniformity of opinion when it comes to other species. This state of affairs is due in part to disagreements about what are the defining characteristics of imitation and in part to the history of research in this area.

Thorndike (1898, 1911) proposed the following definition of imitation: "If one can from an act witnessed learn to do an act, he in some way makes use of the sequence seen, transfers the process to himself; in the common sense of the word, he *imitates*" (1911, pp. 79–80). Using this simple definition, Thorndike argued that the anecdotal evidence for imitation offered by his contemporaries (e.g., Romanes, 1884; Morgan, 1900) could be explained in other ways. One would think it should be relatively simple to determine if an individual learned to imitate an action by observing others performing that action. The problem is that what looks on the surface like imitation sometimes can be explained by other mechanisms. A simple example of this is the spread among birds in the British Isles of the behavior of prying open the wax-board tops of milk bottles to drink the cream from the top[4] (see Box 13.1). Although Fisher and Hinde (1949) noted that it would take "carefully controlled experiments on birds of known history" (p. 347) to determine how this behavior was acquired, at one time this phenomenon was described in a number of textbooks as an example of the cultural transmission of knowledge through imita-tion. Now we know that it occurs through a combination of a social process called local enhancement (or stimulus enhancement), Pavlovian conditioning (sign-tracking), and operant conditioning.

Local Enhancement (Stimulus Enhancement)

Sometimes the mere presence of another individual can promote learning that appears to be due to imitation but is not. The presence of

---

[4]Cream floats to the top in nonhomogenized milk. Most of the milk we purchase today is homogenized.

another individual can draw observers' attention to a particular location or to a particular object. This can increase the probability that observers will contact that object or go to that location. Once there, the observers may perform similar actions, but these are not necessarily imitated.

The social transmission of the behavior of removing the wax-board tops of milk bottles by birds in the British Isles described by Fisher and Hinde (see Box 13.1) involves a mechanism

BOX 13.1

The Opening of Milk Bottles by Birds

Fisher and Hinde offered the following observations about the cultural transmission of how birds open milk bottles.

The bottles are usually attacked within a few minutes of being left at the door. There are even several reports of parties of tits following the milkman's cart down the street and removing the tops from bottles in the cart whilst the milkman is delivering milk to the houses.

The method of opening employed varies greatly. When the milk bottle is closed by a cap of metal foil the bird usually first punctures the cap by hammering with its beak and then tears off the metal in thin strips. Sometimes the whole cap is removed, sometimes only a small hole is made in it. Cardboard caps may be treated in a variety of ways. The whole top may be removed, or only the press-in centre, or the cardboard may be torn off layer by layer until it is thin enough for a small hole to be made in it; the milk may be taken through this hole or the bird may insert its beak in the hole and flick off the remainder of the top. The records show that several different methods may be used in any one district,

and that more than one method may be employed by one individual. For example, Margaret Campbell watched a Great Tit tap out half the small central disc and take a few sips of milk. The bird was then disturbed, but returned in a minute or two. This time it alighted on another bottle "on which the stopper was slightly crooked; it made no attempt to peck but inserted its beak under the raised part and flicked it off in one movement.. .." It is therefore quite certain that the process which has been learnt is the whole business of obtaining milk from milk bottles, and not any particular technique for opening bottles.

From Fisher and Hinde, 1949, pp. 347 and 354. Reprinted with permission of *British Birds*.

called **local enhancement** (Thorpe, 1956, 1965) or **stimulus enhancement** (Heyes, 1994; Spence, 1937): *The presence of the demonstrator draws the observer's attention to a specific location or object and thus increases the probability that the observer will go to that location or contact that object*, in this case, the milk bottles.

Sherry and Galef (1984) took up Fisher and Hinde's challenge (see above) and created a laboratory simulation of the milk bottle situation using small foil-covered plastic tubs filled with cream (the kind restaurants serve with coffee or tea). The design of their experiment is presented in the top panel of Table 13.1. First they tested 16 chickadees individually to determine whether any would peck thorough the foil to get to the milk on their own. The four birds who did so on their own became the demonstrators. The remaining birds were divided into three groups: The birds in the *Tutored Group* watched another bird in an adjacent cage opening tubs five different times. During this time, the observers also had a sealed tub in their own cage, which they could open while watching the demonstrator. A second group *(Open Tub)* had an open tub in their cage on five different occasions. They did *not* observe another bird. The third group *(Closed Tub)* had five trials with a closed tub and no demonstrator. Then all birds in all three groups were given five trials with a sealed tub. Three of the four birds in both the Tutored and Open Tub groups learned to peck through the foil, either in training or in the test (in the case of the *open tub* group, whose first opportunity came during the test). None of the birds in the Closed Tub group pecked through the foil in the test trials.

In a follow-up study, Sherry and Galef (1990) repeated parts of their earlier experiment (with more subjects in each group) and added another group *(Tutor Present*; bottom panel of Table 13.1). In this group, the demonstrator was present in the other cage but it did not have a tub to open, while the observer had a closed tub in his or her cage. There also was a *Tutored* Group and a *Closed Tub* group. Seven of the 14 birds in the *Tutored* Group and 5 of the 16 subjects in the *Tutor Present* group opened tubs during the five test trials; none of the *Closed Tub* subjects did.

These data suggest that imitation is not the only explanation for the spread of a behavior pattern through a population. Two other possibilities come to mind. First, the performance of the *Tutored* Group could have been due to local enhancement; that is, a bird feeding from a food source draws the observer's attention to that food source. However, that does not explain why individuals in the *Open Tub* group learned to peck through the foil. That result appears to be due to sign-tracking: The birds in the *Open Tub* group learned through direct experience that the tub contains food (and thus is a signal for food). Through the mechanism of sign-tracking, they approached and directed feeding movements (pecking) toward that signal. Therefore, removing wax lids or pecking through foil could spread through a population because the open tubs (bottles) left by some birds attract others. Of course, once a bird is successful at piercing the foil or removing the lid, he or she can become efficient at this behavior through hill-climbing (i.e., through operant conditioning). Second, the simple presence of other birds no doubt increases activity and thus increases the chances that birds will discover for themselves how to do it. This latter mechanism is called **social facilitation**: *behavior that is aroused by the mere presence of another member of the species* (Zajonc, 1965). Social facilitation would explain the performance of the birds in the Tutor Present group in Sherry and Galef's second experiment (1990).

Table 13.1 Designs for the Sherry and Galef (1984, 1990) Experiments Demonstrating Local (Stimulus) Enhancement as a Mechanism for Social Learning

1984 experiment			
Pretraining	Training	Test	Results: # opening tubs in test
All 16 birds tested to see whether they would peck through the foil cover to get milk The 4 birds that did served as demonstrators for the other 12	**Tutored group** ($N = 4$): Observers watched demonstrators open milk tubs **Open tub group** ($N = 4$): Had an open tub in their cage (no demonstrator) **Closed tub group** ($N = 4$): Had a closed tub in cage (no demonstrator)	Birds from all 3 groups given 5 trials with a closed tub	**Tutored group:** 3 out of 4 **Open tub group:** 3 out of 4 **Closed tub group:** 0 out of 4
1990 experiment			
Pretraining	Training	Test	Results: # opening tubs in test
Birds tested to see whether they would peck through the foil cover to get milk Those birds that did served as demonstrators	**Tutor present group** ($N = 16$): Another bird present, but it does not have a tub to open **Tutored group** ($N = 14$): Observers watched demonstrators open milk tubs **Closed tub group** ($N = 10$): Had a closed tub in cage (no demonstrator)	Birds from all 3 groups given 5 trials with a closed tub	**Tutor present group:** 5 out of 16 **Tutored group:** 7 out of 14 **Closed tub group:** 0 out of 10

Reprinted from *Animal Behaviour*, 32/3, David F. Sherry and B.G. Galef, Cultural transmission without imitation, 938, ©1984, with permission from Elsevier.

Krebs, MacRoberts, and Cullen (1972) also studied in the laboratory the behavior of a species similar to that described by Fisher and Hinde (1949). They constructed a set of artificial trees on which small feeders of various shapes were affixed. Krebs et al. observed that when a single bird found some food, others quickly joined the successful bird, and all of the birds then directed their searches to that general area or to the type of feeder where the first individual found food; this is another example of local enhancement. Based on these observations, Krebs et al. argued that local enhancement is an adaptive specialization because it increases the chances for finding food: When a number of individuals are searching for food, the chances of one of the group finding food is increased. Once food is found, local enhancement directs others in that group to that location or food source.

Goal Emulation

> When individuals use a tool in a functional manner and do not just copy the behavior they observe, we classify this as goal emulation not imitation.

Another mechanism that looks like imitation is called goal emulation: *reproducing the results obtained by the demonstrator* (Tomasello, 1990). Goal emulation is different from imitation because the observer reproduces the *results* achieved by the demonstrator, *not* the behavior. Using chimpanzees, Tomasello, Davis-Dasilva, Camak, and Bard (1987) demonstrated that the social learning of tool use in chimpanzees is *not* due to imitation. They had juvenile chimpanzees watch another chimp use a metal T-bar to rake in out-of-reach food. At a later time, the observers used the T-bar to rake food, but they did not always use it in the same way the demonstrator did. It was apparent from their behavior that the observers learned through observation that the tool can be used to obtain food, but they were not merely imitating the demonstrator. Tomasello et al. suggested that observation of the demonstrator using the tool made the tool "more salient *in its function as a tool* " (p. 181). Nagell, Olguin, and Tomasello (1993) repeated this experiment with both chimpanzees and 2-year-old children. In both cases, the demonstrator was an adult human. They found that the human children copied the behavior of the demonstrator (imitated), even when the demonstrator used an inefficient method to obtain the food. In contrast, the chimpanzees used the T-bar in various ways independently of what the demonstrator did. The same is true of orangutans (Call & Tomasello, 1994, 1995).

Summarizing his work, Tomasello (1996) concluded that apes attend to the relationship between the tool and the outcome and not the behavior of the demonstrator. Apes clearly have the intelligence to use tools creatively to bring about changes in their environment, and they can learn this by observation, but they do not necessarily imitate the behaviors they observe.

True Imitation

> In order to demonstrate that an individual learns to perform an action by imitation, one has to demonstrate that the observer's performance is not due to any of the mechanisms described above. This can be achieved when there is more than one way to perform the task, the demonstrator performs it in one of the possible ways, and the behavior of the observer matches the behavior of the demonstrator, even if that is not the most efficient way to perform the action. This test is called the bidirectional control or two-action procedure.

Thorpe (1956, 1965) offered the following definition of imitation: "By true imitation is meant the copying of a novel or otherwise improbable act or utterance, or some act for which there is clearly no instinctive tendency" (1956, p. 122). This rather restrictive definition eliminates from consideration as true imitation any behavior that occurs as the result of interaction with another individual but can be explained through some other mechanism. Thus, the social transmission of mobbing cries and fear of snakes does not qualify as imitation because both involve instinctive knowledge, and both can be explained by simpler mechanisms (in this case, observational conditioning of a module from a behavior system). Similarly, birds learning to remove wax-board lids from milk bottles and to peck through the foil tops of milk bottles can be explained as local enhancement, social facilitation, and perhaps sign-tracking, but *not* imitation.

The Bidirectional Control or Two-Action Procedure as a Way to Demonstrate Imitation. Dawson and Foss (1965) proposed a way to satisfy Thorpe's criterion for true imitation. Their technique is sometimes called the bidirectional control method or the two-action procedure. It is an adaptation of the method used by Grindley (1932) to demonstrate instrumental learning in guinea pigs (see Chapter 7). To rule out the effects of Pavlovian conditioning on operant behavior, Grindley showed that he could specify the direction (left or right) toward which his animals turned their heads by making the presentation of the carrot dependent on the direction he (Grindley) selected. This ruled out sign-tracking as the explanation for the conditioned behavior because the conditioned behavior was not directed at a specific signal for food. This two-action or bidirectional procedure can be used to rule out sign-tracking and other stimulus-directed behaviors in studies of imitation. In experiments on imitation, the two-action or bidirectional control procedure *requires that there be more than one way an individual can perform an action (or more than one action) that leads to the outcome. Different observers can watch different demonstrators obtaining the outcome in different ways. Imitation is inferred to be the mechanism for learning if the observers perform the action they observed, even if other ways also work (or work better).*

Dawson and Foss (1965) used the two-action procedure to investigate imitation in budgerigars (parakeets). The task was to remove a red square of thin cardboard from a white pot containing seed. Birds were paired together with one serving as the demonstrator and the other as the observer. The demonstrator learned the task in the absence of the observer and then performed it in the presence of the observer who watched from an adjoining cage. Twenty-four hours later, the observer is given the opportunity to obtain food from the white pot in the absence of the demonstrator. In each pair the observer used the method of the demonstrator (edge the cardboard off with the beak or use foot to dislodge the cardboard). Two months later they were still doing it the same way. Galef, Manzig, and Field (1986) repeated this experiment using more pairs of birds, but their results were both small and transient. On the other hand, Heyes and Saggerson (2002) found strong evidence for imitation in the same species using a task where the demonstrators had to either pull up or push down on a stopper to gain access to food.

Using the bidirectional or two-action procedure, imitation has been demonstrated in a number of different species. For example, Collins (1988) demonstrated imitation of pushing a panel to the left or right in mice, and Zentall and his colleagues demonstrated imitation in pigeons (Kaiser, Zentall, & Galef, 1997; Zentall, Sutton, & Sherburne, 1996) and in quail (Adkins & Zentall, 1996, 1998; Dorrance & Zentall, 2001) where the demonstrated actions were either pecking at or stepping on a treadle to receive food. In later experiments, Zentall and his colleagues demonstrated imitation in pigeons that observed a conspecific demonstrator pushing a screen that blocked the feeder either left or right (Klein & Zentall, 2003) and in dogs that observed a conspecific demonstrator pushing aside either left or right a mesh screen that covered an opening in a wooden panel to gain access to food from the experimenter sitting behind the panel. Voelkl and Huber (2000) arranged for marmosets to observe a demonstrator remove the lids from a set of plastic containers to obtain a mealworm. Some demonstrators accomplished this only with their hands, and others also used their mouths (something marmosets typically do not do). When given the opportunity to open similar containers, the observers used the methods they observed. Voelkl and Huber (2007) repeated this experiment, this time recording the head motions of both their demonstrators and observers opening the canisters. Using detailed motion analyses, they found that the observers precisely copied the movement patterns of the demonstrators.

Because all of these experiments used the bidirectional or two-action procedure, the results cannot be explained by local enhancement, social facilitation, sign-tracking, or goal emulation. These results appear to be due to imitation. However, one must still be careful to attribute behavior to imitation even when using the bidirectional or two-action procedure (see Box 13.2).

BOX 13.2

The Importance of Eliminating Confounds in Experiments

In a series of experiments, Heyes and her colleagues appeared to have demonstrated true imitation in rats using the bidirectional or two-action procedure (Heyes and Dawson, 1990; Heyes, Dawson, & Nokes, 1992; Heyes, Jaldow, & Dawson, 1993, 1994; Heyes, Jaldow, Nokes, & Dawson, 1994). They had hungry rats observe from an adjoining cage a trained demonstrator push a vertical pole either left or right to obtain food. The demonstrator was removed, and the observer was placed in the other cage and allowed to push the rod to obtain food. Although food could be obtained for pushing the rod in any direction, the observers tended to push it in the same direction relative to their own bodies as they had observed the demonstrators do.

However, there is a confound in these experiments. That confound was revealed when the pole was rotated 180° before placing the observer in the cage with the pole and the observers tended to push the pole in the opposite direction from what they had observed the demonstrators

do (Mitchell, Heyes, Gardner, & Dawson, 1999). In another set of experiments, Campbell and Heyes (2002) prevented rats from observing the direction (up or down) that demonstrators pushed a lever attached to the side of the demonstrator's chamber. When placed in the demonstrator's chamber, these rats tended to move the lever in the same direction the demonstrators did even though the "observers" could not observe the direction. In a second experiment, Campbell and Heyes had their observer rats watch a demonstrator in another chamber move the lever either up or down. The observers were then placed in a different chamber where a rat they had not observed moved the lever in the opposite direction from what was observed. These "observers" tended to move the lever in the direction the former inhabitants of that box did rather than in the direction they observed.

The results of these three experiments point to odor cues left by demonstrators on the pole or lever as the major factor in the results of their earlier experiments. It is to Heyes' credit that she continued to look for alternative explanations for her earlier results. Clearly, using the bidirectional or two-action procedure does not guarantee that what one observes is imitation. There is a lesson here for all behavioral scientists: Things may not be what they appear. We need to continue to look for alternative explanations for our data.

TRANSMISSION OF INFORMATION ABOUT WHAT TO DO THROUGH DIRECTED INSTRUCTION

In all of the examples of social learning we have encountered thus far with the exception of the dance in bees, the behavior of the demonstrator is not affected by the presence of an observer; that is, the demonstrator would have performed the same actions if the observer were not present. We referred to this type of communication or social transmission as inadvertent or unintentional. In the case of **instruction**, *the transmission of information from demonstrator to observer is intentional*. We refer to this as directed instruction or teaching.

The transmission of information from one individual to another through directed instruction is called **teaching** (Caro & Hauser, 1992). Learning from directed instruction or teaching is different from the other forms of social learning. First, the transmission of information is *intentional* on the part of the demonstrator. Although it is difficult to determine intention in nonhuman species, it may be inferred when the behavior of the demonstrator is modified by the presence of the observer; that is, the demonstrator does something in the presence of the observer that he or she would not do if the observer were not present.

The second difference between instruction and the other forms of learning we have discussed to this point is the effect of the mode of transmission on the behavior of the observer. Instruction, like other forms of social learning, short-cuts the discovery process and thus produces more rapid learning than might otherwise occur if the individual had to discover what to do on his or her own.

That is the positive side of instruction. However, at least in humans, behaviors learned through verbal instructions frequently become less sensitive to the prevailing conditions. More on that later.

Forms of Instruction

Teaching and instruction refer to the behavior of the teacher. Although our interest here is in the behavior of the pupil, it is important to note that instruction (teaching) can take various forms, many of which have been observed in nonhuman species.

Opportunity Teaching. The most common type of instruction observed in nonhuman species is **opportunity teaching**: *The teacher puts the pupil into a situation that is conducive for the pupil to learn.* Caro (1994) provided a nice example of opportunity teaching in cheetahs. Female cheetahs with cubs 2.5 to 3.5 months old will start to refrain from their usual behavior of killing prey when they catch it and instead release the prey in the presence of their cubs (sometimes after carrying it to the cubs). After 5 to 15 minutes, the mother would then kill the prey. As the cubs grow older, they begin to kill the prey she brings them. Schaller (1967) described a tigress pulling down a buffalo and then leaving it for her cubs to kill. When they failed to do that, she toppled the buffalo for them to try again. Thornton and McAuliffe (2006) and Thornton (2008) described how meerkats use opportunity teaching with their young. Meerkats are small carnivores belonging to the mongoose family that live in the Kalahari Desert in Botswana, Namib Desert in Namibia and southwestern Angola, and in South Africa. They consume a variety of prey including scorpions. By 3 months of age, pups can handle difficult prey. This is facilitated by adults. When young meerkats are present, adult meerkats will kill or disable prey (e.g., removing the sting from a scorpion) before presenting it to pups instead of immediately consuming the prey, which they do when no pups are present. As the pups grow older, they are increasingly given intact prey.

Under laboratory conditions, Caro (1980a, 1980b) studied the development of predatory behavior in domestic cats. Cats usually kill prey immediately, but beginning at about 4 weeks of age, mother cats expose their kittens to live prey. As the kittens grow older, the mother's latency to kill prey herself increases as the predation skill of her offspring improve. In all of these examples, the adults provided opportunities for the juveniles to develop their hunting skills, and the adult's behavior changed as the juveniles became more proficient.

Coaching. The other major class of instruction observed in nonhuman species is called **coaching**: *altering the behavior of the pupil through encouragement or punishment* (Caro & Hauser, 1992). Altmann (1980) described how a baboon mother *encouraged* her infant to walk: "A mother began to take a few steps away from her infant, paused, and looked back at the infant. As soon as the infant began to move slowly toward her, she again moved slowly away. At first, this sequence was repeated every few steps, but soon a mother seemed to be able to initiate a long bout of following, by one such pause" (p. 130). On the other side, there are numerous examples of *punishment (discouragement)* of behaviors by nonhuman teachers. For example, Seyfarth and Chaney (1980) described adult vervet monkeys punishing juveniles for making an inappropriate alarm cry, and Goodall (1986) described adult chimpanzees taking foods that were not part of the group's diet away from infants. Goodall argued that this accounts for differences in food preferences among different troops of chimpanzees.

Demonstration. Closely related to coaching (and perhaps another form of coaching) is **demonstration**: *actively teaching a skill by performing it in front of another individual.* Boesch (1991) provided some examples in chimpanzees. In one case, a mother demonstrated to her son how to hold a nut on an anvil while the youngster hammered it open. In a second example, a mother reoriented a hammer in the hand of her daughter, who then hammered open the nuts. Boesch also observed female chimpanzees providing examples of opportunity teaching by leaving stones and nuts in the vicinity of their offspring and passively allowing their young to take stones and nuts from them.

Physical Guidance. Fouts, Fouts, and Van Cantfort (1989) described how an adult chimpanzee who had been taught sign language by humans molded a juvenile's hand into the sign for food. In the language of behavior modification, this last example is called *physical guidance* or *putting through: physically putting the other individual through the motions.* Caro and Hauser (1992) classified physical guidance (putting through) and demonstration as forms of coaching.

Verbal Instructions. Although all of the methods of instruction described above have been observed in animals, in humans the most common form of teaching is through **verbal instruction:** *telling someone what to do or how to do something.* Skinner (1966, 1969) noted that verbal instructions can take the form of **advice** (*informing someone what will happen under certain circumstances*), **directions** (*telling someone how to do something or where to go to obtain something*), or **commands** (*when a person in control of the outcomes tells someone what to do to obtain or avoid an outcome*). Skinner described the information conveyed by these various forms of verbal instructions as **rules:** *statements of the relationships (contingencies) between events,* and he referred to *behaviors that are guided by a rule* as **rule-governed behaviors.**[5] Instructions, directions, and advice function as occasion setters (or discriminative stimuli) informing us of a behavior-outcome relationship. In the remainder of this chapter we will review the effects of verbal instructions on human behavior.

THE EFFECTS OF VERBAL INSTRUCTIONS ON HUMAN BEHAVIOR

We humans are different from other species in two important ways: we have greater reasoning abilities, and we have the ability to convey to each other what we know through speech and the written word. Although many other species also have methods to communicate among themselves, that ability is most highly evolved in humans. As a result, human behavior is strongly influenced by what we are told (i.e., verbally-mediated knowledge) as well as by what we directly experience when we encounter Pavlovian conditioning and operant conditioning procedures (i.e., contingency-mediated knowledge).

---

[5]In one sense, most Pavlovian conditioned and operant conditioned behaviors are rule-governed because these behaviors reflect an inference process based on personal experience with the contingent relationship between events (CSs and USs in Pavlovian conditioning and behaviors and outcomes in operant conditioning). Because the term "rule-governed" is used by many people to designate operant behaviors under the influence of verbal rules, "verbally-mediated" will be used here to refer to both Pavlovian conditioned and operant conditioned behaviors affected by verbal instructions or that reflect self-generated instructions.

There are two ways that we can learn about relationships between environmental events and about relationships between behaviors and outcomes: we can detect the prevailing contingencies (CS-US or B-O) either through direct experience with them or we can be told by someone else what they are. *Learning based on direct experience with a contingency* is said to be **contingency-mediated learning**, while *learning based on verbal descriptions of the contingency or instructions about what to do* is said to be **verbally-mediated learning**. However, this distinction is not as clean as it appears at first glance. Although humans given false information about the CS-US or B-O contingencies have been observed to perform according to the misleading instructions, humans can learn that the instructions are incorrect and adjust their behavior to the prevailing contingency. On the other hand, in the absence of explicit instructions, humans left to experience the prevailing contingency frequently generate incorrect self-instructions and behave according to these self-instructions and not the contingency. Furthermore, because most of us have a long history of following instructions (Zettle & Hayes, 1982), an authority figure can have strong control over our behavior, even to the point where some people will follow instructions to inflict harm on others (Milgram, 1963). Skinner (1966, 1969) argued that instruction following is also an operant behavior because it can be reinforced or punished like other operants. Therefore, it is accurate to portray human Pavlovian conditioning and operant conditioning as reflecting a mixture of both contingency-mediated and verbally-mediated behaviors. Which of these dominates performance depends on a variety of conditions. We will examine some of these now.

The Effects of Verbal Instructions on Pavlovian Conditioning

Human Pavlovian conditioning is very susceptible to verbal instructions when the CS and US bear no natural relationship to each other. When the CS and US have a natural relationship, Pavlovian conditioning is not easily influenced by instructions.

The majority of Pavlovian conditioning studies of humans in the laboratory involve eyelid conditioning or various indexes of conditioned emotional responses (e.g., changes in heart rate and galvanic skin response [GSR]). In Chapters 2 and 6, we noted that *with arbitrary CSs like circles and triangles, verbal instructions about the CS-US relationship affect the course of conditioning in humans*; that is, emotional responses can be induced by merely informing someone of the impending CS-US contingency (Cook & Harris, 1937; Dawson & Grings, 1968). Furthermore, informing someone that the procedure has changed to extinction also produces a rapid decline in emotional responses (Bridger & Mandell, 1965; Cook & Harris, 1937; Dawson & Grings, 1968; Katz et al., 1971; Wilson, 1968), and providing people with false information about the CS-US contingency will lead them to behave in accordance with that false information, not the contingency in effect (Deane, 1969; Spence & Goldstein, 1961). All of these effects occur with arbitrarily chosen CSs, and all are examples of verbally-mediated behaviors in Pavlovian conditioning.

On the other hand, the effects of information about the CS-US relationship are different when the CS is a snake or spider. Although such information can facilitate the acquisition of conditioned emotional responses with stimuli like snakes and spiders, information that the US will no longer occur has little effect on extinction (Öhman & Hugdahl, 1979). This explains why behavior therapy approaches based on Pavlovian conditioning (as opposed to instructions not to be afraid) are required for the treatment of phobias to those stimuli (Marks, 1987; Öhman & Hugdahl, 1979).

Taken together, these findings suggest that in humans (and perhaps in other vertebrate species) Pavlovian conditioning occurs at two levels. The first level is more primitive, automatic, noncognitive, and highly specialized, and it is less affected by verbal instructions. We see another example of this with patients who receive chemotherapy: they know that it is the chemotherapy and not what they eat that makes them nauseous, yet they still develop CTAs (Bernstein, 1991). The second level can be described as "cognitive relational learning" in which the individual actively processes information about the relationships between events (Dawson & Schell, 1987; Levey & Martin, 1983; Razran, 1955). There is clear evidence for relational learning in other species (see Chapter 5), but in humans we clearly see the effects of verbal mediation. Thus, the important difference between us humans and other species is how easily some CRs can be manipulated by telling us about the CS-US contingency.

The Effects of Verbal Instructions on Operant Conditioning

Because we adult humans have a long history of being rewarded for following instructions, our operant behavior is easily influenced by instructions. On the one hand, verbal instructions lead to rapid learning, but on the other hand, this can make us insensitive to changes in the prevailing contingencies and thus inefficient in our performance of these verbally-mediated behaviors.

Although there can be no doubt that we humans are sensitive to and adjust our behavior based on the outcomes of our actions, it is interesting that in many respects other animal species are better at this (Higgins & Morris, 1984; Perone, Galizio, & Baron, 1988). With members of other species, we can either wait for them to discover the correct action like Skinner (1932c) did in his early work with rats pressing levers for food or use the method of shaping by successive approximations to direct them to the right place (Skinner, 1938). Despite our superior problem-solving abilities, humans do not always do well when left on their own or even when the shaping by successive approximations is used. Frequently, we humans need some verbal instructions when it is not obvious what is required of us.

In avoidance conditioning situations, members of other species can rapidly learn the required avoidance behavior with no intervention when that behavior is *not* counter to their natural tendency in dangerous situations (Bolles, 1972; Bolles & Popp, 1964; Sidman, 1953a). This is not necessarily the case with humans. Ader and Tatum (1961) arranged the following situation: Thirty-six medical students and graduate students were seated next to a table onto which a small red button on a wooden board was fastened. An electrode was placed on their leg and shocks were administered every 5 seconds. These shocks could be avoided by pressing the button in front of them (free-operant avoidance task in which the shock-shock and response-shock intervals were both 5 seconds; see Chapter 7). No instructions were given. Of the 36 subjects in this experiment, only 17 figured out that each press of the button would result in a 5-second shock-free period. It is surprising that so many of Ader and Tatum's subjects did not learn the relationship between pressing the button and avoiding shock: the button was obvious and there certainly was adequate motivation to avoid being shocked. On the other hand, using a different free-operant avoidance task (avoidance of loss of money), Baron and Kaufman (1966) found that instructions prior to the session about the target behavior and its outcomes produced immediate, stable avoidance behavior. Clearly, *verbal instructions can establish operant behavior quickly and efficiently in humans; in the absence of instructions, some humans may not learn what to do.*

Perhaps the most striking difference between humans and members of other species is how adult humans behave under fixed-interval (FI) schedules of reinforcement. As we saw in Chapter 9, rats and pigeons readily adjust their behavior to the demands of fixed-interval schedules, and within a few sessions they exhibit the characteristic fixed-interval scallop or break-and-run pattern (Figure 13.4, left panel). On the other hand, humans given minimal instructions to perform a target behavior and no instructions about the schedule of reinforcement typically exhibit one or the other of the patterns on the right side of Figure 13.4, either a very high rate of behavior that ignores the temporal aspects of the fixed-interval schedule (pattern A) or extremely good temporal discrimination with one or two instances of the target behavior occurring near the end of the intervals (pattern B) (see Weiner, 1964, 1965, 1969, 1970). Sometimes, both patterns will be observed in the same individual in different sessions or even within the same session (Lippman & Meyer, 1967). Pattern A is clearly inefficient because much more behavior is generated than is needed to obtain the reinforcer. On the other hand, pattern B is quite efficient because it tracks the contingency and provides the individual with the maximum amounts of reinforcement possible for the minimum amount of effort.

What accounts for the difference between members of other species and human infants on the one hand and adult humans on the other? Lowe (1979) proposed that this difference is due to the tendency for adult humans to generate their own rules about the situation when none is supplied by the experimenter; that is, their behavior is verbally-mediated. To test this hypothesis, Bentall, Lowe, and Beasty (1985) and Lowe, Beasty, and Bentall (1983) had humans under the age of 2 years work on FI schedules to receive either music or food. The target behavior was touching a cylinder placed in front of them on a highchair. Their pattern of touching looked like that obtained from members of other species on FI schedules.

However, when they tested children over the age of four and adults in similar situations, their behavior resembled the patterns on the right panel of Figure 13.4. Children 2.5 to 4 years old were inconsistent, some showing the pattern of younger children and others the pattern of older children and adults. In a later study, Bentall and Lowe (1987) found that they could induce the adult pattern in children in the 2.5- to 4-year-old

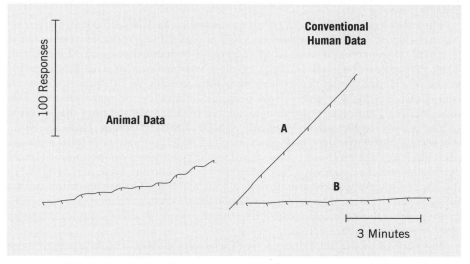

Figure 13.4 Typical cumulative records of performance on fixed-interval schedules of reinforcement by nonhumans and humans under the age of 2 years (left) and humans above the age of 4 years given minimal instructions (right). Pattern A indicates a very high rate of behavior that ignores the temporal aspects of the fixed-interval schedule, and Pattern B an extremely good temporal discrimination with one or two instances of the target behavior occurring near the end of the intervals. Sometimes both Patterns A and B will be observed in the same individual.

From Lowe, 1979, Determinants of human operant behavior. In P. Harzem and M. D. Zeiler (Eds.), *Advances in analysis of behaviour: Volume 1, Reinforcement and the organization of behaviour.* (pp. 159–192). Reproduced with permission of P. M. Lowe.

range by instructing them to perform the target behavior rapidly. These results are consistent with Lowe's hypothesis that verbally proficient humans generate their own rules when none are supplied by someone else. On the other hand, children under the age of 2 years have not developed that capacity; therefore, their behavior is contingency-mediated and reflects both the molar and molecular feedback functions for the schedule.

Rosenfarb, Newland, Brannon, and Howey (1992) studied the effects of self-generated rules on performance. Their subjects were allowed to earn points on two different schedules, each of which was signaled by a different light. When the right light was on, the schedule was an IRT > 5 seconds and when the left light was on the schedule was a fixed-ratio 8 (FR 8). While they were learning this task, some subjects were asked to state what they thought determined how they earned points. These rules were then transmitted to a second set of subjects who could try them out. A third group of subjects was left on their own and neither asked to develop rules nor were they given any. After an hour, all subjects were put on extinction. The subjects given rules (the second group) acquired schedule-typical behavior at the fastest pace, but by the end of extinction, the third group (those not asked to generate nor given rules) reduced their behavior the most on the FR schedule. Therefore, *asking subjects to generate rules facilitates acquisition but retards extinction.* Furthermore, *self-generated rules function similarly to externally acquired rules.* It is interesting, however, that sometimes subjects produced schedule-appropriate behavior before generating the correct rule. This indicates that *self-generated rules are not necessarily independent of the prevailing contingency and provides further evidence that the distinction between contingency-mediated and verbally-mediated behavior is not clear cut.*

The study just described also points to the importance of verbal instructions on human behavior. Lippman and Meyer (1967) provided an early demonstration of the powerful effects verbal instructions can have on human behavior on FI schedules. They gave different groups of adults different information (for most groups, erroneous information) about the schedule they were to work on. In all cases, the actual contingency was FI 20 seconds. Those people told that the contingency depended on their pressing a button after a certain amount of time had elapsed since the last point earned performed like members of other species on FI schedules. However, those told (erroneously) that the contingency involved making a number of button presses performed as if they were on a ratio schedule. Subjects given no instructions either performed as if they were on a ratio schedule throughout the session or switched to the low rate interval pattern after various amounts of time. Those who switched from the ratio pattern to the interval pattern demonstrated that the contingency may eventually override the instructions with sufficient experience. Kaufman, Baron, and Kopp (1966) reported similar findings.

The performance of adult humans on FI schedules indicates that instructions (both self-instructions and instructions from others) may block the individual's making contact with the contingency and produce resistance to change. As we saw in Chapter 8, one is more likely to discover the contingency through hill-climbing when there is sufficient variability in one's behavior to detect that contingency (Joyce & Chase, 1990; LeFrancois, Chase, & Joyce, 1988), but instructions may reduce behavioral variability and make humans less flexible than members of other species when confronting some schedules of partial reinforcement (Davey, 1988).

Weiner (1969) demonstrated that the different patterns described in Figure 13.4 can also be due to previous experience. He exposed one group of adults to an FR 40 schedule and another to an IRT > 20 sec schedule. Following this training, all participants were placed on a series of FI schedules (FI 10 sec, FI 30 sec, FI 60 sec, and FI 300 sec). Those participants who experienced the FR 40 schedule continued to perform the behavior at a high rate even though the schedule changed to a series of increasing FI schedules, even one as long as 300 seconds. On the other hand, those participants who experienced the IRT > 20 schedule continued to perform the behavior very slowly when they were switched to the FI schedules. All participants, both those who had prior experience with FR and IRT < t schedules, were insensitive to changes in the FI schedules.

While members of other species adjust their behavior to changes in schedules and to changes in the interval on FI schedules, humans do not always do so readily.

The Importance of the Distinction Between Verbally Mediated and Contingency-Mediated Behaviors

Contingency-mediated and verbally mediated behaviors may appear similar, but because they are acquired in different ways, there are some important differences between how individuals perform them.

We humans are different from other species in a number of ways, among these are our greater reasoning abilities and the ability to convey to each other what we know through spoken and written words. Although many other species also have methods to communicate among themselves, that ability is most highly evolved in humans. As a result, human behavior is strongly influenced by what we are told as well as by what we experience directly through Pavlovian conditioning and operant conditioning (Davey, 1987, 1988; Lowe, 1979, 1983; Perone et al., 1988), and the differences between the performance of humans and members of other species on the operant conditioning tasks described above appear to be due to the important role that language plays in human experience (Baron & Galizio, 1983; Hayes, Brownstein, Zettle, Rosenfarb, & Korn, 1986; Lowe, 1983). Because most of us have been rewarded in the past for following instructions, we tend to follow instructions (even incorrect instructions). We teach children to follow directions by rewarding those that do and punishing those that do not. Most of us already have a long history of following directions by the time we become adults (Hayes, Zettle, & Rosenfarb, 1989).

Furthermore, we humans actively seek to understand the relationship between events in our environment and between our behavior and outcomes. Rather than approach each situation as if it is entirely novel, we invoke our existing knowledge and inference processes. In the absence of instructions, those of us who are verbally proficient humans (above the age of 4 years) deal with new operant conditioning situations by attempting to figure out the "rules." We have a strong disposition to see causal connections even where none exist. As a result, we tend to maintain nonfunctional patterns of behavior when there is a zero contingency between behavior and reinforcing events (Bruner & Revusky, 1961; Catania & Cutts, 1963; Wright, 1962), and we believe we can control the delivery of reinforcers (when, in fact, we cannot). This is referred to as "the illusion of control" (Alloy & Abramson, 1979; Langer, 1975; Matute, 1996; Wortman, 1975).

When there is adequate feedback, we can adjust our behavior to the demands of the situation through hill-climbing, but when feedback is difficult to ascertain or minimal, or there is little cost for following inaccurate rules (or inaccurate instructions), we tend to persist in behavior patterns that are not efficient or optimal for that situation. Thus, rules (whether self-generated or supplied by others) that appear to us to work remain effective rules while those that do not lose their effectiveness to govern our behavior.

On the other hand, when the individual can ascertain that following instructions results in the loss of positive reinforcement, he or she may adapt his or her behavior to the prevailing contingency (Galizio, 1979; Hayes et al., 1986; Weiner, 1969).

Instructed behaviors (behaviors that occur because someone told you what to do or what the outcomes of that behavior would be) and contingency-shaped behaviors (behaviors acquired through the more gradual process of hill-climbing) may look alike on the surface, but because they were acquired through different routes, there are some rather important differences between them:

1. Instructions produce rapid increases in positively reinforced behaviors in humans (see, e.g., Ayllon & Azrin, 1964; Baron & Kaufman, 1966), and extinction is more effective when it is combined with instructions (see, e.g., Weiner, 1970). Punishment works best with humans when the target behavior is specified and the individual is told why that behavior is undesirable (see, e.g., Parke, 1969; Kazdin, 1980). Instructions can promote performance when they bring us into contact with the prevailing contingencies (Hayes et al., 1986; Schmidt & Young, 1991; Svartdal, 1995). All of this is hardly surprising. Telling you what to do or what the rules are eliminates the need to figure them out yourself through the trial-and-error process of hill-climbing.

2. On the other hand, people instructed to perform a behavior a certain way continue even when the contingency changes or the instructions (or self-generated rules) are incorrect. This is especially true when there is little cost for following inaccurate instructions (Galizio, 1979) or when the contingency is not easy to ascertain (Baron, Kaufman, & Stauber, 1969; Harzem, Lowe, & Bagshaw, 1978; Kaufman et al., 1966; Lippman & Meyer, 1967). Instructions (even self-instructions) tend to reduce behavioral variability and thus can make us less sensitive to the prevailing contingencies (Davey, 1988). This insensitivity to change is less likely when behavior is shaped by successive approximation and by minimal instructions (Catania, Mathews, & Shimoff, 1982; Mathews, Shimoff, Catania, & Sagvolden, 1977; Shimoff, Catania, & Mathews, 1981), or when the penalty for incorrect performance is obvious (Galizio, 1979).

Therefore, the advantage of being able to learn rapidly from instructions (as opposed to discovering through trial and error) is somewhat offset by the insensitivity to the prevailing contingency and to changes in the contingency that instructions produce. Instructed behavior looks more like procedural knowledge than declarative knowledge.

SUMMARY AND CONCLUSIONS

Obtaining knowledge about events and the relationships between events and about how to perform actions efficiently through interactions with others is called *social learning*. Through social learning, individuals are able to short-cut the discovery process and acquire knowledge from other members of their species. This leads to the *cultural transmission of knowledge*; that is, the transfer of knowledge from one generation to another through learning.

Social learning can occur through a variety of mechanisms: Rats, birds, and humans (and most likely members of other species) can learn what foods to eat and not to eat by observing what other members of their species eat. Birds can learn the identity of predators, and apes can learn to fear snakes through the mechanism of observational conditioning, a form of Pavlovian conditioning where the US is a reaction of another individual.

Sometimes individuals learn through *imitation*, although one must be careful when attributing a behavior to imitation because not all observational learning is due to imitation. Behavior that looks like imitation can be due to social (local) enhancement, sign-tracking, social facilitation, or goal enhancement, to name a few possibilities. To conclude that an individual is imitating another, one must be able to show that the behavior in question is not a species-specific behavior evoked by some aspect of the situation. True imitation is said to occur when there are a number of ways to perform the action and the observer only performed it the same way the demonstrator did. One can demonstrate true imitation with the *two-action* or *bidirectional procedure*. In all of these examples of learning through observation, the behavior of the demonstrator was not affected by the presence of an observer; therefore, we say these forms of social learning are *inadvertent* or *unintentional*.

Many times social learning occurs through direct instruction. Examples of this are cheetahs teaching their cubs to kill prey through *opportunity teaching*, baboon mothers encouraging their infants to walk through *coaching*, chimpanzees teaching their young to crack open nuts through *demonstrations*, chimpanzees teaching each other to make signs through *physical guidance*, and humans using *verbal instructions* in the form of advice, directions, and commands to inform each other about contingencies. In all of these situations, one individual is *intentionally* teaching another.

Learning based on direct experience with a contingency is said to be *contingency-mediated*, while learning based on verbal descriptions of the contingency or instructions about what to do is said to be *verbally-mediated*. Verbal instruction has a powerful effect on Pavlovian conditioning with arbitrarily chosen CSs and USs. For example, emotional responses can be induced by merely informing someone of the impending CS-US contingency, and informing someone that the procedure has changed to extinction also produces a rapid decline in the CR, while providing people with false information about the CS-US contingency will lead them to behave in accordance with that false information and not the actual contingency in effect.

Humans learn to perform operant behaviors rapidly and efficiently when given relevant instructions. In the absence of instructions, humans above the age of 4 years deal with new operant conditioning situations by attempting to figure out the "rules," and even if these self-generated rules or the instructions given to them are incorrect, humans tend to persist as long as the cost of inefficient performance is not too great or the behavior-outcome contingency is not obvious. Unfortunately, instructions (even self-instructions) tend to reduce behavioral variability and thus make humans less sensitive to the prevailing contingencies. The advantage of being able to learn rapidly from instructions (as opposed to discovering through trial and error) is somewhat offset by the resistance to change that instructions produce.

1. What is the adaptive value of social learning of food preferences? Why do we describe this as "inadvertent" learning?

2. Why do we classify social transmission of fear as due to Pavlovian conditioning? What are the CS, CR, US, and UR here?

3. How can we demonstrate that something is learned by imitation and not through some other mechanism (e.g., local [stimulus] enhancement, social facilitation, or goal emulation)?

4. Give some examples of instruction *by* animals.

5. How does verbal instruction influence human Pavlovian conditioning and operant conditioning?

6. What is the difference between verbally-mediated and contingency-mediated behaviors? Why is this difference important?

EPILOGUE

It is easy for us who have lived most or all of our lives in a modern industrial and technological society to forget that the industrial revolution began a scant 200 years ago in England and that most of the trappings of our modern society (electrical appliances, automobiles, airplanes, computers, etc.) were invented only within the past 125 years. For most of the million or so years we humans have existed as a separate species, we were foragers, hunting, and scavenging for food instead of buying it at the food market. We can catch a glimpse of what the life of our early human ancestors might have been like by observing groups of people who still engage in a foraging lifestyle.

The difference between us moderns and people who still forage is not one of intellectual capacity. The fossil record indicates that the cranial capacity of humans has not changed in the last 50,000 years. Our modern technological society is the result of the gradual accumulation and transmission of knowledge via books and other storage devices. Members of foraging societies also have accumulated knowledge about such things as how to make weapons and use them to hunt, where and when they are most likely to find food, where and how to dig for food, and how to prepare the food to eat. Like us, they transmit this knowledge to each other using language, but they tend to be preliterate and lack a written language to preserve and transmit that knowledge as efficiently as we do. Clearly, we are not really different from our early human ancestors and our contemporaries who live as foragers; we just live in different niches. We technologically sophisticated humans would have a hard time surviving in their niche without their assistance, and they might have a hard time surviving in ours.

In this book, we have discussed three sources of knowledge: instinctive knowledge obtained by an individual's ancestors that is transmitted through heredity; learned knowledge obtained through personal experience; and learned knowledge transmitted between members of a species through social learning. Cultural transmission of knowledge occurs when knowledge is passed from generation to generation through social learning. Much of the knowledge we humans possess we obtained from other people through direct conversation, formal instruction, the mass media, and the written word. Cultural transmission of knowledge is not restricted to humans; it has been observed in a variety of species. But the original knowledge had to be discovered by someone through direct experience (i.e., Pavlovian conditioning or operant conditioning).

Members of all species possess some instinctive knowledge. In addition to having inborn reflexes, we humans are equipped to make certain forms of causal inferences readily. For example, human infants as young as 27 weeks of age appear to understand what happens to an object when another object bumps into it (like when one billiard ball strikes another; Leslie, 1982; Leslie & Keeble, 1987), and 4-month-old human infants show more delight when moving their leg causes a mobile to move than when the mobile moves independently of their behavior (Watson, 1984). Inferences about how objects in our environment move and interact with each other and about simple cause-effect relationships involving physical objects reflect a process called "intuitive physics." These inferences are the result of inborn perceptual mechanisms that predispose us to make these causal inferences (Michotte, 1963). Hence we refer to this as instinctive knowledge.

Although instinctive knowledge is adequate for survival for many species, particularly those with short life spans or who live in relatively stable environments, it does not provide for rapid adjustment to new circumstances. Learning to identify good and bad things and learning about the causal structure of the environment in which we live frees us from that constraint.

Learning is the name we give to the psychological process by which knowledge is acquired from experience. Although learning (and the knowledge obtained from learning) cannot be directly observed, we can infer that individuals have learned and what they have learned by observing changes in their behavior after they have had certain experiences. The various forms of learning evolved as solutions to problems of survival: Pavlovian conditioning provides us with the ability to learn through direct experience about, and response to, relationships between environmental events; operant conditioning provides us with the ability to adjust our behavior based on the outcomes of these behaviors; and social learning provides us with a mechanism for sharing what we have learned through direct experience.

Individuals appear to be predisposed to acquire some types of knowledge rapidly, even in a single trial. This is particularly true for certain dangerous events. For example, many species are able to quickly learn to avoid foods that make them ill. Which aspect of the food becomes the identifying feature for future avoidance depends on the species: Nocturnal animals like rats tend to avoid foods based on taste, and species that rely primarily on vision to search for food (like birds) tend to avoid foods based on appearances. But experience also plays a role here. Individuals are more likely to avoid novel foods as opposed to familiar foods after becoming ill (an example of the CS preexposure effect; see Chapter 4). This reflects learned knowledge about the familiar foods that in the past have been found to be safe (while the status of the novel foods may not have yet been determined). Humans exhibit all of these phenomena when we suffer gastric distress.

Even when learning does not occur in one trial, innate knowledge can still play a role. For example, pigeons more readily associate visual cues with stepping on a treadle to earn food and auditory cues with stepping on the treadle to avoid shock, and it is easier for pigeons to learn to peck for food than to avoid shock (Foree & LoLordo, 1973, 1975; LoLordo, 1979). This also reflects the niche in which pigeons evolved: Predators of birds are likely to be heard before they are seen, while the food birds eat is located through visual search. Likewise, pigeons approach and eat food, and they flee danger. Humans exhibit similar predispositions; for example, conditioned fear can be more rapidly produced in humans when the CS is a snake or spider than when it is an arbitrarily chosen stimulus like a square or triangle (Marks, 1987). Gould and Marler (1987) called this "learning by instinct" because instinctive knowledge about certain events guides the learning process.

Suffering gastric distress after consuming some food is a Pavlovian conditioning procedure because the two events are experienced in some relationship to each other. We discussed many other examples of Pavlovian conditioning procedures in nature in Chapters 2 and 6. Pavlovian conditioning provides individuals with the ability to learn about predictive relationships between environmental events, even when these predictive relationships did not exist in the species' evolutionary niche. However, the CR that may emerge as a result of experience with Pavlovian conditioning procedures is a biologically preorganized behavior pattern released by a signal (the CS) for a biologically important event (the US). In nature, the adaptive function of these CRs is to help the individual prepare in some way for the occurrence of that biologically significant event (the US). But even when no biologically significant events are present, individuals are capable of associating the occurrence of two "neutral" events and using that information later (the phenomenon of sensory preconditioning; see Chapter 5). Thus although some instances of Pavlovian conditioning are highly specialized for specific situations (like taste aversion learning), the abilities underlying Pavlovian conditioning allow for learning about new relationships, even those involving arbitrarily chosen events.

Performing an action that results in food and doing something that results in avoiding or escaping from danger are examples of operant conditioning procedures. Operant conditioning provides individuals with an additional ability: the ability to use feedback from the outcomes (O) of their actions or behaviors (B) to become more efficient at executing effective actions in that stimulus situation (S) in the future. Through the mechanisms underlying operant conditioning, individuals adapt their behavior to the specific requirements for obtaining a certain outcome in a given stimulus situation. Here, too, some things are easier to learn than others, reflecting the role of instinctive knowledge in the acquisition of stimulus-behavior-outcome (S→[B-O]) relationships. But operant conditioning cannot occur without Pavlovian conditioning. These two types of learning are actually intertwined. Pavlovian conditioning provides individuals with mechanisms to acquire knowledge about predictors of important events (both appetitive and aversive), and operant conditioning provides a way for individuals to become more efficient at either obtaining the appetitive events (positive reinforcers, rewards) or avoiding the aversive ones (negative reinforcers). Thus, the discriminative stimuli in operant conditioning situations are also Pavlovian predictors of the events we call reinforcers.

Despite the differences in procedure between Pavlovian conditioning and operant conditioning, both appear to reflect a process of causal inference and the formation of associations between events (declarative knowledge): Pavlovian conditioning procedures, which involve arrangements between environmental events (CSs and USs), are encoded as CS-US associations, and operant conditioning procedures, which involve relationships between behaviors and outcomes, are encoded as B-O associations. In both cases, associations based on positive contingencies are excitatory, and associations based on negative contingencies are inhibitory. Individuals also encode the absence of a relationship (a zero contingency) as learned irrelevance. Associations contain information about sensory and hedonic attributes of the events, the temporal relationships between these events, the perceived contingency, and the situations in which these relationships are experienced. Furthermore, individuals can also encode hierarchical arrangements of events they experience. Sometimes the context enters into Pavlovian associations as a CS and sometimes it serves as an occasion setter for a CS-US relationship. The context also serves as an occasion setter in operant conditioning.

One can only speculate about the origins of Pavlovian conditioning and operant conditioning (instrumental learning), but it appears that Pavlovian conditioning is the more primitive type for a number of reasons: First, Pavlovian conditioned responses are restricted by the specific CSs and USs and do not allow the individual to adjust his or her behavior to the immediate outcomes of that behavior. Second, Pavlovian conditioned responses can serve as the basis for operant conditioned responses because they are frequently the first behaviors that emerge in some situations. Third, Pavlovian predictors of important events can also serve as operant discriminative stimuli signaling that an important event is about to occur in a given situation. Finally, Pavlovian conditioning has been observed in one-celled organisms; bees and insects may be the simplest organisms to possess the ability we call operant conditioning.

Operant conditioning reflects the feedback mechanism called hill-climbing. As we noted in Chapter 8, hill-climbing occurs in single-celled organisms, but those organisms, while able to learn through Pavlovian conditioning, do not possess memory abilities to store feedback for more than a fleeting moment—that is, just long enough to compare two sensations and make an adjustment to improve one's situation.

Think about what our lives would be like if we did not possess the ability to learn and remember. All we would ever know about the world would be the knowledge we possessed at birth. When we retired at night, we would not know any more about the world than we knew when we woke that morning. We would never learn anything new. We could not become more proficient at doing anything because we could not learn from simple trial and error or from observation. As long as food and shelter were relatively plentiful and easy to obtain, and we instinctively knew how to obtain them and avoid danger, we might survive long enough to reproduce so that our species would survive; however, we would be in real trouble if our environment changed and the knowledge we possessed no longer was sufficient to allow us to find food, shelter, and mates, and to avoid being eaten. But fortunately, we can learn from personal experience and pass the knowledge we obtain to others. That is how we got to where we are today.

GLOSSARY

Adaptation. A process of adjustment to the circumstances in which an individual lives.

Advice. A form of **verbal instruction** in which someone is informed as to what will happen under certain circumstances.

Appetitive events. Things individuals seek out, approach, consume, or do something to obtain. They are also called **positive reinforcers** or **rewards**.

Applied behavior analysis. The systematic application of operant conditioning procedures as therapeutic interventions.

Association. How the experienced connections between experienced environmental events are stored in memory. Associations consist of the mental representations of both the external events experienced and the relationship between these events. Associations are inferred when the presentation of the conditioned stimulus evokes the conditioned response in the absence of the unconditioned stimulus.

Autoshaping (sign-tracking). Behavior that is directed toward or away from a stimulus that signals the occurrence or absence of a significant event (e.g., food, heat, shock).

Aversive events. Things that individuals will do something to get away from. They are also called **negative reinforcers**.

Avoidance conditioning (procedure). The operant conditioning procedure in which a behavior will postpone or cancel a **negative reinforcer** that might ordinarily occur if the behavior did not occur. There are two varieties of avoidance conditioning: **signaled avoidance (discriminated avoidance)** and **unsignaled avoidance (nondiscriminated, free operant,** or **Sidman avoidance)**.

Backward chaining (procedure). A procedure for training individuals to perform a sequence of actions: The last action in the sequence is trained first, and each preceding action is added one at a time until the entire chain of actions is performed.

Backward conditioning (phenomenon). The occurrence of a conditioned response (CR) after exposure to a **backward conditioning procedure**.

Backward conditioning (procedure). The Pavlovian conditioning procedure in which the unconditioned stimulus (US) precedes the conditioned stimulus (CS).

Behavior modification. The systematic application of operant conditioning procedures as therapeutic interventions.

Behavior-outcome (B-O) association. How experience with an operant conditioning procedure is encoded as **declarative knowledge**. This is an association between representations of the behavior and the outcome.

Behavior-outcome contingency. A programmed relationship between some behavior and an outcome for performing that behavior in a certain situation and at a certain time.

Behavior system. An interrelated set of perceptual mechanisms, central control mechanisms, and motor mechanisms organized around biologically important functions such as feeding, drinking, mating, defense, body care, social bonding, and care of young.

Behavior therapy. The systematic application of Pavlovian conditioning procedures as therapeutic interventions.

Behavioral contrast (phenomenon). When an individual is working for two different reinforcers and one of them is changed, the behavior that produces the *unchanged* reinforcer changes in the *opposite* direction than the behavior that produces the changed reinforcer.

Behavioral momentum. The tendency for a behavior to persist when the reinforcement contingency is changed. Behaviors that are more *resistant to change* have more behavioral momentum.

Behavioral variability. The inherent variability in all behavior. Even in an unchanging environment, the individual does not perform a given behavior *exactly* the same way every time.

Bias. Bias occurs in a **concurrent choice situation** when the individual prefers one alternative more than would be predicted from the **empirical matching law**.

Bidirectional control procedure. The procedure used to demonstrate that a behavior is learned through **imitation**. This procedure requires that there be more than one way an individual can perform an action (or more than one action) that leads to the outcome. Different observers can watch different demonstrators obtaining the outcome in different ways. Imitation is inferred to be the mechanism for learning if the observers perform the action they observed, even if other ways also work (or work better). This is also called the **two-action procedure**.

Blocking. The phenomenon whereby prior conditioning with one element of a compound stimulus interferes with conditioning to the other element.

Causal inference. A judgment or conclusion that one event influences, affects, or causes another.

Chaining (procedure). See also **Backward chaining (procedure)**.

Changeover delay (COD). In a **concurrent schedule**, after the individual switches from one schedule to another, the changeover delay determines the length of time the individual must spend performing the behavior on the second schedule before earning a reinforcer on that second schedule.

Coaching. A form of **instruction** in which the behavior of the pupil is altered through encouragement or punishment.

Collateral behavior. A behavior that is not required for the occurrence of the outcome. These behaviors tend to occur on **IRT > t** schedules because they occupy the individual, thereby increasing the chances that the individual will obtain the outcome when the required waiting time has elapsed.

Commands. A form of **verbal instruction** in which a person in control of the outcome tells someone what to do to obtain or avoid that outcome.

Compensatory response. A conditioned response opposite from the unconditioned response. Compensatory responses anticipate the unconditioned response to maintain **homeostasis**.

Concurrent choice (procedure). An individual is given the choice between two or more simultaneously available activities or two or more simultaneously available commodities.

Concurrent schedule of reinforcement. Two or more different schedules of partial reinforcement run concurrently, and the individual can choose which to work on at any given time. The two most common variations are the **side-by-side procedure** and the **schedule-control procedure**.

Conditioned emotional response. A learned emotional response (such as fear) to a stimulus that did not evoke that response before conditioning.

Conditioned excitation. The underlying process that generates the conditioned response in Pavlovian conditioning.

Conditioned excitatory stimulus. A conditioned stimulus that gains the capacity to generate a conditioned response through a **positive CS-US contingency**. The standard symbol for a conditioned excitatory stimulus is **CS+**.

Conditioned inhibition. An underlying process that generates a reaction that is antagonistic to the conditioned response evoked by a positive (excitatory) contingency with the same CS and US.

Conditioned inhibitory stimulus. A conditioned stimulus that gains the capacity to generate a reaction that is antagonistic to the conditioned response evoked by a positive (excitatory) contingency with the same CS and US. A conditioned inhibitory stimulus is produced by a negative CS-US contingency. The standard symbol for a conditioned inhibitory stimulus is CS−.

Conditioned reflex. Pavlov's term for a response to a stimulus that is "conditional" on the individual's experience. Today we call this a conditioned response.

Conditioned reinforcer (secondary reinforcer). Something that derives its ability to function as a reinforcer as a result of experience, specifically as the result of a Pavlovian conditioning procedure. Events become conditioned (secondary) reinforcers when they predict the occurrence of primary reinforcers.

Conditioned response (CR). A response that occurs to a stimulus as a result of exposure to a Pavlovian conditioning procedure. Before conditioning, this response did not reliably occur to this stimulus. Pavlov called this a conditioned reflex.

Conditioned stimulus (CS). A stimulus or event to which a response occurs as a result of exposure to a Pavlovian conditioning procedure. Before conditioning, this stimulus or event did not produce that response (although it may have produced other responses like orienting reflexes).

Conditioned suppression. The disruption of ongoing behavior by the presentation of a fear-provoking event. How much the ongoing behavior is disrupted provides a quantitative index of fear. The quantitative index of conditioned suppression and fear is called the suppression ratio.

Conditions of learning. The conditions of learning are those aspects of a situation that produce long-term changes in behavior. We study the conditions of learning by manipulating various aspects of the situation and observing the effects these may have on the subject's behavior at a later time.

Constant conjunction. Two events have constant conjunction when they occur together consistently.

Contingency. The predictive relationship between the target behavior and the outcome in operant conditioning.

Contingency management. The systematic application of operant conditioning procedures as therapeutic interventions.

Contingency-mediated learning. Learning based on direct experience with a contingency.

Continuous reinforcement schedule. The procedure in which the outcome occurs after each occurrence of the target behavior in operant conditioning.

CS preexposure effect. The retardation of Pavlovian conditioning by familiarity with the conditioned stimulus (in the absence of a US prior to conditioning). This is also called latent inhibition.

CS-US consistency. How often the conditioned stimulus (CS) and the unconditioned stimulus (US) occur in relationship to each other. The more often the US follows the CS and the less often the US occurs in the absence of the CS, the greater the CS-US consistency. See also CS-US contingency.

CS-US contingency. The rule that specifies how likely it is that the US will follow the CS and how likely it is that the US will appear in the absence of the CS. Contingencies in Pavlovian conditioning are specified in terms of two probabilities: the probability that the US will occur when the CS occurs [Pr (US|CS)], and the probability that the US will occur when the CS did not occur [Pr (US|no CS)]. The difference between these two probabilities defines the CS-US contingency.

Cultural evolution. The process by which we humans adapt to our environment by transmitting acquired knowledge from generation to generation through teaching and imitation.

Cultural transmission of knowledge. Learned knowledge acquired through experience transmitted between humans. See also Social transmission of knowledge.

Cumulative record. A graphical representation of the rate of occurrence of a behavior in which the total number of behaviors that have occurred up to each point in time is plotted against time. The device for generating a cumulative record is called a cumulative recorder.

Cumulative recorder. A device for creating a graphical representation of the rate of occurrence of a behavior in which the total number of behaviors that have occurred to each point in time is plotted against time. The output of a cumulative recorder is called a cumulative record.

Declarative knowledge (knowing that). Knowledge of specific information.

Delay conditioning (phenomenon). With a delay conditioning procedure, the conditioned response (CR) occurs shortly before the time that the unconditioned stimulus (US) is scheduled to occur instead of when the CS commences. Pavlov called this a delayed reflex.

Delay conditioning (procedure). The Pavlovian conditioning procedure in which the conditioned stimulus (CS) occurs and remains on until the unconditioned stimulus is presented.

Delayed reflex. Pavlov's name for a conditioned response in delay conditioning or trace conditioning that occurs shortly before the time that the US is scheduled to occur instead of when the CS commences.

Demonstration. Actively teaching a skill by performing it in front of another individual.

Dependent variable. What we observe subjects do after experiencing the independent variable in an experiment. See also Phenomenon.

Differential conditioning. In Pavlovian conditioning, this is the procedure in which one CS (CS+) signals the occurrence of the US, and the other CS (CS–) signals the absence of the US. This procedure is also called discrimination training or differentiation.

Differential reinforcement (procedure). The operant conditioning procedure in which behaviors that satisfy certain criteria are reinforced and all other behaviors are not.

Differential reinforcement of high rates (DRH) schedule. On this operant conditioning schedule of reinforcement, the outcome occurs when the individual performs the target behaviors in rapid succession with less than the specified time (t) between them. This schedule generates high rates of behavior. Because the interresponse time (IRT) between successive behaviors must be *less* than the designated time (t), it is also referred to as an IRT $< t$ schedule.

Differential reinforcement of low rates (DRL) schedule. On this operant conditioning schedule of reinforcement, the individual must perform a behavior, wait at least some specified amount of time (t), and then perform the behavior again in order to receive the outcome. This schedule generates slow rates of behavior. Because the interresponse time (IRT) between successive behaviors must be *greater* than the designated time (t), it is also referred to as an IRT $> t$ schedule.

Differential reinforcement of other behavior (DRO). This is another name for the procedures called omission training and punishment by removal.

Differentiation (phenomenon). The modification of behavior that results from the successful application of the procedure of differential reinforcement.

Directions. A form of verbal instruction in which someone is told how to do something or where to go to obtain something.

Discriminability (of a stimulus). How noticeable that stimulus is from the background.

The discriminability of a stimulus is related to its salience.

Discriminated avoidance (procedure). The operant conditioning procedure in which the impending aversive event is signaled and the target behavior cancels the next occurrence of that event. Discriminated avoidance is also called signaled avoidance.

Discrimination training. See Differential conditioning.

Discriminative stimulus. An event that signals a behavior-outcome relationship in operant conditioning.

Dishabituation. The phenomenon that occurs when presentation of another (usually strong) stimulus results in a temporary increase in responsiveness to the original stimulus. See also Habituation.

Disinhibition. The reappearance of a conditioned response (CR) when a novel or sudden stimulus is presented during the procedure of extinction, or when the CS is presented during the early part of the interstimulus interval during trace and delay conditioning. Disinhibition also occurs during habituation (procedure) when presentation of another (usually strong) stimulus results in a temporary increase in responsiveness to the original stimulus.

Drive. An inferred psychological process that arises from some internal need or bodily state. Drive is an intervening variable invoked to provide a link between the conditions (independent variables) that produce the internal state and the resulting activated behaviors (dependent variable).

Empirical matching law. The observation that individuals match the *relative allocation* of their behavior to the *relative rates, amounts,* or *immediacy* of the alterative outcomes in a concurrent choice situation.

Episodic memory. The system that stores personally experienced events and episodes.

Escape conditioning (procedure). The operant conditioning procedure in which a negative reinforcer (aversive event) is present and the individual does something to terminate it.

Establishing operation (procedure). A procedure that alters how effectively something functions as a reinforcer by changing an individual's internal or external environment.

Evaluative conditioning. A primitive, automatic, noncognitive form of Pavlovian conditioning in which the affective evaluative reaction to an event (the CS) is changed by the affective evaluative reaction to another event (the US) that reliably occurs in close temporal contiguity to the CS. The result is a shift in the evaluation of the CS in the direction of the evaluation of the US.

Evolution by natural selection. The mechanism proposed by Charles Darwin to explain the diversity of life. Evolution by natural selection is based on the following three principles: (1) The observed characteristics of individuals are inherited, (2) Within a species, individuals differ from one another in both their physical structures and behavioral dispositions, and (3) Those characteristics of an individual that favor survival in competition with others and in the face of environmental stresses or changes will be more likely to be transmitted to offspring and thus tend to be preserved.

Excitation. The psychological process generated by a positive contingency.

Excitatory conditioning. The procedure that leads to the occurrence of conditioned responses. See also Positive CS-US contingency.

Excitatory contingency. The Pavlovian conditioning procedure in which the US is *more* likely to occur *following* the CS than in its absence; that is, Pr (US|CS) > Pr (US|no CS). This is also called a positive CS-US contingency.

Experimental hypothesis. The prediction derived from a theory.

Explicit knowledge. Internally-stored information that we can usually relate to others. Declarative knowledge tends to be explicit knowledge.

Explicitly unpaired (procedure). The Pavlovian conditioning procedure in which the US *never* follows CS. The contingency is represented as Pr (US|CS = 0) and Pr (US|no CS) > 0.

External inhibition (phenomenon). In Pavlovian conditioning, the disruption of a conditioned response (CR) by the introduction of an external stimulus or event.

Extinction (operant conditioning phenomenon). As a result of experience with the operant conditioning procedure of extinction, the conditioned behavior occurs less frequently and with less vigor.

Extinction (operant conditioning procedure). After an operant conditioned behavior has been established, the outcome for that behavior is discontinued.

Extinction (Pavlovian conditioning phenomenon). As a result of experience with the Pavlovian conditioning procedure of extinction, the conditioned response (CR) occurs less frequently and with less vigor when the conditioned stimulus (CS) is presented. Pavlov called this phenomenon experimental extinction.

Extinction (Pavlovian conditioning procedure). After a Pavlovian conditioned response (CR) has been established, the conditioned stimulus (CS) is presented without the unconditioned stimulus (US).

Feature-negative discrimination. The Pavlovian conditioning arrangement whereby the presence of an event (the feature) signals that the US will *not* follow the CS. There are two kinds of feature-negative discriminations: simultaneous feature-negative discrimination and serial feature-negative discrimination.

Feature-positive discrimination. The Pavlovian conditioning arrangement whereby the presence of an event (the feature) determines whether the US will follow the CS. There are two kinds of feature-positive discriminations: simultaneous feature-positive discrimination and serial feature-positive discrimination.

Findley procedure. With this concurrent schedule arrangement, individuals can do something in one location to select which schedule they want to work on in another location. Choice is defined both on a moment-by-moment basis and in terms of the relative distributions of time each schedule is on and how much behavior occurs with each schedule. This procedure is also referred to as a schedule control procedure or a switching-key (switching-lever) concurrent schedule.

First-order conditioning. The standard procedure for Pavlovian conditioning in which CS→US.

Fixed-interval schedule of reinforcement (FI *t*). A schedule of reinforcement in operant conditioning in which the first occurrence of the target behavior after a *specified interval of time* has elapsed will produce the outcome; that interval is the *same* for each outcome.

Fixed-ratio schedule of reinforcement (FR *n*). A schedule of reinforcement in operant conditioning in which the individual has to perform the target behavior a *specified number of times* in order to obtain a certain outcome; that number is the *same* for each outcome.

Flooding (procedure). The procedure where individuals are placed in the situation in which an aversive event usually occurs and are prevented from performing the avoidance behavior. The behavior therapy called **implosion therapy** employs flooding to reduce fear.

Free operant avoidance (procedure). The operant conditioning procedure in which the impending aversive event is not signaled and the target behavior cancels the next occurrence of that event. Also called **unsignaled avoidance, nondiscriminated avoidance,** and **Sidman avoidance.**

General process learning ability. The ability to learn about relationships that may not have existed during the evolution of the species.

Generalized empirical matching law. The version of the **empirical matching law** that incorporates bias, overmatching, and undermatching into a general statement about behavior in **concurrent choice** situations.

Generalized theoretical matching law. The version of the **theoretical matching law** that incorporates bias, overmatching, and undermatching into a general statement about the relationship between the relative values of the reinforcers and the relative allocation of behavior in **concurrent choice** situations.

Goal emulation. A form of social learning whereby the observer reproduces the *results* obtained by the demonstrator, *not* the behavior of the demonstrator.

Habituation (phenomenon). The diminution of responsiveness to a particular stimulation as a result of repeated exposure to that stimulation.

Habituation (procedure). The repeated presentation of a stimulus that is not harmful or has no bearing on an individual's welfare.

Hill-climbing. A method for adjusting behavior based on successive comparisons of one's situation. The adjustment is based on whether the behavior improves or worsens one's situation.

Homeostasis. The maintenance of the internal environment within tolerable limits.

Imitation. Learning how to perform an action by observing another individual performing that action.

Implicit knowledge. Internally stored information that we may not be able to relate to others. For example, we may be able to demonstrate that we can do something but may not be able to describe how we did it. **Procedural knowledge** tends to be implicit knowledge.

Implosion therapy. The behavior therapy that employs **flooding** to reduce fear.

Imprinting. Exposure to certain things during specific times in an individual's life leads to long-term attachment or responsiveness to those things.

Incentive. Something an individual will work to obtain. **Positive reinforcers** are sometimes referred to as incentives.

Incentive contrast (phenomenon). An overshooting or undershooting of behavior when an individual experiences change in the incentive value of the reward.

Incentive learning. Learning about the incentive values of foods, fluids, and other things by consuming them and experiencing the aftereffects of these things. If the aftereffects of consumption are experienced as positive, then the consumed object gains positive value, and if the effects are experienced as negative then the consumed object gains negative value. Furthermore, the incentive value that accrues will depend on the individual's state at the time of the consumption.

Incentive motivation. An inferred psychological process that is aroused by a reinforcer (or a signal for a reinforcer). The independent variable is the presentation of something of hedonic value or a signal for that thing, and the dependent measure is the accompanying change in behavior involving that hedonic event.

Incentive value. The incentive value of something is how attractive that thing is to the individual. The incentive value of something depends on its physical characteristics, but it is determined by the individual and depends on his or her species, personal experiences, and physical and psychological states at the moment. We measure incentive value by how the individual behaves toward that object or event.

Independent variable. The things we systematically manipulate in an experiment (what we do to the subjects). See also **Procedure**.

Induced variation. Behaviors generated by the situation. Because different situations can generate different behaviors, we attribute variation in behaviors to the variation in the situations.

Inference. The psychological process by which individuals make judgments and draw conclusions based on the information available to them.

Inhibition. A psychological process generated by a negative contingency that is *antagonistic* to the **excitation** generated by a positive contingency. We use inhibition as an explanation for when the behavior that occurs to a signal for the *absence* of an important event (that is, the CS in a negative contingency) is *opposite* to the behavior that occurs to a signal for the *presence* of an important event (the CS in a positive contingency).

Inhibition of delay (phenomenon). After repeated experience with delay or trace conditioning, the conditioned response tends to occur close to the time the US is scheduled to occur, not when the CS is presented; in other words, the CR is delayed.

Inhibitory conditioning. The procedure that leads to responses that are antagonistic to conditioned responses produced by an **excitatory contingency (positive CS-US contingency).**

Inhibitory contingency. The Pavlovian conditioning procedure in which the US is *more* likely to occur in the *absence* of the CS than in its presence; that is, $\Pr(US \mid CS) < \Pr(US \mid no\ CS)$. This is also called a **negative CS-US contingency.**

Innate. Not acquired through direct experience by that individual.

Instinctive knowledge. Knowledge obtained through the mechanism of heredity and not acquired through direct experience by that individual. See also **Innate.**

Instincts. Stereotyped behavior patterns that are performed in the same way by members of a particular species without practice.

Instruction. The *intentional* transmission of information from demonstrator to observer.

Instrumental learning (instrumental conditioning). The name for those procedures where the learned behavior was "instrumental" in bringing about the occurrence of the outcome. At one time, the terms instrumental learning and instrumental conditioning were reserved for studies of learning in mazes and other apparatuses in which the subjects had to move from one location to another to obtain a reward or to escape aversive stimulation. Today it is used by many people interchangeably with **operant conditioning.**

Internal inhibition. The term used by Pavlov to describe the process that produces experimental extinction. Pavlov viewed internal inhibition as a process antagonistic to the process that produces the original conditioned response. This is similar to what we call today **conditioned inhibition.**

Interresponse time (IRT). The time between successive actions.

Interstimulus interval (ISI). The time between the offset of the conditioned stimulus and the onset of the unconditioned stimulus.

Interval schedule of reinforcement. A schedule of reinforcement in operant conditioning in which the first occurrence of the target behavior after a *specified interval of time* has elapsed will produce the outcome.

Intervening variable. A conceptual link between the independent variable (procedure) and the dependent variable (phenomenon). This conceptual link provides a psychological explanation of the observed relationship between the independent and dependent variables. Psychological processes (like learning, emotion, motivation) are intervening variables.

IRT<*t* schedule. On this operant conditioning schedule of reinforcement, the outcome occurs when the individual performs the target behaviors in rapid succession with less than the specified time (*t*) between them; in other words, the **interresponse time (IRT)** between successive behaviors must be *less* than the designated time (*t*). This schedule generates high rates of behavior and is also referred to as a **differential reinforcement of high rates (DRH) schedule.**

IRT>*t* schedule. On this operant conditioning schedule of reinforcement, the individual must perform a behavior, wait at least some specified amount of time (*t*), and then perform the behavior again in order to receive the outcome; in other words, the **interresponse time (IRT)** between successive behaviors must be *greater* than the designated time (*t*). This schedule generates slow rates of behavior and is also referred to as a **differential reinforcement of low rates (DRL) schedule.**

Kineses. Movements guided by feedback from successive comparisons of one's position based on purely local clues.

Knowledge. Internally stored information about the world and about how to do things.

Latent inhibition. The retardation of Pavlovian conditioning by familiarity with the conditioned stimulus (in the absence of a US prior to conditioning). This is also called the **CS preexposure effect.**

Law of effect (theoretical statement). "Of several responses made to the same situation, those that are accompanied or closely followed by satisfaction to the animal will, other things being equal, be more firmly connected with the situation, so that when it [the situation] recurs, they [the responses] will be more likely to recur; those which are accompanied or closely followed by discomfort to the animal will, other things being equal, have their connections with that situation weakened, so that, when it [the situation] recurs, they [the responses] will be less likely to occur. The greater the satisfaction or discomfort, the greater the strengthening or weakening of the bond [situation-response connection]" (Thorndike, 1911, p. 244).

Learned behavior. Reflects the acquisition of knowledge gained from experience.

Learned helplessness. The retardation of the acquisition of successful avoidance behavior that results from prior experience with a zero contingency with aversive stimuli.

Learned irrelevance. The causal inference that two events are unrelated. Learned irrelevance results from experience with a **zero contingency.**

Learned knowledge. Knowledge obtained through individual experience.

Learned release. The theoretical concept used to explain the function of the conditioned stimulus in Pavlovian conditioning: biologically pre-organized behavior patterns related to the unconditioned stimulus are *released* by signals for the unconditioned stimulus.

Learning (phenomenon). The observed change in behavior at a later time as a result of a prior experience.

Learning (process). The psychological process (or processes) by which knowledge is acquired from experience.

Learning-performance problem. The only way we can study learning is by observing performance, but performance may not always reflect learning.

Limited hold (procedure). When a limited hold is added to **interval schedules of reinforcement,** there is a limited time after the interval has elapsed during which the target behavior must occur in order to obtain the reward. If the target behavior does not occur during that limited time, the opportunity for reward is canceled.

Local enhancement. The presence of the demonstrator draws the observer's attention to a specific location or objects and thus increases the probability that the observer will go to that location or contact that object. Also called **stimulus enhancement.**

Magazine training (procedure). The procedure for teaching animals to approach a food tray when they hear the food dispenser (or food magazine) activate to make food available to them.

Melioration ("making better"). This is an explanation for the **empirical matching law** based on the following two assumptions: (1) Individuals are sensitive to the current behavioral cost of obtaining reinforcers, where behavioral cost is measured in terms of how much time and effort is expended for each reinforcer. (2) Individuals attempt to equalize the behavioral cost of obtaining reinforcement across the various choices and outcomes.

Mental representation. The internal depiction of an experienced environmental event. It is assumed that this depiction is mapped into a neural code.

Method of successive approximations (procedure). See Shaping by the method of successive approximations (procedure).

Molar feedback function. The relationship between the *overall* rate of reinforcement and the *overall* rate of behavior generated by a given schedule of reinforcement.

Molecular feedback function. The moment-to-moment relationship between outcomes and behaviors generated by a given schedule of reinforcement.

Momentary maximizing. This is an explanation for the **empirical matching law** based on the assumption that the momentary probability of being reinforced governs the individual's behavior on a **concurrent schedule of reinforcement**.

Motivation. The psychological process we invoke to explain both the activation and goal-directedness of some behaviors. Motivations can be aroused by changes in internal conditions, by aversive stimulation, or by the goal or signals for the goal. We refer to motivations aroused by changes in internal conditions or aversive stimulation as **drives** and motivations aroused by goals or signals for goals as **incentive motivations**.

Necessary condition. In a cause-effect relationship, a **necessary condition** is something in whose absence the effect cannot occur.

Negative behavior-outcome contingency. The operant conditioning procedure in which the outcome (O) is less likely to occur following a behavior (B) than in its presence; that is, $\Pr(O|B) < \Pr(O|\text{no B})$.

Negative CS-US contingency. The Pavlovian conditioning procedure in which the US is *less* likely to occur following the CS than in its absence; that is, $\Pr(US|CS) < \Pr(US|\text{no CS})$. A negative contingency is also called an **inhibitory contingency**.

Negative occasion setter. A stimulus that informs the individual that the next occurrence of the conditioned stimulus (CS+) will not be followed by the US. In the *presence* of the negative occasion setter, the US will *not* occur; in its *absence*, the US *will* occur. It "sets the occasion" for the *nonoccurrence* of the US.

Negative reinforcers. Events that increase the probability of a behavior when the event is removed or canceled. They are also called **aversive events**.

Negative reinforcement (procedure). The operant conditioning procedure of removing or canceling a **negative reinforcer** following a behavior. With the procedure of negative reinforcement, the individual is less likely to receive the negative reinforcer if he or she performs the target behavior than if he or she does not. There are two varieties of negative reinforcement: **escape conditioning** and **avoidance conditioning**.

Niche. The set of physical and biological conditions in which members of a species live. These include the physical conditions of the environment (e.g., climate, moisture level, terrain for terrestrial species, salinity of water for aquatic species); sources of food, water, and shelter; the availability of potential mates; and the characteristics of predators.

Nondiscriminated avoidance (procedure). The operant conditioning procedure in which the impending aversive event is not signaled, and the target behavior cancels the next occurrence of that event. Also called **unsignaled avoidance**, **Sidman avoidance**, and **free operant avoidance**.

Observational conditioning (procedure and phenomenon). A Pavlovian conditioning procedure in which the conditioned stimulus (CS) is something to which a member of one's own species (a conspecific) exhibits fearful behavior. The unconditioned stimulus (US) is the observed fearful behavior in the conspecific, and the conditioned response (CR) is fear of that thing by the observer.

Occasion setter. A stimulus that provides information as to whether something else will or will not happen ("sets the occasion" for the occurrence or nonoccurrence of that other event).

Omission training (procedure). The operant conditioning procedure in which there is a negative contingency with a positive reinforcer. With the procedure of omission training, the individual is more likely to receive the positive reinforcer if he or she does not perform the target action than if he or she does. Thus, behavior leads to one of the following outcomes: (1) "omission" or loss of an otherwise programmed reward, or (2) loss of access to reward that is otherwise available. Omission training is also called **punishment by removal** and **differential reinforcement of other behavior (DRO)**.

Operant. Skinner's term for behaviors that act on the environment to produce certain effects (outcomes).

Operant conditioning (phenomenon). The observed change in behavior after an individual experiences the **procedure of operant conditioning**. Behaviors followed by the *presentation* of **positive reinforcers** or the *removal or canceling* of expected **negative reinforcers** are *more* likely to occur again, and behaviors followed by the *removal or cancellation* of expected **positive reinforcers** or the *presentation* of **negative reinforcers** are *less* likely to occur again.

Operant conditioning (procedure). The presentation of an outcome when the individual engages in a designated behavior or behavior pattern in a given situation. Outcomes can be the presentation, removal, or cancellation of **positive reinforcers** or **negative reinforcers**.

Opportunity teaching. A form of **instruction** in which the teacher puts the pupil into a situation that is conducive for the pupil to learn.

Optimization (molar maximizing). This is an explanation for the **empirical matching law** based on the assumption that individuals attempt to allocate their behavior to obtain the maximum overall gain for the least amount of effort, and that if an optimal allocation exists, they will find it.

Orienting reflex (OR). An investigatory response to a sudden or novel stimulus. These may occur the first few times the individual experiences the stimulus or event that will be the **conditioned stimulus** in Pavlovian conditioning.

Overmatching. Individuals are said to overmatch on a **concurrent schedule** when they spend *more* time and effort on the schedule with the higher rate of reinforcement than is predicted from the **empirical matching law**.

Overshadowing. When conditioning occurs to one of the stimuli that accompany an unconditioned stimulus at the expense of other simultaneously presented stimuli.

Partial (intermittent) reinforcement schedule. A schedule of reinforcement in operant conditioning in which not every instance of the target behavior is followed by the outcome.

Partial reinforcement extinction effect (PREE). An increase in **resistance to extinction** following experience with a **partial reinforcement schedule**.

Pavlovian conditioning (phenomenon). The individual behaves differently in the future to the **conditioned stimulus** after experiencing a **Pavlovian conditioning procedure**.

Pavlovian conditioning (procedure). Two events occur in some relationship to each other. Typically, one event (the **conditioned stimulus**) precedes the other event (the **unconditioned stimulus**).

Pavlovian conditioning (process). The psychological process that accounts for the phenomenon of Pavlovian conditioning after an individual has been exposed to a **Pavlovian conditioning procedure**.

Phase-specific learning. A form of learning that occurs rapidly when the experiences involve exposure to certain types of stimulation during specific times in the individual's life.

Phenomenon. What we observe happens after individuals experience the **procedure** in an experiment. See also **Dependent variable**.

Physical guidance. Actively teaching a skill by physically putting the other individual through the motions. This procedure is also called **putting through**.

Positive behavior-outcome contingency. The operant conditioning procedure in which the outcome (O) is more likely to occur following a behavior (B) than in its absence. In symbolic form, $\Pr(O|B) > \Pr(O|\text{no } B)$.

Positive CS-US contingency. The Pavlovian conditioning procedure in which the US is *more* likely to occur following the CS than in its absence; that is, $\Pr(US|CS) > \Pr(US|\text{no } CS)$. A positive contingency is also called an **excitatory contingency**.

Positive occasion setter. A stimulus that informs the individual that the next occurrence of the conditioned stimulus (CS+) will be followed by the US. In the *presence* of the positive occasion setter, the US *will* occur; in its *absence*, the US will *not* occur. That stimulus "sets the occasion" for the *occurrence* of the US.

Positive punishment (procedure). Another name for the procedure called **punishment (by application)**.

Positive reinforcement (procedure). The operant conditioning procedure in which there is a **positive behavior-outcome contingency** with a **positive reinforcer** (reward, appetitive event). With the procedure of positive reinforcement, the individual is more likely to receive the positive reinforcer if he or she performs the target behavior than if he or she does not. Positive reinforcement is also called **reward training**.

Positive reinforcer. An event that increases the probability of a behavior when it (the event) is presented following that behavior. Because positive reinforcers are things that individuals will seek out, approach, consume, or do something to obtain, they are also called **appetitive events** or **rewards**.

Post-conditioning devaluation of the US (procedure). A way to study associations based on experience with Pavlovian conditioning. After producing a conditioned response in the conventional manner (with a positive CS-US contingency), we remove the individual from the training situation and *change the hedonic value of the unconditioned stimulus*. If and how this affects the conditioned response gives us information about how the Pavlovian conditioning experience is encoded.

Post-reinforcement pause (PRP). The length of time that an individual pauses after the presentation of each outcome in operant conditioning.

Predatory imminence continuum. This term describes the relationship between the proximity of a predator to an individual and the behaviors that individual will engage in to avoid being the predator's next meal.

Prefiguring. The term used to describe the function of conditioned responses as enabling the individual to optimize interactions with forthcoming biologically important events (food, predators, rivals, mates).

Primary reinforcer. Something that can function as a **reinforcer** with little or no experience required.

Principle. A statement describing the relationship between the procedure and the phenomenon. Principles are stated in terms of observable events (procedures and phenomena). They tell us how the conditions of learning are related to the phenomenon of learning, but they do not tell us anything about the mechanisms or processes underlying learning.

Procedural knowledge (knowing how). Knowledge of how to do something.

Procedure. The arrangement of events presented to the subject in an experiment. See also Independent variable.

Prompting (procedure). Using verbal or physical encouragement to get a behavior to occur.

Punishment [by application] (procedure). The operant conditioning procedure in which there is a positive contingency with a negative reinforcer (aversive event). With the procedure of punishment by application, the individual is more likely to receive the negative reinforcer if he or she performs the target action than if he or she does not. Another name for this procedure is positive punishment.

Punishment [by removal] (procedure). The operant conditioning procedure in which there is a negative contingency with a positive reinforcer. With the procedure of punishment by removal, the individual is more likely to receive the positive reinforcer if he or she does not perform the target action than if he or she does. Punishment by removal is also called omission training and differential reinforcement of other behavior (DRO).

Putting through (procedure). Actively teaching a skill by guiding the individual through the action and then following with reward. This procedure is also called physical guidance.

Random-interval schedule of reinforcement (RI t). In random-interval schedules, the probability of reinforcement becoming available in the next instance of time is determined in the following manner: The probability that the reinforcer will be available in the next 0.5 second interval for the next target behavior is equal to $1/t$. Over time, the average time between reinforcement availability will average

to t. Random-interval schedules are a variation of variable-interval schedules, and the behavior patterns generated by both are similar.

Random-ratio schedule of reinforcement (RR n). In a random-ratio schedule, each behavior has a probability of $1/n$ of being followed by a reinforcer where n is the mean of the ratio requirement. With a random-ratio schedule, the probability of the next instance of the target behavior occurring is always constant at $1/n$. Random-ratio schedules are a variation of variable-ratio schedules, and the behavior patterns generated by both are similar.

Rapid reacquisition. After a period of extinction, the behavior-outcome contingency is reintroduced and behavior is reacquired more quickly than during original acquisition training.

Ratio schedule of reinforcement. A schedule of reinforcement in operant conditioning in which the individual has to perform the target behavior a *specified number of times* in order to obtain a certain outcome.

Ratio strain. Prolonged pauses that occur in various places in ratio schedules when the ratio size is too large or the reinforcer is too meager to maintain performance.

Reinforce (procedure). Create an arrangement between a behavior and a reinforcer. Behaviors are reinforced if they are followed by the *presentation* of a positive reinforcer or the *removal* of a negative reinforcer.

Reinforce (process). The "strengthening" of a behavior as a result of the procedure of reinforcement.

Reinforcement (procedure). The procedure of arranging the temporal relationship between a behavior and a reinforcer.

Reinforcer. An event that increases the rate or probability of occurrence of a behavior when that event is either presented, removed, or canceled following that behavior.

Reinstatement. An effect that occurs after extinction training and refers to the reappearance of the CR when the extinguished CS is presented following exposures to the US.

Relative validity. How well a CS predicts the occurrence of a US relative to how well other CSs predict the occurrence of that same US. The CS with the *highest correlation* with the US has the *highest relative validity*.

Renewal. An effect that occurs after extinction training and refers to a reappearance of the CR when the extinguished CS is presented outside the extinction context.

Reproductive fitness. The measure of success in natural selection: Within a species, those with greater reproductive fitness will produce more offspring that survive to reproduce.

Resistance to extinction. The measure of behavioral persistence during extinction in both Pavlovian conditioning and operant conditioning. In Pavlovian conditioning, resistance to extinction is measured by how long it takes an individual to stop making the CR to a CS that is no longer followed by a US. In operant conditioning, resistance to extinction is measured by how long it takes an individual to stop performing the target behavior when the outcome for that behavior no longer occurs.

Respondent. Skinner's term for a behavior that is elicited by a stimulus. **Conditioned responses** and **unconditioned responses** in Pavlovian conditioning are respondents.

Resurgence. The return of a previously extinguished behavior during extinction of a second behavior.

Retardation of acquisition test for conditioned inhibition. In this test, we attempt to turn a suspected conditioned inhibitory stimulus into a conditioned excitatory stimulus by putting that stimulus into a positive **CS-US contingency**. If that procedure increases the number of trials to produce a conditioned response to that stimulus, that stimulus is an inhibitory stimulus.

Reward. Something individuals seek out, approach, consume, or do something to obtain. It is also called a **positive reinforcer** or an **appetitive event**.

Reward training (procedure). The operant conditioning procedure in which there is a positive behavior-outcome contingency with a **positive reinforcer (reward, appetitive event)**. With the procedure of positive reinforcement, the individual is more likely to receive the positive reinforcer if he or she performs the target behavior than if he or she does not. Reward training is also called **positive reinforcement**.

Rules. A statement of the relationships (contingencies) between events. Rules can be provided by others through instruction or can be self-generated. A rule need not be an accurate reflection of the prevailing contingencies.

Rule-governed behavior. Behavior that is guided by a **rule**.

S→[B-O] association. When experience with an operant conditioning procedure is encoded as a **behavior-outcome (B-O) association**, the representation of the stimulus situation serves as the occasion setter informing the individual that the outcome will follow a certain behavior in that situation.

Salience (of a stimulus). The likelihood that a stimuli will be attended to or noticed by an individual in a given situation. The salience of a stimulus is related to its **discriminability**.

Schedule control procedure. With this **concurrent schedule** arrangement, individuals can do something in one location to select which schedule they want to work on in another location. Choice is defined both on a moment-by-moment basis and in terms of the relative distributions of time each schedule is on and how much behavior occurs with each schedule. Usually this procedure is referred to as a **switching-key** or **switching-lever concurrent schedule**, or the **Findley procedure**.

Schedule of reinforcement. The conditions an individual has to satisfy in order to obtain the reinforcing event in operant conditioning.

Schedule-induced behaviors. Behaviors that emerge when significant events are presented periodically.

Second-order conditioning (phenomenon). Individuals make a conditioned response to a stimulus (CS_2) that was never presented with the US (procedure of second-order conditioning).

Second-order conditioning (procedure). Individuals are given **first-order Pavlovian conditioning** ($CS_1 \rightarrow US$). Then they are given Pavlovian conditioning with a second stimulus (CS_2) that was only paired with CS_1. (CS_2 is never paired with an unconditioned stimulus.)

Secondary reinforcer. See **conditioned reinforcer**.

Semantic memory. The system that stores facts, ideas, and concepts (which are conveyed to us through language).

Sensitization (phenomenon). Enhanced responsiveness to routine events as a result of exposure to a dangerous or painful situation.

Sensitization (procedure). Exposure to a dangerous or painful situation.

Sensory preconditioning (phenomenon). After experiencing two seemingly nonsignificant stimuli together in the absence of a US (sensory preconditioning procedure), training one of these as a conditioned stimulus (presenting it with a US) will produce *a conditioned response* to both that stimulus and *to the other stimulus (even though that other stimulus was never presented with a US)*.

Sensory preconditioning (procedure). Two seemingly nonsignificant stimuli are presented together in the absence of a US prior to Pavlovian conditioning with one of these stimuli as the conditioned stimulus.

Serial feature-negative discrimination. An excitatory conditioned stimulus is followed by a US *except* when that CS is preceded by the feature.

Serial feature-positive discrimination. An excitatory conditioned stimulus is followed by a US *only* when that CS is preceded by the feature.

Shaping by the method of successive approximations (procedure). A procedure for training individuals to perform a certain action by rewarding closer and closer approximations to the final behavior.

Side-by-side procedure. This **concurrent schedule** procedure provides the individual with two or more different behaviors to perform (peck at different keys, press different levers, etc.), each of which occasionally produces reinforcement on a given partial reinforcement schedule. The two schedules operate simultaneously and independently, and the individual is free to choose which schedule to work on at any given point in time. Choice is defined on a moment-by-moment basis and in terms of the relative distributions of time and effort directed toward each alternative. This is also called a **two-key** or **two-lever concurrent schedule**.

Sidman avoidance (procedure). The operant conditioning procedure in which the impending aversive event is not signaled, and the target behavior cancels the next occurrence of that event. Also called **unsignaled avoidance, nondiscriminated avoidance**, and **free operant avoidance**.

Sign-tracking (autoshaping). Behavior that is directed toward or away from a stimulus that signals the occurrence or absence of a significant event (e.g., food, heat, shock).

Signaled avoidance (procedure). The operant conditioning procedure in which the impending aversive event is signaled and the target behavior cancels the next occurrence of that event. Signaled avoidance is also called **discriminated avoidance**.

Simultaneous conditioning (phenomenon). The occurrence of a conditioned response (CR) after exposure to a **simultaneous conditioning procedure**.

Simultaneous conditioning (procedure). The Pavlovian conditioning procedure in which the conditioned stimulus (CS) and the (US) completely overlap.

Simultaneous feature-negative discrimination. An excitatory conditioned stimulus (CS+) is followed by a US *except* when the feature occurs along with that CS.

Simultaneous feature-positive discrimination. An excitatory conditioned stimulus (CS+) is followed by a US *only* when the feature occurs along with that CS.

Social facilitation. Behavior that is aroused by the mere presence of another member of the species.

Social learning. Obtaining knowledge about events and the relationships between events, and how to perform actions efficiently, through interactions with others.

Social transmission of knowledge. Learned knowledge acquired through experience transmitted between members of a species. See also **Cultural transmission of knowledge.**

Spatial contiguity. Events have spatial contiguity when they occur close together in space.

Species-specific defense reactions. Inherited behavior patterns evoked in response to danger.

Spontaneous recovery (phenomenon). Recovery of the target behavior after an interval of time in which there is no stimulation.

Stimulus enhancement. See Local enhancement.

Stimulus generalization (phenomenon). The occurrence of learned behavior in response to stimuli not present during training that are similar to the stimuli that were present during training. The more similar the new stimulus is to the training stimulus, the more likely the learned pattern of behavior will occur in response to that new stimulus.

Stimulus-response (S-R) association. How experience with an operant conditioning procedure is encoded as **procedural knowledge**. According to the Law of Effect, individuals learn to perform a particular activity in a given situation, and the reinforcing event (the event that causes satisfaction) serves to strengthen the link between the stimulus situation and the behavior that occurs just prior to the presentation of the reinforcer. The reinforcing event is *not* encoded here as part of what gets learned.

Sufficient condition. In a cause-effect relationship, a **sufficient condition** is something in whose presence the effect *must* occur.

Summation test for conditioned inhibition. In this test, a suspected conditioned inhibitory stimulus (CS–) is presented along with a known conditioned excitatory stimulus (CS+). A reduction in the conditioned response when the combination of stimuli is presented indicates that the suspected conditioned inhibitory stimulus is indeed inhibitory.

Suppression ratio. A quantitative index of fear based on **conditioned suppression**. The amount of conditioned suppression and the value of the suppression ratio will reflect the level of fear conditioned to the CS. Suppression ratios vary between 0.5 and 0. A ratio of 0.5 indicates *no* conditioned suppression; a ratio of 0 indicates *complete* suppression. Therefore, the lower the ratio, the greater the conditioned suppression (and the greater the conditioned fear).

Surprise. Individuals are surprised when something unanticipated or unexpected occurs, and learning is initiated by unanticipated or surprising events.

Switching-key (switching-lever) concurrent schedule. With this **concurrent schedule** arrangement, individuals can do something in one location to select which schedule they want to work on in another location. Choice is defined both on a moment-by-moment basis and in terms of the relative distributions of time each schedule is on and how much behavior occurs with each schedule. This procedure is also referred to as a **schedule control procedure** or the **Findley procedure**.

Teaching. The transmission of information from one individual to another through directed instruction.

Temporal conditioning (phenomenon). The occurrence of a conditioned response (CR) after exposure to a **temporal conditioning procedure**. That conditioned response tends to occur just before the next unconditioned stimulus is scheduled to occur.

Temporal conditioning (procedure). The unconditioned stimulus (US) is presented at regular intervals. No other event regularly accompanies the US.

Temporal discounting. The tendency to devalue something that cannot be obtained right away. The value of that thing decreases the further away it is in time, but the change in its value is not linear.

Temporal contiguity. Events have temporal contiguity when they occur close together in time.

Temporal precedence (priority). The order of events. In Pavlovian conditioning, this usually refers to the CS occurring *before* the US.

Temporal proximity. The time between the behavior and the reinforcing event (the outcome).

Theoretical matching law. The theoretical statement that the **empirical matching law** is true because "individuals match the *relative allocation* of their behavior to the *relative values* of the alternative outcomes in a **concurrent choice** situation."

Theory. Our proposed explanation, in the language of experimental psychology.

Time schedule of reinforcement. A schedule of reinforcement in which a reinforcer is delivered after a certain time has elapsed independently of the individual's behavior. This is different from an **interval schedule of reinforcement**, which requires the individual to do something (e.g., peck a key or press a lever) after the time has elapsed.

Topography of a behavior. The description of how an individual performs an action.

Trace conditioning (phenomenon). With a **trace conditioning procedure**, the conditioned response (CR) occurs in the interval between the end of the conditioned stimulus (CS) and the time when the unconditioned stimulus (US) is scheduled to occur.

Trace conditioning (procedure). The Pavlovian conditioning procedure in which the conditioned stimulus (CS) is withdrawn some time before the unconditioned stimulus (US) is scheduled to occur.

Trace response. Pavlov's name for a response to the memory trace of the CS (which was no longer present when the US was presented).

Transitive inference. The psychological process by which individuals combine two pieces of information about the relationship between events to infer a third relationship. Second-order conditioning, sensory preconditioning, and the effects of post-conditioning devaluation of the US reflect transitive inference.

Truly random procedure. The Pavlovian conditioning procedure in which the US is *as likely* to occur following a CS as in the absence of the CS; that is, Pr (US I CS) = Pr (US I no CS). This is also called a **Zero CS-US contingency**.

Two-action procedure. The procedure used to demonstrate that a behavior is learned through **imitation**. This procedure requires that there be more than one way an individual can perform an action (or more than one action) that leads to the outcome. Different observers can watch different demonstrators obtaining the outcome in different ways. Imitation is inferred to be the mechanism for learning if the observers perform the action they observed, even if other ways also work (or work better). This is also called the **bidirectional control procedure**.

Unconditioned reflexes. Pavlov's term for what we call today an **unconditioned response**.

Unconditioned response (UR). A response that is reliably elicited to a stimulus or event before Pavlovian conditioning begins. That stimulus is called the **unconditioned stimulus (US)**.

Unconditioned stimulus (US). A stimulus or event that reliably elicits a response before Pavlovian conditioning begins. That response is called the **unconditioned response (UR)**.

Undermatching. Individuals are said to undermatch on a **concurrent schedule** when they spend *less* time and effort on each schedule than is predicted by the **empirical matching law**. The most extreme case of undermatching is to switch back and forth between the two schedules regardless of the relative rates of reinforcement available on those schedules.

Unique cause (necessary and sufficient condition). In a cause-effect relationship, a **necessary and sufficient condition (unique cause)** is something in whose absence the effect *cannot* occur and in whose presence the effect *must* occur.

Unsignaled avoidance (procedure). The operant conditioning procedure in which the impending aversive event is not signaled, and the target behavior cancels the next occurrence of that event. Also called **nondiscriminated avoidance, free operant avoidance,** and **Sidman avoidance**.

US preexposure effect. The retardation of Pavlovian conditioning by presenting the unconditioned stimulus (US) by itself prior to conditioning.

Value (V) of a reinforcer. In the theoretical **matching law**, the value (V) of a reinforcer is defined as the product of its rate of occurrence (R), how much there is (Magnitude), how quickly it follows the target behavior (Immediacy), and other attributes that affect the value of a reinforcer (X); that is, $V = R \times M \times I \times X$.

Variable-interval schedule of reinforcement (VI *t*). A schedule of reinforcement in operant conditioning in which the first occurrence of the target behavior after a *specified interval of time* has elapsed will produce the outcome; that interval varies around a certain average (*t*). Variable-interval schedules are related to **random-interval schedules,** and the behavior patterns generated by both are similar.

Variable-ratio schedule of reinforcement (VR *n*). A schedule of reinforcement in operant conditioning in which the individual has to perform the target behavior a *specified number of times* in order to obtain a certain outcome; that number varies around a certain average (*n*). Variable-ratio schedules are related to **random ratio schedules,** and the behavior patterns generated by both are similar.

Verbal instruction. Telling someone what to do or how to do it.

Verbally mediated learning. Learning based on verbal descriptions of the contingency or about what to do.

Within-compound association. The name given to an association between two stimuli experienced together as a compound.

Yoking (procedure). The purpose of this procedure is to equate the number and pattern of reinforcers available to two individuals. Subjects are "yoked" when behavior of one individual determines the delivery of the reinforcer to both of them.

Zero CS–US contingency. The Pavlovian conditioning procedure in which the US is *as likely* to occur following a CS as in the absence of the CS; that is, Pr (US | CS) = Pr (US | no CS). This is also called a **truly random procedure**.

REFERENCES

Adams, C. D. (1980). Post-conditioning devaluation of an instrumental reinforcer has no effect on extinction performance. *Quarterly Journal of Experimental Psychology, 32,* 447–458.

Adams, C. D. (1982). Variations in the sensitivity of instrumental responding to reinforcer devaluation. *Quarterly Journal of Experimental Psychology, 34B,* 77–98.

Adams, C. D., & Dickinson, A. (1981). Instrumental responding following reinforcer devaluation. *Quarterly Journal of Experimental Psychology, 33B,* 109–122.

Adams, D. K. (1929). Experimental studies of adaptive behavior in cats. *Comparative Psychology Monographs, 6*(27), 1–166.

Ader, R. (1985). Conditioned immunopharmacological effects in animals: Implications for a conditioning model of pharmacotherapy. In L. White, B. Tursky, & G. E. Schwartz (Eds.), *Placebo: Theory, research, and mechanisms* (pp. 306–323). New York: Guilford Press.

Ader, R. (1997). The role of conditioning in pharmacotherapy. In A. Harrington (Ed.), *The placebo effect: An interdisciplinary exploration* (pp. 138–165). Cambridge MA: Harvard University Press.

Ader, R., & Cohen, N. (1982). Behaviorally conditioned immunosuppression and murine systemic lupus erythematosus. *Science, 215,* 1534–1536.

Ader, R., & Cohen, N. (1991). The influence of conditioning on immune responses. In R. Ader, D. L. Felton, & N. Cohen (Eds.), *Psychoneuroimmunology* (2nd ed., pp. 611–646). San Diego, CA: Academic Press.

Ader, R., & Cohen, N. (2001). Conditioning and immunity. In R. Ader, D. L. Felten, & N. Cohen (Eds.), *Psychoneuroimmunology* (Vol. 2, 3rd ed., pp. 3–34). New York: Academic Press.

Ader, R., & Tatum, R. (1961). Free operant avoidance conditioning in human subjects. *Journal of the Experimental Analysis of Behavior, 4,* 275–276.

Adkins, C. K., & Zentall, T. R. (1996). Imitative learning in male Japanese quail (Coturnix japonica) using the two-action method. *Journal of Comparative Psychology, 110,* 316–320.

Adkins, C. K., & Zentall, T. R. (1998). Imitation in Japanese quail: The role of reinforcement of demonstrator responding. *Psychonomic Bulletin & Review, 5,* 694–697.

Alferink, L. A., Critchfield, T. S., Hitt, J. L., & Higgins, W. J. (2009). Generality of the matching law as a descriptor of shot selection in basketball. *Journal of Applied Behavior Analysis, 42,* 595–608.

Alharbi, F., & el-Guebaly, N. (2013). The relative safety of disulfiram. *Addictive Disorders & Their Treatment, 12,* 140–147.

Allen, C. T., & Shimp, T. A. (1990). On using classical conditioning methods for researching the impact of ad-evoked feelings. In S. J. Agras, J. A. Edell, & T. M. Dubitsky (Eds.), *Emotion in advertising: Theoretical and practical explorations* (pp. 19–34). Westport, CT: Quorum Books.

Alloy, L. B., & Abramson, L. Y. (1979). Judgment of contingency in depressed and nondepressed students: Sadder but wiser? *Journal of Experimental Psychology: General, 108,* 441–485.

Alloy, L. B., & Tabachnik, N. (1984). Assessment of covariation by humans and animals: The joint influence of prior expectations and current situational information. *Psychological Review, 91,* 112–149.

Altmann, J. (1980). *Baboon mothers and infants.* Cambridge MA: Harvard University Press.

American Psychiatric Association (2013). *Diagnostic and statistical manual of mental disorders* (5th ed.). Washington, DC: Author.

Amsel, A. (1958). The role of frustrative nonreward in noncontinuous reward situations. *Psychological Bulletin, 55,* 102–119.

Amsel, A. (1992). *Frustration theory: An analysis of dispositional learning and memory.* New York: Cambridge University Press.

Amsel, A., & Roussel, J. (1952). Motivational properties of frustration: I. Effect on a running response of the addition of frustration to the motivational complex. *Journal of Experimental Psychology, 43,* 363–368.

Anderson, J. R. (1990). *Cognitive psychology and its implications* (3rd ed.). New York: Freeman.

Annau, Z., & Kamin, L. J. (1961). The conditioned emotional response as a function of the intensity of the US. *Journal of Comparative and Physiological Psychology, 54,* 428–432.

Anokhin, P. K. (1974). *Biology and neurophysiology of the conditional reflex and its role in adaptive behavior.* Oxford: Pergamon.

Antonitis, J. J. (1951). Response variability in the white rat during conditioning, extinction, and reconditioning. *Journal of Experimental Psychology, 42,* 273–281.

Aparicio, C. F. (2001). Overmatching in rats: The barrier choice paradigm. *Journal of the Experimental Analysis of Behavior, 75,* 93–106.

Appel, J. B., & Hiss, R. H. (1962). The discrimination of contingent from noncontingent reinforcement. *Journal of Comparative and Physiological Psychology, 55,* 37–39.

Arthurs, J., Lin, J.-Y., Amodeo, L. R, & Reilly, S. (2012). Reduced palatability in drug-induced taste aversion: II. Aversive and rewarding unconditioned stimuli. *Behavioral Neuroscience, 126,* 433–444.

Asem, J. S. A., & Holland, P. C. (2012). The effects of high-fat diets on extinction and renewal. *Behavioral Neuroscience, 126,* 493–498.

Ash, D. W., & Holding, D. H. (1990). Backward versus forward chaining in the acquisition of a keyboard skill. *Human Factors, 32,* 139–146.

Asratyan, E. A. (1974). Conditioned reflex theory and motivational behavior. *Acta Neurobiologiae Experimentalis, 34,* 15–31.

Augustine of Hippo. (1982). *The literal meaning of Genesis.* (J. H. Taylor, Trans.). New York: Paulist Press.

Ayllon, T., & Azrin, N. H. (1964). Reinforcement and instructions with mental patients. *Journal of the Experimental Analysis of Behavior, 7,* 327–331.

Ayllon, T., & Michael, J. (1959). The psychiatric nurse as a behavioral engineer. *Journal of the Experimental Analysis of Behavior, 2,* 323–334.

Ayres, J. J. B., Benedict, J. O., & Witcher, E. S. (1975). Systematic manipulation of individual events in a truly random control in rats. *Journal of Comparative and Physiological Psychology, 88,* 97–103.

Ayres, J. J. B., Haddad, C., & Albert, M. (1987). One-trial excitatory backward conditioning as assessed by conditioned suppression of licking in rats: Concurrent observations of lick suppression and defensive behaviors. *Animal Learning and Behavior, 15,* 212–217.

Azrin, N., & Lindsley, O. (1956). The reinforcement of cooperation between children. *Journal of Abnormal and Social Psychology, 52,* 100–102.

Baer, D. M. (1962). Laboratory control of thumbsucking by withdrawal and re-presentation of reinforcement. *Journal of the Experimental Analysis of Behavior, 5,* 525–528.

Baerends, G. P. (1970). A model for the functional organization of incubation behaviour. In G. P. Baerends & R. H. Drent (Eds.), *The herring gull and its egg. Behaviour* (Suppl. 17; pp. 263–312).

Baerends, G. P. (1976). The functional organization of behaviour. *Animal Behaviour, 24,* 726–738.

Baerends-van Roon, J. M., & Baerends, G. P. (1979). *The morphogenesis of the behaviour of the domestic cat, with a special emphasis on the development of prey-catching.* Amsterdam: Elsevier/North-Holland.

Baeyens, F., Crombez, G., De Houwer, J., & Eelen, P. (1996). No evidence for modulation of evaluative flavor-flavor associations in humans. *Learning and Motivation, 27,* 200–241.

Baeyens, F., Crombez, G., Hendrickx, H., & Eelen, P. (1995). Parameters of human evaluative flavor-flavor conditioning. *Learning and Motivation, 26,* 141–160.

Baeyens, F., Crombez, G., Van den Bergh, O., & Eelen, P. (1988). Once in contact, always in contact: EC is resistant to extinction. *Advances in Behaviour Research and Therapy, 10,* 179–199.

Baeyens, F., Eelen, P., Crombez, G., & Van den Bergh, O. (1992). Human evaluative conditioning: Acquisition trials, presentation schedule, evaluation style and contingency awareness. *Behavior Research and Therapy, 30,* 133–142.

Baeyens, F., Eelen, P., & Van den Bergh, O. (1990). Contingency awareness in evaluative conditioning: A case for unaware evaluative conditioning. *Cognition and Emotion, 4,* 3–18.

Baeyens, F., Eelen, P., Van den Bergh, O., & Crombez, G. (1990). Flavor-flavor and color-flavor conditioning in humans. *Learning and Motivation, 21,* 434–455.

Baeyens, F., Eelen, P., Van den Bergh, O., & Crombez, G. (1992). The content of learning in human evaluative conditioning: Acquired valence is sensitive to US-revaluation. *Learning and Motivation, 23,* 200–224.

Baeyens, F., Vansteenwegen, D., Hermans, D., Vervliet, B., & Eelen, P. (2001). Sequential and simultaneous feature positive discriminations: Occasion setting and configural learning in human Pavlovian conditioning. *Journal of Experimental Psychology: Animal Behavior Processes, 27,* 279–295.

Bakal, C. W., Johnson, R. D., & Rescorla, R. A. (1974). The effect of change in US quality on the blocking effect. *Pavlovian Journal of Biological Sciences, 9,* 97–103.

Baker, A. G. (1990). Contextual conditioning during free-operant extinction: Unsignaled, signaled, and backward-signaled noncontingent food. *Animal Learning and Behavior, 18,* 59–70.

Baker, A. G., & Mackintosh, N. J. (1977). Excitatory and inhibitory conditioning following uncorrelated presentations of the CS and US. *Animal Learning and Behavior, 5,* 315–319.

Baker, A. G., Mercier, P., Vallée-Tourangeau, F., Frank, R., & Pan, M. (1993). Selective associations and causality judgments: Presence of a strong causal factor may reduce judgments of a weaker one. *Journal of Experimental Psychology: Learning, Memory, and Cognition, 19,* 414–432.

Balaz, M. A., Gutsin, P., Cacheiro, H., & Miller, R. R. (1982). Blocking as retrieval failure: Reactivation of associations to a blocked stimulus. *Quarterly Journal of Experimental Psychology, 34B,* 99–113.

Balleine, B. (1992). Instrumental performance following a shift in primary motivation depends on incentive learning. *Journal of Experimental Psychology: Animal Behavior Processes, 18,* 236–250.

Balleine, B. W., & Dickinson, A. (1998). The role of incentive learning in instrumental outcome revaluation by sensory-specific satiety. *Animal Learning and Behavior, 26,* 46–59.

Balleine, B. W., & O'Doherty, J. P. (2010). Human and rodent homologies in action control: Corticostriatal determinants of goad-directed and habitual learning. *Neuropsychopharmacology, 35,* 48–69.

Balsam, P. D. (1982). Bringing the background to the foreground: The role of contextual cues in autoshaping. In M. L. Commons, R. Herrnstein, & A. R. Wagner (Eds.), *Quantitative analyses of behavior: Acquisition* (Vol. 3, pp. 145–171). Cambridge, MA: Ballinger.

Balsam, P. D. (1985). The functions of context in learning and performance. In P. D. Balsam & A. Tomie (Eds.), *Context and learning.* Hillsdale, NJ: Lawrence Erlbaum.

Balsam, P. D., Deich, J. D., Ohyama, T., & Stokes, P. D.

(1998). Origins of new behavior. In W. O. O'Donohue (Ed.), *Learning and behavior therapy* (pp. 403–420). Boston: Allyn & Bacon.

Balsam, P. D., & Gibbon, J. (1988). Formation of tone-US associations does not interfere with the formation of context-US associations. *Journal of Experimental Psychology: Animal Behavior Processes, 14,* 401–412.

Balsam, P. D., & Schwartz, A. L. (1981). Rapid contextual conditioning in autoshaping. *Journal of Experimental Psychology: Animal Behavior Processes, 7,* 382–393.

Balsam, P. D., & Tomie, A. (Eds.). (1985). *Context and learning.* Hillsdale, NJ: Lawrence Erlbaum.

Bandura, A. (1986). *Social foundations of thought and action: A social cognitive theory.* Englewood Cliffs, NJ: Prentice-Hall.

Barker, L. M., Best, M. R., & Domjan, M. (Eds.). (1977). *Learning mechanisms in food selection.* Waco, TX: Baylor University Press.

Barnet, R. C., Grahame, N. J., & Miller, R. R. (1993). Temporal encoding as a determinant of blocking. *Journal of Experimental Psychology: Animal Behavior Processes, 19,* 327–341.

Barnet, R. C., & Miller, R. R. (1996). Temporal encoding as a determinant of inhibitory control. *Learning and Motivation, 27,* 73–91.

Barnett, S. A. (1956). Behavior components in the feeding of wild and laboratory rats. *Behaviour, 9,* 24–43.

Barnett, S. A. (1975). *The rat: A study in behavior.* Chicago: University of Chicago Press.

Baron, A., & Galizio, M. (1983). Instructional control of human operant behavior. *The Psychological Record, 33,* 495–520.

Baron, A., & Kaufman, A. (1966). Human free-operant avoidance of "time-out" from monetary reinforcement. *Journal of the Experimental Analysis of Behavior, 9,* 557–565.

Baron, A., Kaufman, A., & Stauber, K. (1969). Effects of instructions and reinforcement feedback on human operant behavior maintained by fixed-interval reinforcement. *Journal of the Experimental Analysis of Behavior, 12,* 701–712.

Baron, A., & Leinenweber, A. (1995). Effects of a variable-ratio conditioning history on sensitivity to fixed-interval contingencies in rats. *Journal of the Experimental Analysis of Behavior, 63,* 97–110.

Barrett, B. H. (1962). Reduction in rate of multiple ticks by free operant conditioning techniques. *Journal of Nervous and Mental Disease, 135,* 187–195.

Bateson, P. P. G. (1978). Sexual imprinting and optimal outbreeding. *Nature, 273,* 659–660.

Baum, M. (1970). Extinction of avoidance responding through response prevention (flooding). *Psychological Bulletin, 74,* 276–284.

Baum, M., & Poser, E. G. (1971). Comparison of flooding procedures in animal and man. *Behavior Research and Therapy, 9,* 249–254.

Baum, W. M. (1982). Choice, changeover, and travel. *Journal of the Experimental Analysis of Behavior, 38,* 35–49.

Baum, W. M. (1993). Performance on ratio and interval schedules of reinforcement: Data and theory. *Journal of the Experimental Analysis of Behavior, 59,* 245–264.

Baum, W. M. (2002). From molecular to molar: A paradigm shift in behavior analysis. *Journal of the Experimental Analysis of Behavior, 78,* 95–116.

Baum, W. M. (2004). Molar and molecular views of choice. *Behavioural Processes, 66,* 349–359.

Baum, W. M. (2012). Rethinking reinforcement: Allocation, induction, and contingency. *Journal of the Experimental Analysis of Behavior, 97,* 101–124.

Baum, W. M., & Rachlin, H. C. (1969). Choice as time allocation. *Journal of the Experimental Analysis of Behavior, 12,* 861–874.

Baumeister, A., Hawkins, W. F., & Cromwell, R. L. (1964). Need states and activity level. *Psychological Bulletin, 61,* 438–453.

Beck, H. P., Levinson, S., & Irons, G. (2009). Finding Little Albert: A journey to John B. Watson's infant laboratory. *American Psychologist, 64,* 605–614.

Benedict, J. O., & Ayers, J. J. B. (1972). Factors affecting conditioning in the truly random control procedure. *Journal of Comparative and Physiological Psychology, 78,* 323–330.

Benhamou, S., & Bovet, P. (1989). How animals use their environment. A new look at kinesis. *Animal Behavior, 38,* 375–383.

Benhamou, S., & Bovet, P. (1992). Distinguishing between elementary orientation mechanisms by means of path analysis. *Animal Behavior, 43,* 371–377.

Benhamou, S., Sauvé, J-P., & Bovet, P. (1990). Spatial memory in large scale movements: Efficiency and limitation of the egocentric coding process. *Journal of Theoretical Biology, 145,* 1–12.

Beninger, R. J., Kendall, S. B., & Vanderwolf, C. H. (1974). The ability of rats to discriminate their own behaviors. *Canadian Journal of Psychology, 28,* 79–91.

Bentall, R. P., & Lowe, C. F. (1987). The role of verbal behavior in human learning: III. Instructional effects in children. *Journal of the Experimental Analysis of Behavior, 47,* 177–190.

Bentall, R. P., Lowe, C. F., & Beasty, A. (1985). The role of verbal behavior in human learning: II. Developmental differences. *Journal of the Experimental Analysis of Behavior, 43,* 165–181.

Bernstein, I. L. (1978). Learned taste aversions in children receiving chemotherapy. *Science, 200,* 1302–1303.

Bernstein, I. L. (1991). Aversion conditioning in response to cancer and cancer treatment. *Clinical Psychology Review, 11,* 185–191.

Bernstein, I. L., & Webster, M. M. (1980). Learned taste aversions in humans. *Physiology and Behavior, 25,* 363–366.

Berridge, K. C. (2000). Measuring hedonic impact in animals and infants: Microstructure of affective taste reactivity patterns. *Neuroscience and Biobehavioral Reviews, 24,* 173–198.

Best, P. J., Best, M. R., & Henggeler, S. (1977). The contribution of environmental non-ingestive cues in conditioning with aversive internal consequences. In L. M. Barker, M. R. Best, & M. Domjan (Eds.), *Learning mechanisms in food selection* (pp. 371–393). Waco, TX: Baylor University Press.

Bijou, S. W. (1955). A systematic approach to the experimental analysis of young children. *Child Development, 26,* 161–168.

Birch, L. L. (1980). Effects of peer models' food choices and eating behaviors on preschoolers' food preferences. *Child Development, 51,* 489–496.

Bitterman, M. E. (1975). The comparative analysis of learning. *Science, 188,* 699–709.

Black, A. H. (1971). Autonomic aversive conditioning in infrahuman subjects. In F. R. Brush (Ed.), *Aversive conditioning and learning* (pp. 3–104). New York: Academic Press.

Blair, M. E., & Shimp, T. A. (1992). Consequences of an unpleasant experience with music: A second-order negative conditioning perspective. *Journal of Advertising, 21*(1), 35–43.

Blaisdell, A. P., Gunther, L. M., & Miller, R. R. (1999). Recovering from blocking achieved by extinguishing the blocking CS. *Animal Learning and Behavior, 27,* 63–76.

Blakely, E., & Schlinger, H. (1988). Determinants of pausing under variable-ratio schedules: Reinforcer magnitude, ratio size, and schedule configuration. *Journal of the Experimental Analysis of Behavior, 50,* 65–73.

Blanchard, R. J., & Blanchard, D. C. (1969a). Crouching as an index of fear. *Journal of Comparative and Physiological Psychology, 67,* 370–375.

Blanchard, R. J., & Blanchard, D. C. (1969b). Passive and active reactions to fear-eliciting stimuli. *Journal of Comparative and Physiological Psychology, 68,* 129–135.

Blanchard, R. J., Fukunaga, K. K., & Blanchard, D. C. (1976). Environmental control of defensive reactions to footshock. *Bulletin of the Psychonomic Society, 8,* 129–130.

Blechert, J., Michael, T., Williams, S. L., Purkis, H. M., & Wilhelm, F. H. (2008). When two paradigms meet: Does evaluative learning extinguish in differential fear conditioning? *Learning and Motivation, 39,* 58–70.

Bliss-Moreau, E., Owren, M., & Barrett, L. F. (2010). I like the sound of your voice: Affective learning about vocal signals. *Journal of Experimental Social Psychology, 46,* 557–563.

Blough, D. S. (1958). New test for tranquilizers. *Science, 127,* 586–587.

Boakes, R. A. (1973). Response decrements produced by extinction and by response-independent reinforcement. *Journal of the Experimental Analysis of Behavior, 19,* 293–302.

Boakes, R. A., & Nakajima, S. (2009). Conditioned taste aversions based on running or swimming. In S. Reilly & T. R. Schachtman (Eds.), *Conditioned taste aversion: Behavioral and neural processes* (pp. 159–178). New York: Oxford University Press.

Boakes, R. A., Poli, M., Lockwood, M. J., & Goodall, G. (1978). A study of misbehavior: Token reinforcement in the rat. *Journal of the Experimental Analysis of Behavior, 29,* 115–134.

Boelens, H., & Kop, P. F. M. (1983). Concurrent schedules: Spatial separation of response alternatives. *Journal of the Experimental Analysis of Behavior, 40,* 35–45.

Boesch, C. (1991). Teaching among wild chimpanzees. *Animal Behaviour, 41,* 530–532.

Bolders, A. C., Band, G. P. H., & Stallen, P. J. (2012). Evaluative conditioning induces changes in sound valence. *Frontiers in Psychology, 3,* 106.

Bolles, R. C. (1970). Species-specific defense reactions and avoidance learning. *Psychological Review, 77,* 32–48.

Bolles, R. C. (1972). Reinforcement, expectancy, and learning. *Psychological Review, 95,* 394–409.

Bolles, R. C. (1985). The slaying of Goliath: What happened to reinforcement theory? In T. D. Johnston & A. T. Piertrewicz (Eds.), *Issues in the ecological study of learning* (pp. 387–399). Hillsdale, NJ: Erlbaum.

Bolles, R. C., Hayward, L., & Crandall, C. (1981). Conditioned taste preferences based on caloric density. *Journal of Experimental Psychology: Animal Behavior Processes, 7,* 59–69.

Bolles, R. C., Holtz, R., Dunn, T., & Hill, W. (1980). Comparison of stimulus learning and response learning in a punishment situation. *Learning and Motivation, 11,* 78–96.

Bolles, R. C., & Popp, R. J. Jr. (1964). Parameters affecting the acquisition of Sidman avoidance. *Journal of the Experimental Analysis of Behavior, 7,* 315–321.

Borrero, J. C., Crisolo, S. S., Tu, Q., Rieland, W. A., Ross, N. A., Francisco, M. T., & Yamamoto, K. Y. (2007). An application of the matching law to social dynamics. *Journal of Applied Behavior Analysis, 40,* 589–601.

Bossert, J. M., Liu, S. Y., Lu, L., & Shaham, Y. (2004). A role of ventral tegmental area glutamate in contextual cue-induced relapse to heroin seeking. *Journal of Neuroscience, 24,* 10726–10730.

Bossert, J. M., Poles, G. C., Wihbey, K. A., Koya, E., & Shaham, Y. (2007). Differential effects of blockade of dopamine D1-family receptors in nucleus accumbens core or shell on reinstatement of heroin seeking induced by contextual and discrete cues. *Journal of Neuroscience, 27,* 12655–12663.

Bousfield, W. A. (1955). Lope de Vega on early conditioning. *American Psychologist, 10,* 828.

Bouton, M. E. (1984). Differential control by context in the inflation and reinstatement paradigms. *Journal of Experimental Psychology: Animal Behavior Process, 10,* 56–74.

Bouton, M. E. (1991). Context and retrieval in extinction and in other examples of interference in simple associative learning. In L. Dachowski & C. F. Flaherty (Eds.), *Current topics in animal learning: Brain, emotion, and cognition* (pp. 25–53). Hillsdale, NJ: Erlbaum.

Bouton, M. E. (1993). Context, time, and memory retrieval in the interference paradigms of Pavlovian learning. *Psychological Bulletin, 114*, 80–99.

Bouton, M. E. (1994). Context, ambiguity, and classical conditioning. *Current Directions in Psychological Science, 3*, 49–53.

Bouton, M. E. (2002). Context, ambiguity, and unlearning: Sources of relapse after behavioral extinction. *Biological Psychiatry, 52*, 976–986.

Bouton, M. E. (2004). Context and behavioral processes in extinction. *Learning and Memory, 11*, 485–494.

Bouton, M. E. (2010). The multiple forms of "context" in associative learning theory. In B. Mesquita, L. Feldman Barrett, & E. Smith (Eds.), *The mind in context* (pp. 233–258). New York: Guilford Press.

Bouton, M. E. (2014). Why behavior change is difficult. *Preventive Medicine, 68*, 29–36.

Bouton, M. E., & Bolles, R. C. (1979). Role of conditioned contextual stimuli in fear extinction in reinstatement of extinguished fear. *Journal of Experimental Psychology: Animal Behavior Process, 5*, 368–378.

Bouton, M. E., & Bolles, R. C. (1985). Contexts, event-memories, and extinction. In P. D. Balsam & A. Tomie (Eds.), *Context and learning* (pp. 133–166).Hillsdale, NJ: Lawrence Erlbaum Associates.

Bouton, M. E., & King, M. D. (1983). Contextual control of the extinction of conditioned fear: Tests for the associative value of the context. *Journal of Experimental Psychology: Animal Behavior Processes, 9*, 248–265.

Bouton, M. E., Mineka, S., & Barlow, D. H. (2001). A modern learning theory perspective on the etiology of panic disorder. *Psychological Review, 108*, 4–32.

Bouton, M. E., & Ricker, S. T. (1994). Renewal of extinguished responding in a second context. *Animal Learning and Behavior, 22*, 317–324.

Bouton, M. E., & Todd, T. P. (2014). A fundamental role for context in instrumental learning and extinction. *Behavioural Processes, 104*, 13–19.

Bouton, M. E., Todd, T. P., Vurbic, D., & Winterbauer, N. E. (2011). Renewal after the extinction of free and operant behavior. *Learning and Behavior, 39*, 57–67.

Bouton, M. E., Winterbauer, N. E., & Vurbic, D. (2012). Context and extinction: Mechanisms of relapse in drug self-administration. In M. Haselgrove & L. Hogarth (Eds.), *Clinical applications of learning theory* (pp. 103–133). East Sussex, UK: Psychology Press.

Bovbjerg, D. H., Redd, W. H., Maier, L. A., Holland, J. C., Lesko, L. M., Niedzweicki, D., . . . Hakes, R. B. (1990). Anticipatory immune suppression and nausea in women receiving cyclic chemotherapy for ovarian cancer. *Journal of Consulting and Clinical Psychology, 58*, 153–157.

Bowlby, J. (1973). *Attachment and loss, Vol. 2: Separation.* New York: Basic Books.

Bowlby, J. (1982). *Attachment and loss: Vol. 1. Attachment* (2nd ed.). New York: Basic Books.

Boyd, R., & Richerson, P. J. (1985). *Culture and the evolutionary process.* Chicago: University of Chicago Press.

Braveman, N. S. (1974). Poison-based avoidance learning with flavored or colored water in guinea pigs. *Learning and Motivation, 5*, 182–194.

Braveman, N. S. (1975). Formation of taste aversions in rats following prior exposure to sickness. *Learning and Motivation, 6*, 512–534.

Braveman, N. S., & Bronstein P. (Eds.). (1985). *Experimental assessments and clinical applications of conditioned food aversions.* New York: New York Academy of Sciences.

Bregman, E. O. (1934). An attempt to modify the emotional attitudes of infants by the conditioned response technique. *Journal of Genetic Psychology, 45*, 169–198.

Breland, K., & Breland, M. (1961). The misbehavior of organisms. *American Psychologist, 16*, 681–684.

Breland, K., & Breland, M. (1966). *Animal behavior.* New York: Macmillan.

Bridger, W. H., & Mandel, I. J. (1965). Abolition of the PRE by instructions in GSR conditioning. *Journal of Experimental Psychology, 69,* 476–482.

Broadbent, D. E. (1961). *Behaviour.* London: Metheun.

Broborg, D. J., & Bernstein, I. L. (1987). Candy as a scapegoat in the prevention of food aversions in children receiving chemotherapy. *Cancer, 60,* 2344–2347.

Brodigan, D. L., & Peterson, G. B. (1976). Two-choice discrimination performance of pigeons as a function of reward expectancy, prechoice delay, and domesticity. *Animal Learning and Behavior, 4,* 121–124.

Brogden, W. J. (1939). Sensory preconditioning. *Journal of Experimental Psychology, 25,* 323–332.

Brogden, W. J., Lipman, E. A., & Culler, E. (1938). The role of incentive in conditioning and extinction. *American Journal of Psychology, 51,* 109–117.

Brontë, A. (1994). *The tenant of Wildfell Hall.* Ware, UK: Wordsworth Editions. (Original work published 1848)

Brooks, D. C., & Bouton, M. E. (1993). A retrieval cue for extinction attenuates spontaneous recovery. *Journal of Experimental Psychology: Animal Behavior Processes 19,* 77–89.

Brooks, D. C., & Bouton, M. E. (1994). A retrieval cue for extinction attenuates response recovery (renewal) caused by a return to the conditioning context. *Journal of Experimental Psychology: Animal Behavior Processes, 20,* 366–379.

Brower, L. P. (1969). Ecological chemistry. *Scientific American, 220*(2), 22–29.

Brown, J. S., & Jacobs, A. (1949). The role of fear in the motivation and acquisition of responses. *Journal of Experimental Psychology, 39,* 747–759.

Brown, P., & Jenkins, H. (1968). Autoshaping of the pigeon's keypeck. *Journal of the Experimental Analysis of Behavior, 11,* 1–8.

Brown, R. M., & Robertson, E. M. (2007). Off-line processing: Reciprocal interactions between declarative and procedural memories. *Journal of Neuroscience, 27,* 10468–10475.

Brownstein, A. J. (1971). Concurrent schedules of response-independent reinforcement: Duration of a reinforcing stimulus. *Journal of the Experimental Analysis of Behavior, 15,* 211–214.

Bruner, A., & Revusky, S. H. (1961). Collateral behavior in humans. *Journal of the Experimental Analysis of Behavior, 4,* 349–350.

Bullock, D. H. (1960). Repeated conditioning-extinction sessions as a function of reinforcement schedule. *Journal of the Experimental Analysis of Behavior, 3,* 241–243.

Bullock, D. H., & Smith, W. C. (1953). An effect of repeated conditioning-extinction upon operant strength. *Journal of Experimental Psychology, 46,* 349–352.

Burish, T. G., Levy, S. M., & Meyerowitz, B. E., (Eds.). (1985). *Cancer, nutrition, and eating behavior: A biobehavioral perspective.* Hillsdale, NJ: Lawrence Erlbaum Associates.

Burkhardt, P. E. (1980). One trial backward fear conditioning in rats as a function of UCS intensity. *Bulletin of the Psychonomic Society, 15,* 9–11.

Buss, D. M. (1995). Evolutionary psychology: A new paradigm for psychological science. *Psychological Inquiry, 6,* 1–30.

Butler, R. A. (1953). Discrimination learning by rhesus monkeys to visual exploration motivation. *Journal of Comparative and Physiological Psychology, 46,* 95–98.

Bykov, K. M. (1959). *The cerebral cortex and the internal organs.* Moscow: Foreign Languages Publishing House.

Byrne, R. W. (2002). Imitation of novel complex actions: What does the evidence from animals mean? *Advances in the Study of Behavior, 31,* 77–105.

Calhoun, J. B. (1962). *The ecology and sociology of the Norway rat.* Bethesda, MD: U.S. Department of Health, Education, and Welfare.

Call, J., & Tomasello, M. (1994). The social learning of tool use by orangutans (Pongo pygmaeus). *Human Evolution, 9*, 297–313.

Call, J., & Tomasello, M. (1995). The use of social information in the problem solving of orangutans and human children. *Journal of Comparative Psychology, 109*, 301–320.

Campbell, D. T. (1956). Adaptive behavior from random response. *Behavioral Science, 1*, 105–110.

Campbell, D. T. (1960). Blind variation and selective retention in creative thought as in other knowledge processes. *Psychological Review, 67*, 380–400.

Campbell, F. M., and Heyes, C. M. (2002). Rats smell: Odour mediated local enhancement, in a vertical movement two action test. *Animal Behaviour, 63*, 1055–1063.

Campbell, H. C., Capaldi, E. D., Sheffer, J. D., & Bradford, J. P. (1988). An examination of the relationship between expectancy learning and preference conditioning. *Learning and Motivation, 19*, 162–182.

Campese, V., & Delamater, A. R. (2013). ABA and ABC renewal of conditioned magazine approach are not impaired by dorsal hippocampus inactivation or lesions. *Behavioural Brain Research, 248*, 62–73.

Campos, J. J., Anderson, D. I., Barbu-Roth, M., Hubbard, E. M., Hertenstein, M. J., & Witherington, D. (2000). Travel broadens the mind. *Infancy, 1*, 149–219.

Cançado, C. R. X., & Lattal, K. A. (2011). Resurgence of temporal patterns of responding. *Journal of the Experimental Analysis of Behavior, 95*, 271–287.

Cannon, D., Berman, R., Baker, T., & Atkinson, C. (1975). Effect of preconditioning unconditioned stimulus experience on learned taste aversions. *Journal of Experimental Psychology: Animal Behavior Processes, 104*, 270–284.

Capaldi, E. D., Campbell, D. H., Sheffer, J. D., & Bradford, J. P. (1987). Conditioned flavor preferences based on delayed caloric consequences. *Journal of Experimental Psychology: Animal Behavior Processes, 13*, 150–155.

Capaldi, E. D., & Powley T. L. (Eds.). (1990). *Taste, experience, and feeding.* Washington, DC: American Psychological Association.

Cappell, H., & LeBlanc, A. E. (1977). Parametric investigations of the effects of prior exposure to amphetamine and morphine on conditioned gustatory aversion. *Psychopharmacology, 51*, 265–271.

Carey, M. P., & Burish, T. G. (1988). Etiology and treatment of the psychological side effects associated with cancer psychotherapy: A clinical review and discussion. *Psychological Bulletin, 104*, 307–325.

Carlton, P. L., & Vogel, J. R. (1967). Habituation and conditioning. *Journal of Comparative and Physiological Psychology, 63*, 348–351.

Caro, T. M. (1980a). Effects of the mother, object play and adult experience on predation in cats. *Behavioral and Neural Biology, 29*, 29–51.

Caro, T. M. (1980b). Predatory behaviour in domestic cat mothers. *Behaviour, 74*, 128–147.

Caro, T. M. (1994). *Cheetahs of the Serengeti plains: Grouping in an asocial species.* Chicago: University of Chicago Press.

Caro, T. M., & Hauser, M. D. (1992). Is there teaching in nonhuman animals? *Quarterly Review of Biology, 67*, 151–174.

Carr, E. G., & McDowell, J. J. (1980). Social control of self-injurious behavior of organic etiology. *Behavior Therapy, 11*, 402–409.

Carr, J. E., Severtson, J. M., & Lepper, T. L. (2009). Noncontingent reinforcement is an empirically supported treatment for problem behavior exhibited by individuals with developmental disabilities. *Research in Developmental Disabilities, 30*, 44–57.

Cason, H. (1925). The conditioned reflex or conditioned response as a common activity of living organisms. *Psychological Bulletin, 22*, 445–472.

Cassidy, J., & Shaver, P. R. (2008). *Handbook of attachment: Theory, research, and clinical applications* (2nd ed.). New York: Guilford Press.

Catania, A. C. (1962). Independence of concurrent responding maintained by interval schedules of reinforcement. *Journal of the Experimental Analysis of Behavior, 5*, 175–184.

Catania, A. C. (1963). Concurrent performances: Reinforcement interaction and response independence. *Journal of the Experimental Analysis of Behavior, 6*, 253–263.

Catania, A. C. (1966). Concurrent operants. In W. K. Honig (Ed.), *Operant behavior: Areas of research and application* (pp. 213–270). New York: Appleton-Century-Crofts.

Catania, A. C., & Cutts, D. (1963). Experimental control of superstitious responding in humans. *Journal of the Experimental Analysis of Behavior, 6*, 203–208.

Catania, A. C., Mathews, B. A., & Shimoff, E. (1982). Instructed versus shaped human verbal behavior: Interactions with nonverbal responding. *Journal of the Experimental Analysis of Behavior, 38*, 233–248.

Catania, A. C., & Reynolds, G. S. (1968). A quantitative analysis of the responding maintained by interval schedules of reinforcement. *Journal of the Experimental Analysis of Behavior, 11*, 327–383.

Channell, S., & Hall, G. (1983). Contextual effects in latent inhibition with an appetitive conditioning procedure. *Animal Learning and Behavior, 11*, 67–74.

Chiamulera, C., Borgo, C., Falchetto, S., Valerio, E., & Tessari, M. (1996). Nicotine reinstatement of nicotine self-administration after long-term extinction. *Psychopharmacology, 127*, 102–107.

Chiamulera, C., Valerio, E., & Tessari, M. (1995). Resumption of ethanol-seeking behaviour in rats. *Behavioural Pharmacology, 6*, 32–39.

Christie, J. (1996). Spatial contiguity facilitates Pavlovian conditioning. *Psychonomic Bulletin & Review, 3*, 357–359.

Chung, S., & Herrnstein, R. J. (1967). Choice and delay of reinforcement. *Journal of the Experimental Analysis of Behavior, 10*, 67–74.

Church, R. M. (1964). Systematic effect of random error in the yoked control design. *Psychological Bulletin, 78*, 21–27.

Clark, F. C., & Taylor, B. W. (1960). Effects of repeated extinction of an operant on characteristics of extinction curves. *Psychological Reports, 6*, 226.

Cleland, C. G., & Davey, G. C. L. (1983). Autoshaping in the rat: The effects of localizable visual and auditory signals for food. *Journal of the Experimental Analysis of Behavior, 40*, 47–57.

Cliffe, M. J., & Parry, S. J. (1980). Matching reinforcer value: Human concurrent variable-interval performance. *Quarterly Journal of Experimental Psychology, 32*, 557–570.

Cohen, J. (1990). Attitude, affect, and consumer behavior. In B. S. Moore & A. M. Isen (Eds.), *Affect and social behavior* (pp. 152–206). New York: Cambridge University Press.

Cohen, N. J., & Squire, L. R. (1980). Preserved learning and retention of pattern analyzing skill in amnesics: Dissociation of knowing how and knowing that. *Science, 210*, 207–210.

Cole, M. R. (2001). The long-term effect of high- and low-rate responding histories on fixed-interval responding in rats. *Journal of the Experimental Analysis of Behavior, 75*, 43–54.

Cole, R. P., Barnet, R. C., & Miller, R. R. (1995). Effect of relative stimulus validity: Learning or performance deficit? *Journal of Experimental Psychology: Animal Behavior Processes, 21*, 293–303.

Cole, R. P., & Miller, R. (1999). Conditioned excitation and conditioned inhibition acquired through backward conditioning. Learning and Motivation, 30, 129–156.

Colgan, P. (1989). *Animal motivation.* London: Chapman & Hall.

Collins, R. L. (1988). Observational learning of a left-right behavioural asymmetry in mice (Mus musculus). *Journal of Comparative Psychology, 102*, 222–224.

Colwill, R. M. (1994). Associative representations of instrumental contingencies. *The Psychology of Learning and Motivation, 31*, 1–72.

Colwill, R. M., & Rescorla, R. A. (1985). Post-conditioning devaluation of a reinforcer affects instrumental responding. *Journal of Experimental Psychology: Animal Behavior Processes, 11*, 120–132.

Colwill, R. M., & Rescorla, R. A. (1986). Associative structures in instrumental learning. In G. H. Bower (Ed.), *The psychology of learning and motivation* (Vol. 20, pp. 55–104). New York: Academic Press.

Colwill, R. M., & Rescorla, R. A. (1988). Associations between the discriminative stimulus and the reinforcer in instrumental learning. *Journal of Experimental Psychology: Animal Behavior Processes, 14*, 155–164.

Colwill, R. M., & Rescorla, R. A. (1990). Evidence for hierarchical structure of instrumental learning. *Animal Learning and Behavior, 18*, 71–82.

Conger, R., & Killeen, P. (1974). Use of concurrent operants in small group research: A demonstration. *Pacific Sociological Review, 17*, 399–416.

Conrad, D. G., Sidman, M., & Herrnstein, R. J. (1958). The effect of deprivation upon temporally spaced responding. *Journal of the Experimental Analysis of Behavior, 1*, 59–65.

Cook. E. W., Hodes, R. L., Lang, P. J. (1986). Preparedness and phobia: Effects of stimulus content on human visceral conditioning. *Journal of Abnormal Psychology, 95*, 195–207.

Cook, M., & Mineka, S. (1990). Selective associations in the observational conditioning of fear in monkeys. *Journal of Experimental Psychology: Animal Behavior Processes, 16*, 372–389.

Cook, M., Mineka, S., Wolkenstein, B., & Laitsch, K. (1985). Observational conditioning of snake fear in unrelated rhesus monkeys. *Journal of Abnormal Psychology, 93*, 355–372.

Cook, S. W., & Harris, R. E. (1937). The verbal conditioning of the galvanic skin response. *Journal of Experimental Psychology, 21*, 202–210.

Coombes, S., Revusky, S. H., & Lett, B. T. (1980). Long-delay taste aversion learning in an unpoisoned rat: Exposure to a poisoned rat as the unconditioned stimulus. *Learning and Motivation, 11*, 256–266.

Corbit, L. H., Chieng, B. C., & Balleine, B. W. (2014). Effects of repeated cocaine exposure on habit learning and reversal by N-acetylcysteine. *Neuropsychopharmacology, 39*, 1893–1901.

Corbit, L. H., Nie, H., & Janak, P. H. (2012). Habitual alcohol seeking: Time course and the contribution of subregions of the dorsal striatum. *Biological Psychiatry, 72*, 389–395.

Corning, W. C., Dyal, J. A., & Willows, A. O. D. (Eds.). (1973). *Invertebrate learning: Volume 1 protozoans through annelids.* New York: Plenum Press.

Cowles, J. T. (1937). Food tokens as incentives for learning by chimpanzees. *Comparative Psychology Monograph, 14*(5), 1–96.

Cowles, J. T., & Nissen, H. W. (1937). Reward-expectancy in delayed-responses of chimpanzees. *Journal of Comparative Psychology, 24*, 345–358.

Crespi, L. P. (1942). Quantitative variation of incentive and performance in the white rat. *American Journal of Psychology, 55*, 467–517.

Crombag, H. S., Bossert, J. M., Koya, E., & Shaman, Y. (2008). Context-induced relapse to drug-seeking: A review. *Philosophical Transactions of the Royal Society, 363*, 3233–3243.

Crombag, H. S., Grimm, J. W., & Shaham, Y. (2002). Effect of dopamine receptor antagonists on renewal of cocaine seeking by reexposure to drug-associated contextual cues. *Neuropsychopharmacology, 27*, 1006–1015.

Culler, E. (1938). Recent advances in some concepts of conditioning. *Psychological Review, 45*, 134–153.

Curio, E. (1988). Cultural transmission of enemy recognition by birds. In T. R Zentall & B. Galef (Eds.), *Social learning: Psychological and biological perspectives* (pp. 75–97). Hillsdale, NJ: Erlbaum.

Curio, E., Ernst, U., & Vieth, W. (1978). Cultural transmission of enemy recognition: One function of mobbing. *Science, 202,* 899–901.

Dadds, M. R., Bovbjerg, D. H., Redd, W. H., & Cutmore, T. R. (1997). Imagery in classical conditioning. *Psychological Bulletin, 122,* 89–103.

Dallery, J., McDowell, J. J., & Lancaster, J. S. (2000). Falsification of matching theories account of single-alternative responding: Herrnstein's k varies with sucrose concentration. *Journal of the Experimental Analysis of Behavior, 73,* 23–44.

Danks, D. (2009). The psychology of causal perception and reasoning. In H. Beebee, C. Hitchcock, & P. Menzies (Eds.), *Oxford handbook of causation* (pp. 447–470). Oxford: Oxford University Press.

Darwin, C. (1901). *The descent of man and selection in relation to sex.* New York: Collier. (Original work published 1871)

Darwin, C. (1962). *The voyage of the Beagle.* Garden City, NY: Doubleday. (Original work published 1860)

Darwin, C. (1964). *On the origin of species by means of natural selection: Or the preservation of favoured races in the struggle for life.* Cambridge: Harvard University Press. Copyright © 1964, 1992 by the President and Fellows of Harvard College. (Original work published 1859)

Darwin, C. (1979). *The expression of the emotions in man and animals.*

New York: St. Martin's Press. (Original work published 1873)

Davey, G. C. L. (1987). An integration of human and animal models of Pavlovian conditioning: Associations, cognitions, and attributions. In G. Davey (Ed.), *Cognitive processes and Pavlovian conditioning in humans* (pp. 83–114). Chichester: Wiley.

Davey, G. C. L. (1988). Trends in human operant theory. In G. Davey & C. Cullen (Eds.), *Human operant conditioning and behavior modification* (pp. 1–14). Chichester: Wiley.

Davey, G. C. L. (1989). *Ecological learning theory.* London: Routledge.

Davey, G. C. L. (1992). Classical conditioning and the acquisition of human fears and phobias: A review and synthesis of the literature. *Advances in Behaviour Research and Therapy, 14,* 29–66.

Davey, G. C. L., & Cleland, G. G. (1982). Topography of signal-centered behavior in the rat: Effects of deprivation state and reinforcer type. *Journal of the Experimental Analysis of Behavior, 38,* 291–304.

Davey, G. C. L., & Cleland, G. G. (1984). Food anticipation and lever-directed activities in rats. *Learning and Motivation, 15,* 12–36.

Davidson, J. R., Hughes, D., Blazer, D. G., & George, L. K. (1991). Post-traumatic stress disorder in the community: An epidemiological study. *Psychological Medicine, 21,* 713–721.

Davis, E. R., & Platt, J. R. (1983). Contiguity and contingency in the acquisition and maintenance of an operant. *Learning and Motivation, 14,* 487–512.

Davis, J. M. (1973). Imitation: A review and critique. In P. P. G. Batson & P. H. Klopfer (Eds.), *Perspectives in ecology* (Vol. 1, pp. 43–72). Boulder, CO: Westview Press.

Davis, M. (1974). Sensitization of the rat startle response by noise. *Journal of Comparative and Physiological Psychology, 87,* 571–581.

Davis, M. (1989). Sensitization of the acoustic startle reflex by footshock. *Behavioral Neuroscience, 103,* 495–503.

Davis, M. (2011). NMDA receptors and fear extinction: Implications for cognitive behavioral therapy. *Dialogues in Clinical Neuroscience, 13,* 463–474.

Davis, M., Myers, K. M., Chhatwal, J., & Ressler, K. J. (2006). Pharmacological treatments that facilitate extinction of fear: Relevance to psychotherapy. *NeuroRX, 3,* 82–96.

Davison, M., & Baum, W. M. (2000). Choice in a variable environment: Every reinforcer counts. *Journal of the Experimental Analysis of Behavior, 74,* 1–24.

Davison, M., & McCarthy, D. (1988). *The matching law: A research review.* Hillsdale, NJ: Erlbaum.

Dawson, B. V., & Foss, B. M. (1965). Observational learning

in budgerigars. *Animal Behaviour*, *13*, 470–474.

Dawson, M. E., Catania, J. J., Schell, A. M., & Griggs, W. W. (1979). Automatic classical conditioning as a function of awareness of stimulus contingencies. *Biological Psychology*, *9*, 23–40.

Dawson, M. E., & Grings, W. W. (1968). Comparison of classical conditioning and relational learning. *Journal of Experimental Psychology*, *76*, 227–231.

Dawson, M. E., & Schell, A. M. (1987). Human autonomic and skeletal classical conditioning: The role of conscious cognitive processes. In G. Davey (Ed.), *Cognitive processes and Pavlovian conditioning in humans* (pp. 27–55). Chichester: Wiley.

Deane, G. E. (1969). Cardiac activity during experimentally induced anxiety. *Psychophysiology*, *6*, 17–30.

De Houwer, J. (2011). Evaluative conditioning: A review of functional knowledge and mental process theories. In T. R. Schachtman & S. Reilly (Eds.), *Associative learning and conditioning theory: Human and non-human applications* (pp. 399–416). New York: Oxford University Press.

De Houwer, J., Baeyens, F., Vansteenwegen, D., & Eelen, P. (2000). Evaluative conditioning in the picture-picture paradigm with random assignment of CSs to USs. *Journal of Experimental Psychology: Animal Behavior Processes*, *26*, 237– 242.

Delamater, A. R. (1997). Selective reinstatement of stimulus-outcome associations. *Animal Learning and Behavior*, *25*, 400–412.

Delamater, A. R., & Westbrook, R. F. (2014). Psychological and neural mechanisms of experimental extinction: A selective review. *Neurobiology of Learning and Memory*, *108*, 38–51.

Dennett, D. (1975). Why the law of effect will not go away. *Journal of the Theory of Social Behavior*, *5*, 169–187.

Dess, N. K., & Overmier, J. B. (1989). General learned irrelevance: Proactive effects of Pavlovian conditioning in dogs. *Learning and Motivation*, *20*, 1–14.

de Toledo, L., & Black, A. H. (1966). Heart rate: Changes during conditioned suppression in rats. *Science*, *152*, 1404–1406.

de Villiers, P. (1977). Choice in concurrent schedules and a quantitative formulation of the law of effect. In W. K. Honig & J. E. R. Staddon (Eds.), *Handbook of operant behavior* (pp. 233–287). Englewood Cliffs, NJ: Prentice-Hall.

de Wit, H., & Stewart, J. (1981). Reinstatement of cocaine-reinforced responding in the rat. *Psychopharmacology*, *75*, 134–143.

de Wit, H., & Stewart, J. (1983). Drug reinstatement of heroin-reinforced responding in the rat. *Psychopharmacology*, *79*, 29–31.

Dews, P. B. (1965). The effect of multiple SΔ periods on responding on a fixed-interval schedule: III Effect of changes in pattern of interruptions, parameters and stimuli. *Journal of the Experimental Analysis of Behavior*, *8*, 427–435.

Dews, P. B. (1978). Studies of responding under fixed-interval schedules of reinforcement: II The scalloped patterns of the cumulative record. *Journal of the Experimental Analysis of Behavior*, *29*, 67–75.

Dias-Ferreira, E., Sousa, J. C., Melo, I., Morgado, P., Mesquita, A. R., Cerqueira, J. J., . . . Sousa, N. (2009). Chronic stress causes frontostriatal reorganization and affects decision-making. *Science*, *325*, 621– 625.

Diaz, E., Ruiz, G., & Baeyens, F. (2005). Resistance to extinction of human evaluative conditioning using a between-subjects design. *Cognition and Emotion*, *19*, 245–268.

Di Ciano, P., & Everitt, B. J. (2002). Reinstatement and spontaneous recovery of cocaine-seeking following extinction and different durations of withdrawal. *Behavioural Pharmacology*, *13*, 397–405.

Dickinson, A. (1976). Appetitive-aversive interactions: Facilitation of aversive conditioning by prior appetitive conditioning in the rat. *Animal Learning and Behavior*, *4*, 416–420.

Dickinson, A. (1980). *Contemporary animal learning theory*. Cambridge: Cambridge University Press.

Dickinson, A. (1985). Actions and habits: The development of behavioral autonomy. *Philosophical Transactions of the Royal Society (London), B308,* 67–78.

Dickinson, A. (1989). Expectancy theory in animal conditioning. In S. B. Klein & R. R. Mowrer (Eds.), *Contemporary learning theories: Pavlovian conditioning and the status of traditional learning theory.* Hillsdale, NJ: Erlbaum.

Dickinson, A. (1994). Instrumental conditioning. In N. J. Mackintosh (Ed.), *Animal learning and cognition* (pp. 45–79). London: Academic Press.

Dickinson, A., & Balleine, B. (1994). Motivational control of goal-directed action. *Animal Learning and Behavior, 22,* 1–18.

Dickinson, A., & Balleine, B. (1995). Motivational control of instrumental action. *Current Directions in Psychological Science, 4,* 162–167.

Dickinson, A., Balleine, B., Watt, A., Gonzalez, F., & Boakes, R. A. (1995). Motivational control after extended instrumental training. *Animal Learning and Behavior, 23,* 197–206.

Dickinson, A., & Brown, K. J. (2007). Flavor-evaluative conditioning is unaffected by contingency knowledge during training with color-flavor compounds. *Learning & Behavior, 35,* 36–42.

Dickinson, A., Hall, G., & Mackintosh, N. J. (1976).

Surprise and the attenuation of blocking. *Journal of Experimental Psychology: Animal Behavior Processes, 2,* 313–322.

Dickinson, A., & Mulatero, C. W. (1989). Reinforcer specificity of the suppression of instrumental performance on a noncontingent schedule. *Behavioral Processes, 19,* 167–180.

Dickinson, A., Nicholas, D. J., & Adams, C. D. (1983). The effect of instrumental training contingency on susceptibility to reinforcer devaluation. *Quarterly Journal of Experimental Psychology, 35B,* 35–51.

Dickinson, A., & Shanks, D. (1985). Animal conditioning and human causality judgement. In L.-G. Nilsson & T. Archer (Eds.), *Perspectives in learning and memory* (pp. 167–191). Hillsdale NJ: Lawrence Erlbaum Associates.

Dickinson, A., & Shanks, D. (1995). Instrumental action and causal representation. In G. D. Sperber, D. Premack, & A. J. Premack (Eds.), *Causal cognition: A multidisciplinary debate* (pp. 5–25). Oxford: Clarendon.

Dickinson, A., Watt, A., & Griffiths, W. J. H. (1992). Free operant acquisition with delayed reinforcement. *Quarterly Journal of Experimental Psychology, 45B,* 241–258.

Domjan, M. (1972). CS preexposure in taste-aversion learning: Effects of deprivation and preexposure duration.

Learning and Motivation, 3, 389–402.

Domjan, M. (1994). Formulation of a behavior system for sexual conditioning. *Psychonomic Bulletin and Review, 1,* 421–428.

Domjan, M., & Akins, C. K. (2011). Applications of Pavlovian conditioning to sexual behavior and reproduction. In T. R. Schachtman & S. Reilly (Eds.), *Associative learning and conditioning theory: Human and non-human applications* (pp. 507–531). New York: Oxford University Press.

Domjan, M., Blesbois, E., & Williams, J. (1998). The adaptive significance of sexual conditioning: Pavlovian control of sperm release. *Psychological Science, 9,* 411–415.

Domjan, M., & Siegel, S. (1971). Conditioned suppression following CS preexposure. *Psychonomic Science, 25,* 11–12.

Donahue, J. W., & Palmer, D. C. (1994). *Learning and complex behavior.* Boston: Allyn & Bacon.

Dorrance, B. R., & Zentall T. R. (2001). Imitative learning in Japanese quail (Coturnix japonica) depends on the motivational state of the observer quail at the time of observation. *Journal of Comparative Psychology, 115,* 62–67.

Doughty, A. H., & Oken, G. (2008). Extinction-induced response resurgence: A selective review. *Behavior Analyst Today, 9,* 27–34.

Dreyfus, L. R. (1991). Local shifts in relative reinforcement rate and time allocation on concurrent schedules. *Journal of Experimental Psychology: Animal Behavior Processes, 17,* 486–502.

Dykman, R. A., Ackerman, P. T., & Newton, J. E. O. (1997). Posttraumatic stress disorder: A sensitization reaction. *Integrative Physiological and Behavioral Science, 32,* 9–18, 75–83.

Eckerman, D. A., Heinz, R. D., Stern, S., & Kowlowitz, V. (1980). Shaping the location of a pigeon's peck: Effect of rate and size of shaping steps. *Journal of the Experimental Analysis of Behavior, 33,* 299–310.

Edmunds, M. (1974). *Defense in animals.* Harlow, Essex: Longman.

Eikelboom, R., & Stewart, J. (1982). Conditioned drug-induced physiological responses. *Psychological Review, 89,* 507–528.

Elkins, R. L. (1973). Attenuation of drug-induced bait shyness to a palatable solution as an increasing function of its availability prior to conditioning. *Behavioral Biology, 9,* 221–226.

Elliott, M. H. (1928). The effect of change of reward on the maze performance of rats. *University of California Publications in Psychology, 4,* 19–30.

English, H. B. (1929). Three cases of the "conditioned emotional response." *Journal of Abnormal and Social Psychology, 34,* 221–225.

Epstein, R., & Skinner, B. F. (1980). Resurgence of responding during the cessation of response-independent reinforcement. *Proceedings of the National Academy of Sciences, 77,* 6251–6253.

Estes, W. K., & Skinner, B. F. (1941). Some quantitative properties of anxiety. *Journal of Experimental Psychology, 29,* 390–400.

Everitt, B. J., & Robbins, T. W. (2013). From the ventral to the dorsal striatum: Devolving views of their roles in drug addiction. *Neuroscience and Biobehavioral Reviews, 37,* 1946–1954.

Ewer, R. F. (1971). The biology and behavior of a free-living population of black rats (Rattus rattus), *Animal Behavior Monographs, 4,* 127–174.

Fanselow, M. S. (1993). Associations and memories: The role of NMDA receptors and long-term potentiation. *Current Directions in Psychological Science, 2,* 152–156.

Fanselow, M. S. (1994). Neural organization of the defensive behavior system responsible for fear. *Psychonomic Bulletin and Review, 1,* 429–438.

Fanselow, M. S., & Lester, L. S. (1988). A functional behavioristic approach to aversively motivated behavior: Predatory imminence as a determinant of the topography of defensive behavior. In R. C. Bolles & M. D. Beecher (Eds.), *Evolution and learning* (pp. 185–211). Hillsdale, NJ: Erlbaum.

Fantz, R. L. (1961). The origin of form perception. *Scientific American, 204,* 66–72.

Fantz, R. L. (1963). Pattern vision in newborn infants. *Science, 140,* 296–297.

Ferster, C. B. (1953). The use of the free operant in the analysis of behavior. *Psychological Bulletin, 50,* 263–274.

Ferster, C. B. (1961). Positive reinforcement and behavioral deficits of autistic children. *Child Development, 23,* 437–456.

Ferster, C. B., & DeMyer, M. K. (1961). The development of performances in autistic children in an automatically controlled environment. *Journal of Chronic Diseases, 13,* 312–345.

Ferster, C. B., & DeMyer, M. K. (1962). A method for the experimental analysis of the behavior of autistic children. *American Journal of Orthopsychiatry, 1,* 87–110.

Ferster, C. B., & Skinner, B. F. (1957). *Schedules of reinforcement.* New York: Appleton-Century-Crofts.

Field, A. (2005). Learning to like (or dislike): Associative learning of preferences. In A. Wills (Ed.), *New directions in human associative learning* (pp. 221–252). Mahwah, NJ: Lawrence Erlbaum.

Findley, J. D. (1958). Preference and switching under concurrent scheduling. *Journal of the Experimental Analysis of Behavior, 1,* 123–144.

Finke, R. A. (1980). Levels of equivalence in imagery and perception. *Psychological Review, 87,* 113–132.

Finke, R. A. (1985). Theories relating mental imagery to perception. *Psychological Bulletin, 98,* 236–259.

Fisher, J., & Hinde, R. A. (1949). The opening of milk bottles by birds. *British Birds, 42,* 347–357.

Fisher, W. W., & Mazur, J. E. (1997). Basic and applied research on choice responding. *Journal of Applied Behavior Analysis, 30,* 387–410.

Flanagan, B., Goldiamond, I., & Azrin, N. H. (1958). Operant stuttering: The control of stuttering behavior through response-contingent consequences. *Journal of the Experimental Analysis of Behavior, 1,* 49–56.

Fleming, A. S., & Gonzalez, A. (2009). Neurobiology of human maternal care. In P. T. Ellison & P. B. Gray (Eds.), *Endocrinology of social relationships* (pp. 294–318). Cambridge MA: Harvard University Press.

Fleshler, M., & Hoffman, H. S. (1962). A progression for generating variable-interval schedules. *Journal of the Experimental Analysis of Behavior, 5,* 529–530.

Foree, D. D., & LoLordo, V. M. (1973). The differential effects of food-getting vs. shock-avoidance procedures. *Journal of Comparative and Physiological Psychology, 85,* 551–558.

Foree, D. D., & LoLordo, V. M. (1975). Stimulus-reinforcer interactions in the pigeon. *Journal of Experimental Psychology: Animal Behavior Processes, 104,* 39–46.

Forman, R. R. (1984). Leg position learning by an insect: I. A heat avoidance learning paradigm. *Journal of Neurobiology, 15,* 127–140.

Formby, D. (1967). Maternal recognition of infant's cry. *Developmental Medicine and Child Neurology, 9,* 293–298.

Fouts, R., Fouts, D. H., & Van Cantfort, T. E. (1989). The infant Loulis learns signs from cross-fostered chimpanzees. In R. A. Gardiner, B. T. Gardiner, & T. E. Van Cantfort (Eds.), *Teaching sign language to chimpanzees* (pp. 280–292). Albany: State University of New York Press.

Fowler, H. (1971). Suppression and facilitation by response contingent shock. In F. R. Brush (Ed.), *Aversive conditioning and learning* (pp. 537–604). New York: Academic Press.

Franks, C. M. (1963). Ease of conditioning and spontaneous recovery from experimental extinction. *British Journal of Psychology, 54,* 351–357.

Franks, J. F., & Lattal, K. A. (1976). Antecedent reinforcement schedule training and operant response reinstatement in rats. *Animal Learning and Behavior, 4,* 374–378.

Freeman, T. J., & Lattal, K. A. (1992). Stimulus control of behavioral history. *Journal of the Experimental Analysis of Behavior, 57,* 5–15.

Furlong, T. M., Jayaweera, H. K., Balleine, B. W., & Corbit, L. H. (2014). Binge-like consumption of a palatable food accelerates habitual control of behavior and is dependent on activation of the dorsolateral striatum. *Journal of Neuroscience, 34,* 5012–5022.

Galef, B. G., Jr. (1977). Mechanisms for the social transmission of food preferences from adult to weanling rats. In L. M. Barker, M. Best, & M. Domjan (Eds.), *Learning mechanisms in food selection* (pp. 123–150). Waco, TX: Baylor University Press.

Galef, B. G., Jr. (1978). Differences in affiliation behavior of weanling rats selecting eating and drinking sites. *Journal of Comparative and Physiological Psychology, 92,* 431–437.

Galef, B. G., Jr. (1985a). Direct and indirect behavioral pathways to the social transmission of food avoidance. In N. S. Braveman & P. Bronstein (Eds.), *Experimental assessments and clinical applications of conditioned food aversions* (pp. 203–215). New York: New York Academy of Sciences.

Galef, B. G., Jr. (1985b). Socially induced diet preference can partially reverse a LiCl-induced diet aversion. *Animal Learning and Behavior, 13,* 415–418.

Galef, B. G., Jr. (1986a). Social identification of toxic diets by Norway rats (Rattus norvegicus).

Journal of Comparative Psychology, 100, 331–334.

Galef, B. G., Jr. (1986b). Social interaction modifies learned aversions, sodium appetite, and both palatability and handling time induced dietary preference in rats (Rattus norvegicus). *Journal of Comparative Psychology, 100,* 432–439.

Galef, B. G., Jr. (1987). Social influences on the identification of toxic foods by Norway rats. *Animal Learning and Behavior, 15,* 327–332.

Galef, B. G., Jr. (1988a). Imitation in animals: History, definitions, and interpretation of data from the psychological laboratory. In T. R. Zentall & B. G. Galef (Eds.), *Social learning: Psychological and biological perspectives* (pp. 3–28). Hillsdale, NJ: Erlbaum.

Galef, B. G., Jr. (1988b). Communication of information concerning distant diets in a social, central-place foraging species: Rattus norvegicus. In T. Zentall & B. Galef (Eds.), *Social learning: Psychological and biological perspectives* (pp. 119–139). Hillsdale, NJ: Erlbaum.

Galef, B. G., Jr. (1989). Socially mediated attenuation of taste aversion learning in Norway rats: Preventing development of "food phobias." *Animal Learning and Behavior, 17,* 468–474.

Galef, B. G., Jr. (1990). An adaptationist perspective on social learning, social feeding, and social foraging in Norway rats. In D. A. Dewsbury

(Ed.), *Contemporary issues in comparative psychology* (pp. 55–79). Sunderland, MA: Sinauer.

Galef, B. G., Jr. (1996). Introduction. In C. W Heyes & B. G. Galef, Jr. (Eds.), *Social learning in animals: The roots of culture* (pp. 3–15). New York: Academic Press.

Galef, B. G., Jr. (1998). Recent progress in studies of imitation and social learning. In M. Sabourin, F. Craik, & M. Robert (Eds.), *Advances in psychological science: Biological and cognitive aspects* (pp. 275–299). Sussex, UK: Psychology Press.

Galef, B. G., Jr. (2005). Social learning. In I. Whishaw & B. Kolb (Eds.), *The behavior of the laboratory rat: A handbook with tests* (pp. 363–370). New York: Oxford University Press.

Galef, B. G., Jr., & Clark, M. M. (1972). Mother's milk and adult presence: Two factors determining initial dietary selection by weanling rats. *Journal of Comparative and Physiological Psychology, 78,* 220–225.

Galef, B. G., Jr., Kennett, D. J., & Stein, M. (1985). Demonstrator influence on observer diet preference: Effects of familiarity and exposure context in R. norvegicus. *Animal Learning and Behavior, 13,* 25–30.

Galef, B. G., Jr., Manzig, L. A., & Field, R. M. (1986). Imitation learning in budgerigars: Dawson and Foss (1965) revisited. *Behavioral Processes, 13,* 191–202.

Galef, B. G., Jr., Mason, J. R., Preti, G., & Bean, N. J. (1988). Carbon disulfide: A semiochemical mediating socially induced diet choice in rats. *Physiology and Behavior, 42,* 119–124.

Galef, B. G., McQuoid, L. M., & Whiskin, E. E. (1990). Further evidence that Norway rats do not socially transmit aversions to toxic bait. *Animal Learning and Behavior, 18,* 199–205.

Galef, B. G., Jr., Rudolf, B., Whiskin, E. E., Choleris, E., Mainardi, M., & Valsecchi, P. (1998). Familiarity and relatedness: Effects of social learning about foods by Norway rats and Mongolian gerbils. *Animal Learning and Behavior, 26,* 448–454.

Galef, B. G., Jr., & Stein, M. (1985). Demonstrator influence on observer diet preference: Analyses of critical interactions and olfactory signals. *Animal Learning and Behavior, 13,* 31–38.

Galef, B. G., Jr., & Wigmore, S. W. (1983). Transfer of information concerning distant foods: A laboratory investigation of the "information-centre" hypothesis. *Animal Behaviour, 31,* 748–758.

Galef, B. G., Jr., Wigmore, S. W., & Kennett, D. J. (1983). A failure to find socially mediated taste aversion learning in Norway rats (R. norvegicus). *Journal of Comparative Psychology, 97,* 358–363.

Galizio, M. (1979). Contingency-shaped and rule-governed

behavior: Instructional control of human avoidance. *Journal of the Experimental Analysis of Behavior, 31,* 53–70.

Gallistel, C. R. (1990a). *The organization of learning.* Cambridge, MA: Bradford Books/MIT Press.

Gallistel, C. R. (1990b). Representations in animal cognition: An introduction. *Cognition, 37,* 1–22.

Gallistel, C. R. (1992). Classical conditioning as an adaptive specialization: A computational model. *The Psychology of Learning and Motivation, 28,* 35–67.

Gallistel, C. R., & Gibbon, J. (2000). Time, rate, and conditioning. *Psychological Review, 107,* 289–344.

Garcia, J., Clarke, J. C., & Hankins, W. G. (1973). Natural responses to scheduled rewards. In P. P. G. Batson & P. H. Klopfer (Eds.), *Perspective in ethology* (pp. 1–41). New York: Plenum.

Garcia, J., Ervin, F. R., & Koelling, R. A. (1966). Learning with prolonged delay of reinforcement. *Psychonomic Science, 5,* 121–122.

Garcia, J., Kimeldorf, D. J., & Hunt, E. L. (1961). The use of ionizing radiation as a motivating stimulus. *Psychological Review, 68,* 383–395.

Garcia, J., Kimeldorf, D. J., & Koelling, R. A. (1955). Conditioned aversion to saccharin resulting from exposure to gamma radiation. *Science, 122,* 157–158.

Garcia, J., & Koelling, R. A. (1966). Relation of cue to consequence in avoidance learning. *Psychonomic Science, 4,* 123–124.

Garcia, J., Kovner, R. K., & Green, K. F. (1970). Cue properties versus palatability of flavors in avoidance learning. *Psychonomic Science, 20,* 313–314.

Garcia, J., Rusiniak, K. W., & Brett, L. P. (1977). Conditioning food-illness aversions in wild animals: Caveant Canonici. In H. Davis & H. M. B. Hurwitz (Eds.), *Operant-Pavlovian interactions* (pp. 273–316). Hillside, NJ: Erlbaum.

Gardner, R. A., & Gardner, B. T. (1969). Teaching sign language to a chimpanzee. *Science, 165,* 664–672.

Gardner, R. A., & Gardner, B. T. (1988). Feedforward versus feedbackward: An ethological alternative to the law of effect. *Behavioral and Brain Sciences, 11,* 429–493.

Garrick, T., Morrow, N., Shalev, A. Y., & Eth, S. (2001). Stress-induced enhancement of auditory startle: An animal model of posttraumatic stress disorder. *Psychiatry, 64,* 346–354.

Gasbarri, A., Pompili, A., Packard, M. G., & Tomaz, C. (2014). Habit learning and memory in mammals: Behavioral and neural characteristics. *Neurobiology of Learning and Motivation, 114,* 198–208.

Gerber, G. J., & Stretch, R. (1975). Drug-induced reinstatement of extinguished self-administration behavior in monkeys. *Pharmacology, Biochemistry and Behavior, 3,* 1055–1061.

Gibbon, J. (1981). The contingency problem in autoshaping. In C. M. Locurto, H. S. Terrace, & J. Gibbon (Eds.), *Autoshaping and conditioning theory* (pp. 285–308). New York: Academic Press.

Gibson, E. J., & Walk, R. D. (1960). The "visual cliff." *Scientific American, 202*(4), 64–71.

Gilbert, R. M. (1970). Psychology and biology. *Canadian Psychologist, 11,* 221–238.

Gillan, C. M., Papmeyer, M., Morein-Zamir. S., Sahakian, B. J., Fineberg, N. A., Robbins, T. W., & de Wit, S. (2011). Disruption in the balance between goal-directed behavior and habit learning in obsessive-compulsive disorder. *American Journal of Psychiatry, 168,* 718–726.

Gillette, K., Martin, G. M., & Bellingham, W. P. (1980). Differential use of food and water cues in the formation of conditioned aversions by domestic chicks (Gallus gallus). *Journal of Experimental Psychology: Animal Behavior Processes, 6,* 99–111.

Ginsburg, S., & Jablonka, E. (2010). The evolution of associative learning: A factor in the Cambrian explosion. *Journal of Theoretical Biology, 266,* 11–20.

Ginton, A., Urca, G., & Lubow, R. E. (1975). The effects of preexposure to nonattended stimuli on subsequent learning: Latent inhibition in adults. *Bulletin of the Psychonomic Society, 5*, 5–8.

Giurfa, M., & Sandoz, J. C. (2012). Invertebrate learning and memory: Fifty years of olfactory conditioning of the proboscis extension response in honeybees. *Learning and Memory, 19*, 54–66.

Gleick, J. (1987). *Chaos: Making a new science.* New York: Viking.

Glickman, S. E., & Sroges, R. W. (1966). Curiosity in zoo animals. *Behaviour, 26*, 151–188.

Gluck, M. A., & Myers, C. E. (1995) Representation and association in memory: A neurocomputational view of hippocampal function. *Current Directions in Psychological Science, 4*, 23–29.

Goddard, M. J. (1999). Renewal to the signal value of an unconditioned stimulus. *Learning and Motivation, 30*, 15–34.

Goddard, M. J., & Jenkins, H. M. (1988). Blocking of a CS-US association by a US-US association. *Journal of Experimental Psychology: Animal Behavior Processes, 14*, 177–186.

Goetz, E. M., & Baer, D. M. (1973). Social control of form diversity and the emergence of new forms in children's block building. *Journal of Applied Behavior Analysis, 6*, 209–217.

Gompertz, T. (1957). Some observations on the feral pigeon in London. *Bird Study, 4*, 2–13.

Gonzalo, A., López, P., & Martín, J. (2013). Adaptive forgetting in Iberian green frog tadpoles (pelophylax perezi): Learned irrelevance and latent inhibition may avoid predator misidentification. *Journal of Comparative Psychology, 127*, 56–62.

Goodall, G. (1984). Learning due to the response-shock contingency in signaled punishment. *Quarterly Journal of Experimental Psychology, 36B*, 259–279.

Goodall, J. (1986). *Chimpanzees of Gombe: Patterns of behavior.* Cambridge MA: Harvard University Press.

Goodwin, D. (1983). Behaviour. In M. Abs (Ed.), *Physiology and behaviour of the pigeon.* London: Academic Press.

Gorn, G. J. (1982). Effects of music in advertising on choice behavior. *Journal of Marketing, 46*, 94–101.

Gould, J. L., & Marler P. (1984). Ethology and the natural history of learning. In P. Marler & H. S. Terrace (Eds.), *The biology of learning* (pp. 47–74). Berlin: Springer-Verlag.

Gould, J. L., & Marler, P. (1987). Learning by instinct. *Scientific American, 256*(1), 74–84.

Gould, S. J. (1977). *Ontogeny and phylogeny.* Cambridge: Harvard University Press.

Gould, S. J. (2002). *The structure of evolutionary theory.* Cambridge, MA: Harvard University Press.

Graham, C. H., & Gagne, R. M. (1940). The acquisition, extinction, and spontaneous recovery of a conditioned operant response. *Journal of Experimental Psychology, 26*, 251–280.

Grastyan, E., & Vereczkei, L. (1974). Effects of spatial separation of the conditioned signal from reinforcement: A demonstration of the conditioned character of the orienting response. *Behavioral Biology, 10*, 121–146.

Gray, N. S., & Snowden, R. J. (2005). The relevance of irrelevance to schizophrenia. *Neuroscience and Biobehavioral Reviews, 29*, 989–999.

Green, L., & Rachlin, H. (1977). On the directionality of keypecking during signals for appetitive and aversive events. *Learning and Motivation, 8*, 515–558.

Greenwald, M. K., Bradley, M. M., Cuthbert, B. N., & Lang, P. J. (1998). Startle potentiation: Shock sensitization, aversive learning, and affective picture modulation. *Behavioral Neuroscience, 112*, 1069–1079.

Grill, H. J. (1985). Introduction: Physiological mechanisms in conditioned taste aversions. *Annals of the New York Academy of Sciences, 443*, 67–88.

Grill, H. J., & Berridge, K. (1985). Taste reactivity as a

measure of neural control of palatability. In J. M. Sprague & A. N. Epstein (Eds.), *Progress in psychobiology and physiological psychology* (Vol. 11, pp. 2–61). New York: Academic Press.

Grill, H. J., & Norgren, R. (1978a). The taste reactivity test: I. Mimetic responses to gustatory stimuli in neurologically normal rats. *Brain Research, 143*, 263–279.

Grill, H. J., & Norgren, R. (1978b). Chronically decerebrate rats demonstrate satiation but not bait shyness. *Science, 201*, 267–269.

Grill, H. J., Spector, A. C., Schwartz, G. J., Kaplan, J., & Flynn, F. W. (1987). Evaluating taste effects on ingestive behavior. In F. M. Toates & N. E. Rowland (Eds.), *Techniques in the behavioral and neural sciences: Feeding and drinking* (pp. 151–188). Amsterdam: Elsevier.

Grillon, C., Morgan, C. A., Davis, M. S., & Southwick, S. M. (1998). Effect of darkness on acoustic startle in Vietnam veterans with PTSD. *The American Journal of Psychiatry, 155*, 812–817.

Grindley, G. C. (1932). The formation of simple habit in guinea pigs. *British Journal of Psychology, 23*, 127–147.

Grunow, A., & Neuringer, A. (2002). Learning to vary and varying to learn. *Psychonomic Bulletin and Review, 9*, 250–258.

Gustavson, C. R. (1977). Comparative and field aspects of learned aversions. In L. M. Barker, M. R. Best, & M. Domjan (Eds.), *Learning mechanisms in food selection* (pp. 23–43). Waco, TX: Baylor University Press.

Gustavson, C. R., Kelly, D. J., Sweeney, M., & Garcia, J. (1976). Prey-lithium aversions: I. Coyotes and wolves. *Behavioral Biology, 17*, 61–72.

Guthrie, E. R. (1935). *The psychology of learning*. New York: Harper.

Guthrie, E. R. (1942). Conditioning: A theory of learning in terms of stimulus, response, and association. In N. B. Henry (Ed.), *The forty-first yearbook of the national society for the study of education: Part II. The psychology of learning*. Chicago: University of Chicago Press.

Guthrie, R. M., & Bryant, R. A. (2005). A study of auditory startle response in firefighters before and after trauma exposure. *American Journal of Psychiatry, 162*, 283–290.

Haberlandt, K., Hamsher, K., & Kennedy, A. W. (1978). Spontaneous recovery in rabbit eyelid conditioning. *Journal of General Psychology, 98*, 241–244.

Hailman, J. P. (1969). How an instinct is learned. *Scientific American, 221*(6), 98–106.

Hall, G. (2009). Preexposure to the unconditioned stimulus in nausea-based aversion learning. In S. Reilly & T. R. Schachtman (Eds.), *Conditioned taste aversion: Behavioral and neural processes* (pp. 58–73). New York: Oxford University Press.

Hall, W. G., Arnold, H. M., & Myers, K. P. (2000). The acquisition of an appetite. *Psychological Science, 11*, 101–105.

Hamlin, A. S., Clemens, K. J., & McNally, G. P. (2008). Renewal of extinguished cocaine-seeking. *Neuroscience, 151*, 659–670.

Hamlin, A. S., Newby, J., & McNally, G. P. (2007). The neural correlates and role of D1 dopamine receptors in renewal of extinguished alcohol-seeking. *Neuroscience, 146*, 525–536.

Hammerl, M., Bloch, M., & Silverthorne, C. P. (1997). Effects of US-alone presentations on human evaluative conditioning. *Learning and Motivation, 28*, 491–509.

Hammerl, M., & Grabitz, H.-J. (1996). Human evaluative conditioning without experiencing a valued event. *Learning and Motivation, 27*, 278–293.

Hammond, L. J. (1980). The effects of contingencies upon appetitive conditioning of free-operant behavior. *Journal of the Experimental Analysis of Behavior, 34*, 297–304.

Harlow, H. F. (1949). The formation of learning sets. *Psychological Review, 56*, 51–65.

Harlow, H. F. (1950). Learning and satiation of response to intrinsically motivated complex puzzle performance by monkeys. *Journal of Comparative and*

Physiological Psychology, 43, 289–294.

Harlow, H. F., & Harlow, M. K. (1965). The affectional systems. In A. M. Schrier, H. F. Harlow, & F. Stollnitz (Eds.), *Behavior of nonhuman primates* (Vol. 2, pp. 287–334). New York: Academic Press.

Harlow, H. F., & Soumi, S. J. (1970). Nature of love— simplified. *American Psychologist, 25,* 161–168.

Harris, B. (1979). What ever happened to Little Albert? *American Psychologist, 34,* 151–160.

Harris, J. A., Jones, M. L., Bailey, G. K., & Westbrook, R. F. (2000). Contextual control over conditioned responding in an extinction paradigm. *Journal of Experimental Psychology: Animal Behavior Process, 26,* 174–185.

Harrison, J. M. (1979). The control of responding by sounds: Unusual effect of reinforcement. *Journal of the Experimental Analysis of Behavior, 32,* 167–181.

Hartman, T. F., & Grant, D. A. (1962). Effects of pattern of reinforcement and verbal information on acquisition, extinction, and spontaneous recovery of the eyelid CR. *Journal of Experimental Psychology, 63,* 217–226.

Harzem, P., Lowe, C. F., & Bagshaw, M. (1978). Verbal control in human operant behavior. *Psychological Record, 28,* 405–423.

Hassler, A. D., Scholz, A. T., & Horral, R. M. (1978). Olfactory imprinting and homing in salmon. *American Scientist, 66,* 347–355.

Hayes, S. C., Brownstein, A. J., Zettle, R. D., Rosenfarb, I., & Korn, Z. (1986). Rule-governed behavior and sensitivity to changing consequences of responding. *Journal of the Experimental Analysis of Behavior, 45,* 237–256.

Hayes, S. C., Zettle, R. D., & Rosenfarb, I. (1989). Rule-following. In S. C. Hayes (Ed.), *Rule-governed behavior: Cognition, contingencies, and instructional control* (pp. 191–220). New York: Plenum.

Hazeltine, E., Grafton, S. T., and Ivry, R. (1997). Attention and stimulus characteristics determine the locus of motor sequence learning: A PET study. *Brain, 120,* 123–140.

Hearst, E. (1989). Backward associations: Differential learning about stimuli that follow the presence versus the absence of food in pigeons. *Animal Learning and Behavior, 17,* 280–290.

Hearst, E., Bottjer, S. W., & Walker, E. (1980). Conditioned approach-withdrawal behavior and some signal-food relations in pigeons: Performance and positive vs. negative "associative strength." *Bulletin of the Psychonomic Society, 16,* 183–186.

Hearst, E., & Franklin, S. R. (1977). Positive and negative relations between a signal and food: Approach-withdrawal behavior to the signal. *Journal of Experimental Psychology: Animal Behavior Processes, 3,* 37–52.

Hearst, E., & Jenkins, H. M. (1974). *Sign-tracking: The stimulus-reinforcer relation and directed action.* Austin, TX: Psychonomic Society.

Hediger, H. (1955). *Studies of the psychology and behavior of captive animals in zoos and circuses* (G. Sircom, Trans.). New York: Criterion Books.

Heinrich, B. (1984). Learning in invertebrates. In P. Marler & H. S. Terrace (Eds.), *The biology of learning* (pp. 135–147). New York: Springer-Verlag.

Heinroth, B. (1976). The foraging specializations of individual bumblebees. *Ecological Monograph, 46,* 105–128.

Heinroth, B. (1979). "Majoring" and "minoring" by foraging bumblebees, Bombus vagans: An experimental analysis. *Ecology, 60,* 245–255.

Hemmes, N. S. (1975). Pigeons' performance under differential reinforcement of low rate schedules depends on the operant. *Learning and Motivation, 6,* 344–357.

Hemmes, N. S., Eckerman, D. A., & Rubinsky, H. J. (1979). A functional analysis of collateral behavior under differential-reinforcement-of-low-rate schedules. *Animal Learning and Behavior, 7,* 328–332.

Hennessey, T. M., Rucker, W. B., & McDiarmid, C. G.

(1979). Classical conditioning in paramecia. *Animal Learning and Behavior, 7,* 417–423.

Hermans, D., Crombez, G., Vansteenwegen, D., Baeyens, F., & Eelen, P. (2003). Expectancy-learning and evaluative learning in human classical conditioning: Differential effects of extinction. In P. L. Gower (Ed.), *Psychology of fear* (pp. 133–156). New York: Nova Science.

Herrick, R. M. (1964). The successive differentiation of a lever displacement response. *Journal of the Experimental Analysis of Behavior, 7,* 211–215.

Herrnstein, R. J. (1958). Some factors influencing behavior in a two-response situation. *Transactions of the New York Academy of Sciences, 21,* 35–45.

Herrnstein, R. J. (1961). Relative and absolute strength of response as a function of frequency of reinforcement. *Journal of the Experimental Analysis of Behavior, 4,* 267–272.

Herrnstein, R. J. (1964). Will. *Proceedings of the American Philosophical Society, 108,* 455–458.

Herrnstein, R. J. (1966). Superstition: A corollary of the principles of operant conditioning. In W. K. Honig (Ed.), *Operant behavior: Areas of research and application* (pp. 33–51). New York: Appleton-Century-Crofts.

Herrnstein, R. J. (1970). On the law of effect. *Journal of the Experimental Analysis of Behavior, 13,* 243–266.

Herrnstein, R. J. (1982). Melioration as behavioral dynamism. In M. L. Commons, R. J. Herrnstein, & H. Rachlin (Eds.), *Quantitative analyses of behavior, Vol. II: Matching and maximizing accounts* (pp. 433–458). Cambridge, MA: Ballinger.

Herrnstein, R. J. (1990a). Rational choice theory: Necessary but not sufficient. *American Psychologist, 45,* 356–367.

Herrnstein, R. J. (1990b). Behavior, reinforcement, and utility. *Psychological Science, 1,* 217–224.

Herrnstein, R. J., & Heyman, G. M. (1979). Is matching compatible with reinforcement maximization on concurrent variable interval variable ratio? *Journal of the Experimental Analysis of Behavior, 31,* 209–223.

Herrnstein, R. J., Loewenstein, G. F., Prelec, D., & Vaughan, W. (1993). Utility maximization and melioration: Internalities in individual choice. *Journal of Behavioral Decision Making, 6,* 149–185.

Herrnstein, R. J., & Loveland, D. H. (1975). Maximizing and matching on concurrent ratio schedules. *Journal of the Experimental Analysis of Behavior, 24,* 107–116.

Herrnstein, R. J., & Prelec, D. (1991). Melioration: A theory of distributed choice. *Journal of Economic Perspectives, 5,* 137–156.

Herrnstein, R. J., & Prelec, D. (1992). A theory of addiction. In G. Lowenstein & J. Elster (Eds.), *Choice over time* (pp. 331–360). New York: Russell Sage Foundation.

Herrnstein, R. J., & Vaughn, W. (1980). Melioration and behavioral allocation. In J. E. R. Staddon (Ed.), *Limits to action: The allocation of individual behavior* (pp. 143–176). New York: Academic Press.

Heth, C. D. (1976). Simultaneous and backward fear conditioning as a function of number of CS-UCS pairings. *Journal of Experimental Psychology: Animal Behavior Processes, 2,* 117–129.

Heth, C. D., & Rescorla, R. A. (1973). Simultaneous and backward fear conditioning in the rat. *Journal of Comparative and Physiological Psychology, 82,* 434–443.

Heyes, C. M. (1994). Social learning in animals: Categories and mechanisms. *Biological Reviews, 69,* 207–231.

Heyes, C. M., & Dawson, G. R. (1990). A demonstration of observational learning in rats using a bidirectional control. *Quarterly Journal of Experimental Psychology, 42B,* 59–71.

Heyes, C. M., Dawson, G. R., & Nokes, T. (1992). Imitation in rats: Initial responding and transfer evidence. *Quarterly Journal of Experimental Psychology, 45B,* 81–92.

Heyes, C. M., & Durlach, P. J. (1990). "Social blockage" of taste aversion learning in Norway rats (R. norvegicus): Is it a social phenomenon? *Journal of Comparative Psychology, 104*, 82–87.

Heyes, C. M., Jaldow, E., & Dawson, G. R. (1993). Observational extinction: Observation of nonreinforced responding reduces resistance to extinction in rats. *Animal Learning and Behavior, 21*, 221–225.

Heyes, C. M., Jaldow, E., & Dawson, G. R. (1994). Imitation in rats: Conditions of occurrence in a bidirectional control procedure. *Learning and Motivation, 25*, 276–287.

Heyes, C. M., Jaldow, E., Nokes, T., & Dawson, G. R. (1994). Imitation in rats: The role of demonstrator action. *Behavioral Processes, 32*, 173–182.

Heyes, C. M., and Saggerson, A. (2002). Testing for imitative and non imitative social learning in the budgerigar using a two object/two action test. *Animal Behaviour, 64*, 851–859.

Heyman, G. M. (1979). Matching and maximizing in concurrent schedules. *Psychological Review, 86*, 496–500.

Higgins, S. T., & Morris, E. K. (1984). Generality of free-operant avoidance conditioning to human behavior. *Psychological Bulletin, 96*, 247–272.

Hilgard, E. R., & Marquis, D. G. (1940). *Conditioning and learning.* New York: Appleton-Century-Crofts.

Hinde, R. A. (1960). Energy models of motivation. *Society of Experimental Biology Symposium, 14*, 199–213.

Hineline, P. N., & Rachlin, H. (1969). Escape and avoidance of shock by pigeons pecking a key. *Journal of the Experimental Analysis of Behavior, 12*, 533–538.

Hobaiter, C., Poisot, T., Zuberbühler, K., Hoppitt, W., & Gruber, T. (2014). Social network analysis shows direct evidence for social transmission of tool use in wild chimpanzees. *PLoS Biology, 12*(9): e1001960. doi:10.1371/journal.pbio.1001960.

Hodos, W., Ross, G. S., & Brady, J. V. (1962). Complex response patterns during temporally spaced responding. *Journal of the Experimental Analysis of Behavior, 5*, 473–479.

Hogan, J. A. (1971). The development of a hunger system in young chicks. *Behaviour, 39*, 128–201.

Hogan, J. A. (1973). How young chicks learn to recognize food. In R. A. Hinde & J. Stevenson-Hinde (Eds.), *Constraints on learning* (pp. 119–139). New York: Academic Press.

Hogan, J. A. (1988). Cause and function in the development of behavior systems. In E. M. Blass (Ed.), *Handbook of behavioral neurobiology* (Vol. 9, pp. 63–106). New York: Plenum.

Hogan, J. A. (1994). Structure and development of behavior systems. *Psychonomic Bulletin and Review, 1*, 439–450.

Hogan, J. A., & Roper, T. J. (1978). A comparison of the properties of different reinforcers. In J. S. Rosenblatt, R. A. Hinde, C. Beer, & M. C. Busnel (Eds.), *Advances in the study of behavior* (Vol. 8, pp. 155–255). New York: Academic Press.

Hogarth, L., Balleine, B. W., Corbit, L. H., & Killcross, S. (2013). Associative learning mechanisms underpinning the transition from recreational drug use to addiction. *Annals of the New York Academy of Sciences, 1282*, 12–24.

Holland, P. C. (1977). Conditioned stimulus as a determinant of the form of the Pavlovian conditioned response. *Journal of Experimental Psychology: Animal Behavior Processes, 3*, 77–104.

Holland, P. C. (1980a). Influence of visual conditioned stimulus characteristics on the form of Pavlovian appetitive conditioned responding in rats. *Journal of Experimental Psychology: Animal Behavior Processes, 6*, 81–97.

Holland, P. C. (1980b). CS-US interval as a determinant of the form of Pavlovian appetitive conditioned responses. *Journal of Experimental Psychology: Animal Behavior Processes, 6*, 155–174.

Holland, P. C. (1981). Acquisition of representation-mediated conditioned food aversions. *Learning and Motivation, 12*, 1–18.

Holland, P. C. (1983). Occasion setting in Pavlovian feature positive discriminations. In M. L. Commons, R. J.

Herrnstein, & A. R. Wagner (Eds.), *Quantitative analyses of behavior: Discriminative properties of reinforcement schedules* (Vol. 4, pp. 183–206). New York: Ballinger.

Holland, P. C. (1984). Origins of behavior in Pavlovian Conditioning. In G. Bower (Ed.), *The psychology of learning and motivation* (Vol. 18, pp. 129–174). New York: Academic Press.

Holland, P. C. (1985). The nature of conditioned inhibition in serial and simultaneous feature negative discriminations. In R. R. Miller & N. E. Spear (Eds.), *Information processing in animals: Conditioned inhibition* (pp. 267–297). Hillsdale, NJ: Erlbaum.

Holland, P. C. (1990). Event representation in Pavlovian conditioning: Image and action. *Cognition, 37*, 105–131.

Holland, P. C. (1992). Occasion setting in Pavlovian conditioning. *The Psychology of Learning and Motivation, 28*, 69–125.

Holland, P. C., & Wheeler, D. S. G. (2009). Representation-mediated food aversions learning. In S. Reilly & T. R. Schachtman (Eds.), *Conditioned taste aversion: Behavioral and neural processes* (pp. 196–225). New York: Oxford University Press.

Hollis, K. L. (1982). Pavlovian conditioning of signal-centered action patterns and autonomic behavior: A biological analysis of function. In J. S. Rosenblatt, R. A. Hinde, C. Beer, & M. C. Busnel (Eds.), *Advances in the study of behavior* (Vol. 12, pp. 1–64). New York: Academic Press.

Hollis, K. L. (1984). The biological function of Pavlovian conditioning. *Journal of Experimental Psychology: Animal Behavior Processes, 10*, 413–425.

Hollis, K. L. (1990). The role of Pavlovian conditioning in territorial aggression and reproduction. In D. A. Dewsbury (Ed.), *Contemporary issues in comparative psychology* (pp. 197–219). Sunderland, MA: Sinauer Associates.

Hollis, K. L. (1997). Contemporary research on Pavlovian conditioning: A "new" functional analysis. *American Psychologist, 52*, 956–965.

Hollis, K. L., Dumas, M., Singh, P., & Fackelman, P. (1995). Pavlovian conditioning of aggressive behavior in blue gourami fish (Trichogaster trichopterus): Winners become winners and losers stay losers. *Journal of Comparative Psychology, 109*, 123–133.

Hollis, K. L., Pharr, V. L., Dumas, M. J., Britton, G. B., & Field, J. (1997). Classical conditioning provides paternity advantage for territorial male blue gouramis (Trichogaster trichopterus). *Journal of Comparative Psychology, 111*, 219–225.

Holman, E. W. (1975). Immediate and delayed reinforcers for flavor preferences in the rat. *Learning and Motivation, 6*, 91–100.

Holman, J., Goetz, E. M., & Baer, D. M. (1977). The training of creativity as an operant and an examination of its generalization characteristics. In B. Etzel, J. Le Blanc, & D. M. Baer (Eds.), *New developments in behavioral research: Theory, method, and application* (pp. 441–471). Hillsdale, NJ: Erlbaum.

Honda, M., Deiber, M. P., Ibanez, V., Pascual-Leone, A., Zhuang, P., & Hallett, M. (1998). Dynamic cortical involvement in implicit and explicit motor sequence learning. A PET study. *Brain, 121*, 2159–2173.

Honey, R. C., & Hall, G. (1991). Acquired equivalence and distinctiveness of cues using a sensory-preconditioning procedure. *Quarterly Journal of Experimental Psychology, 43B*, 121–135.

Hoppitt, W., & Laland, N. (2008). Social processes influencing learning in animals: A review of the evidence. In M. Naguib (Ed.), *Advances in the study of behavior* (Vol. 38, pp. 105–165). New York: Academic Press.

Horner, R. D. & Keilitz, I. (1975). Training mentally retarded adolescents to brush their teeth. *Journal of Applied Behavior Analysis, 8*, 301–309.

Hudson, B. B. (1950). One-trial learning in the domestic rat. *Genetic Psychology Monographs, 41*, 99–145.

Hull, C. L. (1943). *Principles of behavior.* New York: Appleton-Century-Crofts.

Hull, C. L. (1952). *A behavior system.* New Haven, CT: Yale University Press.

Hume, D. (1977). *An enquiry concerning human understanding.* E. Steinberg (Ed.). Indianapolis, IN: Hackett.

Hume, D. (1992). *Treatise of human nature.* Buffalo, NY: Prometheus Press. (Original work published 1739)

Hume, D. (1993). *An abstract of a treatise of human nature.* Indianapolis, IN: Hackett. (Original work published 1740)

Hume, D. (1993). *Enquiries concerning the human understanding and concerning the principles of morals.* Indianapolis, IN: Hackett. (Original work published 1777)

Humphreys, L. G. (1939). Acquisition and extinction of verbal expectations in a situation analogous to conditioning. *Journal of Experimental Psychology, 25,* 294–301.

Immelmann, K., & Soumi, S. J. (1981). Sensitive phases in development. In K. Immelmann, G. W. Barlow, L. Petrinovich, & M. Mann (Eds.), *Behavioral development* (pp. 395–431). London: Cambridge University Press.

Innis, N. K., Simmelhag-Grant, V. L., & Staddon, J. E. R. (1983). Behavior induced by periodic food delivery: The effects of interfood interval. *Journal of the Experimental Analysis of Behavior, 39,* 309–322.

Isaacs, W., Thomas, J., & Goldiamond, I. (1960). Application of operant conditioning to reinstate verbal behavior in psychotics. *Journal of Speech and Hearing Disorders, 25,* 8–12.

Isacoff, S. (2001). *Temperament: How music became a battleground for the great minds of western civilization.* New York: Alfred Knopf.

Jacobs, H. L. (1964). Observations on the ontogeny of saccharine preference in the neonate rat. *Psychonomic Science, 1,* 105–106.

Jenkins, H. M. (1962). Resistance to extinction when partial reinforcement is followed by regular reinforcement. *Journal of Experimental Psychology, 64,* 441–450.

Jenkins, H. M. (1973). Effects of the stimulus-reinforcer relation on selected and unselected responses. In R. A. Hinde & J. Stevenson-Hinde (Eds.), *Constraints on learning* (pp. 189–203). New York: Academic Press.

Jenkins, H. M., Barrera, F. J., Ireland, C., & Woodside, B. (1978). Signal-centered action patterns of dogs in appetitive classical conditioning. *Learning and Motivation, 9,* 272–296.

Jenkins, H. M., & Moore, B. R. (1973). The form of the autoshaped response with food or water reinforcers. *Journal of the Experimental Analysis of Behavior, 20,* 163–181.

Jog, M. S., Kubota, Y., Connolly, C. I., Hillegaart, V., & Graybiel, A. M. (1999). Building neural representations of habits. *Science, 286,* 1745–1749.

Johnson, J. S., & Newport, E. L. (1989). Critical period effects in second language learning: The influence of maturational state on the acquisition of English as a second language. *Cognitive Psychology, 21,* 60–99.

Johnston, T. D. (1981). Contrasting approaches to a theory of learning. *Behavioral and Brain Sciences, 4,* 125–173.

Jones, M. C. (1924). A laboratory study of fear: The case of Peter. *Pedagogical Seminary, 31,* 308–315.

Jones, M. C. (1974). Albert, Peter, and John B. Watson. *American Psychologist, 29,* 581–583.

Jørgensen, C. H., Pedersen, B., & Tønnesen, H. (2011). The efficacy of disulfiram for the treatment of alcohol use disorder. *Alcoholism: Clinical and Experimental Research, 35,* 1749–1758.

Joyce, J. H., & Chase, P. N. (1990). Effects of response variability on the sensitivity of rule-governed behavior. *Journal of the Experimental Analysis of Behavior, 54,* 251–262.

Kagel, J. H., Battalio, R. C., & Green, L. (1995). *Economic choice theory: An experimental analysis of animal behavior.* New York: Cambridge University Press.

Kaiser, D. H., Zentall, T. R., & Galef, B. G., Jr. (1997). Can imitation in pigeons be explained by local enhancement together with trial-and-error learning? *Psychological Science, 8,* 459–460.

Kaitz, M., Lapidot, P., Bronner, R, & Eidelman, A. I. (1992). Parturient women can recognize their infants by touch. *Developmental Psychology, 28,* 35–39.

Kalat, J. W., & Rozin, P. (1973). "Learned safety" as a mechanism in long-delay taste aversion learning in rats. *Journal of Comparative and Physiological Psychology, 83,* 198–207.

Kamin, L. J. (1965). Temporal and intensity characteristics of the conditioned stimulus. In W. F. Prokasy (Ed.), *Classical conditioning: A symposium* (pp. 118–147). New York: Appleton-Century-Crofts.

Kamin, L. J. (1968). Attention-like processes in classical conditioning. In M. R. Jones (Ed.), *Miami symposium on the prediction of behavior: Aversive stimulation* (pp. 9–32). Coral Gables, FL: University of Miami Press.

Kamin, L. J. (1969). Predictability, surprise, attention, and conditioning. In B. A. Campbell & R. M. Church (Eds.), *Punishment and aversive behavior* (pp. 279–296). New York: Appleton-Century-Crofts.

Kamin, L. J., & Schaub, R. E. (1963). Effects of conditioned stimulus intensity on the conditioned emotional response. *Journal of Comparative and Physiological Psychology, 56,* 502–507.

Kanner, L., & Eisenberg, L. (1955). Notes on the follow-up studies of autistic children. In P. H. Hoch & J. Zubin (Eds.), *Psychopathology of childhood* (pp. 227–239). New York: Grune and Stratton.

Kanner, L., Rodriguez, A., & Ashenden, B. (1972). How far can autistic children go in matters of social adaptation? *Journal of Autism and Childhood Schizophrenia, 2,* 9–33.

Kapostins, E. E. (1963). The effect of drl schedules on some characteristics of word utterances. *Journal of the Experimental Analysis of Behavior, 6,* 281–290.

Kapur, S. (2003). Psychosis as a state of aberrant salience: A framework linking biology, phenomenology, and pharmacology in schizophrenia. *American Journal of Psychiatry, 160,* 13–23.

Karpicke, J., Christoph, G., Peterson, G., & Hearst, E. (1977). Signal location and positive versus negative conditioned suppression in the rat. *Journal of Experimental Psychology: Animal Behavior Processes, 3,* 105–118.

Kasprow, W. J., Cacheiro, H., Balaz, M. A., & Miller, R. R. (1982). Reminder-induced recovery of associations to an overshadowed stimulus. *Learning and Motivation, 13,* 155–166.

Katz, A., Webb, L., Stotland, E. (1971). Cognitive influences on the rate of GSR extinction. *Journal of Experimental Research in Personality, 5,* 208–215.

Kaufman, A., Baron, A., & Kopp, R. E. (1966). Some effects of instructions on human operant behavior. *Psychonomic Monograph Supplements, 1,* 243–250.

Kaufman, M. A., & Bolles, R. C. (1981). A nonassociative aspect of overshadowing. *Bulletin of the Psychonomic Society, 18,* 318–320.

Kazdin, A. E. (1980). Acceptability of time-out from reinforcement procedures for disruptive child behavior. *Behavior Therapy, 11,* 329–344.

Kehoe, E. J., Graham-Clarke, P., & Schreurs, B. G. (1989). Temporal patterns of the rabbit's nictitating membrane response to compound and component stimuli under mixed CS-US intervals. *Behavioral Neuroscience, 103,* 283–295.

Kehoe, E. J., & White, N. E. (2004). Overexpectation: Response loss during sustained stimulus compounding in the rabbit nictitating membrane preparation. *Learning and Memory, 11,* 476–483.

Keith-Lucas, T., & Guttman, N. (1975). Robust single-trial delayed backward conditioning. *Journal of Comparative and Physiological Psychology, 88,* 468–476.

Kelleher, R. T., Fry, W., & Cook, L. (1959). Inter-response time distribution as a function of temporally spaced responses. *Journal of the Experimental Analysis of Behavior, 2,* 91–106.

Keller, R. J., Ayres, J. J. B., & Mahoney, W. J. (1977). Brief versus extended exposure to truly random control procedures.

Journal of Experimental Psychology: Animal Behavior Processes, 3, 53–66.

Kelley, H. H. (1967). The processes of causal attribution. *American Psychologist, 28,* 107–128.

Kelly, M. M., & Forsyth, J. P. (2007a). Observational fear conditioning in the acquisition and extinction of attentional bias for threat: An experimental evaluation. *Emotion, 7,* 324–335.

Kelly, M. M., & Forsyth, J. P. (2007b). Sex differences in response to an observational fear conditioning procedure. *Behavior Therapy, 38,* 340–349.

Kerfoot, E. C., Agarwal, I., Lee, H. J., & Holland, P. C. (2007). Control of appetitive and aversive taste-reactivity responses by an auditory conditioned stimulus in a devaluation task: A FOS and behavioral analysis. *Learning and Memory, 14,* 581–589.

Kerkhof, I., Goesaert, E., Dirikx, T., Vansteenwegen, D., Baeyens, F., D'Hooge, R., & Hermans, D. (2009). Assessing valence indirectly and online. *Cognition & Emotion, 23,* 1615–1629.

Killcross, S., & Balleine, B. (1996). Role of primary motivation in stimulus preexposure effects. *Journal of Experimental Psychology: Animal Behavior Processes, 22,* 23–42.

Killeen, P. (1969). Reinforcement frequency and contingency as factors in fixed-ratio behavior.

Journal of the Experimental Analysis of Behavior, 12, 391–395.

Killeen, P. R. (1975). On the temporal control of behavior. *Psychological Review, 82,* 89–115.

Killeen, P. R. (1978). Superstition: A matter of bias, not detectability. *Science, 199,* 88–90.

Killeen, P. R. (1979). Arousal: Its genesis, modulation, and extinction. In P. Harzem & M. D. Zeiler (Eds.), *Advances in analysis of behaviour: Volume 1, Reinforcement and the organization of behavior* (pp. 31–78). New York: Wiley.

Killeen, P. R. (1981). Learning as causal inference. In M. L. Commons & J. A. Nevin (Eds.), *Quantitative analyses of behavior: Discriminative properties of reinforcement schedules* (Vol. 1, pp. 89–112). Cambridge, MA: Ballinger.

Killeen, P. R., Hanson, S. J., & Osbourne, S. R. (1978). Arousal: Its genesis and manifestation as response rate. *Psychological Review, 85,* 571–580.

Kimble, G. A. (1964). Comment on Longo, Klempay, and Bitterman. *Psychonomic Science, 1,* 40.

Kimble, G. A., & Perlmuter, L. C. (1970). The problem of volition. *Psychological Review, 77,* 361–384.

Kimmel, H. D. (1965). Instrumental inhibitory factors in classical conditioning. In W. F. Prokasy (Ed.), *Classical conditioning: A symposium* (pp.

148–171). New York: Appleton-Century-Crofts.

Kirk, G. S., Raven, J. E., & Schofield, M. (1983). *The presocratic philosophers: A critical history with a selection of texts* (2nd ed.). Cambridge: Cambridge University Press.

Kirsch, I. (1997). Specifying nonspecifics: Psychological mechanisms of placebo effects. In A. Harrington (Ed.), *The placebo effect: An interdisciplinary exploration* (pp. 166–186). Cambridge MA: Harvard University Press.

Kish, G. B. (1955). Learning when the onset of illumination is used as reinforcing stimulus. *Journal of Comparative and Physiological Psychology, 48,* 261–264.

Klein, E. D., & Zentall, T. R. (2003). Imitation and affordance learning by pigeons (Columba livia). *Journal of Comparative Psychology, 117,* 414–419.

Kleinknecht, R. A. (1994). Acquisition of blood, injury, and needle fears and phobias. *Behaviour Research and Therapy, 32,* 817–823.

Kline, L. W. (1899a). Method in animal psychology. *American Journal of Psychology, 10,* 256–279.

Kline, L. W. (1899b). Suggestions for a laboratory course in comparative psychology. *American Journal of Psychology, 10,* 399–430.

Knowlton, B. J., Mangels, J. A., & Squire, L. R. (1996). A neostriatal habit learning system in humans. *Science, 273,* 1399–1402.

Konorski, J. (1948). *Conditioned reflexes and neuronal organization.* Cambridge: Cambridge University Press.

Konorski, J. (1967). *Integrative activity of the brain: An interdisciplinary approach.* Chicago: University of Chicago Press.

Konorski, J., & Miller, S. (1937a). On two types of conditioned reflex. *Journal of General Psychology, 16,* 264–272.

Konorski, J., & Miller, S. (1937b). Further remarks on two types of conditioned reflex. *Journal of General Psychology, 17,* 405–407.

Kramer, T. J., & Rilling, M. (1970). Differential reinforcement of low rates: A selective review. *Psychological Bulletin, 74,* 225–254.

Krank, M. D., & MacQueen, G. M. (1988). Conditioned compensatory responses elicited by environmental signals for cyclophosphamine-induced suppression of the immune system. *Psychobiology, 16,* 229–235.

Krebs, J. R., MacRoberts, M., & Cullen, J. M. (1972). Flocking and feeding in great tit Parus major—An experimental study. *Ibis, 114,* 507–530.

Kremer, E. F. (1971). Truly random and traditional control procedures in CER conditioning in the rat. *Journal of Comparative and Physiological Psychology, 76,* 441–448.

Kremer, E. F. (1978). The Rescorla-Wagner model: Losses in associative strength in compound conditioned stimuli. *Journal of Experimental Psychology: Animal Behavior Processes, 4,* 22–36.

Kremer, E. F., & Kamin, L. J. (1971). The truly random control procedure: Associative or nonassociative effects in rats. *Journal of Comparative and Physiological Psychology, 74,* 203–210.

Kuo, Z-Y. (1932). Ontogeny of embryonic behavior in aves: IV The influence of embryonic movements upon behavior after hatching. *Journal of Comparative Psychology, 14,* 109–122.

Laborda, M. A., McConnell, B. L., & Miller, R. R. (2011). Behavioral techniques to reduce relapse after exposure therapy: Applications of studies of experimental extinction. In T. R. Schachtman & S. Reilly (Eds.), *Associative learning and conditioning theory: Human and non-human applications* (pp. 79–103). New York: Oxford University Press.

Lane, H., Kopp, J., Sheppard, W., Anderson, T., & Carlson, D. (1967). Acquisition, maintenance, and retention in the differential reinforcement of vocal duration. *Journal of Experimental Psychology Monograph Supplement, 74* (2, Whole no. 635).

Langer, E. J. (1975). The illusion of control. *Journal of Personality and Social Psychology, 32,* 311–328.

Lantz, A. E. (1973). Effect of number of trials, interstimulus interval, and dishabituation during CS habituation on subsequent conditioning in a CER paradigm. *Animal Learning and Behavior, 1,* 273–277.

Laties, V. G., & Weiss, B. (1963). Effects of a concurrent task on fixed-interval responding in humans. *Journal of the Experimental Analysis of Behavior, 6,* 431–436.

Laties, V. G., Weiss, B., Clark, R. L., & Reynolds, M. D. (1965). Overt "mediating" behavior during temporally spaced responding. *Journal of the Experimental Analysis of Behavior, 8,* 107–116.

Laties, V. G., Weiss, B., & Weiss, A. B. (1969). Further observations on overt "mediating" behavior and the discrimination of time. *Journal of the Experimental Analysis of Behavior, 12,* 43–57.

Lattal, K. A., & Gleeson, S. (1990). Response acquisition with delayed reinforcement. *Journal of Experimental Psychology: Animal Behavior Processes, 16,* 27–39.

Lattal, K. A., St. Peter, C., & Escobar, R. (2013). Operant extinction: Elimination and generation of behavior. In G. J. Madden, W. V. Dube, T. D. Hackenberg, G. P. Hanley, & K. A. Lattal (Eds.), *APA handbook of behavior analysis, vol. 2: Translating principles into practice* (pp. 77–107). Washington, DC: American Psychological Association.

Lattal, K. A., & St. Peter Pipkin, C. (2009). Resurgence of previously reinforced responding: Research and application. *Behavior Analyst Today, 10,* 254–265.

Lattal, K. M., & Lattal, K. A. (2012). Facets of Pavlovian and operant extinction. *Behavioural Processes, 90,* 1–8.

Lattal, K. M., & Nakajima, S. (1998). Overexpectation in appetitive Pavlovian and instrumental conditioning. *Animal Learning and Behavior, 26,* 351–360.

Laverty, L. M. (1980). The flower-visiting behavior of bumblebees: Floral complexity and learning. *Canadian Journal of Zoology, 58,* 1324–1335.

Lavin, M. J. (1976). The establishment of flavor-flavor associations using a sensory preconditioning training procedure. *Learning and Motivation, 7,* 173–183.

Lavin, M. J., Freise, B., & Coombes, S. (1980). Transferred flavor aversions in adult rats. *Behavioral and Neural Biology, 28,* 15–33.

LeBlanc, K. H., Maidment, N. T., & Ostlund, S. B. (2013). Repeated cocaine exposure facilitates the expression of incentive motivation and induces habitual control in rats. *PLoS One, 8,* e61355.

LeClerc, R. (1985). Sign-tracking behavior in aversive conditioning: Its acquisition via a Pavlovian mechanism and its suppression by operant contingencies. *Learning and Motivation, 16,* 63–82.

Lefebvre, L., & Palameta, B. (1988). Mechanisms, ecology, and population diffusion of socially learned food-finding behavior in feral pigeons. In T. Zentall & B. Galef (Eds.), *Social learning: Psychological and biological perspectives* (pp. 141–164). Hillsdale, NJ: Erlbaum.

LeFrancois, J. R., Chase, P. N., & Joyce, J. H. (1988). The effects of a variety of instructions on human fixed-interval performance. *Journal of the Experimental Analysis of Behavior, 49,* 383–393.

Leitenberg, H., Rawson, R. A., & Bath, K. (1970). Reinforcement of competing behavior during extinction. *Science, 169,* 301–303.

Leitenberg, H., Rawson, R. A., & Mulick, J. A. (1975). Extinction and reinforcement of alternative behavior. *Journal of Comparative and Physiological Psychology, 88,* 640–652.

Lejeune, H., & Jasselette, P. (1986). Accurate drl performance in the pigeon: Comparison between perching and treadle pressing. *Animal Learning and Behavior, 14,* 205–211.

Lenneberg, E. H. (1967). *Biological foundations of language.* New York: Wiley.

Leslie A. M. (1982). The perception of causality in infants. *Perception, 11,* 173–186.

Leslie, A. M., & Keeble, S. (1987). Do six-month-old infants perceive causality? *Cognition, 25,* 265–288.

Lett, B. T., & Grant, V. L. (1996). Wheel running induces conditioned taste aversion in rats trained while hungry and thirsty. *Physiology and Behavior, 59,* 699–702.

Lett, B. T., Grant, V. L., Koh, M. T., & Parsons, J. F. (1999). Pairing a flavor with activity in a flat, circular alley induces conditioned taste aversion. *Learning and Motivation, 30,* 241–249.

Levey, A. B., & Martin, I. (1975). Classical conditioning of human "evaluative responses." *Behaviour Research and Therapy, 13,* 221–226.

Levey, A. B., & Martin, I. (1983). Part I. Cognitions, evaluations and conditioning: Rules of sequence and rules of consequence. *Advances in Behaviour Research and Therapy, 4,* 181–195.

Lewontin, R. C. (1978). Adaptation. *Scientific American, 239*(3), 213–230.

Libby, A. (1951). Two variables in the acquisition of depressant properties by a stimulus. *Journal of Experimental Psychology, 42,* 100–107.

Lieberman, D. A. (1993). *Learning: Behavior and cognition* (2nd ed.). Pacific Grove, CA: Brooks/Cole.

Lieving, G. A., & Lattal, K. A. (2003). Recency, repeatability, and reinforcer retrenchment: An experimental analysis of resurgence. *Journal of the Experimental Analysis of Behavior, 80*, 217–234.

Lin, J.-Y., Arthurs, J., & Reilly, S. (2014). Conditioned taste aversion, drugs of abuse and palatability. *Neuroscience and Biobehavioral Reviews, 45*, 28–45.

Linden, D. R., Savage, L. M., & Overmier, J. B. (1997). General learned irrelevance: A Pavlovian analog to learned helplessness. *Learning and Motivation, 28*, 230–247.

Lindsey, A. M., Piper, B. F., & Blackburn, G. L. (1972). The phenomenon of cancer cachexia: A review. *Oncology Nursing Forum, 9*, 38–42.

Lindsley, O. R. (1956). Operant conditioning methods applied to research in chronic schizophrenia. *Psychiatric Research Reports, 5*, 118–139.

Linwick, D., Overmier, J. B., Peterson, G. B., & Mertins, M. (1988). Interaction of memories and expectancies as mediators of choice behavior. *American Journal of Psychology, 101*, 313–334.

Lipp, O. V., Mallan, K. M., Libera, M., & Tan, M. S. (2010). The effects of verbal instruction on affective and expectancy learning. *Behaviour Research and Therapy, 48*, 203–209.

Lipp, O. V., Oughton, N., & LeLievre, J. (2003). Evaluative learning in human Pavlovian conditioning: Extinct, but still

there? *Learning and Motivation, 34*, 219–239.

Lippman, G., & Meyer, M. E. (1967). Fixed-interval performance as related to instructions and to subjects' verbalization of the contingency. *Psychonomic Science, 8*, 135–136.

Lipsitt, L., Reilly, B. M., Butcher, M. J., & Greenwald, M. M. (1976). The stability and interrelationships of newborn sucking and heart rate. *Developmental Psychobiology, 9*, 305–310.

Locurto, C. M., Terrace, H. S., & Gibbon, J. (Eds.). (1981). *Autoshaping and conditioning theory.* New York: Academic Press.

Logan, F. A. (1954). A note on stimulus intensity dynamism (V). *Psychological Review, 61*, 77–80.

Logue, A. W. (1980). Visual cues for illness-induced aversions in the pigeon. *Behavioral and Neural Biology, 28*, 372–377.

Logue, A. W. (1988). A comparison of taste aversion learning in humans and other vertebrates: Evolutionary pressures. In R. C. Bolles & M. D. Beecher (Eds.), *Evolution and learning* (pp. 97–116). Hillsdale, NJ: Erlbaum.

Logue, A. W., & Chavarro, A. (1987). Effect on choice of absolute and relative values of reinforcer delay, amount, and frequency. *Journal of Experimental Psychology: Animal Behavior Processes, 13*, 280–291.

Logue, A. W., Ophir, I., & Strauss, K. E. (1981). The acquisition of taste aversions in humans. *Behaviour Research and Therapy, 19*, 319–333.

LoLordo, V. M. (1979). Selective associations. In A. Dickinson & R. A. Boakes (Eds.), *Mechanisms of learning and motivation* (pp. 367–398). Chichester: Wiley.

Longo, N., Klempay, S., & Bitterman, M. E. (1964). Classical appetitive conditioning in the pigeon. *Psychonomic Science, 1*, 19–23.

Lorenz, K. Z. (1969). Innate bases of learning. In K. Pribram (Ed.), *On the biology of learning* (pp. 13–93). New York: Hartcourt, Brace, and World.

Lovaas, O. I. (1987). Behavioral treatment and normal educational and intellectual functioning in young autistic children. *Journal of Consulting and Clinical Psychology, 55*, 3–9.

Lovaas, O. I. (1993). The development of a treatment-research project for developmentally disabled and autistic children. *Journal of Applied Behavior Analysis, 26*, 617–630.

Lovaas, O. I., Berberich, J. P., Perloff, B. F., & Schaeffer, B. (1966). Acquisition of imitative speech in schizophrenic children. *Science, 151*, 705–707.

Lovaas, O. I., & Favell, J. E. (1987). Protection for clients undergoing aversive/restrictive interventions. *Education and Treatment of Children, 10*, 311–325.

Lovaas, O. I., Freitag, G., Gold, V. J., & Kassorla, I. C. (1965). Experimental studies in childhood schizophrenia: Analysis of self-destructive behavior. *Journal of Experimental Child Psychology, 2,* 67–84.

Lovaas, O. I., Freitag, G., Kinder, M. I., Rubinstein, B. D., Schaeffer, B., & Simmons, J. Q. (1966). Establishment of social reinforcers in two schizophrenic children on the basis of food. *Journal of Experimental Child Psychology, 4,* 109–125.

Lovaas, O. I., Freitag, G., Nelson, K., & Whalen, C. (1967). The establishment of imitation and its use for the establishment of complex behavior in schizophrenic children. *Behavior Research and Therapy, 5,* 171–181.

Lovaas, O. I., Koegel, R., Simmons, J. Q., & Long, J. S. (1973). Some generalization and follow-up measures on autistic children in behavior therapy. *Journal of Applied Behavior Analysis, 6,* 131–166.

Lovaas, O. I., & Simmons, J. Q. (1969). Manipulation of self-destruction in three retarded children. *Journal of Applied Behavior Analysis, 2,* 143–157.

Lovibond, P. F., Preston, G. C., & Mackintosh, N. J. (1984). Context specificity of conditioning, extinction, and latent inhibition. *Journal of Experimental Psychology: Animal Behavior Processes, 10,* 360–376.

Löw, A., Lang, P. J., Smith, J. C., and Bradley, M. M. (2008). Both predator and prey: Emotional arousal in threat and reward. *Psychological Science, 19,* 865–873.

Lowe, C. F. (1979). Determinants of human operant behavior. In P. Harzem & M. D. Zeiler (Eds.), *Advances in analysis of behaviour: Volume 1, Reinforcement and the organization of behaviour* (pp. 159–192). New York: Wiley.

Lowe, C. F. (1983). Radical behaviorism and human psychology. In G. C. L. Davey (Ed.), *Animal models of human behavior* (pp. 71–93). Chichester: John Wiley.

Lowe, C. F., Beasty, A., & Bentall, R. P. (1983). The role of verbal behavior in human learning: Infant performance on fixed interval schedules. *Journal of the Experimental Analysis of Behavior, 39,* 157–164.

Lubbock, J. (1882). *Ants, bees, & wasps.* New York: Appleton.

Lubow, R. E. (1989). *Latent inhibition and conditioned attention theory.* Cambridge, England: Cambridge University Press.

Lubow, R. E. (2009). Conditioned taste aversion and latent inhibition: A review. In S. Reilly & T. R. Schachtman (Eds.), *Conditioned taste aversion: Behavioral and neural processes* (pp. 37–57). New York: Oxford University Press.

Lubow, R. E., & Moore, A. U. (1959). Latent inhibition: The effect of nonreinforced preexposure to the conditioned stimulus. *Journal of Comparative and Physiological Psychology, 52,* 415–419.

Lubow, R. E., Schnur, P., & Rifkin, B. (1976). Latent inhibition and conditioned attention theory. *Journal of Experimental Psychology: Animal Behavior Processes, 2,* 163–174.

Lubow, R. E., & Weiner, I. (Eds.). (2010). *Latent inhibition: Cognition, neuroscience and applications to schizophrenia.* New York: Cambridge University Press.

Luongo, A. F. (1976). Stimulus selection in discriminative taste-aversion learning in the rat. *Animal Learning and Behavior, 4,* 225–230.

Lupfer, G., Egleston, D., & Frieman, J. (2001). *Which attributes of conditioned stimuli elicit behavior systems in rats?* Paper presented at the annual meeting of the Psychonomic Society, Orlando, Florida, November, 2001.

Lupfer, G., Frieman, J., & Coonfield, D. L. (2003). Social transmission of flavor preferences in social and non-social hamsters. *Journal of Comparative Psychology, 117,* 449–455.

Lupfer, G. J., Frieman, J., Wiens, K., & Bennett, J. (2000). *Golden hamsters do not acquire food preferences from littermates.* Poster presented at the meeting of the Psychonomic Society, New Orleans.

Lupfer-Johnson, G., Hanson, K. L., Edwards, L. E., Elder, R. L., & Evans, S. L. (2009). Social cues influence foraging in dwarf hamsters (phodopus campbelli). *Journal of Comparative Psychology, 123,* 226–229.

Lupfer-Johnson, G., & Ross, J. (2007). Dogs acquire food preferences from interacting with recently fed conspecifics. *Behavioural Processes, 74*, 104–106.

MacFarland, D. J. (1970). Behavioral aspects of homeostasis. *Advances in the Study of Behavior, 3*, 1–26.

Machado, A. (1989). Operant conditioning of behavioral variability using a percentile reinforcement schedule. *Journal of the Experimental Analysis of Behavior, 52*, 155–166.

Machado, A. (1992). Behavioral variability and frequency-dependent selection. *Journal of the Experimental Analysis of Behavior, 58*, 241–263.

Mackintosh, N. J. (1971). An analysis of overshadowing and blocking. *Quarterly Journal of Experimental Psychology, 23*, 118–125.

Mackintosh, N. J. (1973). Stimulus selection: Learning to ignore stimuli that predict no change in reinforcement. In R. A. Hinde & J. Stevenson-Hinde (Eds.), *Constraints on learning* (pp. 75–100). New York: Academic Press.

Mackintosh, N. J. (1974). *The psychology of animal learning*. London: Academic Press.

Mackintosh, N. J. (1975). A theory of attention: Variations in the associability of stimuli with reinforcement. *Psychological Review, 82*, 276–298.

Mackintosh, N. J. (1976). Overshadowing and stimulus intensity. *Animal Learning and Behavior, 4*, 186–192.

Mackintosh, N. J. (1977). Conditioning as the perception of causal relations. In R. E. Butts & J. Hintikka (Eds.), *Foundational problems in the special sciences* (pp. 241–250). Dordrect, Netherlands: Reidel.

Mackintosh, N. J. (1983). *Conditioning and associative learning*. Oxford: Oxford University Press.

Mackintosh, N. J. (1985). Varieties of conditioning. In N. M. Weinberger, J. L. McGaugh, & G. Lynch (Eds.), *Memory systems in the brain* (pp. 335–350). New York: Guilford Press.

Mackintosh, N. J., Bygrave, D. J., & Picton, D. M. B. (1977). Locus of the effect of a surprising reinforcer in the attenuation of blocking. *Quarterly Journal of Experimental Psychology, 29*, 327–336.

Mackintosh, N. J., & Cotton, M. M. (1985). Conditioned inhibition from reinforcement reduction. In R. R. Miller, & N. E. Spear (Eds.), *Information processing in animals: Conditioned inhibition* (pp. 89–110). Hillsdale, NJ: Erlbaum.

Mackintosh, N. J., & Dickinson, A. (1979). Instrumental (Type II) conditioning. In A. Dickinson & R. A. Boakes (Eds.), *Mechanisms of learning and motivation* (pp. 143–170). Hillsdale, NJ: Erlbaum.

Mackintosh, N. J., & Reese, B. (1979). One-trial overshadowing.

Quarterly Journal of Experimental Psychology, 31B, 519–526.

MacNab, R. M., & Koshland, D. E. (1972). Gradient-sensing mechanism in bacterial chemotaxis. *Proceedings of the National Academy of Sciences, USA, 69*, 2509–2512.

MacQueen, G. M., & Siegel, S. (1989). Conditional immunomodulation following training with cyclophosphamine. *Behavioral Neuroscience, 103*, 638–647.

Mahoney, K., Van Wagenen, K, & Meyerson, L. (1971). Toilet training of normal and retarded children. *Journal of Applied Behavior Analysis, 4*, 173–181.

Mahoney, W. J., & Ayres, J. J. B. (1976). One-trial simultaneous and backward fear conditioning as reflected in conditioned suppression of licking in rats. *Animal Learning and Behavior, 4*, 357–362.

Malott, R. W., & Cumming, W. W. (1966). Concurrent schedules of interresponse time reinforcement: Probability of reinforcement and the lower bounds of the reinforced interresponse time intervals. *Journal of the Experimental Analysis of Behavior, 9*, 317–325.

Maren, S., Phan, K. L., & Liberzon, I. (2013). The contextual brain: implications for fear conditioning, extinction and psychopathology. *Nature Reviews Neuroscience, 14*, 417–428.

Marinelli, P. W., Funk, D., Juzytsch, W., Li, Z., & Le, A. D.

(2007). Effects of opioid receptor blockade on the renewal of alcohol seeking induced by context: Relationship to c-fos mRNA expression. *European Journal of Neuroscience, 26,* 2815–2823.

Mark, T. A., & Gallistel, C. R. (1994). Kinetics of matching. *Journal of Experimental Psychology: Animal Behavior Processes, 20,* 79–95.

Marks, I. M. (1987). *Fears, phobias, and rituals.* New York: Oxford University Press.

Marler, P. (1976). Sensory templates in species-specific behavior. In J. C. Fentress (Ed.), *Simpler networks and behavior* (pp. 314–329). Sunderland, MA: Sinauer.

Marler, P. (1987). Sensitive periods and the roles of specific and general sensory stimulation in songbird learning. In P. Marler & J. P. Rauschecker (Eds.), *Imprinting and cortical plasticity* (pp. 99–135). New York: Wiley.

Marler, P. (1991). The instinct for vocal learning: Songbirds. In S. Brauth, R. J. Dooling, & W. S. Hall (Eds.), *Plasticity of development* (pp. 36–73). Cambridge, MA: MIT Press.

Marr, M. J. (2009). The natural selection: Behavior analysis as a natural science. *European Journal of Behavior Analysis, 10,* 103–118.

Marshall, B. S., Gokey, D. S., Green, P. L., & Rashotte, M. E. (1979). Spatial location of first- and second-order visual conditioned stimuli in second-order conditioning of the pigeon's keypeck. *Bulletin of the Psychonomic Society, 13,* 133–136.

Martin, G. L., & Pear, J. (2003). *Behavior modification: What it is and how to do it* (7th ed.). Englewood Cliffs, NJ: Prentice Hall.

Martin, I., & Levey, A. B. (1978). Evaluative conditioning. *Advances in Behaviour Research and Therapy, 1,* 57–101.

Martin I., & Levey, A. B. (1985). Conditioning, evaluations and cognitions: An axis of integration. *Behaviour Research and Therapy, 23,* 167–175.

Martin, I., & Levey, A. B. (1987). Learning what will happen next: Conditioning, evaluation, and cognitive processes. In G. Davey (Ed.), *Cognitive processes and Pavlovian conditioning in humans* (pp. 57–82). Chichester: Wiley.

Martin, I., & Levey, A. B. (1994). The evaluative response: Primitive but necessary. *Behaviour Research and Therapy, 32,* 301–305.

Mason, J. R. (1988). Direct and observational learning by red-winged blackbirds (Agelaius Phoeniceus): The importance of complex visual stimuli. In T. Zentall & B. Galef (Eds.), *Social learning: Psychological and biological perspectives* (pp. 99–115). Hillsdale, NJ: Erlbaum.

Mason, J. R., Arzt, A. H., & Reidinger, R. F. (1984). Comparative assessment of food preferences and aversions acquired by observational learning. *Auk, 101,* 796–803.

Mason, J. R., & Reidinger, R. F. (1981). Effects of social facilitation and observational learning on feeding behavior of the red-winged blackbird (Agelaius Phoeniceus). *Auk, 98,* 778–784.

Mason, J. R., & Reidinger, R. F. (1982). Observational learning of food aversions in red-winged blackbirds (Agelaius Phoeniceus). *Auk, 99,* 548–554.

Mathews, J. R., Hodson, G. D., Crist, W. B., & LaRoche, G. R. (1992). Teaching young children to use contact lenses. *Journal of Applied Behavior Analysis, 25,* 229–235.

Mathews, J. R., Shimoff, E., Catania, A. C., & Sagvolden, T. (1977). Uninstructed human responding: Sensitivity to ratio and interval schedules. *Journal of the Experimental Analysis of Behavior, 27,* 453–467.

Matute, H. (1996). Illusion of control: Detecting response-outcome independence in analytic but not naturalistic conditions. *Psychological Science, 7,* 289–293.

Matzel, L. D., Schachtman, T. R., & Miller, R. R. (1988). Learned irrelevance exceeds the sum of CS-preexposure and US-preexposure deficits. *Journal of Experimental Psychology: Animal Behavior Processes, 14,* 311–319.

Mayr, E. (1974). Behavior programs and evolutionary strategies. *American Scientist, 62,* 650–659.

Mazur, J. E. (1981). Optimization theory fails to predict performance of pigeons in a two-response situation. *Science, 214*, 823–825.

Mazur, J. E. (1983). Steady-state performance on fixed-, mixed-, and random-ratio schedules. *Journal of the Experimental Analysis of Behavior, 39*, 293–307.

McAlister, W. R., & McAlister, D. E. (1971). Behavioral measurement of conditioned fear. In F. R. Brush (Ed.), *Aversive conditioning and learning* (pp. 105–179). New York: Academic Press.

McAlister, W. R., & McAlister, D. E. (1992). Fear determines the effectiveness of a feedback stimulus in aversively motivated instrumental learning. *Learning and Motivation, 23*, 99–115.

McConnell, B. L., & Miller, R. R. (2014). Associative accounts of recovery-from-extinction effects. *Learning and Motivation, 46*, 1–15.

McDowell, J. J. (1981). On the validity and utility of Herrnstein's hyperbola in applied behavior analysis. In C. M. Bradshaw, E. Szabadi, & C. F. Lowe (Eds.), *Quantification of steady-state operant behaviour* (pp. 311–324). Amsterdam: Elsevier/North Holland.

McDowell, J. J. (1982). The importance of Herrnstein's mathematical statement of the law of effect for behavior therapy. *American Psychologist, 37*, 771–779.

McDowell, J. J. (1988). Matching theory in natural human environments. *The Behavior Analyst, 11*, 95–109.

McDowell, J. J. (1989). Two modern developments in matching theory. *The Behavior Analyst, 12*, 153–166.

McDowell, J. J. (2004). A computational model of selection by consequences. *Journal of the Experimental Analysis of Behavior, 81*, 297–317.

McDowell, J. J. (2005). On the classic and modern theories of matching. *Journal of the Experimental Analysis of Behavior, 84*, 111–127.

McDowell, J. J. (2010). Behavioral and neural Darwinism: Selectionist function and mechanism in adaptive behavior dynamics. *Behavioural Processes, 84*, 358–365.

McDowell, J. J. (2013a). On the theoretical and empirical status of the matching law and matching theory. *Psychological Bulletin, 139*, 1000–1028.

McDowell, J. J. (2013b). A quantitative evolutionary theory of adaptive behavior dynamics. *Psychological Review, 120*, 731–750.

McDowell, J. J., & Caron, M. L. (2010a). Matching in an undisturbed natural human environment. *Journal of the Experimental Analysis of Behavior, 93*, 415–433.

McDowell, J. J., & Caron, M. L. (2010b). Bias and undermatching in delinquent boys' verbal behavior as a function of their level of deviance. *Journal of the Experimental Analysis of Behavior, 93*, 471–483.

McDowell, J. J., & Dallery, J. (1999). Falsification of matching theory: Changes in the asymptote of Herrnstein's hyperbola as a function of water deprivation. *Journal of the Experimental Analysis of Behavior, 72*, 251–268.

McDowell, J. J., & Wixted, J. T. (1986). Variable-ratio schedules as variable-interval schedules with linear feedback loops. *Journal of the Experimental Analysis of Behavior, 46*, 315–329.

McEachin, J. J., Smith, T., & Lovaas, O. I. (1993). Long-term outcome for children with autism who received early intensive behavioral interventions. *American Journal of Mental Retardation, 97*, 359–372.

McFarland, D. (1989). *Problems of animal behavior.* Harlow, Essex, England: Longman Scientific.

McFarlane, A. C. (1988). The phenomenology of posttraumatic stress disorders following a natural disaster. *Journal of Nervous and Mental Disease, 176*, 22–29.

McFayden-Ketchum, S. A., & Porter, R. H. (1989). Transmission of food preferences in spiny mice (Acomys cahirinus) via nose-mouth interaction between mothers and weanlings. *Behavioral Ecology and Sociobiology, 24*, 59–62.

McKearney, J. W. (1969). Fixed-interval schedules of electric shock presentation: Extinction and recovery of performance under different shock intensities and fixed interval durations. *Journal of the Experimental Analysis of Behavior, 12*, 301–313.

McLaren, I. P., Forrest, C. L., McLaren, R. P., Jones, F. W., Aitken, M. R., & Mackintosh, N. J. (2014). Associations and propositions: The case for a dual-process account of learning in humans. *Neurobiology of Learning and Memory, 108*, 185–195.

McLean, A. P. (2006). The sampling distribution of *k*. *Behavioral Processes, 72*, 300–308.

McNally, R. J. (1987). Preparedness and phobias: A review. *Psychological Bulletin, 101*, 283–303.

Mechner, F. (1959). A notational system for the description of behavioral procedures. *Journal of the Experimental Analysis of Behavior, 2*, 133–150.

Merckelbach, H., Arntz, A., & de Jong, P. (1991). Conditioning experiences in spider phobics. *Behaviour Research and Therapy, 29*, 333–335.

Meuwissen, I., & Over, R. (1990). Habituation and dishabituation of female sexual arousal. *Behavioral Research and Therapy, 28*, 217–226.

Michael, J. (1982). Distinguishing between discriminative and motivational functions of stimuli. *Journal of the Experimental Analysis of Behavior, 37*, 149–155.

Michon, J. A. (1985). The compleat time experiencer. In J. A. Michon & J. L. Jackson (Eds.), *Time, mind, and behavior.* Berlin: Springer-Verlag.

Michotte, A. (1963). *The perception of causality.* London: Methuen.

Mikulka, P. J., Leard, B., & Klein, S. B. (1977). The effect of illness (US) exposure as a source of interference with the acquisition and retention of a taste aversion. *Journal of the Experimental Analysis of Behavior, 3*, 189–210.

Milad, M. R., Rauch, S. L., Pitman, R. K., & Quirk., G. J. (2006). Fear extinction in rats: Implications for human brain imaging and anxiety disorders. *Biological Psychology, 73*, 61–71.

Milgram, N. W., Krames, L., & Alloway, T. M. (Eds.). (1977). *Food aversion learning.* New York: Plenum Press.

Milgram, S. (1963). Behavioral study of obedience. *Journal of Abnormal and Social Psychology, 67*, 371–378.

Miller, G. A. (1981). *Language and speech.* San Francisco: W. H. Freeman.

Miller, H. L., Jr. (1976). Matching-based hedonic scaling in the pigeon. *Journal of the Experimental Analysis of Behavior, 26*, 335–347.

Miller, N. E. (1948). Studies of fear as an acquirable drive. *Journal of Experimental Psychology, 38*, 89–101.

Miller, N. E. (1951). Learnable drives and rewards. In S. S. Stevens (Ed.), *Handbook of experimental psychology.* New York: Wiley.

Miller, N. E. (1959). Liberalization of basic S-R concepts: Extensions to conflict behaviour, motivation, and

social learning. In S. Koch (Ed.), *Psychology: A study of a science* (Vol. 2, pp. 196–292). New York: McGraw-Hill.

Miller, R. R., & Barnet, R. C. (1993). The role of time in elementary associations. *Current Directions in Psychological Science, 2*, 106–111.

Miller, R. R., Barnet, R. C., & Grahame, N. J. (1992). Responding to a conditioned stimulus depends on the current associative status of other cues present during training of that specific stimulus. *Journal of Experimental Psychology: Animal Behavior Processes, 18*, 251–264.

Miller, R. R., Barnet, R. C., & Grahame, N. J. (1995). Assessment of the Rescorla-Wagner model. *Psychological Bulletin, 117*, 363–386.

Miller, R. R., & Matzel, L. D. (1988). The comparator hypothesis: A response rule for the expression of associations. In G. B. Bower (Ed.), *The psychology of learning and motivation* (Vol. 22, pp. 51–92). San Diego, CA: Academic Press.

Miller, R. R., & Matzel, L. D. (1989). Contingency and relative associative strength. In S. B. Klein & R. R. Mowrer (Eds.), *Contemporary learning theories: Pavlovian conditioning and the status of traditional learning theory* (pp. 61–84). Hillsdale, NJ: Erlbaum.

Miller, R. R., & Schachtman, T. R. (1985). Conditioning context as an associative baseline: Implications for response generation and the nature of conditioned inhibition. In R. R. Miller & N. E. Spear (Eds.), *Information processing in animals: Conditioned inhibition* (pp. 51–88). Hillsdale, NJ: Erlbaum.

Miller, S., & Konorski, J. (1969). On a particular form of conditioned reflex. (B. F. Skinner, Trans.) *Journal of the Experimental Analysis of Behavior, 12*, 187–189. (Original publication 1928, Sur une forme particulière des reflexes conditionnels. *Compte Rendu des Seances de la Société de Biologie, 99*, 1155–1157)

Mineka, S., & Cook, M. (1986). Immunization against the observational conditioning of snake fear in rhesus monkeys. *Journal of Abnormal Psychology, 95*, 307–318.

Mineka, S., & Cook, M. (1988). Social learning and the acquisition of snake fear in monkeys. In T. Zentall & B. Galef (Eds.), *Social learning: Psychological and biological perspectives* (pp. 51–73). Hillsdale, NJ: Erlbaum.

Mineka, S., Davidson, M., Cook, M., & Keir, R. (1984). Observational conditioning of snake fear in rhesus monkeys. *Journal of Abnormal Psychology, 93*, 355–372.

Mineka, S., Keir, R., & Price, V. (1980). Fear of snakes in wild and lab-reared rhesus monkeys. *Animal Learning and Behavior, 8*, 653–663.

Mitchell, C. J., Heyes, C. M., Gardner, M. R., and Dawson, G. R. (1999). Limitations of a bidirectional control procedure for the investigation of imitation in rats: Odour cues on the manipulandum. *Quarterly Journal of Experimental Psychology, 52B*, 193–202.

Montgomery, K. C. (1954). The role of exploratory drive in learning. *Journal of Comparative and Physiological Psychology, 47*, 60–64.

Morgan, C. A., Grillon, C., Southwick, S. M., Davis, M., & Charney, D. S. (1996). Exaggerated acoustic startle reflex in Gulf War veterans with posttraumatic stress disorder. *American Journal of Psychiatry, 153*, 64–68.

Morgan, C. L. (1894). *Introduction to comparative psychology*. London: Scott.

Morgan, C. L. (1900). *Animal behaviour*. London: Arnold.

Morgan, M. J., & Nicholas, D. J. (1979). Discrimination between reinforced action patterns in the rat. *Learning and Motivation, 10*, 1–22.

Morrison, S. D. (1976). Control of food intake in cancer cachexia: A challenge and a tool. *Physiology and Behavior, 17*, 705–714.

Morse, W. H. (1966). Intermittent reinforcement. In W. K. Honig (Ed.), *Operant behavior: Areas of research and application* (pp. 52–108). New York: Appleton-Century-Crofts.

Moscovitz, A., & LoLordo, V. M. (1968). Role of safety in the Pavlovian backward fear conditioning procedure. *Journal of Comparative and Physiological Psychology, 66*, 673–678.

Moskowitz, B. A. (1978). The acquisition of language. *Scientific American, 239*(5), 92–108.

Mowrer, O. H. (1939). Stimulus response theory of anxiety. *Psychological Review, 46*, 553–565.

Mowrer, O. H. (1940). An experimental analogue of "regression" with incidental observations on "reaction-formation." *Journal of Abnormal Psychology, 35*, 56–87.

Mowrer, O. H. (1960). *Learning theory and behavior*. New York: Wiley.

Mowrer, O. H., & Aiken, E. G. (1954). Contiguity vs. drive reduction in conditioned fear: Temporal variations in conditioned and unconditioned stimulus. *American Journal of Psychology, 67*, 26–38.

Muenzinger, K. F. (1928). Plasticity and mechanization of the problem box habit in guinea pigs. *Journal of Comparative Psychology, 8*, 45–70.

Munjack, D. J. (1984). The onset of driving phobias. *Journal of Behavior Therapy and Experimental Psychiatry, 15*, 305–308.

Munn, N. L. (1950). *Handbook of psychological research on the rat*. Boston: Houghton Mifflin.

Murray, E., & Foote, F. (1979). The origins of fear of snakes. *Behaviour Research and Therapy, 17*, 489–493.

Murton, R. K. (1971). The significance of a specific search image in the feeding behaviour of the wood-pigeon. *Behaviour, 40*, 10–42.

Myers, C. E., Oliver, L. M., Warren, S. G., Gluck, M. A. (2000). Stimulus exposure effects in human associative learning. *Quarterly Journal of Experimental Psychology, B53*, 173–187.

Myers, K. M., & Carlezon, W. A. (2010). Extinction and drug- and withdrawal-paired cues in animal models: Relevance to the treatment of addiction. *Neuroscience and Biobehavioral Reviews, 35*, 285–302.

Myskiw, J. C., Izquierdo, I., & Furini, C. R. G. (2014). Modulation of the extinction of fear learning. *Brain Research Bulletin, 105*, 61–69.

Nagell, K., Olguin, R., & Tomasello, M. (1993). Processes of social learning in the imitative learning of chimpanzees and human children. *Journal of Comparative Psychology, 107*, 174–186.

Nakajima, M., Nakajima, S., & Imada, H. (1999). General learned irrelevance and its prevention. *Learning and Motivation, 30*, 265–280.

Nakajima, S., Tanaka, S., Urushihara, K., & Imada, H. (2000). Renewal of extinguished lever-press responses upon return to the training context. *Learning and Motivation, 31*, 416–431.

Napier, R. M., Macrae, M., & Kehoe, E.J., (1991). Rapid reacquisition in conditioning of the rabbit's nictitating membrane response. *Journal of Experimental Psychology: Animal Behavior Processes, 18*, 182–192.

Nelson, A., & Killcross, S. (2006). Amphetamine exposure enhances habit formation. *Journal of Neuroscience, 26*, 3805–3812.

Nesbitt, R. E., & Ross, L. (1980). *Human inference: Strategies and shortcomings of social judgment.* Englewood Cliffs, NJ: Prentice-Hall.

Nesse, R. M. (1990). Evolutionary explanations of emotions. *Human Nature, 1*, 261–289.

Neuringer, A. J. (1967). Effects of reinforcer magnitude on choice and rate of responding. *Journal of the Experimental Analysis of Behavior, 10*, 417–424.

Neuringer, A. J. (1986). Can people behave "randomly?" The role of feedback. *Journal of Experimental Psychology: General, 115*, 62–75.

Neuringer, A., Deiss, C., & Olsen, G. (2000). Reinforced variability and operant learning. *Journal of Experimental Psychology: Animal Behavior Processes, 26*, 98–111.

Neuringer, A., Kornell, N., & Olufs, M. (2001). Stability and variability in extinction. *Journal of Experimental Psychology: Animal Behavior Processes, 27*, 79–94.

Nevin, J. A. (1969). Interval reinforcement of choice behavior in discrete trials. *Journal of Applied Behavior Analysis, 12*, 875–885.

Nevin, J. A. (1979). Overall matching versus momentary maximizing: Nevin (1969) revisited. *Journal of Experimental Psychology: Animal Behavior Processes, 5*, 300–306.

Nevin, J. A., Mandell, C., and Atak, J. R. (1983). The analysis of behavioral momentum. *Journal of the Experimental Analysis of Behavior, 39*, 49–59.

Newport, E. L. (1990). Maturational constraints on language learning. *Cognitive Science, 14*, 11–28.

Newport, E. L. (1991). Contrasting concepts of the critical period for language. In S. Carey, & R. Gelman (Eds.), *The epigenesis of mind: Essays on biology and cognition* (pp. 111–130). Hillsdale, NJ: Erlbaum Associates.

Nicolaides, S. (1977). Sensory-neuro-endocrine reflexes and their anticipatory and optimizing role in metabolism. In M. R. Kare & O. Maller (Eds.), *The chemical senses and nutrition* (pp. 123–143). New York: Academic Press.

Nisbett, R., & Ross, L. (1980). *Human inference: Strategies and shortcomings of social judgment.* Englewood Cliffs, NJ: Prentice-Hall.

Nissen, H. W., & Elder, J. H. (1935). The influence of amount of incentive on delayed response performance of chimpanzees. *Journal of Genetic Psychology, 47*, 49–72.

Nordquist, R. E., Voorn, P., de Mooij-van Malsen, J. G., Joosten, R. N. J. M. A., Pennartz, C. M. A., & Vanderschuren, L. J. M. J. (2007). Augmented reinforcer value and accelerated habit formation after repeated amphetamine treatment. *European Neuropsychopharmacology, 17,* 532–540.

Norman, D. A. (1981). Categorization of action slips. *Psychological Review, 88,* 1–15.

Notterman, J. M. (1959). Force emission during bar pressing. *Journal of the Experimental Psychology, 58,* 341–347.

Notterman, J. M., & Mintz, D. E. (1965). *Dynamics of response.* New York: Wiley.

Numan, M., Fleming, A. S., & Levy, F. (2006). Maternal behavior. In J. D. Neill (Ed.), *Knobil and Neill's physiology of reproduction* (pp. 1921–1993). San Diego, CA: Elsevier.

Oberling, P., Bristol, A. S., Matute, H., & Miller, R. R. (2000). Biological significance attenuates overshadowing, relative validity, and degraded contingency effects. *Animal Learning and Behavior, 28,* 172–186.

O'Donohue, W., & Plaud, J. J. (1991). The long-term habituation of sexual arousal in the human male. *Journal of Behavior Therapy & Experimental Psychiatry, 22,* 87–96.

Oehlberg, K., & Mineka, S. (2011). Fear conditioning and attention to threat: An integrative approach to understanding the etiology of anxiety disorders. In T. R. Schachtman & S. Reilly (Eds.). *Associative learning and conditioning theory: Human and non-human applications* (pp. 44–78). New York: Oxford University Press.

Öhman, A., & Hugdahl, K. (1979). Instructional control of autonomic respondents: Fear relevance as a critical factor. In N. Birbaumer & H. D. Kimmel (Eds.), *Biofeedback and self-regulation* (pp. 149–165). New York: Erlbaum.

Öhman, A., & Mineka, S. (2001). Fears, phobias, and preparedness: Toward an evolved module of fear and fear learning. *Psychological Review, 108,* 483–522.

Olazábal, D. E., Pereira, M., Agrati, D., Ferreira, A., Fleming, A. S., González-Mariscal, G., . . . Uriarte, N. (2013a). New theoretical and experimental approaches on maternal motivation in mammals. *Neuroscience and Biobehavioral Reviews, 37,* 1860–1874.

Olazábal, D. E., Pereira, M., Agrati, D., Ferreira, A., Fleming, A. S., González-Mariscal, G., . . . Uriarte, N. (2013b). Flexibility and adaptation of the neural substrate that supports maternal behavior in mammals. *Neuroscience and Biobehavioral Reviews, 37,* 1875–1892.

Ono, K., & Iwabuchi, K. (1997). Effects of histories of differential reinforcement of response rate on variable-interval responding. *Journal of the Experimental Analysis of Behavior, 67,* 311–322.

Orlando, R., & Bijou, S. (1960). Single and multiple schedules of reinforcement in developmentally retarded children. *Journal of the Experimental Analysis of Behavior, 3,* 339–348.

Ornitz, E. M., & Guthrie, D. (1989). Long-term habituation and sensitization of the acoustic startle response in the normal adult human. *Psychophysiology, 26,* 166–173.

Ostlund, S., & Balleine, B. (2008). On habits and addiction: An associative analysis of compulsive drug seeking. *Drug Discovery Today: Disease Models, 5,* 235–245.

Oxoby, R. J., & Finnigan, H. (2007). Developing heuristic-based quality judgments: Blocking in consumer choice. *Psychology & Marketing, 24,* 295–313.

Pacheco-López, G., Engler, H., Niemi, M.-J., & Schedlowski, M. (2009). Taste-immune associative learning. In S. Reilly & T. R. Schachtman (Eds.), *Conditioned taste aversion: Behavioral and neural processes* (pp. 473–496). New York: Oxford University Press.

Page, S., & Neuringer, A. (1985). Variability is an operant. *Journal of Experimental Psychology: Animal Behavior Processes, 11,* 429–452.

Parke, R. D. (1969). Effectiveness of punishment as an interaction of intensity, timing, agent nurturance, and cognitive structuring. *Child Development, 40,* 213–235.

Parker, L. A., & Revusky, S. (1982). Generalized conditioned flavor aversions: Effects of toxicosis training with one flavor on the preference for different novel flavors. *Animal Learning and Behavior, 10,* 505–510.

Patterson, F., & Linden, E. (1982). *The education of Koko.* New York: Holt, Rinehart & Winston.

Pavlov, I. P. (1927). *Conditioned reflexes.* (G. V. Anrep, Trans.). London: Oxford University Press.

Pavlov, I. P. (1932). The reply of a physiologist to psychologists. *Psychological Review, 39,* 91–127.

Pavlov, I. P. (1934). An attempt at a physiological interpretation of obsessional neurosis and paranoia. *Journal of Mental Science, 80,* 187–197.

Pavlov, I. P. (1955). Experimental psychology and psychopathology in animals. In K. S. Koshoyants (Ed.), *I. P. Pavlov selected works* (pp. 151–168). Moscow: Foreign Languages Publishing House. (Original work published 1903)

Pearce, J. M. (1987). *Introduction to animal cognition.* London: Erlbaum.

Pearce, J. M., Colwill, R. M., & Hall, G. (1978). Instrumental conditioning of scratching in the laboratory rat. *Learning and Motivation, 9,* 255–271.

Pearce, J. M., & Hall, G. (1980). A model for Pavlovian learning: Variations in the effectiveness of conditioned but not unconditioned stimuli. *Psychological Review, 87,* 532–552.

Pearce, J. M., Nicholas, D. J., & Dickinson, A. (1981). The potentiation effect during serial conditioning. *Quarterly Journal of Experimental Psychology, 33B,* 159–179.

Pears, D. (1971). *What is knowledge?* New York: Harper & Row.

Pecoraro, N. C., Timberlake, W. D., & Tinsley, M. (1999). Incentive downshifts evoke search repertoires in rats. *Journal of Experimental Psychology: Animal Behavior Processes, 25,* 153–167.

Peele, D. B., Casey, J., & Silberberg, A. (1984). Primacy of interresponse-time reinforcement for rate differences under variable-ratio and variable-interval schedules. *Journal of Experimental Psychology: Animal Behavior Processes, 10,* 149–167.

Penn, D. C., & Povinelli, D. J. (2007). Causal cognition in human and nonhuman animals: A comparative, critical review. *Annual Review of Psychology, 58,* 97–118.

Perez-Cruet, J., Tolliver, C., Dunn, C., Marvin, S., & Brady, J. V. (1963). Concurrent measurement of heart rate and instrumental avoidance behavior in the Rhesus monkey. *Journal of the Experimental Analysis of Behavior, 6,* 61–64.

Perkins, C. C., Jr. (1953). The relations between conditioned stimulus intensity and response strength. *Journal of Experimental Psychology, 75,* 337–392.

Perone, M., Galizio, M., & Baron, A. (1988). The relevance of animal-based principles in the laboratory study of human operant conditioning. In G. Davies & C. Cullen (Eds.), *Human operant conditioning and behavior modification* (pp. 59–85). Chichester: Wiley.

Perry, C., Zbukvic, I., Kim, J. H., & Lawrence, A. J. (2014). The role of cues and contexts on drug-seeking behavior. *British Journal of Pharmacology, 171,* 4636–4672.

Peters, J., Vallone, J., Laurendi, K., & Kalivas, P. W. (2008). Opposing roles for the ventral prefrontal cortex and the basolateral amygdale on the spontaneous recovery of cocaine-seeking in rats. *Psychopharmacology, 197,* 319–326.

Peterson, G. B., Ackil, J. E., Frommer, G. P., & Hearst, E. (1972). Conditioned approach and contact behavior toward signals for food or brain stimulation reinforcement. *Science, 177,* 1009–1011.

Peterson, G. B., Wheeler, R. L., & Armstrong, G. D. (1978). Expectancies as mediators in the differential-reward conditional discrimination performance of pigeons. *Animal Learning and Behavior, 6,* 279–285.

Petscher, E. S., Rey, C., & Bailey, J. S. (2009). A review of empirical support for differential reinforcement of alternative behavior. *Research* in *Developmental Disabilities, 30,* 409–425.

Pickens, C. L. & Holland, P. C. (2004). Conditioning and cognition. *Neuroscience and Biobehavioral Reviews, 28,* 651–661.

Pierce, W. D., & Epling, W. F. (1983). Choice, matching, and human behavior: A review of the literature. *The Behavior Analyst, 6,* 57–76.

Pierce, W. D., Epling, W. F., & Greer, S. M. (1981). Human communication and the matching law. In C. M. Bradshaw, E. Szabadi, & C. F. Lowe (Eds.), *Quantification of steady-state operant behaviour* (pp. 345–352). Amsterdam: Elsevier/North Holland Biomedical Press.

Pinel, J. P. J., Mana, M. J., & Wilkie, D. M. (1986). Postshock learning and conditioned defensive burying. *Animal Learning and Behavior, 14,* 301–304.

Pineno, O., & Miller, R. R. (2004). Signaling a change in cue-outcome relations in human associative learning. *Learning and Behavior, 32,* 360–375.

Pitman, R. K., Rasmusson, A. M., Koenen, K. C., Shin, L. M., Orr, S. P., Gilbertson, M. W., . . . Liberzon, I. (2012). Biological studies of post-traumatic stress disorder. *Nature Reviews Neuroscience, 13,* 769–787.

Platt, J. R., Kuch, D. O., & Bitgood, S. C. (1973). Rats' leverpress duration as psychophysical judgements of time. *Journal of the Experimental Analysis of Behavior, 19,* 239–250.

Plaud, J. J., Gaither, G. A., Henderson, S. A., & Devitt, M. K. (1997). The long-term habituation of sexual arousal in human males: A crossover design. *The Psychological Record, 47,* 385–398.

Pleyers, G., Corneille, O., Luminet, O., & Yzerbyt, V. (2007). Aware and (dis)liking: Item-based analyses reveal that valence acquisition via evaluative conditioning emerges only when there is contingency awareness. *Journal of Experimental Psychology: Learning, Memory & Cognition, 33,* 130–144.

Podlesnik, C. A., Jimenez-Gomez, C., & Shahan, T. A. (2006). Resurgence of alcohol seeking produced by discounting non-drug reinforcement as an animal model of drug relapse. *Behavioral Pharmacology, 17,* 369–374.

Pole, N., Neylan, T. C., Otte, C., Henn-Haase, C., Metzler, T. J., & Marmar, C. R. (2008). Prospective prediction of posttraumatic stress disorder symptoms using fear potentiated auditory startle responses. *Biological Psychiatry, 65,* 235–240.

Porter, R. H., Cernoch, J. M., McLaughlin, F. J., (1983). Maternal recognition of neonates through olfactory cues. *Physiology and Behavior, 30,* 151–154.

Postman, L. (1947). The history and present status of the law of effect. *Psychological Bulletin, 44,* 489–563.

Poulson, C. L. (1983). Differential reinforcement of other-than-vocalization as control procedure in the conditioning of infant vocalization rate. *Journal of Experimental Child Psychology, 36,* 471–489.

Powell, R. W., Kelly, W., & Santisteban, D. (1975). Response-independent reinforcement in the crow: Failure to obtain autoshaping and positive automaintenance. *Bulletin of the Psychonomic Society, 6,* 513–516.

Premack, D. (1959). Toward empirical behavior laws: I. Positive reinforcement. *Psychological Review, 66,* 219–233.

Premack, D. (1962). Reversibility of the reinforcement relation. *Science, 136,* 255–257.

Premack, D. (1965). Reinforcement theory. In D. Levine (Ed.), *Nebraska symposium on motivation* (pp. 123–180). Lincoln: University of Nebraska Press.

Preston, G. C., Dickinson, A., & Mackintosh, N. J. (1986). Contextual conditional discriminations. *Quarterly Journal of Experimental Psychology, 38B,* 217–237.

Prokasy, W. F. (1958). Extinction and spontaneous recovery of conditioned eyelid responses as a function of amount of acquisition and extinction training. *Journal of Experimental Psychology, 56,* 319–324.

Pryor, K. W., Haag, R., & O'Reilly, J. (1969). The creative porpoise: Training for novel behavior. *Journal of the Experimental Analysis of Behavior, 12,* 653–661.

Quick, S. L., Pyszczynski, A. D., Colston, K. A., & Shahan, T. A. (2011). Loss of alternative non-drug reinforcement induces relapse of cocaine-seeking in rats: Role of dopamine D(1) receptors. *Neuropsychopharmacology, 36,* 1015–1020.

Quinsey, V. L. (1971). Conditioned suppression with no CS-US contingency in the rat. *Canadian Journal of Psychology, 25,* 69–82.

Quirk, G. J. (2002). Memory for extinction of conditioned fear is long-lasting and persists following spontaneous recovery. *Learning and Memory, 9,* 402–407.

Rachlin, H. C. (1970). *Introduction to modern behaviorism.* San Francisco: W. H. Freeman.

Rachlin, H. C. (1971). On the tautology of the matching law. *Journal of the Experimental Analysis of Behavior, 15,* 249–251.

Rachlin, H., Battalio, R. C., Kagel, J. H., & Green, L. (1981). Maximization theory in behavioral psychology. *Behavioral and Brain Sciences, 4,* 371–417.

Rachlin, H., Green, L., Kagel, J. H., & Battalio, R. C. (1976). Economic demand theory and psychological studies of choice. In G. Bower (Ed.), *The psychology of learning and motivation* (Vol. 10, pp. 129–154). New York: Academic Press.

Rachman, S. J. (1977). The conditioning theory of fear acquisition: A critical examination. *Behaviour Research and Therapy, 15,* 375–387.

Rachman, S., & Costello, C. (1961) The aetiology and treatment of childrens' phobias. *American Journal of Psychiatry, 118,* 97–105.

Rakison, D. H., & Derringer, J. (2008). Do infants possess an evolved spider-detection mechanism? *Cognition, 107,* 381–393.

Ramsay, D. S., & Woods, S. C. (1997). Biological consequences of drug administration: Implications for acute and chronic tolerance. *Psychological Review, 104,* 170–193.

Randich, A., & Haggard, D. (1983). Exposure to the unconditioned stimulus alone: Effects upon retention and acquisition of conditioned suppression. *Journal of Experimental Psychology: Animal Behavior Processes, 9,* 147–159.

Randich, A., & LoLordo, V. M. (1979a). Associative and nonassociative theories of the UCS preexposure phenomenon: Implications for Pavlovian conditioning. *Psychological Bulletin, 86,* 523–548.

Randich, A., & LoLordo, V. M. (1979b). Preconditioning exposure to the unconditioned stimulus affects the acquisition of a conditioned emotional response. *Learning and Motivation, 10,* 245–275.

Randich, A., & Rescorla, R. A. (1981). The effects of separate presentations of the US on conditioned suppression. *Animal Learning and Behavior, 9,* 55–64.

Randich, A., & Ross, R. T. (1985). Contextual stimuli mediate the effects of pre- and postexposure to the unconditioned stimulus on conditioned suppression. In P. D. Balsam, & A. Tomie (Eds.), *Context and learning* (pp. 105–132). Hillsdale, NJ: Erlbaum.

Rankin, C. H., Abrams, T., Barry, R. J., Bhatnagar, S., Clayton, D. F., Colombo, J., . . . Thompson, R. F. (2009). Habituation revisited: An updated and revised description of the behavioral characteristics of habituation. *Neurobiology of Learning and Memory, 92,* 135–138.

Ratcliffe, J. M., & ter Hofstede, H. M. (2005). Roosts as information centres: Social learning of food preferences in bats. *Biological Letters, 1,* 72–74.

Razran G. (1955). Conditioning and perception. *Journal of Experimental Psychology, 62,* 83–95.

Reed, D. D., Critchfield, T. S., & Martens, B. K. (2006). The generalized matching law in elite sport competition: Football play calling as operant choice. *Journal of Applied Behavior Analysis, 39,* 281–297.

Reed, P., & Clark, C. (2011). Impact of intervening learning on resurgence in humans with autism spectrum disorders. *Learning and Behavior, 39,* 163–170.

Reed, P., & Reilly, S. (1990). Context extinction following conditioning with a delayed reward enhances subsequent instrumental responding. *Journal of Experimental Psychology: Animal Behavior Processes, 16,* 48–55.

Reid, R. L. (1958). The role of the reinforcer as stimulus. *British Journal of Psychology, 49,* 202–209.

Reilly, S. (2009). Central gustatory system lesions and conditioned taste aversion. In S. Reilly and T. R. Schachtman (Eds.), *Conditioned taste aversion: Behavioral and neural processes* (pp. 309–327). New York: Oxford University Press.

Reilly, S., & Schachtman, T. R. (Eds.). (2009). *Conditioned taste aversion: Behavioral and neural processes.* New York: Oxford University Press.

Reiss, S., & Wagner, A. R. (1972). CS habituation produces a "latent inhibition effect" but no active "conditioned inhibition." *Learning and Motivation, 3,* 237–245.

Renne, C. M., & Creer, T. L. (1976). Training children with asthma to use inhalation therapy equipment. *Journal of Applied Behavior Analysis, 9,* 1–11.

Renner, K. E. (1964). Delay of reinforcement: A historical review. *Psychological Bulletin, 61,* 341–361.

Renner, M. J. (1988). Learning during exploration: The role of behavioral topography during exploration in determining subsequent adaptive behavior. *International Journal of Comparative Psychology, 2,* 43–56.

Renner, M. J., & Seltzer, C. P. (1991). Molar characteristics of exploratory and investigative behavior in the rat (rattus norvegicus). *Journal of Comparative Psychology, 105,* 326–339.

Rescorla, R. A. (1966). Predictability and the number of pairings in Pavlovian fear conditioning. *Psychonomic Science, 4,* 383–384.

Rescorla, R. A. (1967a). Inhibition of delay in Pavlovian fear conditioning. *Journal of Comparative and Physiological Psychology, 64,* 114–120.

Rescorla, R. A. (1967b). Pavlovian conditioning and its proper control procedures. *Psychological Review, 74,* 71–80.

Rescorla, R. A. (1968). Probability of shock in the presence and absence of CS in fear conditioning. *Journal of Comparative and Physiological Psychology, 66,* 1–5.

Rescorla, R. A. (1969). Conditioned inhibition of fear resulting from negative CS-US contingencies. *Journal of Comparative and Physiological Psychology, 67,* 504–509.

Rescorla, R. A. (1970). Reduction in the effectiveness of reinforcement after prior excitatory conditioning. *Learning and Motivation, 1,* 327–381.

Rescorla, R. A. (1971a). Summation and retardation tests of latent inhibition. *Journal of Comparative and Physiological Psychology, 75,* 77–81.

Rescorla, R. A. (1971b). Variation in the effectiveness of reinforcement and nonreinforcement following prior inhibitory conditioning. *Learning and Motivation, 2,* 113–123.

Rescorla, R. A. (1972). Informational variables in Pavlovian conditioning. In G. H. Bower & J. T. Spence (Eds.), *Psychology of learning and motivation* (Vol. 6, pp. 1–46). New York: Academic Press.

Rescorla, R. A. (1973). Effect of US habituation following conditioning. *Journal of Comparative and Physiological Psychology, 82,* 137–143.

Rescorla, R. A. (1974). Effect of inflation on the unconditioned stimulus value following conditioning. *Journal of Comparative and Physiological Psychology, 86,* 101–106.

Rescorla, R. A. (1980a). Simultaneous and successive associations in sensory preconditioning. *Journal of Experimental Psychology: Animal Behavior Processes, 6,* 207–216.

Rescorla, R. A. (1980b). *Pavlovian second-order conditioning: Studies in associative learning.* Hillsdale, NJ: Erlbaum.

Rescorla, R. A. (1987). A Pavlovian analysis of goal-directed behavior. *American Psychologist, 42,* 119–129.

Rescorla, R. A. (1988). Pavlovian conditioning: It's not what you think it is. *American Psychologist, 43*, 151–160.

Rescorla, R. A. (1990). Instrumental responses become associated with reinforcers that differ in one feature. *Animal Learning and Behavior, 18*, 206–211.

Rescorla, R. A. (1991). Associative relations in instrumental learning: The Eighteenth Bartlett Memorial Lecture. *Quarterly Journal of Experimental Psychology, 43B*, 1–23.

Rescorla, R. A. (1992). Hierarchical associative relations in Pavlovian conditioning and instrumental training. *Current Directions in Psychological Science, 1*, 66–70.

Rescorla, R. A. (1993). Inhibitory associations between S and R in extinction. *Animal Learning and Behavior, 21*, 327–336.

Rescorla, R. A. (1994). Transfer of instrumental control mediated by a devalued outcome. *Animal Learning and Behavior, 22*, 27–33.

Rescorla, R. A. (1997). Response inhibition in extinction. *Quarterly Journal of Experimental Psychology, 50B*, 238–252.

Rescorla, R. A. (1999). Summation and overexpectation with qualitatively different outcomes. *Animal Learning and Behavior, 27*, 50–62.

Rescorla, R. A. (2001). Experimental extinction. In R. R. Mowrer & S. B. Klein (Eds.), *Handbook of contemporary learning theories* (pp. 119–154). Mahwah, NJ: Lawrence Erlbaum Associates.

Rescorla, R. A. (2004). Spontaneous recovery. *Learning and Memory, 11*, 501–509.

Rescorla, R. A., & Cunningham, C. L. (1978) Within-compound flavor associations. *Journal of Experimental Psychology: Animal Behavior Processes, 4*, 267–275.

Rescorla, R. A., & Cunningham, C. L. (1979). Spatial contiguity facilitates Pavlovian second-order conditioning. *Journal of Experimental Psychology: Animal Behavior Processes, 5*, 152–161.

Rescorla, R. A., Durlach, P. J., & Grau, J. W. (1985). Contextual learning in Pavlovian conditioning. In P. D. Balsam & A. Tomie (Eds.), *Context and learning* (pp. 23–56). Hillsdale, NJ: Erlbaum.

Rescorla, R. A., & Freberg, L. (1978). The extinction of within-compound flavor associations. *Learning and Motivation, 9*, 411–427.

Rescorla, R. A., & Furrow, D. R. (1977). Stimulus similarity as a determinant of Pavlovian conditioning. *Journal of Experimental Psychology: Animal Behavior Processes, 3*, 203–215.

Rescorla, R. A., & Heth, C. D. (1975). Reinstatement of fear to an extinguished conditioned stimulus. *Journal of Experimental Psychology: Animal Behavior Processes, 1*, 88–96.

Rescorla, R. A., & Holland, P. C. (1976). Some behavioral approaches to the study of learning. In M. R. Rosenzweig & E. L. Bennett (Eds.), *Neural mechanisms of learning and memory* (pp. 165–192). Cambridge, MA: MIT Press.

Rescorla, R. A., & Skucy, J. C. (1969). Effect of response-independent reinforcers during extinction. *Journal of Comparative and Physiological Psychology, 67*, 381–389.

Rescorla, R. A., & Wagner, A. R. (1972). A theory of Pavlovian conditioning: Variations in the effectiveness of reinforcement and nonreinforcement. In A. H. Black & W. F. Prokasy (Eds.), *Classical conditioning II: Current research and theory* (pp. 64–99). New York: Appleton-Century-Crofts.

Revusky, S. (1971). The role of interference in association over a delay. In W. K. Honig & P. H. R. James (Eds.), *Animal memory* (pp. 155–213). New York: Academic Press.

Revusky, S. (1977). Learning as a general process with an emphasis on data from feeding experiments. In N. W. Milgram, L. Krames, & T. M. Alloway (Eds.), *Food aversion learning* (pp. 1–51). New York: Plenum.

Revusky, S. (1985). The general process approach to animal learning. In T. D. Johnston & A. T. Piertrewicz (Eds.), *Issues in the ecological study of learning* (pp. 401–432). Hillsdale, NJ: Erlbaum.

Revusky, S. (2009). Chemical aversion treatment for alcoholism. In S. Reilly & T. R. Schachtman (Eds.), *Conditioned taste aversion: Behavioral and neural processes* (pp. 445–472). New York: Oxford University Press.

Revusky, S. H., & Bedarf, E. W. (1967). Association of illness with prior ingestion of novel foods. *Science, 155,* 219–220.

Revusky, S., & Garcia, J. (1970). Learned associations over long delays. In G. H. Bower & J. T. Spence (Eds.), *The psychology of learning and motivation: Advances in research and theory* (Vol. 4, pp. 1–84). New York: Academic Press.

Ricker, S. T., & Bouton, M. E. (1996). Reacquisition following extinction in appetitive conditioning. *Learning and Behavior, 24,* 423–436.

Rimm, D., Janda, L., Lancaster, D., Nahl, M., & Dittmar, K. (1977). An exploratory investigation of the origin and maintenance of phobias. *Behaviour Research and Therapy, 15,* 231–238.

Roitblat, H. L. (1982). The meaning of representation in animal memory. *The Behavioral and Brain Sciences, 5,* 353–406.

Roitblat, H. L. (1987). *Introduction to comparative cognition.* New York: Freeman.

Romanes, G. J. (1882). *Animal intelligence.* London: Kegen, Pail, Trench.

Romanes, G. J. (1884). *Mental evolution in animals.* New York: AMS Press.

Romanowich, P., Bourret, J., & Vollmer, T. R. (2007). Further analysis of the matching law to describe two- and three-point shot allocation by professional basketball players. *Journal of Applied Behavior Analysis, 40,* 311–315.

Rosas, J. M., & Alonso, G. (1996). Temporal discrimination and forgetting of CS duration in conditioned suppression. *Learning and Motivation, 27,* 43–57.

Rosas, J. M., & Bouton, M. E. (1997). Renewal of a conditioned taste aversion upon return to the conditioning context after extinction in another one. *Learning and Motivation, 28,* 216–229.

Rosas, J. M., & Callejas-Aguilera, J. E. (2006). Context switch effects on acquisition and extinction in human predictive learning. *Journal of Experimental Psychology: Learning Memory and Cognition, 32,* 461–474.

Rosas, J. M., Todd, T. P., & Bouton, M. E. (2013). Context change and associative learning. *Wiley Interdisciplinary Reviews: Cognitive Science, 4,* 237–244.

Rosenfarb, I. S., Newland, M. C., Brannon, S. E., & Howey, D. S. (1992). Effects of self-generated rules on the development of schedule controlled behavior. *Journal of the Experimental Analysis of Behavior, 58,* 107–121.

Rosenzweig, M. R., & Bennett, M. C. (1996). Psychobiology of plasticity: Effects of training and experience on brain and behavior. *Behavioural Brain Research, 78,* 57–65.

Ross, R. T., & Holland, P. C. (1981). Conditioning of simultaneous and serial feature positive discriminations. *Animal Learning and Behavior, 9,* 293–303.

Rowell, T. E. (1961). The family group in golden hamsters: Its formation and break-up. *Behaviour, 17,* 81–95.

Rozeboom, W. W. (1958). "What is learned?" An empirical enigma. *Psychological Review, 65,* 22–33.

Rozin, P. (1976). The selection of food by rats, humans and other animals. In J. Rosenblatt, R. A. Hinde, C. Beers, & E. Shaw (Eds.), *Advances in the study of behavior* (Vol. 6, pp. 21–76). New York: Academic Press.

Rozin, P., & Fallon, A. E. (1987). A perspective on disgust. *Psychological Review, 94,* 23–41.

Rozin, P., & Schull, J. (1988). The adaptive-evolutionary point of view in experimental psychology. In R. C. Atkinson, R. J. Herrnstein, G. Lindzey, and R. D. Luce (Eds.), *Stevens' handbook of experimental psychology* (2nd ed., Vol. 1, pp. 503–546). New York: Wiley.

Rozin, P., & Zellner, D. (1985). The role of Pavlovian conditioning in the acquisition of food likes and dislikes. In N. S. Braveman & P. Bronstein (Eds.), *Experimental assessments and clinical applications of conditioned food aversions* (pp. 189–202). New York: New York Academy of Sciences.

Ruddle, H., Bradshaw, C. M., Szabadi, E., & Bevan, P. (1979). Behaviour of humans in concurrent schedules programmed on spatially separated operanda. *Quarterly Journal of Experimental Psychology, 31,* 509–517.

Rushforth, N. B., Burnett, A., & Maynard, R. (1963). Behavior in Hydra: Contraction responses of Hydra pirardi to mechanical and light stimuli. *Science, 139,* 760–761.

Rutter, M. (1966). Prognosis: Psychotic children in adolescence and early adult life. In J. K. Wing (Ed.), *Early childhood autism: Clinical educational, and social aspects.* London: Pergamon Press.

Ryle, G. (1949). *The concept of mind.* London: Hutchinson.

Sahley, C. L. (1984). Behavior theory and invertebrate learning. In P. Marler & H. S. Terrace (Eds.), *The biology of learning* (pp. 181–196). New York: Springer-Verlag.

Sahley, C. L., Martin, K. A., & Gelperin, A. (1990). Analysis of associative learning in the terrestrial mollusc Limax maximus. II. Appetitive learning. *Journal of Comparative Physiology, 167,* 339–345.

Sahley, C. L., Rudy, J. W., & Gelperin, A. (1981). An analysis of associative learning in a terrestrial mollusc: Higher-order

conditioning, blocking and a transient US pre-exposure effect. *Journal of Comparative Physiology, 144,* 1–8.

Sajwaj, T., Twardosz, S., & Burke, M. (1972). Side effects of extinction procedures in a remedial preschool. *Journal of Applied Behavior Analysis, 5,* 163–175.

Samelson, F. (1980). Little Albert, Cyril Burt's twins, and the need for a critical science. *American Psychologist, 35,* 619–625.

Savastano, H. I., & Fantino, E. (1994). Human choice in concurrent ratio-interval schedules of reinforcement. *Journal of the Experimental Analysis of Behavior, 61,* 453–463.

Schachtman, T. R., Brown, A. M., & Miller, R. R. (1985). Reinstatement-induced recovery of a taste-LiCl association following extinction. *Animal Learning & Behavior, 13,* 223–227.

Schachtman, T. R., & Reilly, S. (2011). Things you always wanted to know about conditioning but were afraid to ask. In T. R. Schachtman & S. Reilly (Eds.), *Associative learning and conditioning theory: Human and non-human applications* (pp. 3–23). New York: Oxford University Press.

Schachtman, T. R., Walker, J., & Fowler, S. (2011). Conditioning and advertising. In T. R. Schachtman & S. Reilly (Eds.), *Associative learning and conditioning theory: Human and non-human applications*

(pp. 481–506). New York: Oxford University Press.

Schaffer, H. R., & Emerson, P. E. (1964). Patterns of response to physical contact in early human development. *Journal of Child Psychology and Psychiatry, 5,* 1–13.

Schaller, G. (1967). *The deer and the tiger.* Chicago: University of Chicago Press.

Schmajuk, N. A., & DiCarlo, J. J. (1992). Stimulus configuration, classical conditioning, and hippocampal functioning. *Psychological Review, 99,* 268–305.

Schmidt, R. A., & Young, D. E. (1991). Methodology for motor learning: A paradigm for kinematic feedback. *Journal of Motor Behavior, 23,* 13–24.

Schmidt-Hansen, M., Killcross, A. S., & Honey, R. C. (2009). Latent inhibition, learned irrelevance, and schizotypy: Assessing their relationship. *Cognitive Neuropsychiatry, 14,* 11–29.

Schneider, B. A. (1969). A two-state analysis of fixed-interval responding in the pigeon. *Journal of the Experimental Analysis of Behavior, 12,* 677–687.

Schnur, P. (1971). Selective attention: Effect of element preexposure on compound conditioning in rats. *Journal of Comparative and Physiological Psychology, 76,* 123–130.

Schoenfeld, W. N., & Cole, B. K. (1972). *Stimulus schedules: The t-T systems.* New York: Harper and Row.

Schoenfeld, W. N., Cumming, W. W., & Hearst, E. (1956). On the classification of reinforcement schedules. *Proceedings of the New York Academy of Sciences, 42,* 563–570.

Schreurs, B. G., & Westbrook, R. F. (1982). The effect of changes in the CS-US interval during compound conditioning upon an otherwise blocked element. *Quarterly Journal of Experimental Psychology, 34B,* 19–30.

Schwartz, B. (1974). On going back to nature: A review of Seligman and Hagar's biological boundaries of learning. *Journal of the Experimental Analysis of Behavior, 21,* 183–198.

Schwartz, B. (1980). Development of complex, stereotyped behavior in pigeons. *Journal of the Experimental Analysis of Behavior, 33,* 153–166.

Schwartz, B., & Williams, D. R. (1971). Discrete-trials spaced responding in the pigeon: The dependence of efficient performance on the availability of a stimulus for collateral pecking. *Journal of the Experimental Analysis of Behavior, 16,* 155–160.

Sclafani, A. (1990). Nutritionally based learning flavor preferences in rats. In E. D. Capaldi & T. L. Powley (Eds.), *Taste, experience, and feeding* (pp. 139–156). Washington, DC: American Psychological Association.

Sclafani, A. (2004). Oral and postoral determinants of food reward. *Physiology and Behavior, 81,* 773–779.

Segal, E. F. (1972). Induction and the provenance of operants. In R. M. Gilbert & J. R. Millenson (Eds.), *Reinforcement: Behavioral analyses* (pp. 1–34). New York: Academic.

Seligman, M. E. P. (1972). Phobias and preparedness. In M. E. P. Seligman & J. L. Hagar (Eds.), *Biological boundaries of learning* (pp. 251–262). New York: Appleton-Century-Crofts.

Seyfarth, R. M., & Chaney, D. L. (1980). Vocal development in vervet monkeys. *Animal Behaviour, 34,* 1450–1468.

Shanks, D. R. (1994). Human associative learning. In N. J. Mackintosh (Ed.), *Animal learning and cognition* (pp. 335–374). San Diego: Academic Press.

Shanks, D. R., & Dickinson, A. (1987). Associative accounts of causality judgment. In G. H. Bower (Ed.), *The psychology of learning and motivation* (Vol. 21, pp. 229–261). San Diego, CA: Academic Press.

Sherry, D. F., & Galef, B. G., Jr. (1984). Cultural transmission without imitation. *Animal Behaviour, 32,* 937–938.

Sherry, D. F., & Galef, B. G., Jr. (1990). Cultural transmission without imitation: More about bottle opening by birds. *Animal Behaviour, 40,* 987–989.

Shettleworth, S. J. (1975). Reinforcement and organization of behavior in golden hamsters: Hunger, environment, and food reinforcement. *Journal of Experimental Psychology: Animal Behavior Processes, 1,* 56–87.

Shettleworth, S. J. (1978). Reinforcement and organization of behavior in golden hamsters: Punishment of three action patterns. *Learning and Motivation, 9,* 99–123.

Shettleworth, S. J. (1983). Function and mechanism in learning. In M. D. Zeiler & P. Harzem (Eds.), *Advances in analysis of behaviour, Vol. 3: Biological factors in learning* (pp. 1–39). Chichester: Wiley.

Shettleworth, S. J. (1993). Varieties of learning and memory in animals. *Journal of Experimental Psychology: Animal Behavior Processes, 19,* 5–14.

Shettleworth, S. J. (1994). Biological approaches to the study of learning. In N. J. Mackintosh (Ed.), *Animal learning and cognition* (pp. 185–219). San Diego: Academic Press.

Shimoff, E., Catania, A. C., & Mathews, B. A. (1981). Uninstructed human responding: Sensitivity of low-rate performance to schedule contingencies. *Journal of the Experimental Analysis of Behavior, 36,* 207–220.

Shimp, C. P. (1966). Probabilistically reinforced choice behavior in pigeons. *Journal of the Experimental Analysis of Behavior, 61,* 453–463.

Shimp, C. P. (1969). Optimal behavior in free-response experiments. *Psychological Review, 76,* 97–112.

Shull, R. L. (1971). Sequential patterns in post-reinforcement pauses on fixed-interval schedules of food. *Journal of the Experimental Analysis of Behavior, 15,* 221–231.

Sidman, M. (1953a). Avoidance conditioning with brief shock and no exteroceptive warning signal. *Science, 118,* 157–158.

Sidman, M. (1953b). Two temporal parameters of the maintenance of avoidance behavior by the white rat. *Journal of Comparative and Physiological Psychology, 46,* 253–261.

Sidman, M. (1956). Time discrimination and behavior interaction in a free operant situation. *Journal of Comparative and Physiological Psychology, 49,* 469–473.

Siegel, S. (1972). Conditioning of insulin-induced glycemia. *Journal of Comparative and Physiological Psychology, 78,* 233–241.

Siegel, S. (1975). Conditioning insulin effects. *Journal of Comparative and Physiological Psychology, 89,* 189–199.

Siegel, S. (1977). Morphine tolerance acquisition as an associative process. *Journal of Experimental Psychology: Animal Behavior Processes, 3,* 1–13.

Siegel, S. (1984). Pavlovian conditioning and heroin overdose: Reports by overdose victims. *Bulletin of the Psychonomic Society, 22,* 428–430.

Siegel, S. (1985). Drug-anticipatory responses in animals.

In L. White, B. Tursky, & G. E. Schwartz (Eds.), *Placebo: Theory, research, and mechanisms* (pp. 288–305). New York: Guilford Press.

Siegel, S. (1999). Drug anticipation and drug addiction: The 1998 H. David Archibald lecture. *Addiction, 94,* 1113–1124.

Siegel, S. (2002). Explanatory mechanisms for placebo effects: Pavlovian conditioning. In H. A. Guess, A. Kleinman, J. W. Kusek, & L. W. Engel (Eds.), *The science of the placebo: Towards an interdisciplinary research agenda* (pp. 133–157). New York: BMY Books.

Siegel, S. (2005). Drug tolerance, drug addiction, and drug anticipation. *Current Direction in Psychological Science, 14,* 296–300.

Siegel, S., & Allan, L. G. (1996). The widespread influence of the Rescorla-Wagner model. *Psychonomic Bulletin and Review, 3,* 314–321.

Siegel, S., & Allan, L. G. (1998). Learning and homeostasis: Drug addiction and the McCollough Effect. *Psychological Bulletin, 124,* 230–239.

Siegel, S., Baptista, M. A. S., Kim, J. A., McDonald, R. V., & Weise-Kelly, L. (2000). Pavlovian psychopharmacology: The associative basis of tolerance. *Experimental and Clinical Psychopharmacology, 8,* 276–293.

Siegel, S., & Domjan, M. (1971). Backward conditioning as an inhibitory procedure. *Learning and Motivation, 2,* 1–11.

Siegel, S., Hinson, R. E., & Krank, M. D. (1978). The role of predrug signals in morphine analgesic tolerance: Support for a Pavlovian conditioning model of tolerance. *Journal of Experimental Psychology: Animal Behavior Processes, 4,* 188–196.

Siegel, S., Hinson, R. E., Krank, M. D., & McCully, J. (1982). Heroin "overdose" death: Contribution of drug-associated environmental cues. *Science, 216,* 436–437.

Siegel, S., & Ramos, B. M. C. (2002). Pavlovian psychopharmacology: The associative basis of tolerance. *Experimental and Clinical Psychopharmacology, 10,* 162–183.

Silberberg, A., Hamilton, B., Ziriax, J. M., & Casey, J. (1978). The structure of choice. *Journal of Experimental Psychology: Animal Behavior Processes, 4,* 368–398.

Silby, R. M., & MacFarland, D. J. (1976). On the fitness of behavioral sequences. *American Naturalist, 110,* 601–617.

Silva, F. J., & Timberlake, W. (2000). A clarification of the nature of backward excitatory conditioning. *Learning and Motivation, 31,* 1–20.

Silva, F. J., Timberlake, W., & Cevik, M. O. (1998). A behavior systems approach to the expression of backward associations. *Learning and Motivation, 29,* 1–22.

Silva, F. J., Timberlake, W., & Koehler, T. L. (1996). A behavior systems approach to bidirectional excitatory serial conditioning. *Learning and Motivation, 27,* 130–150.

Simon, H. A. (1956). Rational choice theory and the structure of the environment. *Psychological Review, 63,* 129–138.

Sims, C. R., Neth, H., Jacobs, R. A., & Gray, W. D. (2013). Melioration as rational choice: Sequential decision making in uncertain environments. *Psychological Review, 120,* 139–154.

Siqueland, E. R., & Lipsitt, L. P. (1966). Conditioned head-turning in human newborns. *Journal of Experimental Child Psychology, 3,* 356–376.

Skinner, B. F. (1930). On the conditions of elicitation of certain eating reflexes. *Proceedings of the National Academy of Sciences, 16,* 433–438.

Skinner, B. F. (1932a). Drive and reflex strength. *Journal of General Psychology, 6,* 22–37.

Skinner, B. F. (1932b). Drive and reflex strength: II. *Journal of General Psychology, 6,* 38–48.

Skinner, B. F. (1932c). On the rate of formation of a conditioned reflex. *Journal of General Psychology, 7,* 274–285.

Skinner, B. F. (1933a). On the rate of extinction of a conditioned reflex. *Journal of General Psychology, 8,* 114–129.

Skinner, B. F. (1933b). The abolishment of a discrimination. *Proceedings of the National Academy of Sciences, 19,* 825–828.

Skinner, B. F. (1933c). The rate of establishment of a discrimination. *Journal of General Psychology, 9,* 302–352.

Skinner, B. F. (1935a). The generic nature of the concepts of stimulus and response. *Journal of General Psychology, 12,* 40–65.

Skinner, B. F. (1935b). Two types of conditioned reflex and a pseudo-type. *Journal of General Psychology, 12,* 66–77.

Skinner, B. F. (1936). The reinforcing effect of a differentiating stimulus. *Journal of General Psychology, 14,* 263–278.

Skinner, B. F. (1937). Two types of conditioned reflex: A reply to Konorski and Miller. *Journal of General Psychology, 16,* 272–279.

Skinner, B. F. (1938). *The behavior of organisms.* New York: Appleton-Century-Crofts.

Skinner, B. F. (1945). The operational analysis of psychological terms. *Psychological Review, 52,* 270–277.

Skinner, B. F. (1948). Superstition in the pigeon. *Journal of Experimental Psychology, 38,* 168–172.

Skinner, B. F. (1950). Are theories of learning necessary? *Psychological Review, 57,* 193–216.

Skinner, B. F. (1953). *Science and human behavior.* New York: MacMillan.

Skinner, B. F. (1960). Pigeons in a pelican. *American Psychologist, 15,* 28–37.

Skinner, B. F. (1966). An operant analysis of problem solving. In B. Kleinmuntz (Ed.), *Problem-solving: Research, method, and teaching* (pp. 225–257). New York: Wiley.

Skinner, B. F. (1969). *Contingencies of reinforcement: A theoretical analysis.* New York: Appleton-Century-Crofts.

Skinner, B. F. (1974). *About behaviorism.* New York: Knopf.

Skinner, B. F. (1981). Selection by consequences. *Science, 213,* 501–504.

Skinner, B. F. (1984). Selection by consequences. *Behavioral and Brain Sciences, 7,* 477–510.

Slivka, R. M., & Bitterman, M. E. (1966). Classical appetitive conditioning in the pigeon. *Psychonomic Science, 4,* 181–183.

Small, W. S. (1900). Experimental study of the mental processes of the rat. *American Journal of Psychology, 11,* 133–165.

Small, W. S. (1901). Experimental study of the mental processes of the rat. II. *American Journal of Psychology, 12,* 206–239.

Smith, J. C., Blumsack, J. T., & Bilek, F. S. (1985). Radiation-induced taste aversions in rats and humans. In T. G. Burish, S. M. Levy, & B. E. Meyerowitz (Eds.), *Cancer, nutrition, and eating behavior. A biobehavioral perspective* (pp. 77–101). Hillsdale, NJ: Erlbaum.

Smith, J. C., & Roll, D. L. (1967). Trace conditioning with

X-rays as an aversive stimulus. *Psychonomic Science, 9,* 11–12.

Smith, K. (1984). "Drive": In defense of a concept. *Behaviorism, 12,* 71–114.

Smith, M. C., Coleman, S. R., & Gormezano, I. (1969). Classical conditioning of the rabbit's nictitating membrane response at backward, simultaneous, and forward CS-US intervals. *Journal of Comparative and Physiological Psychology, 69,* 226–231.

Smith, M. F. (1939). The establishment and extinction of the token-reward habit in the cat. *Journal of General Psychology, 20,* 475–486.

Smith, S. M. (2007). Context and human memory. In H. L. Roediger, III, Y. Dudai, & S. M. Fitzpatrick (Eds.), *Science of memory: Concepts* (pp. 111–114). New York: Oxford University Press.

Smith, S., & Guthrie, E. R. (1921). *General psychology in terms of behavior.* New York: Appleton-Century-Crofts.

Spear, N. E., & Riccio, D. C. (1994). *Memory: Phenomena and principles.* Boston: Allyn & Bacon.

Spence, K. W. (1937). Experimental studies of learning and higher mental processes in infra-human primates. *Psychological Bulletin, 34,* 806–850.

Spence, K. W., & Goldstein, H. (1961). Eyelid conditioning performance as a function of emotion-producing instructions. *Journal of Experimental Psychology, 62,* 291–294.

Spooner, A., & Kellogg, W. N. (1947). The backward conditioning curve. *American Journal of Psychology, 60,* 321–334.

Spooner, F., & Spooner, D. (1984). A review of chaining techniques: Implications for future research and practice. *Education and Training of the Mentally Retarded, 19,* 114–124.

Squire, L. R. (1982). The neuropsychology of human memory. *Annual Review of Neuroscience, 5,* 241–273.

Squire, L. R. (1992). Memory and the hippocampus: A synthesis from findings with rats, monkeys, and humans. *Psychological Review, 99,* 195–231.

Squire, L. R. (2004). Memory systems of the brain: A brief history and current perspective. *Neurobiology of Learning and Memory, 82,* 171–177.

Staats, A. W., & Staats, C. K. (1958). Attitudes established by classical conditioning. *Journal of Abnormal and Social Psychology, 57,* 37–40.

Staats, C. K., & Staats, A. W. (1957). Meaning established by classical conditioning. *Journal of Experimental Psychology, 54,* 74–80.

Staddon, J. E. R. (1965). Some properties of spaced responding. *Journal of the Experimental Analysis of Behavior, 8,* 19–28.

Staddon, J. E. R. (1975). Learning as adaptation. In W. K. Estes (Ed.), *Handbook of learning and cognitive processes,*

Vol. 2., Conditioning and behavior therapy (pp. 37–98). Hillsdale, NJ: Erlbaum.

Staddon, J. E. R. (1983). *Adaptive behavior and learning.* Cambridge: Cambridge University Press.

Staddon, J. E. R. (1988). Learning as inference. In R. C. Bolles & M. D. Beecher (Eds.), *Evolution and learning* (pp. 59–78). Hillsdale, NJ: Erlbaum.

Staddon, J. E. R., & Simmelhag, V. L. (1971). The "superstition" experiment: A reexamination of its implications for the principles of adaptive behavior. *Psychological Review, 78,* 3–43.

Stahl, C., & Unkelbach, C. (2009). Evaluative learning with single versus multiple USs: The role of contingency awareness. *Journal of Experimental Psychology: Animal Behavior Processes, 35,* 286–291.

Stahl, C., Unkelbach, C., & Corneille, O. (2009). On the respective contributions of awareness of US valence and US identity in attitude formation through evaluative conditioning. *Journal of Personality and Social Psychology, 97,* 404–420.

Stallings, J., Fleming, A. S., Corter, C., Worthman, C., & Steiner, M. (2001). The effects of infant cries and odors on sympathy, cortisol, and autonomic responses in new mothers and nonpostpartum women. *Parenting: Science and Practice, 1,* 71–100.

Stampfl, T. C., & Levis, D. J. (1967). Essentials of implosion therapy: A learning-therapy-based psychodynamic behavior therapy. *Journal of Abnormal Psychology, 72,* 496–503.

Steiner, J. E., Glaser, D., Hawilo, M. E., & Berridge, K. C. (2001). Comparative expression of hedonic impact: Affective reactions to taste by human infants and other primates. *Neuroscience and Biobehavioral Reviews, 25,* 53–74.

Steinmetz, J. E. (1998). The localization of a simple type of learning and memory: The cerebellum and classical eyeblink training. *Current Directions in Psychological Science, 7,* 72–77.

Stilling, S. T., & Critchfield, T. S. (2010). The matching relation and situation-specific bias modulation in professional football play selection. *Journal of the Experimental Analysis of Behavior, 93,* 435–454.

Stokes, P. D. (1995). Learned variability. *Animal Learning and Behavior, 23,* 164–176.

Stokes, P. D., & Balsam, P. D. (1991). Effects of reinforcing preselected approximations on the topography of the rat's bar press. *Journal of the Experimental Analysis of Behavior, 55,* 213–231.

Stokes, P. D., Mechner, F., & Balsam, P. D. (1999). Effects of different acquisition procedures on response variability. *Animal Learning and Behavior, 27,* 28–41.

Stuart, E. W., Shimp, T. A., & Engle, R. W. (1987). Classical

conditioning of consumer attitudes: Four experiments in an advertising context. *Journal of Consumer Research, 14,* 334–351.

Svartdal, F. (1995). When feedback contingencies and rules compete: Testing a boundary condition for verbal control of instrumental performance. *Learning and Motivation, 26,* 221–238.

Taylor, J. E., & Deane, F. P. (1999). Acquisition and severity of driving-related fears. *Behaviour Research and Therapy, 37,* 435–449.

Temple, J. L., Giacomelli, A. M., Roemmich, J. N., & Epstein, L. H. (2008). Habituation and within session changes in motivated responding for food in children. *Appetite, 50,* 390–396.

Thomas, B. L., Larsen, N., & Ayres, J. J. B. (2003). Role of context similarity in ABA, ABC, and AAB renewal paradigms: Implications for theories of renewal and for treating human phobias. *Learning and Motivation, 34,* 410–436.

Thompson, R. F. (2013). An essential memory trace found. *Behavioral Neuroscience, 127,* 669–675.

Thompson, R. F., & Spencer, W. A. (1966). Habituation: A model phenomenon for the study of neural substrates of behavior. *Psychological Review, 73,* 16–43.

Thorndike, E. L. (1898). Animal intelligence: An experimental study of the associative processes in animals. *Psychological Review*

Monographs Supplement, 2(4), Whole No. 8, 1–109.

Thorndike, E. L. (1901). The mental life of monkeys. *Psychological Review Monographs Supplement, 3*(5), Whole No. 15.

Thorndike, E. L. (1911). *Animal intelligence.* New York: Macmillan.

Thornton, A. (2008). Variation in contributions to teaching by meerkats. *Proceedings of the Royal Society of London (Series B), 275,* 1745–1751.

Thornton, A., & McAuliffe, K. (2006). Teaching in wild meerkats. *Science, 313,* 227–229.

Thorpe, W. H. (1956). *Learning and instinct in animals.* Cambridge, MA: Harvard University Press.

Thorpe, W. H. (1965). *Learning and instinct in animals* (2nd ed.). London: Metheun.

Tiffany, S. T., & Baker, T. B. (1981). Morphine tolerance in the rat: Convergence with a Pavlovian paradigm. *Journal of Comparative and Physiological Psychology, 95,* 747–762.

Timberlake, W. (1983a). The functional organization of appetitive behavior: Behavior systems and learning. In M. D. Zeiler & P. Harzem (Eds.), *Advances in analysis of behaviour (Vol. 3): Biological factors in learning* (pp. 177–221). Chichester: Wiley.

Timberlake, W. (1983b). Rats' responses to a moving object

related to food or water: A behavior-systems analysis. *Animal Learning and Behavior, 11,* 309–320.

Timberlake, W. (1990). Natural learning in laboratory paradigms. In D. A. Dewsbury (Ed.), *Contemporary issues in comparative psychology* (pp. 31–54). Sunderland, MA: Sinauer Associates.

Timberlake, W. (1994). Behavior systems, associationism, and Pavlovian conditioning. *Psychonomic Bulletin and Review, 1,* 405–420.

Timberlake, W., & Grant, D. L. (1975). Autoshaping in rats to the presentation of another rat predicting food. *Science, 190,* 690–692.

Timberlake, W., & Lucas, G. A. (1985). The basis of superstitious behavior: Chance contingency, stimulus substitution, or appetitive behavior? *Journal of the Experimental Analysis of Behavior, 44,* 279–299.

Timberlake, W., & Lucas, G. A. (1989). Behavior systems and learning: From misbehavior to general principles. In S. B. Klein & R. R. Mowrer (Eds.), *Contemporary learning theories: Instrumental conditioning theory and the impact of biological constraints on learning* (pp. 237–275). Hillsdale, NJ: Erlbaum.

Timberlake, W., Wahl, G., & King, D. (1982). Stimulus and response contingencies in the misbehavior of rats. *Journal of Experimental Psychology: Animal Behavior Processes, 8,* 62–85.

Timberlake, W., & Washburne, D. L. (1989). Feeding ecology and laboratory predatory behavior toward live and artificial moving prey in seven rodent species. *Animal Learning and Behavior, 17,* 2–10.

Tinklepaugh, O. L. (1928). An experimental study of representative factors in monkeys. *Journal of Comparative Psychology, 8,* 197–236.

Toates, F. (1986). *Motivational systems.* Cambridge: Cambridge University Press.

Todd, T. P. (2013). Mechanisms of renewal after the extinction of instrumental behavior. *Journal of Experimental Psychology: Animal Behavior Processes, 39,* 193–207.

Todd, T. P., Vurbic, D., & Bouton, M. E. (2014a). Behavioral and neurobiological mechanisms of extinction in Pavlovian and instrumental learning. *Neurobiology of Learning and Motivation, 108,* 52–64.

Todd, T. P., Vurbic, D., & Bouton, M. E. (2014b). Mechanisms of renewal after the extinction of discriminated operant behavior. *Journal of Experimental Psychology: Animal Learning and Cognition, 40,* 355–368.

Todd, T. P., Winterbauer, N. E., & Bouton, M. E. (2012). Effects of the amount of acquisition and contextual generalization on the renewal of instrumental behavior after extinction. *Learning & Behavior, 40,* 145–157.

Todes, D. P. (1997). From the machine to the ghost within: Pavlov's transition from digestive physiology to conditioned reflexes. *American Psychologist, 52,* 947–955.

Todrank, J., Byrnes, D., Wrzesniewski, A, & Rozin, P. (1995). Odors can change preferences for people in photographs: A cross-modal evaluative conditioning study with olfactory USs and visual CSs. *Learning and Motivation, 26,* 116–140.

Tolman, E. C. (1920). Instinct and purpose. *Psychological Review, 27,* 218–233.

Tolman, E. C. (1932). *Purposive behavior in animals and men.* New York: Appleton-Century-Crofts.

Tolman, E. C. (1949a). There is more than one kind of learning. *Psychological Review, 56,* 144–155.

Tolman (1949b). The nature and functioning of wants. *Psychological Review, 56,* 357–369.

Tolman, E. C., & Brunswik, E. (1935). The organism and the causal texture of the environment. *Psychological Review, 42,* 43–77.

Tomasello, M. (1990). Cultural transmission in the tool use and communicatiory signaling of chimpanzees? In S. Parker & K. Gibson (Eds.), *"Language" and intelligence in monkeys and apes: Comparative developmental perspectives* (pp. 274–311). Cambridge: Cambridge University Press.

Tomasello, M. (1996). Do apes ape? In C. W. Heyes & B. G. Galef, Jr. (Eds.), *Social learning in animals: The roots of culture* (pp. 319–346). New York: Academic Press.

Tomasello, M., Davis-Dasilva, M., Camak, L., & Bard, K. (1987). Observational learning of tool-use by young chimpanzees. *Human Evolution, 2,* 175–183.

Tomie, A., Murphy, A. L., & Fath, S. (1980). Retardation of autoshaping following pretraining with unpredictable food: Effects of changing the context between pretraining and testing. *Learning and Motivation, 11,* 117–134.

Trapold, M. A. (1970). Are expectancies based on different positive reinforcing events discriminably different? *Learning and Motivation, 1,* 129–140.

Trapold, M. A., & Overmier, J. B. (1972). The second learning process in instrumental learning. In A. H. Black & W. F. Prokasy (Eds.), *Classical conditioning II: Current research and theory* (pp. 427–452). New York: Appleton-Century-Crofts.

Trowbridge, M. H., & Cason, H. (1932). An experimental test of Thorndike's theory of learning. *Journal of General Psychology, 7,* 245–260.

Tuber, D. S. (1986). Dominance, the bidirectional hypothesis, and Pavlovian backward conditioning in the US-US paradigm. *Animal Learning and Behavior, 14,* 421–426.

Tulving, E. (1972). Episodic and semantic memory. In E. Tulving & W. Donaldson (Eds.), *Organization of memory* (pp. 381–403). New York: Academic Press.

Tulving, E. (1985). How many memory systems are there? *American Psychologist, 40,* 385–398.

Tunney, R. J., & Shanks, D. R. (2002). A re-examination of melioration and rational choice. *Journal of Behavioral Decision Making, 15,* 291–311.

Turnbull, H. W. (1961). *The great mathematicians.* New York: New York University Press.

Urushihara, K. (2004). Excitatory backward conditioning in an appetitive conditioned reinforcement preparation with rats. *Behavioural Processes, 67,* 477–489.

Valentine, C. W. (1930). The innate bases and fear. *Journal of Genetic Psychology, 37,* 393–419.

Valsecchi, P., Choleris, E., Moles, A., Guo, C., & Mainardi, M. (1996). Kinship and familiarity as factors affecting social transfer of food preferences in adult Mongolian gerbils (Meriones unguiculatus). *Journal of Comparative Psychology, 110,* 243–251.

Valsecchi, P., & Galef, B. G., Jr. (1989). Social influences on the food preferences of house mice (Mus musculus). *International Journal of Comparative Psychology, 2,* 245–256.

van Osselaer, S. M. J., & Alba, J. W. (2000). Consumer learning and brand equity. *Journal of Consumer Research, 27,* 1–16.

Vansteenwegen, D., Francken, G., Vervliet, B., De Clercq, A., & Eelen, P. (2006). Resistance to extinction in evaluative conditioning. *Journal of Experimental Psychology: Animal Behavior Processes, 32,* 71–79.

Vaughn, W., Jr. (1981). Melioration, matching, and maximization. *Journal of the Experimental Analysis of Behavior, 36,* 141–149.

Vaughn, W., Jr., Kardish, T. A., & Wilson, M. (1982). Correlation versus contiguity in choice. *Behavioral Analysis Newsletters, 2,* 153–160.

Vervliet, B., Craske, M. G., & Hermans, D. (2013). Fear extinction and relapse state of the art. *Annual Review of Clinical Psychology, 9,* 215–248.

Vestergaard, K., Hogan, J. A., & Kruijt, J. P. (1990). The development of a behavior system: Dustbathing in the Burmese red junglefowl: I. The influence of the rearing environment on the organization of dustbathing. *Behaviour, 112,* 99–116.

Vieth, W., Curio, E., & Ernst, U. (1980). The adaptive significance of avian mobbing III. Cultural transmission of enemy recognition in blackbirds: Cross-species tutoring and properties of learning. *Animal Behaviour, 28,* 1217–1229.

Voelkl, B., & Huber, L. (2000). True imitation in marmosets. *Animal Behavior, 60,* 195–202.

Voelkl, B., & Huber, L. (2007). Imitation as faithful copying of a novel technique in marmoset monkeys. *PLoS ONE 2,* e611. (doi:10.1371/journal. pone.0000611)

Vogel, R., & Annau, Z. (1973). An operant discrimination task allowing variability of reinforced response patterning. *Journal of the Experimental Analysis of Behavior, 20,* 1–6.

Vollmer, T. R., & Bourret, J. (2000). An application of the matching law to evaluate the allocation of two- and three-point shots by college basketball players. *Journal of Applied Behavior Analysis, 33,* 137–150.

Von Frisch, K. (1974). Decoding the language of the bee. *Science, 185,* 663–668.

Vyse, S. A., & Belke, T. W. (1992). Maximizing versus matching on concurrent variable-interval schedules. *Journal of the Experimental Analysis of Behavior, 58,* 325–334.

Wagenaar, W. A. (1970). Generation of random sequences by human subjects: A critical survey of literature. *Psychological Bulletin, 77,* 65–72.

Wagner, A. R., Logan, F. A., Haberlandt, K., & Price, T.

(1968). Stimulus selection in animal discrimination learning. *Journal of Experimental Psychology, 76,* 171–180.

Walls, R. T., Zane, T., & Ellis, W. D. (1981). Forward and backward chaining, and whole task methods: Training assembly tasks in vocational rehabilitation. *Behavior Modification, 5,* 61–74.

Walters, G. C., & Glaser, R. D. (1971). Punishment of instinctive behavior in the Mongolian gerbil. *Journal of Comparative and Physiological Psychology, 75,* 331–340.

Walther, E. (2002). Guilty by mere association: EC and the spreading attitude effect. *Journal of Personality and Social Psychology, 82,* 919–934.

Walther, E., Gawronski, B., Blank, H., & Langer, T. (2009). Changing likes and dislikes through the back door: The US-revaluation effect. *Cognition and Emotion, 23,* 889–917.

Walther, E., & Nagengast, B. (2006). Evaluative conditioning and the awareness issue: Assessing contingency awareness with the four-picture recognition test. *Journal of Experimental Psychology: Animal Behavior Processes, 32,* 454–459.

Wanchisen, B. A., Tatham, T. A., & Mooney, S. E. (1989). Variable-ratio conditioning history produces high- and low-rate fixed-interval performance in rats. *Journal of the Experimental Analysis of Behavior, 52,* 167–179.

Warner, L. H., & Warden, C. J. (1927). The development of a standard animal maze. *Archives of Psychology, 93,* 1–35.

Wasserman, E. A. (1973). Pavlovian conditioning with heat reinforcement produces stimulus-directed pecking in chicks. *Science. 181,* 875–877.

Wasserman, E. A. (1974). Stimulus-reinforcer predictiveness and selective discrimination learning in pigeons. *Journal of Experimental Psychology, 103,* 284–297.

Wasserman, E. A. (1978). The relationship between motor and secretory behaviors in classical appetitive conditioning. *Pavlovian Journal of Biological Science, 13,* 182–186.

Wasserman, E. A. (1990). Detecting response-outcome relations: Toward an underlying understanding of the causal texture of the environment. *The Psychology of Learning and Motivation, 26,* 27–82.

Wasserman, E. A., Franklin, S., & Hearst, E. (1974). Pavlovian appetitive contingencies and approach vs. withdrawal to conditioned stimuli in pigeons. *Journal of Comparative and Physiological Psychology, 86,* 616–627.

Watson, J. B. (1919). *Psychology from the standpoint of a behaviorist.* Philadelphia: Lippincott.

Watson, J. B., & Rayner, R. (1920). Conditioned emotional reactions. *Journal of Experimental Psychology, 3,* 1–14.

Watson, J. S. (1984). Bases of causal inference in infancy: Time, space, and sensory relations. In L. P. Lipset & C. Rovee-Collier (Eds.), *Advances in infancy research* (Vol. 3, pp. 152–160). Norwood, NJ: Ablex.

Weber, J. N., Peterson, B. K., & Hoekstra, H. E. (2013). Discrete genetic modules are responsible for the evolution of complex burrowing behaviour in deer mice. *Nature, 493*, 402–405.

Weiler, I. J., Hawrylak, N., & Greenough, W. T. (1995). Morphogenesis in memory formation: Synaptic and cellular mechanisms. *Behavioural Brain Research, 66*, 1–6.

Weiner, H. (1964). Conditioning history and human fixed-interval performance. *Journal of the Experimental Analysis of Behavior, 7*, 383–385.

Weiner, H. (1965). Conditioning history and maladaptive human behavior. *Psychological Reports, 17*, 935–942.

Weiner, H. (1969). Controlling human fixed-interval performance. *Journal of the Experimental Analysis of Behavior, 12*, 349–373.

Weiner, H. (1970). Human behavioral persistence. *The Psychological Record, 20*, 445–456.

Weingarten, H. P. (1983). Conditioned cues elicit feeding in sated rats: A role for learning in meal initiation. *Science, 220*, 431–433.

Weiss, B., & Laties, V. G. (1961). Behavioral thermoregulation. *Science, 133*, 1338–1344.

Wesp, R. K., Lattal, K. A., & Poling, A. D. (1977). Punishment of autoshaped key-peck responses of pigeons. *Journal of the Experimental Analysis of Behavior, 27*, 407–418.

Westbrook, R. F., Jones, M. L., Bailey, G. K., & Harris, J. A. (2000). Contextual control over conditioned responding in a latent inhibition paradigm. *Journal of Experimental Psychology: Animal Behavior Processes, 26*, 157–173.

White, N. M., Packard, M. G., & McDonald, R. J. (2013). Dissociation of memory systems: The story unfolds. *Behavioral Neuroscience, 127*, 669–675.

Whiten, A., Goodall, J., McGrew, W. C., Nishida, T., Reynolds, V., Sugiyama, Y., . . . Boesch, C. (1999). Cultures in chimpanzees. *Nature, 399*, 682–685.

Whiten, A., & Ham, R. (1992). On the nature and evolution of imitation in the animal kingdom: Reappraisal of a century of research. *Advances in the Study of Behavior, 21*, 239–283.

Wike, E. L. (1966). *Secondary reinforcement: Selected experiments.* New York: Harper & Row.

Wilcoxon, H., Dragoin, W., & Kral, P. (1971). Illness-induced aversions in rat and quail: Relative salience of visual and gustatory cues. *Science, 171*, 826–828.

Wilkenfield, J., Nickel, M., Blakely, E., & Poling, A. (1992). Acquisition of lever-press responding in rats with delayed reinforcement: A comparison of three procedures. *Journal of the Experimental Analysis of Behavior, 58*, 431–443.

Willcocks, A. L., & McNally, G. P. (2011). The role of context in re-acquisition of extinguished alcoholic beer-seeking. *Behavioral Neuroscience, 125*, 541–550.

Williams, B. A. (1988). Reinforcement, choice, and response strength. In R. C. Atkinson, R. J. Herrnstein, G. Lindzey, & R. D. Luce (Eds.), *Stevens' handbook of experimental psychology* (2nd ed., pp. 167–244). New York: Wiley.

Williams, B. A. (1994a). Reinforcement and choice. In N. J. Mackintosh (Ed.), *Animal learning and cognition* (pp. 81–108). San Diego, CA: Academic Press.

Williams, B. A. (1994b). Conditioned reinforcement: Neglected or outmoded explanatory concept. *Psychonomic Bulletin & Review, 1*, 457–475.

Williams, B. A., & McDevitt, M. A. (1996). Inhibition and superconditioning. *Psychological Science, 13*, 454–459.

Williams, B. A., & McDevitt, M. A. (2002). Inhibition and superconditioning. *Psychological Science, 13*, 454–459.

Williams, D. A., Butler, M. M., & Overmier, J. B. (1990). Expectancies of reinforcer location and quality as cues for a conditional discrimination. *Journal of Experimental Psychology: Animal Behavior Processes, 16*, 3–13.

Williams, D. A., Frame, K. A., & LoLordo, V. M. (1992). Discrete signals for the unconditioned stimulus fail to overshadow contextual or temporal conditioning. *Journal of Experimental Psychology: Animal Behavior Processes, 18,* 41–55.

Williams, D. A., & LoLordo. V. M. (1995). Time cues block the CS, but the CS does not block time cues. *Quarterly Journal of Experimental Psychology, 48B,* 97–116.

Williams, D. A., Overmier, J. B., & LoLordo, V. M. (1992). A reevaluation of Rescorla's early dictums about Pavlovian conditioned inhibition. *Psychological Bulletin, 111,* 275–290.

Williams, D., & Williams, H. (1969). Automaintenance in the pigeon: Sustained pecking despite contingent non-reinforcement. *Journal of the Experimental Analysis of Behavior, 12,* 511–520.

Williams, J. M. G., Mathews, A., & MacLeod, C. (1996). The emotional stroop task and psychopathology. *Psychological Bulletin, 120,* 3–24.

Williams, K. A. (1929). The reward value of a conditioned stimulus. *University of California Publications in Psychology, 4,* 31–55.

Willingham, D. B., Salidis, J., & Gabrieli, J. D. E. (2002). Direct comparison of neural systems mediating conscious and unconscious skill learning. *Journal of Neurophysiology, 88,* 1451–1460.

Wilson, G. D. (1968). Reversal of differential GSR conditioning by instructions. *Journal of Experimental Psychology, 76,* 491–493.

Wilson, M. P., & Keller, F. S. (1953). On the selective reinforcement of spaced responding. *Journal of Comparative and Physiological Psychology, 46,* 190–193.

Wilson, P. N., Boakes, R. A., & Swan, J. (1987). Instrumental learning as a result of omission training on wheel running. *Quarterly Journal of Experimental Psychology, 39B,* 161–171.

Winterbauer, N. E., Lucke, S., & Bouton, M. E. (2013). Some factors modulating the strength of resurgence after extinction of an instrumental behavior. *Learning and Motivation, 44,* 60–71.

Wittlin, W. A., & Brookshire, K. H. (1968). Apomorphine-induced conditioned aversion to a novel food. *Psychonomic Science, 12,* 217–218.

Wolf, M. M., Risley, T. R., & Mees, H. (1964). Application of operant conditioning procedures to the behaviour problems of an autistic child. *Behaviour Research and Therapy, 1,* 305–312.

Wolfe, J. B. (1936). Effectiveness of token rewards for chimpanzees. *Comparative Psychology Monograph, 12*(60), 1–72.

Wolpe, J. (1958). *Psychotherapy by reciprocal inhibition.* Stanford, CA: Stanford University Press.

Wolpe, J., & Rachman, S. (1960). Psychoanalytic evidence: A critique based on Freud's case of Little Hans. *Journal of Nervous and Mental Disease, 131,* 135–145.

Wood, D. C. (1973). Stimulus-specific habituation in a protozoan. *Physiology and Behavior, 11,* 349–354.

Woodruff, G., & Williams, D. R. (1976). The associative relation underlying autoshaping in the pigeon. *Journal of the Experimental Analysis of Behavior, 26,* 1–14.

Wortman, C. B. (1975). Some determinants of perceived control. *Journal of Personality and Social Psychology, 31,* 282–294.

Wright, J. C. (1962). Consistency and complexity of response sequences as a function of schedules of noncontingent reward. *Journal of Experimental Psychology, 63,* 601–609.

Wrightman, D. C., & Sistrunk, F. (1987). Part-task training strategies in simulated carrier landing final-approach training. *Human Factors, 29,* 245–254.

Yeo, A. G. (1974). The acquisition of conditioned suppression as a function of interstimulus interval duration. *Quarterly Journal of Experimental Psychology, 26,* 405–416.

Yerkes, R. M., & Morgulis, S. (1909). The method of Pawlow in animal psychology. *Psychological Bulletin, 6,* 257–273.

Yin, H. H., & Knowlton, B. J. (2006). The role of the basal

ganglia in habit formation. *Nature Reviews Neuroscience, 7,* 464–476.

Yin, H. H., Knowlton, B. J., & Balleine, B. W. (2004). Lesions of dorsolateral striatum preserve outcome expectancy but disrupt habit formation in instrumental learning. *European Journal of Neuroscience, 19,* 181–189.

Yin, H. H., Ostlund, S. B., Knowlton, B. J., & Balleine, B. W. (2005). The role of the dorsomedial striatum in instrumental conditioning. *European Journal of Neuroscience, 22,* 513–523.

Zajonc, R. B. (1965). Social facilitation. *Science, 149,* 269–274.

Zajonc, R. B. (1980). Feeling and thinking: Preferences need no inferences. *American Psychologist, 35,* 151–175.

Zajonc, R. B. (1984). On the primacy of affect. *American Psychologist, 39,* 117–123.

Zamble, E. (1973). Augmentation of eating following a signal for feeding in rats. *Learning and Motivation, 4,* 138–147.

Zamble, E., Baxter, D. J., & Baxter, L. (1980). Influences of conditioned incentive stimuli on water intake. *Canadian Journal of Psychology, 34,* 82–85.

Zapata, A., Minney, V. L., & Shippenberg, T. S. (2010). Shift from goal-directed to habitual cocaine seeking after prolonged experience in rats. *Journal of Neuroscience, 30,* 15457–15463.

Zarcone, T. J., Branch, M. N., Hughes, C. E., Pennypacker, H. S. (1997). Key pecking during extinction after intermittent or continuous reinforcement as a function of the number of reinforcers delivered during training. *Journal of the Experimental Analysis of Behavior, 67,* 91–108.

Zeaman, D. (1949). Response latency as a function of the amount of reinforcement. *Journal of Experimental Psychology, 39,* 466–483.

Zeiler, M. D. (1970a). Other behavior: Consequences of reinforcing not responding. *Journal of Psychology, 74,* 149–155.

Zeiler, M. D. (1970b). Time limits for completing fixed ratios. *Journal of the Experimental Analysis of Behavior, 14,* 275–286.

Zeiler, M. (1977). Schedules of reinforcement: The controlling variables. In W. K. Honig & J. E. Staddon (Eds.), *Handbook of operant behavior* (pp. 201–232). Englewood Cliffs, NJ: Prentice-Hall.

Zellner, D. A., Rozin, P., Aron, M., & Kulish, C. (1983). Conditioned enhancement of human's liking for flavor by pairing with sweetness. *Learning and Motivation, 14,* 338–350.

Zener, K. (1937). The significance of behavior accompanying conditioned salivary secretion for theories of the conditioned response. *American Journal of Psychology, 50,* 384–403.

Zentall, T. R. (1996). An analysis of imitative learning in animals. In C. W Heyes & B. G. Galef, Jr. (Eds.), *Social learning in animals: The roots of culture* (pp. 221–243). New York: Academic Press.

Zentall, T. R. (2001). Imitation in animals: Evidence, function and mechanism. *Cybernetic Systems, 32,* 53–96.

Zentall, T. R., Sutton, J. E., & Sherburne, L. M. (1996). True imitative learning in pigeons. *Psychological Science, 7,* 343–346.

Zettle, R. D., & Hayes, S. C. (1982). Rule-governed behavior: A potential theoretical framework for cognitive-behavior therapy. In P. C. Kendall (Ed.), *Advances in cognitive-behavioral research and therapy* (pp. 73–118). New York: Academic Press.

Zironi, I., Burattini, C., Aicardi, G., & Janak, P. H. (2006). Context is a trigger for relapse to alcohol. *Behavioural Brain Research, 167,* 150–155.

Zirpoli, T. J., & Melloy, K. J. (1997). *Behavior management: Applications for teachers and parents* (2nd ed.). Upper Saddle River, NJ: Merrill.

AUTHOR INDEX

Dittmar, K., 443
Domjan, M., 66, 102, 114, 189, 202, 208
Donahue, J. W., 141
Dorrance, B. R., 451
Doughty, A. H., 405
Dragoin, W., 69, 112
Dreyfus, L. R., 362
Dumas, M., 198
Dumas, M. J., 208
Dunn, C., 197
Dunn, T., 259, 260 (figure)
Durlach, P. J., 170, 441
Dyal, J. A., 29
Dykman, R. A., 14

Eckerman, D. A., 295, 297
Edmunds, M., 196 wards, L. E., 438
Edwards, L. E., 438
Eelen, P., 160, 203, 204, 205, 209
Egleston, D., 193
Eidelman, A. I., 188 (box)
Eikelboom, R., 65
Eisenberg, L., 265
Elder, J. H., 239
Elder, R. L., 438
el-Guebaly, N., 66 (box)
Elkins, R. L., 126
Elliott, M. H., 236–237 (figure), 238 (figure), 283, 389
Ellis, W. D., 233
Emerson, P. E., 17
Engle, R. W., 204
Engler, H., 60–61
English, H. B., 53–54, 101
Epling, W. F., 342, 354
Epstein, L. H., 12
Epstein, R., 404
Ernst, U., 444–445 (figure)
Ervin, F. R., 67
Escobar, R., 409
Estes, W. K., 56
Eth, S., 14
Evans, S. L., 438
Everitt, B. J., 403, 404
Ewer, R. F., 191, 193

Fackelman, P., 198
Falchetto, S., 405
Fallon, A. E., 436 (note 1)
Fanselow, M. S., 8, 189, 196, 206
Fantino, E., 349
Fantz, R. L., 243
Fath, S., 126
Favell, J. E., 266 (box)
Ferreira, A., 188 (box)
Ferster, C. B., 262 (box), 264, 296, 297, 300, 307, 310 (figure), 311 (figure), 313 (figure), 317 (figure), 319 (figure), 337, 340
Field, A., 205
Field, J., 208
Field, R. M., 451
Findley, J. D., 337–338, 340
Fineberg, N. A., 403
Finke, R. A., 141
Finnigan, H., 125
Fisher, J., 446, 447 (box)– 448, 449
Fisher, W. W., 342
Flanagan, B., 264
Fleming, A. S., 188 (box)
Fleshler, M., 319
Flynn, F. W., 71
Foote, F., 443
Foree, D. D., 466
Forman, R. R., 431
Formby, D., 188 (box)
Forrest, C. L., 208
Forsyth, J. P., 443–444
Foss, B. M., 451
Fouts, D. H., 455
Fouts, R., 455
Fowler, H., 240
Fowler, S., 204
Frame, K. A., 172–173
Francisco, M. T., 354
Francken, G., 204
Frank, R., 121
Franklin, S., 75, 201, 207
Franklin, S. R., 95, 201
Franks, C. M., 46
Franks, J. F., 405

Freberg, L., 155
Freeman, T. J., 324–325
Freise, B., 440
Freitag, G., 267 (box), 268–269, 416
Frieman, J., 193, 438
Frommer, G. P., 75, 194, 201, 416
Fry, W., 296
Fukunaga, K. K., 196
Funk, D., 406
Furini, C. R. G., 177
Furlong, T. M., 403
Furrow, D. R., 153

Gabrieli, J. D. E., 3
Gagne, R. M., 404
Gaither, G. A., 12
Galef, B. G., Jr., 192, 193, 436, 437 (figure), 438, 439 (figure), 440, 441, 446, 448–449 (table), 451
Galizio, M., 457, 461, 462
Gallistel, C. R., 141, 172, 362, 415
Garcia, J., 29, 67–68 (table/ figure), 111, 113, 202, 203, 208, 391
Gardner, B. T., 28, 262 (box)
Gardner, M. R., 452 (box)
Gardner, R. A., 28, 262 (box)
Garrick, T., 14
Gasbarri, A., 403
Gawronski, B., 204
Gelperin, A., 208
George, L. K., 14 (box)
Gerber, G. J., 405
Giacomelli, A. M., 12
Gibbon, J., 77, 172, 173
Gibson, E. J., 30
Gilbert, R. M., 413
Gilbertson, M. W., 14 (box)
Gillan, C. M., 403
Gillette, K., 69
Ginsburg, S., 26
Ginton, A., 114
Giurfa, M., 208
Glaser, D., 71, 202

White, N. E., 133
White, N. M., 8
Whiten, A., 31–32, 435, 436, 446
Wiens, K., 438
Wigmore, S. W., 437 (figure), 438, 439 (figure)
Wihbey, K. A., 406
Wike, E. L., 249
Wilcoxon, H., 69, 112
Wilhelm, F. H., 204
Wilkenfield, J., 285, 381, 382 (figure)
Wilkie, D. M., 102, 197
Willcocks, A. L., 405
Williams, B. A., 135, 284, 342, 347, 354
Williams, D., 74, 76, 215, 301
Williams, D. A., 163, 172–173, 173–174, 390
Williams, D. R., 185, 189, 201, 297
Williams, H., 74, 76, 215, 301
Williams, J., 208
Williams, J. M. G., 443
Williams, K. A., 247
Williams, S. L., 204
Willingham, D. B., 3

Willows, A. O. D., 29
Wilson, G. D., 54, 456
Wilson, M., 360–361 (table)
Wilson, M. P., 296, 297
Wilson, P. N., 260–262 (box), 261 (table), 263 (figure)
Winterbauer, N. E., 404, 406, 409
Witcher, E. S., 104
Witherington, D., 30
Wittlin, W. A., 113
Wixted, J. T., 321–322
Wolf, M. M., 231
Wolfe, J. B., 246–247
Wolkenstein, B., 442
Wolpe, J., 52, 443
Wood, D. C., 12
Woodruff, G., 185, 189, 201
Woods, S. C., 65, 200
Woodside, B., 183 (figure)–184 (figure), 185, 189, 201, 207
Worthman, C., 188 (box)
Wortman, C. B., 461
Wright, J. C., 461
Wrightman, D. C., 233
Wrzesniewski, A., 204

Yamamoto, K. Y., 354
Yeo, A. G., 96
Yerkes, R. M., 19 (figure), 218
Yin, H. H., 403
Young, D. E., 295, 462
Yzerbyt, V., 204

Zajonc, R. B., 203, 448
Zamble, E., 201
Zane, T., 233
Zapata, A., 403
Zarcone, T. J., 331
Zbukvic, I., 177
Zeaman, D., 283
Zeiler, M., 307, 310
Zeiler, M. D., 297, 377–379, 420, 423
Zellner, D., 203
Zener, K., 182, 185
Zentall, T. R., 436, 446, 451
Zettle, R. D., 456, 461, 462
Zhuang, P., 3
Ziriax, J. M., 360
Zironi, I., 406
Zirpoli, T. J., 232
Zuberbühler, K., 435

SUBJECT INDEX

Blocking
  defining, 123, 137, 470
  of hedonic qualities of US,
    150 (table)–151
  passage of time and, 173–174
Blue gourami behavior
    (examples)
  defense of territory, 197–198
    (figure), 199 (figure)
  reproductive fitness, 208
Break and run pattern, 309,
  311–312, 316

Caregiving behavior system,
    in humans, 187 (box)–188
    (box)
Catatonic patient, shaping to
    talk, 231 (box)–232 (box)
Cat behavior (examples)
  conditioned reinforcers, 247
  instrumental learning,
    218–221, 219 (figure),
    220 (box)–221 (box), 271
  predatory behavior, 186, 454
Causal inference
  conditions for promoting,
    375
  defining, 81, 82, 470
  differences from evaluative
    conditioning, 205
  effects of temporal proximity
    and contingency on, 383
  human behavior examples,
    83 (box)–84 (box)
  learned irrelevance and, 116
  overshadowing and, 112
  See also Inference; Operant
    conditioning, as
    inference task; Pavlovian
    conditioning, as
    inference task
Cause-and-effect relationships,
  465–466
Chaining, 233, 470
Changeover delay (COD),
  339, 470
  over-/undermatching and,
    352–353

Chaos theory, 418
Cheetahs, opportunity teaching
    and, 454
Chemotherapy, conditioned
    taste aversions and, 66–67,
    112–113, 209, 457
Chicken behavior (examples)
  behavior-outcome
    contingencies,
    380 (box)–381 (box)
  instrumental learning, 222
  sign-tracking, 75
  See also Bird behavior
    (examples)
Chimpanzee behavior
    (example)
  coaching, 454
  conditioned reinforcers,
    246–247
  demonstration, 454–455
  goal emulation, 450
  opportunity teaching, 455
  physical guidance (putting
    through), 455
  relativity of effectiveness of
    reinforcers, 239
Choice, concurrent choice
    situation, 340, 349–350,
    355, 362. See also
    Matching
Circus animal training, putting
    through procedure and,
    232
Classical conditioning,
  37 (note 1)
Coaching, 454, 470
Cognitive abilities, 32
Cognitive relational
    learning, 457
Collateral behavior, 297, 470
Commands, 455, 470
Commission work, schedules of
    partial reinforcement and,
    312, 314
Compensatory response
  defining, 199, 470
  function of, 200
  See also Mirroring

Complete temporal
    contiguity, 96
Compound CS, 111
Concurrent choice,
    340, 349–350, 355,
    362, 470
Concurrent schedules of
    reinforcement
  defining, 470
  empirical matching law and,
    337–339, 338 (figure)
  schedule-control procedure,
    337–338 (figure), 340,
    342, 346, 362, 363
  side-by-side procedure, 337,
    338 (figure), 339, 362
Conditioned drug reactions,
    60–65
  as context specific, 168, 200
  conditioned
    immunosuppression
    and, 60–62 (table)
  functions of, 199–200
  heroin overdose survival,
    64 (box)
  mimicking drug effect and,
    60–62 (table)
  mimicking/mirroring
    differences and, 64–65
  mirroring drug effect and,
    62–64
  placebo effects and, 62
  See also Drugs
Conditioned emotional
    response
  appetitive events and,
    206 (table)
  autonomic nervous system
    and, 197
  aversive events and,
    206 (table)
  defining, 470
  extinction and, 52, 54, 93
  fear as intervening variable
    in, 50, 55, 59
  human behavior example
    of, 50–55, 51 (box)–52
    (box), 206, 443

Contingency- *vs.* verbally
mediated behaviors,
461–462
Continuous reinforcement
schedule, 305–306, 471
Control, illusion of, 461
Crows, browsing subsystem of,
194. *See also* Bird behavior
(examples)
CS preexposure effect
as context specific,
168, 170–171
CTA learning and, 113–114
(table)
defining, 471
learned irrelevance and, 118
negative CS-US contingency
and, 115
positive CS-US contingency
and, 115
salience and, 113–115,
114 (table)
temporal proximity and, 115
zero CS-US contingency
and, 113
CS-US contingency, Pavlovian
conditioning and, 86–96
defining CS-US
contingency, 471
effects of contingencies,
90–92 (figure), 91 (table)
negative, CS predicts absence
of US, 88–89, 90 (table)
positive, CS predicts
occurrence of US,
87–88, 89–90 (table)
summary of various
contingencies,
89–90 (table)
varying degree of
contingency and, 92–96,
93 (figure), 94 (figure/
table), 95 (figure)
zero, CS predicts nothing
about occurrence of US,
89, 90 (table)
See also Negative CS-US
contingency; Positive

CS-US contingency;
Zero CS-US
contingency
Cues, relative validity of, 121
Cultural evolution, 31, 472
Cultural transmission of
knowledge, 28–29, 435,
465, 472. *See also* Social
transmission of knowledge
Cumulative record, 226–227
(figure), 229 (figure), 472
Cumulative recorder,
226 (figure), 472

Darwin, Charles, 24 (box)–26
(box), 413
Declarative knowledge
(knowing that)
defining, 2–3, 4 (figure), 472
instrumental learning/
operant conditioning as,
384–385
obtained during cultural
transmission, 29
operant conditioning and,
383, 385–386, 402
Pavlovian conditioning and,
144–148, 145 (table),
146 (figure), 147 (figure),
385–388, 386 (table),
387 (table/figure)
procedural knowledge *vs.*,
143
transition to procedural
knowledge and,
400 (table)–401 (figure)
Delay conditioning, 46, 47
(figure), 96, 172, 381, 472
Delayed reflex, 46, 472
Demonstration, 454–455, 472
Dependent variable
conditioned emotional
responses and, 59
defining, xxii, 7, 9 (table), 472
Descartes, René, 40
*Diagnostic and Statistical Manual
of Mental Disorders, Fifth
Edition* (DSM-5), 264

Differential conditioning
(discrimination training),
162 (table)–164, 166, 167,
183–184, 249, 472
Differential outcomes effect, 391
Differential reinforcement
behavioral topographies and,
293–295, 294 (figure)
defining, 293, 472
interresponse times and,
295–297, 300
molecular feedback and, 321
novel activities and, 297–298
of high rates schedule, 297,
325, 326 (figure)
of low rates schedule, 296,
324, 325, 326 (figure)
of other behavior, 250–251,
259 (note 8)
See also Differentiation;
Reinforcement
Differentiation
behavior variability and,
417–418
defining, 472
of behavior by reinforcement
and extinction, 292–293
See also Differential
reinforcement
Direct variable, 307, 310
Directed instruction, 453–455
Directions, 232, 455, 472
Discriminability (of stimulus)
defining, 472
salience and, 110 (figure)–111
schedules of partial
reinforcement and,
328–330
Discriminated avoidance,
255–256 (figure), 473
Discrimination training. *See*
Differential conditioning
Discriminative stimulus
defining, 271, 299, 473
operant conditioning and,
273, 383, 393–396,
394 (table), 395 (figure),
397 (table/figure)

Dishabituation, 12, 473. *See also* Habituation
Disinhibition, 45, 46, 49, 172, 174, 176–177, 182, 473
Dog behavior (examples)
  conditioned emotional reactions, 207
  imitation, 451–452
  sensory preconditioning, 154
  social transmission of food preferences, 438
  successive approximations and jumping, 231
  Type II conditioned reflex, 270
  See also Dog behavior (examples), conditioned salivation
Dog behavior (examples), conditioned salivation
  basic procedure, 18–19 (figure), 41 (figure), 84
  differential conditioning, 183 (figure)–185 (figure)
  differential conditioning/ discrimination training, 162 (table)–163
  disinhibition, 45, 172, 182
  inhibition of delay, 172
  involvement of entire behavior system, 182–185, 183 (figure)–184 (figure)
  motor behavior, 182–183
  passage of time as CS for events, 172
  post-conditioning devaluation, 143–144 (table)
  schedules of partial reinforcement, 306
  second-order conditioning, 48 (table), 152 (table)–153
  simultaneous feature-negative discrimination training, 162 (table)

summation test, 164
trace conditioning, 46, 47 (figure), 69, 182
unconditioned stimuli, 43
unrestrained dogs, 182, 183 (figure)–185 (figure)
Dolphins, successive approximations and jumping by, 231
Drive, defining, 282, 473
Drugs
  devaluation procedures and, 402–403
  melioration *vs.* optimization of choice in, 361
  reinstatement and, 405
  size of US preexposure and tolerance to, 168
  student attitudes toward, 343–346, 345 (figure)
  withdrawal from, 62–63
  See also Conditioned drug reactions

Eating reflex, 225–228 (figure), 226 (figure)–227 (figure), 229 (figure)
Empirical matching law
  applied to single behavior, 364–366, 367 (figure), 368 (box)–369 (box)
  bias and, 351 (figure)–352
  concurrent schedules of reinforcement and, 337–339, 338 (figure)
  defining, 473
  development of, 339–342 (figure), 341 (table)
  deviations from, 351–354
  extensions of, 343–350
  generalized, 350, 475
  overmatching and, 352 (figure)–353
  ratio schedules and, 348–349
  relative immediacy of reinforcement and, 347–348

relative magnitude of reinforcement and, 346–347
relative time allocation and, 343–346, 344 (figure), 345 (figure)
sensitivity to attributes of choices, 352–354
summary of matching relationships, 349–350
undermatching and, 352 (figure)
Episodic knowledge, 4 (figure)
Episodic memory, 3, 473
Epistemology, 2 (note 1)
Escape conditioning, 250, 254–255, 473
Establishing operation, 243, 246, 391, 473
Evaluative conditioning, 203–205, 209, 473
Evolution by natural selection, 24–26, 473
Evolution of learning, 21–29
  doctrine of evolution by natural selection, 24–26
  knowledge and natural selection, 28–29
Excitation
  conditioned, 90, 163–165
  defining, 161 (note 3), 473
Excitatory association, extinction and, 175, 176 (figure)
Excitatory conditioning
  avoidance behavior and, 91
  defining, 90, 473
  in absence of US, 134, 135 (figure), 136
  latent inhibition and, 113 (note 2)
  sensory preconditioning and, 154
  zero contingencies and, 116
  See also Positive CS-US contingency

genetic transmission of, 27
induced behaviors and, 415
learned release and, 186
learning and, 32, 466
natural selection and, 54–55,
    205, 436
operant conditioning
    and, 287
salience of stimuli and,
    109, 111
social learning and, 435, 440
use of problem box to
    minimize influence of,
    379 (note 1)
See also Instinctive knowledge
Instinctive knowledge
defining, 26–27,
    465–466, 476
imprinting and, 31
in species with short life
    spans, 81
natural selection and, 28
sign-tracking and, 76
transmission of, 28–29,
    30, 81, 442, 451
See also Innate knowledge
Instincts, 27, 476
Instructed behaviors,
    contingency-based
    behaviors *vs.*, 462
Instructed learning, effect of
    investment in parenting
    on, 30
Instructions, 432, 453–455, 476
Instrumental conditioning,
    73–74, 215 (note 1)
Instrumental learning
    (instrumental
    conditioning)
as declarative knowledge,
    384–385
defining, 476
first laboratory experiments
    on, 217–225
mazes and, 222 (figure)–225,
    223 (box)–225 (box)
operant conditioning and,
    215–216, 383–385

Pavlovian conditioning *vs.*,
    271–274
problem boxes and,
    218–222, 219 (figure),
    220 (box)–221 (box)
Interim behaviors, 423
Internal inhibition,
    45, 164 (note 4),
    175–176 (figure), 476
Interoceptive context, 175
Interreinforcer interval (IRI),
    310–311, 312, 315, 318,
    320, 321
Interresponse time (IRT),
    295–297, 309, 476
Interstimulus interval (ISI),
    96, 98, 191, 476
Interval schedules of
    reinforcement
defining, 476
fixed-interval (FI *t*), 316–318,
    317 (figure), 458–461,
    459 (figure)
limited holds and, 320
random-interval (RI *t*),
    319 (figure), 481
ratio schedules *vs.*, 402
variable-interval (VI *t*),
    318–320, 319 (figure)
See also Partial (intermittent)
    reinforcement schedule
Intervening variable
associative strength as,
    127, 129
conditioned emotional
    responses and, 50, 55, 59
defining, 8–9 (table), 476
drive as, 292
learning as, 33
See also Motivation
IRT< *t* schedules, 297, 476–477
IRT> *t* schedules, 295–296, 477

Japanese quail, reproductive
    fitness and, 208

Kinematic feedback, 295
Kineses, 287, 289, 477

Knowledge
cultural transmission of,
    28–29, 435, 465
defining, 2–3, 477
explicit, 3, 4 (figure)
implicit, 3, 4 (figure)
inherited, 109, 127–128
instinctive, 26–27, 28, 31,
    81, 465–466
learned, 26, 28–29, 465
natural selection and,
    26, 28–29, 81
See also Declarative
    knowledge (knowing
    that); Innate knowledge;
    Operant conditioning,
    representations
    of knowledge in;
    Pavlovian conditioning,
    representations
    of knowledge in;
    Procedural knowledge
    (knowing how);
    Social transmission of
    knowledge
Knowledge of
    performance, 295
Knowledge retrieval, 32

Lamarck, Jean Baptiste de,
    25 (box)
Language immersion, 18
Language learning in humans
as phase-specific learning, 18
cultural evolution and, 31
effect of parenting on, 30
similarities to song learning
    in birds, 28
Latent inhibition, 113 (note
    2), 477. *See also* CS
    preexposure effect;
    Inhibition
Law of Effect, 235, 363, 370,
    383, 384, 420, 420 (note 1),
    427, 477
Learned behavior, defining,
    2, 477
Learned helplessness, 256, 477